Quantitative economic policies and interactive planning

A reconstruction of the theory of economic policy

Quantitative economic policies and interactive planning

A reconstruction of the theory of economic policy

ANDREW HUGHES HALLETT
Erasmus University, Rotterdam

HEDLEY REES
University of Bristol

CAMBRIDGE UNIVERSITY PRESS
Cambridge
London New York New Rochelle
Melbourne Sydney

Published by the Press Syndicate of the University of Cambridge
The Pitt Building, Trumpington Street, Cambridge CB2 1RP
32 East 57th Street, New York, NY 10022, USA
296 Beaconsfield Parade, Middle Park, Melbourne 3206, Australia

First published 1983

Printed in Great Britain at
the University Press, Cambridge

Library of Congress catalogue card number: 82–4204

British Library Cataloguing in Publication Data

Hughes Hallett, Andrew
Quantitative economic policies and interactive planning. —
1. Economic policy—Mathematical models
I. Title II. Rees, Hedley
338.9′001′8 HD82

ISBN 0 521 23718 1

Contents

Preface

This book is about techniques of quantitative economic planning, and their application in political economies. It is about the theory of economic policy and identifying both the scope and the limitations for policy intervention. It explores the problems of policy evaluation with the help of econometric models; ranging from simple forecasting exercises to the multiobjective stochastic and dynamic optimisations of optimal control, and from determining particular policy values to evaluating the potential of alternative policy regimes or the benefits of error correction mechanisms.

The book has been written to challenge the 'physical analogy and algorithm' approach to economic policy design which has dominated the literature in the past. We develop methods for determining quantitative policies designed specifically to cope with uncertainties about an economy's dynamic responses, about the future exogenous influences and the variables which policy makers may take as exogenous, about preference orderings on the policies' expected outcomes, and about the appropriate degree of risk aversion. Some of the traditional methods of policy design may be familiar as techniques. But their application (as opposed to algorithmic details) to designing consensus policies in a political environment is not well understood.

Our aim is to provide techniques for making rational policy choices consistent with the degree of uncertainty and the variations in individual preferences, expectations, or information sets, found in social systems. This kind of *strategic planning* recognises that political realities restrict acceptable choices within the physical constraints of the economy. Since any knowledge of the economy and the degree of control over it will be both uncertain and limited, policy makers must negotiate, within a system of preferences, over likely outcomes if they are to exploit an economy's ability to achieve certain objectives more efficiently than would 'natural forces' and current measures. Policies emerge from interactive bargaining and experimenting with different options which allow for the reactions of other decision makers. Policy makers are not expected to try to override physical bottlenecks, uncertainty, or the reactions of others, by issuing detailed commands. But experience has shown that governments of different persuasions are distinguished by the extent to which they intervene in their economy, rather than by whether or not they intervene. We have therefore focused on how a policy authority may best plan its own activities and their impact on other sectors of the economy. If it turns out that nothing is to be gained by intervention then that will be revealed by strategic planning exercises.

The experimental nature of strategic planning, whether based on conditional forecasts or conditional optimisations, necessarily makes the coverage of the book ambitious. Each of the traditional techniques, such as forecasting, simulation, multiplier analysis, must be introduced to deal with a different element in the solution to a fully specified policy problem. The argument here is condensed for those traditional techniques; and optimisation (or control theory) is then presented as a direct generalisation of them, rather than just an alternative activity. Of course, it is impossible to avoid setting out efficient computational forms of those techniques in part I. But part II extends those techniques to provide certain qualitative properties in the quantitative solutions; specifically error correction properties, robustness to model and information errors, collective decisions for cooperating and noncooperating agents, modifications for increasing uncertainty, and performance indicators for designing new policy packages. Our experience, and that of many colleagues, convinced us that these extensions to traditional methods were necessary, rather than desirable, if the theory of economic policy is to be made operational in practice. The popular analogy between steering the economy and controlling a physical system is counter-productive because it suggests that selecting policies is a technical matter in which the policy maker scarcely plays a decisive role; and it is misleading because it hinders consideration of these qualitative properties.

No book of this kind is written without accumulating intellectual and administrative debts. Attributing specific intellectual debts is difficult. We have profited from association with the PREM (as it was) group at Imperial College London, from colleagues in Bristol and Rotterdam, from meetings of the Econometric Society and the Society for Economic Dynamics and Control, and from seminars in Oxford and London. Jean-Pierre Ancot, Angus Deaton, Chris Gilbert, and Jean Paelinck all helped improve the text, and have provided excellent hospitality to match. Andries Brandsma, Jarig van Sinderen and Nico van der Windt between them read and commented on the whole manuscript. Marja de Jong and Lisa Vucic typed it with efficiency and indispensable good humour, as Mary Harthan did for its ancestors. But our greatest debt is to Claudia Becker, who, like the good policy maker, intervened in an imperfect system to ensure the book's eventual production.

Rotterdam and Bristol
August 1981.

AJHH
HJBR

Part I

Techniques

1

The opportunity for economic planning

1.1 The components of choice

Economic plans are almost always presented in terms of policy targets on the one hand, and policy achievements on the other. Policy debates and planning documents have generally, if not entirely, been concerned with the properties of the economic policies advocated, with the importance of those properties for achieving certain objectives, and with the obstacles standing in the way of those desired achievements. The examination of what policy choices are actually available is pressed firmly into second place, with the result that the feasibility and expediency of the plan are left largely unexplored. At best this leads to poor policy selections, and at worst it is dangerous. If only a few very simple options are considered, no serious thought can be given to how well the plan matches the preferences, or to assessing the scope or limitations for intervention. There will be no check whether instruments exist to achieve the required results and how they would have to be used; no estimates of the risks run should the chosen policies fail (given the uncertainty over how the economy works and what exogenous events must be faced); and no contingency plans to cope with the consequences of uncertain events.

Planning consists of a good deal more than a description of the aims and the preferred path to those objectives. In our view, policies cannot be properly evaluated, still less justified, unless the constraints and conditions under which they operate are made clear. The failure to appreciate those constraints and conditions, because they are neither well defined nor made explicit, is responsible both for the misunderstandings of the opportunity for economic planning, and for the inconsistencies, frequent alterations and eventual failures of the policies themselves which have been such a common experience. Unlike preferences, correct conditioning information, or risk aversion, the *opportunities* for policy choice can be observed directly provided we have the means to relate different options to different outcomes (i.e. some econometric or other economic model). Policy choice is straightforward provided these options are generated systematically, and that we have the means to relate each to an explicit specification of the assumptions and components of the decision mechanism which underlies it. These assumptions will be loosely grouped into the four components of a planning model: the econometric model, the conditioning information, the preferences and risk aversion. We start by considering the opportunity for choosing economic policies. In Chapter 2 we examine the nature of the planning problem. Then we move onto the planning techniques themselves, taking up each component in turn. The first step is to find ways of predicting the consequences, and associated uncertainties, of different specifications of the conditioning information (Chapters 3 and 4). Next, we see how properties of a model and its controllability can affect policy evaluations (Chapters 5 and 6). The third step is to investigate the role played by preferences and risk aversion (Chapters 7 and 8). In the second part we describe ways of experimenting with specifications of those parts of the policy problem which are not directly observable. We investigate:

(a) risk reduction and error sensitivities (Chapter 9)
(b) collective preferences for cooperating policy makers (Chapter 10)
(c) expectations, and the assumptions of exogeneity for multiple non-cooperating policy makers (Chapter 11)
(d) degrees of uncertainty (Chapter 12)
(e) the evaluation of obstacles and the contribution of new or existing instruments (Chapter 13).

The final chapter argues that optimisation is an efficient way of searching for a policy recommendation when parts of the problem are difficult to specify correctly a priori. It not only provides the opportunity for sound economic planning, but also the policies are derived in a form which is answerable to, and capable of justification by, informed opinion.

We must stress from the start that this kind of planning is not intended to produce the rigid instructions typical of command economies, although the techniques put forward might be so used by others. It is not even necessarily concerned with centralised planning. It can, and has, been applied to market regulation and to multiplayer decentralised planning. The planning techniques involve a search for policies to achieve preset policy goals in which market behaviour and adaptive behaviour are both allowed for. Policy makers are expected to intervene in the steering of their economy because governments have the responsibility to plan their own affairs properly since that impinges on everybody else. But they do not need to plan for everybody else. The aim is to define the limits to what can be done and to respond optimally to events both anticipated and unexpected. This is a matter of negotiating with the political and economic environment rather than seeking to control it.

1.2 Some historical perspectives

The idea that governments should accept some responsibility for the management of the economy has been widely accepted only since the war. First low unemployment was taken as a target. Then the level of economic activity and balanced trade were added as targets. Econometric models concentrated on modelling the consumption demand to support that activity – first as short-run, and then long-run phenomena. In the 1950s the problems were perceived to be economic growth, productivity, the interactions of demand components and demand management. Production functions, derived labour and investment demands, and growth models with cyclical behaviour made their appearance among econometric models. By 1960 many countries were experiencing labour shortages, and econometric models began to explore labour supply and its impact on wage and price movements. In the later 1960s trade imbalances and investment cycles renewed the interest in models of those sectors of an economy. Inflation in the 1970s further encouraged disaggregation into submodels, e.g. of the energy sector. Later, as inflation persisted, the monetary sector (and expectations) inevitably became the focus of attention. Then rising unemployment prompted a reexamination of production (supply) determination, and of disequilibrium behaviour in various markets.

At this stage econometric models had got too large to be accurate or reliable. So, at a time when nonintervention is popularly argued to be the best solution to economic difficulties, it is no surprise to find a return to sequences of small and simple models. Nevertheless low inflation, growth, the foreign trade balance, money supply regulation, currency stability, industrial structure, a fair income distribution over people and regions, and investment policies – all of these, conflicting or not, are still the targets of economic policy. The main policy instruments include various types of direct and indirect taxation, interest rates, hire purchase conditions, other forms of credit availability and debt management, investment incentives, the exchange rate, import restrictions, many kinds of government expenditure both current and capital – including the phasing of public investment programmes – taxes on imports and/or exports, and a wages–prices policy. Typically, unforeseen shocks have come from world trade conditions, import prices or supplies, or events in a dominating commodity market, and perhaps the weather.

Therefore, policy makers apparently have no difficulty in specifying policy goals. West German planners, for instance, are required by law to announce their target values each year (for a 5 year horizon) for GNP growth, unemployment, the foreign trade position, and inflation. They are not required to state how they intend to reach those goals, but in practice some general indications will be given in relation to the perceived obstacles and past successes. The Germans come nearest to being the exception which 'proves' our first conclusion: that policy makers have clear ideas about their ideal target values but that they show little ability to formulate the plans to fit those targets.

These criticisms are harsh but not unwarranted as, to take one example, the history of planning in Britain shows only too clearly. The form and content of official British planning since the war can be found in the lively account by Budd (1978). The overriding impression is that the plans contained every exhortation to reach specified goals (one plan is described as a cross between a sermon and a call to arms) but almost totally without indicating how these goals were to be achieved. Whereas policy makers have never had difficulty in either naming the main targets or (since 1960) in putting desired values on those targets, the policy instruments have in most cases not even been discussed (see the plans of 1945–51, the 'stop–go' plans of 1961–4, the National Plan of 1964–6, the New Industrial Strategy of 1975–9, etc.). Hence the technical feasibility of the planned developments remained untested. Nor was there any check on whether sufficient instruments capable of achieving the stated objectives even existed (as in the case of the incomes policies of 1967–9 and 1972–5, which had been planned as instruments).

Since the way in which the available instruments were to be used was never set out, the repeated failures come as no surprise. Nevertheless, the catalogue of muddle, inconsistencies, and policy switches is rather overwhelming. Partly this reflects the painful discovery that the plans, whose success had been taken for granted, were infeasible; and partly the fact that the trade-offs available between objectives had never been examined so that consistent choices could not be made. In that case success with one target inevitably implies unexpected and unsatisfactory outcomes in another. If attention is switched to the most awkward failure, economic policies become directed to just suppressing failures one after another. The classic example is the 1967 devaluation. In 1965 4% growth was chosen as first priority in the National Plan apparently without properly evaluating the implications for the financial and balance of payments targets. By 1966 defence of the exchange rate had come to dominate all other policy choices. But devaluation became unavoidable in 1967, and policies were at once directed at removing the balance of payments deficit. In a similar way, inconsistent choices appear as a result of conflicts between short-run and long-run policy measures when the dynamic constraints, and trade-offs over time, are overlooked. The obvious example is the 'stop–go' policies of demand management (1961–4), which may have exaggerated the cycles they were designed to remove and which certainly foundered on the balance of payments constraint they were intended to circumvent. The habit of forecasting only 1–2 years ahead (which appears still to dominate planning, the latest medium-term strategies notwithstanding) makes these inconsistencies hard to avoid. Finally, all these plans were set out with an unreal degree of certainty; that is to say there was no assessment of the risk that they might fail, and no contingency plans to deal with those failures or the consequences of uncertain events. Policies could not be modified from their ideal values in the face of perceived risks, nor did it prove possible to revise the plans thereafter consistently with the desired strategy. The New Industrial Strategy of 1975 provides the most blatant example. Fear that uncertainties would invalidate a plan had, by that stage, led to a return to exhortation and unrealistic targets and to the dismissal of any considerations of feasibility or how the instruments would be used (this was called being flexible). Apparently the possibility of incorporating an explicit error correction mechanism from the start was not raised.

It is not that policy makers were unaware of the dangers of infeasible plans and a lack of instruments; or of not examining the available trade-offs between dynamic policy choices; or of the need for risk avoidance and policy revisions. The point is that they have not had the means to describe, still less analyse, these aspects of their policy problem. This has led them to ignore any such difficulties – clearly an unsatisfactory basis for any decision making. Selection techniques to make these inputs to policy choice explicit are therefore necessary. If some of the inputs to the resulting planning model cannot easily be specified a priori (and this is certainly true of preferences, risk, and conditioning information, but less so of the econometric model) they will at least be explicit in each candidate policy considered. Only then are the crucial elements in the specification of the plan underlying any policy choice open to criticism and debate. Such open discussion is indispensable if policy makers are to make responsible policy choices, as well as to be answerable for them.

1.3 Econometric models in economic planning

Although national macro-econometric models may have taken the centre of the stage they should not be allowed to dominate the many econometric models of other economic processes. Models have been successfully constructed for individual industries and individual sectors within an economy, for particular markets (in world and/or national terms), and for regional and urban subeconomies. The techniques which we discuss can be applied to any of these models. In principle these techniques can also be applied to any social process capable of description by a set of simultaneous equations.

The first econometric models were constructed by Tinbergen for the Dutch, British and United States economies (Tinbergen (1968)) at the time of the second world war. These models, together with the advances in economic theory and the realisation of the interdependence and very complex dynamics governing the behaviour of economic variables, inspired many subsequent models. A second impulse to the development of econometric models has been the increasing commitment by governments, over the same period, to certain social and economic goals. As these commitments become more extensive and more specific the problem of determining how they can be simultaneously achieved – or if to do so is even feasible – becomes more acute. The model specifies the dynamic constraints which must be allowed for in achieving any of these goals. The government may use a model to sketch the consequences – and the associated uncertainties – of various possible policy packages, or sets of likely events, over some planning horizon before choosing its preferred strategy. At its simplest this may merely involve forecasting the variables of interest, but it could involve the optimisation of an objective function with respect to policy variables which are constrained by the model.

An important sufficient condition for the construction and use of econometric models has been the development of numerical analysis techniques. We have potentially to analyse the performance of a large system of nonlinear simultaneous difference equations (seldom of low order) under a wide variety of different circumstances and over several time periods. Optimisation, estimation, equation solution, and approximation techniques are all involved. One constraint has been the very large quantity of information which has to be processed in these operations. Another is the considerable reliance placed on the availability of long and reliable time series of a large number of economic variables. Recent advances in computer technology and numerical analysis have now largely removed the computational constraint even for the largest problems. But, despite some improvements, the difficulty of reliable data remains and all too frequently causes trouble in the shape of model errors. Similarly, economic theory cannot yet guarantee a model free of specification errors. Inevitably there must be approximations where the mechanisms of economic behaviour are imperfectly understood. In particular it has proved difficult to capture the speed and form of dynamic responses with any accuracy. In addition, the model's parameters must be estimated on a restricted sample of recent data. They cannot therefore be perfect estimates in the sense that they describe the behaviour of the variables valid for all circumstances. They can only describe the responses found in the kind of situations observed in this sample of recent history.

In practice there has been no shortage of econometric models for analysing all the different problems which have interested policy makers. In the US the simple economy wide models estimated by Klein (1950) led to the medium-sized models of Klein and Goldberger (1955) (25 equations with annual data), and of Michigan University (Suits (1962), Hymans and Shapiro (1974)) with 47 equations and quarterly data and which has been updated and expanded in several versions. There has been a tendency for the size and detail of models to grow, enabling econometricians to explain many detailed components of the economy which otherwise would remain exogenous. The scope of the models for policy analysis has therefore markedly increased. In this class of large general purpose models is the Brookings model (Duesenberry et al. (1965, 1969)) with several hundred equations and exogenous variables requiring the estimation of several thousand coefficients; the well known Wharton model (Evans and Klein (1968)) in its various versions of between 70 and 200 equations; and, more recently, the Hickman–Coen model (Hickman and Coen (1976)). However, models are now more often designed for specific jobs. In the class of specific models are the Data Resources Inc. model (Eckstein et al. (1974)) for components of demand (expenditures) and supply; the OBE model (Hirsch (1973)) for government policy detail; the MPS model (Ando et al. (1972)) for detail on the monetary sector. All comprise a few hundred equations. Thus the disaggregation of models has proceeded over time, by sector detail, and by purpose of construction.

In the UK the range is more restricted. A small model was constructed at Oxford (Klein et al. (1961)); a descendant of that is the forecasting and policy analysis model of the London Business School (Ball et al. (1975)) comprising about 100 equations plus a very detailed fiscal sector. The Treasury and the Bank of England both operate large models, and there is a medium model in use at the National Institute for Economic and Social Research (Ormerod (1979)). These are models for short- and medium-term analysis. Quite a different approach is taken by the long run growth model maintained at Cambridge (Barker (1976)), which is based on interindustry accounting and the linear expenditure system.

Further examples of macro-econometric models exist, but are used to varying extents, in nearly every other country. Models for alternative economic systems, e.g. Russia, are also available (Green and Higgins (1978)). The final step of linking various national models to give an explanation of world trade flows has been undertaken and is operative in project LINK (Ball (1973)).

Models have also been constructed for developing economies with specific representation of their aid, investment or supply constraints, and particular market problems. Most extensive, perhaps, are those for India (see Desai (1973)) but there are many others. These models often concentrate on interindustry accounting identities but they are gradually becoming more sophisticated in representing the behavioural relations as well.

Many micro-econometric models appear in the form of regional planning and urban planning models (see Paelinck and Klaassen (1979) and references therein).

Although they attract less publicity, commodity models are widely used to explain the movements in a given market. Quite often they are world market models and involve considerable institutional and specialised knowledge of the particular market. They can be used by individual agents for planning: e.g. for the consequences for exchange rate policy, for foreign trade flows, or for stock control and price stabilisation problems. These models have detailed explanations of the supply and demand of the given commodity and perhaps its immediately competitive and complementary goods. They usually concentrate on problems of price formation, disequilibrium analysis, or the operation of cartels. Such diverse crops as tea, coffee, cocoa, jute, water melons, meat, sugar and onions have been treated. Metals such as copper, tin, zinc, tungsten have also been considered. It is a small step to construct these kinds of models to analyse supply and demand for some product within one economy – some examples are the car industry, rail transport, or textile industry models. Models of particular sectors are perhaps more common. The best known are those of the energy sector; the agricultural sector; housing; the financial sector; investment behaviour; complete demand systems; or even wages, prices and the labour market.

There is therefore no shortage of experience to help design an econometric model to plan for the many and varied objectives of policy makers. But, whether or not they come up with a reliable model, policy makers will certainly be constrained by a lack of corresponding experience in specifying the three remaining inputs for an economic decision model.

1.4 On model design

Perhaps it is obvious from this diversity of econometric models, and the variety of tasks to which they are put, that there will never be one model – nor indeed one best model – for an economic process. It is not that models are frequently revised as new information and research becomes available. But a model's specification must vary according to the use for which the model is intended; and policy makers certainly appear to have set themselves a wide range of objectives. The fact that specifications vary with uses is essentially a consequence of the size and information constraints which prevent the ideal model being realised. Both data and the underlying economic theory differ in their availability and reliability for different variables and their components; and different levels of aggregation and detail are required for different tasks. Models designed for one purpose cannot generally be expected to be effective for some other.

One major problem is to decide on the level of disaggregation. Disaggregation over time gives a finer description of the structure of lags in the economic processes and is more useful for analysing business cycle developments and other short-run policy impact and timing problems. On the other hand, the data available for the disaggregated variables may be less reliable or even may not be available at all. Disaggregation by sector obviously depends heavily on what is required from the model, and what is necessary for an accurate explanation of each variable. Thus, consumption may be split into durable, non-durable and services components on the argument that the speeds of adjustment of these expenditure changes are radically different, as are the determinants for each; yet they are much the same for each item within each member of that classification. Aggregation would cause much accuracy and precision to be lost. Similarly investment is often split into residential, business, plant and machinery, and government components. Imports and exports and employment are also often split into components by demand categories; and so on.

One may want a disaggregated model to give information on quite detailed components of the economy, to enable it to reflect changes due to structural shifts, external shocks or any possible policy shifts which may imply considerable disaggregation. Many instruments operate at a micro level; for example, Dorrington and Renton (1975) have investigated the effects of tax structure changes on the UK economy. Balanced budget GDP was found to change 26% more for given equal changes in the supertax rate as compared to those in a single person's tax allowance. More marked changes follow from the same changes in family allowances. A very detailed model is required for such exercises. So disaggregation decisions also follow from the intended use of the model.

On the other hand, too much disaggregation may be counter-productive because the quality and coverage of the data become inferior. Unreliable or inconsistent runs of data will produce poor results. Aggregation not only uses more reliable data but also benefits from cancellation of errors so the fit is better (Grunfeld and Griliches (1960)). But what is the advantage of that if none of the information on policy (or structural) shifts mentioned in the previous paragraph can be captured, and *changes* of direction are missed? It is rather easy to guess the major components of an economy on a 'no change' or 'same change as last period' basis since the economy evolves rather slowly. If the future does indeed have a similar structure to the past, false models will continue to predict the future as well as they did the past. Yet success with such aggregated 'back of the envelope' calculations may mean rather little, not only because it is uninformative on the details of the economy but also because such calculations neither contain information on, nor account for, the economic responses of that economy.

The argument of this section is illustrated in a general way by the popular dispute over whether large forecasting models are appropriate for policy analysis and prescription. Models good for forecasting are not necessarily the best for policy selection – although of course a perfect model would be ideal for both. Criteria for successful forecasting models typically demand accuracy, low forecasting errors, and detail on many closely related endogenous variables.

In contrast, models suitable for control exercises may be simpler than successful forecasting models since:

(i) Control exercises only require good forecasts of the few targets, and an accurate measure of their linkage with the instruments.

(ii) The targets tend to be the economic aggregates. If we disaggregate, inevitably some parts of the model will be worse specified than others and a 'noisier' system will result.

(iii) Any model incorporates approximations in its specification. Variables may be omitted or be treated as exogenous instead of endogenous, or the form and length of the lag structure may be approximated. There is no reason to suppose that the approximations suitable for a short-run problem of detail (e.g. forecasting) will also be suitable in a longer-run problem concentrating on dynamic structures (e.g. selecting policies for future growth).

(iv) A forecast error is irremediable. But the closed loop feedback controls described in Chapter 7 contain an explicit error correction mechanism. Although we cannot prevent the shocks which cause the forecasting errors, we can ensure that they cause minimal damage to the policy choices thereafter. Uncertainty and risk may therefore be modelled differently for different purposes.

Economic theory and econometric practice seldom lead directly to a model specification suitable for a particular purpose. It will be necessary to tailor the theoretical model for the uses desired of it. Consider an industrial economy in which the government is interested in forecasting and policy analysis. Traditional economic theory suggests we start with a description of dynamic equilibrium behaviour in which

(a) $S = Y - C(Y), \quad I = I(r)$ (goods markets) (1.1)

and $S = I$, or a financed gap

(b) $M_D = m_1(Y) + m_2(r, p)$ (money markets) (1.2)

and $M_s = M_D$, or a financed gap

(c) $Y = Y(N), \quad w = Y'(N), \quad w - w_0 + W(N)$ (labour markets) (1.3)

and $Y = wN$, or a financed income – full employment gap.

Here S = savings, Y = aggregate demand, I = investment, r = interest rate, M_D = demand for money, p = price level, M_s = money supply, N = labour force, w = wages (sticky below w_0). The bracketed terms denote functions, where $Y'(.)$ is a first derivative and $C(Y)$ consumption expenditure. Now there are three possible definitions of GDP:

(i) GDP = aggregate value added in sector outputs (supply)
(ii) GDP = aggregate demand (consumption, investment, trade, etc.)
(iii) GDP = aggregate incomes (wages, profits, rents, etc.)

Ex post they must be identical, but they can differ ex ante to show the total financing required to bridge the three gaps. So the next stage is to consider the specification of the financing necessary in the short term, and of the adjustment processes (in each set of markets) which will close the gaps in the medium term. That may involve short-run models of the demand or supply of goods (goods markets), of the money supply used to support these demand and supply levels (money markets), or of the incomes available to support demand and supply (labour markets). Disaggregation within each market or sector represented by (1.1), (1.2) or (1.3) allows us to see which components are adjusting and how. Modelling these adjustment processes explicitly produces a dynamic model of short-run disequilibrium behaviour. Then a model of the government's decision making (including its information set, attitudes to risk, targets, and preferences) must be explicitly introduced in order to see how the adjustment processes can be influenced by the setting of policy instruments. Surprisingly few models used for policy evaluation actually describe these aspects of planning behaviour directly, with the result that they cannot provide either reliable descriptions or sensible prescriptions for any of their variables. This is reflected in the common experience (sometimes popularised as Goodhart's Law) that 'all good econometric models break down when applied to policy analysis'.

A model designed in this manner will certainly incorporate short-run adjustment behaviour which is consistent with an appropriate long-run (moving) equilibrium. Short-run policy measures deduced from it are therefore necessarily consistent with the long-run goals of full employment, price stability, and balanced trade (internally and externally) implied by the elimination of the gaps in (1.1) to (1.3). The way is therefore open to policy analysis.

In this book we have a great deal to say about modelling all these components of planning behaviour; but rather less about the model itself because that is exhaustively covered in other texts. The development of (1.1)–(1.3) to a full estimated model designed for forecasting and policy analysis will be found in general texts, such as Evans (1969).

1.5 Policy experiments

One theme running through this book is that the different techniques for analysing an economy which use a model also yield useful information on the properties of that model. The same holds for policy evaluation techniques studied in this book, and the characteristics of preferences, information sets, and risk aversion revealed by particular policy selections or rejections. So one reason for adopting these techniques is to get that information; the other being to actually select policies. There is then a serious issue of experimental design in order to ask the right questions of the model. Such experiments are vitally important since they are the nearest we may come to testing alternative specifications of the components of the planning model as (a) there is no possibility of manipulating the economic system under repeatedly identical experimental conditions (indeed there is no possibility of 'live' experiments, let alone of experimental design), (b) there is an inherent randomness in human behavioural reactions not found in physical systems, (c) there are observation and measurement problems which can never be fully overcome, (d) we must use restricted samples for study.

Obviously there is no reason to expect nature (or indeed governments) to perform the crucial controlled experiments which will enable us to distinguish between alternative specifications of these components. In that case 'laboratory' experiments, not 'live' ones, must be conducted. The whole planning model should be subjected to severe testing during its construction *and* the derivation of policy recommendations, with the aim of correcting specifications which would appear later to have led to mistaken policy proposals. Policy experiments can provide diagnostic tests of a *planning* model in a similar way to that in which forecasting and simulation experiments test an *econometric* model. It is rather more difficult to set up rigorous statistical tests as there is no obvious underlying distribution theory. But it is in the nature of our experience of economic variables that the econometric models which explain those variables should be better understood and the testing of them much more advanced. Tests on the other three components are therefore both more difficult and more pressing. Nevertheless, they can be transformed into tests on the economic and policy variables. So, while the construction of an econometric model is inevitably bound up with the using of that model, policy experiments are equally bound up with the specification of a planning model. One learns by doing; specification and uses are an interactive process which leads iteratively to a complete specification of the planning model, which while not perfect is at least an adequate approximation of the true decision structure and an approximation whose shortcomings are well understood.

2

The theory of economic policy

2.1 A representation of the planning system

2.1.1 The model

Let us assume that an agreed model has been specified, estimated and tested. Assume also that we have satisfied ourselves that the model is an accurate enough representation of the processes we wish to analyse. For the moment consider that model to be linear

$$\beta Y + \Gamma X^{+} = U \tag{2.1}$$

where Y is a $g \times T$ matrix of endogenous variables, X^{+} is a matrix of T observations on all predetermined variables; β and Γ are respectively $g \times g$ and $g \times h^{+}$ matrices of coefficients; and U represents $g \times T$ random errors. The variables in (2.1) cover some time span, $t = 1 \ldots T$, which is of interest for planning purposes. We write the structural model form (2.1) in individual time periods

$$\beta Y_t + \Gamma X_t^{+} = U_t \qquad t = 1 \ldots T \tag{2.2}$$

where Y_t and U_t are g-vectors from Y and U, and $X_t^{+\prime} = [Y'_{t-1} \ldots Y'_{t-l}, X'_t \ldots X'_{t-k}]$ where X'_t denotes the transpose of X_t.

Thus, there are up to l lags in endogenous variables and k in the h purely exogenous variables, X_t. In order to separate the lags out in the structural form, we replace (2.2) with

$$\sum_{j=0}^{l} \beta_j Y_{t-j} + \sum_{j=0}^{k} \Gamma_j X_{t-j} = U_t. \tag{2.2a}$$

The restricted reduced form of our model follows from (2.1),

$$Y = \Pi X^{+} + V \text{ where } \Pi = -\beta^{-1}\Gamma \text{ and } V = \beta^{-1}U. \tag{2.3}$$

A particular form of (2.3) corresponding to (2.2a) is

$$Y_t = \sum_{j=1}^{l} \Pi_{1j} Y_{t-j} + \sum_{j=0}^{k} \Pi_{2j} X_{t-j} + V_t \tag{2.4}$$

or again

$$Y_t^+ = \Pi_1^* Y_{t-1}^+ + \Pi_2^* X_t^+ + V_t^+ \tag{2.5}$$

where $Y_t^{+\prime} = (Y_t' \ldots Y_{t-l+1}')$, $X_t^{+\prime} = (X_t' \ldots X_{t-k}')$ and $V_t^{+\prime} = (V_t', 0 \ldots 0)$, and

$$\Pi_1^* = \begin{bmatrix} \Pi_{11} \ldots \Pi_{1l} \\ I_{g(l-1)} \quad 0 \end{bmatrix} \text{ and } \Pi_2^* = \begin{bmatrix} \Pi_{20} \ldots \Pi_{2k} \\ 0 \;\ldots\; 0 \end{bmatrix}.$$

Therefore, without loss of generality we can redesignate any linear simultaneous difference equation model of arbitrary order as

$$Y_t = \Pi_1 Y_{t-1} + \Pi_2 X_t + V_t. \tag{2.6}$$

For the purpose of analysis, an lth order difference equation system has been reduced to a first order one at the cost of a number of very sparse matrices. Hereafter we represent models in the first order form in the knowledge that this is a perfectly general form for a dynamic model.

2.1.2 The notation system

The notation system employed here describes complete sets of variables (Y, X, etc.) by capital letters, and subsets of them (y, x, etc.) by lower case letters. Thus u_t is the nonzero subset of U_t if there are identities in (2.1). If we consider p players in a policy game then $X_t' = (x_t^{(1)\prime} \ldots x_t^{(p)\prime}, n_t')$ where the last 'player' is nature. This convention extends only to the variables in (2.1). It may be convenient to regard y_t and x_t as the leading elements of Y_t and X_t but in practice it is more flexible to accept the elements in these vectors in an arbitrary order. We use the model (2.6) except where noted otherwise.

With respect to the remaining notation of this book, we adopt the convention of declaring quantities in 'common' for the duration of the book, or 'locally' for the duration of a chapter. The quantities mentioned so far are in 'common', plus those in sections 7.2.1 to 7.2.4 below. In addition, we use the lag operator L (L^{-1} the lead operator); the superscript '$+$' to denote augmentation with extra elements; the superscript '$*$' on variables to denote optimised values; and '$\sim$' over a variable to denote deviations from desired values. Lastly, $\rho(.)$ denotes spectral radius, and $r(.)$ rank.

2.1.3 The classification of variables

We may classify all the variables in the planning system according to a particular use of the model; namely policy targets (chosen from Y_t), policy instruments (from X_t), 'data' or noncontrollable variables (from X_t and U_t), and nontargets (from Y_t). The targets may be primary or technical, respectively, if they directly affect the welfare of the community or if they have no such direct impact (such as the balance of payments) but have indirect consequences through monetary conditions. Typically the targets will be a small subset of m variables, y_t, contained within Y_t. Likewise there are only n variables, x_t, in X_t which take whatever value is assigned to them by a decision maker. These are the policy instruments currently open to the decision maker in question; the planners, the government, the market regulation authority, an entrepreneur or consumer, etc., depending on the context. If the values chosen for x_t are conditioned by economic circumstances (Y_t) then x_t is endogenised as the policy makers' preferred reactions. The remaining $h-n$ variables, N_t, are non-controllables being exogenous both to the model and the decision maker. Some of the variables in N_t may be instruments in the hands of other economic agents who are capable of influencing the economy (other policy makers, trade-unions, business interests, pressure groups, foreign trading governments, etc.), while others may be considered 'acts of God' (the weather, political events, or the world trade level). Thus we partition $X_t' = (x_t' \vdots N_t')$ and Π_{2j} of (2.4) conformably as $(\Pi_{2j} \vdots \Pi_{3j})$, $j = 0 \ldots k$; and likewise Π_2 in (2.6) as $(\Pi_2 \vdots \Pi_3)$. Hereafter the form of the variables (X_t, or x_t and N_t) determines whether Π_2 refers to (2.6) or to the submatrix in $(\Pi_2 \vdots \Pi_3)$ conforming to $(x_t' \vdots N_t')$. Finally the nontargets are those $g-m$ elements of Y_t which may take any value without *direct* penalty to the community. It should be noted that both N_t and U_t will be unknown when plans and forecasts for period t must be formulated, so that any calculations will have to be conditioned on some anticipated values for them. The degree of uncertainty about those future values may differ significantly. Finally, the classification of variables is necessarily dependent on the specification of the problem at hand; it will vary in different applications and over different time horizons.

2.2 The policy problem

The original exposition of the theory of economic policy was given by Tinbergen (1952). To set this up we need an idealised version of the planning problem involving (2.1). The shortcomings of the approach will then be noted. Solutions to these problems will be set out in later chapters. We shall follow an integrated sequence of techniques for policy evaluation, from the very simple ad hoc to complete policy optimisation, until we come to a method of achieving Tinbergen's aims.

2.2.1 The specification of a policy problem

It will be noted that many of the targets suggested in Chapter 1 are probably conflicting, if not actually inconsistent. They may be rivals within the same planning period or over different periods. To resolve such conflicts we postulate an index of overall performance of the economy denoted by $w(y_t)$ which we shall try to optimise. The function $w(y_t)$ expresses the trade-offs between those targets which the community or planners agree to accept, or reveal themselves as prepared to accept. The specification of $w(y_t)$ will naturally present problems and this will be discussed later. Since trade-offs are involved the performance index is only an ordinal measure, but as such it may be interpreted as an index of social welfare.

We shall assume that a satisfactory classification of the endogenous variables into targets and non-targets, and exogenous variables into instruments and data variables, has been agreed upon by the policy makers and their advisors, and we shall also assume that they do have complete control over the instruments. The latter is a very strict and, in some cases, possibly unrealistic assumption.

Consider a planning horizon of one period ahead. In this case all values of lagged variables are also known, and the policy formulation problem consists of four steps:

(a) The setting of m values of the targets to be achieved.
(b) The forecasting of the future values of the data variables. All calculations will be conditioned on these values.
(c) The derivation of n values of instruments to achieve the targets.
(d) The setting of the instruments at these values.

Now, if we can agree on the values in steps (a) and (b) it should be simple to manage step (c). Notice policy determination uses the model in the opposite way to conventional forecasting or simulation in which we insert values on the right of (2.6) and solve for the endogenous variables. Moreover, our objectives can be relations between variables (such as the balance of payments, the income shares accruing to different sectors of the community) if those relations are first included as extra structural equations. We later contemplate modifying our policies to counteract past mistakes, especially those made because of the uncertainty in (b) and in the Πs estimated in (2.6), or because failures in implementation are recorded for administrative reasons. It may also be necessary to restrain the instrument values to remain within acceptable bounds.

The difficulties in dealing with step (b) are not easily resolved since by definition we have little information on how these data variables are formed and hence little idea on how to set their values. If we did know more about them they could be endogenous to the system. N_t could perhaps be forecasted by some naive model, by a 'committee of experts', or by other external information (e.g. published plans). U_t is by definition a purely random structural error and is traditionally specified to have a zero mean. But in any event we could always solve the policy problem several times, each time conditioned on different values of data variables selected according to some subjective, or previously estimated, probability distribution associated with each variable. We could then investigate the several policy outcomes and select by some preassigned criterion the one we like best, or that which had the highest probability of actually occurring (Chapters 7 and 8). Therefore it is also worth investigating whether or not the policy outcomes are sensitive to variations in the data variables (done in Chapter 9).

The setting of target values is comparatively easy. In the nature of things, if we are interested in a particular variable as a target we will have some idea on the value we think it ought to take. Politicians usually pick out a target because it has not taken the values they think it should. Thus the classification of variables and the setting of desired target values go together in the specification of the policy formulation problem.

Disagreements may arise, however, over the relative priorities to be assigned to targets and their values. This problem is important because it becomes necessary to favour one target over another when the potential stochastic shocks from the various uncertainties associated with (b) cause markedly different disturbances in those targets. We shall also need to discriminate between the possible deterministic solutions when $n \neq m$.

2.2.2 Static controllability

We optimise $w(y_t)$ by choice of x_t values for each $t = 1 \ldots T$ separately. The linkage between y_t and x_t must be explicit. For this purpose a version of (2.2) must be constructed where the non-targets are dropped and where N and U are known:

$$B_0 y_t = -C_0 x_t + b_t \tag{2.7}$$

where b_t is a known vector including assumed values for U_t and N_t. Equation (2.7) is a reparameterised version of (2.2), with the nontarget equations substituted out of the system and X_t partitioned between x_t and N_t. For example, let y_t be the leading m elements of Y_t and partition $\beta_0 = \begin{bmatrix} \beta_{01} & \beta_{02} \\ \beta_{03} & \beta_{04} \end{bmatrix}$, with β_{01} of order m, and β_{04} of order $g - m$. Then $B_0 = \beta_{01} - \beta_{02}\beta_{04}^{-1}\beta_{03}$; and let $(C_0 \vdots C_1)$ represent the partitioning of $-(I \vdots \beta_{02}\beta_{04}^{-1})\Gamma_0$ corresponding to x_t and N_t. Thus $b_t = -(I \vdots \beta_{02}\beta_{04}^{-1}) \times \left(\sum_1^l \beta_j Y_{t-j} + \sum_1^k \Gamma_j X_{t-j} - U_t \right) + C_1 N_t$.

A planning horizon of one period means x_t is set without accounting for its impacts on the feasible performance in periods $t+1, \ldots, T$. This myopic strategy might be suggested since we can implement only x_t at the current planning interval. We aim to solve

$$\min_{x_t} \{w(y_t)\} \tag{2.8}$$

subject to (2.7) and conditional on the knowledge of b_t and $(\beta \vdots \Gamma)$. There are two possible approaches. We can minimise $w(y_t)$ to give the optimal or ideal target values, y_t^*, and obtain x_t^* from

$$x_t^* = -C_0^{-1}(B_0 y_t^* - b_t); \tag{2.9}$$

or we can substitute

$$B_0^{-1}(-C_0 x_t + b_t) \tag{2.10}$$

into $w(y_t)$ and minimise to give x_t^* directly. Now (2.9) exists only if $n = m$ (actually if C_0 is nonsingular). That is the condition for the existence of x_t^* values which yield arbitrary ideal target values, y_t^*, exactly for *any* set of preferences. Equation (2.10) tells us essentially the same thing, although this solution always exists. Since $w(y_t)$ has zero gradients in m directions at its minimum but the constrained minimisation produces n first order conditions, we can fit x_t^* to the implied unconstrained minimisers of $w(y_t)$ only if $n \geqslant m$. Thus, if $n > m$ then we have some surplus instruments which could be transferred to N_t. But if $n < m$ there is no solution by (2.9), and only an inferior optimum by (2.10) in the sense that the desired target values cannot be achieved exactly.

The basic theorem of Tinbergen is that $n = m$ ($n \geqslant m$) is required to uniquely (non-uniquely) solve the economic policy problem. In such cases the model is said to be perfectly *statically controllable*. There are, however, several drawbacks to this analysis:

(i) We cannot guarantee to have sufficient independent instruments ($n \geqslant m$); indeed we shall show that for a full definition of the policy problem this condition is never satisfied (section 10.3.1).

(ii) This myopic strategy ignores the dynamics of the economy, which form an essential aspect of policy design. Given $n \geqslant m$ and neither uncertainty nor penalties on using the instruments then a myopic strategy is justified since a sequence of single period instrument choices achieves the desired targets in each period. But in all other cases we must account for the (probable) future consequences of current decisions which cannot be eliminated exactly by later instrument choices. This means the optimisation must include all constraints, at every t, in order to fix each lag in Y_t at its optimal value and then optimise for the whole set (Y_t^*, x_t^*), $t = 1 \ldots T$, at once.

(iii) We have no idea what values to use for u_t and N_t, given that they are unknown when x_t is set. There may be a related problem of uncertainty over $(\beta \vdots \Gamma)$.

(iv) There is no established theory or experience to indicate the appropriate specification of $w(y_t)$; neither its functional form and arguments, nor the relative priorities for the various y_t elements at each t.

(v) The classification (Y_t, x_t) does not allow instruments to be model coefficients. Yet we will find some so-called instruments are in fact partially endogenous; e.g. tax yields where the real instrument is a tax rate.

(vi) It would be more realistic to place inequality bounds on the feasible and permissible values of x_t; say $x_{min} \leqslant x_t \leqslant x_{max}$. Alternatively it would be more realistic to place costs on changing instrument values. These might represent administrative and informational costs, and more importantly political costs since governments will be risk averse and naturally loath to have to introduce large, frequent, or unpopular variations in their instruments. There are also costs to reversals of policy. Thus both y_t and x_t should be included in the objective function. Then, except by chance, the unconstrained optimum (that is the ideal position) will lie outside the boundary of the feasible set.

(vii) On the other hand, we can follow the same approach if the model were nonlinear, and solutions to (i) – (vi) have been found. Given the many numerical optimisation techniques available, this complication is of a different nature and of an order simpler to resolve than the shortcomings mentioned above.

2.3 Characteristics of the solution to the policy problem

To illustrate the policy problem we employ a small example:

$$Y = Z + C + G \tag{2.11}$$
$$C = a(Y - T) \qquad 0 < a < 1$$

where in real terms, $Y = \text{GDP}$, $C = \text{consumption}$, $T = \text{net tax bill on incomes}$, $G = \text{government expenditure}$, and $Z = \text{all other components of GDP}$. Let $\Delta Y = Y - Y^d$ where Y^d is the target value for Y. We have $Y = (Z + G - aT)/(1 - a)$

so $$\Delta Y = \frac{\Delta G}{1 - a} \text{ or } \Delta Y = \left[\frac{-a}{1 - a}\right]\Delta T. \tag{2.12}$$

The required policy *changes* are $\Delta G = \Delta Y(1 - a)$ or $\Delta T = -\Delta Y(1 - a)/a$. However, it is clear that the tax yield is not a valid instrument in that it is itself affected by the level of Y in the economy which is a target. To some extent T is a target as well as an instrument; the correct instrument is the tax *rate*.

2.3.1 Partially endogenous instruments and other nonlinearities

Suppose in addition $T = t_0 + t_1 Y$, for $0 < t_1 < 1$, and that the desired level of Y^d is to be achieved by altering t_1 or t_0 to produce the necessary tax yield T^d. We have a policy problem where instruments are coefficients and the associated 'instrument' variables are partly endogenous. Including coefficients in the list of instruments increases realism, but it complicates the calculation of policy values and changes the flexibility of policy responses. For the additive (variable type) instruments t_0 and G,

$$\Delta Y = \frac{a\,\Delta t_0}{1-a(1-t_1)} \quad \text{or} \quad \Delta Y = \frac{\Delta G}{1-a(1-t_1)}. \tag{2.13}$$

The values of t_0 or G which yield Y^d follow from (2.13). They imply the tax policy

$$\Delta T = \frac{(1-a)\,\Delta t_0}{1-a(1-t_1)}$$

or

$$\Delta T = \frac{t_1\,\Delta G}{1-a(1-t_1)}. \tag{2.14}$$

So the larger the value of t_1 $(0 < t_1 < 1)$ the more damped the response of Y to changes in G or t_0 due to the offsetting changes in tax yields. If we ignore these automatic stabilisers, as (2.12) does, we shall compute policies which are too weak to achieve the required targets. In this case the required policies depend only on the level of the other potential instruments.

But if, instead, we change the multiplicative (coefficient type) instrument then

$$\Delta Y = \frac{-aY\Delta t_1}{1-a(1-t_1)} \quad \text{and} \quad \Delta T = \frac{(1-a)(Z+G-at_0)}{(1-a(1-t_1))^2}\Delta t_1. \tag{2.15}$$

Evidently the required policy now also depends on the *level* of economic activity. Different policies will be computed for the target Y depending on the levels of Z and G in addition to t_1. This is because, despite the linearity of our model, the decision variables (targets plus instruments) enter the model non-linearly via the product $t_1 Y$. Policy instruments with nonlinear impacts cause three new difficulties:

(i) Although the $n \geqslant m$ rule still generally applies we are no longer able to solve the model via a linear reduced form.

(ii) When solving the resulting nonlinear equations we have to establish whether or not a solution exists, and then worry about the possibility of having to pick one of the potentially multiple solutions.

(iii) The relations which determine the required instrument as a function of the desired target vary with the level of economic activity as well as other instruments.

Now consider a price vector normalised on the price of $Z + G$. Suppose the government raises an expenditure tax on C, giving a final price P as $P(1 - t_3) = 1$ for $t_3 =$ the expenditure tax rate. Then $X = PC + Z + G$

where $X = \text{GDP}$ in nominal terms. Setting $t_0 = 0$ leaves real disposable income as $D = (1 - t_1)Y/P = (1 - t_1)(1 - t_3)\, Y = Y - T$. From this we compute that

$$\text{either} \quad \Delta Y = \frac{-a(1 - t_3)(Z + G)}{[1 - a(1 - t_1)(1 - t_3)]^2} \Delta t_1 \tag{2.16}$$

$$\text{or} \quad \Delta Y = \frac{-a(1 - t_1)(Z + G)}{[1 - a(1 - t_1)(1 - t_3)]^2} \Delta t_3 . \tag{2.17}$$

The impact of changing one tax rate depends on the level set for the other. Not only does the *required policy* alter with the level of economic activity but the *effectiveness* of any instrument also varies with both the level of economic activity and the state of the other instruments. There is a potential danger that we may be required to set one instrument in a way which renders the other one largely ineffective.

We have used $\Delta T = t_1 \Delta Y + Y \Delta t_1$ here. The second term is the *discretionary* policy change and the first its endogenous consequence. Expanding the model to provide this extra information has led to more complicated policy calculations. Three points arise from this. The model must be appropriate to the instruments and targets that the government is considering. The desire to stay with simple policy selection techniques must not lead us to simplify or aggregate the model to the point that it can no longer correctly answer the questions we put to it. Second, the calculations involved rapidly become too complicated for 'back of the envelope' style calculations even for these simple models. Third, the tax rate settings are interdependent so that the distribution of the tax burden between t_1 and t_3 itself influences the outcome.

2.4 Redundant instruments and infeasible plans

One aspect of policy determination, yet to be brought out, is the influence of the problem definition. We refer to the selection of the targets from the endogenous variables, together with their desired values, and the selection of instruments to be used. Later the problem definition will include setting the planning horizon, ideal values for the instruments, and the particular exogenous (possibly random) events to be countered.

2.4.1 On the effectiveness of instruments

The first point at issue is the effectiveness of instruments for reaching the desired target values. Section 2.2 makes it clear that the desired targets can always be attained provided that they refer to independently determined variables (B_0 nonsingular in (2.10)), and that there are sufficient independent instruments steering the economy ($n \geqslant m$

and C_0 nonsingular in (2.9)). But, even then, if C_0^{-1} contains large elements then the chosen instrument set is ineffective; small adjustments to y_t require large swings in x_t values, which will be unacceptable if not administratively infeasible. Again, if B_0^{-1} is large, moderate changes in y_t demand either small alterations to x_t or large alterations which are almost completely offsetting. The instruments are increasingly ineffective for the problem in hand. Such precise 'fine tuning' may not be realistic, and it certainly cannot counteract the large impacts of the unknown non-controllables.

The problem of ineffective instruments covers each of these possibilities. Consider the earlier example, but with foreign trade and investment added, and expenditure taxes dropped,

$$\begin{aligned}
Y &= C + I + G + E - M \\
C &= a(Y - T) \\
T &= t_0 + t_1 Y \\
M &= m_1 C + m_2 G \qquad 0 < m_1, m_2 < 1 \\
I &= bY + Z \qquad 0 < b < 1
\end{aligned} \tag{2.18}$$

where $E =$ exports, $M =$ imports, and $I =$ investment expenditures. Suppose Y and M are targets, and t_0 and G the instruments. Then

$$\begin{pmatrix} \Delta Y \\ \Delta M \end{pmatrix} = d^{-1} \begin{bmatrix} (m_1 - 1)a & (1 - m_2) \\ m_1 a(b - 1) & m_2(1 - b) + a(m_1 - m_2)(1 - t_1) \end{bmatrix} \begin{pmatrix} \Delta t_0 \\ \Delta G \end{pmatrix} \tag{2.19}$$

provided that $d = 1 - a(1 - t_1)(1 - m_1) - b \neq 0$. Although the static controllability condition ($n \geqslant m$) is satisfied here, one of these instruments becomes redundant if the matrix of (2.19) (equivalent to C_0 in (2.9)) is singular. Its determinant is $a(m_1 - m_2)(1 - b + a(m_1 - m_2)(1 - t_1))/d^2$, so this happens unless $m_1 \neq m_2$. Consequently the instruments become ineffective as $(m_1 - m_2) \rightarrow 0$.

A related case of redundant instruments arises when t_1 replaces G. Now (2.19) is replaced by

$$\begin{pmatrix} \Delta Y \\ \Delta M \end{pmatrix} = \begin{bmatrix} d(m_1 - 1)a & (m_1 - 1)a[(m_1 - 1)at_0 + (1 - m_2)G + Z + E] \\ dm_1 a(b - 1) & m_1 a(b - 1)[(m_1 - 1)at_0 + (1 - m_2)G + Z + E] \end{bmatrix} \begin{pmatrix} \Delta t_0 \\ \Delta t_1 \end{pmatrix}^{d^{-2}} \tag{2.20}$$

whose matrix is singular for all (rather than particular) values of the model's parameters. One instrument is always redundant in this case (despite $n \geqslant m$) because it is not possible to engineer the necessary two separate effects through the single channel of T. In other words, Tinbergen's theorem and static controllability should be stated in terms of the nonsingularity of C_0 rather than as $n \geqslant m$.

The point made here is that the effectiveness of policy instruments is often more important than their number. But instruments ineffective in one situation do not necessarily remain so in another.

2.4.2 On infeasible plans

Thus (2.19) and (2.20) illustrate two cases of ineffective instruments due to (near) redundancy. The economy becomes unmanageable because of the inadequate means of control. The solution is to extend the scope for policy interventions – by legislation if necessary. There are cases (e.g. (2.20)) of insufficient intervention channels; and they call for the creation of new policy instruments. There are cases (e.g. (2.19)) where the structure of economic reactions annihilates the independent impacts of the instruments. This calls for 'changing the rules of the game' by engineering structural shifts in those reactions (or by creating new instruments).

But cases of ineffectiveness due to near redundancy should be distinguished from those due to infeasibility. Cases with $d = 0$ reflect a redundant equation in (2.18) and consequently linear dependence between the two targets Y and M. Unless their desired values satisfy an identical linear relation, these targets cannot both be realised by any instrument values. Hence the plans are infeasible. The plans become near-infeasible as $d \rightarrow 0$ and will require large and offsetting instrument movements if both targets are to be met, whereas conventionally small movements would be sufficient for either instrument to reach each target alone. Only if the desired target values closely follow the original dependency within the model do we have the case where small policy adjustments are called for. In fact $d \simeq 0$ is not so unlikely. A country with $a = 0.85$, $t_1 = 0.1$, $m_1 = 0.05$, and $Z = 0$ needs only a mild capital inflow, if public and private savings are directed to investment, to produce $d = 0$.

It may be possible to alter the economic structure (for example, legislation could shift t_1 and hence d), but otherwise we can only determine the instrument values which would set the targets as close to their desired values as possible. A related infeasibility arises when the planner also has ideal values for the instruments (i.e. those he would set given a free hand and released from the constraints of the model). The two sets of ideal values cannot generally satisfy the model; this infeasibility can only be resolved by getting 'as close as possible' to the ideal.

2.4.3 On the use of instruments

Consider (2.19) again for the conventional case of $d > 0$. Suppose that $m_1 > m_2$; and that we plan for growth in GNP ($\Delta Y > 0$) plus the imports to facilitate that ($\Delta M > 0$). The individual instrument settings are unambiguous and have the expected signs (either $\Delta t_0 < 0$ or $\Delta G > 0$). However, used together the instruments are determined from

$$\Delta t_0 = \frac{d}{a(m_1 - m_2)}\left[m_2\left(\Delta Y + \frac{\Delta M}{1-b}\right) - \frac{\Delta M}{1-b}\right]$$

and
$$\Delta G = \frac{d}{(m_1 - m_2)}\left[m_1\left(\Delta Y + \frac{\Delta M}{1-b}\right) - \frac{\Delta M}{1-b}\right]. \tag{2.21}$$

The combination of instruments may mean that one of them is used perversely (in comparison to its individual impact). By (2.21) that happens whenever $\Delta Y/\Delta M$ lies outside the closed interval $[(1-m_1)/(m_1(1-b)), (1-m_2)/(m_2(1-b))]$ i.e. whenever the planned ΔY is large or small enough compared to ΔM. If ΔY is relatively large then Δt_0 is 'perverse'; and if ΔY is relatively small ΔG is 'perverse'. Moreover, in only one of these cases can any contribution to balancing the budget be made at the same time.

Thus, in any given situation the way we use the instruments may alter with the targets set, as well as with the parameters, or level of activity, in the system. In particular it may be necessary to use one instrument in a perverse manner: overshooting with one instrument and pulling back with another.

2.5 The need for optimisation

Up to this point we have assumed that each target must be achieved. An obvious way out of the ineffective instruments problem is to compromise; i.e. to 'trade' targets and to try to get as 'close' as possible to them, although this means that none will be satisfied exactly. We balance the failure to reach one target against the comparative success in reaching another. To do that requires the minimisation of a loss function which penalises the failure to reach each desired target by the relative importance of making that failure zero.

Another suggestion is to set aside n of the m independent targets, where n is the total number of independent instruments, as the most important. These are achieved in the usual way, while the remaining $m-n$ are allowed to take whatever values they must. We call the first set 'fixed targets' which will be achieved, and the second set 'flexible targets' which are aimed for but cannot be achieved exactly. This, of course, is simply a particular case of the compromise solution with infinite penalties given to the fixed targets and zero weights to the flexible targets.

We may only be able to use instruments up to their acceptable, or administratively and technically feasible, boundary values. So with relatively ineffective instruments we may be unable to control the targets completely because the large instrument changes necessary to secure small target improvements will be ruled out. Again a loss function approach needs to be introduced. Until now our policy problem has assumed that instrument changes are costless. This is patently not the case. There are costs, administrative and informational, to a tax rate change. An interest rate increase has expensive consequences for debt management. Most obviously, the government will count very carefully the political costs of an instrument change especially when it directly affects the voting public, as does a tax change. It will naturally try to avoid introducing either large, frequent, or unpopular variations in any of the instruments. That is to say that a risk averse government will err on the side of caution rather than make a mistake which will have to be corrected with another policy change later. There may also be economic costs as well as political costs to frequent alterations or reversals of policy. There is a well known argument that economic development and investment can only take place against the background of stable and gradually evolving economic conditions and policies. All of this amounts to saying that there are also desired values of instruments; and instruments are only pure instruments provided they remain within reasonably narrow limits. The simple and obvious solution is to include deviations of instruments from their desired values in the loss function. In this sense the distinction between targets and instruments is less clear than their names might suggest.

Finally, there are two very important problems which we have so far ignored. The first relates to the fact that we are usually dealing in models with estimated parameters which are not known with certainty. The second oversight refers to the fact that we have not dealt anywhere with multiperiod problems, i.e. we have assumed that we would like to achieve some particular target now, but have not built in a desired growth path up to some planning horizon. It is vital for planners to formulate a set of policy trajectories that are coordinated, consistent and optimal over several periods taken together. This implies their joint optimisation from the present to the planning horizon. In fact the model will display the dynamics of the economy which, we have argued, are an essential feature of the economic process. Both model and optimisation are in fact more complicated computationally than the foregoing examples would suggest.

2.6 Conclusions

In what follows, various methods for dealing with the problems raised in this chapter will be discussed. If we are committed to the 'optimisation' of policies then a formal approach is the obvious one to use. There is, however, a strong history of ad hoc methods in policy formulation, and that is often an acceptable alternative. The techniques of simulation and multiplier analysis will be looked at next. After that we move on to the analytical methods of optimising policies.

3

Forecasts in planning

3.1 Introduction

The previous chapter serves as an introduction to the process of economic planning with an econometric model. We are now going to consider the first step in the development of an economic policy package. This is to forecast the most likely time path of the economy over some chosen time period (say the present term of office of the government). In practice, particular attention will presumably be paid to certain target variables, although we shall not initially couch it in these terms. In this chapter we survey the main difficulties in constructing conditional forecasts of economic variables. Later chapters will discuss how this information can be used to design policy measures to meet a predetermined set of objectives laid down by the planners.

3.2 Forecasting and the reduced form model

We start from the proposition that a policy advisor must first be able to forecast where the present course is leading; and, second, he must have the means of gauging what (and when) the responses will be to any particular policy adjustment. Only then is it possible to search through possible policy adjustments to select that which is most consistent with the objectives. Thus the ability to make a forecast (the best single estimate of the future time path of the economy) and to make projections (the best estimates of that time path under a variety of assumptions for the values of exogenous variables, including the available policy instruments) is an essential prerequisite for planning and policy evaluation.

On the other hand, in making forecasts or projections it is necessary to exercise sufficient caution in order to allow for the potential errors and uncertainties in the key judgements involved. Thus our interest in forecasting and projection techniques is with the best point forecasts, with assessing the sources and likely margins of error (confidence bounds), and with the possibility of combining forecasts from different sources. Naturally any forecasts will be conditional on the assumptions covering the exogenous variables. So forecasts and nonstochastic simulations will be distinguished only by whether exogenous variables are set respectively at their expected (or most likely) values, or at values in various other scenarios whose consequences we would like to evaluate. Having done this, the design of policy measures will consist of deciding on those scenarios and on ways of discriminating between their results.

For expository purposes we shall drop the distinction between x_t and N_t in this chapter. We use (2.6)

$$Y_t = \Pi_1 Y_{t-1} + \Pi_2 X_t + V_t \tag{3.1}$$

remembering that this reduced form model will cover a dynamic linear model with l lags in endogenous variables and k in the exogenous variables.

The most natural vehicle to use for forecasting is the reduced form since each equation can be solved independently to give the forecast for each endogenous variable. In most forecasting exercises the following assumptions are implicit:

(1) Future values of the exogenous variables are known without error over the whole forecasting period.
(2) The error term V_t has mean zero, and hence the best estimate of the future values of the endogenous variables is given when $V_t = 0$.
(3) The structural model (2.1) is an adequate representation of the economy and will continue to remain so over the forecast period.

We shall follow convention and initially assume these assumptions to be true, but later we relax them and consider the effects on the forecasts.

At time t, the one step ahead forecast of Y_t (i.e. the forecast of Y_{t+1} made at the end of period t) will be obtained from (3.1) as

$$Y_{t+1,t} = \Pi_1 Y_t + \Pi_2 X_{t+1} \tag{3.2}$$

where it is assumed for the present that X_{t+1}, Π_1 and Π_2 are known.

Extending this result, the f step ahead forecast (i.e. the forecast of Y_{t+f} made at time t) will be

$$Y_{t+f,t} = \Pi_1 Y_{t+f-1} + \Pi_2 X_{t+f}. \tag{3.3}$$

However, Y_{t+f-1} is not observed and hence has to be replaced by its forecast value $Y_{t+f-1,t}$ which in turn contains $Y_{t+f-2,t} \cdots Y_{t+2,t}, Y_{t+1,t}, Y_t$; i.e. the process of obtaining $Y_{t+f,t}$ is a recursive process involving all previous endogenous variable forecasts. If $f < l$ then some of the lagged endogenous variables will be observable, giving (in terms of (2.4)):

$$Y_{t+f,t} = \sum_{j=1}^{f-1} \Pi_{1j} Y_{t+f-j,t} + \sum_{j=f}^{l} \Pi_{1j} Y_{t-j} + \sum_{j=0}^{k} \Pi_{2j} X_{t+f-j}. \tag{3.4}$$

If $f \geqslant l$ then the middle term of (3.4) vanishes.

In general the values of the parameters will be estimated rather than known precisely. In addition we cannot pretend, at t, that we actually know the future values of the exogenous variables although we may have a fairly good idea of some of them. Forecasts for many variables which are traditionally regarded as exogenous such as government expenditure, or transfer payments in various forms, are obtainable from known government policy which necessarily has to be planned some time in advance. Other exogenous variables, such as labour supply, may not change rapidly from year to year, hence in principle one can make good estimates of future values, especially for the near future. Many econometricians would however regard it as much too optimistic to consider being able to predict the values of all the exogenous variables in a model (especially a large model) with any accuracy and would point to the unexpected effects of the oil price rise of 1973 or the frequent changes in government policy resulting in cancellation of projects as the battle against inflation has proceeded.

Fortunately one can adopt the alternative approach of 'conditional' forecasting; i.e. the forecasts produced are explicitly recognised as being conditional on the values of the exogenous variables that were used. Thus one can produce forecasts conditional on unchanged government policy, or a growth of 5% in world trade, or a growth of 2% in GNP, etc. If the future is very uncertain several forecasts can be produced, each conditional on different assumptions. The choice between the forecasts is then left to the user's judgement.

3.3 The composition of forecast errors

Evidently there are four potential sources of error in our forecast $Y_{t+f,t}$ when compared to the actual realisation Y_{t+f}:

(a) from the stochastic disturbances $V_{t+f} \neq E(V_{t+f}) = 0$.

(b) from the parameter estimates $\hat{\Pi} = (\hat{\Pi}_1 \vdots \hat{\Pi}_2) \neq (\Pi_1 \vdots \Pi_2) = \Pi$; although $\hat{\Pi}$ may be consistent (for large samples $\hat{\Pi} \to \Pi$) it will not coincide with Π itself.

(c) when X_{t+f} is unknown at t, $X_{t+f,t} \neq X_{t+f}$ will be used as its anticipated value in (3.3).

(d) from $Y_{t+f-j,t} \neq Y_{t+f-j}$ in (3.4), representing the cumulative effects of past forecast errors.

Of these errors, (a) represents *specification errors* (poor specification and data inaccuracies) and errors due to purely random behaviour; (b) contains *estimation errors* (inappropriate specification or estimation techniques) and sampling variability; (c) contains *information errors*; and (d), relative to (a), (b) and (c), covers *errors due to the dynamic structure.*

The seriousness of the errors of types (c) and (d) can be evaluated, and to some extent eliminated, by inserting the actual values of variables where possible, which in practice means 'forecasting' within historical periods. But the inherent variability of economic processes means the errors in (a) and (b) can never be completely avoided. Thus we distinguish ex post from ex ante forecasts:

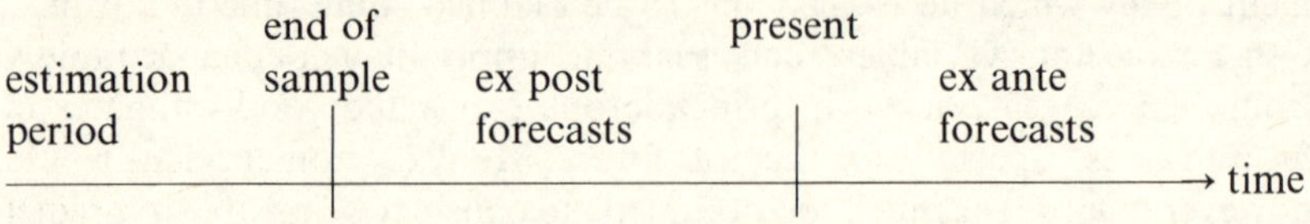

Figure 3.1 Types of forecasts

Ex ante forecasts are those conditional on $X_{t+f,t}$; ex post are unconditional given X_{t+f}; both are conditional on $\hat{\Pi}$. Lagged dependent variables should be replaced by their realisations in ex post forecasts when a series of one step predictions is the aim. Otherwise, using forecasts generated in earlier steps for the lagged variables in (3.4) gives a better picture of the ex ante forecasting power of our model. Then comparing those results to the case where lagged endogenous variables are replaced by their realisations (where possible) gives a measure of the errors in the dynamic structure of the model. Having done that, the next step is to compare ex ante and ex post forecasts to give a measure of the information errors detailed above.

Revising forecasts raises many of the same points. If the ex ante forecast horizon is $t+f$, we have all four sources of error at period $t+1$. At $t+2$, X_{t+1} and $\hat{V}_{t+1} = Y_{t+1} - Y_{t+1,t}$ will be known, so that the forecasts for $t+2 \ldots t+f$ can be repeated with actuals for Y_{t+1} (i.e. use (3.4) for $t+1$ and insert $\hat{V}_{t+1}$) and X_{t+1}, plus any revisions to $X_{t+i,t}$ for $i = 2 \ldots f$. These revised forecasts are conditioned on all the information available at $t+2$, rather than that at the start of the exercise. The errors under the headings (a), (c) and (d) above will at least have been reduced.

Thus, by conditional forecasts we mean $E(Y_{t+f}|\Omega_t)$ where Ω_t is the information set at t consisting of $\hat{\Pi}_1$, $\hat{\Pi}_2$; plus X_{t-j}, Y_{t-j} (which includes past errors $\hat{V}_{t-j}$), $j \geqslant 0$; and $X_{t+j,t}$ for $0 < j \leqslant f$. An investigation of the forecasting performance of a model can provide valuable experimental evidence on the success of its specification; and should lead to further improvements in that specification.

3.4 Optimal forecasts

Suppose we wish to forecast beyond the sample period T, where (somewhat improbably) the exogenous variables are known. If the economy is represented by (3.1) where $\Pi_1 = 0$ and X_{t+f}, for $f = 1, 2 \ldots$, are contained within Ω_T then (irrespective of any estimate we may or may not already have made for Π_2) the optimal forecast of Y_{T+f} made at T is

$$Y_{T+f,T} = \hat{\Pi}_2 X_{T+f} + (Y - \hat{\Pi}_2 X)\Sigma^{-1} W \tag{3.5}$$

where $\hat{\Pi}_2$ is the ordinary least squares estimate of Π_2 based on a sample of $1 \ldots T$, and $\Sigma = E(V'V)$ and $W = E(V'V_{T+f})$ are variance and auto-covariance estimates (Goldberger (1962)). Variables without subscripts are matrices of sample observations as defined for (2.3). This forecast is optimal in the traditional econometric sense of being best linear unbiased, i.e. $E(Y_{T+f}|\Omega_T) = Y_{T+f,T}$, subject to the forecast error variances, $E[(\hat{v}_i)'_{T+f}(\hat{v}_i)_{T+f}]$, being minimised for each $i = 1 \ldots g$. We normally consider the case of V_t being serially uncorrelated so that the last term of (3.5) vanishes. In that case the use of $E(V_t) = 0$ in (3.3) is indeed justified.

Several questions now arise: what happens to the variance of the forecast errors when $\Pi_1 \neq 0$ (examined in section 3.7 below), when another estimator is used for Π_2 (section 3.4.3), or when X_{T+f} is uncertain (section 3.5)? In each case how do we construct confidence intervals about $Y_{T+f,T}$ for interval forecasts (sections 3.4.2 and 3.6)? A second line of questions stems from the optimisation criterion taken here: is a combination of forecast error variances more appropriate, or could the forecasts be improved in combination with forecasts from other sources? These various extensions are examined in sections 3.8 to 3.11 below.

3.4.1 Forecast error variances

We derive the variance–covariance matrix of these optimised forecast errors, from $T+1$ to $T+f$, by taking (3.1) with $\Pi_1 = 0$ and stacking variables:

$$\text{vec}(Y^{(f)\prime}) = (I_g \otimes X^{(f)})\text{vec}(\hat{\Pi}_2') + \text{vec}(V^{(f)\prime}) \tag{3.6}$$

where $X^{(f)} = \begin{pmatrix} X'_{T+1} \\ \vdots \\ X'_{T+f} \end{pmatrix}$ is known. Naturally $Y^{(f)} = (Y_{T+1} \cdots Y_{T+f})$ and $V^{(f)}$ likewise. Hence, if V_t is serially uncorrelated and $\hat{V}_{T+j} = Y_{T+j} - Y_{T+j,T}$,

$$\begin{aligned}\text{Var}(\text{vec}(\hat{V}^{(f)\prime})) &= (I \otimes X^{(f)})\text{Var}(\text{vec}(\hat{\Pi}_2'))(I \otimes X^{(f)})' + \Sigma \otimes I \\ &= \Sigma \otimes (X^{(f)}(X'X)^{-1}X^{(f)\prime} + I) \qquad (3.7)\end{aligned}$$

where $X'X$ and Σ (with typical element σ_{ij}) are sample values. Thus the variance of the forecast errors in the ith variable, for $T+1$ to $T+f$, is

$$\text{Var}(\hat{V}_{i.}^{(f)}) = \sigma_{ii}(X^{(f)}(X'X)^{-1}X^{(f)\prime} + I) \tag{3.8}$$

which depends on the variance–covariance matrix of the ith reduced form parameter estimates and that of V_i, and on all exogenous variable values.

On the other hand the variance of all forecast errors in one period, $T+j$, is

$$\begin{aligned}\mathrm{Var}(\hat{V}^{(f)}_{.T+j}) &= \Sigma(X^{(f)}(X'X)^{-1}X^{(f)\prime}+I)_{jj}\\ &= \Sigma(X_{T+j}(X'X)^{-1}X'_{T+j}+I)\end{aligned} \tag{3.9}$$

which depends on the variance and covariances of all $\hat{\Pi}_2$ and V elements, but only on X_{T+j}. Thus the forecast is always subject to an error which at the very least has a standard error equal to the standard error of regression. In addition the forecast error will have a larger variance the greater the variability of the estimated parameters and the greater the value of the exogenous variables. In other words, better forecasts arise from better fitting models, and those with a larger variance in X within the sample. Of course, exactly the same expressions, (3.7)–(3.9), apply when all variables are measured as deviations from their sample means. Thus, since the matrices in (3.7) are positive (semi) definite, the variance–covariance matrix of forecast errors is minimal (i.e. Σ itself) when $X^{(f)}$ contains the sample means in every column.[1] So the best forecasts are obtained when $X^{(f)}$ lies near the average of the fitting period. This explains why we stress that planning and forecasting techniques of subsequent chapters are reliable only when the model is used in circumstances not radically different from those at the time of its construction.

3.4.2 Confidence intervals

Although policy makers both in government and industry have an obvious need for point forecasts as described above, they also need a statement of the expected accuracy of those forecasts. There is, for example, a great difference between a forecast inflation level of 4% p.a. accurate to within 1% p.a., and the same figure accurate to within 10% p.a.

Continuing with the idealised model (3.6), we may estimate (3.7) by

$$\Phi = \hat{\Sigma}\otimes[X^{(f)}(X'X)^{-1}X^{(f)\prime}+I] \tag{3.10}$$

where $\hat{\Sigma}=(T-h)^{-1}(Y-\hat{\Pi}_2X)'(Y-\hat{\Pi}_2X)$ is obtained from the sample. If $V_{T+j}\sim N(0,\Sigma)$ then $\mathrm{vec}(\hat{V}^{(f)})=\mathrm{vec}(Y^{(f)}-\hat{Y}^{(f)})$ is normally distributed with mean zero and the variance in (3.7). Replacing Σ with $\hat{\Sigma}$ means

$$V^{(f)\prime}\Phi^{-1}V^{(f)}\left(\frac{T-h-g+1}{(T-h)g}\right)\sim F_{(g,T-h-g+1)} \tag{3.11}$$

from which confidence ellipsoids may be constructed. This is usually done by projecting the expression in (3.11) on the coordinate axes to give forecast confidence intervals as (see Hymans (1968))

$$(y_i)_{T+j,T}\pm(c\Phi_\kappa)^{1/2}\quad i=1\ldots g \text{ for each }\quad j=1\ldots f \tag{3.12}$$

1 A direct proof of this is in Pindyck and Rubinfeld (1976).

where $c = ((T-h)g/(T-h-g+1))F^{(\alpha)}_{(g,T-h-g+1)}$ for the $\alpha\%$ probability level, Φ_κ is the κth diagonal element from Φ, and $\kappa = ij$.

3.4.3 Restricted reduced form parameters

How far do these results carry over to the case where restricted rather than unrestricted reduced form parameters are used? We can assume that we start from consistent estimates of the structural coefficients. Then $\hat{\Pi}_2$ is a consistent estimate and, if $X^{(f)}$ is still fixed, we have asymptotically best and unbiased forecasts in the same sense as (3.5). $\hat{\Sigma}$ may still be used if it is obtained by inserting the restricted reduced form $\hat{\Pi}_2$ estimate. So (3.10) remains a consistent estimate of the required matrix. The optimality of forecasts remains intact for large samples. But, by the same token, the variance formulae (3.7)–(3.11) are incorrect for small T as the simplifications following the OLS version of $\hat{\Pi}_2$ no longer apply.

Since we only have asymptotic optimality, and consistent variance formulae at best, there is little to be gained by going for the correct expression to replace (3.10). It could, however, be computed by inserting

$$\mathrm{Var}(\mathrm{vec}(\hat{\Pi}_2')) \simeq J'\Delta J \quad \text{where} \quad J = (\beta^{-1})' \otimes \begin{pmatrix} \Pi_2 \\ \cdots \\ I \end{pmatrix} \tag{3.13}$$
$$\text{and} \quad \Delta = \mathrm{Var}(\mathrm{vec}(\beta \vdots \Gamma))$$

into (3.7) (Goldberger, Nagar and Odeh (1961)). To evaluate (3.13) requires consistent estimates, and an asymptotic variance–covariance matrix. One should also be aware that the variance approximated by (3.13) may not always exist (i.e. when $\hat{\Pi}_2$ is derived from two or three stage least squares structural estimates, Sargan (1976)). We shall follow this line no further. However, it is generally argued that the restricted reduced form estimates are preferable as they are more efficient and contain more information on the specification of the model. But that does presuppose that the specification (and estimation) is accurate for, if not, this reduced form is inferior.

3.4.4 The criterion for optimal forecasts

The forecasting method of (3.3) when $\Pi_1 = 0$ is justified on the usual grounds of minimum mean square error

$$E(Y_{T+j}|\Omega_T) = Y_{T+j,T} \text{ and } \min \mathrm{Var}((\hat{v}_i)_{T+j}|\Omega_T) \text{ for } \begin{cases} i = 1 \ldots g \\ j = 1 \ldots f \end{cases}. \tag{3.14}$$

On the other hand, the forecast error covariance matrix (3.7) is not necessarily minimised, except in the sense of individual variances. If one is more interested in some elements of Y_{T+j} than others, then it may be possible to do better than (3.14). In forecasting economic performance this must be the typical situation. Governments are nearly always more interested in what will happen in election years than in nonelection years. They are always more interested in targets than nontargets; for example, at the time of writing the British government is more concerned with inflation and unemployment than with the balance of payments.

The criterion in (3.14) may therefore look rather too simple, particularly with respect to the implied equal quadratic penalties on all forecast errors in $\hat{V}_{T+j}$. Some penalty function with different and time varying relative costs on prediction errors, such as $w = \sum_{j=1}^{f} E(\hat{V}'_{T+j} Q_j \hat{V}_{T+j})$ or perhaps a nonquadratic function $w = E\{\sum_j w_j(\hat{V}_{T+j})\}$, would be more realistic. However, (3.3) remains the optimal forecast provided w is symmetric about $\hat{V}_{T+j} = 0$ with continuous monotonically increasing first derivative; and the conditional probability density function of Y_{T+j} is symmetric, continuous and unimodal (Granger and Newbold (1977)).

The symmetry of the density function for Y_{T+j} has proved rather acceptable; normality is traditionally accepted for the random errors of an econometric model without much question. The symmetry of w is much more difficult. Indeed it is easy to think of counter-examples where to underpredict is significantly more costly than to overpredict by the same amount; such as in the danger of running out of some buffer stock. Notice however that the quadratic nature of the cost or preference function plays no role here. It is the symmetry, not the particular functional form, which may be the drawback to this criterion and to (3.3).

These are important points to remember when we come to construct explicit preference functions for policy evaluation in later chapters. Of course, the use of such a preference function is to assess the value of particular sets of forecasts, rather than to determine the technique by which they are produced.

3.5 Conditional forecasting: stochastic exogenous variables

Within the context of the above analysis, the first relaxation in the basic assumptions we can usefully make is that the exogenous values are fixed and known with certainty. Feldstein (1971) investigates the case where future exogenous values are estimated. The values are denoted by $\hat{X}$ (they need not be conditioned on Ω_T) and are assumed to be unbiased with covariance matrix

$$\left.\begin{aligned} E(\hat{X}) &= X \\ E(\hat{X} - X)(\hat{X} - X)' &= \Psi \end{aligned}\right\}$$

and in addition

$$E(\hat{X} - X)(\hat{\Pi}_2 - \Pi_2) = 0$$

which will be true if the errors in the process generating the exogenous values are independent of the errors in the process generating the Ys, which is only another way of saying that the Xs are truly exogenous. Unfortunately, this still excludes the important case of lagged endogenous variables.

Under these assumptions on the behaviour of the 'forecast' exogenous values, the endogenous forecast values are given as before:

$$Y_{T+f,T} = \hat{\Pi}_2 \hat{X}_{T+f}, \tag{3.15}$$

will still be unbiased since

$$E(Y_{T+f}|\Omega_T) = E(\hat{\Pi}_2)E(\hat{X}_{T+f}) = Y_{T+f,T}. \tag{3.16}$$

Indeed these conditional forecasts may be treated in exactly the same fashion as the unconditional forecasts of the previous sections since $\hat{X}_{T+f}$, rather than X_{T+f} itself, is now contained within Ω_T. Hence the conditional variances in (3.14) are minimised; and we have conditional optimality in (3.15). The unconditional forecast error covariance matrices, however, differ from those in (3.7) and following. Instead, the forecast error variances and covariances are now

$$\begin{aligned}\text{Cov}[(\hat{v}_i)_{T+F}, (\hat{v}_j)_{T+f}] = \hat{X}'_{T+f}\Theta_{ij}\hat{X}_{T+f} + (\Pi_2)'_{i.}\Psi(\Pi_2)_{j.} \\ + \text{tr}(\Theta_{ij}\Psi) + h^2\sigma_{ij}\end{aligned} \tag{3.17}$$

where Θ_{ij} is the (i, j)th submatrix of $\Theta = \text{Var}(\text{vec}(\hat{\Pi}'_2))$, and $i, j = 1, \ldots, g$. In (3.17) we have the (i, j)th element of the (f, f)th submatrix of the counterpart to Φ of (3.10). We can insert (3.13) or $\hat{\Sigma} \otimes (X'X)^{-1}$ as appropriate for Θ. It is straightforward to derive forecast confidence intervals for this case by inserting (3.17) for the corresponding element of Φ in (3.12).

The importance of these results is not just that the variances and covariances of the forecast error can be calculated but that they enable us to give an indication of the extent of error which is imposed by assuming that the exogenous series are known with certainty. (3.17) has two extra positive terms over (3.7).

3.6 Confidence bounds and the non-normality of forecast errors

The distribution theory derived earlier depended on the assumption of normality of the disturbances, since normally distributed disturbances give rise to normally distributed parameter estimates by OLS and hence to normally distributed forecasts if the exogenous variables take fixed values. That theory may be extended in an asymptotic sense for certain other parameter estimates. If, however, the exogenous variables are stochastic the forecast variable is not usually distributed normally.

The problem is that the forecast is now produced by the sum of the products of two random variables, $\hat{X}$ and $\hat{\Pi}$. The resulting distribution is complicated and not generally normal, although it might be approximated by a normal distribution. The difficulty is that then the construction of confidence intervals (and the implied tests) as described at (3.11) is invalid. Moreover, it will not generally be possible to derive the new distribution of the forecast errors; so it is not possible to construct exact confidence intervals. Nor is it possible to evaluate (3.11) as an approximation.

An alternative approach is to use Tchebychev inequalities to give outer bounds to the confidence interval, erring on the conservative side. The inequality is

$$P(|(\hat{v}_i)_{T+f}| \geqslant q\sigma_{iT}^{(f)}) \leqslant \frac{1}{q^2} \tag{3.18}$$

for any real number $q > 0$; and $(\sigma_{iT}^{(f)})^2 = \mathrm{Var}((y_i)_{T+f})$. That is, the probability that $(y_i)_{T+f}$ lies within q standard deviations of the true value is less than $1/q^2$. If we know that the distribution of the forecast error is well behaved in that it is unimodal and symmetric, then (3.18) can be replaced by

$$P(|(\hat{v}_i)_{T+f}| \geqslant q\sigma_{iT}^{(f)}) \leqslant \frac{4}{9}\cdot\frac{1}{q^2} \tag{3.19}$$

which makes the limits much closer but they are still on the conservative side. Details and further refinements can be found in Cramer (1946). Thus, by choice of q, (3.18) or (3.19) will give tolerance bounds containing the associated confidence bounds. In practice $\hat{\sigma}_{iT}^{(f)}$ will be inserted but this estimate, compared to a true value, is unlikely to affect such conservative tolerance bounds. The extension of (3.18) to provide the convex set containing the confidence ellipsoids of (3.11) is

$$P\left(\sum_{i=1}^{gf}\sum_{j=1}^{gf}\Phi^{ij}(\hat{v}_i^{(f)})(\hat{v}_j^{(f)}) \geqslant q^2\right) \leqslant \frac{gf}{q^2} \tag{3.20}$$

where $\Phi = \mathrm{Var}(\mathrm{vec}\ \hat{v}^{(f)'})$, and Φ^{ij} is the typical element of Φ^{-1}.

3.7 Forecast error variances with dynamic models

The most complicated, and unfortunately the most common, situation is the presence of lagged endogenous variables in the forecasting equation. The effect of these variables is to upset all the analytical results we have developed so far. The one step ahead predictor, given Ω_T, is

$$Y_{T+1,T} = E(Y_{T+1}|\Omega_T) = \sum_{j=1}^{l} \hat{\Pi}_{1j} Y_{T+1-j} + \sum_{j=1}^{k} \hat{\Pi}_{2j} X_{T+1-j} + \hat{\Pi}_{20} \hat{X}_{T+1}. \tag{3.21}$$

Confidence limits are thus easily established in exactly analogous fashion to that of section 3.5, since Ω_T contains Y_{T-j}, X_{T-j} and $\hat{X}_{T+1}$, for $j \geqslant 0$, just as before. The forecast error variance formulae derived in (3.17) apply.

Difficulties only arise when we come to consider forecasts further ahead since in this case we are introducing forecast values for the lagged endogenous variables. These are random variables with complicated distributions. Following (3.21), the forecast two steps ahead can be written

$$Y_{T+2,T} = \hat{\Pi}_{11} Y_{T+1,T} + \sum_{j=2}^{l} \hat{\Pi}_{1j} Y_{T+2-j} + \sum_{j=2}^{k} \hat{\Pi}_{2j} X_{T+2-j} + \sum_{j=0}^{1} \hat{\Pi}_{2j} \hat{X}_{T+2-j}. \tag{3.22}$$

The variance of the forecast errors in this case contains terms similar to (3.17) with, in addition,

$$\begin{aligned}
&\hat{\Pi}'_{11} \operatorname{Var}(\hat{V}_{T+1}) \hat{\Pi}_{11} + 2 \sum_{j=2}^{l} \sum_{i=2}^{l} Y'_{T+2-j} \operatorname{Cov}(\hat{\Pi}_{1j}, \hat{\Pi}_{1i}) Y_{T+2-i} \\
&+ 2 \sum_{j=2}^{l} \operatorname{Cov}(\hat{\Pi}_{1j} Y_{T+2-j}, \hat{\Pi}_{11} \hat{V}_{T+1}) \\
&+ 2 \sum_{j=2}^{l} \sum_{i=2}^{k} \operatorname{Cov}(\hat{\Pi}_{1j} Y_{T+2-j}, \hat{\Pi}_{2i} X_{T+2-i}) \\
&+ 2 \sum_{j=2}^{k} \operatorname{Cov}(\hat{\Pi}_{2j} X_{T+2-j}, \hat{\Pi}_{11} \hat{V}_{T+1}) \\
&+ 2 \sum_{j=0}^{1} \sum_{i=2}^{l} \operatorname{Cov}((\hat{\Pi}_{2j} \hat{X}_{T+2-j} - \Pi_{2j} X_{T+2-j}), \hat{\Pi}_{1i} Y_{T+2-i}) \\
&+ 2 \sum_{j=0}^{1} \operatorname{Cov}((\hat{\Pi}_{2j} \hat{X}_{T+2-j} - \Pi_{2j} X_{T+2-j}), \hat{\Pi}_{11} \hat{V}_{T+1}).
\end{aligned} \tag{3.23}$$

Even the first term here ignores the fact that $\hat{\Pi}_{11}$ is a random variable, so that (3.23) should contain yet more terms.

It is important to note that it is not the sheer complexity of (3.23) which causes the problems. Modern computers could evaluate the resulting expressions even from a general f-step ahead prediction from a full model, although one may run up against problems of expense. The real problem in evaluating (3.23) lies in the sort of information needed. The information necessary for the covariances in (3.23) is not, of course, produced at the model estimation stage; and there is really no analytical way of so doing when anything other than an unrealistically simplified simultaneous equation model is being considered. Estimates of the confidence intervals for the general dynamic model are therefore too complicated to evaluate for any but the simple case of a one step ahead predictor. The alternative is to determine those limits by stochastic simulation methods (this will be covered in Chapters 4 and 5) or to use asymptotic approximations. This latter approach is only valid for linear models and has been developed by Schmidt (1974, 1978) although there are similar results for time series methods, such as those due to Box and Jenkins (1970) where confidence limits are discussed, and these results have been extended by Yamomoto (1976), Bhansali (1974) and Broomfield (1972).

Nevertheless, none of these results shed any light on the distribution of the forecast errors. They can only be used in the Tchebychev approximation (or some other) when confidence intervals are to be constructed.

3.8 On combining forecasts

Confidence intervals may be important, but in dynamic models they are very difficult to construct. Moreover, the optimality in our forecasting theory is forfeit in such cases. It is here that the question of the gain to combining forecasts from different sources arises. Forecasting from an econometric model is sensible (if not 'optimal') from an economic point of view. It conforms to the perceived structure of an evolving economy, derived from economic theory and from the observed behaviour of that economy. It produces the forecasts which are mutually consistent both across sectors and over time; only genuinely exogenous variables remain (in principle) exogenous but a wide information set is used in each forecast; and it can capture the effects of structural shifts (and data revisions) elsewhere in the economy. But forecasting this way is not optimal statistically. We might produce single equation forecasts (for each variable) which, intelligently constructed, give statistically near optimal forecasts based on the restricted information set of past values. Granger and Newbold (1977) review the Box–Jenkins, and similar, forecasts of this type. But they do not necessarily conform to the known and observed behavioural patterns of the economy, nor to economic theory; nor will the forecasts be constrained to be mutually consistent. The information set involved in their construction is limited, and any information used, exogenous to the forecast variable itself, must be forecast without recognising that it may in fact have been endogenous to the system. Such forecasts are not necessarily economically sensible.

These are two different forecasting techniques, based on different information sets, each of which contains useful information absent in the other. One offers an economic input but lacks statistical properties; the other has statistical properties but lacks an economic foundation. When disagreements appear (as they often do) as to which is the 'correct' forecasting methodology, it is because of a confusion over which characteristics are appropriate. A combination of forecasts can often improve over either individual one by trading their information contents and properties against one another. If two unbiased[2] one step forecasts of Y_t, $\hat{Y}_t$ and $\hat{\hat{Y}}_t$, have error variances σ_1^2 and σ_2^2, respectively, then

$$Y_t^* = c^*\hat{Y}_t + (1 - c^*)\hat{\hat{Y}}_t \text{ where } c^* = \frac{\sigma_2^2 - \rho\sigma_1\sigma_2}{\sigma_1^2 + \sigma_2^2 - 2\rho\sigma_1\sigma_2} \tag{3.24}$$

is the best combination forecast, having the minimal achievable forecast error variance

$$\sigma^{*2} = \frac{\sigma_1^2\sigma_2^2(1 - \rho^2)}{\sigma_1^2 + \sigma_2^2 - 2\rho\sigma_1\sigma_2} \leqslant \min(\sigma_1^2, \sigma_2^2). \tag{3.25}$$

Equality follows in (3.25) only if $\hat{Y}_t$ and $\hat{\hat{Y}}_t$ are based on exactly the same information set (ρ is the correlation coefficient between the two forecast *errors*); e.g. $\rho = \sigma_1/\sigma_2$ etc. It is still worth combining them if one forecast is significantly inferior to the other even when their errors are closely related; e.g. when σ_1/σ_2 is large and $\rho > 0 (< 0)$ and large, one modifies Y_t^* away from $\hat{Y}_t$ (from $\hat{\hat{Y}}_t$) on the grounds that the latter 'is always wrong'; $c^* \notin (0, 1)$. The largest improvements occur as $|\rho| \to 1$ for, although each of the forecasts is hardly inferior to the other, the probable association of their errors (the sign and size of ρ) show which way to adjust Y_t^* in relation to $\hat{Y}_t$ and $\hat{\hat{Y}}_t$ if the probability of 'being wrong' is to be reduced compared to that in the component forecasts. Hence, the more the information contained in the components differs, whether producing related forecast errors or not, the better we can do by combining.

In order to use (3.24) we must estimate $\hat{\sigma}_1$, $\hat{\sigma}_2$ and $\hat{\rho}$. This can be done using the track record of the two forecasting techniques. Granger and Newbold discuss several possible procedures. The empirical evidence suggests that simple estimates (ignoring $\hat{\rho}$) may be best. Examples quoted there show that the standard error of inventory forecasts from the Wharton

2 The forecasts in this chapter have all been asymptotically unbiased. What follows is due to Granger & Newbold (1977).

econometric model can be reduced by about 60% on combination with Box–Jenkins forecasts (themselves improved by 35%).

It is also possible to combine several forecasts together, using a vector of weights

$$c^* = \Sigma^{-1} i/(i'\Sigma^{-1} i) \tag{3.26}$$

where $E(ee') = \Sigma$, $e' = (e_1 \dots e_p)$, for the jth forecast error e_j and the unit vector i. It appears that in practice only marginal gains are made in combining the third (or further) forecasts.

There is therefore considerable potential value in combining forecasts, particularly where optimal or near optimal forecasts are not available in practice (i.e. for almost all econometric models) and the information contained in the individual forecasts is very different. It is certainly worthwhile to consider combining forecasts whether they come from different techniques, as here, or from different econometric models, or from other more informal sources (including 'expert' opinion).

3.9 Forecasting with autocorrelated errors

Suppose the general dynamic linear model originally specified is (2.2a), but the structural errors obey the scheme

$$U_t = \sum_{j=1}^{q} P_j U_{t-j} + a_t \tag{3.27}$$

$$\text{where } E(a_t a_s') \begin{cases} = 0, t \neq s \\ = \Sigma, t = s. \end{cases}$$

As is well known the serial correlation structure of the error term causes problems at the estimation stage but it is not always appreciated that similar problems may arise at the forecasting stage.

Following (3.4) we can leave the model in the original variables and produce forecasts from the reduced form

$$\begin{aligned} Y_{t+f,t} = \sum_{j=1}^{f} \hat{\Pi}_{1j} Y_{t+f-j,t} + \sum_{j=1}^{l} \hat{\Pi}_{1j} Y_{t+f-j} \\ + \sum_{j=0}^{k} \hat{\Pi}_{2j} X_{t+f-j} + \hat{V}_{t+f,t} \end{aligned} \tag{3.28}$$

where the error term is included because we can now do better than merely using its expected value. Although $E(U_{t+1}) = 0$, $E(U_{t+1}|\Omega_t) = \sum_1^q P_j \hat{U}_{t-j+1} \neq 0$, and Ω_t contains

$$\hat{V}_{t-j} = Y_{t-j} - \sum_{i=1}^{l} \hat{\Pi}_{1i} Y_{t-i-j} - \sum_{i=1}^{k} \hat{\Pi}_{2i} X_{t-i-j} \quad j \geqslant 0. \tag{3.29}$$

But $\hat{V}_{t+f} = \beta_0^{-1}\hat{U}_{t+f}$ so, if $f = 1$, then by (3.27)

$$\hat{V}_{t+f,t} = \beta_0^{-1} \sum_{j=1}^{q} P_j \hat{U}_{t+f-j} \tag{3.30}$$

is the best estimate of the reduced form errors. If $f \neq 1$,

$$\hat{V}_{t+f,t} = \beta_0^{-1}\left(\sum_{j=1}^{f-1} P_j U_{t+f-j,t} + \sum_{j=f}^{q} P_j \hat{U}_{t+f-j}\right) \tag{3.31}$$

where forecast values of the error term have been produced by extrapolating (3.27).

The sole difference between (3.28) and the standard forecasting formulae (3.4) is that a 'constant', $\hat{V}_{t+f,t}$, has been introduced in order to take into account the predictability of a non-zero error. The forecast error variance follows the lines of (3.23) but will be more complicated again since $Y_{t+1,t}$ and V_t are now correlated.

In fact, even if the structural disturbances are not serially correlated the same points apply to any dynamic model, or one where there is some autoregressive structure in the exogenous variables. This is because in any forecasting exercise the residuals from the forecasting equations are serially correlated and heteroscedastic. Their predictability from past realisations can be used to correct each of the forecasts $Y_{t+f-j,t}$, on the right of (3.28), for that part of the forecast error which can be expected in advance even when $E(V_{t+f}) = 0$. Take for instance the linear dynamic model (2.6) with X_t known:

$$Y_t = \Pi_1 Y_{t-1} + \Pi_2 X_t + V_t. \tag{3.32}$$

Then $Y_t = \hat{Y}_t + \hat{V}_t$, where $\hat{V}_t = Y_t - \hat{\Pi}_1 \hat{Y}_{t-1} - \hat{\Pi}_2 X_t$ are the errors in the forecasts $\hat{Y}_t = \hat{\Pi}_1 \hat{Y}_{t-1} + \hat{\Pi}_2 X_2$, and where $\hat{\Pi}_1$ and $\hat{\Pi}_2$ are consistent estimates of Π_1, Π_2 such that $\hat{\Pi}_i = \Pi_i + \Delta_i$. Hence, since $Y_0 = \hat{Y}_0$, back-substituting yields $\hat{Y}_t - Y_t = -\sum_{j=1}^{t} \Pi_1^{t-j}(\Delta_2 X_j + \Delta_1 \hat{Y}_{j-1} - V_j)$. Now

$$\hat{V}_t = \sum_{j=1}^{t} \Pi_1^{t-j}(V_j - \Delta_2 X_j - \Delta_1 \hat{Y}_{j-1}) \tag{3.33}$$

is a moving average involving past values of V_t, X_t and $\hat{Y}_t$. As such, $\hat{V}_t$ must be heteroscedastic and serially correlated in any forecasting process for more than one step ahead.

Thus, given a forecasting error $\hat{V}_t = Y_t - \hat{\Pi}_1 Y_{t-1} - \hat{\Pi}_2 X_t$, expost forecasts at t, $E(\hat{V}_{t+j}|\Omega_t) \neq 0$, are available sequentially via (3.33) for $j = 1 \ldots f$. We cannot compute these conditional expectations exactly since the Δ_i terms are unknown. But if we did have them, we could improve $Y_{t+f,t}$ of (3.28) by replacing $Y_{t+f-j,t}$ with $Y_{t+f-j,t} + \hat{V}_{t+f-j,t}$ on the right;

or *equivalently* use (3.28) as it is and then insert a forecast adjustment $\hat{V}_{t+f,t} = \sum_{j=1}^{f} \hat{\Pi}_{1j} \hat{V}_{t+f-j,t} \neq 0$.

Nevertheless, given some idea of Δ_1 and Δ_2, we could, in fact, make an informed guess at $E(\hat{V}_{t+j}|\Omega_t)$ by inserting estimated values into (3.33). The informed guess would assign values to Δ_1 and Δ_2 from prior knowledge, economic theory, previous estimates of Π_1 and Π_2 – or, most important, from experience of how the economy actually works. Such a guess would also come from knowledge of any institutional changes or structural shifts which could not be incorporated in the model through reestimation. It might possibly be estimated by an observed $\hat{V}_t$ using the idea of sequential revisions to forecasts which was mentioned earlier.

The same points obviously apply, even if $\Pi_1 = 0$, when $X_t = P^* X_{t-1} + \varepsilon_t$ say, where $E(\varepsilon_t) = 0$ and $E(\varepsilon_t \varepsilon_s') = 0$, $t \neq s$. For then we can define the pseudo system

$$\begin{pmatrix} Y_t \\ X_t \end{pmatrix} = \begin{bmatrix} 0 & \Pi_2 P^* \\ 0 & P^* \end{bmatrix} \begin{pmatrix} Y_{t-1} \\ X_{t-1} \end{pmatrix} + \begin{pmatrix} \Pi_2 \varepsilon_t + V_t \\ \varepsilon_t \end{pmatrix} \tag{3.34}$$

which is of the same form as (3.32). Normally we get both cases together since future exogenous values are usually formed by some sort of extrapolation from the information available at the time the forecast was made. The extrapolation may be simply a linear extrapolation from the last available observation or it might be something more sophisticated taking in extra information, e.g. on anticipated government expenditure, or world trade.

We have now shown that the forecast errors are serially correlated whenever $\Pi_1 \neq 0$, or $P_j \neq 0$, or $P^* \neq 0$. In each case, we should make some adjustments to the forecasts in (3.28), in principle via (3.30) or (3.33). But it may be hard to make exact, or even realistic, adjustments with these formulae. In that case adjustments to the constant term for each forecast is an informal way of doing the same thing.

3.10 Forecasting with extraneous information

It is worth examining more closely the possibility of informally adjusting forecasts which has been thrown up in both of the last two sections.

The technique of forecasting from an econometric model has the appearance of a mechanistic process which has eliminated the role of personal judgement as far as possible. If the values of the exogenous variables were known or agreed then the forecasts would be reproducible by other econometricians. The evaluation of the forecasts from the model, and the comparison of the performance of different models, would be straightforward.

In practice adjustments are inevitably made to mechanistic forecasts for a variety of reasons. First, as we have seen, the input of values of future exogenous variables calls for considerable elements of judgement. Secondly, a change in structure of all or part of the economy may have taken place since the model was originally specified, Ideally one would want to respecify and reestimate the model, but this may often be impracticable in the case of large econometric models. Thirdly, an event might occur for which there is no provision in the list of variables. For example dock strikes, harvest failures or sudden changes in the supply situation caused by something like the oil price rises of the 1970s cannot always be fed directly into the model even though their effects may be quite substantial. Fourthly, nearly all published data are subject to revisions and sometimes those revisions are quite substantial for the most recent figures. As the latest figures are most subject to revisions, one is forecasting from an uncertain base and certainly any extrapolation of the figures could well produce inaccurate forecasts. The problem of data revision is an important practical problem which, not being amenable to theoretical analysis, is at present either ignored or handled in an ad hoc manner.

These four factors mean that either a revision of the model must be undertaken or some form of adjustment must be used. Often model builders are unable, or unwilling, to reestimate since, even if the model could be respecified, one would either use data which refer to the very short period after the change in structure, or take a longer time series which also included information on the behaviour before the change. The relationship so estimated will not generally represent the present situation but will be at best an average of the position before and after the change. At worst the respecified relationship will not fit, and neither will the old relationship. This sort of situation is by no means a rarity; the history of econometric models is littered with once rigid, reliable relationships which are no longer capable of producing accurate predictions.

For these reasons it is common practice to scrutinise the econometric forecast and where appropriate to make adjustments to the forecast values. These adjustments contain qualitative information which is usually a distillation of the forecaster's experience of the actual performance of the variable under study. Viewed in this light the potential information set is vast, and the number of ways of organising it enormous, but some of it is of a very informal nature. Thus the optimal forecasting theory is useful theoretically, but not as an exclusive mode of operating. Few forecasters have in fact judged these forecasts to be the best, given all the available conditioning information. Either the value of the constant term is altered (hence the term 'intercept adjustment'), or the error term is given a non-zero 'expectation' in the forecast (hence the term 'add factor').

There are several ways of rationalising this. First, the forecaster may regard his modified forecasts as a more realistic outcome of events. In this case there is no need to justify the adjustments because the role of the econometric model is to perform an accounting exercise. The initial forecasts are adjusted and then run through the model to find any incompatibilities. The adjusted figures are further revised and run through the model. The process stops when the adjusted values are simultaneously compatible with all the equations in the model. The forecasting exercise is a judgemental one (starting from a mechanical forecast) subject only to consistency constraints imposed by the model. An elegant exposition of this approach is given by Worswick (1975). But that forecast is also equivalent to a mechanical forecast, just with a different set of exogenous values and one can always adjust the constant terms to represent this.

An alternative interpretation, and the one we adopted in previous sections, is to regard the adjustment process as being open to analysis. One case is model misspecification, estimation biases, or a change in structure which means that the parameters associated with certain variables in the model are no longer correct. The forecast errors will then be correlated systematically. The adjustment is made by (3.33) when we have an idea of Δ_1 and Δ_2, or by (3.28) where the constant is adjusted to act as an informal predictor of the error term. However, estimation of the associated autoregressive structure is usually not possible within the information constraints, in which case an ad hoc version is used where the predicted error is the average of the last two or three observed terms. Examples of this appear in Evans, Haitovsky, Treyz and Su (1972). Another case arises with incorrect values of past or future exogenous, or past endogenous, variables. When forecast errors (or intuition) reveal such a case but it is not clear what the correct values should have been, the intercepts in the forecasting equations should be adjusted while waiting for improved estimates of the input variables to become available.

The use of these informal constant adjustments leaves open the question of how to construct them in a sensible and accountable fashion. Young (1979) describes various residual analysis methods, in which the adjustments are generated as the sample means of structural residuals, or as projections of simple autoregressive or time trends fitted to the structural residual (perhaps with dummies for 'special events'). This is equivalent to 'tuning' the model, which, if it is not to be misused, requires a strong prior notion of what its dynamic properties should be, or of what the outcomes will be. It requires both considerable experience with the model and familiarity with the economy. Osborne and Teale (1979) show to what lengths one can find oneself going in order to bring the forecasts back on line.

Perhaps the best justification for these informal adjustments is the simplest of all. They can merely be a representation of the modifications to the econometric forecast when it is combined with an intuitive or judgemental forecast provided by the forecaster himself (based on extraneous information). If no attempt was made to optimise the combination, and if the informal forecast was not formulated precisely, the combined forecast would appear to come from a constant shift in each equation. We have seen the benefits of combining forecasts can be substantial, particularly when the information contained in each is significantly different. So this is a case where combining forecasts is particularly worthwhile; model and forecaster together are more powerful than either individually.

3.11 Nonstochastic simulations

Simulation means solving a set of simultaneous difference equations. In this, simulation and forecasting employ similar techniques, and, in fact, we can treat nonstochastic simulation as a form of forecasting. We have called forecasting making the single best estimate of the future based on what you think is going to happen, and prediction the forecasting of what would have happened conditional on alternative assumptions in terms of the exogenous variables or the model's parameters. Thus putting several simulations together can provide a form of interval estimate of the future. Simulation is therefore a way of experimenting with the model to see the probable consequences of possible courses of action, particularly with respect to policy variables.

Simulation with the stochastic terms in the model is also possible. So we must distinguish two sorts of simulation – *stochastic* and *nonstochastic*. Stochastic simulation is where we simulate the model using a random sample of the stochastic terms, e.g. we might take 100 or 1000 drawings from $f_u(u_t)$ for $u_{t+1} \sim N(0, \sigma^2)$ and compute the density function $f_y(Y_{t+1})$, plus its mean, variance, etc. We might also take drawings from $f_\Pi(\hat{\Pi})$ or $f_x(\hat{X}_{t+1})$. From this we can assess the impact of the various stochastic terms; or rather the dangers of ignoring them by setting stochastic terms at their expected values. In view of the difficulties of obtaining confidence intervals this is the only realistic way of assessing the probability distribution $f_y(Y_{T+1})$. Stochastic simulation is for assessing the properties and performance of the model when analytic solutions are impracticable, and deterministic simulations do not provide the information sought. The robustness of the economy to stochastic shocks, or the construction of confidence intervals for a dynamic model, are examples.

In nonstochastic simulation X_t are no longer forecast values, but experimental values. That is merely to extend section 3.5 to the model (3.1), where alternative values of $\hat{X}_t \notin \Omega_t$ are used. Those exogenous variables which are not objects of the experiment are held constant or allowed to follow a neutral growth path which reflects the past movements. Suppose we wish to experiment with variable X_{1t}, then rewriting (3.2) we have

$$Y_t = \hat{\Pi}_1 Y_{t-1} + \hat{\Pi}_2^{(1)} \hat{X}_{1t} + \hat{\Pi}_2^{(2)} X_{2t}. \tag{3.35}$$

We obtain the simulated values of Y_t using the previous simulated values in Y_{t-1}, or the actual observed values if we are simulating an 'alternative' history. For each simulation, a new trajectory will be specified for $\hat{X}_{1t}$, $t = 1 \ldots T$. Several examples will appear in what follows.

Two points must be born in mind when interpreting nonstochastic simulation results. Equation (3.33) establishes that the forecast error variance generally increases with the number of steps ahead:

$$\text{Var}(\hat{V}_t) = \sum_{j=0}^{t} \Pi_1^{t-j} \text{Var}(V_j) + \text{other variances} \tag{3.36}$$

when V_j is serially uncorrelated (it is uncorrelated with $\Delta_2 \hat{X}_j + \Delta_1 \hat{Y}_{j-1}$ when out of the estimation period). Similarly expressing the forecast $\hat{Y}_t$ in terms of Y_0 and $\hat{X}_{t-j}$, $j = 1 \ldots t$, shows $\text{Cov}(\hat{Y}_t, \hat{V}_t) = 0$ if V_j and $\hat{X}_j$ are uncorrelated (asymptotically) and $E(\Delta_i) = 0$, for $i = 1, 2$. Then

$$\text{Var}(Y_t) = \text{Var}(\hat{Y}_t) + \text{Var}(\hat{V}_t). \tag{3.37}$$

Hence the behaviour of the actual and simulated series is not the same in that $\text{Var}(\hat{Y}_t) < \text{Var}(Y_t)$. This result extends to more general autocovariance differences between Y_t and $\hat{Y}_t$ as shown by Granger and Newbold (1977). So simulations (and forecasts) have in any case a lower variance than realisations. One should not be too easily persuaded of the precision of their projections.

3.12 Conclusion

Having identified the problems behind production of confidence intervals for forecasts it comes as no surprise to find that in general they are very seldom calculated. Most econometricians are content to report point forecasts, perhaps differing assumptions, and to leave the forecast variability unmentioned.

There are perhaps three reasons for this. Firstly, the theory has been developed using the linearities of the model. The exact analytical forecast bands depend crucially on the linearity of the reduced form equations. Secondly, the assumption that the predetermined variables are known with certainty is manifestly not true in general. Yet the confidence bands for dynamic models, with stochastic exogenous values, are extremely complicated. Thirdly, there are often, at least in the minds of the model builders, more pressing tasks. There is the undoubted problem of specification of the equations in the model, and there is an obvious reluctance to spend large amounts of computer time on simulations for constructing confidence intervals when there are still estimation deficiencies.

Despite these difficulties it is important to produce approximate intervals because policy makers need to know how much reliance can be placed on any forecast figure, especially if the forecaster is forecasting levels and the policy maker is reacting to forecast *changes* in levels. There is an obvious possibility for a forecast increase in unemployment to be compatible with an actual fall when the forecast variability is taken into account (and not necessarily with small probability).

Once confidence limits for the forecasts are obtained, the resulting forecasts can be tested. This is the subject of Chapter 5. If the actual observations lie outside the confidence limits then, apart from type I errors, the possible explanations are:

(a) Parameter values have changed
(b) Variance of error term has changed
(c) Variance/covariance matrix of the parameters has changed
(d) The structure of the economy has changed
(e) Exogenous variable behaviour has changed or was incorrectly specified
(f) Original model was misspecified.

We usually think of (a), (d) and (f) as reasons why a forecast would be incorrect but the others are equally valid in the context of simulation results. We have stressed the dynamic aspects here. The importance of getting the lag structure right (and forecasting is one way of testing this) is equivalent to paying more attention to the time series aspects of economic modelling.

4

The analysis of dynamic responses

4.1 Nonlinear models and stochastic simulation

Chapter 3 introduced the concept of deterministic simulation with a linear model by producing forecast paths of endogenous variables under various assumptions about the likely behaviour of the exogenous variables. Since any time path for the exogenous variables can be input, and also estimated parameter values can be changed, we are in fact experimenting with the model as a proxy for experimenting on the real world. We are, however, bound by the accuracy and specification of the estimated model. In particular, it must be remembered that the specification and estimation of the model depends crucially on what has been observed behaviour in the past, and as an approximation to the real world it seldom contains information about changes that are substantially different from those which have occurred.

The advantages of simulation generally outweigh any difficulties on this score. It is a quick, direct, and flexible approach in which any number of different experiments may be attempted with a given model. It enables us to investigate the effects of whole policy packages in one go.

Since simulation is essentially an experimental method it should be subject to good experimental design. The amount of information obtained will be dependent on the way the simulation exercise is attempted. This can be especially important when using large econometric models since they typically involve heavy computer costs, particularly where they contain nonlinearities. Details, and the application of variance reduction techniques by which efficient stochastic simulation studies are achieved, can be found in Kleijnan (1975) and Hendry and Harrison (1974).

The technique of simulation has more than one use. The principal headings are:

(1) The establishment of confidence limits for forecasts from dynamic linear or nonlinear models.

(2) The comparative evaluation of models to test their plausibility as a description of the real world.

(3) The examination of the effects of proposed policy changes, in terms of the size and timing of their impacts,
(4) The computation of multipliers, to evaluate the coordination and phasing of policy measures, or to assess the impacts on current and future targets of exogenous shocks.

Chapter 3 has covered topic (1) for linear models; (2) will be discussed in Chapter 5. The remaining topics are the subject of this chapter. Nonlinear models are also considered. The 'ad hoc' techniques of the previous chapter were introduced because the general dynamic analysis of a simultaneous equation model is difficult. We therefore start by analysing the dynamic properties of a model. This removes the necessity of treating only a few particular situations. We will be able to describe the effects of any given shock or changes in exogenous conditions, particularly policy variables, in current and subsequent planning periods. A rudimentary multiperiod policy analysis is possible.

4.2 Simulation and the search for policies

A simple and highly practical example of nonstochastic simulation as a method for assessing alternative policy packages is provided by De Wolff and Sandee (1959). In 1958 the Dutch Social and Economic Council was asked to consider the implications of a reduction of the existing subsidies on milk consumption and of increases in the level of controlled rents existing at the time, under the additional restriction that the existing policies on wages and prices should not be violated to any great extent. The simulations of the possible policies were carried out on the policy model of the Central Planning Bureau. At the time the government felt that it had six variables under its control for policy purposes. They were government expenditure, nominal wage rates (through an incomes policy), indirect taxes (containing the milk subsidies as a negative tax), wage and profit tax rates, and controlled rents. These instruments could, of course, only be altered within certain limits determined by what was considered politically acceptable.

The target variables were the balance of payments $(E - M)$, consumer prices (P_c) and the government deficit (S_g). By simulating the model with boundary values of the instruments based on past experience of policy changes, a set of conditional forecasts for the target variables was produced giving the feasible areas for possible policy packages projected onto the coordinate policy axes, marked A in Figure 4.1.

As a result of discussions and bargaining between the different elements represented in the Council it was felt that the boundaries on the instruments were too large; and the fact that the balance of payments was already

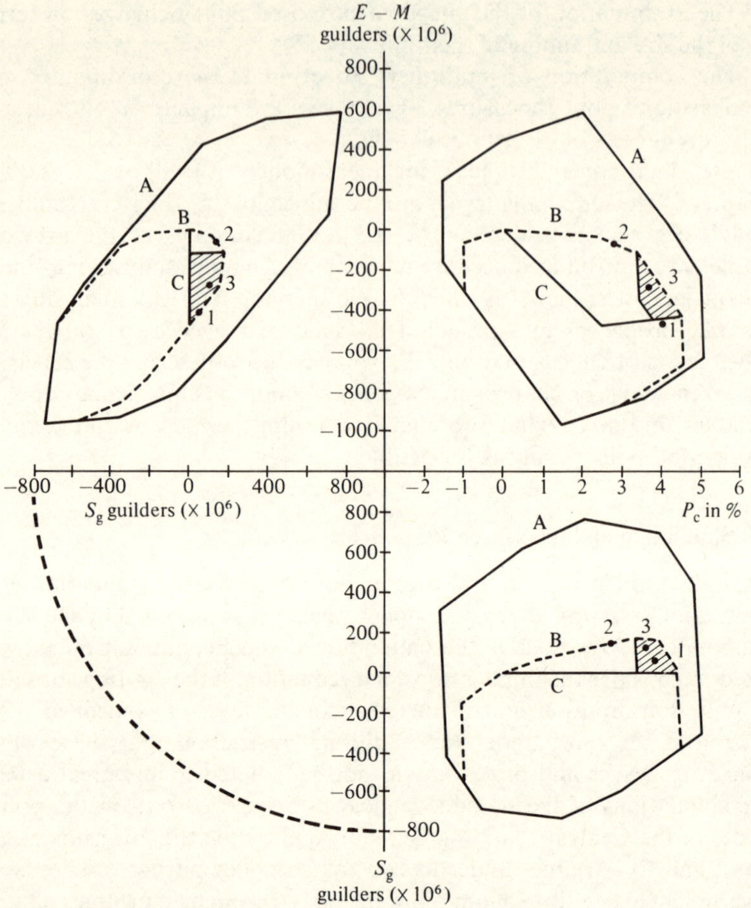

Figure 4.1 Feasible policy sets in Dutch economic planning
$E - M$ = Balance of payments
S_g = Budget deficit
P_c = Consumer prices

in surplus meant that any increase in taxation would be unacceptable politically. However, it was agreed that the reduction of milk subsidies and increases in rents could be passed off as structural improvements provided they were compensated for by an increase in wage rates. Simulating those restrictions gave area B in figure 4.1. Further restrictions were introduced by the government who stipulated no increase in the government deficit.

The simulations of the model with these further restrictions produced an acceptable area (marked C) for policy, much smaller than the original area except with respect to prices. But the Council could not reach a unanimous decision. The rent increase was agreeable to everybody. The abolition of the milk subsidy was, however, less popular; some wanted partial reductions, others none. Some wanted wage increases to compensate for the milk subsidy reduction, others wanted wage increases and then *extra* compensation. The common ground here can be captured by inserting restrictions on the instruments; rents and taxes up at most by 25% and 100 million guilders respectively. This gave the shaded areas of figure 4.1. Within these deliberations three distinct policies emerged:

(1) No decrease in milk subsidies, an increase in wages of 4% and then extra wages in compensation for the rent increase.
(2) No wage increase except for compensation for rent increases and milk subsidy reductions.
(3) In between these two extremes, half the members of the Council agreed on some increases in wages and compensation for rent increases and milk subsidy reductions.

Of these choices, policy 3 lies between 1 and 2, and only 1 and 3 lie within the acceptable area just constructed. 2 lay outside the area for every target variable though it was within a feasible area if the restrictions on instrument variations could be relaxed.

The lesson of the study is clear. Firstly, the discussions of the Council would probably have been better structured with the results of this simulation exercise. Secondly, a simulation exercise which is designed to produce optimal policy packages needs some way of discriminating between alternative packages. This, in theory, is provided by some sort of welfare function, a topic we shall discuss in greater detail in Chapter 10 with this example of interactive bargaining in policy selection very much in mind. Thirdly, policies are typically selected from a search to identify what is feasible and what is the acceptable common ground.

Notice that there are very clearly defined 'rules of the game' which each member of the planning body accepts by agreeing to participate in the policy debate. At each bargaining round, each planner has his own view of the acceptable policy set. Bargaining establishes a collectively acceptable set as the intersection of the individual ones. This new acceptable set is the starting point in the next round of discussions. Participation in competitive bargaining therefore implies a contraction rule, and thus ultimately provides a compromise decision.

4.3 Model forms: final forms

We started by assuming a structural form for our econometric model (2.1). That starting point is inevitable, since the model must be specified from economic theory by tracing the observed influence of one variable upon another – a necessary view for a complex system observed only at aggregated intervals of time. Since we perforce lack the ability to experiment with the system – indeed we lack the ability to design a satisfactory experiment – all our theorising and hypothesis testing will be in terms of the structural form, rather than on direct links between exogenous and endogenous variables, and their dynamics, derived from observed behaviour.

It is relatively easy to compute and compare the consequences of exogenous changes in a single equation. It is not difficult to deduce the stability and cyclical characteristics of a single dynamic equation. But in an equation system we must somehow deduce these things as a combination of the properties of individual equations. Fortunately (2.1) has a solution, the reduced form (2.3), where the intermediate steps between variables are substituted out. The immediate impacts of exogenous changes are exposed, which is useful for simulation and policy analysis one step ahead. But the full causality flows of the economy are substantially bound up in the memory of past events contained in the lagged variables.

We can solve the difference equation system (2.4) for any number of periods ahead in order to bring out separately the dynamic characteristics of the model as a whole. The result is the final form of the model. Here the intermediate dynamics (lagged endogenous variables) are substituted out, exposing the direct links between any given input variable, present or past, and the contemporaneous or subsequent outputs. All the delayed impacts of exogenous changes are made explicit. But it is still difficult to separate how much of the output behaviour is due to the dynamics, from that due to a particular realisation of input changes. For that reason we return, in Chapter 8, to another model representation: the state-space form.

Consider the development of (2.6) over T periods.

$$Y_t = \Pi_1^T Y_{t-T} + \sum_{i=0}^{T-1} \Pi_1^i \Pi_2 X_{t-i} + \sum_{i=0}^{T-1} \Pi_1^i V_{t-i} \tag{4.1}$$

in terms of the 'initial condition' Y_{t-T} which contains information on the endogenous variables from T to $T+l$ periods earlier. It shows the dependence of Y_t on all present and past exogenous variables and random errors, plus the start up conditions. To extract the same information for the current Y_t only, we take out the first g rows of (2.6); the remaining rows refer to lags in Y_t. Because each X_{t-i} contains lags, the impact of one period's exogenous variable is spread over k terms of the first sum of (4.1).

If we let $T \to \infty$ we have the final form. If Π_1 is such that $\lim_{T\to\infty} \Pi_1^T = 0$ we have

$$Y_t = \sum_{i=0}^{\infty} \Pi_1^i \Pi_2 X_{t-i} + \sum_{i=0}^{\infty} \Pi_1^i V_{t-i} \tag{4.2}$$

since the sums converge to a finite limit given finite values for (X_{t-i}, V_{t-i}). Otherwise the system is said to be explosive or unstable. Y_t is dependent on the entire history of (X_{t-i}, V_{t-i}) and displays the current and delayed impacts of exogenous variables on endogenous ones. The same is true for (4.1), for a restricted history and a start up condition. We define (4.2) as the final form; and (4.1) as the *T*-period final form. The way is now open for policy analysis.

4.4 Multiplier analysis

If we compute the final form (4.2), we can measure the impact of any exogenous variable, or stochastic shock, on any endogenous variable of the current or any future period.[1] Taking the terms in the summations in the same sequence as the index *i*, we get the impacts of steadily increasing intervals of delay. Finally as $i \to \infty$ we get the very long-run impacts. For cumulative effects we sum those impacts over *i*. So we can compute all the alterations to any endogenous variable resulting from changes of specified amounts in any exogenous variables. Nonstochastic simulations will provide projected outcomes conditional on specified future policies. We can therefore aim to compute sequences of policy changes to achieve more acceptable expected outcomes for the target variables, in which *all* the direct and indirect (immediate, short-run and long-run) effects are taken into account. And from (4.1) we can compare policies for their efficiency in achieving either of these objectives at successive points of time.

The key here is obviously the sequence of matrices

$$\Pi_2, \Pi_1\Pi_2, \Pi_1^2\Pi_2, \ldots \tag{4.3}$$

We define *impact multipliers* as $\partial y_{it}/\partial x_{jt}$, given t and for $i = 1 \ldots g$ and $j = 1, \ldots, h$. These multipliers show the instantaneous changes in endogenous variables resulting from a unit change in any exogenous variable. *Interim multipliers* are defined as $\partial y_{i\tau}/\partial x_{jt}$ for any $t < \tau, i = 1 \ldots g$ and $j = 1 \ldots h$. They measure the incremental change at τ in an endogenous variable $\tau - t$ periods after a unit change in some exogenous variable. *Dynamic multipliers* give the total effect up to some r periods delay; that is the sum of the impact and each interim multiplier to that point, $\sum_{\tau=t}^{r} \partial y_{i\tau}/\partial x_{jt}$. As $r \to \infty$ we get the *total* (equilibrium or final) multipliers

1 The appendix to Chapter 7 shows an efficient way to compute this.

$\sum_{\tau=t}^{\infty} \partial y_{i\tau}/\partial x_{it}$ for changes at t. Because of the stacking of lags in Y_t and X_t, impact multipliers may be read off as the (i, j)th element of the leading $g \times h$ submatrix of Π_2. Likewise interim multipliers are computed as the (i, j)th element from the first g rows of

$$\sum_{j=1}^{\min(k,i)} \Pi_1^{i-j} \begin{pmatrix} \Pi_{2j} \\ 0 \end{pmatrix}. \tag{4.4}$$

Dynamic multipliers follow from (4.4) summed from $i = 0$ to $\tau - t$, and total multipliers as the corresponding element of

$$\sum_{i=0}^{\infty} \sum_{j=0}^{\min(k,i)} \Pi_1^{i-j} \begin{pmatrix} \Pi_{2j} \\ 0 \end{pmatrix} \tag{4.5}$$

assuming $\lim_{i \to \infty} \Pi_1^i = 0$. But for analytic purposes, it is simpler to take those elements from the $g \times h$ submatrix in the top left position of $\sum_{i=t}^{r} \Pi_1^{i-t} \Pi_2$ and $(I - \Pi_1)^{-1} \Pi_2$ respectively. The multipliers are derived from the reduced form parameters and successive members of the final form parameter matrices.

Thus, in a linear model, the multipliers are independent of the level of economic activity, the size of changes in x_{jt}, t or τ. But they are not independent of $\tau - t$. In a nonlinear model, explicit differentiation will show each multiplier to be a function of the economic variables. This is easily seen from an analytic linear approximation to any nonlinear model. So in that case multipliers depend on the level of economic activity and the size of exogenous changes, as well as $\tau - t$.

4.5 Multipliers and policy evaluation

The definitions given above refer to once and for all changes in exogenous variables. Sustained changes can be easily treated by summing the multipliers over, say, p periods. For example

$$dy_{ip} = \sum_{j=1}^{h} \sum_{s=t}^{p} \sum_{\tau=s}^{p} \frac{\partial y_{i\tau}}{\partial x_{js}} dx_{js}. \tag{4.6}$$

Similarly by summing over i in (4.6) we have the total effects of changes in one instrument on some set of targets; but by summing over j we have the total effects of several instruments on one target, which is of particular interest because we can then examine the effects of policy packages as well as of individual policies.

If targets are combinations of endogenous variables, rather than single variables, we can insert that linear combination among the structural equations before evaluating the multipliers. Suppose the government wishes to aim for a particular budget surplus or deficit. We insert among the identities of the structural form $B = T^* - G^*$ where T^* = taxation and G^* = government expenditure. Then we can simply compute the multipliers as described, so that if $y_{it} = B$, $x_{jt} = T^*$ and $x_{kt} = G^*$ we have the impact effect

$$dy_{it} = \frac{\partial y_{it}}{\partial x_{jt}} dx_{jt} + \frac{\partial y_{it}}{\partial x_{kt}} dx_{kt} \tag{4.7}$$

and dynamic effects similarly by (4.6). As an example, Suits (1962) reports that for the Michigan University model of the US economy

$$\Delta B = 0.462\Delta T^* - 0.376\Delta G^* \tag{4.8}$$

By setting ΔB at its desired value we can find a wide variety of ΔT, ΔG combinations to give ΔB. Changing y_{it} to GNP in (4.7), Suits also found that

$$\Delta GNP = 1.304\Delta G^* - 1.119\Delta T^*. \tag{4.9}$$

So by setting a desired GNP value we can solve (4.8) and (4.9) simultaneously to give the T^*, G^* combination required. In this way we can aim to use policy packages to produce target packages.

Repeating these calculations for several time periods produces the Tinbergen theory of economic policy again, generalised to the dynamic case. Consider a planning interval of $t = 1 \ldots T$. Then (4.6) implies

$$\begin{pmatrix} Y_1 \\ \vdots \\ Y_T \end{pmatrix} = \begin{pmatrix} R_1 & & 0 \\ \vdots & \ddots & \\ R_T & \cdots & R_1 \end{pmatrix} \begin{pmatrix} X_1 \\ \vdots \\ X_T \end{pmatrix} + \begin{pmatrix} S_1 \\ \vdots \\ S_T \end{pmatrix} + \begin{pmatrix} \Pi_1 Y_0 \\ \vdots \\ \Pi_1^T Y_0 \end{pmatrix} \tag{4.10}$$

where R_1 contains the impact multipliers of X_t on Y_t and $R_i (i \geqslant 2)$ are the interim multipliers for $T - t = i$ of the same. $S_i (i \geqslant 1)$ are all the other effects on Y_i in period i, excluding any delayed impacts of the initial conditions which are themselves summarised in Y_0. Immediately we see that, if each X_t contained sufficient instruments ($h \geqslant g$), we could solve (4.10) for the required changes in those instruments to give a desired set of changes in targets based on some expected values for future values of variables in S_i.

4.5.1 The time profile of policy impacts

Multipliers describe the dynamic responses of any particular target to changes in some instruments. The time profile of these responses is of interest; some show a cycle with or without sign changes, some rise to a peak and fall back, while others converge monotonically to a new level of activity. The long-run effects are usually rather different from the

Klein's annual model of the US economy (1921–40) (Klein 1950)

$$C = 16.786 + 0.02\Pi + 0.225\Pi_{-1} + 0.8(W_1 + W_2) + U_C$$
$$I = 17.784 + 0.231\Pi + 0.546\Pi_{-1} - 0.146K_{-1} + U_I$$
$$W_1 = 1.599 + 0.42(Y + T - W_2) + 0.164(Y + T - W_2)_{-1} + 0.135t + U_W$$
$$Y = C + I + G - T$$
$$\Pi = Y - W_1 - W_2$$
$$K = K_{-1} + I$$

C = consumption, I = investment, W_1 = private wage bill, W_2 = government wage bill, Y = national income, Π = profits, K = capital stock, D = income distribution, T = tax bill, G = government expenditure, t = time (1931 = 1); and U_C, U_I and U_W are random disturbances.

impact effects. Naturally this information is useful for judging the effects of a policy, but it is more useful for planning a time path of that policy variable to achieve a desired sequence of target values. It is then but a short step to comparing two instruments for effectiveness in achieving some target values or trajectories, or to determine the correct moment to switch between policies.

Theil and Boot (1962) compute the multipliers for the Klein's model I (table 4.1). The first row contains impact multipliers, and thereafter interim multipliers. Total multipliers are presented in table 4.2. All these multipliers show damped cyclical characteristics with the cycle length of about 14 years; and all, but those for K, have roughly the same phase relationship. The endogenous variables are more sensitive to unit changes in T and G than in W_2. The damping factor appears to be quite strong. The initial signs are as we would expect. Increasing G raises all endogenous variables whereas raising T depresses them; and raising W_2 raises C and Y but depresses the rest. The cumulative effects are seen to be rather smaller but of the same signs as the impact effects.

4.5.2 Partially endogenous instruments

It is vitally important that the multipliers should be computed with instruments correctly specified as partially endogenous (variables and parameters) where appropriate. We have already shown how this can alter the multipliers and policy implications in Chapter 2, and argued that it will be of considerable empirical significance. Goldberger (1959) estimates the built-in flexibility of the economy as the proportional reduction in fluctuations due to the automatic stabilisers in the tax functions. The result is $\alpha = 1 - \partial Y/\partial Y^* = 0.35$ for the US economy using the Klein–

Table 4.1 *Impact and interim multipliers for Klein's model I (all figures are multiplied by 1000).*

Lag in years	C	Π	W_1	I	Y	K	C	Π	W_1	I	Y	K
			Unit increase in W_2						*Unit increase in T*			
0	666	−224	−162	−52	614	−52	−188	−1281	−204	−296	−1484	−296
1	−234	−160	−225	−152	−386	−203	−1014	−1026	−881	−894	−1908	−1190
2	−172	−80	−168	−76	−248	−280	−1006	−570	−954	−518	−1524	−1708
3	−79	−8	−76	−5	−84	−285	−543	−116	−516	−88	−631	−1796
4	6	45	9	48	54	−237	−28	235	−9	254	226	−1542
5	67	74	69	77	144	−160	368	441	384	456	825	−1086
6	98	81	100	83	181	−77	590	506	601	517	1107	−569
7	102	71	103	72	174	−5	641	460	647	466	1107	−102
8	86	51	87	52	138	47	561	344	563	346	907	243
9	60	28	59	28	87	74	403	199	402	198	601	442
10	30	6	29	6	36	80	218	62	215	59	277	500
11	4	−10	3	−11	−7	70	49	−46	45	−30	−1	450
12	−15	−20	−16	−20	−36	50	−79	−114	−83	−117	−196	332
13	−26	−23	−27	−23	−49	26	−154	−140	−157	−143	−297	189
14	−29	−21	−29	−21	−50	5	−179	−133	−181	−135	−314	54
15	−25	−16	−25	−16	−41	−10	−163	−104	−164	−105	−268	−51
16	−18	−9	−18	−9	−28	−20	−123	−64	−123	−64	−187	−115
17	−10	−3	−10	−3	−13	−22	−72	−25	−71	−24	−96	−139
18	−2	2	−2	2	−0	−20	−23	7	−22	8	−15	−131
19	3	5	4	5	9	−15	16	29	17	30	45	−101
20	7	6	7	6	13	−9	40	38	41	39	79	−61

(*Continued*)

Table 4.1 (*Continued*)

Lag in years	C	Π	W_1	I	Y	K	C	Π	W_1	I	Y	K
			Unit increase in G						*Unit increase in t*			
0	671	1118	811	259	1930	259	154	− 52	195	− 12	143	− 12
1	1170	801	1127	759	1928	1017	− 11	− 52	3	− 39	− 49	− 50
2	859	403	838	382	1241	1399	− 43	− 33	− 38	− 28	− 72	− 79
3	396	40	380	24	420	1423	− 31	− 11	− 29	− 9	− 40	− 89
4	− 31	− 226	− 45	− 239	− 270	1184	− 7	7	− 6	8	1	− 80
5	− 335	− 372	− 346	− 383	− 718	801	14	19	14	20	34	− 60
6	− 490	− 407	− 498	− 415	− 905	387	27	24	27	25	52	− 35
7	− 511	− 357	− 515	− 361	− 872	25	31	24	32	24	55	− 11
8	− 432	− 257	− 434	− 258	− 691	− 233	29	19	29	19	48	8
9	− 298	− 140	− 297	− 139	− 437	− 372	22	12	22	12	34	10
10	− 150	− 32	− 147	− 29	− 179	− 401	13	5	13	5	18	24
11	− 18	49	− 15	53	34	− 349	5	− 1	4	− 1	3	23
12	77	98	80	101	178	− 248	− 2	− 5	− 2	− 5	− 7	18
13	130	114	133	116	246	− 132	− 7	− 7	− 7	− 7	− 14	11
14	144	104	145	105	249	− 27	− 9	− 7	− 9	− 7	− 15	4
15	127	78	127	79	206	52	− 8	− 6	− 8	− 6	− 14	− 1
16	92	46	92	46	138	98	− 7	− 4	− 7	− 4	− 10	− 5
17	51	15	50	14	65	112	− 4	− 2	− 4	− 2	− 6	− 7
18	12	− 10	11	− 11	2	102	− 2	− 0	− 2	0	− 2	− 7
19	− 17	− 25	− 18	− 26	− 43	76	0	1	0	1	1	− 5
20	− 34	− 31	− 35	− 32	− 66	44	2	2	2	2	4	− 4

Source: Theil and Boot (1962), Review of the International Statistical Institute, 30, 136–152

Table 4.2. *Total multipliers of Klein's model I*

	C	Π	W_1	I	Y	K
W_2	0.536	– 0.192	– 0.271	0	0.536	– 1.025
T^*	– 0.569	– 1.237	– 0.333	0	– 1.569	– 6.564
G^*	1.323	0.965	1.358	0	2.323	5.123

Goldberger model, where ∂Y is the long-run change in GNP due to some change in an instrument and ∂Y^* is the same when tax yields are constrained to remain constant. In terms of impact multipliers alone $\alpha = 0.113$, so the automatic stabilisers take some time to become fully effective (the time interval is a year). The tax impact multiplier drops from 1.38 to 1.22 on allowing for automatic stabilisation.

4.6 Nonlinear models: simulation, forecasts and multipliers

So far we have worked entirely in terms of linear models. This was essentially for ease of exposition since linear models yield analytic results in general. The multiplier analysis, and the forecasting or simulation processes are obviously simplified by the fact that policy impacts are invariant to the time origin, the level of economic activity, or the size of policy changes.

But in a nonlinear context there are two issues: how to solve sets of nonlinear simultaneous equations, since there is now generally no analytic reduced form representation of the model; and, given that, whether the same forecasting or simulation procedures (particularly with respect to the stochastic variables) are still legitimate. We represent the dynamic non-linear model by

$$y_{it} = f_i(y_{1,t} \dots y_{g,t}, y_{1,t-1} \dots y_{g,t-l}, x_{1t} \dots x_{h,t-k}) + u_{it} \tag{4.11}$$

for $i = 1 \dots g$.

The procedure adopted for simulation in practice is usually similar to that outlined for the linear case. The extrapolated values of the exogenous values, the estimated parameter values, and the expected values of the random terms are put into (4.11). We cannot now use the reduced form to solve for the endogenous variables in these nonlinear equations. Instead we resort to the Gauss–Seidel or associated methods (defined in the appendix to this chapter) to compute numerical counterparts to the reduced or final forms. By altering the exogenous values we can generate any number of conditional forecasts, or multiplier evaluations.

4.6.1 Multipliers in nonlinear models

For nonlinear models, multipliers must be evaluated by simulation. If we want to investigate the impact of changing x_{jt}, in period $t \leqslant \tau$, on $y_{i\tau}$, i.e. $\partial y_{i\tau}/\partial x_{jt}$, we solve the model to evaluate $y_{i\tau}$ with and without some change δx_{jt}. The difference between the simulated value incorporating that change and the original 'control' solution is a measure of $\delta y_{i\tau}$. The multiplier is simply evaluated as $\delta y_{i\tau}/\delta x_{jt}$ which is a numerical approximation to $\partial y_{i\tau}/\partial x_{jt}(i = 1 \ldots g; j = 1 \ldots h; \tau$ and $t = 1 \ldots T)$ provided δx_{jt} is a small change. Naturally $\partial y_{i\tau}/\partial x_{jt}$ is a function whose evaluation depends on the levels of the variables in the 'control' (benchmark) solution of the model. Hence the problems which arise with evaluating multipliers in this context are: (i) that multipliers are dependent on the state of economic activity including the levels of y_{it} and x_{jt} as well as all other variables: (ii) the multiplier values obtained will be dependent on the sign and size of the change in x_{jt}. The fact that a nonlinear model's multipliers will depend on the 'control' solution chosen cannot be avoided; all we can do is to remember the effects. We are left with the difficulty of deciding on a suitable control solution which could represent actual sample values of exogenous variables. It is not enough simply to maintain the exogenous variables at fixed levels over the simulation period since that is neither plausible, nor does it elicit the dynamic responses to exogenous changes.

It is instructive, therefore, to see just how sensitive multipliers may be to levels of economic activity and the size of policy changes in a nonlinear model. We illustrate these points from an exercise by Morishima and Saito (1972) who constructed a ten equation model of the US economy for 1902–52. Since this is a very long-run model it can be specified appropriately in log linear form in order to capture the observed exponential growth. The economic targets are national income (Y) and employment (N); and the instruments real cash balances (M/P, where $P =$ prices) and autonomous investment expenditure (I). Comparisons are made of the relative effectiveness of fiscal and monetary policies in the different sets of economic circumstances which the American economy faced over this period.

We shall not comment on the realism of the model, nor on the realism of the implicit assumption that the government indeed has control of those instruments. Nevertheless, before proceeding to policy analysis it is necessary to validate the model – that is, to check that the model is an adequate description of the economy whose policy options require analysis. Morishima and Saito perform a series of tests on their model. They examine the ex post (1952–60) forecasting performance, and forecasted turning points. Throughout they (implicitly) compare their model's performance with that of the Klein–Goldberger model and the naive model which predicts no change. Finally they compare their computed impact multipliers with those of five other models. A detailed discussion of model validation techniques follows in Chapter 5; we need only draw attention to them here as an integral part of any policy evaluation exercise. The complete model may be written in a reduced form corresponding to (2.6)

$$\log Y_t = \Pi_1 \log Y_{t-1} + \Pi_2 \log X_t + V_t. \tag{4.12}$$

For impact elasticity multipliers we may pick out, from Π_2, the coefficient representing $\partial \log Y/\partial \log I$, $\partial \log Y/\partial \log M$, $\partial \log N/\partial \log I$ and $\partial \log N/\partial \log M$. Using the fact that

$$\frac{\partial \log Y}{\partial \log M} = \frac{\partial \log Y}{\partial \log(M/P)} \cdot \frac{\partial \log(M/P)}{\partial \log M} = \frac{\partial \log Y}{\partial \log(M/P)}\left[1 - \frac{\partial \log P}{\partial \log M}\right] \tag{4.13}$$

we can get values for $\partial \log Y/\partial \log(M/P)$, the impact multiplier for the real quantity of money on income, and similarly for $\partial \log N/\partial \log(M/P)$. To get absolute impact multipliers we note that, for example,

$$\frac{\partial \log Y}{\partial \log I} = \frac{I}{Y} \cdot \frac{\partial Y}{\partial I} \tag{4.14}$$

and by several substitutions from the structural and reduced form equations of the model we arrive at the multipliers of interest; in this case $\partial Y/\partial I = 1/(1 - 0.282\ C/Y)$ where C = consumption expenditure.[2]

In a similar way we get

$$\frac{\partial N}{\partial I} = \frac{1}{(1.107 - 0.312 C/Y)} \cdot \frac{N}{Y}$$

$$\frac{\partial Y}{\partial (M/P)} = \frac{PY}{M} \cdot \frac{0.16 C/Y}{1 - 0.349 C/Y} \quad \text{and}$$

$$\frac{\partial N}{\partial (M/P)} = \frac{NP}{M} \cdot \frac{0.16 C/Y}{1.107 - 0.386 C/Y}.$$

These multipliers vary with the average propensity to consume, C/Y, labour productivity, Y/N, or similar ratios, each of which will vary over time and the economic cycle. Taking a proportion of the labour force in employment (N/0.57L) as an indicator of cyclical movements, scatter diagrams of computed values of the multipliers (here reproduced for

2 The details are given by Morishima and Saito (1972). In this example I incorporates the 'autonomous' investment flows which finance the current account foreign trade gap; I is $I + B$ in the Morishima–Saito notation.

$\partial Y/\partial I$ and $\partial N/\partial I$ only in figures 4.2 and 4.3) separate into three and four distinct historical periods respectively, and show some obvious trends. $\partial Y/\partial I$ separates the first world war era (1902–29) from the depression period (1930–40) and the postwar period (1946–52). It shows a distinct tendency to rise and fall with unemployment. This tendency is apparent throughout, but it is weaker in the thirties and stronger postwar. In fact, the higher is unemployment the more effective is this multiplier for promoting expansion, yet less so when it was needed in the thirties than it was after the war, which may explain the different problems in managing demand which the planners encountered in those periods.

We can see that, productivity apart, the same pattern would hold for $\partial N/\partial I$. But productivity has risen on a long-term trend, with short-run fluctuations. It rises in booms and declines in depressions. Similar short-run fluctuations appear in the average propensity to consume (down in booms and up in depressions) which was responsible for the negative relationship in each grouping of figure 4.3. These two short-run effects reinforce each other to produce a more distinct separation of short-run

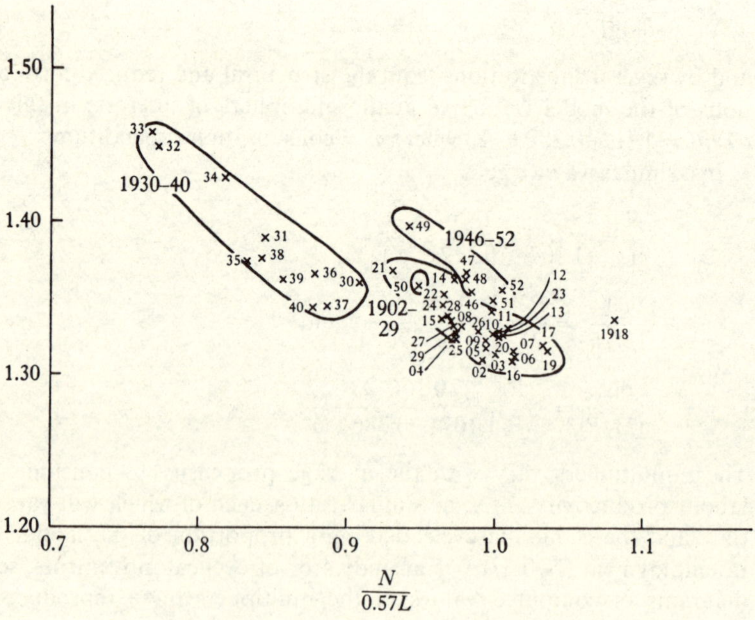

Figure 4.2 Scatter diagram of ($\partial Y/\partial I$) on ($N/0.57L$) of the Morishima/Saito model
Source: Morishima and Saito (1972), p. 40.

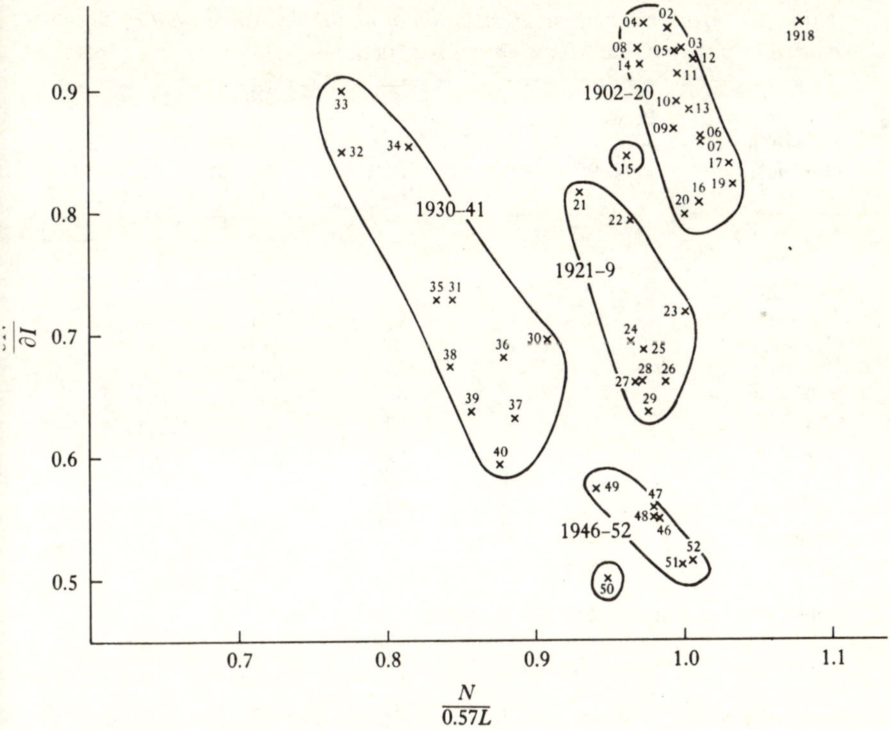

Figure 4.3 Scatter diagram of $(\partial N/\partial I)$ on $(N/0.57L)$ of the Morishima/Saito model
Source: Morishima and Saito (1972), p. 42.

behaviour (the negative relationship within each group) from long-run responses (the positive relation between the groups). The secular trend in N/Y, absent from C/Y, is in fact strong enough to separate a pre first world war era (1902–20) from the twenties (1921–9). Thus, the employment multiplier rises with unemployment, but its effectiveness has suffered a secular decline over the period. Not surprisingly, we reach the same conclusions over the difficulties of managing employment as we did for the management of demand above. It is interesting that both these conclusions on short-run (but not longer-run) policy effectiveness were predicted by Keynes.

A similar analysis of $\partial Y/\partial(M/P)$ and $\partial N/\partial(M/P)$ is also possible. That may be depicted in terms of the relative effectiveness of fiscal policies (as above) to these monetary policies, over the various eras identified. The average values of the ratios $\{\partial Y/\partial I\}/\{\partial Y/\partial(M/P)\}$ were computed

Table 4.3 *Marginal rate of substitution of public investment policy for monetary policy in the Morishima/Satio model*

Employment ratio in %	Period 1902–9	1910–20[a]	1921–9	1930–40	1947–52
75.0–77.4	—	—	—	6.59	—
77.5–79.9	—	—	—	—	—
80.0–82.4	—	—	—	5.97	—
82.5–84.9	—	—	—	5.31	—
85.0–87.4	—	—	—	5.14	—
87.5–89.9	—	—	—	4.92	—
90.0–92.4	—	—	—	4.39	—
92.5–94.9	—	—	3.82	—	5.40
95.0–97.4	3.69	3.77	3.80	—	—
97.5–99.9	3.49	3.68	3.69	—	5.29
100.0–102.4	3.42	3.48	3.49	—	4.82
102.5–104.9	—	3.21	—	—	—

[a]Excluding 1918.
Source: Morishima and Saito (1972), p. 45.

according to a classification into five periods and 12 different levels of employment – see table 4.3. It can be seen that fiscal policy becomes steadily more effective relative to monetary policy as unemployment increases (reading vertically) and also over time (reading horizontally), although individually both are becoming less effective (figures 4.2 and 4.3). Fiscal policy is relatively more effective in all cases studied.

Morishima and Saito go on to evaluate the interim multiplier counterparts to the impact multipliers above, but they do not establish if the above conclusions carry over to this dynamic framework. We now have rather more information than from a linear model, but one should always be careful in interpreting the results of policy comparisons. There is no suggestion that it is equally easy or cheap to arrange a unit change in either instrument; but if such a unit change is achieved then fiscal policy is more effective. Secondly, these particular conclusions are only relevant to impact multipliers; they make no statements on the dynamic effects. In that context the fact that M/P is a stock but I is a flow will make a difference since comparable policies would imply a sustained change in the latter but a once and for all change for the former. That sort of difference can be important. An increased budget deficit may be a powerful instrument but it has to be financed now and in the future. Finally, multipliers may show one policy to be more effective, but to determine if it is also 'best' requires some statement of preferences.

4.6.2 Nonstochastic simulation and nonlinear models

There remains the question of whether our nonstochastic simulation (forecasting, multiplier analysis) process is legitimate for nonlinear models in the sense of producing unbiased, and approximately optimal, conditional forecasts $E(Y_{t+f}|\Omega_t)$ for an arbitrary Ω_t. The nonlinear model case is difficult to analyse precisely because of the nonlinearities involved. But the situation can be illustrated by using a model which is nonlinear in endogenous variables but linear in parameters. This form has many applications since the most common form of nonlinearity to appear in models is that caused by price deflators. The advantage of restricting the econometric model to this type is that it allows a reduced form to be obtained.

The behaviour of the model under these circumstances is best explained by a simple example. Consider

$$y_{1t} = ax_t + u_{1t} \tag{4.15}$$

$$y_{2t} = b\exp(y_{1t}) + u_{2t} \tag{4.16}$$

where u_{1t} and u_{2t} are normally distributed with zero mean and serially uncorrelated with variances σ_1^2 and σ_2^2, then the nonstochastic simulation solution would be provided by

$$y_{1t} = ax_t, \qquad y_{2t} = b\exp(ax_t) \tag{4.17}$$

for given x_t, a and b. Then substitute (4.16) into (4.15)

$$y_{2t} = b\exp(ax_t)\exp u_{1t} + u_{2t}. \tag{4.18}$$

Now $E(\exp(u_{1t})) = \exp(\sigma_1^2/2)$ is a general result for lognormal distributions. Hence

$$\exp(u_{1t}) = \exp(\sigma_1^2/2) + u_{3t} \tag{4.19}$$

where $E(u_{3t}) = 0$. Consequently

$$y_{2t} = c\exp(ax_t) + u_{4t} \tag{4.20}$$

where $c = b\exp(\sigma_1^2/2)$, and $u_{4t} = u_{2t} + b\exp(ax_t)u_{3t}$ and $E(u_{4t}) = 0$. Equations (4.15) and (4.20) make up the reduced form of the model and $E(u_{4t}) = 0$; but u_{4t} is heteroscedastic with respect to x_t and is generally serially correlated.

This example illustrates an important general point. A deterministic solution based on expectations of random exogenous variables does not produce the conditional expectation of the endogenous variables. If we carry out a nonstochastic simulation exercise on the model as given above, it will not agree with the solution to the reduced form; setting $u_{4t}=0$ is not the same as setting $u_{1t}=u_{2t}=0$ in the structural form. We may set each additive disturbance, u_{it} of (4.13), at its expected value of zero, but that is only one component in each reduced form disturbance v_{it}; the remainder being within the right-hand side endogenous variables. If we aim for unbiased forecasts $E(y_{it}|\Omega_t)$ we should account for the fact that $f_i(E(u_{jt})) \neq E(f_i(u_{jt}))$; or equivalently we cannot just replace the right-hand side endogenous variables with their expectations in order to generate that for y_{it}. The same would be true for the estimates of the parameters being replaced by their expectations in a model nonlinear in parameters. And in the general nonlinear model we must necessarily work through the structural form. Thus, the multipliers cannot generally be interpreted as the model's 'expected responses'.

Both nonstochastic simulation and multiplier analysis yield values which cannot agree in general with historically observed values because the act of setting the error term to zero eliminates an element in the solution of the model. The importance of this point clearly depends on the degree of nonlinearity in the model and on the parameters of the distribution of the error term. One way out of this difficulty is to use the stochastic simulation technique described in section 4.7 below.

Despite the results indicated here it has been found that the differences between deterministic simulation and the mean of the stochastic simulations for a nonlinear model are not usually large. It would, however, be a mistake to assume that we could neglect the effects of nonlinearity. As Wallis and Salmon (1980) point out, the specification and estimation of most models (particularly large macro models) is biased towards linearity. Models are frequently constructed which are linear in parameters and are estimated using ordinary least squares (thus neglecting simultaneity). Secondly, inconsistent parameter estimates will cause prediction bias in both deterministic and stochastic simulation. In general we are unable to separate the error due to parameter inconsistency and that due to nonlinearity. In fact, using the standard techniques for testing and validating a model we may move away from the true model to one which performs better in terms of deterministic simulation.

4.7 Issues in implementing simulation studies

4.7.1 The representation of specific policies

A comprehensive simulation study which covers many of the uses mentioned at the start is due to Fromm and Taubman (1968). The object of the exercise was to examine some policy proposals by using the Brookings model. It illustrates many of the difficulties met with in the implementation (as opposed to the calculations) of simulation exercises for policy analysis. The main part of the study was an evaluation of the effects of the 1965 reduction in excise taxes, followed by the evaluation of alternative policy proposals by computing the relevant multipliers, both impact and interim.

One difficulty with studying a specific policy measure is that the policy changes may not be represented by relevant variables in the actual model. The change in excise taxes was no exception since the impact of the measures was not across the board but varied from item to item. The Brookings model assumes that firms use a mark up pricing mechanism but the extent to which the tax changes are passed on, and the point at which the tax is imposed, will have quite a large impact on prices. In addition, because the Brookings model is disaggregated as far as sectors but not down to individual commodities, implicit tax rates for the sectors had to be constructed from the information on each of the products affected.

The method for incorporating excise tax cuts therefore is to feed the effects into the price mechanism and then let the model allocate these effects on real disposable income, assets, etc., by means of deflators. However, the results of a simulation exercise are not always unambiguous. As exogenous changes such as population increases or technological advances appear, there is an exogenous growth in the tax base which implies that additional amounts of tax are given up in tax reductions, i.e. the effects of the excise tax reductions keep growing in the future. If this method of simulating the economy were being compared with increases in government expenditure, then in order to achieve a comparable effect the level of government expenditure must also be increased.

In order to evaluate the multipliers necessary for the policy comparisons we naturally come up against the question of the exact form of fiscal and monetary changes. On the fiscal side the tax yield is not a controlled variable. The variables under the government's control are the tax rate, tax allowances, and the size of tax bands. On the monetary side the interest rate is to some extent under government control and this affects the components of final demand by indirect action through the financial sector. In neither of these cases is it sensible to evaluate multipliers in the traditional way described in sections 4.3 and 4.5. The effects of a fiscal or monetary policy measure must first of all be translated into value terms, and then the multiplier can be evaluated. Fromm and Taubman define a real input multiplier as the increase in real output flow realised per constant dollar of additional resource input. This is an unambiguous measure for linear models, but not for nonlinear models where the impact on real output will depend on the values of the other variables in the model.

The effect of changing tax rates is to increase the amount of government revenue. These revenues, however, depend on the size of the tax base which is subject to change – maybe in response to the change in tax rates itself. We therefore have to consider a fixed tax base and define the impact tax rate multiplier on GNP as $\Delta GNP/((TP - TP')/PC)$ where ΔGNP is the change in GNP caused by the changing tax rates, and TP and TP' are the revenues collected from the *original tax base* at the old and new rates. The revenues are deflated by PC, the implicit price deflator for personal consumption before the tax rate changes. In any simulation experiment these quantities eventually settle down after several quarters and the value of the multiplier stabilises.

The case of changes in excise taxes is similar to that for income taxes except that the degree to which tax changes are passed on to consumers is important.

4.7.2 The use of 'control' solutions

A similar simulation study was performed by Klein (1969) on the effect of the 1964 income tax cut in the US. Once again the Brookings model was used with a tax sector designed specifically for the purpose. After the actual tax cut took place production and consumer expenditure grew and unemployment fell. On the other hand federal tax receipts fell as did net exports. Government expenditure grew. The problem is to determine how much of these changes was due to tax cuts, as distinct from other exogenous changes in the economy.

A 'status quo' or 'control' solution is produced by simulating the model with all the observed exogenous values and original parameters, except for those associated with the tax cuts. These are retained as before the change. The resulting endogenous series give the model's view of what would have happened without the tax cuts. A comparison of the results with a simulation of the model including the tax cuts provides a measure of their effects. Note that the comparison is not made with the actual *observed* values after the tax cut. This difference would be due to the effects of the tax cut *and* the errors in the model specification.

The results of the simulation show that the effects of the tax cuts are to increase GNP by some $10 billion over the no-tax-cut situation by the end of 1964. Unemployment is reduced by 0.5 per cent, consumer expenditure increases, as do wage receipts, and personal taxes fall. The simulations were then repeated on the Wharton model. A comparison of the assessment of the impact of the tax cuts from the two different models is, of course, only possible at the descriptive level. There are no theoretical statistical tests available for such a 'messy' problem where the models are so different in construction. Output changes are smaller in the Wharton model but unemployment changes are larger. It is, however, in the time paths that the models differ. The Wharton model predicts a larger initial gain in GNP but thereafter tails off, and it is the Brookings model which eventually produces the larger effect.

The step of a comparison between the simulation of two different models is an important one. The idea is to produce some sort of 'consensus' position from the results of different models. This is made necessary by the difficulty of testing any particular model. In addition, by comparing the results of different models we can learn something about their strengths and weaknesses and perhaps even why one model predicts certain variables better than another model. As a valuable spin-off we can make some evaluation of the performances of the econometric models and how they might be improved. This consensus position, of course, also underlies the combination of forecasts or simulations noted in section 3.8.

4.8 Stochastic simulation

As we have seen the formulation of confidence intervals for assessing forecasting accuracy is important. For linear models with a dynamic structure it is unfortunately a difficult analytic procedure with only asymptotic results to show for the effort. For nonlinear models even those results are out of the question. In these circumstances it is natural to turn to simulation methods. That is not the only use of stochastic simulation; we shall also see it being used to assess the performance of the model, to assess the reliability of certain policy instruments, and to look at their robustness. Considering (3.1) again, instead of setting V_t to zero we now generate a set of random values having the same behaviour as the observed series V_t, i.e. we generate a series having the same mean, variance and auto-covariance. When the model is simulated one of the random V_t vectors is added in, as in equation (3.1). This procedure is known as *stochastic simulation.* A new series of endogenous values is produced for every random number series we generate.

McCarthy (1972) shows how quick and easy generating the required set of random variables can be. If $\hat{V}$ is the matrix of equation residuals, i.e. it is a $g \times T$ matrix where T is the length of the estimating sample which has produced the residual estimates, and e is a $(T \times 1)$ vector of independent normal $N(0, 1)$ variates generated by the computer, then the residuals for a simulation are given by $T^{-1/2}(\hat{V}e)$.

The generated $(g \times 1)$ vector will give a residual for each equation in the model. Furthermore these generated residuals will have the same expected covariance matrix as the sample residuals. The method can also be modified fairly simply to obtain residuals which have the same *serial* covariance properties as the sample period residuals.

We can apply this same technique to provide random drawings from the probability density functions associated with $X_{t+j,t}$ and $\hat{\Pi}$, and which may have been estimated from sample data. Stochastic simulation studies may examine the effects of shocks from one, or all, of these sources.

4.8.1 On stochastic simulation results

An example of stochastic simulation which illustrates many of these points is provided by Nagar (1969). The simulation was performed on a condensed linear version of the Brookings model of the US economy.

The model was subjected to a stochastic simulation exercise of the form described over the period 1953:3 to 1962:4; a period which overlaps the estimation period. The disturbances were generated to be normally distributed with zero means and a covariance matrix which was the same as that produced by the residuals from the estimation period. In addition it was assumed that the disturbances were serially independent.

Twenty simulated values for each of the thirty eight quarters were obtained for the five variables, real GNP, real personal consumption, unemployment, real business gross investment, and real private residential construction. The mean, variance, maximum and minimum values for each quarter were recorded.

The mean stochastic solution (the estimated conditional expectation) was always near to the nonstochastic solution where the error terms are taken as zero. This should not be too surprising since the model is totally linear. Hence the difference in any quarter between the average stochastic solution and the nonstochastic solution is attributable solely to the generated disturbances having a non-zero mean for that quarter. If the model was nonlinear then this would not necessarily be true. One would probably be worried if the divergence between the nonstochastic and average stochastic solutions were too great but some divergence is certainly to be expected.

The simulated results also show that the quarter to quarter simulations tend to be unstable. The range of simulated values seems rather high and the changes from quarter to quarter are also rather large. These factors have two causes. Firstly, any major shock to the system, in the sense that a generated disturbance is large, is transmitted from equation to equation via the endogenous variables. In the real world, extreme observations tend to cause behavioural relationships to change and hence these shocks are often damped by temporary substitutions or inertial phenomena. This implies a temporary change in structure of the economy which the model, having fixed parameters, does not possess. Secondly, the assumption of serial independence leads to simulated values which can exhibit large quarterly changes. It is worth noting that Nagar found that prediction errors built up fast in these simulations. The model tracked well for the first 8 quarters, but by then the forecast error variances were large. It is possible to compute those variances and associated confidence bounds by direct stochastic simulations with a large number of replications; and this study shows that it is worthwhile to do so.

At the beginning of this chapter we noted that the results of any simulations were only valid if the values generated by the simulation exercise were of the same order as those observed in the sample estimation period. It is, however, fairly clear that in any simulation exercise of a reasonable size there will be some generated disturbances which will be large, particularly if they are generated to be serially independent. The results of a simulation in which large disturbances occur should obviously be treated with caution though the effects of a large disturbance may well be missed if the whole experiment is done internally in the computer with only a summary of results being produced. Nagar concludes that one should modify the simulation procedure whenever a large error, say in excess of two standard deviations, occurs. The modification in its simplest form would be to ignore the value and generate another, though if serially correlated disturbances are being generated this should not be necessary. In other words, one can only use a given model in a restricted set of circumstances. To go beyond those circumstances (represented here by extreme shocks) requires a new version of the model. One might regard any particular specification as a low order approximation to some more complicated 'true' specification.

4.8.2 Stochastic simulation and the reliability of policies

Further insight into the effects of stochastic simulation and the uses to which simulation can be put is provided by Haitovsky and Wallace (1972) This essentially was a study to compare monetary and fiscal policies by simulation with two macroeconometric models of the US economy, the FRB–MIT model and the Wharton model. A number of interesting issues arise which are principally concerned with the stochastic nature of the economy and the effects of different policies on target variables. Friedman (1953) has pointed out that if the link between the policy variable and the target variable lies through random variables then policies affect the stability or variance of the target variable, and policies which depend on reactions to recent observations (discretionary policies) may lead to increased instability in target variables. Stability depends on the degree to which connections between instruments and targets are random.

A second issue, that of the choice of instruments, depends on how that randomness is distributed. In a deterministic framework it is straightforward to assess the relative effects of different policies and to choose the one which is most effective. If the effect is not enough we use a larger instrument change. In the stochastic world this is no longer true – a larger change is likely to produce greater instability. The most sensible way out is to use a package or combination of policies which will have the desired effect even if there is only one target variable being considered. This is the way that most 'real life' policies are constructed, and it is easy to see why once one leaves the safe predictable world of the deterministic model. Haitovsky and Wallace choose as target variables the rate of growth of output and prices. These targets are achieved by using monetary and fiscal variables as instruments and these are brought into operation in a discretionary sense by the use of *ad hoc* policy rules which depend on the levels of unemployment and the rate of increase of prices.

The simulation introduces random variation in three ways:

(a) additive random error terms
(b) stochastic parameter values
(c) stochastic non-instrument exogenous variables.

The additive disturbances are assumed to be serially independent and the parameters are generated to be normally distributed about the point estimates with the estimated variance/covariance matrix (this is achieved by McCarthy's method described earlier). The exogenous variables are generated by a third order autoregressive model which had been fitted to sample data. The 'exogenous' instrument values are allowed to change on each run as dictated by the policy rules mentioned.

For each simulation, comprising 16 quarters, the parameter values are first generated, then the non-instrument exogenous values and the disturbances for each quarter. The model is solved for the endogenous variables quarter by quarter, at each point reassessing the values of the instrument variables in the light of the automatic policy rules established initially.

Growth rates in output and prices are computed for each simulation as well as the 'within simulation' and 'across simulation' standard errors. These latter statistics can be used to rank policies for their effects on the stability of the targets.

In addition a nonstochastic solution was produced and compared to the stochastic solution outcomes. In contrast with other studies it was found that the mean of the stochastic solutions was significantly different from the nonstochastic solution on a number of occasions, a possibility already noted.

4.9 The search for a policy recommendation

4.9.1 'Ready reckoners'

Multiplier analysis, in a linear model at least, is an alternative to nonstochastic simulation. Without solving the model for each possible exercise, we can examine the consequences of an infinite number of alternative scenarios in the exogenous variables. By referring to tables of multipliers for *unit* changes in the exogenous variables of the model in question, multiplying by the proposed changes, and then summing over variables and time, we can determine the effects on any contemporaneous or future endogenous variables. This is the technique for the design, and evaluation, of policy options used in the UK. Taking the current agreed forecast as a benchmark, deviations from that, resulting from a unit disturbance in each policy instrument individually, are computed for each target and each time period (see HMSO (1978)). Because the model is nonlinear these calculations have to be made by simulation. The result is a table of 'ready reckoners' (multipliers) which can be used in any desired linear combination to show the deviations thereby achieved from the benchmark solution. By manipulating these linear combinations, we endeavour to construct the most desirable set of deviations from the benchmark solution. Equation (4.6) showed such a linear combination, with the policy changes dx_{js} to be determined.

The advantage of this approach is that any number of options can be generated from one table of 'ready reckoners', and we need only multipliers of the chosen targets and instruments, a small subset from the solution of the full model (see table 6.4 below). Nevertheless, to obtain the multipliers in the first place is an extensive operation, and the quantity of 'ready reckoners' is still large given that they have to be manipulated by hand. This approach is rather clumsy for searching through all the linear combinations. It would be preferable to use some systematic and efficient search procedure to locate the best combination. This is the aim of the policy optimisation techniques described later.

Two technical problems are that policy selection by these means makes no allowance for uncertainty, yet that may have substantial effects. We shall consider stochastic simulation to resolve these problems. Secondly, in a nonlinear model the 'ready reckoners' will be dependent on the levels of the policy variables they are designed to select. An iterative approach in which the multipliers are periodically reevaluated is called for; but in practice this is seldom done. It is usually claimed that the multipliers are insensitive to those small policy changes acceptable to the policy makers. Certainly this has been claimed to be the case for the British Treasury model (HMSO (1978)). It is also claimed in Dutch economic planning. On the other hand, detailed analysis of the Dutch Government's planning model shows that for certain policy combinations this sensitivity was considerable, although that did not in fact lead to any significant sensitivity in the policy choices (Brandsma, Hughes Hallett and Van der Windt (1981)). Therefore, in practice, claims for near-linearity must be substantiated in each case, at least for a realistically defined 'acceptable' set of policy choices.

In the case of nonlinear models one extra caveat about the use of simulation and ready reckoner results should be stressed. One of the most common ways in which nonlinearities arise in the model (and the economy) is through asymmetrical responses. The result is that policy changes are not reversible; often an increase in a policy variable does not bring about the mirror image of a decrease in that policy variable.

4.9.2 The necessity of interactive planning procedures

Policy selection through an interactive bargaining process can profitably be refined by combining multiplier and simulation analyses. Economic advisors naturally tend to examine the consequences of candidate policies, and to select desirable policy values for some target, in terms of a model's dynamic responses. They will pick an instrument for its efficiency, per unit change, in achieving some target without awkward side effects. The necessary changes in that instrument follow directly; and, as we have seen, the same procedure applies to constructing policy packages for several periods by taking weighted sums of multipliers. But the less technically minded policy maker assesses the problems he faces, and his preferred solution, in the form of the simulated outcomes of various possible scenarios. This is partly because his function must be further removed from the technical details of any model, and partly because he must necessarily also be concerned with those judgemental factors which the model cannot capture (political issues, risk aversion, the value of intervention, coordination, confidence, etc.). Alternatives in the levels or variances of simulated trajectories, the reduction of fluctuations, and the timing of changes in those trajectories, are the natural currency of his discussion.

There is, therefore, a natural division between 'technicians' who understand the technical structure of the economy, and the statistical basis of their model, but have less grasp of the political and economic possibilities; and the 'policy makers' for whom the reverse applies. We emphasise this division by distinguishing, respectively, the feasible from the acceptable policy space. If neither party has a clear perception of *both* policy sets (and both are essential ingredients to policy formulation) then it will be necessary to confront a choice from one set with its evaluation within the other. Interaction is necessary to extract experimentally the requisite information for making a final choice. This necessity manifests itself in the traditional planners' argument that they must see what possibilities for policy exist before choosing between them; and in the function of advisors to provide the information to guide decision making, but not to make decisions. If this were not the case, then policy making would be a cold and mechanical process in which policy makers state the goals and the advisors provide the model. The rest is no more than arithmetic and switching on the computer. The continuing and increasingly sophisticated policy debate belies that view, which is both unnecessary and untenable even for the most fervent advocate of econometric models.

One of our chief concerns in this book is to present models as the means to conduct controlled policy 'experiments' so that informed and considered decisions can be made, but not necessarily from the range of options generated by the model and advisors. Reality, and the reasons just given, dictate that interactive planning is an inescapable fact, and that policy selection techniques must necessarily be set within such a framework. This we do formally and in some detail in Chapter 10, picking up the points made so far in this section. Of course we find more reasons there, such as the need for policy makers to discover experimentally an appropriate numerical specification for their relative preferences in a given situation, and the need to reconcile different preferences and different perceptions of the feasible choices between multiple planners.

The interactions of the De Wolff and Sandee example at the start of this chapter have become formalised in Dutch planning practice as an interactive procedure combining multiplier analysis and simulation. The advisors use ready reckoners ('spoorboekjes') to construct candidate policies and the policy makers react in terms of modifications to the simulated outcomes. The policy makers start by stating what changes in goals and instrument values, about an agreed central projection, they regard as favourable. Then the advisors (the staff of the Central Planning Bureau) build up their policy suggestion from the multipliers; the resulting policy changes are simulated through the model for presentation to the policy makers. The latter reply by indicating the alterations to the current suggestions which they judge to be improvements. Interaction then follows on a daily basis until a final suggestion is accepted. The planning horizon is 5 years, and the whole exercise is conducted with an (implicit) linearisation of the medium model about the central projection. We return to a formal model of this interactive procedure in Chapter 10.

Appendix: Techniques for solving large nonlinear equation systems

Since solving systems of nonlinear equations underlies most of the techniques discussed in this book, it is necessary to describe numerical methods for their solution. We review here some iterative schemes based on the Gauss–Seidel method. We look at its convergence conditions, and pick out some variants designed to exclude nonconvergence as far as possible while exploiting any potential accelerations.

Consider the nonlinear system

$$Y_t = f(Y_t, Z_t, u_t) \tag{A4.1}$$

where Y_t, u_t and Z_t are vectors of endogenous variables, structural errors and predetermined variables respectively. From now on we omit the time indices. A linear approximation to the endogenous part of (A4.1) gives

$$Y = BY + b \tag{A4.2}$$

where $B = (\partial f/\partial Y)_Y$ and b is a vector of predetermined elements including conditional expectations. A first order iteration, designed to provide a solution Y^* to (A4.1), is at step s

$$Y^{(s+1)} = G^{(s)}Y^{(s)} + c \tag{A4.3}$$

for an arbitrary start $Y^{(0)}$. The best known example of (A4.3) is,

$$y_i^{(s)} = \alpha f_i(y_1^{(s)} \ldots y_{i-1}^{(s)}, y_{i+1}^{(s-1)} \ldots y_g^{(s-1)}) + (1-\alpha)y_i^{(s-1)} \tag{A4.4}$$

for $\quad i = 1 \ldots g.$

In this case

$$G^{(s)} = (I - \alpha L^{(s+1)})^{-1}(\alpha U^{(s)} + (1-\alpha)I) \tag{A.4.5}$$

where

$$L_{ij}^{(s+1)} = \begin{cases} B_{ij}^{(s+1)} & j < i \\ 0 & \text{otherwise} \end{cases} \quad \text{and} \quad U_{ij}^{(s)} = \begin{cases} B_{ij}^{(s)} & j > i \\ 0 & \text{otherwise.} \end{cases}$$

$B^{(s)}$ is B evaluated at $Y^{(s)}$ and $c = (I - \alpha L^{(s+1)})^{-1}b$. The parameter α is subject to the user's choice. (A4.4) is known as the SOR (successive overrelaxation) method, but reduces to Gauss–Seidel if $\alpha = 1$.

The difficulty with (A4.4) is that the convergence theory is incomplete, and what exists can only be established by a limiting argument which has no real prospect of being extended. For a general linear equation system ($B^{(s)} = B$ all s), an $\alpha > 0$ small enough exists such that (A4.4) converges only if the roots of B are less than unity in real part. It diverges if $\alpha \notin (0, 2)$. These results are not operational since no results on setting α (or the equation ordering, which also influences convergence) are available.[3]

The difficulties in using (A4.4) are more pronounced for nonlinear equations, since its convergence analysis is iteration dependent. We can only say that for a neighbourhood about Y^*, and an interior point

3 All these results, and the associated convergence tests, are given in Hughes Hallett (1981).

$Y^{(0)}$, $\alpha > 0$ small enough exists to permit convergence if $B^* = (\partial f/\partial Y)_{Y^*}$ has roots less than unity in real part. Inevitably therefore SOR will be used on a 'hit or miss' basis without the possibility of a priori convergence checks, accurate accelerations, or even any guarantee that $Y^{(0)}$ is within the relevant neighbourhood. If convergence difficulties are encountered, it is unclear how they may be resolved. However, iterations formed by combining the acceleration

$$Y^{(s+1)} = \alpha Y^{(s+(1/2))} + (1-\alpha)Y^{(s)} \tag{A4.6}$$

with $Y^{(s+(1/2))} = G^{(s)}Y^{(s)} + b$, using $G^{(s)} = (I - L^{(s+1)})^{-1}U^{(s)}$, reduce the need for 'hit or miss' strategies. In practice it appears to offer almost all the acceleration of (A4.4) with an optimal α (Hughes Hallett (1982a)). This method is known as Fast Gauss–Seidel (FGS). It may prove important to exploit FGS as an acceleration of Gauss–Seidel; HMSO (1978) reports that the policy evaluation exercises conducted at the British Treasury were curtailed by the time and expense involved in solving their model.

Let $\lambda_j = a_j + ib_j, j = 1 \ldots g$, be the roots of $G^{(s)}$ where $i = \sqrt{-1}$. Write $r_j^2 = (a_j - 1)^2 + b_j^2, \gamma_j = -2(a_j - 1)/r_j^2$ and $\gamma = \min_j(\gamma_j)$. FGS is convergent (at each step) if and only if $a_j < 1$ all j. The optimal value of α is then

$$\alpha^* = \min\left[\min_k(\alpha_k \mid \tfrac{1}{2}\gamma_k \leqslant \alpha_k \leqslant \gamma), \tfrac{1}{2}\gamma_{k-1}\right] > 0 \tag{A4.7}$$

where

$$\alpha_1 = \min_{j=1\ldots g}[1 - a_j] \quad \text{and} \quad \alpha_k = \min_{j>k-1}\left[\frac{2(a_{k-1} - a_j)}{r_j^2 - r_{k-1}^2}\right].$$

There are two reasons for recommending FGS in place of SOR. The convergence theory is complete and operational for the general equation system; and we can set α automatically (that is without intervention by the user) as part of the solution technique, by using the information on $G^{(s)}$ contained in past iterates of $Y^{(s)}$. The latter step minimises the chance of convergence difficulties (unless $a_j > 1$, some j). That is important in nonlinear systems because the iteration matrix, and thus the convergence characteristics, vary with the iteration number. There is no other way in which our convergence results may be accurately applied a priori.

If (A4.1) were linear the iterates of (A4.3) correspond exactly to the steps in the power method for locating the eigenvalues of G; i.e. $\rho(G^{(s)}) = \lim_{s\to\infty}|y_i^{(s)}/y_i^{(s-1)}|$. If we assume a real dominant root and estimate its sign to be that of

$$(y_i^{(s)} - y_i^{(s-1)})(y_i^{(s-1)} - y_i^{(s-2)}) \gtrless 0. \tag{A4.8}$$

If the remaining roots of G are negligible α^* is estimated automatically as

$$\alpha_s = (1 \pm |y_i^{(s)}/y_i^{(s-1)}|)^{-1}. \tag{A.4.9}$$

The sign taken in (A4.9) is opposite to that found at (A4.8). The subscript i indicates that element of $Y^{(s)}$ which failed the convergence test by most. A number of variations on the theme of (A4.9) can be introduced. They are examined and tested in Hughes Hallett and van Sinderen (1980).

5

Evaluating a model's performance

5.1 Methods of evaluation

The concept of model validation is a very general one. The idea is to put the estimated model through a battery of tests to see how it performs. In one sense this approach should be unnecessary since a model is usually built with a specific purpose in mind; hence there will be an implicit loss function. However, this typically is not given and probably is never formulated. Instead we get a battery of criteria selected by the model builders themselves, perhaps in the hope that model users will find some measure which will suit their purpose. The criteria adopted are not always statistical because the complexity of simultaneous equation models is such that the requisite statistical theory is not generally available.

The tests used are, therefore, often descriptive tests and the model is said to be validated if it performs reasonably well on most counts. It is, however, quite possible that the model needs to be validated for certain characteristics only, depending on the purpose for which the model was built. It will be, for example, necessary to evaluate the forecasting performance of a model built solely for forecasting purposes, but its ability to reproduce realistic business cycle type oscillations may be of less interest. This latter property would, however, be required if the model was to be used for the analysis of stabilisation policies.

The untutored view of the model building process is that one takes the body of relevant economic theory, uses this to formulate the model, or models, and proceeds to estimation. All that remains to be done is to test the alternative models by using the standard statistical tests on each equation and to discard those which contradict the data, leaving the true model. This is too simplistic. Firstly, it is possible to produce several different models which are consistent with both the theory and the data when the standard statistical tests are applied. Secondly, the scope of these tests is rather narrow in that they typically are conducted on an equation by equation basis. At no time is there any attempt to take an overall look at the model. Every equation is treated separately in its own right, and often is estimated by itself. In a large model this is clearly not an optimal procedure since not all equations will be of an equal standard. The specification of some equations will be better than others because the requisite economic theory is clearer and better researched. The quality of data is also known to vary from variable to variable, both in the accuracy of measurement and in the definitional characteristic which determines whether the variable measures the quantity it is supposed to measure.

The previous chapters have shown that it is not the separate equations of the model which are of interest but the behaviour of the model taken as a whole. This must be investigated because it is quite possible that a model consisting of many equations (200 or more in the larger models) each of which, by itself, performs excellently, will either prove to be unstable or to have other unacceptable characteristics when considered as a whole. The techniques which have proved most useful in model validation come under the following headings:

(1) Evaluation of forecasting performance
(2) Multiplier analysis
(3) Simulation behaviour
(4) Frequency response characteristics
(5) Standard statistical testing

All these techniques, except perhaps for the last, also appear in other contexts. What remains to be done is to adapt the methods to model validation. The path typically followed is to assess the extent to which the model conforms with *a priori* notions about the behaviour of the economy, or if it is in agreement with other research findings. Otherwise the final model estimates obtained may simply have been the product of 'data mining'.

If a regressor variable in any relationship changes its behaviour from the sample period then this will produce incorrect forecasts if the variable enters the model in the incorrect functional form or with the wrong lag structure. Of course, the presence of mis-specification does not guarantee poor forecasts. If the behaviour of the regressor variables is the same as in the sample period then the estimated relationship will yield good forecasts even though the specification is not correct.

The idea that specification error might be responsible for poor forecasting performance rather than genuine 'changes in structure' is a point which is strongly argued by Hendry (1979). Evidence for this can be found in the time series literature, e.g. Granger and Newbold (1977) where there are a large number of examples of simple extrapolative time series methods producing better forecasts than complex simultaneous equation models. If a genuine change in structure had occurred then one would expect that extrapolative methods would suffer in the same way as econometric models.

This result is apparently the opposite of the result due to Pierce (1975) who showed that ex ante forecasts from an econometric model, where the exogenous variables are modelled by a vector ARMA process, have smaller mean squared error than the implied univariate ARMA model for the endogenous variables. Autoregressive moving average (ARMA) processes, both univariate and vector, are covered in Box and Jenkins (1970). However, as Wallis and Salmon (1980) point out, the result depends on a number of assumptions which may well not be true. Most importantly, the model is assumed to be correctly specified (and linear), and secondly an ARMA representation may not be a good one for exogenous variables since they often exhibit discontinuities.

The other source of evidence for mis-specification can be seen directly in the published results of econometric models where frequently there is strong evidence of autocorrelated errors. See, for example, the models reported in Hickman (1972) which account for the findings in Cooper (1972). Granger and Newbold (1977) point out that the econometric models reported in Renton (1975) frequently have R^2 values larger than their Durbin–Watson statistics.

5.2 Assessment by statistical tests

Early econometric models were small, parsimonious in parameters and linear. The reasons for this were partly the paucity of data (typically only annual observations were available) and partly the lack of computing power. In this environment t-tests, F-tests and Durbin–Watson statistics were the standard tools. In recent years more data have become available, especially with the advent of quarterly observations, and computing power has progressed by leaps and bounds. Along with the increased computing power have come the non-linear and dynamic models which are now standard. Estimation methods can be maximum likelihood, or variations on it, and this makes feasible a range of versatile, and asymptotically equivalent, tests of which the likelihood ratio test is the best known. The Lagrange Multiplier test (Aitcheson and Silvey (1960)), the Wald test (Wald (1943)) and the likelihood ratio test enable us to construct fairly complex diagnostic tests on non-linear models, phrased in terms of restrictions on parameters and without the usual normality assumptions. Coincidentally, advances in the time series literature have deepened our understanding of the ways (and importance) of specifying the dynamic form of the structural model and the possibilities (and necessities) of using more complicated error structures.

To cover this literature in full would require more space than we have available, but a few comments are in order. Firstly, the small sample properties of these asymptotic tests are not yet known, neither is their robustness to errors in variables given the finite samples which we have available. Secondly, although they enable one to test fairly sophisticated hypotheses at the estimation stage, there are areas where the economic theory is weak and the alternative hypotheses, against which the maintained hypotheses are tested, are often rather low in economic content. In fact, it is usually so difficult to formulate an alternative hypothesis, which is not so vague as to be meaningless, that the adoption of the alternative on rejection of the maintained hypothesis often produces nonsensical results.

Having made these points, however, it is clear that this literature has important implications for the initial specification and diagnostic testing of the econometric model. Mizon (1977) has produced a framework for determining the dynamic form of a model by specifying firstly a general model with many lags and then proceeding with a series of asymptotic tests to reduce the order of the lags until a satisfactory model is reached. Further work is proceeding in this area based on these asymptotic tests, e.g. Mizon and Hendry (1980). Sargan (1980) investigates further the dynamic specification of the model, and Godfrey (1976, 1978) looks at the specification of error dynamics. Breusch and Pagan (1980) survey the general use of the Lagrange Multiplier test in applied econometrics. There have also been applications of these tests to the choice of linear or non-linear functional forms by means of non-nested tests. General references are Pesaran and Deaton (1978), Godfrey and Wickens (1981), and the survey of Mizon and Richard (1982). If non-nested tests between two alternatives are used there is always the possibility that both null and alternative hypotheses will be rejected, thus indicating mis-specification but not suggesting what improvements should be made.

It is perhaps worth noting that nearly all models contain some fundamentally untestable hypotheses which give the model its special flavour. One model may be a 'disequilibrium model', another may be monetarist, and so on. Each model builder has his own persuasions and beliefs and these will be built in, untested, to his model. This is not necessarily bad practice but it carries with it the danger that the model 'finds' results which are the inevitable consequence of the assumptions built into the model.

Lastly, an alternative way of dealing with statistical testing in non-linear models is to linearise them. The full battery of standard statistical tests for model adequacy is then available for use on the linearised model.

These tests are now exact tests, rather than asymptotic; however, the validity of the chosen linearisation is unknown so the results may be no better than the asymptotic non-linear results.

Three general problems emerge from this approach: (a) most tests can be applied only to single equations; there is no equivalent statistical theory to cover the general model as a whole; (b) the distribution theory underlying the tests is only asymptotic at best; hence the tests may lack power with the restricted samples of economics; and (c) there may be considerable difficulties in formulating general alternative hypotheses which are both theoretically well defined and capable of being estimated with sufficient precision to make an adequate test.

5.3 Assessment by forecasting

In the absence of a fully adequate statistical testing framework for sample estimates of a model, an alternative is provided by looking at the forecasting performance of the model under discussion and perhaps comparing it with that of another model. Descriptive comparisons are necessary since the requisite non-nested statistical tests have not been developed; and in view of the results of Chapter 3 it is easy to see why. But there are measures of forecasting performance which can be considered in isolation. Unfortunately the straightforward comparison of forecasts from two different models to see which performs better is by no means an easy task.

Each model will produce forecasts for a fairly large number of endogenous variables, and it would be very surprising to find that one model completely dominated the other in all variables. It is, in fact, also uncommon to find that both models have the same endogenous variables or indeed that the same variables have identical definitions. In addition, the variance of a forecast series will be less than the variance of the actual series (section 3.11), which accounts for the often noted tendency of forecasts to underpredict boom conditions and overpredict in times of recession. Granger and Newbold (1977) also show that one would expect other differences between the actual and forecast series as their spectra do not have the same shape. The conclusion must be that the series of actual observations and their forecasts will not be directly comparable since they do not exhibit the same behaviour. Forecast evaluations should be seen in this light.

A second problem concerns the cost functions implicit in many of the evaluation procedures. Many of the measures are based on mean squared error (MSE) calculations, which imply a quadratic cost function. This may or may not be appropriate. However, any symmetric and monotonically increasing cost function will *rank* predictors in the same way.

The mean squared error measure, if $e_t^{(1)} = y_t - y_{t,t-1}$ is the error for a one step ahead predictor, is

$$D^2 = \frac{1}{T} \sum_{t=1}^{T} (e_t^{(1)})^2 \tag{5.1}$$

which can be decomposed into (variance of forecast error) + (bias of forecast)^2. Other variations on this measure include mean absolute error (MAE) which is defined as

$$MAE = \frac{1}{T} \sum_{t=1}^{T} |e_t^{(1)}|. \tag{5.2}$$

Since most methods of evaluation of a set of forecasts depend on the comparison of the forecasts with the subsequent actual observations it is not surprising that many researchers (Mincer and Zarnowitz (1969), Theil (1961) and Klein (1971)) should suggest plotting a scatter diagram, or that the relationship

$$y_t = \alpha + \beta f_t + e_t \tag{5.3}$$

(where $f_t = y_{t,t-1}$) should be estimated by least squares. For consistent estimates we must be able to assume that f_t and e_t are uncorrelated, which will be true for optimal forecasts, but will not be true in most practical forecasting exercises. Secondly, we need the assumption that e_t is not serially correlated, which is also generally not true (shown in section 3.9). So that the parameter estimates in (5.3) and their associated standard errors will be biased.

The indication of a good set of forecasts is obviously $\alpha = 0$ and $\beta = 1$ (the so-called 'line of perfect forecasts'). In view of properties of their parameter estimates this hypothesis cannot be tested and in any event the condition $\alpha = 0$, $\beta = 1$ can only be considered a necessary, not sufficient, condition for forecast efficiency (see Hatanaka (1974)). On a descriptive level, if the estimated coefficients are significantly different from these values there are then the following possibilities. Firstly, if $\alpha = 0$ is rejected but not $\beta = 1$, then the forecasts are subject to a constant bias of α. A constant adjustment correction could easily be made to the forecasts. Secondly, if $\beta = 1$ is rejected but not $\alpha = 0$, then the forecasts are proportionately biased. This failing would have to be corrected by a multiplicative factor and suggests that one should look again at some of the parameter values in the equation producing the forecast. In general, however, the results are not at all informative about ways of improving the forecasts. This analysis can be extended to forecasts with any lead time, though in this case even optimal forecasts will produce autocorrelated errors (Box and Jenkins (1970)).

A different way to look at the above analysis is to use the expected squared forecast error, which can be written as

$$E(y_t - f_t)^2 = (\mu_y - \mu_f)^2 + (\sigma_f - \rho\sigma_y)^2 + (1 - \rho^2)\sigma_y^2 \tag{5.4}$$

where ρ is the correlation between y_t and f_t. Since the y_t series is given, the object is to choose a forecast series f_t which minimises the expected squared error. This will be achieved by finding a series f_t for which ρ is as large as possible and where

$$\mu_f = \mu_y \text{ and } \sigma_f = \rho\sigma_y \tag{5.5a, b}$$

These two conditions are exactly those conditions which make $\alpha = 0$, $\beta = 1$; and in addition the second condition shows again that the forecast variance is necessarily less than the series variance. It should be noted that finding a forecast series with a high correlation coefficient with y_t is not sufficient for defining a good forecast. We need, in addition, the condition (5.5a).

Other methods of testing a forecast series using the mean squared error approach are due to Theil (1961). The mean squared error can be estimated as

$$D_T^2 = (\bar{y} - \bar{\hat{y}})^2 + (S_{\hat{y}} - rS_y)^2 + (1 - r^2)S_y^2 \tag{5.6}$$

where $\bar{y}$ and $\bar{\hat{y}}$ are the sample means of the series and its forecast, S_y and $S_{\hat{y}}$ are the sample standard deviations and r is the sample correlation coefficient between the two series.

The purpose of this formula is to show the mean squared error comprises three parts representing the bias, variance and covariance components. If any of these represent a large part of the MSE then this is the factor which is causing error in the forecast series. The suggestion is that the optimal forecast is one for which the first two components tend to zero. It has, however, been pointed out by Jorgenson, Hunter and Nadiri (1970) that this is not appropriate for the decomposition (5.6). We saw in Chapter 3 that for the reduced form

$$Y_t = \Pi_2 X_t + V_t \tag{5.7}$$

the optimal forecast is

$$Y_{t+f,t} = \hat{\Pi}_2 X_{t+f} \tag{5.8}$$

where $\hat{\Pi}_2$ is the OLS estimator, and the forecast error in $(y_i)_{t+f}$ has expectation zero and variance

$$\sigma_{ii}^2[I + X_{t+f}(X'X)^{-1}X'_{t+f}].$$

In addition, the mean value of $e_f = (y_i)_{t+f} - (y_i)_{t+f,t}$ is

$$\bar{e}_f = e'_f \iota / f$$

where ι is the column vector with each element unity.

Hence $$E(\bar{e}_f^2) = \iota'[I + X_{t+f}(X'X)^{-1}X'_{t+f}]\iota\sigma_{ii}^2/f \tag{5.9}$$

using (3.8), where f observations on y_i have been forecasted.

The bias component of Theil's decomposition has expectation different from zero – in fact this expectation is greater than σ^2/f and increases with the distance of X_{t+f} from the mean of the sample values of the exogenous variables. Hence, even for the unique, minimum variance, unbiased linear predictor there is no reason for the bias component to be zero.

Secondly, one would not expect there to be equality between the variance components of the actual and predicted series because, as we have seen, it is not possible to get that equality. Granger and Newbold (1977) give a specific example of a first order autoregressive series $z_t = \alpha z_{t-1} + u_t$ which has optimal predictor $\hat{z}_{t+1} = \alpha z_t$. It then follows that the variance component is $((1-\alpha)/(1+\alpha))D_T^2$ which can take any value as $-1 < \alpha < 1$.

The conclusion must be that the decompositions which Theil suggests are probably misleading.

Other methods of forecast evaluation centre round statistics constructed from the mean squared error. Theil's inequality coefficient is such a statistic and is defined in Theil (1961) as

$$U_1 = D_T \Big/ \left[\left(\frac{1}{T} \sum f_t^2 \right)^{1/2} + \left(\frac{1}{T} \sum y_t^2 \right)^{1/2} \right]. \tag{5.10}$$

According to (5.10) the best forecast is a predicted series which minimises U_1. The unfortunate aspect of this measure is that U_1 is made smaller by choosing a predicted series with a large variance, and is therefore capable of producing misleading results. The situation would not arise if we were dealing with optimal forecasts where the error terms are uncorrelated with the forecasts since here the predicted variance is bounded above by the actual series variance. If the error terms are correlated with the forecasts there are no such restrictions.

Another statistic suggested by Theil is

$$U_2^2 = D_T^2 \Big/ \frac{1}{T} \sum (y_t - y_{t-1})^2 \tag{5.11}$$

which is intended to test the accuracy of the forecast (measured by D_T^2) against the accuracy of the 'naive' 'no change' predictor, i.e. $y_{t,t-1} = y_{t-1}$

(measured by the denominator). Of course, there is no reason why one should stop at this 'naive' predictor. There are many other equally plausible alternatives

e.g. $$\Delta y_{t,t-1} = \Delta y_{t-1} \tag{5.12}$$

or $$\Delta y_{t,t-1} = y_{t-1} - \alpha y_{t-2} \tag{5.13}$$

and indeed the net has been cast still wider by comparing forecasts with autoregressive models and Box – Jenkins autoregressive moving average models, although these could no longer be called naive since they involve fairly detailed specification and estimation procedures. Similar suggestions have been made by Mincer and Zarnowitz (1969).

Unfortunately, although this sort of test is fairly easy to apply and although it carries the implication of a fairly desirable feature – namely that if the econometric forecast cannot do better than a naive forecast then it is not much good – there is no indication of the steps one should take if the forecast does worse than the naive forecast, nor is it clear exactly what has been gained if it proves to be superior.

We have suggested looking at a combination of the forecast and the naive forecast to see whether an optimal combination improves the forecast. If $f_t^{(1)}$ is the model forecast and $f_t^{(2)}$ is the naive forecast then the combined forecast is $y_t = cf_t^{(1)} + (1-c)f_t^{(2)} + e_t$ and the value of c can be determined by ordinary least squares and tested for significance. If c is significantly different from 1 then the naive forecast has added some worthwhile information to the original forecast and hence helps to indicate the ways in which the original model could be improved.

The general conclusion must be that the descriptive methods for evaluating forecasts leave much to be desired. Although easy to apply and superficially appealing they should be treated with extreme caution.

Secondly, there is no general possibility of rigorous statistical testing here. The best we can do is to check that actual values stay within the tolerance bounds about the forecast values which were derived in Chapter 3. This makes a kind of structural stability test.

There is still the question of what role intercept adjustments should be allowed to play in these forecast tests. Suppose now that the full sample was used for estimation, ex ante forecasts made with the model, and after a few time periods actual observations, both of the endogenous and exogenous variables, become available enabling ex post forecasts to be made for this period. We would expect the ex post forecast to differ from the ex ante forecast for any one *or more* of the following reasons:

(1) the ex ante exogenous variable values were incorrectly assessed at the time the forecast was made,

(2) the forecast has an influence on policy management; hence ex ante forecasts produce policy changes which result in new exogenous values,
(3) ex ante forecasts are subject to intercept adjustment, often on a subjective basis.

This third point is the one which causes most difficulty. Having used the correct exogenous values to produce the ex post forecasts any subjective ex post intercept adjustment is not feasible since the actual endogenous variable values are known. Three different forecast series are then possible: firstly, the straight ex post forecasts; secondly, the ex post forecasts with mechanical intercept adjustments designed to cope with non-zero error processes due to serial correlation or biased forecasts; and, thirdly, ex post forecasts with intercept adjustments of the ex ante forecasts. The last of these options should prove to be the optimal procedure if the original intercept adjustments were made to take into account events for which there was no provision in the variables in the model. If, however, the econometrician used the intercept adjustment procedure to achieve an endogenous value which he considers appropriate, i.e. he has an idea in advance of the value of the endogenous variable he wishes to obtain, then the procedure will obviously not be optimal. In an interesting study Evans, Haitovsky and Treyz (1972) analyse these possibilities using the Wharton and OBE econometric models and reach some rather disturbing conclusions. The true ex ante forecasts (i.e. the ex ante forecasts with the relevant adjustment) are often found to be superior to the ex post forecasts (which use the true exogenous values) in all the three forms outlined above. That is, the true ex ante forecasts are superior to the mechanical ex post forecasts, the ex post forecasts with mechanical intercept adjustments and, perhaps most surprisingly, the ex post forecasts with the ex ante intercept adjustments for the Wharton model. This last point obviously suggests that the value of the intercept adjustment depends on the econometrician's *a priori* idea of the value of the endogenous variable and not on the effects of events not catered for by the model.

In addition Evans, Haitovsky, Treyz and Su (1972) found that the true ex ante forecasts were better than all other ex ante forecasts, i.e. the unadjusted ex ante forecasts and mechanically adjusted ex ante forecasts. This perhaps should not be too surprising. The econometric model cannot take into account all the various influences on the endogenous variables and hence the guiding hand of the econometrician will improve matters. The superiority of ex ante over ex post may have three possible causes:

(a) the original (subjective adjustments) are such that they offset errors in the predictors of exogenous variables;

(b) the data reported is naturally faulty, i.e. the observed exogenous values are not true values but are subject to distortion. Evans, Haitovsky, Treyz and Su suggest this might be important for government expenditure;
(c) the equations of the model are mis-specified and any errors in predictions of exogenous variables offset this mis-specification. In particular Evans et al. suggest that the fiscal policy multipliers are overstated.

Both (b) and (c) do not appear to be very damaging in the sense that the errors, once identified, can be corrected. If (a) is the root cause then it suggests that the apparently good performance of econometric models is due to the econometrician and not to the model, as noted by Samuelson (1975).

5.4 Multipliers in model checking

An important use of multipliers is in model validation. In the same way that we have prior expectations from economic theory, previous estimates or observation of economic behaviour on the signs, sizes, and relations between many structural coefficients, we will have similar prior expectations for the multipliers. In the case of structural coefficients, our prior information can be rather precise, and the estimated coefficients can be the subject of hypothesis tests; or it can be much more informal, an expected sign and possibly relative size. An estimated model which fails to reflect that prior knowledge should perhaps be rejected. Prior knowledge on multipliers is unlikely to be precise since economic theory and observed economic behaviour chiefly refer to structural events. But the informal information we have should be used, even if hypothesis testing is not feasible. Multipliers must be of a reasonable size (impact, interim and dynamic multipliers) in the light of both economic theory and observed economic behaviour. Starting with some rough ideas on satisfactory sizes for a few estimated multipliers, it is rather easy to check that other multipliers are of a plausible relative size. We can also check relative sizes of various multipliers at one or more periods of delay for one target–instrument combination. In that way any casual information relating to the sensitivity of targets or effectiveness of instruments, and how the responses build up or decay relative to earlier responses, is used. If the model's dynamic responses cannot correspond with our observation of actual economic events we should doubt the model. However, it is quite possible that this casual information will be restricted to the signs of various multipliers (and possibly changes of sign). In particular, then, we must check the sign pattern in the estimated dynamic multipliers. Rules for using multipliers in model checking are evidently similar to using structural coefficients for model checking.

The main problem in using multipliers for model checking is weakness of the prior knowledge. To help on that score multipliers may be compared to their counterparts in other models which are known to perform well as representations of the relevant aspects of the economy. An obvious difficulty is that the precise definitions of targets or instruments will vary across models and that, with differences in specification, will account for some differences in the multipliers. But if 'correct' or reliable policy inferences are to be drawn from a model then its multipliers must be broadly similar (same sign and of a similar magnitude) to those of models whose ability to mimic the performance of the economy is already proven. Naturally this 'trial by models' is only safety in numbers, with no guarantee that any of the values are accurate; but it is useful when the prior information is weak. We have a consensus estimate of the true multipliers and thus a yardstick less sensitive to the quirks of a particular specification.

Moreover, if on any of these tests some multiplier or, more generally, the behaviour of some target is found to be unsatisfactory or sensitive to small specification or data changes (and this is frequently the case for some multipliers), we can use the various multipliers as components in the dynamic responses to pinpoint exactly which impulse variables (or equations) or which part of the lag structure are causing the problem.

5.5 Assessment by simulation

Non-linear models introduce complexities into model evaluation in that analytic results are generally not obtainable. A tool which will enable us to overcome this problem, as it has done before, is simulation. To make full use of simulation for model evaluation we require a set of observed values over the simulated period, hence the simulations will be ex post. We have already pointed out that over this simulation period the model's performance can be inadequate because of any *one or more* of the following: (a) data errors, (b) specification errors, (c) errors of regression, (d) parameter estimate sampling errors. The problem is to distinguish which is the source of errors in any particular case. Only some are genuine model errors, and with finite samples of imperfect data our ability to correct such errors is limited.

5.5.1 Simulation case studies

Evidently nonstochastic simulations can be used to evaluate the model's performance. However, stochastic simulations can produce extra information, especially for non-linear models.

An early simulation study on the characteristics of stochastic simulation was provided by Adelman and Adelman (1959). This paper was an attempt to assess how good a representation of the US economy was the non-linear dynamic Klein–Goldberger model (Klein and Goldberger (1955)) when viewed not as single equations but as a system. A prime requirement was that the simulated endogenous values should display behaviour which corresponded fairly closely with the observed values. This correspondence involves not only having values which track accurately but also values which exhibit the same dynamic and cyclical behaviour.

The model contains some 25 equations in all. Certain changes and linearisations were made to the original model but the basic specifications of the equations were maintained. The object was to simulate the model over a period of 100 years and the necessary exogenous values were generated by a linear extrapolation of the previously observed values.

The model proved to be exceptionally stable. Non-stochastic simulations produced linear simulation paths, with initial starting values disappearing rapidly. Large simulated shocks were made to the government expenditure variable with a similar result: the model, although initially jolted, rapidly returned to the stable path first experienced. Thus the non-stochastic simulation did not produce results which accord with observed fluctuations.

The answer must, of course, lie with the introduction of stochastic simulations to the system. These were applied in two ways. First, the exogenous variables were subjected to random shocks which produced three to six year cycles of the type normally observed in the actual economy, but with very small amplitude. Since the size of the shocks to the exogenous values were thought to be realistic in size a second approach was taken which accords with our definition of stochastic simulation given earlier. When random disturbances are added to each equation the behaviour of the simulated series was in much better agreement with the observed values. Oscillations were generated with amplitude and periods similar to the actual series.

Although the series may appear similar from observation, Adelman and Adelman attempted a more thorough analysis. The behaviour of simulated series was subjected to the business cycle analysis then operated by the National Bureau of Economic Research. Turning points for each of the series were noted and thus, by taking a consensus of these, a reference cycle established to represent business cycles. The results obtained for the reference cycle are shown in table 5.1.

Thus the behaviour appears very similar. In addition the proportions of cycles which lead or lag the business cycle are similar, as are the sorts of series which lead, or lag, or are coincident with the business cycle.

Table 5.1 *Business Cycle Analysis; US economy.*

	Simulated	Actual economy
Average cycle length (years)	4.0	4.0
Average expansion length (years)	2.6	2.1
Average contraction length (years)	1.5	1.8
% coincident with peaks of business activity	51%	58%
% coincident with troughs of business activity	52%	52%

In general, stochastic simulation confirms that the Klein–Goldberger model is an adequate representation of the economy since it produces results which are in close accord to the actual observed behaviour. That is something which cannot be said for the excessively stable non-stochastic simulation results.

There is an obvious sense in which the Nagar study, cited in Chapter 4, is also a test of the model's performance – particularly with respect to the fast build-up of forecast error variances, and to the inability of the model to withstand large shocks. This kind of evidence may well be used to improve the model design if it is to be used for policy evaluation. Models typically go wrong when large changes occur in the economy. Subjecting the model to large shocks may be a way of assessing the model's sensitivity to these changes. The more 'laboratory' testing that can be done on the model the less likely we are to accept a model which will subsequently produce predictive failures.

5.5.2 The information content

Simulation seems to be an obvious way of experimenting with an econometric model and, if the rather specific nature of each simulation exercise is taken into account, it is a powerful method of analysis. It is perhaps worth pausing to assess the extra information that can be obtained from this exercise over and above the results from an analytic study, however simplified. Using the estimated reduced form and a non-stochastic simulation to produce a series $\hat{Y}_t^*$ we get

$$\hat{Y}_t^* = \hat{\Pi}_1 \hat{Y}_{t-1}^* + \hat{\Pi}_2 X_t \tag{5.14}$$

where $\hat{Y}_0^* = Y_0$ and the values of the exogenous variables are assumed known. So

$$(I - \Pi_1 L)(\hat{Y}_t^* - Y_t) = \Delta_2 X_t + \Delta_1 \hat{Y}_{t-1}^* - V_t \tag{5.15}$$

where L is the lag operator, and Δ_1 and Δ_2 are as defined in Chapter 3.

Assuming that t, Y_0 and X_{t-j} are all given it follows that

$$\text{plim}\ \hat{Y}_t^* = Y_t - \sum_{i=1}^{t} \Pi_1^{t-j} V_j = Y_t^*. \tag{5.16}$$

Hence the assessment of the model by looking at the generated time paths of a non-stochastic simulation exercise obviously makes sense. Equation (5.16) shows that the dynamic properties of the model, assuming it is correctly specified, will be reflected in the behaviour of $\hat{Y}_t^*$. Nevertheless, in small samples a direct comparison of $\hat{Y}_t^*$ and the actual observation Y_t is not necessarily informative because the two series can have significantly different characteristics.

A linear model, in principle, can be solved analytically. Thus forecasts and their confidence bands, multipliers, and the solution path of the endogenous variables can all be obtained from a model with given, or estimated, parameters. In these circumstances neither stochastic nor deterministic simulation can be expected to yield any extra information, a fact noted by Howrey and Kelijan (1971). There are, however, circumstances when simulation would be worth employing. The analytic solution of large linear (linearised or nonlinear) models can sometimes be very expensive in computer time since large models require manipulation of large matrices. Simulation, on the other hand, is much less costly computationally since there are no matrix multiplications or inversions if the Gauss–Seidel method of solution is adopted. In addition we have already seen the use of simulation for the computation of confidence limits for forecasts from a dynamic linear model with a lead time greater than one period.

Model evaluation so far has been couched in terms of model specification (statistical tests, multiplier values) or of forecasting performance. Of the possible sources of model error noted at the beginning of this section, the effects of the variability of data, error terms or parameter estimates have not been considered. In the absence of analytic results simulation is the only answer. Some of these points have been tackled by Sowey (1973) and Nagar (1969).

More recently Fair (1980b, 1981) has attempted to produce a structured framework using stochastic simulation to investigate the performance of the model taking into account these variabilities. By changing the sources of stochastic variation in the model simulation he investigates the predictive accuracy of the model. The procedure Fair outlines is as follows. Using the methods of section 4.8, obtain drawings from a normal distributions with the same mean and variance – covariance matrix as the estimated residuals. Using these random numbers, generate an endogenous variable series as if forecasting. The averages of these forecasts at each time point will define a mean simulation path. The distribution of the forecast around this mean simulation path gives an estimate of the forecast variance, conditional on the variables, parameters or error terms that have been chosen for stochastic simulation. The resulting distributions allow a pseudo-statistical forecast test of the true deterministic forecast in the usual way outlined in section 5.3. The simulation at this stage can be stochastic with respect to the error terms, the parameter estimates or the exogenous variables – or all three. In this way simulation can be used as a flexible and informative tool.

The fourth factor causing model inadequacy was model specification. Fair suggests that the effect of mis-specification can be tackled by using a second estimate of the forecast variance. This estimate is constructed by noting that the difference between the mean simulation path and the actual value of the endogenous variable gives a measure of the mean forecast error. The square of this provides a new estimate of the forecast variance. The expected difference between the two estimates would be zero if the model was correctly specified. Any mis-specification is likely to cause a systematic divergence between the two estimates because the estimated variance–covariance matrices that are used for the stochastic simulation will not, in general, be unbiased estimates of the true variance–covariance matrices. This will, in general, affect both forecast variance estimates, an effect which may cancel out although Fair suggests this is unlikely. The path of the difference between the two variances has some important information on the extent and effect of model mis-specification, although the exact effects of mis-specification are not known.

It is clear that there is more work to be done in this area and that simulation is the only satisfactory tool for tackling the sources of model error which were indicated above.

5.6 Assessment by spectral methods

We have looked at the possibility of assessing the worth of a model by its forecasting performance, the values of the multipliers it generates, and its behaviour under stochastic simulation. The unfortunate consequence is that we are likely to get three different answers since we have essentially imposed three different types of input on the model; respectively a single realisation of exogenous values, steps in the exogenous values, and a white noise disturbance input with randomly varied exogenous values. A method which allows investigation of the model without making the answer conditional on the input would be very valuable. Frequency response analysis using spectra and cross-spectra is just such a method. The method is, however, restricted to linear or linearised models once again, although they may be dynamic.

A good summary of spectral analysis and its applications to econometrics is in Nerlove (1964). The aim is to transform the time series behaviour of a variable into the frequency domain. This has the effect of decomposing the auto-covariances of the time series into the component variances associated with different cycle lengths (frequencies). If we graph the result, that is spectral power against frequency, we can pick out those cycles particularly strong in the variable from the relative maxima. Naturally a purely random variable has no cycles and hence a spectrum equal to a constant at all frequencies.

For our purposes we may treat the exogenous variables as fixed by history, and *compute* the spectral matrix conditional on that fixed realisation. The computations are valid only for a stable system so we regard (2.6) as deviations from an equilibrium trend (and interpret X_t the same way) with $\rho(\Pi_1) < 1$. Then Y_t is a stationary ergodic stochastic process. Most problems considered in spectral analysis concern techniques of estimation, length of data series, and the properties of the estimates – the balance between consistency and efficiency. Although we could in principle obtain spectra by simulations of sufficient length using the model, they would then be subject to sample variability which may not be desirable. Here we calculate the theoretical spectra implied by (2.6) and avoid the uncertainty of interpretation due to sampling variability and the properties of the particular estimation techniques. But, of course, the spectra obtained are those of the model, which is at most an estimate of the economy. They may be certain for the model, but they are subject to sampling variability with respect to the economy although the statistical properties are far too complicated to consider analysing. Simulation, which is the only alternative for nonhistoric policy rules, nonlinear models or short data series, also suffers from the same difficulty.

Under these conditions the spectral representation of Y_t is[1]

$$Y_t = \int_{-\pi}^{\pi} e^{i\omega t} \, dY(\omega) \tag{5.17}$$

where

$$Y(\omega) = \frac{1}{2\pi}\left[\omega Y_0 - \sum_{t \neq 0} \frac{e^{-i\omega t}}{it} Y_t\right]; \quad i = \sqrt{-1}. \tag{5.18}$$

Then the spectral matrix of Y_t is defined as

$$F^y(\omega) = E\{dY(\omega)\overline{dY(\omega)}\} \tag{5.19}$$

1 The approach which follows is similar to that in Howrey (1972) or Nerlove (1964).

where $\overline{dY(\omega)}$ is the conjugate transpose of $dY(\omega)$.

The basic linear dynamic model (2.6) has representation

$$(I - \Pi_1 L)Y_t = \Pi_2 X_t + V_t \tag{5.20}$$

where L is the lag operator. Hence, if we regard X_t as fixed, the dynamic behaviour of Y_t comes from the term $(I - \Pi_1 L)^{-1} V_t$.

The spectral representation of V_t can be written

$$V_t = \int_{-\pi}^{\pi} e^{i\omega t} dV(\omega) \tag{5.21}$$

and the spectral matrix $F^v(\omega)$ is

$$F^v(\omega) = E\{dV(\omega)\overline{dV(\omega)}\}.$$

Now

$$Y_t = (I - \Pi_1 L)^{-1} V_t = (I - \Pi_1 L)^{-1} \int_{-\pi}^{\pi} e^{i\omega t} dV(\omega) \tag{5.22}$$

which, by interchanging the order of operations, gives

$$Y_t = \int_{-\pi}^{\pi} T(\omega) e^{i\omega t} dV(\omega); \quad T(\omega) = (I - \Pi_1 e^{-i\omega})^{-1}. \tag{5.23}$$

Hence, by equating terms

$$dY(\omega) = T(\omega) dV(\omega)$$

and

$$F^y(\omega) = E(dY(\omega)\overline{dY(\omega)}) = T(\omega)F^v(\omega)\overline{T(\omega)}. \tag{5.24}$$

Under the previous assumptions V_t is a purely random variable with zero autocovariances. Hence if $\Sigma = E(V_t' V_t)$

$$F^v(\omega) = \Sigma/2\pi \tag{5.25}$$

although it is open to us to make any assumptions we like if it will help in model evaluation. The spectral matrix $F^y(\omega)$ can then be computed using the estimated values of Σ and Π_1, $F^v(\omega)$ and equation (5.24).

The analysis of the dynamic properties of the system can be approached firstly through the diagonal elements of the spectral matrix which give the power spectra of the endogenous variables.

We would hope that the output spectra from the frequency response analysis would indicate some of the properties of the endogenous variable implied by the model. The usual experience, however, is that the 'typical spectral shape' predominates and that the components indicating the implied cyclical nature of the series, particularly the long cycles, tend to be swamped. In addition the output spectra from different models for the same variable tend not to be readily distinguishable one from another. An example of this approach will be given in Chapter 6, but see also Howrey (1972) and Chow (1975).

The off-diagonal terms of $F^y(\omega)$ contain different information. The (p, j)th element of $F^y(\omega)$, denoted $F^y_{pj}(\omega)$, is known as the cross-spectrum between y_{pt} and y_{jt} ($F^y_{pp}(\omega)$ is the spectrum of y_{pt}). Typically this term is complex and is difficult to use directly. However, we can extract three measures which have proved to be of use in econometrics. Firstly, we define the *gain* by

$$g^y_{pj}(\omega) = |F^y_{pj}(\omega)| / F^y_{jj}(\omega) \tag{5.26}$$

where $|.|$ denotes the modulus of a complex number. This is intuitively equivalent to the regression coefficient between the pth and jth endogenous variable at frequency ω. As such it allows us to investigate the links between y_{pt} and y_{jt} at frequency $\omega \in [0, \pi]$. (e.g. long run relations for small ω, short run for ω near π). The information in the gain function can be compared with the observed behaviour of the actual series y_{pt} and y_{jt} as a method of model evaluation.

The second measure is that of *coherence* and is defined by

$$C^y_{pj}(\omega) = |F^y_{pj}(\omega)|^2 / (F^y_{jj}(\omega) F^y_{pp}(\omega)). \tag{5.27}$$

This is equivalent to the correlation coefficient between y_{pt} and y_{jt} at frequency ω and, as such, gives similar information to the gain.

The third measure is the *phase shift*

$$\Psi^y_{pj}(\omega) = \tan^{-1}(\mathrm{Im}(F^y_{pj}(\omega)) / \mathrm{Re}(F^y_{pj}(\omega))) \tag{5.28}$$

where Im(.) and Re(.) denote imaginary and real parts of a complex number respectively. The phase shift measures the phase difference between y_{pt} and y_{jt} at frequency ω. It is generally not a very informative measure because there is usually some form of feedback between endogenous variables (see Granger and Newbold (1977)). However, there are occasions when the model is recursive and the link between variables is a direct causal one. In these circumstances the phase shift function can indicate whether one series is leading another and by how much. See Chow (1975) for examples.

In principle we may note that the spectral density matrix $F^y(\omega)$ may be computed directly from estimates of Π_1, which would be preferable if its eigenvalues had already been computed. Chow (1975) shows that

$$F^y(\omega) = \frac{1}{\pi} W \Theta(\omega) W' \tag{5.29}$$

where $\Theta(\omega)$ has elements

$$\Theta_{pj}(\omega) = \frac{(W^{-1}\Sigma W^{-1'})}{(1-\lambda_p e^{-i\omega})(1-\lambda_j e^{i\omega})} \tag{5.30}$$

$p, j = 1, 2 \dots l$, for $\omega \in [0, \pi]$. The similarity transform $\Pi_1 = W\Lambda W^{-1}$ defines the indexing of eigenvalues, $\Lambda = \text{diag}(\lambda_i)$. In fact, as Λ and W need to be computed only once this is a considerable advantage both in computation efficiency and numerical accuracy. Indeed if we are only interested in the spectra of a few targets among Y_t we can avoid the computation of the whole $F^y(\omega)$ matrix.

6

Stability and contracyclical policies

6.1 Introduction

Contracyclical policies have been a preoccupation of postwar governments in most industrialised countries. They have often been criticised for their lack of success, and even for their ability to exacerbate the economy's cyclical behaviour. If policies are to respond to cyclical movements, then we must measure the stability and characteristics of those cycles, how they combine in different variables, and the sources of the oscillations. We must also check that removing fluctuations of one frequency does not induce new fluctuations with a different frequency.

The stability and cyclical properties of an econometric model are examined in sections 6.2 and 6.3, and the sources of oscillatory behaviour in section 6.4. Then we explore how cycles are formed in specific variables, and the relations between them in section 6.5. Techniques for setting instruments in response to these cycles are introduced by means of different control rules of the servo-mechanism type (sections 6.6 and 6.7).

However, this policy analysis presupposes that the model can be controlled to reach preassigned objectives – including those of a contracyclical nature. In the Tinbergen result we have seen that this cannot be guaranteed for arbitrary target values without static controllability. Now the question is, can desired contracyclical properties be induced (as opposed to specific target values)? This leads to a general discussion of controllability; and of its stochastic extension, stabilisability, which guarantees that the effects of random shocks to the system can be damped out (sections 6.8 and 6.9). Before we go on to discuss how best to design policies to meet certain objectives, we should check that our system is in fact capable of delivering such achievements.

6.2 Stability tests

We first pursue the theme of the stability of our system (2.1), raised in section 3.10 and in use since section 4.4. The system is stable if the set of endogenous variables converges on some fixed constants following an arbitrary finite disturbance to an exogenous variable, as the interval since that shock tends to infinity. More precisely, since our system is stochastic, the multivariate distribution of endogenous variables must converge stochastically on a limiting multivariate distribution with a fixed mean such that

$$\lim_{t\to\infty} E[(y_{it} - E(y_{it}))^2] < \infty, \quad i = 1 \ldots g.$$

In practice this definition encompassess convergence on an equilibrium or any other growth path (the exogenous variables will doubtless display some growth paths) if the variables in the definition are measured as deviations from those paths. All this means is that the effects, on current endogenous variables, of any disturbance to the growth paths in the past eventually become arbitrarily small. It is obvious from (4.4) and (4.5) that our definition is satisfied if $\lim_{i\to\infty} \Pi_1^i = 0$. And that follows as a standard result for any difference equation, such as (2.6), if $\rho(\Pi_1) < 1$ where $\rho(.)$ denotes spectral radius: Varga (1962), theorem 1.4. Hence one possible method for testing the stability of the difference equation system (2.5) is to check that all eigenvalues of Π_1 lie within the unit circle. Note that both

$$|\Pi_1 - \lambda I| = 0; \text{and } |\Pi_{1l} + (-\lambda)\Pi_{1l-1} + \ldots + (-\lambda)^{l-1}\Pi_{11} + (-\lambda)^l I| = 0 \quad (6.1)$$

give lg identical values, but the second is more efficient for computation (Bowden (1972)).

6.3 Cyclical analysis

Although stability in (2.5) may be tested as easily by computing the eigenvalues of Π_1 as by other methods, the eigenvalues have the added advantage that they reveal the cyclical characteristics of the model. Let Π_1 have roots λ_i where $|\lambda_1| \geqslant \ldots \geqslant |\lambda_{lg}|$. Consider the dominant root of Π_1

$$\lambda_1 = a \pm ib = r(\cos\theta \pm i\sin\theta) \quad (i = \sqrt{-1}). \quad (6.2)$$

Then $r = (a^2 + b^2)^{1/2}$ is the amplitude of the dominant cycle, and $1/r$ is the damping factor per time period. The period of the cycle is $2\pi/\theta$ and its frequency is $\theta/2\pi$ where θ (measured in radians) is obtained from $\cos\theta = a/r$. Thus the model will display a cyclical growth path in the aftermath of any deviation from an equilibrium position if $b \neq 0$. But the model is strictly stable if $r < 1$, weakly stable if $r = 1$, or unstable if $r > 1$.

Table 6.1 *Some dominant cycle characteristics*

Model/Economy	Hendry (2SLS) UK	Klein I (2SLS) USA	Kmenta/Smith USA
root	$0.979 \pm 0.0073i$	$0.759 \pm 0.351i$	$0.8475 \pm 0.0809i$
r (damping factor)	0.979 (1.02)	0.836 (1.196)	0.8513 (1.175)
cycle length ($2\pi/\theta$)	13.1 years	14.6 years	17.9 years
reference	Hendry (1974)	Kenkel (1976)	Kmenta & Smith (1973)

Table 6.2 *Some component cycle characteristics*

Klein I	roots = 0.334, 0; i.e. geometric decay superimposed on the 14.6 year damped cycle
Kmenta/Smith	roots = $0.5834 \pm 0.1156i$, 0.2081; i.e. a small and fast decaying ($r = 0.5956$) 8.04 year cycle, also a fast geometric decay, superimposed on the 17.9 year cycle

Through the eigenvalues of Π_1 we can test not only a model's stability, but we can also compare the cyclical properties of its growth path (damping factor; cycle length) with the observed behaviour of the true economy. We can either do this for the dominant cycle resulting from the dominant root, or for any of the lesser roots whose cycles are superimposed on the dominant cycle. That deals with the inherently oscillatory (or otherwise) behaviour of endogenous variables, and their component cycles as a consequence of some exogenous shock (see tables 6.1 and 6.2). However, two elements vital for policy analysis are missing; (a) how do those cycles combine, and (b) how did they arise in the first place? With answers to those questions we shall be in a position to design instrument trajectories to counteract the observed cycles.

Most economic variables display oscillatory patterns. In comparing cycles, as in the Adelman and Adelman (1959) study, we would want to investigate damping factors, cycle length, turning points, leads and lags, length of expansion and contraction periods, all for a reference cycle in the model and the observed data. But finding similar cycles does not necessarily mean they have the same origins. A second unresolved problem is how to analyse the decomposition of the time path of any variable; that is the relative amplitude and phase relations between component cycles, and how those components combine. We aim for more than just a validation of the characteristics of the model and information on its inherent cycles. We need the ability to predict the effect on the current level of a target after some earlier exogenous change through the multipliers, and the cyclical consequences of some action or strategy in X_t or V_t. For planning we need to know where the resulting peaks and troughs in the target values will be, and whether the phase relations between them have been altered.

The point at issue is to be able to predict whether the cyclical consequences of policies will coincide with the cyclical responses to external events, thus exaggerating peaks and troughs; or vice versa so the peaks and troughs are moderated. In the case of random shocks to the economy this is the only way a contracyclical policy may be designed. Indeed, arguments are frequently directed at governments who, due to misguided policies or varied forms of administrative delays, have in fact been destabilising rather than stabilising (criticisms associated with Dow (1964) or Friedman and Meiselman (1963)). It is obviously important that we consider the coordination and timing of policies, both among themselves so that they do not clash and cancel out, and in relation to the development of the economy so that they modify rather than exaggerate cycles.

6.4 The sources of oscillatory behaviour

In (4.1) there are three potential sources of oscillations in Y_t:

$$\text{(i)} \quad \Pi_1^T Y_{t-T}, \quad \text{(ii)} \sum_j \Pi_1^j \Pi_2 X_{t-j}, \quad \text{(iii)} \sum_j \Pi_1^j V_{t-j}. \tag{6.3}$$

The first displays the general solution, the homogeneous part of the difference equation system with a known initial vector. By writing the similarity transform

$$\Pi_1^T = W\Lambda^T W^{-1} \quad \text{where} \quad \Lambda = \text{diag}(\lambda_j) \tag{6.4}$$

it is obvious that each endogenous variable is a linear combination of the powers of all the eigenvalues, each, and thus all, of whose complex values will impart some oscillatory behaviour.

In a stable system this source of inherent, or natural, oscillatory behaviour will be negligible for large T, and indeed may decay rapidly even for moderate T. From any initial position, other things unchanged, the model will exhibit those cycles associated with each λ_j in its growth path.

Whatever oscillations from the first source are observed, the same characteristics will also be observed from the second source. There are two aspects here. Inherent oscillations in the interim multipliers follow as part of the difference equation solution. But those cyclical effects are then summed together, weighted by the specific sequence $X_{t-j}, j = 0 \dots T-1$. The realisation of X_{t-j} may contain cycles, in addition to those from the multipliers, which can be transferred to the endogenous variables. In a stable system those cycles will again be damped. Of course, even if the multipliers exhibit no cyclical behaviour it is quite possible that the X_{t-j} are such that cycles are produced in Y_t. One has only to think of the regular and frequent reversals of policies which characterise some governments' economic management. Indeed this point is implicit in the criticism that policies have exaggerated any natural cycles. On the other hand X_t might be chosen to annihilate the inherent cycles.

We could refer to cycles due to λ_j as 'internally generated' and to those resulting from a particular X_{t-j} realisation as 'externally generated'. One example of the former type is the traditional multiplier–accelerator model. The latter occurs in a contracyclical policy where any built-in stabilisers are ignored, or if combined administrative delays are not allowed for in policy calculations but last approximately half a cycle.

In the third source we see immediately that cycles may also be generated in two ways. If λ_j is complex we have again the internally generated cycles. And we can get 'externally generated' cycles as above, even if λ_j are real, if by bad fortune the random errors V_{t-j} happen to combine together in a particular way. It is a well known result of Slutsky (1937) that certain linear combinations of random variables will result in cyclical behaviour. Since this is the result of uncontrollable factors rather than misguided policies, it is rather important to know how to counteract it with suitable policies. Suppose

$$EV_t = 0 \quad \text{and} \quad E(V_{t-i}V'_{t-j})\begin{cases} = 0 \text{ if } i \neq j \\ = \Phi \text{ otherwise} \end{cases}$$

and let $P_t = \sum_{j=0}^{T} \Pi_1^j V_{t-j}$. (6.5)

We have

$$E(P_t P'_t) = \Phi_0 = \Phi + \Pi_1 \Phi \Pi'_1 + \dots + \Pi_1^{T-1} \Phi \Pi_1^{T-1\prime}. \tag{6.6}$$

Then

$$\begin{aligned} E(P_t P'_{t-1}) &= \Pi_1[\Phi + \Pi_1 \Phi \Pi'_1 + \dots + \Pi_1^{T-2} \Phi \Pi_1^{T-2\prime}] \\ &= \Pi_1 \Phi_0 - \Pi_1^T \Phi \Pi_1^{T-1\prime}. \end{aligned} \tag{6.7}$$

Thus, if $\lim_{T\to\infty} \Pi_1^T = 0$, we have for large T

$$E(P_t P'_{t-q}) \simeq \Pi_1^q \Phi_0 \qquad q \geqslant 0 \tag{6.8}$$

so the autocovariances are determined by λ_j and Φ_0. Therefore, if λ_j

are complex, P_t tends to cycle. Even if $0 < \lambda_j < 1$ is real there is an increased likelihood that P_t will have the same sign and be of similar size to P_{t-q}, the more so the larger $\max_j |\lambda_j|$ and the smaller q. The probability of regular persistent oscillations will only decrease as $|\lambda_j|$ and/or Φ_0 decrease. In that case the persistence of the effects of large shocks is reduced. But little has been achieved if stabilisation policy rules aimed at reducing the roots of the system in modulus, $|\lambda_j|$, merely increases the output variance. Similarly little is achieved if stabilisation policy effectively removes cycles, say the short period ones, from the model at the expense of increasing the power of others of longer period.

6.5 Cycles in specific variables

We have traced the sources of cycles observed on endogenous variables and analysed the components of internally generated cycles for amplitude, rate of decay and cycle length. That information is useful background for planning but is really more suited to model validation. What is required for planning is an analysis of how those cycles manifest themselves in the individual variables and the relation between the cycles in individual variables. Take, for example, the transformation of Π_1^T given in equation (6.4),

$$Y_t = \Pi_1^T Y_{t-T} = W\Lambda^T W^{-1} Y_{t-T} \tag{6.9}$$

$$\therefore y_{kt} = \sum_j \sum_h \lambda_j^T w_{kj} w^{jh} y_{h,t-T} \quad k, h = 1 \dots g \tag{6.10}$$

where w^{kh} is the (k, h)th element of W^{-1}.

If λ_j is complex then so is the eigenvector, $w_{.j}$, associated with it. Each variable will be following an oscillatory path which is a linear combination of the components of the inherent cycles of the model. But it is difficult to analyse the cycles in y_{kt} in terms of the component cycles. Therefore, the manifestation of individual component cycles, chiefly the dominant cycle, in the growth path of individual variables is usually studied. Policy makers are generally concerned with the dominant or other politically 'sensitive' cycles.

To analyse the effects of one variable on another rewrite Π_1 in (6.4) as

$$\Pi_1 = W\Lambda W^{-1} = \sum_{j=1}^{gl} \lambda_j w_{.j} w^{j.} \tag{6.11}$$

where $w_{.j}$ is column j of W associated with the root λ_j; and $w^{j.}$ is row j from W^{-1}. Without loss of generality assume that the dominant root is a complex conjugate pair:

$$\lambda_1, \lambda_2 = a \pm ib = r(\cos\theta \pm i \sin\theta). \tag{6.12}$$

So the associated elements of the eigenvectors in (6.11) are

$$w_{\cdot 1}w^{1\cdot} = P + iQ \text{ and } w_{\cdot 2}w^{2\cdot} = P - iQ \tag{6.13}$$

where P and Q are $gl \times gl$ matrices. Now substituting (6.12) and (6.13) in (6.11) gives the contributions of the dominant roots to Π_1; and the (m, n)th element of the resulting matrix can be written

$$(\lambda_1 w_{\cdot 1}w^{1\cdot} + \lambda_2 w_{\cdot 2}w^{2\cdot})_{mn} = 2rs_{mn}(\cos(\theta + \psi_{mn})) \tag{6.14}$$

where $s_{mn} = (P_{mn}^2 + Q_{mn}^2)^{1/2}$ and $\psi_{mn} = \tan^{-1}(Q_{mn}/P_{mn})$. Moreover, by de Moivre's theorem λ_1^t, λ_2^t may be written as

$$\lambda_1^t, \lambda_2^t = r^t(\cos t\theta \pm i\sin t\theta)$$

so that, for the dominant cycle, any power T of Π_1 gives

$$(\lambda_1^T w_{\cdot 1}w^{1\cdot} + \lambda_2^T w_{\cdot 2}w^{2\cdot}) = 2r^T s_{mn}\cos(T\theta + \psi_{mn}). \tag{6.15}$$

Suppose there are multiple pairs of complex conjugate eigenvalues then each of the component cycles associated with the complex roots can be expressed in the form (6.15). For the interim multipliers, $\Pi_1^T\Pi_2$, which give the second source of oscillation in (6.3) we compute (6.15) as before but now putting

$$w_{\cdot 1}w^{1\cdot}\Pi_2 = P + iQ \quad \text{and} \quad w_{\cdot 2}w^{2\cdot}\Pi_2 = P - iQ. \tag{6.16}$$

Thus each endogenous variable follows a cyclical pattern composed of all the impulses; one from each current and past $X_{t-i}(0 \leqslant i \leqslant T)$ and the initial condition Y_{t-T}. And each component impulse is a linear combination of all the inherent component cycles (one from each complex conjugate pair of roots) in the form of (6.15), using (6.13) for initial conditions and (6.16) for the effects of subsequent exogenous factors. The characteristics of any one component cycle are composed of the general amplitude r, the cycle length $2\pi/\theta$, a scaling of the amplitude by s_{mn} in the part of the cycle in the mth target variable generated by the nth impulse variable, and a relative phase shift ψ_{mn} imposed by variable n on variable m. Note that only general, rather than specific, characteristics depend on the length of delay since a disturbance. Some examples of the cyclical characteristics, computed for the dominant cycle and exogenous impulses, in the Klein I model are given in table 6.3.

To interpret the results so far consider the behaviour of a particular target m in response to the value of a particular exogenous variable n (or initial endogenous condition) after t periods and in terms of one particular cycle which is given by the roots λ_1, λ_2. The amplitude is now r^t times the initial amplitude but the effect in target variable m attributable to variable n is scaled up or down by s_{mn}. The length of the cycle is still $2\pi/\theta$ in m (as

Table 6.3 *Interim multipliers of Klein's model I; amplitude and phase shifts relative to the dominant root*

	W_2	T	G	W_2	T	G
	s_{mn} (amplitudes)			ψ_{mn} (phase differences)[a]		
C	0.152	0.974	0.760	0.288	0.211	0.288
Π	0.104	0.666	0.520	0.640	0.564	0.640
W_1	0.153	0.979	0.764	0.301	0.224	0.301
I	0.105	0.675	0.527	0.656	0.579	0.656
Y	0.253	1.622	1.266	0.438	0.361	0.438
K	0.206	1.323	1.033	2.065	1.988	2.065

[a]Measured in radians.
Source: Theil and Boot (1962)

it will be for any other variable $m = 1, 2 \ldots g$) and we can work out the present stage of the cycle from $\cos(t\theta)$. But that cycle in variable m has had its peaks (troughs) advanced by $(\psi_{mn} - \psi_{jn})/\theta \geqslant 0$ periods (retarded if $\psi_{mn} < \psi_{jn}$) relative to any other target j. In the Klein I model, for example, table 6.1 shows that the dominant cycle carries the maximum effect of 0.836 of the initial impulse after 1 year; but since it is 1/14.6 of the way through its cycle (measured from the last peak) it is actually only at 0.9078 of its potential peak level. In table 6.3, the instruments T and G cause scaled up cycles in Y and K. Meanwhile W_2 has a much smaller effect on all targets. Also, phase shifts attributable to the instruments are almost all less than a year, except for the cycle in K due to impulses from W_2 which is

$$(2.065 - 0.438)/0.43 = 3.78$$

years in advance over that in Y. But the cycle in K due to T is only

$$(2.065 - 1.988)/0.43 = 0.18$$

years behind that in K due to W_2. Similarly the cycle in K due to W_2 is 4.74 years in advance over the model's dominant (reference) cycle.

Given any reference cycle we may determine the strength of the cycle in the mth target t periods after a single impulse from the nth exogenous variable. Then, if we wish, we can sum directly over all cycles $(1 \ldots gl)$ for the given m, n and t to show the combined effects of all cycles generated by n (t periods ago) on m. But the more interesting cases are more difficult; namely, aggregation over $t = 0 \ldots T$ to give the accumulated effects of repeated impulses from a cycle in the (m, n) case; or aggregation over $n = 1 \ldots h$ to give the combined effects of various instruments on m. All require weighted sums, the weights being the actual values of the impulse variables times the associated eigenvectors as in (6.16). However, this is not particularly useful as the position of any variable, in response to a sequence of impulses, is more easily determined by simulation and a knowledge of the basic component cycles. Cyclical analysis alone cannot suggest directions in which policies could usefully be modified, nor how much scope there is for policy intervention to improve expected outcomes. The combination of many cycles over several periods means that systematic searches to rank policy alternatives are quite out of the question in practice. For the planners concerned with a particular cycle, the useful information is made available by writing the result as (6.15).

It is therefore quite straightforward, but extremely tedious computationally, to check on the cyclical consequences of any policy sequence; and in fact to plan, to a limited degree, their timing and coordination so that they are complementary rather than competitive with each other, but vice versa with respect to the inherent cycles in the model.

6.6 Policy rule types

We have just shown that multipliers may be expressed as linear combinations of the various cycles. In fact, since the model's t-period final form is

$$Y_t = \Pi_1^t Y_0 + \sum_{j=0}^{t-1} \Pi_1^j \Pi_2 X_{t-j} + \sum_{j=0}^{t} \Pi_1^j V_{t-j} \tag{6.18}$$

we can try to get any prescribed values Y_t^d, $t = 1 \ldots T$, *either* by selecting suitable values of X_{t-j} for $j = 0 \ldots t$, $t = 1 \ldots T$; *or* by suitable alterations to the structural parameters (some or all of them) and thus to Π_1 and Π_2; *or*, of course, by combinations of both options. That statement assumes that there are no other restrictions on the permissible alterations of a sufficient number of instruments or parameters. But, in practice, there will be.

Yet another approach would be to obtain policy values from three different types of policy rule in which the instruments are endogenised (Philips (1954, 1957)). If A_t is a matrix of coefficients and Y_t is a component of (2.4) rather than the augmented vector of (2.5):

(1) Proportional rules: $X_t = A_t Y_t$ (6.19)

(in continuous time $X_t = A_t Y_t$)

(2) Integral rules: $X_t = A_t(L) Y_t$ (6.20)

(in continuous time $X_t = \int_{-\infty}^{t} A_\tau Y_\tau d\tau$)

where $L^i Y_t = Y_{t-i}$ and $A_t(L)$ is a matrix polynomial in the lag operator.

(3) Derivative rules: $X_t = A_t \Delta Y_t$ (6.21)

$$\left(\text{in continuous time } X_t = A_t \frac{d}{dt}(Y_t)\right)$$

Evidently integral rules contain the other two as special cases. This means that, given an integral control rule, we may separate out the three components to write it as a proportional plus derivative plus integral (the remaining components) rule. A constant (with respect to Y_t but not with respect to t) may also be added to any of them. Moreover, A_t may be dependent on t (see for example the optimal feedback rule at (8.20) below). Equation (6.19) is only one version of proportionality. Perhaps a more conventional rule (and realistic for discrete time problems) is

$$X_t = A_t Y_{t-1}. \tag{6.22}$$

Consider (6.20), truncated after q periods, as a control rule:

$$X_t = A_t(L)Y_t \quad \text{where } A_t(L) = A_{t1}L + \ldots + A_{tq}L^q. \tag{6.23}$$

This implies that the endogenous variables behave, via (2.4), as[1]

$$Y_t = \sum_{j=1}^{l} (\Pi_{1j} + \Pi_{20}A_{tj})Y_{t-j} + \sum_{j=l+1}^{q} \Pi_{20}A_{tj}Y_{t-j} + \sum_{j=1}^{k} \Pi_{2j}X_{t-j} + V_t. \tag{6.24}$$

Of course, any of these control rules can be reformulated in terms of earlier forecasts of Y_t (i.e. $Y_{t,j}$) and their prediction errors. If those errors are mostly uncorrelated shocks, then (6.20) as a weighted average of past errors tends to smooth the path of the economy. In addition, only the n instruments, rather than the $h-n$ noncontrollables, may be set in a control rule in practice. Thus if x_t is a proper subset of X_t, we must partition $X'_t = (x'_t \vdots N'_t)$ and Π_{2j} as $(\Pi_{2j} \vdots \Pi_{3j})$; then insert these definitions into (6.24) and collect terms.

Our problem then is to choose A_t suitably with respect to the inherent cycles of the model and the characteristics and levels of the desired trajectories in the targets Y_t given, at least, expected values for V_i, for $i \geqslant t$. This is the approach favoured by the monetarists in advocating control by planned growth in the money supply, or that favoured by the Cambridge Group in advocating control by planned growth in budget and trade balances. Both are often characterised by A being set exogenously and invariant to t; otherwise (as in optimal control) we use A_t as a function of

1 We have taken $q \geqslant l$ in (6.24). If $q < l$ then the first two terms reduce to $\sum_{j=1}^{l} (\Pi_{1j} + \Pi_{20}A_{tj}) \times Y_{t-j}$ where $A_{tj} = 0$ for $j = q+1 \ldots l$.

expected variables, and behavioural reactions to them, and it may be revised and recomputed in the light of events. Choosing x_t is equivalent to choosing some A_t and vice versa.

Hence in these policy rules we are contemplating different decision rules which the government might introduce in order to set instrument values as functions of the state of the economy – the actual target outcomes in the immediate past. The introduction of such rules changes the model from (2.4) to (6.24) and in this way we alter the parameters of the controlled reduced model form by making instruments endogenous.

A study by Gandolfo and Padoan (1981) provides an interesting illustration of how policies may be designed in the form of a control rule, with this aim of modifying an economy's dynamic properties. A 14-equation continuous time model of the Italian economy is used for the cyclical analysis. The empirical model is estimated by means of a quarterly approximation to it over the period 1960–79 inclusive. The eigenvalues of the dynamic structure show three component cycles (of lengths 14, 5, and $1\frac{1}{2}$ years respectively) super-imposed on a dominant growth path with slow exponential decay[2]. Then the sensitivities (in the form of partial derivatives) of these eigenvalues to changes in those model parameters, which are associated with partially endogenous policy instruments, are evaluated numerically. For example, increasing the speed at which the monetary authorities adjust the rate of change in money stock to its desired values is stabilising, i.e. the eigenvalues move further from the values which indicate instability. However, increasing their speed of reaction to movements in international reserves moves the eigenvalues which gave the 5 year cycle in such a way as to produce unstable cycles (a policy induced cycle). A similar thing happens if prices are adjusted faster in response to changes in the money stock or if producers react faster to changes in the level of inventories. These examples all refer to the speed of adjustment in a partial adjustment model and so to the coefficients on lagged dependent variables in (2.4). Consequently, they may be regarded as potential adjustments to be engineered in elements of Π_1 of (2.4), to give (6.24). Thus policy selection reduces to picking $A_t(L)$ such that $\Pi_1 + \Pi_2 A_t(L)$ makes just that change. Any restrictions on the acceptable changes in instrument values must be translated into restrictions on the freedom to choose $A_t(L)$.

The control rule approach to setting policy instruments should be distinguished from the case where the policy maker has control over some structural model parameters. The latter are quite common in tax rate parameters, or liquidity ratio terms, of partially endogenous instruments.

2 Since this example deals with a differential rather than difference equation system, we replace each λ_i in the earlier sections of this chapter by $\lambda_i - 1$ in order to perform the same analysis. The eigenvectors are unchanged.

As we saw in Chapter 2, partially endogenous instruments of this type introduce a nonlinear choice problem.

6.7 Stabilisation policies I

After the criticisms of the policy formulation problem in Chapter 2, other computational schemes for acceptable policies have been left deliberately loose. In earlier chapters a sequence of trial and error methods has been suggested for the selection of policy variable values. We extend this sequence in Chapter 7 to its logical end in one form of the optimal control problem. In this chapter we have initiated a parallel course for selecting ad hoc policy rules. In Chapter 8 we also bring that sequence to its logical end in the optimal control problem and further show how the two solutions (the direct computation of instrument values, and the selection of policy rule parameters) are identical.

In the light of (6.24), in order to get a particular sequence of instrument values we need to select $A_t = [A_{t1} \vdots \ldots \vdots A_{tq}]$ such that $\Pi_1 + \Pi_{20} A_t$ imparts the desired cyclical and growth properties to the 'controlled' model[3]

$$Y_t = (\Pi_1 + \Pi_{20} A_t) Y_{t-1} + (0, \Pi_{21} \ldots \Pi_{2k}) X_t + V_t. \tag{6.25}$$

That is to pick A_t so that $\Pi_1 + \Pi_{20} A_t$ has specified eigenvalues, given Π_1 and Π_2, Y_t^d, X_{t-j} for $j \geqslant 1$, and $E(V_t)$. Clearly having desired eigenvalues is only a partial solution. We also need suitable eigenvectors to set the scale and phase terms. But eigenvalues are sufficient for our purpose here.

Evidently this is not an easy problem to solve. We must see how the cyclical and growth characteristics alter with a, b in $\lambda = a \pm ib$; then how a, b alter with the coefficients of their characteristic equation; and finally how that alters with A_t given arbitrary Π_1 and Π_{20} matrices.

Consider the cycle determined by $\lambda_1 = r(\cos\theta + i \sin\theta)$ which could be the solution to

$$\lambda^2 + c\lambda + d = 0; \quad c = -2a; \quad d = r^2. \tag{6.26}$$

Baumol (1961) defines the locus of (c, d) combinations offering the same degree of stability as λ_1, where λ_1 has fixed amplitude $r = r_0$ (say), by

$$\sqrt{d} = r_0 \text{ for } c^2 < 4d, \text{ and } r_0 c = d \text{ for } -2r_0 \leqslant c \leqslant 2r_0. \tag{6.27}$$

This gives a series of concentric triangles of 'iso-stability' lines (figure 6.1). An interior point of a triangle implies greater stability than a boundary

3 It is understood hereafter that Π_1, Π_{20} and A_t are augmented by rows and columns of zeroes, so that $\Pi_1 + \Pi_{20} A_t$ is defined as a matrix of order $g[\max(l, q) - 1]$ derived from (2.6).

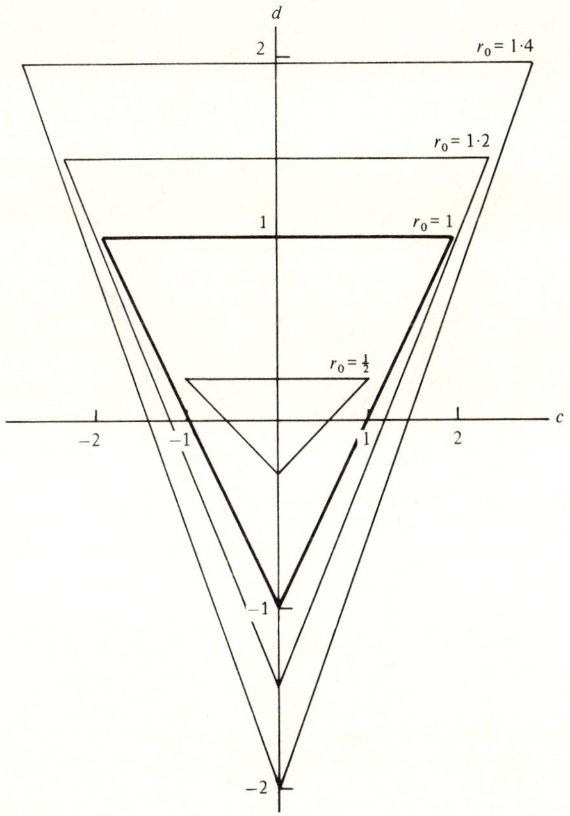

Figure 6.1 Iso-stability lines from (6.27)

point. Evidently we are interested in shifting c, d towards the origin. But how we shift them can influence the ratio $c{:}d$, and therefore the cycle length and θ. 'Iso-frequency' lines are defined as the locus of (c, d) combinations implying the same θ value (figure 6.2). They are given by

$$c^2 = 4d \cos \theta_0 \quad \text{for} \quad \theta = \theta_0. \tag{6.28}$$

Thus, if the ratio $|c:d|$ increases, cycles get longer; and vice versa. Indeed, writing $2\pi/\theta$ for cycle length and

$$d\theta = \frac{\partial \theta}{\partial a} da + \frac{\partial \theta}{\partial b} db$$

we find, since $\dfrac{\partial \cos^{-1} x}{\partial x} = -(1 - x^2)^{-1/2}$ with $x = a/r$,

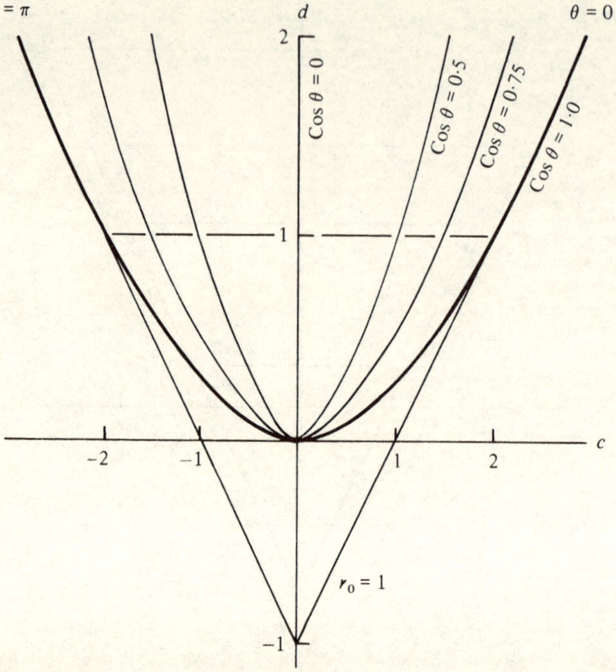

Figure 6.2 Iso-frequency lines from (6.28)

$$\frac{\partial \theta}{\partial a} = -b(a^2 + b^2)^{-1} \quad \text{and} \quad \frac{\partial \theta}{\partial b} = a(a^2 + b^2)^{-1}. \tag{6.29}$$

So we can always arrange to reduce $|c|$ and $|d|$ such that θ increases or decreases as desired.

If we consider λ_1 to be the only root of interest, then (6.26) is the characteristic equation of a system

$$Y_t + cY_{t-1} + dY_{t-2} = e_t. \tag{6.30}$$

But a system with g endogenous variables with maximum lag l gives a characteristic polynomial of order gl. Only in the very simplest models will (6.30) be an equation in the system (2.4), for example the multiplier – accelerator model (Baumol (1961)), where e_t is the exogenous part on the right of (2.4). Any analysis on (6.26)–(6.30) is strictly for illustration only. Generally we rewrite (2.4) in lag operator form

$$Y_t = (I - \Pi_1(L))^{-1}(\Pi_2(L)X_t + V_t) \tag{6.31}$$

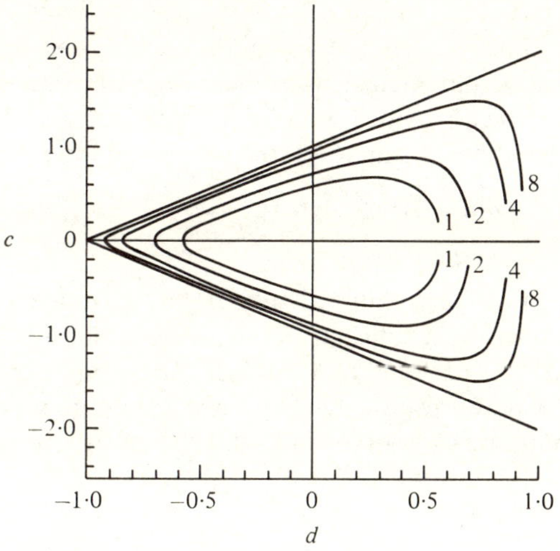

Figure 6.3 Iso-frequency loci for (6.33); *Source*: Howrey (1967)

and assuming stability so that the inverse exists,

$$|I - \Pi_1(L)|\, Y_t = adj(I - \Pi_1(L))(\Pi_2(L)X_t + V_t) \qquad (6.32)$$

where $|.|$ denotes a determinant and *adj* (.) the adjoint matrix. This shows each endogenous variable in terms of *gl* of its own lagged values. So we may also regard (6.26)–(6.30) as an approximation of the behaviour of any equation in (6.32) in the sense of how the cycle of interest behaves. Evidently, in view of the determinant of (6.32), the cyclical behaviour of each endogenous variable will be predominantly determined by a second order difference equation for each member of (6.32) where higher order lags can be neglected. So the dominant cyclical behaviour of each can be more (but probably less) satisfactorily approximated by neglecting lags greater than Y_{t-2} in (6.32).

Howrey (1967) shows that (6.30) implies

$$V(Y_t) = \frac{1 + d}{(1 - d)[(1 + c)^2 - d^2]} V(e_t), \quad \text{if} \quad V(.) = \text{variance} \qquad (6.33)$$

which for stable systems may be graphed in the $(c–d)$ space for various values of the variance ratio $V(Y_t){:}V(e_t) = \sigma$ (figure 6.3). Now consider changing c and d by application of a policy rule of the (6.20) type. Clearly (i) the minimum variance system has $c = d = 0$ (which implies maximum stability with lower limit $\sigma = 1$); (ii) this will change the cycle length, perhaps undesirably; (iii) the attempt to increase stability may, for some c, d values, actually increase the variance ratio. An example is where c is fixed but $d < \frac{1}{2}$ is reduced which, in terms of $\lambda_1 = a + ib$, means a is fixed and b is reduced leading to a lengthening of the cycle. Increasing $|c|$ increases the variance ratio; but increasing $|d| = r^2$ may increase or decrease it. Stability is increased provided c and d are decreased such that the ratio $|c:d|$ is bounded above. From (6.33) the upper and lower bounds on c are

$$1 \pm (\sigma^* - \sigma(d-1))^{1/2} \quad \text{where} \quad \sigma^* = 1 + d + \sigma(d^3 - d^2 - d + 1). \tag{6.34}$$

This means the ratio $|a:b|$ must also be bounded; a given reduction in b being accompanied by a sufficient reduction in a. Otherwise attempts to increase the stability of the system will increase the variance of the system.

Clearly this kind of result extends to any system, so we do not have to rely on the approximation of (6.30) to (6.32). For (6.32) implies

$$\lim_{t \to \infty} V(e_t) = V(Y_t)|I - \Pi_1(L)|^2 = V(Y_t) \prod_{j=1}^{gl} (1 - \lambda_j)^2 \tag{6.35}$$

where $V(.)$ is now a variance–covariance matrix. It is quite possible for example to consider altering coefficients in $\Pi_1(L)$ such that λ_1 only is affected. Writing $\bar{\lambda}_1$ for the complex conjugate, the relevant term in (6.35) is

$(1 - \lambda_1)^2 (1 - \bar{\lambda}_1)^2 = [(1-a)^2 - b^2]^2 + 4(1-a)^2 b^2$ with relative minima at $b \pm (3(1-a)^2)^{1/2}$. So $V(Y_t)$ could always be increased by such ill advised changes to $\Pi_1(L)$.

Evidently (6.33) and (6.35) imply minimum variances in the targets if $b = c = 0$ or $\Pi_1(L) = 0$. So for that objective we should set A_t to destroy the autoregressive structure of (2.4). But it is widely argued in academic literature, in policy documents of all kinds, and in the press, that frequent reversals of the trends in the main economic variables – targets and instruments alike – are undesirable. That is held to be upsetting and damaging to business confidence and labour relations, with consequent depressing effects on economic performance; as well as being indicative of uncertainty both in trading conditions and in the process of policy formulation. The damage comes from that uncertainty. Indeed, if we actually achieved that minimum variance, variations in Y_t would equal the random shocks to the system, in opposition to those comments which reveal a common preference for long smoothed cycles. It is clear that it is generally easier to adapt to slowly developing fluctuations, in the main highly predictable, than to completely random fluctuations even if they are of smaller variance. However, the minimum variance policy neutralises all the dynamic multipliers so any desired movements in the trend in the targets must be fully accounted for by changes in the current instruments. This may not be feasible. Finally there will be limits to the freedom of choice for A_t in terms of feasibility, institutional considerations and political acceptability.

Thus, there is generally a trade-off between using instruments to improve the target outcomes and to reduce the target's variances; and between improving stability with smoothed fluctuations and reduced target variances. The objectives of stabilisation policies can be quite different from those in the policy formulation problem, however the desired trajectories are defined. It is not clear, therefore, what constitutes an ideal stabilisation policy. Given some constraints, it is presumably not a policy directed exclusively at reducing any one of r (the roots), θ (the cycle length), or $V(Y_t)$ the target variances. It would in fact be some compromise between them. In other words we must check (see section 6.10) that a contracyclical policy rule (directed at some specific cycle) has not merely increased the power of some other shorter or longer cycles.

6.8 Stabilisation policies II

The question now arises: with different objectives to stabilisation policy, is it certain that we can pick the ideal A_t in general and thereby get any characteristics we want for the controlled system? If not, what freedom do we have to impose the characteristics we want? Evidently we are asking for a control rule analog to static controllability (the Tinbergen theorem) and, where that fails, for whatever weakened version may be available.

We cannot always choose A_t so as to arbitrarily change (annihilate) the model's dynamic structure at t, and thus achieve arbitrary targets $Y_t^d, t = 1, \ldots, T$. To achieve an arbitrary matrix $(\Pi_1 + \Pi_{20} A_t)$ in (6.25) requires sufficient instruments; i.e. at least $h \geqslant g$ and $l = k = 0$ so Π_{20} is nonsingular. This possibility only exists if there are at least as many instruments as endogenous variables at each decision point, which reproduces the Tinbergen result.

If, however, we pick A_t to set the eigenvalues of $(\Pi_1 + \Pi_{20} A_t)$ at desired positions in the complex plane we get a weakened version of controllability. It is a consequence of the following theorem (Wonham (1974)): for any real matrices C (of order g) and D (of order $g \times h$) and arbitrary (desired) complex numbers $\mu_j, j = 1, \ldots, g$, then, provided $r(D, CD, \ldots, C^{g-1}D) = g$ where $r(.)$ denotes rank, a real matrix A exists such that $C + DA$ has eigenvalues $\mu_j, j = 1, \ldots, g$.

Hence, subject to the mentioned rank condition which will be explained below, we can impose any desired dynamic properties for the controlled economy; but not any arbitrary dynamic structure. The result is independent of the values for g, h, l and k given the restrictions of this rank condition (obviously h is restricted, but $h < g$ is now possible) if $C = \Pi_1, D = \Pi_{20}$ and A_t is taken for A. If, for the moment, we ignore the stochastic terms, choosing each X_t via A_t means cyclical/growth patterns stem entirely from $(\Pi_1 + \Pi_{20}A_t)$ which, by (6.4), splits into two parts – eigenvalues (μ_j) and eigenvectors (W). Without static controllability we can pick μ_j and thus impose any desired cyclical and growth characteristics on the system as a whole, but not how those characteristics combine to form any particular target variable through W, which sets the scale and phase relationships. Therefore, we cannot ensure that particular variables hit their target values at each point, although we can obviously set μ_j so that all variables eventually hit their desired values. That is a longer run controllability of the dynamic structure. We shall now try to make this degree of 'controllability' precise.

6.9 Dynamic controllability and stabilisability

We are proposing to pick $A_t, t = 1, \ldots, T$, to impose certain dynamic properties such that a desirable outcome is assured by some future date, rather than at every point along the way. One would aim to damp out the effects of a shock or policy error within T periods, or to reduce the target variances by that date. This is less ambitious than trying to do the same at every t; and it is a more natural policy design.

Translating this proposition into terms of target values we get: given any initial state, Y_0, can the arbitrary values Y_T^d be achieved at least by some future date T? This weaker version of Tinbergen's theorem only makes sense in terms of expectations. A model having this property is said to be *dynamically* (*point*) *controllable*. Formally, the system

$$Y_t = \Pi_1 Y_{t-1} + \Pi_2 X_t \tag{6.36}$$

is dynamically controllable over $T \geqslant g$ if, and only if, $r(\Pi_2, \Pi_1\Pi_2, \ldots, \Pi_1^{g-1}\Pi_2) = g$ (Turnovsky (1977), p. 333). Notice that this expression contains all the impact and interim multipliers up to g periods ahead. But if we are only interested in m targets out of g we may say the system is controllable with respect to them if, and only if, $r(R_1, \ldots, R_m) = m$ where R_i is the relevant m rows from the matrices $\Pi^{i-1}\Pi_2$ for only $i = 1, \ldots, m$. The reduction in dimension from g to m may be useful in making the concept operational because g typically exceeds m by a large amount – see table 6.4. It may be very much easier to control that part of the system which is of interest, rather than the whole of it.

In section 6.8 we have control rule analogs to Tinbergen's theorem and, in its weakened version, of controllability. In the latter case we can

Table 6.4 *Some representative planning exercises*

Reference	Targets (m)	Instruments (n)	Model equations (g)	Maximum endogenous lag (l)	Planning horizon (T)	Maximum order of optimisation (nT)	Minimum state dimension (γ)
van den Bogaard and Theil (1959)	3	3	7	1	4	12	7
Friedman (1973)	3–7	2–5	88	10	5–8	10–40	880
Pindyck (1973)	5	3	12	6	20	60	72
Bray (1975)	6	6	25	7	16	96	175
Holbrook (1974)	3	3	61	1	6	18	61
Preston et al. (1976)	6	3	734	16	12	36	11744
Athans et al. (1977)	2	2	84	18	16	32	1512
Klein (1977)	4	3	76	10	17	51	760
Ghosh et al (1981)	2	1	30	41	40	40	1230
Brandsma et al. (1981)	7	5	130	6	5	25	780

have less instruments than targets, e.g. $\Pi_1 = \begin{pmatrix} 2 & 3 \\ 4 & 0 \end{pmatrix}$, $\Pi_{20} = \begin{pmatrix} 1 \\ 0 \end{pmatrix}$ imply (6.36) is a controllable system. Notice that point controllability only implies that the economy will pass through Y_T^d at T; it won't necessarily stay there, or follow any specified trajectory thereafter, unless Y_T^d represents an equilibrium state. But if T represents an election (or party congress) then what happens thereafter is of secondary importance, and in any case we can use controllability again. Again one may want one's opponent in a policy game (Chapter 11) to 'capitulate' by T.

The existence of a policy trajectory to move the targets along a preassigned path for a preassigned period requires *dynamic (path) controllability* (see Buiter and Gersovitz (1981) for details):

$r\begin{pmatrix} \Pi_2 \ldots \Pi_1^{2g-2}\Pi_2 \\ \ddots \quad \vdots \\ 0 \quad \Pi_2 \cdots \Pi_1^{g-1}\Pi_2 \end{pmatrix} = g^2$. But this latter is, to some extent, irrelevant because it continues to treat the system as deterministic. Shocks in a stochastic system will knock the economy off its preassigned path despite path controllability. A weaker proposition of guaranteed stability after Y_T^d has been reached (in the sense of controllability) would be more useful. Then the economy would tend to return to equilibrium even with fixed policies. For this we are only interested in the eigenvalues of $(\Pi_1 + \Pi_{20}A_t)$ in (6.25) – and those are in our gift given controllability. Choosing eigenvalues as above means we can choose $\mu_j < 1$, $j = 1 \ldots gl$ as a special case. That is, given point controllability, we can pick A_t such that $\rho(\Pi_1 + \Pi_{20}A_t) < 1$. This is known as the *stabilisability criterion*. If a system is point controllable, it is also stabilisable. How to pick A_t accordingly – or indeed to approach Y_T^d – remains to be seen (Chapter 8).

Thus stabilisability is necessary as a stochastic extension of controllability, to check that policies do indeed exist which will meet our objectives. But because the individual characteristics (determined by the eigenvectors W) cannot be picked at will for each t, stabilisation of a stochastic system is not the same thing as steering it. For example, we might pick policies (and A_t) at each t by specifying suitably smooth desired target and instrument values, and getting as close (in some sense) to them as possible. That is the standard control theory approach. But, as we have seen, that does not necessarily damp out the dynamic effects of random shocks, nor does it necessarily reduce the variance of the targets. Stabilisation can be more than just a problem in control theory.

Finally, there are two allied concepts to be mentioned, although they will not be used hereafter. The model at (6.36) is said to be *observable* if, and only if, $r(I, \Pi_1', \ldots (\Pi_1^{g-1})') = g$; (Aoki (1976)). It means that all characteristics of the system become known after g periods in the sense that the variance of the conditional probability distribution $p(Y_t|Y_{t-1})$ remains bounded throughout. This would become important in cases of errors in measuring the economy's state. *Instrument instability* is a problem where ever greater instrument changes are needed to counteract the effects of past policies necessary to achieve past targets. However, if this condition is unacceptable it reflects inadequate penalties to the use of instruments. Chapter 10.3 shows that raising those penalties leads towards simulating x_t^d values. Secondly, this condition does not arise in a model that is controllable (Aoki (1976)).

Notice, all the conditions (except the last) discussed in this section reflect properties of the model, not of any policy selection technique.

6.10 A spectral approach to cyclical policy analysis

The problem with the foregoing cyclical analysis is that we have no easy method to see how the cycles combine in a particular endogenous variable, nor (which is much more important) can we see the power of any of the individual cycles in a particular variable. The first we dispose of by arguing that we should investigate only the dominant cycle, and even if we could solve the difficulty of how cycles combine we would have no more information than that available from simulation. The second can be solved by computing the spectral matrix of Y_t as outlined in Chapter 5. The use of that method is illustrated by the following example.

The spectral matrix of the (linearised) Klein–Goldberger model has been computed by Howrey (1971). The exogenous tax version of the model ($\rho(\Pi_1) = 0.9815$) and the endogenous tax version ($\rho(\Pi_1) = 0.9941$) were both employed. The results are given in figure 6.4 for three endo-

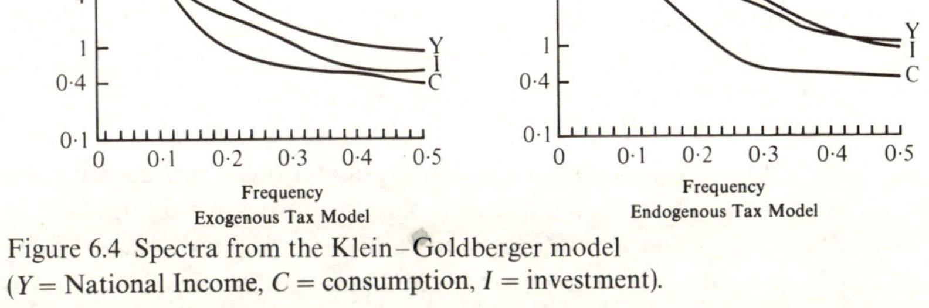

Figure 6.4 Spectra from the Klein–Goldberger model
(Y = National Income, C = consumption, I = investment).

genous variables. The most obvious feature is the strong dominance of the long cycles and trends in both figures. This is the 'typical shape' of spectra of economic variables (Granger (1966)). We can consider the endogenous tax model as showing the performance of the model (economy) under a policy rule for taxation, as compared to the exogenous tax model being the 'uncontrolled' model (economy). This particular rule has evidently removed a lot of power in the longer cycles. The peak corresponding to the long cycles (frequencies 0 to 1) is much reduced, although each variable still has a trend. The relative sensitivity to cycles in the three variables remains the same (Y most, C least). The actual power is if anything decreased at each frequency, so the target variances have been reduced, although the tax function, being imprecise, has contributed to their variances. A worrying feature is that this rule has somewhat increased the power of shorter cycles (a small peak has appeared at $\frac{1}{6}$th cycle per period, frequencies 1.5 to 3).

The cross spectra can be used to compute coherences, gains, and phase shifts for each cycle. Examples of the first and the last for 20 year and 4 year cycles are given in table 6.5. Introducing the policy rule generally reduces the coherences at 20 years and increases them at 4 years. Similarly a number of leads and lags are increased in both cycles. Thus the automatic stabilisation policy is found to somewhat reduce the variances of the targets but at the expense of removing the strength of the long cycles and increasing the strength of shorter cycles. And the variables behave more similarly (barring increased leads and lags) with respect to the business cycle rather than the long swing cycle natural to the model. That may increase difficulties of short-run control. The spectral technique has provided considerably more information than the earlier methods, and also suggests in this example that automatic stabilisation has made the economy more difficult to control for other purposes.

The important application of this spectral approach is for making numerical comparisons of the effects of various policy rules; particularly for total variance and the extent to which cycles have had power increased or reduced (raising or lowering the peaks). So we can see if the policies have been stabilising or destabilising in any sense. We have just had a realistic example of stabilisation, and variance reduction, being achieved at the cost of increased high frequency oscillations. This raises again the question of what stabilisation should be taken to mean. In view of the evident conflict in objectives, some compromise must be obtained in terms of r, θ and $V(Y_t)$. Plans either to minimise deviations from equilibrium or desired growth paths, or to reduce $V(Y_t)$ alone are not adequate.

It is tempting to aim to choose A_t in (6.23) to put peaks and troughs in the spectrum at desired positions. The spectrum of (6.30), as an ap-

Table 6.5 *Coherence and phase relationships for selected variables in the linearised Klein–Goldberger model*[a]

Variable	Exogenous Tax Yield Model				Endogenous Tax Yield Model				Simulation phase relationship
	Coherence		Phase (months)		Coherence		Phase (months)		
(1)	(2) $f = 1/20$	(3) $f = 1/4$	(4) $f = 1/20$	(5) $f = 1/4$	(6) $f = 1/20$	(7) $f = 1/4$	(8) $f = 1/20$	(9) $f = 1/4$	(10)
National income	0.99	0.97	4.7	0.2	0.98	0.89	4.2	2.2	Coincident
Consumption	0.99	0.63	− 2.8	0.3	0.98	0.57	− 5.6	− 0.1	Coincident
Investment	0.99	0.76	− 0.1	− 0.8	0.79	0.89	9.0	− 0.4	Coincident
Private employee compensation	0.99	0.85	− 5.7	− 2.4	0.99	0.95	− 7.5	− 6.3	Coincident
Farm income	0.65	0.05	− 0.5	6.2	0.40	0.20	4.2	10.2	Irregular
Nonwage nonfarm income	0.99	0.58	17.1	1.5	0.84	0.55	42.8	6.8	Coincident
Number of wage and salary earners	0.99	0.72	7.7	0.3	0.97	0.86	4.5	0.9	Coincident
Corporate profits	0.99	0.72	16.7	2.0	0.86	0.87	42.5	6.6	Coincident
Corporate savings	0.99	0.64	19.9	2.4	0.54	0.59	40.6	7.2	Coincident
Corporate surplus	0.96	0.64	− 34.1	− 3.6	0.55	0.59	− 13.3	1.2	Coincident
Capital stock	0.98	0.71	− 42.4	− 6.6	0.69	0.86	− 30.6	− 5.9	Coincident
Depreciation	0.98	0.11	− 35.7	− 3.2	0.76	0.30	− 22.7	− 5.3	Leading
Individual liquid assets	0.76	0.15	28.4	23.0	0.53	0.09	17.5	19.5	Leading
Business liquid assets	0.49	0.03	− 21.1	− 16.8	0.57	0.70	2.4	− 15.0	Coincident (inverted)
Price level	0.79	0.25	− 31.0	0.6	0.21	0.75	− 80.1	4.9	Coincident
Agricultural prices	0.78	0.18	− 30.7	1.0	0.19	0.41	− 73.9	4.8	Coincident
Wage rate	0.87	0.19	− 45.1	− 8.8	0.43	0.61	− 5.9	− 6.6	Lagging

[a] The coherence and phase calculations shown in this table are based on the relationship of gross national product and the corresponding variable shown in column (1) of the tables. The coherence at 1/40 of a cycle per year is shown in column (2) and the coherence at 1/4 of a cycle per year is shown in column (3). The phase differences at these frequencies are shown in columns (4) and (5). A positive entry indicates that the variable in question leads gross national product while a negative entry indicates that the variable lags GNP.

Source: Howrey (1971).

proximation to (2.4), exhibits turning points at

$$\theta = \cos^{-1}\left(\frac{-c(1+d)}{4d}\right) \tag{6.37}$$

where

$f_Y(\theta) = |1 + ce^{-i\theta} + de^{-2i\theta}|^{-2} f_h(\theta)$ is from (5.24); Howrey (1967).

We get maxima if $c > 0$ and minima if $c < 0$. Graphing this for several values of θ in $(c-d)$ space gives figure 6.5. Consider the area enclosed by the curved lines. Outside these we have a monotonic increasing or decreasing spectrum. Thus c increasing, with d fixed, means a peak at higher frequencies ($d \geqslant 0$), or a trough at lower frequencies ($d < 0$). For d increasing, with c fixed, the peak is moved to higher (lower) frequencies if $c < 0 (c > 0)$; and vice versa if $c \leqslant 0$ for the minimum. But to generate this analysis will be difficult as there will be multiple turning points for higher order equations than (6.30). We could take results from (6.30) as an appropriate approximation or we could attempt to work with a more complicated version of figure 6.5. But it is not likely to be worth the effort as to return from adjusted coefficients in (6.30) for each endogenous variable to $\Pi_1 + \Pi_{20}A_t$ via the determinant, and thus to A_t, is a very complicated business indeed.

If we retreat to (5.30), we may consider picking A_t to change eigenvalues

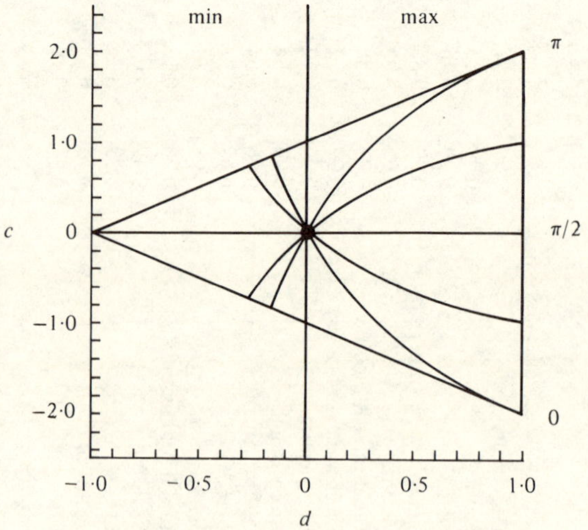

Figure 6.5 Iso-frequency loci for (6.37); *Source*: Howrey (1967)

from those of Π_1 to those of $\Pi_1 + \Pi_{20}A_t$ such that $F^Y(\theta)$ takes on the desired shape. That is exactly where we were before. The problem, remains changing the eigenvectors in W. Picking the peaks and troughs in $F^Y(\theta)$ will be just as difficult, although we can set the parameters of those schemes to give some approximation to the desired shape of $F^Y(\theta)$. In other words, the spectral approach should be retained to evaluate the effects of any policy rule rather than as a design tool.

7

Control theory: a rehabilitation of the theory of economic policy

7.1 Introduction

In this chapter and the next we turn from 'ad hoc' policy selections to policies which are, according to a suitable criterion, explicitly optimised. We also make some assessment of the algorithms which may be used to compute them. We shall show how these optimal policies can be computed such that most of the objections to Tinbergen's theory of economic policy (discussed in Chapter 2) are overcome.

In sections 7.2 and 7.3 we solve the policy choice problem for the case of unequal numbers of targets and instruments, where policy variables are constrained to be within permissible boundaries, and where the alterations to instruments incur costs to welfare. In sections 7.4 and 7.5 we treat uncertainty and dynamic planning problems explicitly. The specification of the objective function, however, is a subject for later chapters. The outcome is a solution of a control theory type, complete with all the distinguishing features of closed loop feedback control and optimal policy revisions in the wake of uncertainty (section 7.6). Finally, we examine the structure of the optimal policy revisions in terms of the innovations to the system since the start of the planning period (section 7.7 and 7.8). Section 7.9 gives a numerical example to illustrate the dynamic policy selection in action.

In this chapter we approach the problem as a direct optimisation of the instrument values. We shall obtain the same results in the following chapter by deriving the optimal feedback law, i.e. optimising $A_t(L)$ of (6.20), in order to generate those values.

7.2 A model of planning behaviour

In constructing a model of a self-managed economy we suppose that the planners make rational choices, in their own or the public interest, when selecting the values for the variables under their control. The assumption of rational choices of course implies no more than that some known preference ordering exists over values of all the variables of interest to the planners, and that this preference ordering should satisfy a minimal set of axioms of choice: *reflexivity* and *completeness* to yield a properly defined set of options; *transitivity* so that a rational and consistent ordering exists; and *convexity* for the existence of an optimal choice. Self-interest maximising choices are made on this basis. Secondly, it is supposed that the planners know their ideal values for the instruments and targets (i.e. that they can define their own policy goals), and that they know that they face certain constraints. It is not assumed that they necessarily know the constraints correctly, but that they at least have some perception and expectations for them and that they choose policies on that basis.

In Chapter 1 we emphasised that policy makers have – in their publications, or through public acceptance – formed rather clear ideas of their policy goals and associated target values. But, as the remainder of this book makes apparent, they have the greatest difficulty in formalising their policy selection problem. Consequently this set of assumptions, but no more than that, seems appropriate for an economic planning model.

7.2.1 The variables and constraints

The planning system contains variables of three kinds: an m-vector of policy objectives (targets) y_t; an n-vector of policy instruments, x_t; and a vector of variables exogenous both to the economic system and to the planners, s_t. We consider a planning horizon T, with discrete decision intervals $t = 1 \dots T$. Let $y' = (y'_1 \dots y'_T)$, $x' = (x'_1 \dots x'_T)$, and $s' = (s'_1 \dots s'_T)$. We write the set of policy variables $z' = (y', x')$. Suppose the planners have selected ideal but generally infeasible trajectories for z as $z^{d'} = (y_1^{d'} \dots y_T^{d'}, x_1^{d'} \dots x_T^{d'})$. Let $\tilde{z} = z - z^d$. The problem of policy choice may now be formulated as one of optimising some function of preferences over the goals and instruments in the planning system, subject to constraints imposed by the feasible performance of the economy itself. The constraints facing the planners, or at least their perception of them, may be represented by a dynamic, time varying and causal model:

$$y_t = f_t(y_{t-1} \dots y_{t-l}, x_t \dots x_{t-k}, s_t). \tag{7.1}$$

Those constraints must be reformulated to include the dynamic responses of the economy for each planning interval, up to and including the planning horizon. So we take such a model and write it with its t-period final forms stacked up for $t = 1 \dots T$. The initial condition of each variable will be known in $Z_{t=0}$. Thus

$$y = Rx + s \tag{7.2}$$

where

$$R = \begin{pmatrix} R_{11} & & 0 \\ \vdots & \ddots & \\ R_{T1} & \dots & R_{TT} \end{pmatrix}. \text{ So } R_{ij} = \begin{cases} \partial y_i/\partial x_j \text{ for } i, j = 1, \dots, T \text{ and } i \geqslant j, \\ 0 \text{ otherwise,} \end{cases}$$

evaluated at some x and s. R_{ij} is $m \times n$ matrix of impact or interim multipliers of the instruments in period j on current or subsequent targets. Summing by rows, $\sum_{j=1}^{i} R_{ij}$ gives the dynamic multipliers after i periods, for each planning interval $i = 1 \dots T$. Targets in this model cannot, as yet, be directly influenced by anticipated instruments. But that restriction will be relaxed for the noncausal models of Chapter 11.

Evidently (7.2) may be constructed for nonlinear models by numerical evaluations of the relevant multipliers. This is discussed in the appendix to this chapter. On the other hand, in a time invariant linear model the instruments will have an impact on targets which is invariant with respect to the trajectories of x and s (and thus invariant to t) for a given length of delay. Hence $R_{ij} = R_{i-j+1}$ for all $i \geqslant j = 1 \dots T$. In that case R simplifies to

$R = \begin{pmatrix} R_1 & & 0 \\ \vdots & \ddots & \\ R_T & \dots & R_1 \end{pmatrix}$; where the submatrices can be calculated directly by the methods of Chapter 4. Multipliers for the model as a whole are:

$$\begin{aligned} R_i^* &= \sum_{j=1}^{\min(k,i)} \Pi_1^{i-j} \begin{pmatrix} \Pi_{2,j-1} \\ 0 \end{pmatrix} \text{ for } i = 1 \dots T \\ &= \Pi_1 \sum_{j=1}^{\min(k,i-1)} \Pi_1^{i-j-1} \begin{pmatrix} \Pi_{2,j-1} \\ 0 \end{pmatrix} \\ &= \begin{cases} \Pi_1 R_{i-1}^* & \text{if } i-1 > k \\ \Pi_1 R_{i-1}^* + \begin{pmatrix} \Pi_{2,i-1} \\ 0 \end{pmatrix} & \text{if } i-1 \leqslant k \end{cases} \end{aligned} \tag{7.3}$$

with the impact multipliers $R_1^* = \begin{pmatrix} \Pi_{20} \\ 0 \end{pmatrix}$. Thus $\lim_{i\to\infty} R_i^* = 0$ if $\rho(\Pi_1) < 1$; that is in a stable system. However, we only require multipliers to link the targets with the instruments. But it is obvious from the fact that powers of Π_1 appear in these expressions that each multiplier involves components from all the augmented dimensions of Y_t^+ in (2.5). Moreover, we are unable to cut down on these dimensions since each *interim* multiplier contains an accumulation of up to l feedthrough effects from *every* past multiplier's impact. Only after we have combined these accumulations over each present and past exogenous disturbance which still affects the subset of targets y_t, can nonpolicy variables be discarded. We are not interested in the multipliers associated with components of Y_t^+ which are actually lagged values or nontargets. Hence, from R_i^* we can delete the last $g(l-1)$ rows (corresponding to the lags in Y_t^+), and then the $g-m$ rows of what remains corresponding to the nontargets in Y_t. That gives R_i from R_i^*. These same deletions also apply to nonlinear models, in the form (7.2), after the full set of multiplier evaluations.

7.2.2 The noncontrollable elements

It is traditional to decompose s as $s = \sigma + Su$ where $S = \begin{bmatrix} S_{11} & & 0 \\ \vdots & \ddots & \\ S_{T1} & \dots & S_{TT} \end{bmatrix}$ corresponds to R. For nonlinear models this decomposition would not be used, for reasons which will appear later. The submatrices $S_{ij} = \partial y_i / \partial u_j$, $i \geqslant j$, are the multipliers with respect to $u' = (u_1' \dots u_T')$ where u_t is the set of structural equation errors at period t. Once again, a time invariant linear model $S_{ij} = S_{i-j+1}$ holds for all $i \geqslant j = 1 \dots T$; where

$$S_i^* = \Pi_1^{i-1} \beta^{-1} \quad i = 1 \dots T \tag{7.4}$$

and S_i is obtained from S_i^* by discarding the same rows as were deleted from R_i^* to give R_i. The columns in S_i^* corresponding to the model's nonstochastic equations can also be discarded when forming S_i.

If we start the construction of (7.2) from the model (2.4), we make no distinction between policy instruments and noncontrollable variables. But, since policy instruments alone are subject to choice, we must partition X_t' as $(x_t' \vdots N_t')$. Hence the matrices $\Pi_{2,j-1}$ in (7.3) refer to the leading submatrix in the partitioning $(\Pi_{2,j-1} \vdots \Pi_{3,j-1})$. Consequently, $\sigma' = (\sigma_1' \dots \sigma_T')$ is derived from

$$\sigma_1^* = \Pi_1 Y_{t=0} + \Pi_2 x_{t=0} + \Pi_3 N_{t=0} \quad \text{and}$$

$$\sigma_i^* = \Pi_1 \sigma_{i-1}^* + \Pi_3 N_i + \sum_{j=i}^{l} \begin{pmatrix} \Pi_{1j} \\ 0 \end{pmatrix} Y_{i-j} + \sum_{j=i}^{k} \begin{pmatrix} \Pi_{2j} \\ 0 \end{pmatrix} x_{i-j} \quad i = 2 \dots T \tag{7.5}$$

where σ_i is obtained from σ_i^* by the same row deletions as were made to R_i^*. If $N' = (N_1' \dots N_T')$ then

$$s = \begin{pmatrix} \Pi_1 \\ \vdots \\ \Pi_1^T \end{pmatrix} Z_{t=o} + KN + Su \tag{7.6}$$

where

$$K = \begin{pmatrix} K_{11} & & 0 \\ \vdots & \ddots & \\ K_{T1} & \dots & K_{TT} \end{pmatrix} \tag{7.7}$$

and $K_{ij} = \partial y_i / \partial N_j$ are multipliers analogous to R_{ij}. In a linear model

R_i and K_i could in fact be obtained simultaneously from (7.3) if $(\Pi_{2,j-1} \vdots \Pi_{3,j-1})$ replaces $\Pi_{2,j-1}$. N_t is not subject to choice, so no generality is lost if lagged noncontrollable variables are treated as separate variables, with separate entries, in N_t. We still do not distinguish instruments in the hands of other agents from other noncontrollables.

Notice the initial conditions, $Z'_{t=0} = (Y'_{t=0}, (\Pi_2 X_{t=0})')$, contain lags back to l and k periods earlier. So in fact we have been dealing with the same augmented reduced form model as found in other texts (e.g. Chow (1975), pp. 153, 154):

$$Z_t = \begin{pmatrix} \Pi_1 & \Pi_2^{**} \\ 0 & I^* \end{pmatrix} Z_{t-1} + \begin{pmatrix} R_{tt} \\ 0 \\ I \\ 0 \end{pmatrix} x_t + \begin{pmatrix} K_{tt} \\ 0 \end{pmatrix} N_t + \begin{pmatrix} S_{tt} \\ 0 \end{pmatrix} u_t \tag{7.8}$$

where Π_1 and Π_2^{**} can also be time varying. In terms of (2.6) $\Pi_2^{**} = \begin{pmatrix} \Pi_{21} \dots \Pi_{2k} \\ 0 \; \dots \; 0 \end{pmatrix}; I^* = \begin{pmatrix} 0 & 0 \\ I_{n(k-1)} & 0 \end{pmatrix}$ is of order $nk; R_{tt} = \Pi_{20}$; $K_{tt} = \begin{pmatrix} \Pi_3 \\ 0 \end{pmatrix}$; and $S_{tt} = \begin{pmatrix} \beta^{-1} \\ 0 \end{pmatrix}$. On the other hand, (7.2) with (7.6) is the model format used by Theil (1964).

7.2.3 The condensed model form

We rewrite (7.2) as:

$$H\tilde{z} = b \tag{7.9}$$

with $H = [I \vdots -R]$ and $b = s - Hz^d$. We then define the feasible set, F, of $\tilde{z}$ values as $F \equiv \{\tilde{z} \in E^{(n+m)T} \mid H\tilde{z} - b = 0\}$. Naturally, since $mT < (n+m)T$, F is not empty.

The dimensions of the optimisation problem have now been reduced from $\{gl + nk\}T$ to $(m+n)T$ choice variables; where $g \geqslant m$, $l \geqslant 1$, and $k \geqslant 0$. Since the economy's dynamic responses have been made explicit for (7.9), we need only to retain those relevant to the policy problem in hand. Other dynamic optimisation methods leave those responses implicit in a reduced form model such as (7.8). They must carry the full set of nontargets, and all the lags of the model, throughout each of the T stages of the optimisation.

The reader should bear in mind the significance of model condensation for computational efficiency. Table 6.4 shows g and h increase with model size and complexity, yet m and n tend not to do so. In fact $g - m$ tends to be a very substantial proportion of the model size, and that is generally multiplied up by $l > 1$. However, the reduction of dimensions was achieved after R and s were obtained, so it is essential that the benefits are not lost in the calculations necessary to obtain R and s. Efficient computational schemes are set out in the appendix to this chapter. For large models it is probably most efficient to evaluate the relevant multipliers by nonstochastic simulations over the interval $[1, T]$ of individual unit shocks in each element of x, given fixed values for N and u. Although this is applied to the nonlinear case in the appendix, it is always available for linear models as well.

Our experience has been that model condensation makes policy optimisation a feasible proposition for large scale models; and cheap enough to be applied even as a routine matter. It is to stress this advantage which justifies any concentration on the algorithms themselves. In the appendix to the following chapter we indicate the computational burden of two large but conventional applications, and attempt some comparisons with other optimisation techniques.

7.2.4 The preference system

The precise specification of the appropriate preference system is a very difficult task for any planning exercise. A comprehensive discussion is deferred to Chapter 10. Here we merely define the form of the preference function to be used.

Optimal policies are almost always derived by picking policy values to minimise a normalised quadratic function of the policy variables,

$$w = \tfrac{1}{2}\tilde{z}'Q\tilde{z} + q'\tilde{z} \tag{7.10}$$

while also satisfying the constraints imposed by the economy as modelled by (7.8) or (7.9).

But since true collective preferences cannot be perfectly known a priori (and Chapter 10 examines in detail why this is), if indeed they even exist, we can at most specify the true performance index implicitly:

$$w = w(\tilde{z}) \tag{7.11}$$

and then take (7.10) to be a quadratic approximation at some feasible value $\tilde{z}^*$. This implicit preference ordering is at least reflexive, complete, transitive and convex. For convenience (7.11) is also assumed continuous and twice differentiable over F; so that Q is symmetric and positive definite. Both Q and q are then functions of $\tilde{z}^*$; $Q = \left[\dfrac{\partial^2 w}{\partial z\, \partial z'}\right]_{\tilde{z}^*}$ and

$q = -Q\tilde{z}^* + \left[\dfrac{\partial w}{\partial z}\right]_{\tilde{z}^*}$. Finally Q will be partitioned, $Q = \begin{pmatrix} A & C' \\ C & B \end{pmatrix}$ conformably with z; and $q' = (q_1', q_2')$ likewise.

Now (7.10) contains implicit ideal values $z^d - Q^{-1}q$. So without loss of generality the linear term can be removed:

$$w = \tfrac{1}{2}(\tilde{\zeta}' Q \tilde{\zeta} - q' Q^{-1} q) \tag{7.12}$$

where $\tilde{\zeta} = \tilde{z} + Q^{-1}q$. By definition genuine ideal values are the unconstrained maximum of (7.11) and (7.10). Therefore a consistent specification of (7.10), where z^d are indeed genuine ideal values, *either* has $q = 0$ *or* has z^d replaced by the artificial values $z^d + Q^{-1}q$. However, if we retain the genuine z^d with $q \neq 0$, the preferences are asymmetric about z^d with $\partial w/\partial z = q$ at z^d. Presumably q would be chosen so that all elements of $\tilde{z}$ have the more 'desirable' sign. In such a case we bias (7.10) to give results which are unavailable from a quadratic approximation to (7.11) at $\tilde{z}^*$. Thus, we may make the transformation of (7.12) without loss of generality, but not without impunity for the interpretation of z^d as ideal values.

7.3 The optimal policies

The planning problem is to pick $\tilde{z}^*$ as

$$\tilde{z}^* = \min_z \{w(\tilde{z}) \mid H\tilde{z} - b = 0\}. \tag{7.13}$$

Define mT Lagrange multipliers, μ. We take a second order approximation to (7.13) in terms of $\tilde{z}$ where, for full generality, we shall continue to use (7.10) but with z^d as genuine ideal values. A model linearisation, as in (7.2), is also implied. The policy choice is then

$$\min_z \{L(\tilde{z}, \mu) \mid L = w + \mu'(H\tilde{z} - b)\}. \tag{7.14}$$

The first order conditions for (7.14) are:

$$\begin{pmatrix} Q & -H' \\ -H & O \end{pmatrix} \begin{pmatrix} \tilde{z} \\ \mu \end{pmatrix} + \begin{pmatrix} q \\ b \end{pmatrix} = 0 \tag{7.15}$$

yielding

$$\tilde{z}^* = Q^{-1}(H'(HQ^{-1}H')^{-1}(HQ^{-1}q + b) - q)$$

and

$$\mu^* = (HQ^{-1}H')^{-1}(HQ^{-1}q + b) \tag{7.16}$$

where also

$$L(\tilde{z}, \mu) = \frac{1}{2}\begin{pmatrix} \tilde{z} \\ \mu \end{pmatrix}' \begin{pmatrix} Q & -H' \\ -H & O \end{pmatrix} \begin{pmatrix} \tilde{z} \\ \mu \end{pmatrix} + \begin{pmatrix} q \\ b \end{pmatrix}' \begin{pmatrix} \tilde{z} \\ \mu \end{pmatrix}. \tag{7.17}$$

$\tilde{z}^*$ is invariant to scalar transformations in (Q, q) but μ^* is directly proportional to such a transform. Now let $\Theta = Q^{-1}H'(HQ^{-1}H')^{-1}$ and $P = I - \Theta H$ for subsequent use.

The compact formula for $\tilde{z}^*$ in (7.16) is in fact identical to those provided by Theil (1964) for $\tilde{x}^*$ and $\tilde{y}^*$ individually:

$$\tilde{x}^* = -(H^{*\prime}QH^*)^{-1}H^{*\prime}\left(Q\begin{pmatrix} b \\ \cdots \\ o \end{pmatrix} + q\right) \text{and } \tilde{y}^* = R\tilde{x}^* + b \quad (7.18)$$

where $H^{*\prime} = (R' \vdots I)$. Thus $\tilde{y}^* = \left[I - R(H^{*\prime}QH^*)^{-1}H^{*\prime}Q\begin{pmatrix} I \\ \cdots \\ O \end{pmatrix}\right]b - R(H^{*\prime}QH^*)^{-1}H^{*\prime}q$. The associated constrained objective function is

$$L(\tilde{x}) = \tfrac{1}{2}\tilde{x}'H^{*\prime}QH^*\tilde{x} + \tilde{x}'H^{*\prime}\left(Q\begin{pmatrix} b \\ \cdots \\ o \end{pmatrix} + q\right) + \tfrac{1}{2}b'Bb + q_1'b \quad (7.19)$$

in place of (7.17). Let $M = H^{*\prime}QH^*$; $m_1 = H^{*\prime}\left(Q\begin{pmatrix} b \\ \cdots \\ 0 \end{pmatrix} + q\right)$, and $m_0 = \tfrac{1}{2}b'Bb + q_1'b$.

The second order conditions sufficient for a strict minimum in both of the constrained objectives are of course satisfied if Q is positive definite. Then this policy selection exists, and is unique to the extent that (7.10) is valid. However, whereas (7.16) is restricted to cases with such a definite statement of preferences, (7.18) can also be used when the specification of $w(\tilde{z})$ is more vague or even incomplete. It is only necessary that M should be of full rank. Thus preferences may be undefined for all but nT of the variables, provided no constraint is redundant. Hence, even when $m > n$, it is possible to solve problems having no penalties on the use of instruments;[1] or problems having no penalties on the targets; and all the combinations between these extremes. Similarly, deleting from (7.9) and (7.10) any variables which are not penalised allows (7.16) to be used provided at least mT variables remain.

Another reason for preferring (7.18) is because it uses only one matrix inversion of order nT rather than the two, of order $(m+n)T$ and mT respectively, in (7.16). The important consideration here is numerical accuracy. Inaccuracies which result from inverting large or illconditioned matrices are notorious; and in this context the danger is sharpened since each implemented z_t^* will turn out to be a function of z_i^*, $i = 1 \ldots t-1$, so error propagation is a serious threat to later policies (see equation (7.39) below).

The methods of policy selection discussed above are, in fact, an application of a standard mathematical programming technique to the policy

1 If $n \geqslant m$ and there are no instrument penalties, optimisation is redundant as the system has perfect static controllability.

problem. As we go on to examine uncertainty, policy revisions and the implied feedback control rule we shall find that this standard technique assumes the characteristics of conventional control theory methods.

7.4 Uncertainty

The policy selection method discussed in the preceding section goes a long way to reconstructing Tinbergen's theory of economic policy choice. The remaining difficulties are uncertainty, and the specification of a preference function. Within the former problem there are three issues:

(i) uncertainty in the variables (i.e. due to N_t and u_t: additive uncertainty);

(ii) uncertainty in the parameters (i.e. due to R, K and S: multiplicative uncertainty); and

(iii) the fact that the parameters of the probability density functions of the uncertain components will vary over time.

7.4.1 Uncertainty in variables

The optimising value of $\tilde{z}^*$ depends explicitly on b – and through that on N_t and u_t – so that its choice must be conditioned on some values for those variables. To that end we replace b by its expectation, conditional on all the information at the moment of calculating (7.16) or (7.18). This may be justified by the *certainty equivalence theorem*:

$$\min_z \{E(w) | H\tilde{z} - b = 0\} = \min_z \{w | H\tilde{z} - E(b) = 0\} \tag{7.20}$$

where $E(.)$ denotes the expectation operator.

Proof:

$$E(w) = \tfrac{1}{2}E(\tilde{z}'Q\tilde{z}) + q'E(\tilde{z}) \tag{7.21}$$

where of course $E(\tilde{z}) = \begin{bmatrix} E(\tilde{y}) \\ \tilde{x} \end{bmatrix} = \begin{bmatrix} R\tilde{x} + E(b) \\ \tilde{x} \end{bmatrix}$. But

$$w(E(\tilde{y}), \tilde{x}) = \tfrac{1}{2}\begin{bmatrix} R\tilde{x} + E(b) \\ \tilde{x} \end{bmatrix}' Q \begin{bmatrix} R\tilde{x} + E(b) \\ \tilde{x} \end{bmatrix} + q'E(\tilde{z}). \tag{7.22}$$

Now

$$E(\tilde{z}'Q\tilde{z}) = E(R\tilde{x} + b)'B(R\tilde{x} + b) + 2(R\tilde{x} + E(b))'C'\tilde{x} + \tilde{x}'A\tilde{x}. \tag{7.23}$$

Hence

$$E(w(\tilde{y}, \tilde{x})) - w(E(\tilde{y}), \tilde{x}) = \tfrac{1}{2}\{E(b'Bb) - E(b)'BE(b)\} \neq 0. \tag{7.24}$$

It is because (7.24) is independent of $\tilde{z}$ that the theorem follows.

Hence if we wish to maximise the expectation of (7.10) subject to (7.9) we have a strategy to deal with uncertain variables. We get the same $\tilde{x}^*$ if, instead, we maximise (7.10) subject to (7.9) with $E(b)$ replacing b.

Comments: The wisdom of the arbitrary substitution of $E(w)$ for w, in recognition of the uncertainties in b, may well be thought questionable. We shall not enter that debate here. Even so, this certainty equivalence result obviously would not hold if any one of the following happens to be true, since extra terms involving $\tilde{x}$ would be introduced into (7.24):

(i) If the objective were any other nonlinear function but quadratic;

(ii) R were not considered fixed; which includes cases of uncertainty in the parameters. For example, suppose $\tilde{x}$ remains nonstochastic. Then stochastic parameters would introduce an extra term of

$$E(\tilde{x}'R'BR\tilde{x}) - \tilde{x}'E(R)'BE(R)\tilde{x} \neq 0 \tag{7.25}$$

in (7.24) which depends on $\tilde{x}$.

(iii) There are nonlinearities in the target–instrument linkages. Note, however, that nonlinearities in any components of b do not affect this theorem.

Looking back at (7.16) and (7.18), we find $\tilde{x}^*$ is a linear function of b (which itself is linear in N and u) so $\tilde{x}^*$ is fixed if the expectations of N and u are. That is the natural situation for u; $E(u) = 0$. And it may be the case for N. But if $E(N)$ were obtained from an auxiliary model or other forecasting methods, or u were known to be serially correlated, then the certainty equivalents may be stochastic; and thus $\tilde{x}^*$ stochastic. Chapter 12 extends the theorem for this case.

A strength of the certainty equivalence theorem is that we can completely avoid specifying probability density functions, $f(u)$ and $f(N)$, for u and N. That might be very hard to do, and would at best be arbitrary and of uncertain validity. In fact, it is only assumed here that $\int_{-\infty}^{\infty} uf(u)du$ and $\int_{-\infty}^{\infty} Nf(N)dN$ both converge to some fixed nonstochastic values. These values (as well as our estimates of them) may well be time varying, and the density functions (subjective or not) can alter as we progress through the planning periods.

It is sometimes said that Su summarises the random components of b, and σ the deterministic ones. This is misleading. The values in N will typically be forecasted with an auxiliary model and/or by using other extraneous information, but those in u by postulating its probability density function. The certainty equivalence strategy makes no distinction between the uncertainty in N and u. Their separation is only to allow the monitoring of the success of the different auxiliary forecasting techniques which may be employed.

7.4.2 Uncertainty in the parameters

We still have the possibility of uncertainty in R, S, and K. The elements of R might be uncertain for several reasons. The dynamic responses of targets to instruments are to some extent genuinely random. The structural parameters may be thought to be stochastic, following some multivariate distribution with estimated (asymptotic) means and variances. Or it may be that they are fixed but impossible to estimate precisely, due to the sampling variability in a finite data set. Again it may be that they vary over time according to some well defined, but imperfectly known, scheme.

In any event, the model's parameters are likely to be uncertain but in rather complicated ways. The probability density function characterising the uncertainty in Π_1 and Π_2 is not generally known (and its moments may not exist) when the latter are restricted reduced form estimates. And even if some features of those density functions (such as the means and variances) are known, the associated characteristics for R will not be known because of the nonlinear transformations and convolutions necessary to derive the latter. It is effectively impossible to characterise this type of uncertainty precisely, so we may as well be content with some approximations. The approximations will be applied in two parts: (i) an approximation to $E(R)$; (ii) an approximation to the correct decision, given some satisfactory estimate of $E(R)$. We shall avoid any attempt at approximating the distribution of R.

First, $E(R)$ is approximated by taking the estimated means of the structural parameter matrices β and Γ, creating Π_1 and Π_2 from them, and thus R via (7.3). We may accept the resulting approximation as adequate, but possibly the stochastic simulation of (7.3), given the asymptotic distribution of (β, Γ), would improve it. Checks on the accuracy of either estimate are impossible without knowledge of the exact distribution of R.

Next, by analogy with the certainty equivalence strategy, we replace R by $E(R)$ throughout (7.16) and (7.18). As a justification of this let $dR = R - E(R)$ and consider the terms in (7.25):

$$\begin{aligned}\tilde{x}'E(R'BR)\tilde{x} &= \tilde{x}'E(R)'BE(R)\tilde{x} + 2\tilde{x}'E(R)'BE(dR)\tilde{x} + E(\tilde{x}'dR'BdR\tilde{x}) \\ &= \tilde{x}'E(R)'BE(R)\tilde{x} + \tilde{x}'E(dR'BdR)\tilde{x} \qquad (7.26)\end{aligned}$$

when $E(dR) = 0$, i.e. we have unbiased estimates. Since β and Γ will be consistently estimated at best, (7.26) is strictly true only asymptotically. But the error in this third approximation is probably very small compared to ignoring the last term of (7.26), which will be the next step. Repeating the certainty equivalence theorem for this case, and using (7.26), yields:

$$\tfrac{1}{2}\{E(b'Bb) - E(b)'BE(b) + \tilde{x}'E(dR'BdR)\tilde{x}\} \neq 0 \qquad (7.27)$$

in place of (7.24). This expression does depend on $\tilde{x}$. If, furthermore, R and b are correlated we must add

$$\tilde{x}'[E(R'Bb) - E(R)'BE(b)] = \tilde{x}'E(dR'Bdb) \tag{7.28}$$

to (7.27). So if, in addition to any other approximations, we may neglect the last term of (7.26) as being of an order smaller than the rest then (7.27) is approximately independent of $\tilde{x}$. This requires that the sum of variances and covariances of R weighted in the scale of target preferences be small. In this sense the certainty equivalence result continues to hold approximately by inserting $E(H)$ for H on the right of (7.20). Similarly we need small correlations between R and b if (7.28) is also to vanish.

Notice that this neglect of the last term of (7.26) – and of that in (7.28) – would also be implied by taking first order approximations to $\tilde{x}'E(R'BR)\tilde{x}$ and $\tilde{x}'E(R'Bb)$ about $E(R)$ and $E(b)$. Hence this strategy of treating the parameters in the optimal decision rules as if they were fixed at their expected values can be justified as correct up to a linear approximation – a strategy termed *first order certainty equivalence.*

In summary, the policy choice which optimises $E(w)$, subject to (7.9), is (7.16) with $E(H)$ and $E(b)$ for H and b respectively. The optimality of this choice is exact for the additive uncertainty in b, but is only correct up to a linear approximation for the multiplicative uncertainty of R. Nevertheless, that approximation becomes arbitrarily good as the variances in R fall, or as the priorities on targets with uncertain responses fall. This approximation is relaxed in Chapter 12.

Comments: There is of course also multiplicative uncertainty within b. Here uncertainty has two sources; from the multipliers in K and S and in the variables N and U. Again we may approximate E(b) by stochastic simulation or by inserting the mean of each uncertain element into (7.6). But there is now no approximation corresponding to first order certainty equivalence, because the choice problem is not complicated by the nonlinear form of these uncertainties within b.

We make no attempt to specify the distributions of R, K and S (any more than we do for N and u) because the relevant distributions are generally unknown, and because evaluating the convolutions of all the density functions which go to make up R and b is out of the question. The set of approximations used here is the price paid to gain the major advantage of this strategy: the freedom to handle uncertainties without any knowledge of the distributions which characterise them.

If nothing else, this discussion should have underlined how difficult it is to derive exact results under uncertainty. An informal approach may be more valuable in practice. Therefore we shall consider the evaluation of the sensitivity of policies to shocks from various sources of uncertainty; also methods for constraining risk and endogenising the determination of the choices of other players within a policy game.

7.5 Dynamic optimisations and multiperiod certainty equivalence

The certainty equivalence theorem specified that all expectations for b and R should be conditioned on the latest information available at the moment of a policy's calculation. Let Ω_t denote the information set known to the planners with certainty at the *start* of decision period t. As before we write the conditional expectation of some variable, ξ, as $E(\xi|\Omega_t)$ or $E_t(\xi)$. For a subvector ξ_i we write $E(\xi_i|\Omega_t)$ as $E_t(\xi_i)$ or $\xi_{i,t}$ if $i \geqslant t$, but as ξ_i if $i < t$.

7.5.1 The selection strategy

In order to preserve each policy decision as a rational choice, a dynamic strategy requires that the latest information available should condition each decision at the moment of its implementation. Fortunately, at each planning period, the planners need only implement the policies in the subvector $\tilde{x}_t^*$ of (7.16). It is therefore rational to adopt the strategy of reoptimising (7.13), at each t, for the remaining $T - t + 1$ periods. That means inserting historical values in (7.16) where possible, and the best single forecasts where not, in order to compute the best single estimate for $\tilde{z}^*$. Likewise, the same reasoning implies that $E_t(w)$ is an appropriate objective at each t, being the best single estimate of w itself.

Thus, for each $t = 1 \ldots T$ we reoptimise $\tilde{z}_{(t)}^{*\prime} = (\tilde{z}_t^{*\prime} \ldots \tilde{z}_T^{*\prime})$ by means of (7.16) for a $T - t + 1$ horizon, but implement its leading subvector only. The remaining subvectors may be thought of as forecasts of the future plans, and due for later revisions before their implementation. This selection strategy is based on certainty equivalence, and involves a sequence of T static optimisations, with decreasing horizons of $T - t + 1$ and changing $E_t(b)$ values, to make up the dynamic optimisation. Each policy vector, $\tilde{z}_{(t)}^*$, computed in this fashion is said to be *first period certainty equivalent* with respect to t. Each leading subvector, $\tilde{z}_t^*$, from successive first period certainty equivalent policy vectors is conditioned on the latest information available at the moment of its calculation. Thus the policies actually implemented, $\tilde{z}_t^*$, form a *multiperiod certainty equivalent* sequence. These sequential optimisations are sketched in figure 7.1. Ω_t itself contains: (i) all past values (from $t - 1$ backwards) of the variables in the system, (ii) the current estimates (i.e. based on data of up to period $t - 1$) of the model parameters in H, b, etc., and (iii) the current forecasts of the future variables, $E_t(u_i)$ and $E_t(N_i)$, $i = t \ldots T$. At any t, the previously

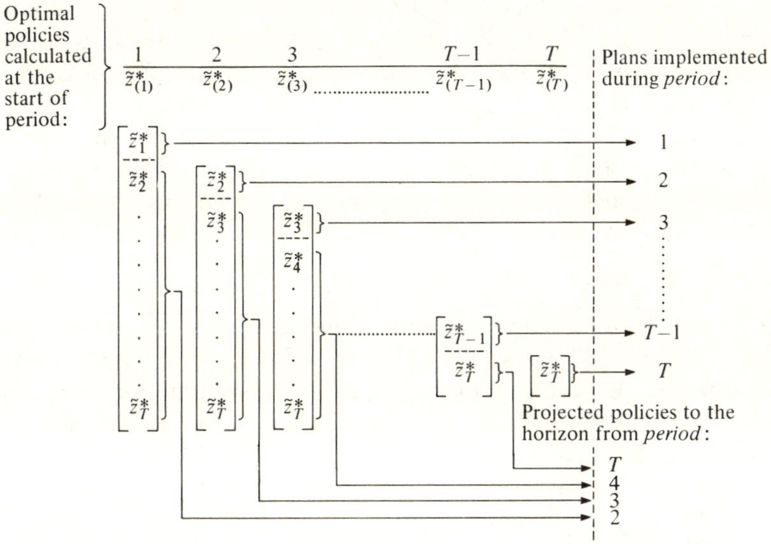

Figure 7.1 A schematic view of the sequence of optimal policy calculations over the planning interval $t = 1 \ldots T$.

uncertain values, N_i and u_i and hence b_i for $i \leqslant t-1$, will have become known. Based on the success or failure of the forecasts made in the past, such as $E_{t-1}(b_j)$ for $j < t$, we may also wish to revise our current view of the future, $E_t(b_j)$ for $j \geqslant t$. Inserting all this new information gives $E_t(b)$ in place of $E_{t-1}(b)$. Moreover, the use of $E_t(H)$ clearly permits the sequential reestimation of the model's parameters based on an increasing sample, although this is less frequently done in applications.

Consequently Ω_t will almost certainly differ from Ω_{t-1}. The conditional expectations, for use in the certainty equivalence theorem, are only independent of t if all realisations of the stochastic variables have been predicted without error, and if we find no cause to revise our current expectations of their future values. Moreover, if this is to apply to the realisations of u (i.e. the structural equation residuals) then the set of multipliers must also be exactly estimated. There is no likelihood that these conditions will all be fulfilled even approximately. Indeed the size of information, data and estimation errors are all too frequently a matter of embarrassment in economics.

7.5.2 The reoptimisations

Now we turn to the reoptimisation process itself. At t, $\tilde{z}_{(t)}$ alone is subject to choice. The remaining variables are fixed at historical realisations, and as such they act as additional constraints on the revised optimisers of (7.13). The implications of this for calculating the revised optimal policies are most easily seen by working in two stages; first in terms of w, and then in terms of the constraint set.

We shall take the simplest approach of substituting known historical values into (7.14). But an alternative would be to reoptimise (7.14) with extra lagrangian terms for the constraints of the historical realisations. For the first stage, let

$$\tilde{y}' = (\tilde{y}_0^{*\prime}, \tilde{y}'_{(t)}) \text{ and } \tilde{x}' = (\tilde{x}_0^{*\prime}, \tilde{x}'_{(t)}) \tag{7.29}$$

be the partitioning of policy variables with respect to time, past and future. Thus $\tilde{z}_0^{*\prime} = (\tilde{y}_0^{*\prime} \vdots \tilde{x}_0^{*\prime})$ are actual realisations and $\tilde{z}'_{(t)} = (\tilde{y}'_{(t)} \vdots \tilde{x}'_{(t)})$ remain to be optimised. We can partition $\mu' = (\mu'_0 \vdots \mu'_{(t)})$ to separate the constraints in y_0 from those in y_t. Next partition each submatrix of Q with respect to time, past and future; thus

$$Q = \begin{pmatrix} B & C' \\ C & A \end{pmatrix} \text{contains } A = \begin{pmatrix} A_1 & A_2 \\ A'_2 & A_{(t)} \end{pmatrix}, B = \begin{pmatrix} B_1 & B_2 \\ B'_2 & B_{(t)} \end{pmatrix} \text{and}$$

$$C = \begin{pmatrix} C_1 & C_2 \\ C_3 & C_{(t)} \end{pmatrix}$$

conforming to the partitioning of $\tilde{z}' = (\tilde{y}' \vdots \tilde{x}')$ defined by (7.29). Expanding $\frac{1}{2}\tilde{z}'Q\tilde{z}$, and collecting terms, we find there are now three components

$$\tfrac{1}{2}\tilde{z}'Q\tilde{z} = \tfrac{1}{2}\tilde{z}_0^{*\prime}Q_1\tilde{z}_0^* + \tilde{z}_0^{*\prime}Q_2\tilde{z}_{(t)} + \tfrac{1}{2}\tilde{z}'_{(t)}Q_{(t)}\tilde{z}_{(t)} \tag{7.30}$$

where

$$Q_1 = \begin{pmatrix} B_1 & C'_1 \\ C_1 & A_1 \end{pmatrix}, Q_{(t)} = \begin{pmatrix} B_{(t)} & C'_{(t)} \\ C_{(t)} & A_{(t)} \end{pmatrix}, \text{and } Q_2 = \begin{pmatrix} B_2 & C'_3 \\ C_2 & A_2 \end{pmatrix}.$$

Similarly $q'\tilde{z} = q'_1\tilde{z}_0^* + q'_{(t)}\tilde{z}_{(t)}$. The constant term of (7.30) may be ignored in the reoptimisations, but the linear term has $(q'_{(t)} + \tilde{z}_0^{*\prime}Q_2)$ in place of the original $q'_{(t)}$. Thus the objective function at each reoptimisation is of the same form as at the previous stage but with modifications to *both* Q and q; and hence the remaining *implicit* ideal values via (7.12). Thus we follow a 'point of aim' which moves according to realisations, and achievements, so far.

For the second stage, partition $H = \begin{pmatrix} I_{m(t-1)} & O & \vdots & -R_0 & O \\ O & I_{m(T-t)} & \vdots & -R_t^+ & -R_{(t)} \end{pmatrix}$

and $b = \begin{pmatrix} b_0 \\ b_{(t)} \end{pmatrix}$ with respect to the past and future. The submatrices of R are

$$R_0 = \begin{pmatrix} R_1 & & O \\ \vdots & \ddots & \\ R_{t-1} & \cdots & R_1 \end{pmatrix}, R_t^+ = \begin{pmatrix} R_t & \cdots & R_2 \\ \vdots & & \vdots \\ R_T & \cdots & R_{T-t+2} \end{pmatrix} \text{ and } R_{(t)} = \begin{pmatrix} R_1 & & 0 \\ \vdots & \ddots & \\ R_{T-t+1} & \cdots & R_1 \end{pmatrix}.$$

Among the constraints, the first $m(t-1)$ have been satisfied exactly by the realised policies which were necessarily feasible. Therefore

$$H\tilde{z} - b = \left(\frac{0}{\tilde{y}_{(t)} - R_t^+ \tilde{x}_0^* - R_{(t)}\tilde{x}_{(t)} - b_{(t)}} \right) \tag{7.31}$$

where the lower subvector is the constraint to be satisfied in the optimisations which remain. Of that subvector, $b_{(t)}$ and $R_t^+ \tilde{x}_0^*$ are both invariant to the choice of $z_{(t)}$. Hence the outstanding constraints are also of the same form as previously, but with $b_{(t)}$ replaced by $b_{(t)} + R_t^+ \tilde{x}_0^*$.

Consequently the recalculation of the policies at $t = 2 \ldots T$ is of the same form as (7.16) for $t = 1$. That is to say the reoptimisation of $\tilde{z}_{(t)}$ boils down to setting Q, H, q and b as those submatrices and subvectors indicated by the subscripts (t) in (7.30) and (7.31). Then we must add

$$Q_2'\tilde{z}_0^* \text{ to } q_{(t)} \text{ and } R_t^+ \tilde{x}_0^* \text{ to } b_{(t)}. \tag{7.32}$$

In practice these additions would be made recursively at each t, involving only $\tilde{x}_{t-1}^*, \tilde{z}_{t-1}^*$, and respectively the associated (leading) columns of $R_{(t-1)}$ and the associated submatrices from $Q_{(t-1)}$.

With these modifications complete we have, in the notation of (7.16) but using the submatrices etc. from (7.30) to (7.32),

$$\tilde{z}_{(t)}^* = \Theta_{(t)} E_t(b_{(t)}) - P_{(t)} Q_{(t)}^{-1} q_{(t)}. \tag{7.33}$$

The sequence of policy revisions in (7.33) ensures that each subvector $\tilde{z}_t^*$, *at the moment of its implementation*, is multiperiod certainty equivalent.

7.5.3 On time consistency

To obtain $E_t(b_{(t)})$ for (7.33) requires the insertion of

$$N' = (N_1' \ldots N_{t-1}', E_t(N_t') \ldots E_T(N_T'))$$

and

$$u' = (u_1' \ldots u_{t-1}', E_t(u_t') \ldots E_t(u_T'))$$

into (7.6). Plans are therefore revised both because our expectations change ($E_t(N_t) \neq E_{t-1}(N_t)$ say) and because of corrections made for the 'mistakes' in earlier calculations ($N_{t-1} \neq E_{t-1}(N_{t-1})$). Each $\tilde{z}_t^*$ will likewise be first order certainty equivalent if the model is reestimated at each t, and $E_t(H)$ is inserted into (7.33).

By inspection of (7.12) it is immediately obvious that the first adjustment of (7.32) is equivalent to a shift in the implicit desired values from $z^d_{(t)}$ to $z^d_{(t)} - Q^{-1}_{(t)} Q'_2 \tilde{z}^*_0$. It is also obvious that the second adjustment in (7.32) is equivalent to an updating of the 'initial' state from period $t-1$ to t. To ignore these adjustments is to implicitly change objectives or to ignore past achievements. We call (7.32) the time consistency constraints because they imply each z^*_t would remain unchanged from its initial evaluation if there were no information revisions ($\Omega_1 = \ldots = \Omega_T$).

7.6 On feedback control rules and uncertainty

The policy revisions depend on the unanticipated components in the additions to Ω_1. They may also result from a changed view of the likely future components in *b*. It is important to understand the determinants of the revisions to the optimal solution. What information is used by the policy maker, and how? We draw out the distinction between feedbacks from measurements of the past, and closed loop controls which react in addition to new probabilistic information about the future.

7.6.1 Policy rule types

An integral control rule, in terms of the complete set of endogenous variables, takes the form

$$x^*_t = G_t(L)Y_t \tag{7.34}$$

where $G_t(L)$ is a time varying polynomial matrix function of the lag operator,

$$G_t(L) = G_{t0} + G_{t1}L + G_{t2}L^2 + \ldots$$

with $G_{t0} = 0$ at all t. But if such a control rule were to be applied in practice, it would be necessary to restrict $G_t(L)$ to a finite number of terms. We must also add an adjustment to (7.34), at each t, in order to capture the influence of any anticipated exogenous events on the chosen values for x^*_t. Such a policy selection rule is a *feedback rule* of the integral control type:

$$x_t = G_t(L)Y_t + g_t \text{ and } G_t(L) = G_{t1}L + \ldots + G_{tp}L^p \tag{7.35}$$

where feedback effects are cut off after p periods. (7.35) is also a slight modification in that the initial conditions (Y_{t-p-1} etc.) within g_t are not restricted to having also obeyed such a feedback rule; they could have been achieved by some other route.

We now write our general policy rule (7.33) as an integral rule. At t, structural equation errors u_j, $j = 1 \ldots t-1$, will be known to the policy maker in the form

$$\hat{u}_j = \beta(Y_j^* - \hat{Y}_j) \tag{7.36}$$

where Y_j^* is the actual realisation of the endogenous variables in the model for period j. $\hat{Y}_j$ is the expectation of them at j; that is conditioned on the model's specification, estimates $E_j(H)$, the actual realised values of the instruments and noncontrollables up to period j, plus actual realised values of the stochastic errors up to period $j-1$. Thus $Y_j^* - \hat{Y}_j$ represents an estimate of the innovations due to u_j. The full set of innovations arrive in the form $E_t(b) - E_j(b)$ and/or $E_t(H) - E_j(H)$ for each $j = 1 \ldots t-1$. For the purpose of this section we suppose the model contains no identities.

Now substituting for the current evaluation of $\hat{Y}_j$, for $j = 1 \ldots t-1$:

$$\begin{pmatrix} \hat{u}_1 \\ \vdots \\ \hat{u}_{t-1} \end{pmatrix} = (I_{t-1} \otimes \beta)\left(\tilde{Y}_0^* - R_0^* \tilde{x}_0^* - \sigma_0^* - S_0^* \begin{pmatrix} \hat{u}_1 \\ \vdots \\ \hat{u}_{t-1} \end{pmatrix} + Y_0^d\right). \tag{7.37}$$

R_0^* and R^* are constructed analogously to R_0 and R except that the submatrices used are R_i^* rather than R_i. Y_0^d is y_0^d augmented with zeroes. Likewise $S_0^* = \begin{bmatrix} 0 & & \\ S_2^* & & 0 \\ \vdots & \ddots & \\ S_{t-1}^* & \cdots & S_2^* 0 \end{bmatrix}$, and $\sigma_0^{*\prime} = (\sigma_1^{*\prime} \ldots \sigma_{t-1}^{*\prime})$ which contains actual realisations. These quantities are also from (7.2) before its concentration on the targets. Next define the nonsingular matrix $F = I + (I \otimes \beta)S_0^*$. Then

$$\begin{pmatrix} \hat{u}_1 \\ \vdots \\ \hat{u}_{t-1} \end{pmatrix} = F^{-1}(I \otimes \beta)(\tilde{Y}_0^* - R_0^* \tilde{x}_0^* - \sigma_0^* + Y_0^d). \tag{7.38}$$

Reverting to (7.33), we now find

$$\begin{aligned} \tilde{z}_{(t)}^* = {} & \Theta_{(t)}\{E_t(\sigma_{(t)}) - y_{(t)}^d + R_{(t)}x_{(t)}^d \\ & + R_t^+ \tilde{x}_0^* + S_t^+ F^{-1}(I \otimes \beta)(\tilde{Y}_0^* - R_0^* \tilde{x}_0^* - \sigma_0^* + Y_0^d)\} \\ & - P_{(t)}Q_{(t)}^{-1}(Q_2' \tilde{z}_0^* + q_{(t)}) \\ = {} & \{\Theta_{(t)}(S_t^+ F^{-1}(I \otimes \beta) \vdots R_t^+ - S_t^+ F^{-1}(I \otimes \beta)R_0^*) \\ & - P_{(t)}Q_{(t)}^{-1}Q_2^{*\prime}\}\begin{bmatrix} \tilde{Y}_0^* \\ \tilde{x}_0^* \end{bmatrix} + d_{(t)} \end{aligned} \tag{7.39}$$

where the vector $d_{(t)}$ contains all terms not involving either $\tilde{Y}_0^*$ or $\tilde{x}_0^*$ (i.e. past achievements). S_t^+ corresponds to R_t^+, and $Q_2^{*\prime}$ is just Q_2' with submatrices B_2' and C_3 augmented with columns of zeroes corresponding to the nontargets in $\tilde{Y}_0^*$. The presence of nontargets in (7.39) is expected since, although they were deleted from (7.9), their determinants remain connected up through simultaneity.

For convenience, the control rule in (7.39) determines $\tilde{y}_{(t)}^*$ as well as $\tilde{x}_{(t)}^*$; but the lower subvector contains the feedback rule for x_t^* alone. Backsubstituting for each $\tilde{x}_{t-i}^*(i = 1 \ldots t-1)$ in turn by previous versions of (7.39) yields a feedback rule in the same form as (7.35). The corresponding expressions for $G_t(L)$ and g_t are too complicated to be worth computing. The point is that $z_{(t)}^*$ follows a truncated integral feedback control rule containing proportional, differential, and integral terms. So each z_t^* value is computed from a linear, time varying, $(t-1)$-order iterative scheme. Both the iteration matrix and the forcing function vary with the step number, through the changes and deletions in H, b, Q and q, and because the point of truncation in the integral controller is extended at each step. This feedback rule makes explicit an optimal policy's dependence on past achievements back to $t = 1$.

7.6.2 Feedback vs closed loop control rules

An open loop control law is one in which every policy may be computed exactly at the first planning period irrespective of how the system actually develops. Clearly, for $t \geqslant 2$ (7.35) is not of this form since Y_{t-1} cannot be known with certainty before period t. The open loop policy nearest to (7.39) is

$$x_t^0 = G_t(L)Y_{t,1} + g_{t,1} = G_t(L)E(Y_t|\Sigma R_i E_1(x_i), E_1(s_t)) + E_1(g_t). \quad (7.40)$$

In contrast a *closed loop control* rule is a feedback control in which the policies are a function of the latest information (*including* probabilistic information) available on the state of the system, and which are computed, at all times, in the knowledge that they will be revised in the light of that information as soon as it becomes available. In continuous time, we require x_t to satisfy (7.20) in terms of the conditional expectations $E_t(.)$,

$$x_t^c = G_t(L)Y_{t,t} + g_{t,t} = \int_{-\infty}^{t}\int_Y\int_X G_\tau(Y_\tau, X_\tau)f_t(Y, X)dXdYd\tau \quad (7.41)$$

where $f_t(Y, X)$ is the joint density function of Y and all exogenous elements X, as seen at t, for $-\infty < \tau \leqslant T$. Consequently (7.41) cannot be computed before t. Now it is obvious that this type of rule must improve on open loop policies because it utilises measurements from the controlled system to reduce uncertainty. That is to say, in $G_\tau(.,.)f_t(.,.)$ realisations are involved for Y_τ, $-\infty < \tau < t$, and the corresponding elements of X are known exactly. However, assuming a linear control rule and since $f_t(Y, X) = f_t(Y \mid X) f_t(X)$, (7.41) is governed by the future values X_τ, $t \leqslant \tau < T$ which are known only in the probabilistic sense of $X_{\tau,t}$. The information in (7.41) divides into the updated past measurements (known with certainty), and the updated conditioning information (known only in a probabilistic sense). The latter includes expected future policy settings, other expected events, and the distribution of future outcomes. Thus, although (7.41) is passive about searching for information, it does use what is presently known at each point about the information which will be obtained later; and it does 'anticipate' continuing to do so at each future moment. Hence (7.41) 'anticipates' the closing of the loop by using the currently expected future measurements from the system.

It is this characteristic of incorporating the latest 'anticipations' of future measurements, which distinguishes closed loop controls from the simpler *feedback controls*. The latter conditions $f_t(.\mid.)$ and $G_\tau(.,.)$ on

$$X_\tau \text{ for } -\infty < \tau < t, \text{ and } E_1(X_\tau) \text{ for } \tau \geqslant t \tag{7.42}$$

i.e. it uses the latest measurements of the past, but it fails to 'anticipate' future measurements or the closing of the loop[2]. That is a much weaker use of probabilistic information. The policy settings would be inferior unless nothing happens to influence our anticipations – which is implausible because if past measurements cause the current policy choice to be revised they must inevitably cause the expected future choices to be revised.

Now the implemented policies within (7.39) are a type of closed loop control, containing feedback components in the first term but 'anticipations' in $d_{(t)}$. However, these policy calculations do not reflect (7.41) precisely since we work in discrete time. It is obviously only possible to solve (7.41) in closed form in continuous time. We might approximate (7.41) by the open loop policy (7.40), or, better, decide to revise (7.40) at a certain number of points between $t = 1$ and $t = T$. That would lead to the *sequential open loop policies*

$$x_t^s = G_t(L) E_j(Y_t) + g_{t,j} \tag{7.43}$$

where $1 \leqslant j < t$ and there are $j = 1 \ldots J < T$ revision points. Sequential open loop policies when $t - j$ and J are not at extreme values with respect to the constraints of the data have been treated as a separate policy rule class by Athans et al. (1977). In terms of (7.16), the re-optimisations described by (7.33) and (7.32) could be undertaken at infrequent (but

2 An obvious example is tax receipts which are automatic stabilisers in the economy. They automatically smooth a cycle, but they cannot guide its future (such as attempting to remove it) which is nevertheless anticipatable.

perhaps regular) intervals. Between revisions the latest policy calculation will be implemented at each decision point.

Obviously closed loop is the limiting form of sequential open loop, i.e.

$$\lim_{\substack{(t-j)\to 0 \\ J \to \infty}} \{x_t^s\} = x_t^c \text{ for } t \in [1, T]. \tag{7.44}$$

In our context, fresh information is available, at best, only discretely at each time interval so the formal distinction between x_t^s and x_t^c is somewhat blurred. However, we refer to policies as closed loop when $t-j$ is a minimum and J a maximum, as constrained by data availability and frequency with which decisions may be taken. Policies are then revised at every period of the decision model, and automatically, which captures the spirit of x_t^c, rather than of x_t^0 or x_t^s. We finish up with

$$x_t = G_t(L)E(Y_t | \sum_i R_i E_t(x_i), E_t(s)) + g_{t,t} \tag{7.45}$$

as a closed loop control.

Notice that the discussion from (7.40) to (7.44) has not considered the uncertainty in R, and with respect to $E_1(R)$ we have open loop control. In principle the ideas here may be extended for that case (Chapter 12). Thus, in terms of (7.33), the implemented policy components, $\tilde{z}_t^*$, constitute closed loop controls; whereas each $\tilde{z}_{(t)}^*$ is a sequentially updated open loop control, updated to t.

7.6.3 Comments on feedback controls

Formal policy selection methods are often roundly criticised for producing policies which are unreliable in the face of the many and significant uncertainties facing the planner. Naturally the idea of rationally chosen policy values attracts less criticism, although policies selected by simulation are no less subject to model and information errors than those which are optimised. The value of a closed loop policy rule is precisely that it specifies from the start that policies shall be corrected, at each t, to counteract the unavoidable information and model errors. They also allow future expectations to be revised in the light of the errors revealed in the past expectations. Alternative policy rules fail to exploit these opportunities for revising the policies for the remainder of the period.

The figure for $\hat{u}_t$ is of course a catch-all for errors resulting from the inevitable shortcomings in specification and estimation, in addition to genuine stochastic shocks. The model is a certain representation of an uncertain (because it is unknown) true economy. So model mis-specifications merely serve to increase the impact of model errors. Model errors also result from uncertainties in estimation. Given a finite sample and probably measurement errors, the estimated model is actually an uncertain representation of an uncertain economy. Badly determined parameter estimates also increase the impact of the stochastic terms in (7.36). In addition $\hat{u}_t$ may cover for data revisions, and also cases of administrative delays in implementing the chosen policies if progressively revised values of $\hat{u}_i$ are used in computing $z^*_{(t)}$ for any $t > i + 1$.

Hence the larger are these innovations and their impacts on policies, the greater is the need to modify policies via a closed loop feedback rule. Therefore it is precisely because (7.36) is a *calculated residual*, and not just an observed stochastic disturbance, that an optimal closed loop feedback rule is so important in forming economic policies. Indeed (7.40) and (7.44) would coincide if there were no uncertainty.

7.6.4 On error elimination

Equation (7.39) shows, inter alia, the current policy x^*_t as a function of past states $\tilde{Y}^*_i$ and $\tilde{x}^*_i$ for $i = t - 1 \dots 1$. In Chapter 6 we mentioned the possibility of choosing x^*_t by picking the best feedback matrices $A_t(t)$ in the control rule (6.20). For that we must first specify the order of the polynomial in $A_t(L)$. The properties of control rules necessary to do this are discussed by Salmon (1981). To be able to eliminate the error between the current state (z_t) and its desired value (z^d_t) generally requires that state to be determined by a difference equation system at least of the form $(I - L)^p z_t = B(L) z_{t-p}$, where $B(L)$ is a matrix polynomial in the lag operator L, and where $p - 1$ equals the order of difference equation system determining z^d_t. If they follow systems of equal order the error will tend to a constant; if z_t follows a lower order system the error will explode. Now z_t is here determined by the 'controlled' model (e.g. (6.24)); but since the underlying model (2.6) has dynamics of arbitrary order it will generally be necessary to ensure that $A_t(L)$, which determines x^*_t, is of sufficient order. Evidently, for t large enough, the optimal control rule always satisfies this condition; (7.39) contains the required rule whenever $t \geqslant p$. From this we conclude (given $T > p$):

(i) an integral control rule is necessary to solve a general policy problem;
(ii) the big policy adjustments occur in early periods ($t < p$) because (7.39) lacks sufficient power to eliminate the failure $\tilde{z}_t$ even in the long run so, other things being equal, the failures initially tend to increase; and
(iii) smoother policy adjustments will appear later ($t > p$) as (7.39) has more than sufficient power.

Large stochastic shocks may obscure points (ii) and (iii) by exaggerating the realised failures. But more vigorous policy changes in early periods (which will be observed in the numerical examples below) are therefore an unfortunate necessity.

7.7 Contingent (discretionary) policies: optimal control without certainty equivalence

For analytic purposes it is often convenient to decompose the objective function (7.10) into mutually exclusive deterministic and stochastic components. From there we can determine the dependence of the implemented values of optimal policy on the innovations as well as the deterministic components. The choice resulting from this alternative approach reproduces (7.18). This analysis also provides a general measure of the importance of stochastic control, and gives a preview of the stochastic properties of optimally chosen policies.

7.7.1 The decomposition of objectives and policy choices

Consider the policy problem at $t = 1$ under additive and first order multiplicative uncertainty. Split b into its deterministic and stochastic components: $b = E_1(b) + \eta$, where $E_1(\eta) = 0$. Likewise $z = E_1(z) + \xi$ where $E_1(\xi) = 0$. Then a model such as (7.9) decomposes as

$$HE_1(\tilde{z}) = E_1(b) \text{ and } H\xi = \eta. \tag{7.46}$$

Similarly the objective function, $E_1(w)$, decomposes to

$$\begin{aligned} E_1(w) &= \tfrac{1}{2}E_1(\tilde{z})'QE_1(\tilde{z}) + q'E_1(\tilde{z}) + \tfrac{1}{2}E_1(\xi'Q\xi) \\ &= w(E_1(\tilde{z})) + \tfrac{1}{2}\operatorname{tr} QV_1(\tilde{z}) \end{aligned} \tag{7.47}$$

where $V_1(\tilde{z}) = E_1(\xi\xi')$ is the conditional variance of z. However, the policy problem remains that of (7.17). We can write

$$\begin{aligned} E_1(L(\tilde{z}, \mu)) = &\frac{1}{2}\begin{pmatrix} E_1(\tilde{z}) \\ E_1(\mu) \end{pmatrix}' \begin{pmatrix} Q & -H' \\ -H & O \end{pmatrix} \begin{pmatrix} E_1(\tilde{z}) \\ E_1(\mu) \end{pmatrix} \\ &+ \begin{pmatrix} q \\ E_1(b) \end{pmatrix}' \begin{pmatrix} E_1(\tilde{z}) \\ E_1(\mu) \end{pmatrix} \\ &+ \tfrac{1}{2}E_1\begin{pmatrix} \xi \\ v \end{pmatrix}' \begin{pmatrix} Q & -H' \\ -H & O \end{pmatrix} \begin{pmatrix} \xi \\ v \end{pmatrix} + E_1(\eta'v) \end{aligned} \tag{7.48}$$

where $\mu = E_1(\mu) + v$ and $E_1(v) = 0$. The policy problem therefore involves minimising two disjoint positive definite quadratic forms,

$$\min_{\tilde{z}}\{E_1(L(\tilde{z}, \mu))\} = \min_{E_1(\tilde{z})}\{w_d(E_1(\tilde{z}), E_1(\mu))\} + \min_{\xi}\{(w_s(\xi, v))\} \tag{7.49}$$

where $w_d(.)$ contains the first two terms of (7.48), and $w_s(.)$ the latter two. The overall optimal choice is the sum of the optimiser of the deterministic part of the objective, $w_d(.)$, and of the stochastic part $w_s(.)$. These two elements of the policy choice are also deterministic and stochastic respectively, and may be determined independently.

First we can best pick $E_1(\tilde{z})$ in the manner of (7.16) since $E_1(b)$ is known ex ante:

$$E_1(\tilde{z}) = \Theta E_1(b) - PQ^{-1}q,$$
$$\text{with } E_1(\mu) = (HQ^{-1}H')^{-1}(E_1(b) + HQ^{-1}q). \tag{7.50}$$

This is the deterministic control. It is the optimal open loop strategy conditional on Ω_1. Thus the deterministic part of the policy problem is best solved by a first period certainty equivalent policy choice for (7.14).

Secondly, without the certainty equivalence theorem (which says that in fact the same policy choice will minimise the whole of $E_1(L(\tilde{z}, \mu))$ we must pick ξ so as to minimise $w_s(\xi, v)$. In view of (7.47) that optimisation problem reduces to minimising $\frac{1}{2}\mathrm{tr}QV_1(\xi)$ subject to the stochastic constraints in (7.46). The difficulty here is that we cannot pick actual values for ξ ex ante. Indeed, ξ is a function of η and is therefore a random variable not under our direct control. But we can pick the transformation of η, so as to determine ξ in such a way as to guarantee minimal stochastic disturbances to $\tilde{z}^*$ as measured by $E_1(\xi' Q\xi)$. Hence our strategy becomes one of selecting the transformation of η so that, whatever realisations of it in fact come to pass, the stochastic component of our criterion is minimised. In this sense, the impacts of stochastic shocks on our system are optimally controlled.

In a linear-quadratic optimisation the required transformation on ξ will be linear: say $\xi_x = G\eta$ so that $\xi = \left[H^*G + \begin{pmatrix} I \\ \cdots \\ 0 \end{pmatrix}\right]\eta$, where $\xi' = (\xi'_y, \xi'_x)$ is conformable to the partitioning in z. Rather than pick the ξ values themselves, we pick G which minimises their conditional variance, $V_1(\xi)$, in terms of $\mathrm{tr}\, QV_1(\xi)$. Reformulating the stochastic constraints in terms of that variance, the stochastic part of the policy choice in (7.49) becomes

$$\min_{G,\, V_1(\xi)} \left\{ L = \tfrac{1}{2}\mathrm{tr}\, QV_1(\xi) - \mathrm{tr}\Lambda\left[V_1(\xi) - \left(H^*G + \begin{pmatrix} I \\ \cdots \\ 0 \end{pmatrix}\right)\Sigma_1\left(H^*G + \begin{pmatrix} I \\ \cdots \\ 0 \end{pmatrix}\right)'\right]\right\} \tag{7.51}$$

where $\Sigma_1 = E_1(\eta\eta')$ and Λ is a symmetric $(n+m)T$ order matrix of lagrangian multipliers. The necessary conditions are as follows:

$$\partial L/\partial G = H^{*\prime}\Lambda\left(H^*G + \begin{pmatrix} I \\ \cdots \\ 0 \end{pmatrix}\right)\Sigma_1 = 0 \tag{7.52}$$

yielding $G^* = -(H^{*\prime}\Lambda H^*)^{-1} H^{*\prime}\Lambda\begin{pmatrix} I \\ \cdots \\ 0 \end{pmatrix}$ as the optimal choice. Next $\partial L/\partial V_1(\xi) = 0$ implies $\frac{1}{2}Q = \Lambda$ at the optimum. Finally $\partial L/\partial\Lambda = 0$ shows the optimised variance to be

$$V_1^*(\xi) = [I - H^*(H^{*\prime}\, QH^*)^{-1}\, H^{*\prime}\, Q] \\ \times \hat{\Sigma}_1 [I - H^*(H^{*\prime}\, QH^*)^{-1}\, H^{*\prime}\, Q]' \tag{7.53}$$

where $\hat{\Sigma}_1 = \begin{pmatrix} I \\ \cdots \\ 0 \end{pmatrix}\Sigma_1(I \vdots 0)$ and $V_1^*(\xi) = V_1(\tilde{z}^*)$.

We can combine these results; the complete solution to (7.49) is

$$\tilde{z}^* = \left[H^*G^* + \begin{pmatrix} I \\ \cdots \\ 0 \end{pmatrix} \right](E_1(b) + (I \vdots 0)Q^{-1}q + \eta) = \tilde{z}_d^* + \tilde{z}_s^* \tag{7.54}$$

where $\tilde{z}_s^* = \left[H^*G^* + \begin{pmatrix} I \\ \cdots \\ 0 \end{pmatrix} \right]\eta$ is the stochastic, and innovations dependent, term. The remainder, $\tilde{z}_d^*$, is the deterministic open loop term.

7.7.2 The statistical properties of optimal policies

The presence of $\tilde{z}_s^*$ in (7.54) stresses a degree of arbitrariness in the first period certainty equivalent policy choices which has not been apparent so far. Although it may seem natural to set η at its expected value of zero, that is evidently a procedure born entirely of asserting certainty equivalence. Any other arbitrary, but fixed, assumed value for η would evidently do just as well. But certainty equivalent policies are the *unbiased* ones, in the sense that they coincide with the current expectation of the ex post optimal choice (7.16):

$$\tilde{z}_d^* = E_1(\tilde{z}^*). \tag{7.55}$$

Unbiasedness means that on average certainty equivalent policies coincide with the actual realisation of the optimal policies in (7.16). So on average, rather than in individual cases, planners would choose the most preferred policies despite the uncertainty over b's realisation. The difficulty is that z_d^* does not provide unambiguously the best estimate of (7.16). For instance, it does not generally have maximum precision. The simplest measures of precision are mean square errors. In this context a small mean square error, or variance, in $\tilde{z}^*$ means that the latter's realisations are more likely to turn out to be clustered more closely about $\tilde{z}_d^*$. Then the implemented policy has a higher probability of being suboptimal by a smaller amount than other selections.

Of course, the amount of potential suboptimality (rather than its probability) depends on the curvature of w. So a low variance is of particular benefit for a variable whose marginal preference function is sharply curved. In such cases one can rationally forego some expected gain in w, in order to secure less uncertainty about a desirable outcome. Although we have seen that $\tilde{z}^*$ minimises the weighted sum of variances and co-variances, $\text{tr}QV_1(\tilde{z}^*)$, that does not necessarily imply that it also minimises $V_1(\tilde{z}^*)$. It turns out that the difference between $V_1(\tilde{z}^*)$ and the variance–covariance matrix of any other policy decision is negative semi-definite only if $Q^{-1} = V_1(\tilde{z}^*)$ happens to be chosen, which is hardly likely. Thus $\tilde{z}^*_d$ is an unbiased, but not a minimum mean square error, estimator of $\tilde{z}^*$, the true but unknown optimal choice.[3]

Thus, (7.47) highlights the potential conflict between obtaining a highly desirable outcome in $E_1(\tilde{z})$ and obtaining a reliable outcome as measured by elements of $V_1(\tilde{z})$. One may not wish to trade (penalise) failures in $E_1(\tilde{z})$ at the same rate as those in $V_1(\tilde{z})$ values. But the trade-offs are set by one single Q for both terms in (7.47). Consequently we may have to adjust Q in order to compromise between ambition and risk aversion. This is the approach taken in Chapters 9 and 10. Alternatively, we may recognise that the indeterminancy of (7.54) reflects the arbitrariness of imposing $E_t(w)$ as a surrogate for w. In that case we can either find ways of using η to induce greater precision, or we can abandon $E_t(w)$ in favour of some other surrogate for w which takes more account of risk aversion. Since this last possibility can always be expressed as $w(\tilde{z})$ and then approximated by (7.10), it supplies a formal justification for making adjustments to Q when w is replaced by $E_t(w)$ as the objective.

7.7.3 Contingent (innovations dependent) policies

Replacing $E_1(.)$ by $E_t(.)$ throughout (7.46) to (7.55), for $t = 2 \ldots T$, means that we could derive the first order certainty equivalent policy, $z^*_{(t)}$, as (7.54) with $E_t(b_{(t)})$ and $\eta_{(t)} = 0$. The time consistency additions of (7.32) would still apply.

On the other hand, we could just update the second term of (7.54) so that the subvectors of η, η_j, are evaluated as $\eta_j = b_j - E_1(b_j)$ if $j \leqslant t-1$; but $\eta_j = E_t(b_j) - E_1(b_j)$ if $j \geqslant t$. That term specifies the innovations to be included in our chosen policies since the open loop policy calculation $\tilde{z}^*_d$. In general, the choice at any moment t is dependent on the developments since an earlier choice at $j < t$:

$$\tilde{z}^*_{(t)} = \tilde{z}^*_{d(t/j)} + \tilde{z}^*_{s(t/j)}. \tag{7.56}$$

Here $\tilde{z}^*_{d(t/j)}$ and $\tilde{z}^*_{s(t/j)}$ are the subvectors of $\tilde{z}^*_d$ and $\tilde{z}^*_s$ corresponding to

3 Notice the parallel with the preoccupation of econometric estimators with unbiasedness at the expense of efficiency.

$\tilde{z}_{(t)}$, but obtained from (7.54) with $E_j(b_{(t)})$ and $\eta = E_t(b_{(t)}) - E_j(b_{(t)})$ respectively.[4] Thus each current policy is the sum of the relevant subvector of the open loop (as seen from j) choice, plus a correction contingent on all the innovations since then.

7.7.4 A measure of the relative importance of stochastic control

Substituting (7.50) and (7.53) into (7.47) splits the optimised objective into its deterministic part $w_d^* = \frac{1}{2}E_t(b)'(HQ^{-1}H')^{-1}E_t(b) + q'\Theta E_t(b)$ and its stochastic part $w_s^* = \frac{1}{2}\operatorname{tr} QV_t^*(\xi)$, where

$$w^* = w_d^* + w_s^*. \tag{7.57}$$

A comparison of w_d^* and w_s^* reveals whether the main benefit lies in picking a trajectory which correctly exploits the anticipated developments in the system; or whether the chief difficulty lies in being able to correct for the impacts of the shocks to the system which threaten to invalidate that chosen trajectory. In other words, we can measure the importance of stochastic control. For further comparisons, the counterpart to w_s for open loop policies is $\frac{1}{2}\operatorname{tr}B\Sigma_1$. Suboptimal open loop policies will imply, in addition, $w_d > w_d^*$.

The point to stress here is that this is an *ex ante* measure of the importance of stochastic control. It may be computed ex ante for any decision (including the first). It therefore indicates the importance of stochastic control independently of whatever particular realisations of the stochastic variables may in fact be encountered. That must be contrasted with measures derived from comparing open and closed loop policies ex post. Those measures depend on the particular stochastic realisation observed. They therefore show how important stochastic control actually was in one particular case, and depend on whether the policy maker was 'lucky' or not. Of course the general ex ante measure above is the appropriate one for assessing risk and the scope for its reduction.

7.8 The superiority of contingent rules for policy selection

We have argued that closed loop controls are essential to preserve $E_t(w)$ at the optimum throughout $t = 1, \ldots, T$. We now demonstrate the theoretical inferiority of other control rule types; and we show the optimality of the policy revisions in a closed loop strategy in terms of the innovations. Again, for simplicity, we confine our attention to additive uncertainty.

4 A version of (7.56) reappears at (7.69) below. That shows the computed policies follow a first order iteration from $\tilde{z}^*_{(1)}$ with the innovations as forcing function.

7.8.1 The optimality of policy revisions

The penalty (loss) to implementing any policy x, other than x^* given by (7.18), is

$$w(\tilde{x}^*) - w(\tilde{x}) = -\tfrac{1}{2}(x - x^*)'M(x - x^*) < 0. \tag{7.58}$$

The sign follows from the positive definiteness of M (guaranteed by that of Q) for *any* $x \neq x^*$ (a difference in at least one element).[5]

To demonstrate the gains to policy revisions we use the constrained objective function (7.19):

$$w(\tilde{x}) = m_0 + m_1'\tilde{x} + \tfrac{1}{2}\tilde{x}'M\tilde{x}. \tag{7.59}$$

Consider, first, the choice of policies at the start of period $t = 1$. (7.18) shows $\tilde{x}^* = -M^{-1}m_1$ is the ex post optimal choice. Faced with the uncertainty in b we replaced it with $E_1(b)$; i.e. we in fact chose $\tilde{x}^*_{(1)} = -M^{-1}E_1(m_1)$ and implemented its leading subvector, $\tilde{x}^*_1$. Then

$$w(\tilde{x}^*) - w(\tilde{x}^*_{(1)}) = -\tfrac{1}{2}\begin{bmatrix} E_1(b) - b \\ \hline 0 \end{bmatrix}' QH^*M^{-1}H^{*\prime}Q\begin{bmatrix} E_1(b) - b \\ \hline 0 \end{bmatrix} \tag{7.60}$$

which is independent of $\tilde{x}$. Next consider the choice of policies at the start of period $t = 2$. Now the leading subvector of $\tilde{x}^*_{(1)}$ is $\tilde{x}^*_0$. The criterion $E_2(w)$ can be represented by returning to the original criterion and conditioning that on Ω_2, and in particular on the fact that $\tilde{x}_1 = \tilde{x}^*_0$ is now forced by history. We include the latter constraint in the reoptimisation of $\tilde{x}$ by defining the Lagrangian multipliers, λ. Then

$$E_2(w(\tilde{x})) = E_2(m_0) + E_2(m_1)'\tilde{x} + \tfrac{1}{2}\tilde{x}'M\tilde{x} - \lambda'(\tilde{x}_1 - \tilde{x}^*_0) \tag{7.61}$$

where the last term, being nonstochastic, must hold exactly. This expression is minimised by

$$\tilde{x}^0 = M^{-1}\left(E_2(m_1) - \begin{pmatrix} \lambda \\ \cdots \\ 0 \end{pmatrix}\right) = E_2(\tilde{x}^*) + (M^{-1})_{.1}\lambda \tag{7.62}$$

where $(M^{-1})_{.1}$ is columns 1 to n of M^{-1}, and $(M^{-1})_{ij}$ is the ijth submatrix of M^{-1}, of order n, partitioned with respect to time; $i, j = 1 \ldots T$. Now $E_2(\tilde{x}^*)$ is the second period certainty equivalent of the, as yet, unknown and uncertain ex post optimal choice. Since $\tilde{x}^0_1 = \tilde{x}^*_0$ is forced by the constraint,

$$\lambda = (M^{-1})^{-1}_{11}(\tilde{x}^*_0 - E_2(\tilde{x}^*_1)). \tag{7.63}$$

5 Theil (1964), p. 145, derives (7.58). It measures the loss to implementing incorrect policies, but not the difference in value between two policies after some disturbance in the information set.

So

$$\tilde{x}^0 - E_2(\tilde{x}^*) = (M^{-1})_{.1}(M^{-1})_{11}^{-1}(\tilde{x}_0^* - E_2(\tilde{x}_1^*)) \neq 0. \tag{7.64}$$

Inspection of $(M^{-1})_{.1}(M^{-1})_{11}^{-1}$ shows that the first subvector in (7.64) is not revised. But only in the special case of *both* Q and R being block diagonal with respect to time are the remaining subvectors not revised. These revisions operate on the full x vector; that is without deletions from Q, H, b, q, etc. All the revisions which take place are in terms of the innovations to the ex post optimal instrument values as perceived at $t = 2$; i.e. in terms of $E_2(b) - E_1(b)$.

This revised policy improves on the previous one if

$$w(\tilde{x}^*) - w(\tilde{x}_{(1)}^*) - \{w(\tilde{x}^*) - w(\tilde{x}^0)\} = w(\tilde{x}^0) - w(\tilde{x}_{(1)}^*) < 0 \tag{7.65}$$

where $\tilde{x}^0$ is given in (7.62). Returning to (7.58), and using (7.64) to give

$$\tilde{x}^0 - \tilde{x}^* = \tilde{x}^0 - \tilde{x}_{(1)}^* - (\tilde{x}^* - \tilde{x}_{(1)}^*) = (M^{-1}\Psi - I)(\tilde{x}^* - \tilde{x}_{(1)}^*) \tag{7.66}$$

where $\Psi = \begin{pmatrix} (M^{-1})_{11}^{-1} & 0 \\ 0 & 0 \end{pmatrix}$, we find (7.65) on the left becomes

$$\tfrac{1}{2}(\tilde{x}^* - \tilde{x}_{(1)})'(\Psi' M^{-1}\Psi - M)(\tilde{x}^* - \tilde{x}_{(1)}) < 0 \tag{7.67}$$

which is the loss due to not making the revisions. The strict inequality follows in (7.67) provided $\Psi' M^{-1}\Psi - M$ proves to be negative definite. This is easily checked since $\Psi' M^{-1}\Psi = \Psi$ and $(M^{-1})_{11}^{-1} = M_{11} - M_{12}M_{22}^{-1}M_{12}'$ when the symmetric matrix M is partitioned as $\begin{pmatrix} M_{11} & M_{12} \\ M_{12}' & M_{22} \end{pmatrix}$ conformable to $\begin{pmatrix} x_1 \\ x_{(2)} \end{pmatrix}$. Thus $\Psi' M^{-1}\Psi - M$ can be written as the negative definite matrix $-(M_{12} \vdots M_{22})' M_{22}^{-1}(M_{12} \vdots M_{22})$, since M is positive definite.

This result may now be applied to show the superiority of the revised policies over unrevised or open loop choices.

7.8.2 An expression for the policy revisions

The term on the left of (7.64) shows the deviation of the revised policy from the current expectation of the ex post optimal choice:

$$\tilde{x}^0 - E_2(\tilde{x}^*) = M^{-1}(\tilde{x}_{(1)}^* - E_2(\tilde{x}^*)) \tag{7.68}$$

So

$$\tilde{x}^0 = M^{-1}\Psi E_1(\tilde{x}^*) + (I - M^{-1}\Psi)E_2(\tilde{x}^*) \tag{7.69}$$

since $\tilde{x}_{(1)}^* = E_1(\tilde{x}^*)$. The revised policies are a weighted average of the previous policy calculation and what we now think would have been optimal, given hindsight (up to Ω_2) and no constraints from history ($\tilde{x}_1^*$). In this form the policy revisions follow a first order iterative updating scheme. The idempotency of $M^{-1}\Psi$ might suggest the revised policy lies closer to $E_2(\tilde{x}^*)$ than $E_1(\tilde{x}^*)$ did. However this is not guaranteed. Counter examples are easily constructed since $\| M^{-1} \|_2 = \rho[I + (M_{22}^{-1}M_{21})'(M_{22}^{-1}M_{21})] > 1$ applies in (7.68). Nevertheless, it may hold in many cases, particularly when R_1 and $Q_{(2)}$ are large (making M_{22}^{-1} small).

Hence, if disturbances 'blow us off course', it is necessary to chart a new course from the current position to the horizon. That revised course will lead us closer to z^d than the unrevised course would have done; but it is not just an updated expectation of our original attempted route, nor is it even necessarily closer than the unrevised course to that updated expectation. It is a genuine new course, rather than just the quickest way back to what we now think would have been the correct route.

7.9 An illustration

To give the flavour of a typical application take that of Van den Bogaard and Theil (1959). The problem and model are summarised in table 7.1.

The problem envisaged is that facing President Roosevelt on assuming office in 1932. The great economic slump had started in 1929. He had been elected on the 'New Deal' policies and was therefore pledged to the reflation of the economy and ending of the chronic unemployment and poverty. In order to solve the depression within his presidency (and naturally to secure his reelection in 1936) it is suggested that at a minimum he requires to return economic activity, per head, to its previous peak of the 1929 level. Current welfare is loosely represented by a consumption target, future welfare by an investment one; and the distribution of income variable between wages and capital (to reflect the 'New Deal' commitment to organised labour) completes the list of targets. Naturally this is rather crude, but it is similar to what happens in practice in strategic economic planning. Having set, at a high political level, the overall strategy, the detailed tactics can be fitted into that strategy in a subsequent exercise.

The problem above may be solved by control methods as follows. The desired trajectories of targets are set as:

$$C^d_{32+i} = C_{32} + \tfrac{1}{4}i(C^d_{36} - C_{32}) \quad i = 1 \ldots 4 \tag{7.70}$$

where the subscript denotes the year. By the above $C^d_{36} = C_{29}(1+\alpha)^7$; C_{32} is known and α = rate of growth of population (observed at 1%).

Table 7.1 *Klein's model I of the US economy as in the policy problem of Van den Bogaard and Theil (1959)*

$C = 16.786 + 0.02\Pi + 0.225\Pi_{-1} + 0.8(W_1 + W_2) + U_C$
$I = 17.784 + 0.231\Pi + 0.546\Pi_{-1} - 0.146K_{-1} + U_I$
$W_1 = 1.599 + 0.42(Y + T - W_2) + 0.164(Y + T - W_2)_{-1} + 0.135t + U_W$
$Y = C + I + G - T$
$\Pi = Y - W_1 - W_2$
$K = K_{-1} + I$
$D = W_1 - 2\Pi$ where
C = Consumption, I = Investment, W_1 = private wage bill,
W_2 = government wage bill, Y = national income, Π = profits
K = capital stock, D = income distribution, T = tax bill,
G = government expenditure, t = time (1931 = 1).

Targets are C, I, D } over a 4 year horizon 1933–6
Instruments are W_2, T, and G }

The objective function contains $A = B = I; C = 0$; and $q = 0$; and desired values:

	1933	1934	1935	1936
C	49.69	53.78	57.88	61.97
I	− 3.1	0	3.1	6.2
D	11.25	7.5	3.75	0.0
W_2	5.04	5.25	5.47	5.69
T	7.40	7.64	7.87	8.11
G	10.44	10.87	11.30	11.73

Investment was observed at about $0.1C$ throughout the twenties; thus

$$I^d_{36} = 0.1C^d_{36} \text{ and } I^d_{32+i} = I_{32} + \tfrac{1}{4}i(I^d_{36} - I_{32}) \quad i = 1 \ldots 4. \quad (7.71)$$

Similarly W_1, the private wage bill, averaged twice profits in 1929. So defining

$$D = W_1 - 2\Pi \text{ gives } D^d_{36} = 0 \text{ and}$$

$$D^d_{32+i} = D_{32} + \tfrac{1}{4}i(D^d_{36} - D_{32}) \quad i = 1 \ldots 4. \quad (7.72)$$

The Klein I model was used for this exercise. The instruments available in that model were the government wage bill (W_2); government expenditure (G) and the tax bill (T). The last instrument is rather unrealistic as it is not fully under the government's control. The tax rate is exactly under their control, but the tax bill depends as well on the level of income, which is another endogenous variable in the model, and hence is partly endogenous to any control problem.

It is argued that for stability in the economy the instruments should be changed continuously and gradually; for example the government wage

Table 7.2 *The optimal behaviour and its consequences 1933–6 (billions of 1934 dollars)*

		Instruments			Targets (realised)			
	Year	W_2	T	G	C	I	D	Y
Realised values	1932	5.3	8.3	10.2	45.6	– 6.2	15.0	41.3
Optimal behaviour & consequences	1933	6.15	8.67	14.21	49.57	– 4.71	6.78	50.40
	1934	5.65	8.38	13.17	52.73	– 1.75	6.41	55.77
	1935	6.07	7.41	13.81	56.68	0.87	1.83	63.95
	1936	6.30	6.95	13.29	64.41	6.07	– 6.76	76.82
Deviations from desired values	1933	1.12	1.27	3.78	– 0.12	– 1.61	– 4.47	0.77
	1934	0.39	0.74	2.30	– 1.05	– 1.75	– 1.09	– 1.25
	1935	0.60	– 0.47	2.51	– 1.20	– 2.23	– 1.92	– 0.45
	1936	0.62	– 1.17	1.56	2.44	– 0.13	– 6.75	5.04
Deviations from realised values	1933	0.55	3.27	4.91	3.07	0.39	0.68	5.10
	1934	– 0.35	1.58	3.17	4.03	1.25	0.41	6.87
	1935	– 0.03	0.21	3.31	5.38	2.17	– 3.37	10.65
	1936	– 1.10	– 1.35	2.99	6.71	3.97	– 8.36	15.02

bill, W_2, should only expand with the rate of economic growth. Similarly G, T are constrained to be near their recent historical positions by what changes are feasible and politically acceptable, and by what shocks the economy can withstand. Desired levels are therefore obtained for instruments as projections for the observed trends in them over the period 1920–32. The trends were obtained by the auxiliary regressions over that period.

$$\left.\begin{aligned} W_2 &= 3.5 + 0.215(t - 1926) \\ T &= 5.7 + 0.24(t - 1926) \\ G &= 1.4 + 0.43(t - 1926) \end{aligned}\right\} \rightarrow \begin{matrix} (W_2^d)_{32+i} \\ T^d_{32+i} \\ G^d_{32+i} \end{matrix} \qquad i = 1 \ldots 4. \qquad (7.73)$$

Now we have to set up the objective function. The specification of that function always poses problems. The two difficulties are: which functional form should be used, and what weights or rate of change of penalties as 'failures' increase? An objective of (7.10) with $Q = I$ and $q = 0$ is used because it is simple, and it allows a linear decision rule and the certainty equivalence theorem to be used. All target and instrument failures are therefore equally penalised in all planning periods.

For the results obtained, see tables 7.2–7.5. Not only is the depression removed by 1936, but in fact also the targets are notably exceeded by that stage in C (and in the implicit target of Y). However, overall, the targets are generally slightly underachieved earlier, and instrument

Table 7.3 *Forecasts of future optimal behaviour (in billions of 1934 dollars per year)*

	1933	1934	1935	1936	1933	1934	1935	1936	1933	1934	1935	1936
			W_2				T				G	
1933	6.15				8.67				14.21			
1934	6.27	5.65			8.49	8.38			13.89	13.17		
1935	6.21	5.97	6.07		7.68	7.47	7.41		13.69	13.64	13.81	
1936	6.38	6.32	6.36	6.30	7.03	6.91	6.96	6.95	13.28	13.34	13.34	13.29

values overshot. Compared with Roosevelt's historical performance the optimal plans are favourable. Only in *D* is there an inferior performance. That suggests we have attached insufficient weight to the target *D* if the preferences are to represent those of the Roosevelt administration.

The instruments are also used in a way interestingly different from history. Chiefly there is higher taxation (but decreasingly so), together with, more noticeably, higher government expenditure. Thus there is an

Table 7.4 *Forecasts of optimised future targets and national income (in billions of 1934 dollars per year).*

		1933		1934		1935		1936	
C									
	1933	47.36	*49.57*						
	1934	51.76		52.71	*52.73*				
	1935	56.35		56.67		56.51	*56.68*		
	1936	60.71		60.77		60.72		60.81	*64.41*
I									
	1933	− 6.14	*− 4.71*						
	1934	− 2.32		− 1.48	*− 1.75*				
	1935	0.96		0.95		0.73	*0.87*		
	1936	3.63		3.42		3.45		3.51	*6.07*
D									
	1933	8.27	*6.78*						
	1934	5.03		5.34	*6.41*				
	1935	1.91		1.96		1.94	*1.83*		
	1936	0.04		0.07		0.05		0.07	*− 6.76*
Y									
	1933	46.76	*50.40*						
	1934	54.83		56.01	*55.77*				
	1935	63.32		63.78		63.64	*63.95*		
	1936	70.31		70.63		70.57		70.68	*76.82*

Note: The figure in italics is the actual outcome.

Table 7.5 *The optimal policy revisions compared*

	1933						1934					
	C	I	D	W_2	T	G	C	I	D	W_2	T	G
1. Historical	46.5	– 5.2	6.16	5.63	5.4	9.3	48.7	– 3.0	6.0	5.32	6.8	10.0
2. Open loop	47.36	– 6.14	8.27	6.15	8.67	14.21	51.76	– 2.32	5.03	6.27	8.49	13.89
3. *Intended* Closed loop	47.36	– 6.14	8.27	6.15	8.67	14.21	52.71	– 1.48	5.34	5.65	8.38	13.17
4. Differences (2–3)	0	0	0	0	0	0	– 0.94	– 0.84	– 0.31	0.61	0.11	0.72
% Differences with respect to desired values	0	0	0	0	0	0	– 1.8	– 28.0[a]	– 4.3	11.6	1.4	6.6
	1935						1936					
	C	I	D	W_2	T	G	C	I	D	W_2	T	G
1. Historical	51.39	– 1.3	5.2	6.0	7.2	10.5	57.7	2.1	1.6	5.16	5.5	10.3
2. Open loop	56.35	0.96	1.91	6.21	7.68	13.69	60.71	3.63	0.04	6.38	7.03	13.28
3. *Intended* Closed loop	56.51	0.73	1.94	6.07	7.41	13.81	60.81	3.51	0.07	6.30	6.95	13.29
4. Differences (2–3)	– 0.16	0.23	– 0.03	0.14	0.27	– 0.12	– 0.1	0.12	– 0.03	0.08	0.08	– 0.01
% Differences with respect to desired values	– 0.003	7.4	– 0.8	2.7	3.4	– 1.1	– 0.002	2.1	1.9[a]	1.4	1.0	– 0.008

$w^* = 48.865$ (open loop) $w^* = 43.36$ (closed loop). The historical evaluation of $w(\tilde{z})$ was 175.5.

[a] for comparison the historical values were taken, as the desired value was zero.

expenditure policy, spending more than the desired or actual values. Notice also that although the tax bill increases, it falls as a proportion of GNP so that average tax *rates* must have fallen.

In table 7.3, the diagonal elements are policies actually implemented. In the lower triangles are the forecasts of future policies made in each of the plans. Thus 6.27 is the 1933 plan's forecast of 1934's value of W_2. By the start of 1934 the new information, previously uncertain, causes the optimal value of W_2 in 1934 to be revised to 5.65. Reading across we have progressive revisions of a plan, and reading down forecasts of a different variable in the future according to the version of the plan computed at the date of the column head.

Table 7.4 is similar to table 7.3, but for the targets and GNP. The leading figure in each column is the expected outcome (what we plan to have for those variables) of the policies actually implemented so far; lower figures are forecasts in the sense of table 7.2. The actual outcome (what actually happens to the targets) is observable only when that year's plans are fully implemented because it depends further on the realisation of the random error registered during that year. That actual outcome is the figure in italics.

Finally table 7.5 summarises the differences between open and closed loop control policies and historical policies. These differences are not insignificant in proportion to the desired values. They tend to be rather varied in size but to decline rapidly. The larger revisions are all introduced at the first opportunity (1934) – while there is still some flexibility in the system. In this case targets can be revised up, and the instruments down. Certainly the revisions cannot be ignored. In terms of the objective function, the closed loop control value is 88% of the open loop value. And the closed loop value is less than 25% of the historical evaluation of $w(\tilde{z})$. It should be borne in mind that this example shows only the revisions due to the certainty equivalents of u being different to actual outcomes. In this model N consists of a time trend, and hence introduces no uncertainty. In more complex models with more uncertain variables, one may expect the improvements of closed loop control over open loop to be more marked.

7.10 Conclusions

In this chapter we have produced a technique for computing optimal policies which largely obviates the objections to the original Tinbergen theory. We have paid particular attention to the dynamic revisions and their optimality, uncertainty, and the fact that these policies constitute a closed loop control. The importance of such a feedback rule in economic problems was underlined.

The value of using a closed loop feedback control law may be reinforced by the analogy of driving from one's house to a restaurant. If I carefully study the map before setting off and memorise the relevant distance and the directions, plus calculations of the speeds to apply at each moment and the timing of direction changes, and I then drive blindfold I would follow open loop control. The probability of arriving unscathed would be extremely small as the monitoring of progress, revised expectations of traffic conditions, etc., and the correction of mistakes, would be impossible. Closed loop control only requires that, in addition, I should drive with open eyes, using any traffic reports. Mistakes can then be rectified and unexpected obstacles avoided. But sometimes, after a very good meal and too much to drink, the return journey from the restaurant resembles open loop control – as does the more sensible course of taking a taxi home! The scheme proposed here for policy formulation actually involves repeated open loop control calculations for forecasting each policy, but a closed loop calculation for the implemented policies (i.e. we both study the directions and drive with eyes open).

Our conclusion therefore is to argue in favour of error correction mechanisms in economic policy calculations as a point of design. It was an interesting observation made by Manove (1971) in another context, that improving the 'institutional' procedures for the calculation of policies may have far-reaching effects in terms of improving their accuracy, stability and robustness even when they cannot be completed with complete accuracy or when they depend on partial or inconsistent information.

Appendix: Computational issues and nonlinear models

(1) The efficient computation of the final form of a linear model

Evidently the size of Π_1, and the raising of it to large powers, is the major obstacle to the efficient computation of R and s. It is however possible to take advantage of its sparseness without losing generality. And R and s need only be obtained once, however many optimisations are required.

Consider first R before the deletion of any rows; we need R_i, $i = 1 \ldots T$. We know from (7.3) that for $i = 1 \ldots T$

$$R_i^* = \Pi_1 \sum_{i}^{\min(k,i-1)} \Pi_1^{i-j-1} \begin{bmatrix} \Pi_{2,j-1} \\ 0 \end{bmatrix}$$

$$= \begin{cases} \Pi_1 R_{i-1}^* & \text{if } i-1 > k \\ \Pi_1 R_{i-1}^* + \begin{bmatrix} \Pi_{2,i-1} \\ 0 \end{bmatrix} & \text{if } i-1 \leqslant k. \end{cases} \qquad \text{(A7.1)}$$

Given the structure and sparseness of Π_1, only the leading g rows of R_i^* require computation – the subsequent rows are just R_{i-1}^* repeated (followed by zeroes if $i \leqslant l-1$; or with the last $g(i-l)$ rows omitted if $i \geqslant l+1$). We can do better without forming Π_1 by defining

$$\begin{aligned} R_i^{+\prime} &= [\hat{R}_i' \ldots \hat{R}_1' \; 0] \text{ if } i \leqslant l-1 \\ &= [\hat{R}_i' \ldots \hat{R}_{i-l-1}'] \text{ otherwise} \end{aligned} \tag{A7.2}$$

where $\hat{R}_i$ is the first g rows of R_i^*. This discards the rows corresponding to lags in Y_t^+. (A7.1) becomes, for $i \geqslant 2$,

$$\hat{R}_i = \begin{cases} \displaystyle\sum_{j=1}^{\min(l,\,i-1)} \Pi_{1j}\hat{R}_{i-j} + \Pi_{2,i-1} & \text{when } i-1 \leqslant k \\ \displaystyle\sum_{j=1}^{\min(l,\,i-1)} \Pi_{1j}\hat{R}_{i-j} & \text{if } i-1 > k \end{cases} \tag{A7.3}$$

with $\hat{R}_1 = \Pi_{20}$.
Thus we have to use at most a $g \times n$ matrix R_i^+, in addition to $\Pi_{11} \ldots \Pi_{1l}$, and $\Pi_{20} \ldots \Pi_{2k}$. Next R_i, $i = 1 \ldots T-l$, are the $m \times n$ submatrices (i.e. nontargets are now deleted) of each $\hat{R}_i$. They may be created immediately *after* $\hat{R}_{i+l}$ is inserted in R_{i+l}^+. Lastly R_i, $i = T-l+1 \ldots T$, are taken from the final R_t^+. Moreover, storage is necessary for R_i^+ only.

By exactly the same arguments S may be computed from

$$\hat{S}_i = \sum_{j=1}^{\min(l,\,i-1)} \Pi_{ij}\hat{S}_{ij} \quad i = 1 \ldots T \quad \text{for} \quad i \geqslant 2 \tag{A7.4}$$

with $\hat{S}_1 = \beta^{-1}$. We have to use a matrix S_i^+ analogous to R_i^+ and store only the appropriate m rows from $\hat{S}_i$ and S_i. We do the same again using $\hat{\sigma}_i$, and σ_i^+, to get finally σ_i itself with only m elements. It may be easier to replace $\Pi_{2,i-1}$ by $(\Pi_{2,i-1} \vdots \Pi_{3,i-1})$ in (A7.3), i.e. no partitioning between x_t and N_t, to obtain $(R_i \vdots K_i)$ together. The rest of σ_i^+ is straightforward from (7.6).

(2) Policy optimisation with nonlinear models

We return to deriving (7.2) from the general nonlinear model (7.1). The required multipliers can be evaluated numerically by simulating a series of individual unit shocks to each instrument in each period (δx_{ti}, $i = 1 \ldots n$ *and* $t = 1 \ldots T$). The changes in targets ($\delta y_{t+\tau,j}$, $j = 1 \ldots m$ *and* $\tau = t \ldots T$ for each $t = 1 \ldots T$) are inserted as the various submatrices $R_{\tau t}$ of R. Any model solution technique (Chapter 4) may be used. One difficulty is to decide on the benchmark trajectories in x and s – the multiplier evaluations should be valid for all candidate policy values (and external events) under consideration. Since those candidates are not known a priori, it will be necessary to design some iterative scheme in which R is determined at some trial x and s; then a new policy chosen, R reevaluated, and so on until the trajectories used in the linearisations match with the policy choice itself. A number of algorithms have been designed for policy optimisation with nonlinear models, but that described here (alternating phases of linearisation about the previous policy calculation, the optimisation by (7.16), then a new linearisation, and so on) is essentially Holbrook's (1974) approach. The reader may consult Brandsma, Hughes Hallett and Van der Windt (1981) for the necessary computational details. We note the following general points:

(a) That procedure is a form of the variable metric optimisation technique.

(b) Convergence from an arbitrary start can be guaranteed. It is often argued that the multipliers are insensitive to variations in x, so iterations are not important. This has not always been the case, and is only half the story since convergence depends on the sensitivity of R to x *and* of x to R. Typically iterations are necessary for those policies which are very important in $w(\tilde{z})$. No statements on the insensitivity of multipliers can be made independently of the preference structure. Also R may be insensitive to individual policy changes, but it is noticeably more sensitive to packages of all policies changing together. The latter may be more representative of reality.

(c) Policy revisions require the repetition of the iterations since the revised policy must be conditioned on the new expectation (evaluation) of the future responses of the model. Full allowance has not yet been made for the uncertainty over the correct multiplier values (i.e. they are potentially a function of s) even at convergence, but there is no difficulty in extending the algorithm for that case in the form of (12.2) below.

(d) Iterations of this kind are essential in order to allow for uncertainty; certainty equivalence holds (locally) at convergence. Direct optimisation techniques have no mechanism for determining appropriate values to be assumed for the uncertain variables. We know certainty equivalence does not apply, unless the model is effectively linear or uncertainty small. Further, (7.47) shows direct optimisation of $E_t(w)$ to be infeasible because of all the transformations/convolutions necessary to obtain $E_t(\tilde{z})$ and $V_t(\tilde{z})$ for each candidate policy, and because $w_d(.)$ and $w_s(.)$ are no longer separable with respect to $E_t(\tilde{z})$ and ξ.

8

Control theory: alternative methods for policy optimisation

8.1 The motivation

Concentration on the policy formulation problem proposed in Chapter 2 has led to a general mathematical programming solution. This perhaps is the natural way to conceive of the stochastic policy problem because it consists of selecting the policy values themselves.

However, an alternative approach would be to stress the importance of a closed loop feedback control rule, and then to calculate an appropriate form of the general decision rule (7.41). Appropriate in this context means the explicit optimisation of the feedback matrices in $G_t(L)$, and of g_t, given an objective function and equality constraints representing the dynamics of economic behaviour. That rule can then be used to generate the policy values. This approach is perhaps natural to the administrator whose responsibility it is to run the economy, rather than to the policy maker who is accountable for specific policy measures. The administrator's natural interest is in the execution of policy; i.e. in the properties of robustness, continuity, the power to damp down shocks, and so on.

There is a certain duality between techniques which select policy values directly (without accounting for the properties of the control rule implied), and techniques which select a control rule directly. This chapter examines the latter group of techniques, as a complement to Chapter 7 which dealt with the former group. Dynamic programming (section 8.3), state-space models (section 8.6), and Pontryagin's discrete 'minimum principle' solutions (section 8.7) are introduced. These optimisation techniques need to be examined because they are the best known solution methods of control theory. Indeed, in most treatments of the subject they are the only solutions provided. But for their optimality, they depend on a particular decision structure (section 8.2). The question of what happens in the absence of this special decision structure is deferred until Chapter 11. In sections 8.4 and 8.5 we shall show that, in circumstances where this particular decision structure applies, the techniques of this chapter and the last all give identical solutions. Nothing is gained by using the best instrument values rather than the best control rule. We can then show the relations between the various techniques available for controlling the economy (sections 8.8 and 8.9).

8.2 The principle of optimality and time nested decisions

The policy problem has variables of three kinds: targets, y_t; instruments, x_t; and noncontrollables, N_t and u_t. They are related through the model (2.4). Algorithms to solve the policy optimisation problem

$$\min_{x_t} \{w(\tilde{z}) | Y_t = \Sigma\Pi_{1i}Y_{t-i} + \Sigma\Pi_{2i}x_{t-i} + \Pi_3 N_t + V_t\} \quad \text{for each } t = 1 \ldots T \tag{8.1}$$

are also of three kinds: those solving a sequence of static optimisations, those applying dynamic programming techniques, and those using Pontryagin's minimum principle. The first uses the model converted from (2.4) to stacked t-period final forms (with nontargets and all lags deleted); that is (7.2). The last requires it in state-space form (e.g. Pindyck (1973)). But for dynamic programming it may either be transformed to a first order linear difference equation in $Z'_t = (Y'_t \ldots Y'_{t-l+1}, x'_t \ldots x'_{t-k+1})$ with forcing function linear in x_t, Chow (1975), or be set in state-space form (Bray (1975)).

We return to (7.8), rewritten as

$$Z_t = \Pi_4 Z_{t-1} + \Pi_5 x_t + a_t + V_t \tag{8.2}$$

where $a_t = \begin{bmatrix} K^*_{tt} \\ 0 \end{bmatrix} N_t$ and $V_t = \begin{bmatrix} S^*_{tt} \\ 0 \end{bmatrix} u_t$ and Z_t is defined as above. In addition $\Pi_4 = \begin{bmatrix} \Pi_1 & \Pi^{**}_2 \\ 0 & I^* \end{bmatrix}$; $\Pi'_5 = (\Pi'_{20} 0 \ldots 0 \, I_n 0 \ldots 0)$; $I^* = \begin{bmatrix} 0 & 0 \\ I_{n(k-1)} & 0 \end{bmatrix}$ of order nk.

The *principle of optimality* states: 'An optimal policy has the property that whatever the initial state and initial decision the remaining decisions must constitute an optimal policy with respect to the state resulting from the first decisions' (Bellman (1961), p. 57). If this is to be used to derive optimal policies it must hold for each of the policies z^*_t, for $t = 1 \ldots T$. For that, it is necessary to have an objective function ($w(\tilde{z})$ in this instance) which is *Markovian*; that is, 'After any number of decisions, t, we wish the effect of the remaining $T - t$ stages of the decision process upon the total return (the criterion $w(\tilde{z})$) to depend only on the state of the system at the end of the tth decision *and* the subsequent decisions' (Bellman (1961), p. 54).

Both statements are satisfied by the optimal policies chosen by the method of Chapter 7 (equation (7.33)).

Proposition 8.1: The optimal policies in the form of the leading subvectors $\tilde{z}_t^*$, from $\tilde{z}_{(t)}^*$ of (7.33) for $t = 1 \ldots T$, satisfy the principle of optimality; and moreover the sequence $E_t(w) = E(w|\Omega_t)$ is a Markovian objective.

Proof: By (7.30) and the discussion following, the objective optimised by (7.33) is

$$E(w|\Omega_t) = \tfrac{1}{2}\tilde{z}_0^{*\prime} Q_1 \tilde{z}_0^{*} + \tilde{z}_0^{*\prime} Q_2 \tilde{z}_{(t)} + \tfrac{1}{2}\tilde{z}_{(t)}' Q_{(t)} \tilde{z}_{(t)} + q_1' \tilde{z}_0^* + q_{(t)}' \tilde{z}_{(t)} \tag{8.3}$$

where $\tilde{z}_0^*$ is fixed. This is a Markovian function by construction, since the last 'initial' state and the past decisions are accurately incorporated in Ω_t *provided* the time-consistency constraints of (7.32) are observed at each step. Therefore, the list of leading subvectors from (7.33) follow the principle of optimality, because the outstanding policies are explicitly and simultaneously reoptimised in terms of a Markovian objective at each and every t.

Now we reformulate the policy problem in terms of (8.2). Suppose we take a time separable version of $w(\tilde{z})$ as a special case; i.e. $w = \sum_{t=1}^{T} w_t(\tilde{z}_t)$, with the quadratic approximation[1]

$$w = \tfrac{1}{2}\sum_t \tilde{z}_t' Q_t \tilde{z}_t. \tag{8.4}$$

The decisions now become recursively dependent, rather than fully interdependent as in (7.16). They are determined by minimising a *constrained* objective function which is nested (backwards) with respect to time:

$$w = \sum_{t=1}^{T} w_t(x_t \ldots x_1, Z_0, a_t \ldots a_1, V_t \ldots V_1) \tag{8.5}$$

by back substitutions from (8.1) into (8.4). Thus decisions can be determined in the same time nested sequence:

$$\min_{\substack{z_t \\ t=1,\ldots,T}} \left\{ \sum_t w_t(\tilde{z}_t) \right\} = \min_{z_1} \left\{ w_1(\tilde{z}_1) + \bar{w}_{T-1}^*(\tilde{z}_{(2)}^*) \right\} \tag{8.6}$$

$$= \min_{z_1} \left\{ w_1(\tilde{z}_1) + \min_{z_2} \left\{ w_2(\tilde{z}_2) + \ldots + \min_{z_t} \left\{ w_t(\tilde{z}_t) + \bar{w}_{T-t}^*(\tilde{z}_{(t+1)}^*) \right\} \cdots \right\} \right\}.$$

Here $\quad \bar{w}_{T-t}^*(\tilde{z}_{(t+1)}^*) = \min\limits_{z_{t+1} \ldots z_T} \left\{ \sum_{t+1}^{T} w_j(\tilde{z}_j) \right\}$

are the evaluations *at* t of the prior $(T - t + 1)$ stage constrained optimisation process.

Performing the indicated minimisations therefore yields a sequence of

1 If $q_t \neq 0$, some t, we apply the transformation of (7.12).

decisions, which, at the moment when they are to be implemented, are dependent on one another through a backwards recursion. However, the time nested structure of (8.6) is not found in the constrained objective (7.17), unless Q satisfies (8.4) *and* R is block triangular (section 11.6 sets this out in detail).

8.3 Policy optimisation by dynamic programming

Given the time nested structure of (8.6), if we can generate a *sequence* of policies $\tilde{z}_t^* \ldots \tilde{z}_T^*$ at planning period t which are optimal for any initial condition z_{t-1} and, if we repeat the procedure over $t - T \ldots 1$, we shall finish up with a sequence of z values which is optimal for the whole period (given an arbitrary initial condition Z_0). Such optimal policies would be obtained analytically by expressing each choice as a function of its initial conditions, and then optimising and backsubstituting over each period in turn. But they would be implemented in a forward sequence by inserting the realised initial condition (and new expectations of a_t, V_t, etc., as required). This ensures each decision, $\tilde{z}_t^*$, is conditioned on Ω_t.

We specifically exploit the time nesting in (8.6) by first solving the policy problem analytically for the last period T, contingent on any initial condition Z_{T-1}. We obtain an expression for an optimal x_T^* in terms of Z_{T-1}. Then we solve the T and $T-1$ period problems together for any Z_{T-2} inserting the result just obtained for x_T^* as a function Z_{T-1}. The latter will be optimised by the choice of an optimal x_{T-1}^* (given any Z_{T-2}) and therefore may be substituted out using (8.2). In the more familiar context of maximum likelihood estimation this is the same operation as concentration – we concentrate the relevant objective function on x_{T-1}. Then we go to the T, $T-1$, $T-2$ period problems; and so on until we have an optimal x_1^*, given that $x_2^* \ldots x_T^*$ are optimised functions of it (through (8.2)) for any Z_0. Thus, at any t, whatever the outcome at period $t-1$, x_t^* to x_T^* are optimal because $x_{t+1}^* \ldots x_T^*$ are restricted to be optimal functions of x_t, and because x_t^* is optimal by construction.

8.3.1 The dynamic programming algorithm

Using conditional expectations in (8.4) and then (8.2), $\min_{x_T} E_T(w_T(Z_{T-1}))$ will be the last period problem, to be solved first. But having replaced z_t by Z_t in (8.2) we must augment Q_t by adding rows and columns of zeros corresponding to the nontargets and lagged values in Z_t; say Q_t^+. Then

$$E_T(w_T) = \tfrac{1}{2}E_T(Z'_T H_T Z_T - 2Z'_T h_T + f_T) \qquad (8.7)$$

where $H_T = Q_T^+$, $h_T = H_T \hat{Z}_T^d$ and $f_T = \hat{Z}_T^{d\prime} H_T \hat{Z}_T^d$, and $\hat{Z}_T^d$ is z_T^d augmented by zeros conformable to Q_T^+. When x_T^* comes to be evaluated, a_T and V_T will still be unknown; and (8.7) must be constrained by (8.2). We take $E_T(a_T)$ to be known at T; likewise that $E_T(V_T)=0$. Note $E_T(Z_{T-1})=Z_{T-1}$ is known at T. We also presume $E_T(a_T' V_T)=0$. Then

$$\begin{aligned}E_T(w_T)=\tfrac{1}{2}[&(\Pi_4 Z_{T-1}+\Pi_5 x_T)' H_T(\Pi_4 Z_{T-1}+\Pi_5 x_T)\\&+2(\Pi_4 Z_{T-1}+\Pi_5 x_T)'(H_T E_T(a_T)-h_T)\\&-2E_T(a_T)' h_T+f_T+E_T(V_T' H_T V_T)+E_T(a_T' H_T a_T)].\end{aligned} \tag{8.8}$$

Solving $\partial E_T(w_T)/\partial x_T=0$ we find the unique optimal policy, to be chosen at the start of period T, is

$$x_T^*=G_T Z_{T-1}+g_T \tag{8.9}$$

where

$$G_T=-(\Pi_5' H_T \Pi_5)^{-1}(\Pi_5' H_T \Pi_4)$$

and

$$g_T=-(\Pi_5' H_T \Pi_5)^{-1}\Pi_5'(H_T E_T(a_T)-h_T). \tag{8.10}$$

Then putting (8.9) back into (8.8)

$$\begin{aligned}E_T(w_T^*(Z_{T-1}))=\tfrac{1}{2}\{&Z_{T-1}'(\Pi_4+\Pi_5 G_T)' H_T(\Pi_4+\Pi_5 G_T)Z_{T-1}\\&+2Z_{T-1}'(\Pi_4+\Pi_5 G_T)'[H_T(\Pi_5 g_T+E_T(a_T))-h_T]\\&+g_T'\Pi_5' H_T \Pi_5 g_T+2g_T'\Pi_5'(H_T E_T(a_T)-h_T)\\&-2E_T(a_T)' h_T+f_T+E_T(V_T' H_T V_T)\\&+E_T(a_T' H_T a_T)\}.\end{aligned} \tag{8.11}$$

Next we solve the problem for the last two periods together. We follow exactly the same steps in order to solve for x_{T-1}, given any Z_{T-2}, having eliminated both x_T^* and Z_{T-1} via (8.9) and (8.2) combined. This leaves an expression involving only x_{T-1} and Z_{T-2}. The time nested structure of (8.6) implies

$$\bar{w}_{T-t}=w_t(\tilde{z}_t)+\sum_{j=t+1}^{T} w_j^*(\tilde{z}_j^*)=w_t(\tilde{z}_t)+\bar{w}_{T-t-1}^*(\tilde{z}_{(t+1)}^*). \tag{8.12}$$

Consequently at $T-1$,

$$\begin{aligned}E_{T-1}(\bar{w}_{T-1})=\tfrac{1}{2}E_{T-1}(&Z_{T-1}' Q_{T-1}^+ Z_{T-1}\\&-2Z_{T-1}' Q_{T-1}^+ \hat{Z}_{T-1}^d+\hat{Z}_{T-1}^{d\prime} Q_{T-1}^+ \hat{Z}_{T-1}^d)\\&+E_T(w_T^*(Z_{T-1})).\end{aligned} \tag{8.13}$$

Therefore inserting (8.11) and collecting terms

$$E_{T-1}(\bar{w}_{T-1})=\tfrac{1}{2}E_{T-1}(Z_{T-1}' H_{T-1} Z_{T-1}-2Z_{T-1}' h_{T-1}+f_{T-1}) \tag{8.14}$$

where now

$$H_{T-1} = Q^+_{T-1} + (\Pi_4 + \Pi_5 G_T)' H_T (\Pi_4 + \Pi_5 G_T) \qquad (8.15)$$

$$h_{T-1} = Q^+_{T-1} \hat{Z}^d_{T-1} + (\Pi_4 + \Pi_5 G_T)'(h_T - H_T(\Pi_5 g_T + E_T(a_T))) \qquad (8.16)$$

$$f_{T-1} = \hat{Z}^{d'}_{T-1} Q^+_{T-1} \hat{Z}^d_{T-1} + (E_T(a_T) + \Pi_5 g_T)' H_T (E_T(a_T) + \Pi_5 g_T) - 2(E_T(a_T) + \Pi_5 g_T)' h_T + f_T + E_T(V_T' H_T V_T). \qquad (8.17)$$

The constrained objective function (8.14) has exactly the same form as its predecessor (8.7). So x^*_{T-1} will be of the same form as (8.9), except that $T-1$ replaces T throughout in the subscripts. The same happens in reformulating (8.11) for $E_{T-1}(\bar{w}^*_{T-1}(\tilde{z}^*_{(T-2)})$. So we can go on to the $E_{T-2}(\bar{w}_{T-2})$ problem simply by repeating (8.13) to (8.17). Now the subscripts change from $T-1$ to $T-2$ throughout; and so on back to x^*_1 as function of the known Z_0 value.

To implement this scheme we need to do the following:

(i) Set $H_T = Q^+_T$, $h_T = H_T \hat{Z}^d_t$

(ii) Compute (8.10), and store for future use.

(iii) For each $t = T-1 \ldots 1$ compute the following two pairs in turn:

$$H_t = Q^+_t + (\Pi_4 + \Pi_5 G_{t+1})' H_{t+1} (\Pi_4 + \Pi_5 G_{t+1})$$

and

$$h_t = Q^+_t \hat{Z}^d_t + (\Pi_4 + \Pi_5 G_{t+1})' (h_{t+1} - H_{t+1}(E_t(a_{t+1}) + \Pi_5 g_{t+1})) \qquad (8.18)$$

and then

$$G_t = -(\Pi_5' H_t \Pi_5)^{-1} (\Pi_5' H_t \Pi_4) \quad \text{and}$$

$$g_t = -(\Pi_5' H_t \Pi_5)^{-1} \Pi_5' (H_t E_t(a_t) - h_t). \qquad (8.19)$$

If Q is positive definite then all Q_t are. Thus the inverses all exist in (8.10) and (8.19), and the policies are unique. The (G_t, g_t) sequence is now stored. In practice, the h_t and g_t sequences in (8.18) and (8.19) will be recomputed separately for $t = T \ldots i$, for each $i = T-1 \ldots 1$ in turn, where $E_i(a_i, h_t, g_t)$ replaces $E_t(a_t, h_t, g_t)$ throughout, since at i the latter quantities will be unknown and our estimates of them will vary with each i.

(iv) Starting with $Z_0 = Z^*_0$ known, compute first the policy then the outcome for each $t = 1 \ldots T$ in forward sequence

$$x^*_t = G_t Z^*_{t-1} + g_t \qquad (8.20)$$

accompanied by

$$Y^*_t = \Pi_6 Z^*_{t-1} + \Pi_{20} x^*_t + a_t + V_t \qquad (\Pi_6 \text{ the first } g \text{ rows of } \Pi_4). \qquad (8.21)$$

In principle (8.20) and (8.21) will use actual values for Z^*_{t-1}. That provides for closed loop control. However, if the outcome of the policy calculations of the previous step is used, we generate forecast policies; and that provides for open loop control. First period certainty equivalent policies at t are obtained by inserting actual Z^*_{j-1} values for $j \leqslant t$ and values calculated via (8.20) and (8.21) thereafter.

8.3.2 Static and dynamic optimisation algorithms

At this point it is important to draw attention to a fundamental difference which distinguishes dynamic programming (and subsequently the Pontryagin approach) from the algorithm of Chapter 7.

The obvious difference is that in Chapter 7 we optimised the current expectation of *all* outstanding policy variables together, and repeated that for each $t = 1 \ldots T$. Here, to get feedback rules we optimised the current expectation of *only* the current policy variables, repeated for each $t = T \ldots 1$; and then obtained policy values forwards. So in Chapter 7 forecasts of future policies are computed automatically at each step, but here they would require extra calculations. Both techniques involve T optimisations. But the former optimises $z_{(t)}$ (i.e. $n + m$ variables simultaneously over $T - t + 1$ periods), and the latter Z_t (i.e. $gl + nk$ variables separately for each t).

Chapter 7 introduced a *static algorithm*: that is one which converts a T-period dynamic optimisation problem into T static optimisation problems, to be solved sequentially for the complete interval from t to T, for each t in turn. The optimisations are constrained by (7.2) and the policies are recomputed as the plans roll forward, so we are not committed to them in advance. That ensures that each objective is Markovian (proposition 8.1), and thus the sequence of *implemented* policies necessarily satisfies the principle of optimality looking forwards. There is no need for any other check on optimality since the outstanding policies are simultaneously reoptimised at each step.

But working directly from (8.6) has provided a *dynamic algorithm*: that is one which exploits the time nested structure of (8.6) to replace the $(T - t + 1)$ optimisations, outstanding at t, with a sequence of $T - t + 1$ single period optimisations. It happens that these sequences are, except for one important aspect of g_t to be explained in section 8.4 below, identical in each set of the $(T - t + 1)$ optimisations (i.e. G_t, and in part g_t, are invariant to Ω_t given a known model and preferences). So it turns out that these sets of single period optimisations from 1 to T may be computed (at $t = 1$) as one set in sequence backwards from T to 1. To do that means obtaining (8.20) for $t = T$; and this will be used when we get to period T.

Then to derive (8.20) at $T-1$, we have to assume that the rule for T is optimal not only for use at T but also as a stepping stone to deriving the rule for use at $T-1$. Only then can we insert the previous rule in (8.4) to produce (8.11) for subsequent optimisations back to $t=1$, and still expect the sequence of rules to be optimal *as a set*, as well as individually. It is important to distinguish (8.20) at t for use at t (where Z_{t-1} is a known realisation), from (8.20) at t for use as a stepping stone to deriving rules for $t-1$ and earlier (when Z_{t-1} is assumed invariant to the chosen x_t – the relevant partial derivatives were set to zero at (8.8) – although neither have actually been determined at that stage). For the optimality of the latter a time nested structure in (8.6) is crucial, because it ensures the necessary backwards Markov property. Markovian objectives are necessary for steps $T, T-1 \ldots 1$ of the recursions, so that the principle of optimality is guaranteed to apply to each stepping stone rule looking backwards. Chapter 11 establishes these conditions formally, and discusses some interesting cases where they are violated.

Then, in a second phase, a dynamic algorithm produces policy values from these rules used in forward sequence. This phase is of course the same as that in the static algorithm, and depends on the same forwards application of the principle of optimality and hence the same forward Markov property.

The distinguishing feature of a dynamic algorithm is this inner sequence of backwards optimisations at t, associated with $x_j, t \leqslant j \leqslant T$, which are the necessary stepping stones for deriving the optimal decision rule for x_t for immediate use. That inner sequence may avoid the reoptimisations of (7.30)–(7.33), but it entails a second application of the principle of optimality and hence the time nesting in (8.6).

8.3.3 The equality of dynamic programming and static optimisations

It is useful to note that the solutions given by (7.18) and (8.20) are identical when used with (8.2) and (8.4) (Norman (1974)). Notice we deal only with first order certainty equivalent choices at this stage. Chapter 12 considers a generalisation.

We can demonstrate this proposition by writing out (7.18) at $t=T$, and substituting for H^* and $E_T(b_{(T)})$, respectively, by $(\Pi'_{20} \vdots I)$ and $E_T(b_T + \sum_2^T R_i \tilde{x}_{t-i})$ from (7.32). Thus at period T, $H^{*\prime} Q_T H^* = \Pi'_5 Q_T^+ \Pi_5$ and, since $Z_{T-1} = \sum_0^{T-1} \Pi_4^{i-1} \Pi_5 x_{T-i-1} + \Pi_4^{T-1} Z_0 + \sum_0^{T-2} \Pi_4^{i-1}(a_{T-i-1} + V_{t-i-1})$, then $\Pi'_5 Q_T^+(\Pi_4 Z_{T-1} + E_T(a_T) - \hat{Z}_T^d) = H^{*\prime} Q_T \begin{pmatrix} E(b_T) \\ \cdots \\ 0 \end{pmatrix}$. Now consider (7.18) at $t = T-1$. Substitute for x_T via (8.20) and (7.1), and then use similar substitutions to the previous step and include $R_2 = \Pi_{11} R_1 + \Pi_{21}$ where $R_1 = \Pi_{20}$. Collecting terms and solving for x^*_{T-1} produces

$$\tilde{x}^*_{T-1} = -(M_1 - M_2 M_4^{-1} M_3)^{-1}[(R'_1 \vdots R'_2 \vdots I \vdots 0) - M_2 M_4^{-1}(0 \vdots R'_1 \vdots 0 \vdots I)]$$
$$\times \left(\begin{array}{cc|cc} B_{T-1} & 0 & C'_{T-1} & 0 \\ 0 & B_T & 0 & C'_T \\ \hline C_{T-1} & 0 & A_{T-1} & 0 \\ 0 & C_T & 0 & A_T \end{array}\right)\begin{pmatrix} b_{T-1} \\ b_T \\ 0 \\ 0 \end{pmatrix} \tag{8.22}$$

where

$$M_1 = R'_1 B_{T-1} R_1 + C_{T-1} R_1 + R'_2 B_T R_2 + R'_1 C'_{T-1} + A_{T-1}$$
$$M_2 = R'_2 B_T R_1 + R'_2 C'_T \text{ and } M_3 = M'_2$$
$$M_4 = A_T + R'_1 C'_T + C_T R_1 + R'_1 B_T R_1 = \Pi'_5 Q^+_T \Pi_5$$

and $M = \begin{pmatrix} M_1 & M_2 \\ M_3 & M_4 \end{pmatrix}$. The leading matrix of (8.22) is $(\Pi'_5 H_{T-1} \Pi_5)^{-1}$ since by (8.18) and (8.19) we can write $H_{T-1} = Q^+_{T-1} + \Pi'_4 H_T \Pi_4 + (\Pi'_4 H_T \Pi_5) G_T$, and hence $\Pi'_5 H_{T-1} \Pi_5 = M_1 - M_2 M_4^{-1} M_2$ using the structures of Π_4 and Π_5. Multiplying out the rest we get $\{(R'_1 B_{T-1} + C_{T-1}) b_{T-1} + R'_2 B_T b_T + R'_2 Q_T \Pi_5 (G_T Z_{T-1} + g_T)\}$. Using the structure of Π_4 and Π_5, we find $R'_1 B_T b_T + C_T b_T = -M_4(G_T Z_{T-1} + g_T)$ follows from (8.20) at T. But the matrix products are components of $\Pi'_5 H_{T-1}$ (using H_{t-1} as above). Hence, substituting for $E_{T-1}(b_T), E_{T-1}(b_{T-1})$ as above, and for Z_{T-1} by (8.2), and collecting terms, yields (8.20) at $T-1$ in straightforward but tedious steps. The demonstration is completed by induction back to $t = 1$. At each step the subscript T denotes quantities from periods $T \ldots t+1$ taken together, and $T-1$ those of period t.

8.4 Certainty equivalence, feedback and closed loop controls

8.4.1 Some characteristics of the dynamic programming solution

(a) Equation (8.20) provides a closed loop feedback control which is an example of the integral control rule (7.35). It implies a first order difference equation system in Z^*_t or a max (l, k) order system in the policy variables themselves. Inserting (8.20) into (8.2) yields

$$Z^*_t = (\Pi_4 + \Pi_5 G_t) Z^*_{t-1} + a_t + V_t + \Pi_5 g_t \tag{8.23}$$

rather than the $(t-1)$th order system of (7.39). But of course we can back substitute for each x^*_{t-i-1}, $0 \leqslant i \leqslant k$, on the right of (8.20); and then repeat the operation until (G_1, g_1) have been introduced. This leaves a $(t-1)$th order feedback rule similar to that contained in (7.39). The rule is time dependent.

(b) The equation determining H_t, (8.18), is known as the Ricatti equation. Together with h_t it shows that implicit penalties, which vary systematically throughout the planning period, are assigned to the policy variables. These penalties differ from those set in (8.4); in particular since the pattern of zeros in Q_t^+ is lost in $H_t(t \leqslant T-1)$ *implicit* penalties are being assigned to the nontargets and lagged values of the model.

(c) The form of these implicit penalties is illustrated by (8.14). The relative penalties assigned to failures at $T-1$ are those originally specified in (8.4) plus those associated with the minimised failures at T. These additions are designed to offset the policies, which would be optimal for period $T-1$ as a one period optimisation, in a direction tending to eliminate the currently anticipated policy failures of period T. The amount of offsetting depends on the relative importance of periods T and $T-1$. The same holds for periods t and $t-1$, except that the penalties we start with are those originally specified plus the accumulation of offsetting penalties up to T. Notice also that $E_{T-1}(E_T(a_T)) = E_{T-1}(a_T)$ has been used in (8.18). So the offsetting penalties are supposed to reflect the future policy failures anticipated at the moment that the preceding policy was calculated.

8.4.2 Certainty equivalence and the tracking gains

The dynamic programming solution has been obtained without invoking certainty equivalence. The steps (8.8) to (8.20) are derived directly from $E_t(\bar{w}_t)$, $t = T \ldots 1$. However, it is obvious that multiperiod certainty equivalence applies to the additive uncertainties since, if we assume it and repeat steps (8.8) to (8.17) for each t, we get precisely the same decision rules. The only alterations concern the terms quadratic in a_t and V_t which do not affect the optimisations.

Multiperiod certainty equivalence is desirable for each decision rule as it is implemented. But, at $t \leqslant T-1$, each rule depends on the future rules used as stepping stones. With respect to those future rules, we need first period (as seen from t) certainty equivalence in the current rule. Implementing the expectation operator $E_t(.)$ in (8.14) will introduce $E_t(a_{t+1}) = E_t(E_{t+1}(a_{t+1}))$ into (8.18). In addition $E_t(h_{t+1})$ and $E_t(g_{t+1})$ should replace h_{t+1} and g_{t+1} since both depend on a_{t+1}, which is unknown at t. Extending this to each $E_t(\bar{w}_t)$, when all future values of a_i, hence h_i and g_i, are unknown, means that the set of tracking gains, g_i, have to be recomputed for all $t \leqslant i \leqslant T$, at each t. That is, g_t depends on h_t and h_t on $h_{t+1} \ldots h_T$ which in turn are determined in part by the uncertain

$a_{t+1} \ldots a_T$. Thus in implementing this computational scheme we must insert $E_t(a_{t+1}) \ldots E_t(a_T)$ throughout the recursions (8.18) and (8.19), in order to finish up with $E_t(h_t)$ in g_t. Only then does (8.20) have first period certainty equivalence, at each t, with respect to the stepping stone rules used from T to $t+1$. Only then, therefore, does each *implemented* rule provide multiperiod certainty equivalent policies.

Consequently, unless our expectations never change after $t = 1$, we must recompute T sets of tracking gains (with $T - t + 1$ members per set). The formula remains fixed, only $E(a_t, h_t$ and $g_t)$ alters. The feedback matrices, G_t, are unaffected unless we wish to alter the model (as we should if first order certainty equivalence is kept up to date) or the preferences (given the success and failures so far). Therefore, in principle, there are T reoptimisations (of order $T - t + 1$) underlying the sequence of rules in (8.20); and the reoptimisations equivalent to (7.30)–(7.33) are not avoided.

8.4.3 Closed loop feedback control

Each set of tracking gains in (8.20) optimises $E_t(\sum_{j=t}^{T} w_j)$ as opposed to $\sum_{j=t}^{T} E_j(w_j)$. It is of course impossible to optimise the latter at any $t < T$. Only when $g_i, i \geqslant t$, is recomputed at each t, and x_t^* alone implemented of the implied x_i^* sequence, do the implemented policies display closed loop control. Otherwise they are open loop with respect to V_j and $N_j, j \geqslant t$, but feedback with respect to V_j and $N_j, j < t$, if Z_{t-1}^* is an actual realisation; or fully open loop if $E_1(Z_{t-1}^*)$ is used. Thus (8.20) automatically corrects for all past errors, but makes no provision for changed expectations unless the tracking gains are recomputed. The use of probabilistic information to condition (8.20) anew at each t distinguishes a closed loop control from a feedback control.

So once again we have innovations dependent policies where the innovations are both unanticipated changes in Ω_t *and* adjustments to the expectations:

$$E_t(x_t^*) = E_i(x_t^*) + G_t[Z_{t-1}^* - E_i(Z_{t-1}^*)] + E_t(g_t) - E_i(g_t) \quad i < t. \tag{8.24}$$

Thus we have *open loop* rules $x_t = f_{t,1}(\Omega_1)$, *feedback* rules $x_t = f_{t,1}(\Omega_t)$, and *closed loop* rules $x_t = f_{t,t}(\Omega_t)$ where $f_{t,1}(.)$ and $f_{t,t}(.)$ are optimal functions subject to Ω_1 and Ω_t respectively. It would be foolish to ignore adjustments to the expectations in problems where uncertainty is too important. But there are no additional complications if the model (8.2) has time varying parameters. We may subscript Π_4 and Π_5 with t throughout (8.18), (8.19) and (8.20). This, of course, parallels the case where multipliers R_{ij} are time dependent in (7.2).

8.5 Steady state solutions and stabilisability

8.5.1 Steady state solutions and stabilisation

Suppose $Q_t = Q, t = 1 \ldots T$, and Π_4 and Π_5 are time invariant. Then (8.18) and (8.19) are time invariant if a steady state exists for H, since that implies a steady state for G. Let $\Pi_4 + \Pi_5 G = D$. If D is time invariant, then

$$H_1 = Q + D'H_2D = Q + D'QD + D^{2'}QD^2 + \ldots + D^{T-1'}H_TD^{T-1}. \tag{8.25}$$

Hence a steady state, $H_1 = H_2 = \ldots$, indeed exists as the solution to

$$H - D'HD = Q \tag{8.26}$$

when both $T \to \infty$ and $\rho(D) < 1$. These conditions are equivalent to specifying that the controlled system, (8.23), shall be stable for any t. In fact (8.26) amounts to Lyapounov's second method for testing the stability of a difference equation system: i.e. $\rho(D) < 1$ if and only if H exists to solve (8.26) for an arbitrary hermitian, positive definite Q. On the other hand, given $\rho(D) < 1$ then a solution always exists; and moreover, then $\bar{H}$ also exists to solve

$$\bar{H} - D'\bar{H}D = I. \tag{8.27}$$

Let $\bar{H}$ have eigenvalues λ_i. Then $\lambda_i \geqslant 1$, and D has eigenvalues $[(\lambda_i - 1)/\lambda_i]^{1/2} < 1$.[2] Hence shocks to the system (8.23) are damped out with an exponential decay. Since a simple transformation connects (8.26) and (8.27), $Q \neq I$ merely serves to reduce the shocks faster in some variables than in others.

Thus, the upshot of (8.26) is clearly that a steady state exists if and only if the system can be made stable (and vice versa) given any disturbances – which is reasonable! In fact, from the discussion of Chapter 6, the conditions for a steady state solution are identical to those for stabilisability. We have therefore justified our stabilisability criterion. In addition, if G has been obtained by, say, (8.19), then the system has been stabilised within our chosen scale of preferences.

8.5.2 Optimal control vs stabilisation

Establishing that a system is stabilisable does not, however, ensure that it is also dynamically controllable (in view of Chapter 6) – although that is likely in practice. Stabilisability may be the stochastic counterpart to controllability, but not its generalisation.

2 For Lyapounov's second method, (8.27), and the eigenvalues of D, see Tausky (1964), theorems 4–7. Lyapounov's first method was discussed in section 6.2

One obvious question is, how may G be chosen so that $\max_i(\lambda_i) \simeq 1$? This would be appropriate if stabilisation is the objective because the damping out of policy failures is at its swiftest. It would be most satisfactory to choose G such that $D = 0$, but that is only possible if $n = m = g$, if $l = 1$, $k = 0$, and if x_t does not enter the preference function. Then $\Pi_5 = \Pi_{20}$ is nonsingular and we have static controllability (as in Tinbergen's theorem). Otherwise the next best choice for G is to minimise $D'\bar{H}D > 0$ (since $\bar{H}$ is positive definite) which yields (8.19) with $\bar{H}$ for H. But this analysis is based on $T \to \infty$ whereas for most applications a rather shorter horizon is of interest. It will also be important to damp out the effects of repeated stochastic shocks. Moreover, it is unlikely that the conditions necessary for one G to suffice for all periods obtain. Hence the best general choice for G will be to minimise $D'H_tD$ for each t, i.e. (8.19) itself.

These remarks amount to saying that in a stochastic system the complete annihilation of a general dynamic structure is not possible without static controllability. But, if a steady state exists, then it is possible to destroy that structure arbitrarily well for T large enough. In other words, there may be a lot more to stabilisation than optimal control techniques alone can supply.

8.5.3 Steady state solutions and sliding windows

If a steady state does exist, it applies to (8.20) with small t values since (8.19) is solved backwards. If current actions have negligible impacts at T, they may be computed independently of their consequences at T. That is to say the distant future does not matter until we are close to T. It can also be shown that if $\hat{Z}_t^d$ is time invariant, then g_t reaches a steady state (Chow (1975)). There can be computational simplifications in policy optimisation for the long run, although it is an empirical matter to decide when T is 'large enough'.

The same simplifications are available for the static algorithm of Chapter 7. Return to (7.39) and note that when $T \to \infty$ and $\rho(\Pi_1) < 1$, the lower blocks of R_t^+ and S_t^+ tend to zero. Hence R has a block of zeros at the bottom left. To see this write $R = \begin{pmatrix} R_1 & 0 \\ R_2 & R_1 \end{pmatrix}$ and $R_2 = 0$; where R_2 contains the multipliers which are negligible (the distant future) and R_1 the rest. Given Q is still time separable and time invariant (i.e. $Q_2^* = 0$ in (7.39)), we see that (7.39) shows a null feedback matrix in the lower block (corresponding to R_2). Let z_1 likewise be the variables of the near future and z_2 those of the distant future. But then $R_t^+ = 0$ and $S_t^+ = 0$, which establishes our result. Moreover, in this case the result also extends to the case where Q is time-varying but separable between the two periods.

Therefore: (i) policy optimisation with a stable linear model and where T is large, may be performed by the method of Chapter 7 with a truncated horizon; and (ii) if that horizon is truncated at $T_1 < T$, say, then optimal policies are given by (7.16). They are reoptimised at each $t = 2 \ldots T - T_1$, with horizon $T_1 + t$, by using a constant Θ and PQ^{-1} in (7.16); the upper block of the matrix in (7.39) being time invariant. Only b needs to be updated according to (7.32). But if Q is also time varying, Θ and PQ^{-1} will need the new Q values inserted. These policies are sometimes said to be optimised via a sliding window. For $t > T - T_1$, (7.33) must be used as normal.

8.6 The state-space model form

The state-space model representation is popular in the control theory literature, and it is needed for Pontryagin's minimum principle solution to policy optimisation.

In Chapter 6 we saw that, even with a model in its final form, it is difficult to separate that part of an endogenous variable's time path due to the model's inherent dynamics and their cumulative effects, from that part due to a particular input realisation. The state-space form of the model achieves such a separation by inserting some artificial variables (state variables) as a link between impulses and the consequent evolution of the outputs. The result is a representation of the model as two equation systems. One system summarises the dynamics. It describes how the previous state (and hence all past states) influences the current state, plus any influences since the past state was formed; a kind of system memory. This generalises the fact that any distributed lag model may be written as a combination of the latest impulses and the last state (including lagged instrument as well as lagged dependent variable effects). For the conventional model the complication is to find transformed variables such that the latest impulse is that of the immediate preceding period. Instantaneous impulses need to become part of the next state so that they may be manipulated as instruments. For extremely short decision intervals – particularly for continuous time problems – this is obviously an important point for the design of the controls. But for the longer intervals found in economics it is of doubtful significance since then the extended reduced form (8.2) could equally well serve as a state-space representation. The second equation system recovers the output of the model from the state variable and other current influences.

To present the model in this form we obviously have to make further expansions to the matrices and vectors representing the model. Two equation systems must be stored. It is therefore particularly important to select a state-space form with minimal dimensions. Preston and Wall

(1973) have shown that for (2.4) the minimal dimension is $\gamma = g(\max(l, k))$. No unique state-space representation of (2.4) exists, but a simple minimal dimension representation is given by Aoki (1976). Let $a_t = \Pi_3 N_t + V_t$. If $l < k$ define $m \times n$ matrices $\Pi_{1i} = 0, i = l+1 \ldots k$; but if $k < l$ define $m \times n$ matrices $\Pi_{2i} = 0$, $i = k+1 \ldots l$. Define[3] the state vector p_t to have subvectors $p_t^{(i)}$, $i = 1 \ldots l$:

$$p_t^{(1)} = Y_t - \Pi_{20} x_t - a_t \tag{8.28}$$

$$p_{t-1}^{(i+1)} = p_t^{(i)} - \Pi_{1i} Y_{t-1} - \Pi_{2i} x_{t-1}, \quad i = 1 \ldots l-1. \tag{8.29}$$

Using (8.28) to eliminate Y_{t-1} from (8.29) we have, for $i = 1 \ldots l-1$,

$$p_t^{(i)} = \Pi_{1i} p_{t-1}^{(1)} + p_{t-1}^{(i+1)} + (\Pi_{1i}\Pi_{20} + \Pi_{2i}) x_{t-1} + \Pi_{1i} a_{t-1}. \tag{8.30}$$

Now substituting state subvectors out on the right in (8.29), by means of (8.30) and the expression obtained for $p_t^{(i)}$ at the previous step, yields:

$$\begin{cases} p_t^{(1)} = Y_t - \Pi_{20} x_t - a_t \\ \vdots \\ p_{t-l+1}^{(l)} = Y_t - \Pi_{11} Y_{t-1} \ldots - \Pi_{1,l-1} Y_{t-l+1} - \Pi_{20} x_t \ldots - \Pi_{2l} x_{t-l+1} - a_t. \end{cases} \tag{8.31}$$

Now (2.4) shows also that $p_{t-l+1}^{(l)} = \Pi_{1l} Y_{t-l} + \Pi_{2l} x_{t-l}$ so that, adjusting the time subscripts once again, we apply (8.28) to get

$$p_t^{(l)} = \Pi_{1l} p_{t-1}^{(1)} + (\Pi_{1l}\Pi_{20} + \Pi_{2l}) x_{t-1} + \Pi_{1l} a_{t-1}. \tag{8.32}$$

Collecting (8.30) and (8.32) together we have the two equation systems

$$p_t = F p_{t-1} + E x_{t-1} + \bar{\Pi} a_{t-1} \tag{8.33}$$

and

$$Y_{t-1} = (I_g \vdots 0) p_{t-1} + \Pi_{20} x_{t-1} + a_{t-1} \tag{8.34}$$

where $p_t' = (p_t^{(1)'} \ldots p_t^{(l)'})$; $F = \Pi_1^{*\prime}$ (notation of (2.5)); $E' = (E^{(1)'} \ldots E^{(l)'})$ with $E^{(i)} = \Pi_{1i}\Pi_{20} + \Pi_{2i}$, $i = 1 \ldots l$; and $\bar{\Pi}' = (\Pi_{11}' \ldots \Pi_{1l}')$. (8.33) contains the dynamic constraints, and (8.34) allows the targets to be recovered. We select optimal policies by solving

$$\min_{p_{t+1}, x_t} \{ w \mid p_{t+1} = F p_t + E x_t + \bar{\Pi} a_t \} \quad \text{for } t = 1 \ldots \mathrm{T} \tag{8.35}$$

provided that $w(\tilde{z})$ is also transformed so that the derivatives and origin of w correspond to the new choice variables p_{t+1} and x_t. Let (8.34) become

$$\tilde{Y}_t = (I \vdots 0) p_t + \Pi_{20} \tilde{x}_t + b_t \text{ for } b_t = a_t - Y_t^d + \Pi_{20} x_t^d$$

3 We presume $l > k$. If not replace l by k in p_t. Notice that in this section Y_t is from (2.4), not (2.6).

or

$$\tilde{Y} = \{I_T \otimes (I_g \vdots 0) \vdots I_T \otimes \Pi_{20}\}\xi + b; \tag{8.36}$$

where

$$b' = (b'_1 \ldots b'_T) \text{ and } \xi' = [p'_1 \ldots p'_T, \tilde{x}'_1 \ldots \tilde{x}'_T].$$

8.7 Policy optimisation by Pontryagin's minimum principle

The first step in this approach is the transformation of our econometric model from (2.4) to the state-space form. This is because, in order to apply Pontryagin's minimum principle, we must write the model in the general form

$$p_{t+1} - p_t = f(p_t, x_t, a_t). \tag{8.37}$$

We define $F^* = F - I$, and convert (8.33) to this format.

8.7.1 On the preference structure

Consider an objective function of the form (7.10). We have to transform that to the penalties implied for p and $\tilde{x}$. It is natural to specify the relative penalties on deviations from desired values of the targets but the policy maker cannot have any idea on weights for p_t which are purely artificial variables. Suppose the policy maker specifies Q^+ and q^+ (i.e. partitioned conformably to z and augmented by zeroes for lagged values and nontargets). Substituting for Y via (8.36) will lead to

$$w = \tfrac{1}{2}\xi' Q \xi + q'\xi + q_0 \tag{8.38}$$

where $\xi' = (p' \vdots \tilde{x}')$ and $Q = \begin{pmatrix} B & C' \\ C & A \end{pmatrix}$; $q' = (q'_1, q'_2)$ and $q_0 = \tfrac{1}{2}b'B^+b + q_1^{+\prime}b$.

Partitioning Q^+ and q^+ defines the transformations as:

$$B = (I \otimes (I \vdots 0))' B^+ (I \otimes (I \vdots 0)); \; C = (C^+ + (I \otimes \Pi'_{20})B^+ \vdots 0);$$

$$A = A^+ + (I \otimes \Pi'_{20})B^+(I \otimes \Pi_{20}) + C^+(I \otimes \Pi_{20}) + (I \otimes \Pi'_{20})C^{+\prime};$$

$$q'_1 = (q_1 + B^+b)'(I \otimes (I \vdots 0)); \text{ and}$$

$$q'_2 = (q_1^+ + b)'(I \otimes \Pi_{20}) + (q_2^+ + C^+b)'.$$

If B^+, C^+ and A^+ have the T^2 submatrices, say B^+_{ij}, C^+_{ij} and A^+_{ij} for $i, j = 1, \ldots, T$ (of orders $m, n \times m$, and n respectively), then B, C and A have T^2 submatrices, of orders $\gamma, n \times \gamma$ and n respectively, given by

$$B_{ij} = \begin{bmatrix} B^+_{ij} & 0 \\ 0 & 0 \end{bmatrix}; \quad C_{ij} = (C^+_{ij} + \Pi'_{20}B^+_{ij} \vdots 0);$$

and $A_{ij} = A^+_{ij} + \Pi'_{20}B^+_{ij}\Pi_{20} + C^+_{ij}\Pi_{20} + \Pi'_{20}C'^+_{ij}$. A similar arrangement is observed in q.

Therefore:

(a) $C_{ij} \neq 0$, unless $C^+_{ij} = -\Pi'_{20}B^+_{ij}$ all $i, j = 1 \dots T$ which cannot generally be true; $C_{ij} \neq C^+_{ij}$ unless $\Pi_{20} = 0$. Further, C_{ij} has no simple structure even if C^+_{ij} has.

(b) $A_{ij} \neq A^+_{ij}$ all $i, j = 1 \dots T$ independently of C^+_{ij} nor has it any simple structure (such as diagonal) even if A^+_{ij} has, unless $\Pi_{20} = 0$.

(c) $q \neq 0$ even if $q^+ = 0$.

It is worth noting that the special structure of $C = 0$ and A diagonal is often used in applications despite these results for (8.38).

If we specialise (7.10) to (8.4)

$$w = \sum_{t=1}^{T} (\tfrac{1}{2}\tilde{Z}'_t Q^+_t \tilde{Z}_t) \tag{8.39}$$

then we can draw exactly the same conclusions for the sequence of weighting matrices B_t, C_t, A_t, and q_t, obtained from Q^+_t.

8.7.2 The Pontryagin algorithm

Consider (8.39) as the original objective function. Transforming that in terms of the state variables yields:

$$w = \sum_t (\tfrac{1}{2}\xi'_t Q_t \xi_t + q'_t \xi_t) + q_0 \text{ where } \xi'_t = (p'_t \vdots \tilde{x}'_t) \tag{8.40}$$

which is a specialised version of (8.38). Removing q_t by (7.12) leaves

$$w = \tfrac{1}{2}\sum_t \tilde{\xi}'_t Q_t \tilde{\xi}_t + \text{constant} \tag{8.41}$$

where $\tilde{\xi}_t = \xi_t - \xi^d_t$, and $\xi^d_t = \begin{pmatrix} 0 \\ x^d_t \end{pmatrix} - Q_t^{-1} q_t$ to be redesignated $\begin{pmatrix} p^d_t \\ x^d_t \end{pmatrix}$ hereafter.

To maximise (8.41), constrained by (8.37), we form the Lagrangian

$$L = \sum_{t=1}^{T} \{\tfrac{1}{2}\tilde{\xi}'_t Q_t \tilde{\xi}_t - \lambda'_{t+1}(F^* p_t + Ex_t + \bar{\Pi} a_t) + \lambda'_{t+1}(p_{t+1} - p_t)\}$$

$$= \sum_{t=1}^{T} H_t(p_t, x_t, \lambda_{t+1}) + \sum_{t=1}^{T} \lambda'_{t+1}(p_{t+1} - p_t) \tag{8.42}$$

where λ_{t+1} is a γ-vector of dynamic lagrange multipliers (costate variables). The expressions $H_t(p_t, x_t, \lambda_{t+1})$ are called the Hamiltonian functions.

The necessary conditions[4] (to be solved for the unknowns p_t, x_t, λ_{t+1})

4 Q_t positive semi-definite ensures the sufficiency of these conditions. We write λ_{t+1} to match p_{t+1}. These necessary conditions constitute Pontryagin's minimum principle. Notice the aim is to choose x_t to minimise each H_t, not L itself. The changing effect of the constraints is carried in $\Delta\lambda_{t+1}$, which provides the dynamic link between periods. This is why it is necessary to separate the dynamics from current constraints. Further details are found in Bernavie (1972), Chapter 5.

for $t = 1 \dots T$ are:

$$p_{t+1} - p_t = \frac{-\partial H_t}{\partial \lambda_{t+1}} = F^* p_t + E x_t + \bar{\Pi} a_t \tag{8.43}$$

and

$$\frac{\partial H_t}{\partial x_t} = 0, \text{ i.e. } \tilde{x}_t = A_t^{-1}(E'\lambda_{t+1} - C_t \tilde{p}_t) \tag{8.44}$$

and

$$\begin{aligned} \lambda_t - \lambda_{t+1} &= -\frac{\partial H_t}{\partial p_t} = -B_t \tilde{p}_t + F^{*\prime}\lambda_{t+1} - C_t' \tilde{x}_t \\ &= -(B_t - C_t' A_t^{-1} C_t)\tilde{p}_t + (F^{*\prime} - C_t' A_t^{-1} E')\lambda_{t+1}. \end{aligned} \tag{8.45}$$

A start to solving this system is provided by $0 = \partial L / \partial p_{T+1} = -\lambda_{T+1}$ (confirming that no binding constraints exist on variables after period T). Insertion into (8.45) yields

$$\lambda_T^* = K_T p_T^* + k_T \text{ with } K_T = -(B_T - C_T' A_T^{-1} C_T)$$

and

$$k_T = -K_T p_t^d. \tag{8.46}$$

Now, by (8.45) we have

$$\begin{aligned} \lambda_{T-1}^* = &-(B_{T-1} - C_{T-1}' A_{T-1}^{-1} C_{T-1})\tilde{p}_{T-1}^* \\ &+ (F' - C_{T-1}' A_{T-1}^{-1} E')\lambda_T^*. \end{aligned} \tag{8.47}$$

Meanwhile inserting (8.44) and (8.46) into (8.43) yields

$$\begin{aligned} p_T^* &= (I - E A_{T-1}^{-1} E' K_T)^{-1} (F - E A_{T-1}^{-1} C_{T-1}) p_{T-1}^* + g_{T-1} \\ &= G_{T-1} p_{T-1}^* + g_{T-1} \end{aligned} \tag{8.48}$$

where

$$\begin{aligned} g_{T-1} = &(I - E A_{T-1}^{-1} E' K_T)^{-1} (\bar{\Pi}\, a_{T-1} \\ &+ E(A_{T-1}^{-1}(E' k_T + C_{T-1} p_{T-1}^d)) + x_{T-1}^d). \end{aligned}$$

Hence, using (8.46) and (8.48), (8.47) can also be written as

$$\lambda_{T-1}^* = K_{T-1} p_{T-1}^* + k_{T-1} \tag{8.49}$$

with

$$\begin{aligned} K_{T-1} = &-(B_{T-1} - C_{T-1}' A_{T-1}^{-1} C_{T-1}) \\ &+ (F' - C_{T-1}' A_{T-1}^{-1} E') K_T G_{T-1} \end{aligned}$$

and

$$\begin{aligned} k_{T-1} = &\ (B_{T-1} - C_{T-1}' A_{T-1}^{-1} C_{T-1}) p_{T-1}^d \\ &+ (F' - C_{T-1}' A_{T-1}^{-1} E')(k_T + K_T g_{T-1}). \end{aligned}$$

Finally, by (8.44)

$$x_{T-1}^{*} = L_{T-1} p_{T-1}^{*} + l_{T-1} \tag{8.50}$$

where

$$L_{T-1} = A_{T-1}^{-1} (E' K_T G_{T-1} - C_{T-1})$$

and $$l_{T-1} = A_{T-1}^{-1} (E'(K_T g_T + k_T) + C_{T-1} p_T^d) + x_{T-d}^d.$$

Therefore we have backwards recursions in K_t, k_t, G_t, g_t, L_t and l_t by replacing T by t throughout (8.48) to (8.50).

This algorithm generalises somewhat on Pindyck (1973) since $\Pi_{20} \neq 0$ and $C_t \neq 0$. It is also efficient computationally. Both inverses exist provided Q_t^+ are positive definite. First, $A_t = (\Pi'_{20} \vdots I) Q_t^+ \begin{pmatrix} \Pi_{20} \\ \hline I \end{pmatrix}$ which is then symmetric and positive definite. Likewise K_T is symmetric and negative semi-definite since its nonzero components are taken from a principle minor of $\left[\begin{pmatrix} I & \Pi_{20} \\ 0 & I \end{pmatrix}' \begin{pmatrix} Q_T^+ \end{pmatrix} \begin{pmatrix} I & \Pi_{20} \\ 0 & I \end{pmatrix} \right]^{-1}$. Hence the inverse in G_{T-1} is a negative definite matrix. Expanding that inverse

$$\begin{aligned} K_{T-1} = & -(B_{T-1} - C'_{T-1} A_{T-1}^{-1} C_{T-1}) \\ & -(F - E A_{T-1}^{-1} C_{T-1})'(K_T + K_T E(A_{T-1} \\ & - E' K_T E)^{-1} E' K_T)(F - E A_{T-1}^{-1} C_{T-1}). \end{aligned} \tag{8.51}$$

Thus K_{T-1} is negative semidefinite, and the inverse in G_{T-2} is negative definite. By induction all the inverses exist.

The use of (8.51) in place of (8.49) means that G_t and g_t may be eliminated, since K_{t+1} $(G_t \vdots g_t)$, for use in L_t and l_t, are automatically computed using the last two brackets of (8.51). Moreover, the largest matrix to be inverted is of order n rather than γ. These savings can be substantial, (i) because there will be relatively few instruments but the dimension of the state vector in a large scale model with many lags will be large, and (ii) because the number of inversions has been halved.

Hence for $t = T-1 \ldots 1$ we compute K_{t+1}, L_t, k_{t+1}, l_t. Then, with p_0 constructed from (8.28), (8.29), (8.33) and x_0, we compute p_t^* (for each $t = 1 \ldots T-1$) and then x_t^* (also Y_t^* and λ_t^* if required), via (8.48) and (8.50) respectively. Finally

$$\tilde{x}_T^{*} = A_T^{-1} C_T \tilde{p}_T^{*} \quad \text{by (8.44).} \tag{8.52}$$

8.7.3 Comments

(a) Naturally each a_t would be replaced by $E_i(a_t)$, $t \geqslant i$, for $i = 1 \ldots T$ in (8.50) and (8.52). But a_t in (8.48) for computing p_{t+1}, for use in (8.50) and

(8.52), would be an actual value. Thus the points made earlier to distinguish a feedback rule from a closed loop control apply once again. We require the recalculation of l_t, for $t \geqslant i$ and each $i = 2 \ldots T$. Then we have, for $t = 1 \ldots T$, quadratic functions of the additive uncertainty:

$$\min_{x_t} E_t\left[H_t + \lambda'_{t+1}\Delta p_{t+1}\right] = \left[\min_{x_t} H_t\left\{p_t, x_t, \lambda_{t+1}, E_t(a_t)\right\} + \lambda'_{t+1}\left\{E_t(a_t)\right\}\Delta p_{t+1}\left\{E_t(a_t)\right\}\right]. \tag{8.53}$$

So each x_t^* by (8.50) optimises $E_t\sum_{j=t}^{T} w_j$ and is first period certainty equivalent with respect to t; and the list of implemented policies will be multiperiod certainty equivalent. Of course open loop controls are also available if $E_1(p_{t-1}^*)$ is inserted on the right of (8.50).

(b) Time varying parameters may easily be fitted into (8.33) and (8.34) and hence (8.43)–(8.52).

(c) The policy decision rule, (8.50), is a type of integral control rule, implying a time varying closed loop control. To extract the coefficients of this integral policy rule in terms of the policy variables themselves is more difficult.

8.8 Problems of generality

8.8.1 The dynamic programming vs the Pontryagin algorithms

Problems over the generality of the Pontryagin approach have been raised by Uebe and Fischer (1978) and Chow (1975). The first point is that A_t, defined following (8.50), is nonsingular provided only that A_t^+ is positive semi-definite and $\Pi_{20} \neq 0$. Given that, there is no necessity to control all instruments in this algorithm; the control of one in each period is sufficient. A_t is of course identical to the generally invertible matrix which occurs in the dynamic programming algorithm at (8.19). And A_t is still of order n.

Second, notice that if $C_T = 0$ (requiring both $C_T^+ = 0$ and $\Pi_{20} = 0$ in general) then $x_t^* = x_T^d$ since no penalties are associated with $p_{T+1}^* \neq p_{T+1}^d$. The last plan requires no optimisation, and there is no penalty on the final state of the economy. That is implausible and dangerous. This situation is well known as the problem of transversality, and will be treated in the next section.

It is now clear that the question of the generality of this algorithm, and the matter of transforming objective function parameters when state-space models are used, turns on $\Pi_{20} \neq 0$. But if $\Pi_{20} = 0$ then our state-space form is identical to the reduced form.

8.8.2 Static vs dynamic algorithms

An interesting feature is that both the dynamic programming and the Pontryagin algorithms require at least one instrument to be controlled, for nonsingularity in (8.19) and (8.54). They cannot be applied to cases where targets alone attract penalties. They therefore could not be applied to solve the Tinbergen formulation of the policy problem, nor to problems where controllable targets are the sole item of interest. So there is a genuine loss of generality compared to (7.18) which can handle either case. Even if policy problems with no particular desired values or penalties for the instruments are considered unrealistic (but utility maximisation in demand theory, and profit maximisation in production theory, show they are not so uncommon) one would still be interested in such examples as part of the experimenting necessary to select the best policies. This will be discussed in section 10.3. One may not be interested in policies per se, but want to see the potential scope or limitations to policy making in certain circumstances. The policy maker will want to know how well (or badly) he could do before considering a subset of the options to make his final decision. We have in fact been arguing that policy selection is typically such an experimental process. For a proper judgement of the options it will be necessary to be able to optimise without instrument penalties in order to see how close one may come to the policy goals given a free hand.

8.8.3 Algorithm structure

The relations between the various policy optimisation algorithms are summarised in table 8.1.

8.9 Extensions: the transversality problem

We have pointed out that, in a dynamic model, policy optimisation implies optimising y_t^* and x_t^* directly as measured by their contributions to w, but also indirectly in terms of their contributions to those future target values which themselves contribute to later components in w. But when we get to within l periods of period T, one by one these indirect penalties no longer apply (similarly within k periods, x_t has fewer indirect effects). For example, if we want to penalise each unit failure in all variables equally, we would set $Q = I$. But the contribution to w from choosing some given value for $\tilde{z}_T$ is then $\tilde{z}'_T\tilde{z}_T$; whereas choosing the same value for $\tilde{z}_1$ it is $\tilde{z}'_1\tilde{z}_1 + \sum_{t=2}^{T}(R_t\tilde{x}_1)'(R_t\tilde{x}_1)$, in terms of (7.9), which is considerably larger. It is simply that the future consequences of $\tilde{z}_T$ do not enter w,

Table 8.1 *Discrete time control algorithms*

	Static algorithms	Dynamic programming	Dynamic, Pontryagin
1. Objective at t	$E_t(w)$ of (7.11)	$E_t(w)$ of (8.4)	$E_t(w)$ of (8.39)
2. Time separable restrictions in $w(\tilde{z})$?	No	Yes	Yes
3. Model form	Stacked final forms; and condensation	Augmented reduced form; or state-space form; no condensation	State-space; no condensation
4. Transformations in Q, q?	No	Only if state-space model form used	Yes
5. (a) Lagrangians	(7.16)	Chow (1975)	(8.48)–(8.52) and (8.34)
(b) Substitution of constraints	(7.18)	(8.20)	Not distinct from dynamic programming with state-space model form
6. Control rule (a) Feedback form	Via (7.32) and N_{t-1} $\hat{u}_{t-1}$ in $E_t(b_{(t)})$: see (7.39)	via Z^*_{t-1}	via p^*_{t-1}
(b) Closed loop form	via feedback and $E_t(b_{(t)})$ using the $E_t(N_j, U_j), j \geqslant t$, components	via feedback and recomputing $g_j, j \geqslant t$, each t, in (8.19)	via feedback and recomputing $l_j, j \geqslant t$, each t, in (8.50)
7. Restrictions on active variables (i.e. those penalised) $t = 1, \ldots, T$	any min(m, n) variables from (y_t, x_t) and $n \geqslant 1$	any n variables from (Y_t, x_t), at least one from x_t, and $n \geqslant 1$	any n variables from (Y_t, x_t), at least one from x_t, and $n \geqslant 1$

whereas in a dynamic model those from $\tilde{z}_1$ do. That means the smaller $T - t$, the larger the $\tilde{x}_t$ failures we can afford to pick (to secure better outcomes) since unit failures in $\tilde{y}_t$ attract lower and lower penalties. In fact we have already seen this effect in action in comment (c) of section 8.4.1 above.

For illustration suppose consumption (C_t^*) and investment (I_t^*) are targets, and the model's investment function contains a distributed lag on capital stock. Then it would improve w to raise C_T^* at the expense of reducing I_T^* since the former affects w directly but the other has mainly future consequences through capital stocks and thus future investment, production and consumption. Those future consequences are not penalised. So it apparently pays to have a party at T and run down the capital stock by increasing consumption. Elections provide excellent illustrations!

In fact T often represents an election, party congress, or plan completion date. Unfortunately politicians (or, indeed, any planner paid by results) may suffer strongly from this kind of moral hazard (as the empirical results of Chapter 10 confirm). One solution is to add or subtract weights in later components of Q in order to offset these transversality effects. But that requires a very detailed knowledge of the combined effects of the multipliers (R_i) and the uncertain additive components (b_i) for a long period after T. It is not a practical proposition.

Another possibility is to specify Q_t, and z_t^d for a number of periods beyond T (at least to $T + \max(k, l)$) and then run the planning exercise to this extended horizon, although x_{T+i}^* are not implemented. Obviously this is an approximate solution, and does not stop those weights being set irresponsibly.

The third possibility is to constrain the state in which the economy is to be found at $T + 1$. In terms of the Pontryagin algorithm, let p_{T+1}^* be the required final state. It would be constructed from the required values of the economic variables on a certainty equivalent basis in (8.28), (8.29) and (8.33). It is therefore possible for p_{T+1}^* to be revised during the exercise. Inserting p_{T+1}^* directly into (8.42) we lose the $\lambda_{T+1} = 0$ condition. Now (8.43)–(8.45) must be solved simultaneously at $t = T$ (where p_{T+1}^* appears on the left of (8.43)). In fact (8.45) and (8.44) become

$$\lambda_T^* = -(B_T - C_T' A_T^{-1} C_T)\tilde{p}_T^* + (F' - C_T' A_T^{-1} E')\lambda_{T+1} \tag{8.54}$$

$$x_T^* = A_T^{-1}(E'\lambda_{T+1} - C_T p_T^*) + x_T^d - A_T^{-1} C_T p_T^d. \tag{8.55}$$

But solving (8.43) for λ_T eliminates λ_{T+1}; leaving (8.46) and (8.52), respectively, with

$$K_T = -[I - (F' - C_t' A_T^{-1} E')D^{-1}]^{-1}(B_T - C_T' A_T^{-1} C_T) \tag{8.56}$$

and $k_T = [I - (F' - C_T' A_T^{-1} E')D^{-1}]^{-1}[(B_T - C_T' A_T^{-1} C_T)p_T^d - e_T]$

where $e_T = (F' - C_T' A^{-1} E')D^{-1}(B_T - C_T' A_T^{-1} C)\{p_T^d - (F - EA_T^{-1} C_T)^{-1}(p_{T+1}^* - \bar{\Pi} a_T + E(A_T^{-1} C_T p_T^d - x_T^d))\}$

Then $\tilde{x}_T^* = L_T \tilde{p}_T^* + l_T$ with (8.57)

$$L_T = A_T^{-1}(E'D^{-1}K_T - C_T) \text{ and } l_T = A_T^{-1}E'D^{-1}k_T + x_T^d - A_T^{-1}C_T p_T^d + (F' - C_T' A_T^{-1} E')^{-1} e_T.$$

In (8.56) and (8.57) we have used

$$D = (F' - C_T' A_T^{-1} E')[I + (F' - C_T' A_T^{-1} E')^{-1}(B_T - C_T' A_T^{-1} C_T) \cdot (F - EA_T^{-1} C_T)^{-1} E A_T^{-1} E'].$$

D^{-1} exists by the arguments following (8.50) provided $(F' - C_T' A_T^{-1} E')^{-1}$ exists. Armed with (8.56) and (8.57) we can continue for $T - 1 \ldots 1$ as before.

One difficulty may be the specification of p^*_{T+1}. If it is not an equilibrium condition for the model it may be difficult to guarantee its feasibility when T is relatively small. The controllability condition should also be checked.

To extend (7.16) similarly requires attaching $\lambda'_{T+1}(z_{T+1} - z^*_{T+1})$ in place of $\frac{1}{2}\tilde{z}'_{T+1} Q_{T+1} \tilde{z}_{T+1}$ to a $T+1$ period problem.

8.10 An application

To illustrate how these algorithms work out in practice, we take a sample of results from Pindyck (1973). The exercise describes the stabilisation of the postwar American economy on a short-run horizon. A 12 equation quarterly model is controlled over the five year period 1957.1 to 1962.1. Potential targets are consumption, nonresidential and residential investment, unemployment, wages, prices, rates of interest, and GNP or disposable income. Potential instruments are money supply, government expenditure, and a surtax variable. The algorithm used is similar to (8.42)–(8.52); except that $\Pi_{20} = 0$. Hence $C = 0$. There will therefore be transversality problems.

We need to specify the elements of $w(\tilde{z})$. Some targets are justifiably 'intermediate'. If each demand component is assigned a weight reflecting our preferences, then implicitly GNP has had its weight assigned and we would be altering our scheme of priorities on the demand components if we assigned an extra weight to GNP. Similarly rates of interest may be assigned zero weights, as here, although both kinds of investment have their own weights. But if a direct target (e.g. investment) is very insensitive to the intermediate target (e.g. the rate of interest) then the implicit weight on the latter is extremely small. Thus those implicit weights are not independent of the model's parameters. So we may nevertheless wish to weight those intermediate targets separately. We may also weight direct and indirect targets separately in order to cater for differing sensitivities to stochastic shocks.

In this example weights are first set to give equal penalties for each percentage deviation from the desired values in consumption (C), nonresidential and residential investment (INR, IR), prices (P), unemployment (U), government expenditure (G) and the change of money supply (ΔM); and twice that for the surtax yield (T) so as to restrain vigorous taxation changes. One demand component, inventory investment, has a zero weight so the implicit weight on GNP is lower than the common weight on percentage deviations; likewise disposable income (YD). Inspection of the wages equation shows wages to be insensitive to these direct targets, so its implicit weight is also much lower than the common weight.

Desired values are chosen to reflect the assumed objective of economic

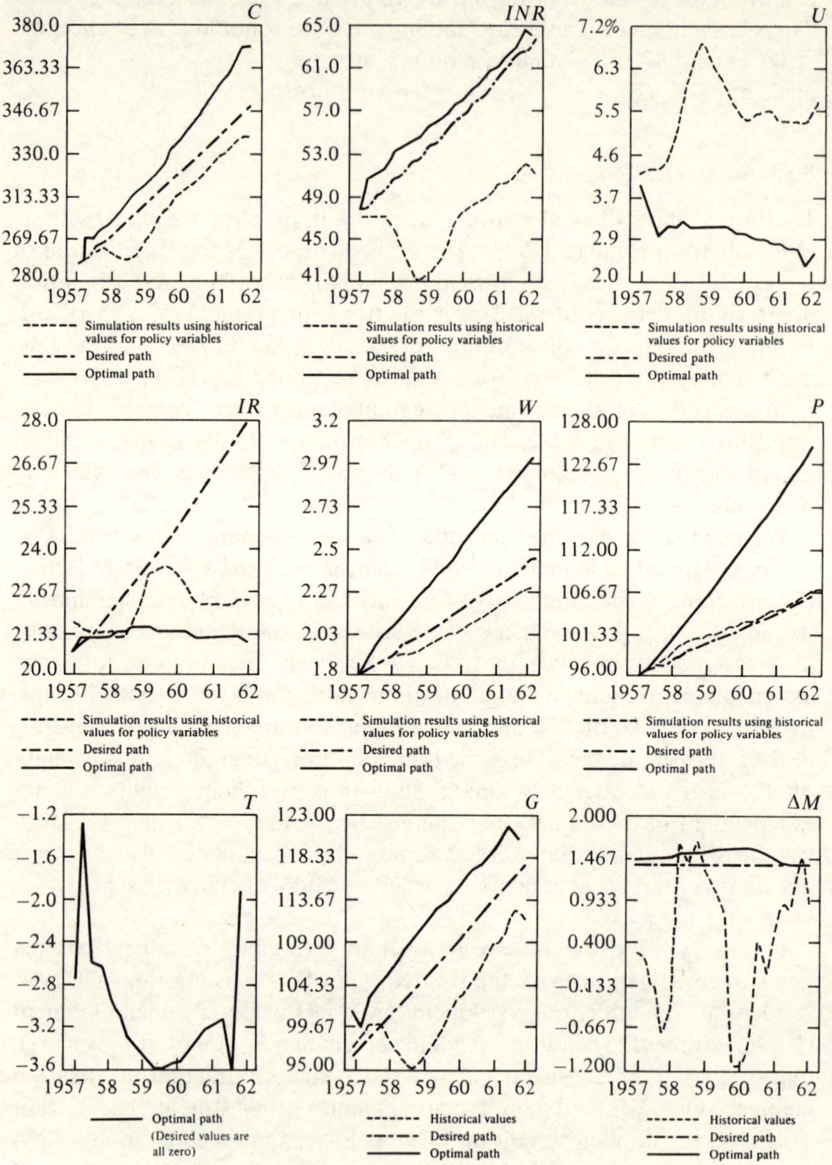

Figure 8.1 Optimal policies for the US economy 1957–61 (Run 1)

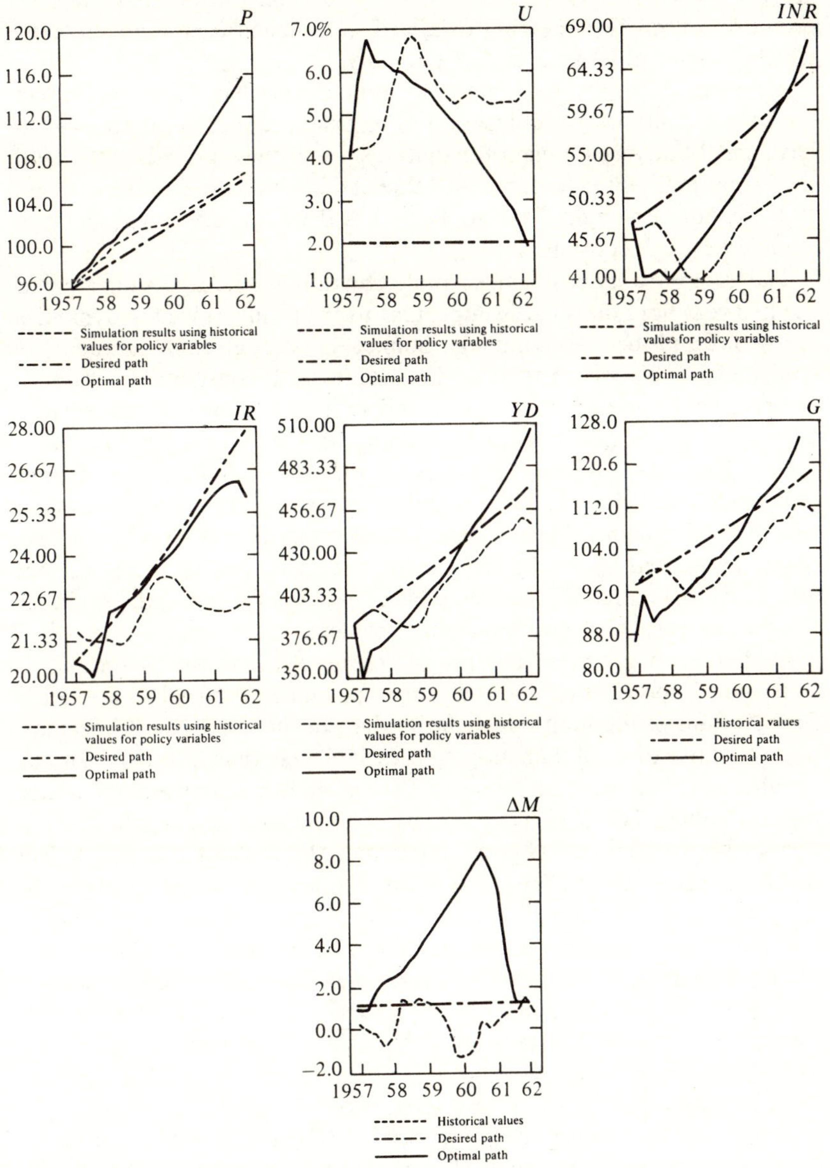

Figure 8.2 Optimal policies for the US economy 1957–61 (Run 2)

stabilisation about smooth growth paths at approximately historical growth rates. Finally a set of values for the noncontrollables must be provided. In this case the only variable is full capacity disposable income which is assumed to grow at $3\frac{1}{2}\%$ annually.

Although this objective function is quite admissible it does not reflect the only definition of 'stabilisation'. For example it is quite possible to have small but very frequent fluctuations about these growth paths; and thereby a small objective function value and low variances in the policies. But the policies might have to be reversed every period leading to a complete lack of continuity.

The transversality problem is handled by running the algorithm beyond the five year horizon. That is important to the results since the dynamics are strong and there are long lags. Some results are given in figure 8.1. *C*, *INR* and *YD* all exceed their desired values with considerable evidence of being smoothed. *U* falls to 3%. This reduction comes about because GNP and its components are high, being fuelled by an aggressive fiscal policy. That has resulted in more price and wage inflation than desired (*P* up to 5%, and *W* up to 12%), together with rising rates of interest in the face of a rising demand for money (with the consequence that *IR* falls far below its desired values by the end of the plan). The variables subject to long lag structures are the ones which go off track at the end, providing further examples of the transversality problem.

Evidently, to get more acceptable results, fiscal variables should be constrained closer to their desired values and monetary variables liberated. Examination of the multipliers shows that, in the short run, targets are more sensitive to fiscal than monetary variables; so that, if roughly similar penalties were imposed on their use, the optimal strategy would be to use fiscal variables. This is clear in the results; ΔM has been stabilised and is very ineffective, whereas *G* grows faster than desired and *T* is extensively used with such abrupt changes as to be of doubtful political feasibility in an economy tied to annual budgets. This suggests higher weights on *T*, and that they should be extremely large for 3 of the 4 quarters so as to permit changes but once a year. A new set of weights is therefore introduced to raise the (implicit) penalties on *P*, *IR*, and *T* and reduce them on ΔM. The results in figure 8.2 show some of the desired modifications. *IR* behaves as desired; inflation was lower but still rises at the end of the plan. ΔM was more extensively used, and *T* less. Expansion of ΔM and an initial reduction in *YD* keeps interest rates down so that *IR* expands. Inspection of the unemployment equation shows *U* to be sensitive to changes in *YD*, rather than to *YD* itself, so that a low but growing *YD* will cause the inevitable initial rise in *U* (to 7%) to be reversed (finishing below 3%) without any particular inflationary pressure. This reduction in YD is obtained by an initially low G which then expands. Fiscal policy is observed to have rapid effects but monetary policy to operate with long lags.

Thus the changed weights have produced more acceptable results, but at a price in U. Other weights could now be tried. However, it is more important to emphasise that the planning exercise has led us to discover more about the working of the model (and economy), especially in terms of the speed and strengths of response to policy changes. This is valuable knowledge which is hard to gather together by, say, multiplier analysis. Since, conditional on Q, this behaviour is optimal it shows exactly which are the effective constraints imposed by the model, and by how much they constrain our freedom of action. It may also prompt improvements to the model's specification. Since the emphasis is on dynamic behaviour, where economic theory and observation have least to offer for specifying individual components of the model, it is useful to exploit any respecifications indicated in these 'tests'. The specification of the preference structure is also likely to be a trial and error process.

8.11 Concluding remarks

Any of the algorithms of this chapter may be reformulated into continuous time. It may not be an issue of great interest in economic applications – except perhaps in theoretical specifications – but it does give further insight in the state-space form. The welfare function becomes $\sum_{t=0}^{T} w_t(p_t, x_t)\Delta t$, and $(p_{t+1} - p_t)/\Delta t$ appears in the left of (8.37). As $\Delta t \to 0$ we have $\int_0^T w(p_t, x_t)dt$ and $\dot{p}_t = -(p_t, x_t, s_t)$. State-space forms are therefore appropriate for continuous time problems. The static algorithm cannot be applied to continuous time problems.

On the other hand, the dynamic programming and Pontryagin solutions have been derived under restrictive conditions. It turns out (Chapter 11 contains the details) that they cannot sensibly be generalised to handle preferences where $w(\tilde{z})$ is not additively time separable. Moreover, they cannot offer coherent and optimal policies when there are endogenously generated expectations, or multiple policy makers. These are particularly severe restrictions because they rule out some characteristic problems of economic policy selection; in particular those where the system reacts to anticipated targets, or contains adaptive behaviour for reducing future uncertainties, or contains decentralised decision making. The analogy between social and physical systems is too weak to permit the application of technology designed for regulating physical systems to problems of social behaviour.

Appendix: Comparative computational costs

(a) Since (8.2) came from (2.6), the dynamic optimisations of (8.6) are constrained by a first order linear difference equation in $gl + nk$ variables, with a forcing function linear in x_t, a_t and V_t. Therefore one likely difficulty with the dynamic programming approach is its dimensionality. Dynamic algorithms make each policy choice explicitly in relation to an arbitrary previous *state* of the economy, rather than of just the previous choices and forcing function values. That makes it impossible to drop any elements from the $(gl + nk)$-vector Z_t to reduce the order of the T optimisations. The future targets are only implicit in the model (8.2), so no model condensation can take place if current optimisations are to account for future target values.

(b) Matrix inversions involve arithmetic operations roughly in proportion to the cube of the order of the matrix. In (8.18) we have T inversions of order n; at (7.18) they are of order $nT, \ldots, n$ for closed loop control. On the other hand, H_t is a $(gl + nk)$ square matrix, built up from similarly dimensioned matrices. H_t is also a component in G_t. It becomes a full matrix for $t \leqslant T - 1$ so that the advantage of sparseness in Q_t^+, Π_4 and Π_5 is lost in the H_t, G_t sequence. To obtain the instrument values by (8.20) costs roughly $T(n^3 + (gl + nk))[2(gl + nk)^2 + n(gl + nk) + 5gn] + (\Sigma t)(gl + nk)[2(gl + nk) + 3n]$ arithmetic operations, compared to $n\{[n^2 + 2(n + m)^2](\Sigma t^3) + [n^2 + n + m](\Sigma t^2)\}$ using (7.18). Obviously (8.20) is more expensive for large g, l, or k, and (7.18) more expensive for large T. In view of table 6.4, (7.18) is preferable for the problems typically encountered in economic planning. The calculations of R and b in (7.18) are ignored because, even for linear models, they may always be obtained by the nonstochastic simulation method described in the appendix to chapter 7; and it may be done as a separate exercise from the optimisations.

(c) Comparing the Pontryagin approach with dynamic programming shows the inversions require the same computation in either case. The remaining operations may be less for the Pontryagin algorithms since $\gamma \leqslant gl + nk$ if $l \geqslant k$, or if $g(k - l) \leqslant nk$ when $l < k$. So it depends on which variables have the longer distributed lags. Typically they are in the endogenous variables, making the Pontryagin algorithm preferable. But (8.48), (8.50) and (8.52) cost roughly

$$\Sigma t[n^3 + \gamma(2\gamma^2 + n\gamma + 5gn)] + (\Sigma t)\gamma(2\gamma + 3n) \text{ operations.}$$

(d) It is hard to construct comprehensive comparisons of different algorithms, but the remarks above help to bring the advantages of model condensation into focus. For example, using (7.16) and the simulation approach of the appendix to Chapter 7, Brandsma, Hughes Hallett and

Van der Windt (1981) compute optimal policies for the nonlinear model used in Dutch economic planning. This is a large scale application with $T = 5, g = 130, l = 6, k = 0, m = 7, n = 5$ and $r = 67$ (in principle $l = 14$, but all lags exceeding T form part of the initial conditions). A closed loop solution (including the evaluation of R and s) took 31.5 secs CPU time, using 11,987 words (equivalent 48,000 bytes) of storage on a DEC 20 system of 256K words capacity. In this case, (7.18) has an advantage, over the better of (8.20) and (8.50), of 1:11 for the maximum order of optimisation, and of 1:1000 in computational burdens. A case apparently less favourable to (7.18) (i.e. having a large T value and a high m/g ratio: $T = 40, g = 30, l = k = 41, m = 2, n = 1$) is in Ghosh, Gilbert and Hughes Hallett (1981) where these advantages are, respectively, 1:10 and 1:554.

These remarks suggest that policy optimisation is perhaps comparable to several regressions using a standard package, and is certainly a routine job. Dimensionality and computational cost should prove no barrier. This is a conclusion of some interest since the Report of the Committee on Policy Optimisation recently argued that, although policy optimisation with the large econometric models in use today might be technically feasible, it was unlikely to be either computationally practicable or cheap (HMSO (1978)).

Part II

Interactive planning

9

Robust policies under uncertainty: sensitivity and perturbations

9.1 On sensitivity analysis

Policy makers are often suspicious of optimal control methods. It is easy to reject the technique outright because one does not trust the model in its structure, the quality of its estimates, its ability to forecast accurately, or the accuracy of its exogenous information; or because one cannot precisely specify the economic priorities in the form of an objective function. It is necessary therefore to see if optimal policy selections are sensitive to any of these problems and, if so, to which item, so that we can concentrate on its specification. Methods are given here to compute alterations to the policies due to changes of a given size in any of the parameters, or due to random shocks in the problem.

We can also regard this chapter as a framework for experimenting with the economic and political specification, in a search for the appropriate policy design. We begin by observing that the difficulties in policy optimisation caused by dimensionality and nonlinearities, which have tended to dominate recent literature, admit a technical solution. In contrast, the uncertainty surrounding the exogenous information and the model is inescapable. It may well be that the latter problem is anyway a much greater obstacle to the successful application of optimisation techniques (or any others) for designing economic policies. The policy makers themselves certainly appear to think so (Chapter 14).

9.2 The scope for data perturbations

Both the uncontrolled variables and the estimated model are uncertain at the moment of calculating policies. This has been allowed for only to the extent of multiperiod and first order certainty equivalence respectively, without regard for the degree of uncertainty and risks involved. It therefore becomes imperative to know the possible consequences of the uncertainties; to have assessed the potential damage; and to be able to form plans or design policies that are robust against these uncertainties. Optimal policies, having a more elaborate computational apparatus, may be more sensitive than others to those difficulties. Certainly anyone concerned with policy making is left in little doubt by the planning authorities that it is the wide degree of uncertainty which makes it difficult for them to accept particular policy recommendations. So it can be as important to be able to compute these sensitivities as it is to be able to compute the associated policy proposals. In section 9.3 we derive the basic sensitivity results we need. We show the sensitivity of optimal policies to changes or errors in the external information. By errors in the external information we mean errors (stochastic shocks) in the assumed values of the disturbances, u, and the exogenous variables, N.

It is equally important to be able to compute sensitivities to model errors as represented by stochastic shocks to the model parameters (section 9.4). Reliable results require the sensitivities to variations in the multipliers to be small. These computed parameter sensitivities can also represent the effect of linearisation errors in the optimal policies for a nonlinear model which has been obtained by the linear approximation process in Chapter 7.

In section 9.5 we look at sensitivities to errors in specifying the preferences and aspirations of the policy maker (represented by (Q, q) and z^d respectively). Again that is information supplied externally; but by the policy maker as a result of introspection, his own value judgements, and bargaining between himself, his colleagues and various pressure groups in the light of what is perceived as feasible. It is not information based on statistical estimates, nor on potentially contestable behavioural assumptions and imperfect measurement of the economic situation.

Information on the sensitivity of policy choices enables us to pinpoint where trouble is likely to arise, as well as to assess the seriousness of that trouble. Only then can we concentrate resources for specification and information gathering where they are most effective in improving policy selection.

Of course simulation and forecasting exercises are no less afflicted with these kinds of errors. To accept the results of one simulation experiment as preferable to another implies some preference ordering is being employed. The specification of relative priorities over policy variables is a less contentious issue when they are used to discriminate between only a few quite distinct options. But policy optimisation uses it to discriminate between a continuum of options. It is worth recalling that the set of policies which are acceptable to policy makers in practice is usually a small subset of the feasible set; that policies which are serious candidates for selection tend to be clearly differentiated only politically, rather than numerically. This suggests that *optimal* policies will be relatively insensitive to the preference parameters.

On the other hand, policy recommendations derived from simulation studies are also sensitive to disturbances in the model's parameters. The outcome of a simulation experiment typically depends crucially on the values taken by a few key parameters in the context of a single model. Uncertainty about those parameters can radically alter the policy conclusions drawn. Ormerod (1979) demonstrates the sensitivity of employment, prices, and the balance of payments, over 24 quarters, to five such disturbed parameters in a 130 equation model of the British economy, in which devaluation, income tax and other basic policy variables are involved. Similarly, the sensitivity of policy simulations to different 'standard' models of the US economy appears in the results of Christ (1975). Here the GNP and price responses to government expenditures and the monetary base (or interest rates) are studied. In both references policy responses often (but not always) show similar time profiles and equilibrium positions, but they arrive there by very different routes. These sensitivities can therefore be taken as a scale of comparison for the sensitivity of short-run optimised policies.

9.3 The comparative statics of optimal policies: stochastic shocks

We define the sensitivity of z_i to a_j (some data of the policy choice problem) as the (i, j) th element of $\partial z/\partial a$, the change in z per unit disturbance in a:

$$dz = (\partial z/\partial a)\, da \tag{9.1}$$

In what follows $\partial z/\partial a$ is a matrix arranged so that its (i, j)th element is $\partial z_i/\partial a_j$. The vectorising operation in this chapter stacks a matrix into an extended vector by rows; for example $\text{vec}(H)' = (H_1 \ldots H_{mT})$ where H_i is row i from H. The set of all sensitivities derived in this chapter is collected together in table 9.8 (p. 220).

We can start from (7.15) which contains the first order conditions to (7.14):

$$\begin{bmatrix} Q & -H' \\ -H & O \end{bmatrix} \begin{bmatrix} \tilde{z}^* \\ \mu^* \end{bmatrix} + \begin{bmatrix} q \\ b \end{bmatrix} = 0. \tag{9.2}$$

Therefore

$$\begin{bmatrix} Q & -H' \\ -H & O \end{bmatrix} \begin{bmatrix} dz^* \\ d\mu^* \end{bmatrix} = \begin{bmatrix} dH'\mu^* \\ dH.\tilde{z}^* - db \end{bmatrix} \tag{9.3}$$

where for the moment z^d is taken as fixed. Now

$$db = ds - dH.z^d \tag{9.4}$$

Inserting (9.4) into (9.3) gives, where $\Phi = -PQ^{-1}$,

$$\begin{bmatrix} dz^* \\ d\mu^* \end{bmatrix} = -\begin{bmatrix} \Phi & \Theta \\ \Theta' & (HQ^{-1}H')^{-1} \end{bmatrix} \begin{bmatrix} dH'\mu^* \\ dH.z^* - ds \end{bmatrix}. \tag{9.5}$$

If partial derivatives have their usual interpretation as sensitivities 'while other quantities are assumed to remain fixed', we have the individual sensitivities

$$\frac{\partial z^*}{\partial s} = \Theta \tag{9.6}$$

and hence (7.6) implies

$$\frac{\partial z^*}{\partial u} = \Theta S; \frac{\partial z^*}{\partial N} = \Theta K \tag{9.7}$$

and

$$\partial z^* = -\Phi \partial H' \mu^* - \Theta \partial H.z^* \text{ so } \frac{\partial z^*}{\text{vec}(\partial H)} = -[\mu^{*\prime} \otimes \Phi + \Theta \otimes z^{*\prime}] \tag{9.8}$$

and

$$\frac{\partial \mu^*}{\text{vec}(\partial H)} = -[\mu^{*\prime} \otimes \Theta' + z^{*\prime} \otimes (HQ^{-1}H')^{-1}] \quad \text{and}$$

$$\frac{\partial \mu^*}{\partial s} = (HQ^{-1}H')^{-1}. \tag{9.9}$$

Moreover, starting from w^*, the optimal performance index, using first (9.2) and then the upper subvector of (9.5) premultiplied by H (note $H\Phi = 0$ and $H\Theta = I$), we have

$$dw^* = (\tilde{z}^{*\prime}Q + q')dz^* = \mu^{*\prime}H.dz^* = -\mu^{*\prime}(dH.z^* - ds). \tag{9.10}$$

Assuming at least one constraint is binding, $\mu^* \neq 0$. One value of ds, which compensates w^* so that $dw^* = 0$ given dH, is

$$ds = dH.z^*. \tag{9.11}$$

But ds in (9.11) cannot uniquely imply $dw^* = 0$. For example, any (dH, ds) combinations leading to the orthogonality of μ^* and $ds - dH.z^*$ also imply $dw^* = 0$. Whether or not such values are likely, the only combination of (dH, ds) which keeps the old z^* within the feasible set when w^* is compensated, given that the structure of H is maintained, is that in (9.11) because

$$y = (R + dR)x^* + (s + ds) = y^* \tag{9.12}$$

This is the only case where the old z^* is still available for choice and thus could also be the compensated choice.

It is now possible to relate the perturbations in w^* to those in z^* via

$$dw^* = \left(\frac{\partial w^*}{\partial z^*} \cdot \frac{\partial z^*}{\partial a}\right) da. \tag{9.13}$$

But (9.10) raises the interesting point that the sensitivity of w^* to a given shock can be less than those in z^*. The possibility of mutually compensating shocks from model shocks (those of H) exists, or from H and s together, but not from the information errors (those of N and u) alone. The possibilities for cancelling shocks between components of z^* are more complicated, but it turns out that they cannot be fully compensating. We examine this possibility more closely in Chapter 13.

Using (9.10), we can write

$$\frac{\partial w^*}{\partial s} = \mu^{*\prime}. \tag{9.14}$$

Similarly,

$$\frac{\partial w^*}{\text{vec}(\partial H)} = -\mu^{*\prime} \otimes z^{*\prime}. \tag{9.15}$$

At this point we have sensitivities for each choice variable (z^*, μ^*, w^*) to each possible stochastic shock (s, and H). Notice that the sensitivity matrices of z^* and μ^* to additive uncertainty (in s) are invariant to the state of economic activity or the size of the shock. But the sensitivities to multiplicative uncertainties (in H) are dependent on the level of z^* and furthermore depend on H, which restricts their usefulness for calculating the disturbances due to large shocks in a given H. Both of these latter dependencies also apply to the sensitivities of w^* for additive as well as multiplicative uncertainties.

9.4 The sensitivity of open loop policies

The sensitivities just derived describe all the perturbations to each choice variable as a consequence of alterations in the conditioning information, exogenous to policy choice and not subject to independent specification by the policy makers. That covers both the current and future expected noncontrollable variable (external information), and the model's estimated parameters (the bounds of feasible economic performance). In view of the discussion of uncertainty in Chapter 7, these are the random variables of the policy choice problem. They are therefore uncertain as well as unknown, rather than just unknown in the way that the parameters of the preference function usually are.

However, sensitivities to model errors in the form of disturbances to the multipliers, dH, are not necessarily useful. The policy maker will also need to evaluate the sensitivities to errors (or disturbances) in the model's structural form; i.e. in β and Γ. It will be straightforward to convert (9.6)–(9.9) and (9.14)–(9.15) to that form.

In passing note that u is in an ambiguous position. As a random structural disturbance it represents random variations in the behaviour of the economic agents, and should therefore be treated as an information variable on a par with N. But it is also a catch-all for structural equation errors (recall section 7.6.2) including model mis-specification, measurement errors, omitted variables, and so on. So we shall consider sensitivities to additive and to multiplicative shocks separately. If the former are called information errors, it is because they represent the errors in an incorrect description of economic responses as well as incorrect predictions and random behaviour.

9.4.1 Sensitivities to additive uncertainty

The impact of pure information errors is given by $\partial z^*/\partial N$; and that from the 'information' and model errors represented by u is given in $\partial z^*/\partial u$. These sensitivity matrices are computed automatically during the policy optimisation calculations themselves. Some numerical examples are given in table 9.2 (p. 210) for the problem of Chapter 7. Likewise we also have

$$\frac{\partial \mu^*}{\partial u} = (HQ^{-1}H')^{-1}S \quad \text{and} \quad \frac{\partial \mu^*}{\partial N} = (HQ^{-1}H')^{-1}K \tag{9.16}$$

$$\frac{\partial w^*}{\partial u} = \mu^{*\prime}S \quad \text{and} \quad \frac{\partial w^*}{\partial N} = \mu^{*\prime}K. \tag{9.17}$$

Optimal policies are disturbed in a similar manner by both noncontrollable events and random errors.

9.4.2 Sensitivity to changes in the model parameters

In this section a method is proposed for calculating changes in z^* due to perturbations in the structural model parameters. This may be used to cover the errors and biases in estimation, or the fact that the parameters are genuinely stochastic, or the local effects of mis-specification of the model. The changes might also reflect reestimation or alternative versions of the model. The evaluation of these sensitivities is likely to be complicated since small changes in even one parameter $(\beta\vdots\Gamma)$ can imply that every element of R, S, K, etc., changes.

The sensitivities in (9.8) show the variations in optimal policy choices with respect to changes in the model's multipliers. Such sensitivities are useful for assessing the errors due to linearising a nonlinear model, or the gains to policy selection by reevaluating the linear approximation at (7.2). We can convert these to sensitivities with respect to structural parameters by evaluating:

$$\frac{\partial z^*}{\operatorname{vec}(\partial H)} \cdot \frac{\operatorname{vec}(\partial H)}{\operatorname{vec}(\partial \Pi^*)} \cdot \frac{\operatorname{vec}(\partial \Pi^*)}{\operatorname{vec} \partial(\beta \vdots \Gamma)} \tag{9.18}$$

where $\Pi^* = (\Pi_{11} \ldots \Pi_{1l}, \Pi_{20} \ldots \Pi_{2k})$. The leading sensitivity matrix here is given by (9.8). In the appendix to this chapter the two remaining terms in (9.18) are shown to be

$$\left[I_{nT} \otimes \begin{pmatrix} 0 \\ \cdots \\ -I_{mT} \end{pmatrix} \right] \begin{bmatrix} E_1 \\ \vdots \\ E_T \end{bmatrix} [-\beta^{-1} \otimes (\Pi^{*\prime} \vdots I)] = E \tag{9.19}$$

where

$$E_t' = [D_{t,1}' \ldots D_{1,1}' \; 0 \vdots \ldots \vdots D_{t,g}' \ldots D_{1,g}' \; 0] \tag{9.20}$$

and $D_{t,j}$ contains rows $(j-1)n$ to jn from $D_t = AP^*D_{t-1} + I_g \otimes (R_{t-1}^{*\prime} \vdots 0)$, for $j = 1 \ldots g$ and $t = 1 \ldots T$, where $D_1 = I \otimes (0 \vdots I)$. A and P^* are given following (A9.5) of the appendix. The zero blocks have $n(T-t)$ columns. Although little insight is gained from (9.18), computations using these formulae are straightforward. Some results, for the problem of Chapter 7, are given in table 9.2. Equation (9.18) applies to the case of identical parametric shocks in every period. For cases in which shocks occur in period t only, the tth row block of R alone is affected; thus only $D_1 \ldots D_{T-t+1}$ need be computed, and only E_t is nonzero in (9.19). These sensitivities depend, in each case, on the level of economic activity, and the strength of the dynamic responses at the point of their evaluation.

We have deliberately set up E in order to capture the effects of shocks to the parameter of any variable in the system at any individual period, even where that variable has until now been excluded from an equation. This is to facilitate the evaluation of sensitivities to changes in the model specification (including the creation of new instruments) during the planning period. It is only necessary to include extra columns in $(\Pi^{*\prime} \vdots I)$ containing the new coefficients. The resulting sensitivity is, of course, approximate unless the disturbances are quite small.

By similar arguments we obtain, via (9.18),

$$\frac{\partial \mu^*}{\operatorname{vec} \partial(\beta \vdots \Gamma)} = (HQ^{-1}H')^{-1}E \tag{9.21}$$

and
$$\frac{\partial w^*}{\text{vec}\,\partial(\beta\vdots\Gamma)} = \mu^{*\prime}E. \tag{9.22}$$

9.4.3 The sensitivity of deterministic and stochastic elements of choice

The sensitivity analysis above has been constructed so that it is applicable *both* to the deterministic (certainty equivalent) policy choices – in which case $E_t(b)$, and thus $E_t(z^*)$, $E_t(\mu^*)$ etc., would be inserted into the formulae given between (9.7) and (9.22) – *and* to the combined deterministic and stochastic elements, when suitable realisations for b, z^* and μ^*, would have to be inserted. The sensitivities of the stochastic components alone follow by subtraction. (We refer to the decomposition between deterministic and stochastic components in section 7.7.) A case in point is (9.15) where

$$dw_d^* = dE_t(w^*) - dw_s^*$$

and

$$\partial w_d^*/\text{vec}(\partial H) = -\,E_t(\mu^*)' \otimes E_t(z^*)'. \tag{9.23}$$

Since the partial derivatives are continuous and the implied integration uniformly convergent

$$\partial E_t(w^*)/\text{vec}(\partial H) = E_t(\partial w^*/\text{vec}(\partial H)) = -\,E_t(\mu^{*\prime} \otimes z^{*\prime}). \tag{9.24}$$

Hence the corresponding sensitivity of w_s^* is the difference between (9.23) and (9.24), where (9.24) can be evaluated from $(HQ^{-1}H')^{-1}\Sigma\Theta'$ for $E_t(bb') = \Sigma$. Similar examples could be computed for the sensitivities of z_d^* and z_s^* and μ_d^* and μ_s^*. However, in all cases but $\partial w^*/\text{vec}(\partial H)$ and $\partial w^*/\text{vec}(\partial Q)$, table 9.8 (p. 220) shows that calculations performed for the certainty equivalent solution in fact supply all the required sensitivities.

The disturbance to $E(z^*)$ of (9.24) is only exact when H is unknown or in error, but not random. If it were random we still need to evaluate the expectations of the relevant sensitivity and of the sensitivity of the (first period *and* first order) certainty equivalent solution. The reader may satisfy himself that very complicated expressions are obtained; some of them appear in a different form in sections 12.2 to 12.4.

All the quantities mentioned so far may be computed by the planner ex ante, to show the scale of the problems he faces, and the scope available for overcoming them. The ex ante optimal quantities ($E_t(z^*)$, $E_t(w^*)$, z_d^*, w_d^*, z_s^*, w_s^*, etc.) indicate the reliability of those decisions as they are made. But sensitivities of the ex post optimal quantities (z^*, w^*) can only show the potential inaccuracies in a particular decision.

9.4.4 On the sensitivity of the policy revision mechanism

The sensitivities given by (9.6)–(9.9) and (9.14)–(9.15) refer to open loop policy choices. However, they can be applied to any arbitrary point $1 \leqslant t \leqslant T$ in the sense of showing the effect of disturbances about $E_t(b)$ and $E_t(H)$. Obviously, for a given t, those disturbances can only occur in $b_{(t)}$ and $H_{(t)}$. For any $t > 1$ we can use the same formulae with $\Theta, \Phi, \tilde{z}^*, H, Q, \mu^*, S, K$ replaced by their counterparts subscripted by (t) – as if we were working from (7.33) – to give the perturbations to $\tilde{z}^*_{(t)}, \mu^*_{(t)}$, and $E_t(w^*)$. In that case $\tilde{z}^*_0$ and μ^*_0 are fixed, so the terms in (7.32) drop out. Recomputing these sensitivities successively from $t = 1$ to $t = T$ gives closed loop policy sensitivities alongside the closed loop policics themselves.

But these are not the only perturbations in z^* which might concern us. If we wish to assess the reliability of a policy package, we should test its sensitivity in anticipation of the likely future shocks. That is a different problem because the adjustments to $b_{(t)}$ and $q_{(t)}$ in (7.32) now affect the sensitivity calculations. For example, Chapter 7 showed that a revised policy is closer to z^d, in terms of $E_t(w)$, than its preceding calculation. Yet, with respect to a shock at t, z^*_0 will be suboptimal. It might have been preferable to have followed a different path (even if the expectations to date have all been realised) to head off the expected impact of this shock. We stress this distinction because the latter optimal path (reflecting the sensitivity to likely future shocks) may appear rather more variable than the former path (the sum of z^*_0 and the sensitivity to shocks actually experienced). Risk aversion is more than just knowing how best to *react* to shocks. Many – those most prominently concerned with policy making in practice, as well as the anti-intervention lobby within the economics profession – would rate continuity and gradualism most highly as characteristics of a plan (see, for example, HMSO (1978), Richardson (1978), Wass (1978)). They would welcome a system in which the sensitivities of the outstanding policies were reduced as we progress through periods (1, T). And they would further constrain those sensitivities so as to increase the likelihood of period on period policy continuity, even at the expense of the likelihood that the realised z^* will be close to $E_t(z^*)$, or w^* to $E_t(w^*)$. For them, once in the wrong place it is better to move away gradually than to rush straight back to the overall correct path.

Obviously this is a characteristic to be introduced via w. In Chapter 10 we shall show that this is a matter of setting intertemporal weights in Q. But, even so, in specifying $w(\tilde{z})$ a priori, we can only set Q to trade the *probability* of potential disturbances with the desire to stick with z^d. Hence we need: (a) rules to check on and increase the robustness of policies, either period on period or overall; and (b) the means to arrive at a compromise Q which sets the terms of trade between robustness in z^* and the outcome of $\tilde{z}$, as well as the terms of trade between the individual policy failures in $\tilde{z}$.

9.5 Changes in the objective function parameters: nonstochastic shocks

The planner will need an assessment of the sensitivity of z^* to changes in Q and q when he is uncertain of his relative priorities over policy variables and/or time. It will help him decide on which elements to concentrate his attention in specifying Q, q or z^d; or, in the case of the interactive algorithm of Chapter 10, on which of the deviations from desired values of the variables he should first concentrate.

9.5.1 Changes in the preference structure

We obtain directly from (7.16)

$$\frac{\partial z^*}{\partial Q_{ij}} = -[I - Q^{-1}H'(HQ^{-1}H')^{-1}H]Q^{-1}\frac{\partial Q}{\partial Q_{ij}}\tilde{z}^*$$

and similarly

$$\frac{\partial z^*}{\partial q_k} = \Phi\frac{\partial q}{\partial q_k} \quad i, j, k = 1, \ldots, (n+m)T.$$

Hence

$$\frac{\partial z^*}{\mathrm{vec}(\partial Q)} = \tilde{z}^{*\prime} \otimes \Phi \text{ and } \frac{\partial z^*}{\partial q} = \Phi. \tag{9.25}$$

The values of these sensitivities depend on the level of preferences about which the changes take place; and the first one also on the level of economic activity. Selected sensitivities of (9.25) for the example in Chapter 7 are presented in table 9.4. The sensitivities $\partial\mu^*/\mathrm{vec}(\partial Q)$ and $\partial\mu^*/\partial q$ are derived directly from (7.16) in a similar fashion:

$$\frac{\partial \mu^*}{\mathrm{vec}(\partial Q)} = \tilde{z}^{*\prime} \otimes \Theta' \text{ and } \frac{\partial \mu^*}{\partial q} = \Theta'. \tag{9.26}$$

At the same time we find by means of (9.13), using (9.10) and (9.25),

$$dw^* = \left(\frac{\partial w^*}{\partial z^*}\cdot\frac{\partial z^*}{\mathrm{vec}(\partial Q)} + \frac{\partial w^*}{\mathrm{vec}(\partial Q)}\right)\mathrm{vec}(dQ) = \tfrac{1}{2}(\mathrm{vec}\,\tilde{z}^*\tilde{z}^{*\prime})'\,\mathrm{vec}\,(dQ) \tag{9.27}$$

or $\partial w^*/\partial Q = \frac{1}{2}\tilde{z}^*\tilde{z}^{*\prime}$; under the restriction $dQ_{ij} = dQ_{ji}$ when $i \neq j$. Similarly

$$dw^* = \left(\frac{\partial w^*}{\partial z^*}\cdot\frac{\partial z^*}{\partial q} + \frac{\partial w^*}{\partial q}\right)dq = \tilde{z}^{*\prime}dq. \tag{9.28}$$

Finally we need to know the effects of changing z^d, the 'aspiration' parameters. The planners may very well want to experiment with changing aspirations in the light of what they perceive to be feasible; or in the light of the 'best' that they find they can secure, in contrast to what they may originally have hoped for. These are exactly the types of modifications which we aim to cater for in the interactive algorithm of Chapter 10, which selects the required policy without a prior specification of $w(\tilde{z})$. Indeed studies cited there reveal empirical evidence that both (Q, q) and z^d are often revised during planning exercises in the light of the performance achieved in earlier steps. From (7.16)

$$\frac{\partial z^*}{\partial z^d} = P \quad \text{and} \quad \frac{\partial \mu^*}{\partial z^d} = (HQ^{-1}H')^{-1}H. \tag{9.29}$$

Hence $\partial w^*/\partial z^d = \mu^{*\prime} H$. This completes the derivation of the full set of sensitivities.

9.5.2 Sensitivities for the complete system

For the complete control problem we have

$$\begin{aligned} dz^* = {} & P dz^d + \Theta[S\, du + K dN] \\ & - [\mu^{*\prime} \otimes \Phi + \Theta \otimes z^{*\prime}] E \operatorname{vec} d(\beta \vdots \Gamma) \\ & + \Phi dq + (\tilde{z}^{*\prime} \otimes \Phi) \operatorname{vec}(dQ). \end{aligned} \tag{9.30}$$

With the exception of E, the components of (9.30) are all obtained during the calculation of the optimal policies themselves. The sensitivities of the multiperiod certainty equivalent (closed loop) policy sequence are likewise obtained by using the sequence of these components subscripted (t), as defined in Chapter 7, and extracting the relevant $(n+m)$ rows from each.

We defer consideration of the sensitivity of z_i^*, $i = 1 \ldots (n+m)T$, to changes in the list of decision variables until Chapter 13.

9.6 The welfare loss from information and model errors

It is important to have a general measure of the loss in overall performance due to implementing suboptimal policies. The welfare loss associated with any disturbance to the policies caused by model or information errors is one special case where (ex post) suboptimality is induced. Comparisons with policies having no pretence of optimality, even ex ante, are also of interest. It may be natural to worry first about the potential errors in any implemented policies compared to the ex post optimal ones; but the disturbances in μ^* and w^* are also important.[1] Indeed if $w(\tilde{z})$ were correctly specified (although we may have reason to doubt this in practice) then the disturbances in z^* would be of no consequence; those in w^* would be all important as a measure of the damage caused by implementing $E_t(z^*)$ rather than z^*.

We measure welfare losses for *any* suboptimal policies by (7.58); for $z \neq z^*$,

$$w(\tilde{z}^*) - w(\tilde{z}) = -\tfrac{1}{2}(x - x^*)' M(x - x^*). \tag{9.31}$$

Thus z might be $z^*_{(1)}$, and z^* the ex post optimal policy. Or, to assess the *potential* loss due to any of the stochastic shocks of section 9.4, extract $dx^* = x - x^*$ from (9.7) or (9.18). Changes attributable to disturbances registered in particular periods are obtained by setting the remainder of $x - x^*$ to zero; changes due to particular variables likewise. We can also use (9.31) to show numerically the benefits of optimally revising policy choices and the advantage of closed loop controls. It is, however, necessary to make sure that x^* and M correspond to one another when computing the approximate losses due to implementing unperturbed policies after H or Q change.

There is one sense in which the parameter sensitivity of optimal policies may be less than that of policies chosen by other means. Le Chatelier's principle states: 'If a system, which is in stable equilibrium, has one of its conditions disturbed the system will adjust in such a way as to tend to annul the changed condition.' Consequently, the implied error in optimal choices which do not account for a changed parameter is less than that in simulated outcomes which do not account for the change. This proposition follows whenever the multipliers change from H^1 to H^2 (implying minimisers $\tilde{x}^1$ and $\tilde{x}^2$ respectively) if the associated objective function evaluations imply[2]

$$w(\tilde{x}^2, H^2) - w(\tilde{x}^2, H^1) - [w(\tilde{x}^1, H^2) - w(\tilde{x}^1, H^1)] \leqslant 0.$$

This is easily verified in our case by (7.19), giving $-\tfrac{1}{2}(x^1 - x^2)'(M^1 + M^2) \cdot (x^1 - x^2) \leqslant 0$ in obvious notation. By rearranging terms, we see that the absolute value of the loss to using x^1 when it is wrong is less than to using x^2 when it is wrong. Hence in this sense an optimal policy is a mini-

1 From (9.14) we see μ^* has its usual interpretation of the marginal improvement to w^* from a unit relaxation in the constraints. It is therefore not of separate interest here. However, in Chapter 13 we find it is useful in aiding the design of policy selections with improved qualities of robustness.

2 By theorem 1, Eichhorn and Oetli (1972). A special case of this result is the negativity condition associated with the Slutsky matrix of demand theory.

max risk policy; although this may be cold comfort since neither of the losses need be small.

9.7 Results of the sensitivity analysis of the policy problem of Chapter 7

Tables 9.2 to 9.7 contain a sample of results from a sensitivity analysis of the policy optimisation example discussed in Chapter 7. The main conclusions are that z^* is clearly least sensitive to changes in Q, and most sensitive to parameter shocks. But, overall, the policy choices are fairly robust to the likely random shocks. This is because of the potential cancelling between the sensitivities of different shocks occurring simultaneously. In this context it can be important to account for the correlations between shocks. Moreover, because of similar substitutions between the perturbations in variables, w^* is disturbed considerably less by these shocks than are the elements in z^*.

The perturbations displayed in detail here are those for 1933 – i.e. for the first set of policies in the closed loop solution. The same calculations have been done for each policy revision, and hence for the complete closed loop policies, but they are not reproduced since no significant modifications to the results in tables 9.2 to 9.7 were found. The perturbations are expressed as relative and as absolute changes; and in either case as confidence intervals from the relevant marginal (for individual shocks) and joint (for multiple shocks) density functions.

The policy problem is defined in table 7.1 (p. 156). In tables 9.2–9.4 perturbations are expressed as a percentage of that variable's original optimised value, with the absolute change ($ billion, 1934 prices) in brackets. All figures refer to the 1933 policy choice (first period certainty equivalence at 1933, with $T = 4$).

Finally, we have assumed all errors to be nonindependently and jointly normally distributed with estimated variances given in table 9.1 (p. 210) and means given in table 7.1 (p. 156). Equation errors are presumed to be independently distributed of parameter errors. Strictly the construction of confidence intervals for the parameter shocks case is illegitimate (the sensitivities themselves are functions of the random quantities $\tilde{z}^*$ and H, and the parameters are no more than asymptotically normal). But they are used for illustration, more precise results being unavailable.

(i) The sensitivity to Q (table 9.4, p. 211): Confidence intervals for information errors (table 9.5, p. 212) or model (parameter) errors (table 9.6, p. 212) are much larger than the perturbations due to unit changes within Q. Similarly comparing tables 9.2 and 9.3 with table 9.4 (pp. 210–11) shows that individual shocks tend to cause greater perturbations than

Table 9.1 *The parameter and structural error variances in the model of table* 7.1

Error variances	U_c	U_I	U_W	
original	1.3	1.42	0.61	
orthogonalised	1.35	1.9	0.075	
Parameter variances:	$i=0$	$i=1$	$i=2$	$i=3$
α_i original	1.645	0.009	0.0014	0.0083
α_i orthogonalised	2.1175	0.0038	0.00165	0.0003
β_i original	52.31	0.0245	0.0213	0.0012
β_i orthogonalised	52.4	0.0277	0.0126	0.00
γ_i original	1.285	0.0014	0.0015	0.0008
γ_i orthogonalised	0.744	0.00	0.001	0.00

Sources: Theil (1964), and Leenders and Rothenburg (1964).

Table 9.2 *Perturbations to optimal policy choices due to individual shocks from structural equation errors in 1933: shocks at ± twice their standard errors (5% probability bounds of the marginal density functions)*

	C	I	D	W_2	I	G
U_C	3.68(1.85)	1.28(.062)	1.08(.07)	18.79(1.149)	6.58(.568)	11.33(1.62)
U_I	.36(.178)	51.3(2.46)	1.13(.076)	3.2(.197)	9.2(.79)	8.14(1.16)
U_W	1.89(.925)	2.6(.124)	11.22(.76)	14.13(.87)	13.75(1.186)	2.64(.38)

Table 9.3 *Perturbations to optimal policy choices due to individual shocks from parameters throughout 1933–6: shocks at ± twice their standard errors (approx. 5% probability bounds of the marginal density functions)*

	C	I	D	W_2	T	G
α_0	3.6(1.72)	2.1(0.13)	11.6(0.96)	13.5(0.83)	4.2(0.36)	19.3(2.74)
α_1	2.7(1.26)	2.1(0.13)	10.0(0.83)	8.8(0.54)	1.7(0.15)	16.7(2.37)
α_2	0.7(0.32)	0.5(0.03)	2.1(0.17)	2.3(0.14)	0.3(0.02)	5.6(0.8)
α_3	7.3(3.47)	6.7(0.41)	32.5(2.69)	35.1(2.16)	6.7(0.58)	51.3(7.29)
β_0	4.1(1.96)	227.0(13.96)	67.1(5.55)	10.6(0.65)	49.9(4.33)	77.1(10.96)
β_1	0.7(0.35)	49.0 (3.03)	15.7(1.3)	4.1(0.25)	9.3(0.81)	18.7(2.67)
β_2	0.4(0.18)	31.3 (1.92)	11.6(0.96)	3.4(0.21)	5.8(0.5)	12.8(1.82)
β_3	3.7(1.76)	226.0(13.92)	76.5(6.33)	14.6(0.9)	50.2(4.36)	81.2(11.54)
γ_0	2.8(1.32)	0.8(0.05)	24.1(2.0)	11.7(0.72)	24.8(2.15)	11.8(1.68)
γ_1	3.9(1.84)	0.8(0.05)	42.3(3.5)	13.0(0.8)	41.7(3.62)	23.3(3.31)
γ_2	3.9(1.87)	1.0(0.06)	44.4(3.67)	12.0(0.74)	44.4(3.85)	25.3(3.59)
γ_3	0.1(0.06)	0.0(0.0)	1.6(0.13)	0.3(0.02)	1.6(0.14)	0.5(0.07)

Table 9.4 *Proportional disturbances due to unit changes in elements of* $Q; dQ_{ij} > 0$.

(*a*) Total number of elements exceeding $|0.6\tilde{z}_i^*|$ and less than $|0.1\tilde{z}_i^*|$ are, respectively, 8 and 465 out of 576; where

	C	I	D	W_2	T	G
Mean sensitivity	0.02(− 0.007)	0.71(− 0.044)	11.6(− 0.96)	0.7(+ 0.42)	0.9(+ 0.02)	2.75(+ 0.08)
Standard deviation sensitivity	0.02(0.01)	14.6(0.9)	16.9(1.4)	11.4(0.68)	10.4(0.21)	19.2(0.57)
and $|0.6\tilde{z}_i^*|$ represents	0.2 (0.07)	15.6(0.96)	32.6(2.7)	10.7(0.66)	8.8(0.76)	15.5(2.2)
but $|0.1\tilde{z}_i^*|$ represents	0.03(0.012)	2.6(0.16)	5.4(0.45)	1.8(0.109)	1.4(0.13)	2.6(0.37)

(b) The largest sensitivities in 1933 solution: those exceeding $|0.6\tilde{z}_i^*|$ were C perturbed through Q_{13} 2.2% (1.1); I through Q_{13}, 29.1% (1.4); D though Q_{22} and Q_{33} by 14.2% (0.96) and 41.8(2.82); G through Q_{33} by 22.8%(1.54). There are no other closed loop elements in this category

Table 9.5 *$d\tilde{z}_i^*$ as a function of all (orthogonalised) structural equation errors; standard errors and probabilities of joint density functions:*

Variable	z_i^*	SE	Confidence interval	$p(dz_i^*) \leqslant \|0.1z_i^*\|$	$p(dz_i^*) \leqslant \|0.25z_i^*\|$
C	47.36	0.969	± 4.1(1.94)	0.9999	0.9999
I	− 6.14	1.432	± 46.6(2.86)	0.3328	0.7154
D	8.27	0.475	± 11.5(0.95)	0.9182	0.9999
W_2	6.15	0.617	± 20.1(1.23)	0.6826	0.872
T	8.67	0.583	± 1.3(1.16)	0.8612	0.9995
G	14.21	1.067	± 14.9(2.13)	0.8164	0.9988

The confidence intervals are expressed as a % of the original optimised value (and the absolute change); the other changes are absolute figures.

Table 9.6 (a) *$d\tilde{z}_i^*$ as a function of all (orthogonalised) parameter errors; standard errors and probabilities of various joint density functions*

Variable	z_i^*	SE	Confidence interval	$p(dz_i^*) \leqslant \|0.1z_i^*\|$	$p(dz_i^*) \leqslant \|0.25z_i^*\|$
C	47.36	1.81	± 7.6 (3.63)	0.9912	0.9999
I	− 6.14	7.27	± 236.8 (14.54)	0.0680	0.1664
D	− 8.27	3.37	± 81.4 (6.74)	0.1974	0.4600
W_2	6.15	0.82	± 26.7 (1.64)	0.5468	0.9398
T	8.67	2.82	± 65.1 (5.64)	0.2434	0.5588
G	14.21	6.25	± 87.9 (12.50)	0.1820	0.4314

Confidence intervals are expressed as a % of the original optimised value (and the absolute change); the other changes are absolute figures.

Table 9.6 (b) *Standard errors or parameter errors in individual equations (absolute changes)*

	C	I	D	W_2	T	G
equation 1 (α_i);	1.18	0.09	0.67	0.55	0.23	1.93
equation 2 (β_i):	1.05	7.27	2.88	0.40	2.23	5.76
equation 3 (γ_i):	0.95	0.02	1.63	0.46	1.71	1.47

Table 9.7 *Some losses due to information and model errors: % loss in* w^* *due to implementing unperturbed open loop policies*

Changed z^* caused by	losses within: 1st period	2nd period	3rd period	4th period	losses over whole plan
Table 9.2, $U_C \pm$ twice its standard error	15.6	15.1	13.3	9.1	8.2
Table 9.2, $U_I \pm$ twice its standard error	16.2	15.6	13.5	8.5	6.93
Table 9.2, $U_W \pm$ twice its standard error	15.8	15.3	13.5	9.4	5.63
Table 9.5, confidence intervals	18.4	—	—	—	6.6
	estimated losses of 1st period		estimated average loss per period over whole plan		
Table 9.6(b) – α_i, confidence intervals	9.7		6.6		
Table 9.6(b) – β_i, confidence intervals	51.1		66.0		
Table 9.6(b) – γ_j, confidence intervals	28.4		36.4		
Table 9.6(a) – all equations, confidence intervals	76.3		111.6		

unit changes in Q. Not only are the largest values in table 9.4 smaller than these confidence limits, they are also few in number. Indeed, the representative figures from table 9.4 (means and standard errors) are actually smaller by factors of 10 or more. Within table 9.4, I, D and G are the variables most affected by changing Q – but I and G only rather erratically.

The conclusion here is to suggest that more effort be put into accurate model specification and estimation, and less into the fine detail of the relative weights in Q. Probably only a few points need careful specification. Within reason, therefore, roughly specified preferences and trade-offs give similar results to those from a very careful specification – both in optimised variable and welfare index. This is a useful conclusion – in so far as it extends to other problems[3] – because the specification of Q is the area of our least experience and knowledge. This conclusion goes against conventional wisdom that errors in specifying the objective function pose the most serious difficulty in policy optimisation (see HMSO (1978)).

(ii) Sensitivity to information errors: Broadly, the calculations neces-

3. Confirmed below at (9.36). Also Chapter 10, and the references there, cite corroborative evidence.

sary for table 9.2 revealed positive du increases y_1^* and depresses x_1^*. These sensitivities are of rather similar sizes for each error, but targets are more sensitive than instruments in absolute values. Perhaps likely shocks from U_I affect the targets most, and those from U_C affect them least; and vice versa for instruments. C, I and G are the most affected variables. In terms of relative disturbances, U_W affects the targets most (apart from U_I on I); and U_C and U_W the instruments most. On this basis it is rather unclear where respecification is most urgently required.

The reliability of z^* cannot be judged from considering single random shocks. Table 9.5 shows dz^* for all errors varying simultaneously. I, of the targets, is least robust both absolutely and relatively, but of the instruments it is G absolutely and W_2 relatively. From the signs on the elements of the sensitivity matrix we find there is a higher chance of offsetting stochastic shocks on D than on W_2. This is some measure of the relative robustness of each z_i^* to the component shocks. We also found that orthogonalising (by principal components) the errors makes little difference because of their low covariances. Table 9.5 summarises these points, and confirms the general robustness of z^* (excepting I).

(iii) Sensitivity to model errors: Evidently z^* is more disturbed by shocks in the parameters (tables 9.3 and 9.6) than structural errors at equivalent probability levels or by errors in Q. In fact this conclusion might be expected in general since dz^* can also be approximated as the product of the sensitivity to information errors, the current $\tilde{z}_i^*$ value, and the parameter shock (Hughes Hallett (1979a)). So this conclusion fails only when the likely parameter shock is smaller than the variable's optimal failure. z_i^* is therefore sensitive to parameter shocks in equations to whose information errors it is sensitive. That is evident from tables 9.3 and 9.6. The targets are somewhat more sensitive than instruments; and targets are naturally most sensitive to the parameters of their own structural equation. Finally, $d\gamma_i > 0$ and $d\alpha_i > 0$ raises targets and depresses instruments; $d\beta_i > 0$ raises all but G.

Tables 9.3 and 9.6 show where the specification of the model should be improved. The sensitivity to β_i is largest.[4] These parameters are badly determined in themselves and that equation as a whole is likely to cause large dz^* values. Only variations in $\alpha_0, \alpha_1, \alpha_2, \beta_1, \beta_2, \gamma_0$ and γ_3 have rather little effect. Generally T, G and I tend to be badly affected.

To orthogonalise the parameter shocks was important here. Ignoring

4 (9.19) is not multi-variate normally distributed. To apply the normal distribution for tables 9.3 and 9.6 we must apply an ordinary central limit theorem so the results are to be interpreted as asymptotic, $T \rightarrow \infty$. But then the probability model describing the distribution of dz_i^* is only a linear approximation about z^* to the true distribution.

their covariances the standard errors computed for table 9.6(a) were (in the same ordering) 2.88, 10.02, 5.29, 1.48, 4.23 and 9.45. But again the possibilities of substitution are such that the robustness of each z_i^* to its components varies considerably; *I*, *T* and *G* are least robust. The chances of cancelling shocks are higher from α_i and γ_i, and within W_2 and *G*.

(iv) the robustness of w^*: Two variables being substitutes means that w^* is largely unaffected when a noticeable increase in one can be compensated by a decrease in the other. Substitution possibilities also exist between a variable's own values over time. At (9.11) we established some theoretical cases where this will happen. By (9.30) we see that z^* can be robust because of mutual cancelling between the various shocks which may in probability strike each variable – especially where the various stochastic terms have high covariances of a suitable sign. But w^*, being the sum of quadratic terms in z^*, can be robust through the cancelling and substitution possibilities between z^* elements themselves; that is over and above any robustness within z^*.

The outcomes of these possibilities are illustrated by table 9.7. Given the sum of the perturbations in individual variables, a lot of substitution has taken place. However, in confirmation of table 9.3, uncertainty in β_i causes more damage than other uncertainties. Hence w^* may display sensitivity characteristics quite different from those of z^* – and, if $w(\tilde{z})$ is correctly specified, it is this robustness of w^* which mainly concerns us.

9.8 Robust policies

If, in any particular application, policy sensitivities turn out to be unacceptably large the question naturally arises: is $w(\tilde{z})$ correctly specified? In order to represent preferences faithfully, $w(\tilde{z})$ must, after all, also include a component to constrain the sensitivities of the implied choice within acceptable limits. We may investigate how the respecification of *Q* can induce greater robustness. But, since that has less effect on the policy choice than the other specification changes, this is a secondary use of $w(\tilde{z})$; the primary use remains setting the priorities for reaching the targets.

9.8.1 The connection between preference parameters and risk averse policies

It is obviously important to allow for parameter uncertainty, as well as for information uncertainty, if one wants to make z^* robust. In the example above that was more important. But whether this is more conveniently done by first order certainty equivalence (as we have done so far) and using the optimal revisions to compensate for the consequent mistakes by feeding back the measured $\hat{u}_t$, or by an explicit procedure as in Chapter 12, is an empirical question.

On the other hand, the precise specification of $w(\tilde{z})$ will be less vital for computing the optimal policies than a correctly specified and well estimated model. So, if the stumbling block to policy selection by optimisation is model or information errors then the policy maker should set Q to create policy choices which are robust to those errors.[5] These parameters are under his control and can be used to reflect his risk aversion. We shall construct rudimentary (but ad hoc) methods of inducing explicit risk aversion into the policy choices. We have already shown that the criterion $E_t(w)$, in place of w, leads to unbiased optimal policy choices; but choices without specific restraint on their precision. We may now look for rules of thumb which improve the robustness of those choices by alterations to the specified preference function. Naturally this approach to handling risk aversion is no more than a stop-gap. A full analysis, which will not be attempted, would consider alternatives to $E_t(w)$ as the criterion, given the specification of w itself.

Now Q is symmetric and positive definite; and by inspection P is idempotent. Thus Φ is symmetric and not of full rank. It is moreover negative semidefinite since writing $Q^{-1} = L'L$, where L is triangular and non-singular, implies

$$\Phi = -L'(I - L^{*\prime}(L^*L^{*\prime})^{-1}L^*)L = -L'P^*L \text{ where } L^{*\prime} = LH'. \tag{9.32}$$

It follows from these properties, and (9.25), that:

$$\text{(i)} \quad \frac{\partial z_j^*}{\partial Q_{ij}} \text{ has the opposite sign to } \tilde{z}_i^* \tag{9.33}$$

for $\begin{cases} j = 1 \ldots (n+m)T \text{ and each} \\ i = 1 \ldots (n+m)T \text{ in turn;} \end{cases}$

$$\text{(ii)} \quad \left|\frac{\partial z_k^*}{\partial Q_{ij}}\right| \leqslant \max\left\{\left|\frac{\partial z_j^*}{\partial Q_{ij}}\right|, \left|\frac{\partial z_k^*}{\partial Q_{ik}}\right|\right\} \tag{9.34}$$

for $\begin{cases} j, k = 1, \ldots, (n+m)T \text{ and each} \\ i = 1, \ldots, (n+m)T; \end{cases}$

$$\text{(iii)} \quad \frac{\partial z_j^*}{\partial q_j} \leqslant 0 \text{ and } \left|\frac{\partial z_j^*}{\partial q_k}\right| \leqslant \max\left\{\left|\frac{\partial z_j^*}{\partial q_j}\right|, \left|\frac{\partial z_k^*}{\partial q_k}\right|\right\} \tag{9.35}$$

for $j, k = 1 \ldots (n+m)T$.

5 In order to preserve the implicit ideal targets, changes in q are ruled out

Hence from (9.32), and for any norm $\|.\|$, since $\|A\| = \rho(A)$ for any hermitian matrix A, and $\|L\|^2 = \|Q^{-1}\|$ (Fröberg (1972), p. 73), we have

$$\|\Phi\| \leqslant \|P\|\,\|Q^{-1}\| = \frac{1}{\rho} \tag{9.36}$$

where ρ is the smallest eigenvalue of Q. Since Q is symmetric we can make either sensitivity in (9.25) arbitrarily small by manipulating the normalising constant in (Q, q). But the norms of Θ, P, K, E etc. (applied to (9.7) and (9.18)) are all invariant to that normalisation. Hence, the sensitivities to changes in the preference structure, (9.25), can be made to be smaller than those to information or model errors. Optimal control is therefore particularly effective for testing the specification of a model, and its associated information set, for suitability as a policy evaluation tool.

9.8.2 Rules for shifting z*

Without loss of generality we can take $\rho = 1$. Then, since $\|\Phi\| \leqslant 1$,

$$\max_k \left|\frac{\partial z_k^*}{\partial Q_{ij}}\right| < |\tilde{z}_i^*| \quad i, k, j = 1 \ldots (n+m)T. \tag{9.37}$$

Hence we know

(i) $dQ_{kk} > 0$ reduces $|\tilde{z}_k^*|$, i.e. z_k moves towards z_k^d, $k = 1 \ldots (n+m)T$

(ii) $dQ_{kj} > 0$, given k, disturbs any $|\tilde{z}_i^*|$ less than $|\tilde{z}_k^*|$, where $i, j = 1 \ldots (n+m)T$ and $i \neq k$. However, the sign of the change in $\tilde{z}_i^*$ is uncertain if $i \neq j$. If $i = j \neq k$, then $|\tilde{z}_i^*|$ is reduced if $\tilde{z}_i^*$ and $\tilde{z}_k^*$ have the same sign, otherwise it is increased.

(iii) under (i) and (ii) and given k, it is possible to get sign changes in $\tilde{z}_i^*$ only if $i \neq k$.

(iv) by (ii) dQ_{kk} achieves the largest disturbances in $|\tilde{z}_k^*|$.

These rules suggest how adjustments to Q can be used to shift z^* values from any trial position to a preferable policy set. Generally we should start with the diagonal elements Q_{kk}, where k indexes the largest failures in descending $|\tilde{z}_k^*|$ values. We can always adjust Q_{kk} so $|\tilde{z}_k^*|$ is reduced but not by so much that another $|\tilde{z}_i^*|$ overtakes it. We can go as far as possible to get a preferred outcome ($Q_{jk}, j \neq k$, may also be used). But only nT arbitrary adjustments, dz^*, are possible since Φ has rank nT at most. Arbitrary adjustments are always possible such that $z^* + dz^*$ is also feasible, because then $Hdz^* = 0$ and $H(\Phi, dz^*) = 0$, although $r(H) = mT$, while $r(\Phi) = nT < (n+m)T$. Then $dz^* = (\tilde{z}^{*\prime} \otimes \Phi)\,\mathrm{vec}(dQ)$ has multiple solutions for dQ. In other words, we may use Q to shift z^* arbitrarily about F, the feasible set, but not arbitrarily about policy space.

9.8.3 Rules for inducing robustness in z*

If now $a = u$, or vec N, or vec$(\beta \vdots \Gamma)$ then

$$\frac{\partial}{\partial Q_{ij}}\left(\frac{\partial z^*}{\partial a}\right) = -\Phi_{.i}\left(\frac{\partial z^*}{\partial a}\right)_{j.} \qquad i,j = 1 \ldots (n+m)T \tag{9.38}$$

so that

$$\partial(\partial z^*/\partial a)/\text{vec}(\partial Q) = -(\text{vec}\,\Phi)\left(\text{vec}\frac{\partial z^*}{\partial a}\right)'. \tag{9.39}$$

This implies

$$\|\partial(\partial z^*/\partial a)/\text{vec}(\partial Q)\| \leqslant \left\|\frac{\partial z^*}{\partial a}\right\| \tag{9.40}$$

and that $\partial(\partial z_i^*/\partial a)/\partial Q_{ij}$ has the same sign as $\partial z_j^*/\partial a$ element for element; $i, j = 1 \ldots (n+m)T$. Thus for more risk aversion:

(i) set the sign of dQ_{kk} opposite to the sign of the sensitivity of z_k^*
(ii) if $\partial z_j^*/\partial a_k > 0$ set $dQ_{ij} < 0$ to reduce the sensitivities $|\partial z_i^*/\partial a_k|$
(iii) we can reduce a sensitivity but not change its sign
(iv) rules (i) and (ii) in section 9.8.1 apply to sensitivities as well as the failures $\tilde{z}_i^*$ and $\tilde{z}_k^*$.

So the objective of minimising $|\tilde{z}|$ is not necessarily compatible with increasing its robustness.

These rules suggest how Q should be adjusted to reflect increased risk aversion in the face of the inevitable stochastic shocks. But a systematic manipulation of $\tilde{z}^*$ via Q awaits the formal analysis of the following chapter.

9.8.4 Rules for inducing robustness in *w**

We can easily extend these rules of thumb to include rules for stabilising w^* in the face of stochastic shocks, via (9.27) and (9.28). Clearly $\partial w^*/\partial Q$ is positive semi-definite. So reducing the penalty on the largest failure will introduce the greatest degree of robustness ($dQ_{ii} < 0$ where $\max_j |\tilde{z}_j^*| = \tilde{z}_i^*$ indicates the index i). More useful perhaps is to adjust the off-diagonal elements $dQ_{ij} = dQ_{ji} < 0(>0)$ if $\tilde{z}_i^* \tilde{z}_j^* > 0(<0)$. A sequence of robustness inducing changes in Q are implied.

The problem is that these robustness inducing rules are diametrically opposed to the objective of reducing $|\tilde{z}^*|$ – whatever the metric. By section 9.8.2 above, this is true for all Q_{ii} adjustments and for all Q_{ij} adjustments with respect to the larger of $|\tilde{z}_i^*|$ and $|\tilde{z}_j^*|$. It may also be true for increasing the robustness of $\tilde{z}^*$, although that is not certain.

Consequently we have a conflict of objectives. Under the criterion $E_t(w)$, risk aversion over the realisation of $w(\tilde{z})$ and the objective of minimising $|\tilde{z}|$ are mutually exclusive. In an uncertain world one has to exploit the trade-off between robustness and optimisation, or between security and success. Because $E_t(w)$ is an arbitrary surrogate for w, its use may require some modifications to Q which would not be appropriate in w itself. This is a very important conclusion, and explains why, in the subsequent chapters, we take so much trouble to stress ways of inducing 'adequate amounts' of risk aversion, robustness, or 'acceptability' into our policy selections. Ultimately it might be necessary to modify (or abandon) $E_t(w)$, in favour of some other function of w, in order to exploit this trade-off between security and success.

9.9 Conclusions

This chapter has treated the sensitivity and robustness of optimal policies from a linear quadratic control problem under two sorts of uncertainty. We have been able to compute the sensitivity of optimal policies to various kinds of model and information errors; and have shown that they are usually more of an obstacle to successful policy selection than is a mis-specification of the preferences. A number of rules have been proposed to improve the robustness of computed policies – in response to an obvious requirement for reliability in the selected policies. We have made use of the parameters controlling the preference function – principally Q. This is not to argue that these rules should dictate the choice of Q(or z^d). On the contrary, the planner should have the full freedom to specify preferences as he wants them. But if the issue of reliable policies in an uncertain world is so important to planners, and one is left in no doubt that it is in practice, then risk aversion will be one component of their preferences. And since planners are so often unsure of how to specify (7.10) exactly, there must be scope for interaction between z^* and (7.10), especially where the latter is indeed some approximation to the true preferences. It is easy enough to see how to use those interactions to get more or less of some policy, but it is not so obvious in which direction to adjust policy values to induce more robustness to each selection.

We have also observed that it will be necessary to exploit a trade-off between ambition and risk aversion in choosing policies. Both objectives require a more systematic treatment; and this is the aim of the interactive algorithms of the following chapter. We conclude that, even if z^* is less sentitive to Q, the design of the objective function is central to the design of reliable policies with a given model and information set.

Table 9.8 *The sensitivities summarised*

1.	(a) $\frac{\partial z^*}{\partial s} = \Theta; \quad \frac{\partial z^*}{\partial u} = \Theta S; \quad \frac{\partial z^*}{\partial N} = \Theta K$
	(b) $\frac{\partial z^*}{\mathrm{vec}(\partial H)} = S_u; \quad \frac{\partial z^*}{\mathrm{vec}\, \partial(\beta{:}\Gamma)} = S_u E$
	(c) $\frac{\partial z^*}{\mathrm{vec}(\partial Q)} = \tilde{z}^{*\prime} \otimes \Phi; \quad \frac{\partial z^*}{\partial q} = \Phi$
	(d) $\frac{\partial z^*}{\partial z^d} = P$
2.	(a) $\frac{\partial \mu^*}{\partial s} = (HQ^{-1}H')^{-1}; \quad \frac{\partial \mu^*}{\partial u} = (HQ^{-1}H')^{-1}S; \quad \frac{\partial \mu^*}{\partial N} = (HQ^{-1}H')^{-1}K$
	(b) $\frac{\partial \mu^*}{\mathrm{vec}(\partial H)} = [\mu' \otimes \Theta' + z^{*\prime} \otimes (HQ^{-1}H')^{-1}]; \quad \frac{\partial \mu^*}{\mathrm{vec}\partial(\beta{:}\Gamma)} = (HQ^{-1}H')^{-1}E$
	(c) $\frac{\partial \mu^*}{\mathrm{vec}(\partial Q)} = \tilde{z}^{*\prime} \otimes \Theta'; \quad \frac{\partial \mu^*}{\partial q} = \Theta'$
	(d) $\frac{\partial \mu^*}{\partial z^d} = (HQ^{-1}H')^{-1}H$
3.	(a) $\frac{\partial w^*}{\partial s} = \mu^{*\prime}; \quad \frac{\partial w^*}{\partial u} = \mu^{*\prime} S; \quad \frac{\partial w^*}{\partial N} = \mu^{*\prime} K$
	(b) $\frac{\partial w^*}{\mathrm{vec}(\partial H)} = -\mu^{*\prime} \otimes z^{*\prime}; \quad \frac{\partial w^*}{\mathrm{vec}\partial(\beta{:}\Gamma)} = \mu^{*\prime} E$
	(c) $\frac{\partial w^*}{\partial Q} = \frac{1}{2}\tilde{z}^*\tilde{z}^{*\prime}; \quad \frac{\partial w^*}{\partial q} = \tilde{z}^{*\prime}$
	(d) $\frac{\partial w^*}{\partial z^d} = \mu^{*\prime} H$

where $\Theta = Q^{-1}H'(HQ^{-1}H')^{-1}$, $P = I - Q^{-1}H'(HQH')^{-1}H$, $\Phi = -PQ^{-1}$

$$S_u = -\mu^{*\prime} \otimes \Phi - \Theta \otimes z^{*\prime} = -\mu^{*\prime} \otimes \Phi - \frac{\partial z^*}{\partial s} \otimes z^{*\prime}$$

$$E = \left[I \otimes \begin{pmatrix} 0 \\ \cdots \\ -I \end{pmatrix} \right] \left[\begin{pmatrix} E_1 \\ \vdots \\ E_T \end{pmatrix} \right] [-\beta^{-1} \otimes (\Pi^{*\prime} {:} I)]$$

Appendix: Sensitivities to model errors

We need to evaluate (9.18),

$$\frac{\partial z^*}{\mathrm{vec}(\partial H)} \cdot \frac{\mathrm{vec}(\partial H)}{\mathrm{vec}(\partial \Pi^*)} \cdot \frac{\mathrm{vec}(\partial \Pi^*)}{\mathrm{vec}\,\partial(\beta \vdots \Gamma)}. \tag{A9.1}$$

Equation (9.8) supplies the left hand term. The evaluation of the two right hand components is straightforward but exceptionally tedious and hardly illuminating. In order to preserve the structure of H whatever the parametric shocks encountered, we write

$$\frac{\mathrm{vec}(\partial H)}{\mathrm{vec}(\partial \Pi^*)} = \frac{\mathrm{vec}(\partial H)}{\mathrm{vec}(\partial R)} \cdot \frac{\mathrm{vec}(\partial R)}{\mathrm{vec}(\partial \Pi^*)} = \left[I_{mT} \otimes \left(\frac{0}{-I_{nT}} \right) \right] \cdot \begin{bmatrix} E_1 \\ \vdots \\ E_T \end{bmatrix}. \tag{A9.2}$$

The first term on the right of (A9.2) is obvious; but the second presents some problems. Note from (7.3) that $\partial R_1^*/\partial(\Pi_1)_{jk} = 0$ for $j, k = 1 \ldots g(l-1)$ and Π_1 from (2.6). In that notation there are no instrument lags; hence $\partial R_1^*/\partial(\Pi_2)_{jk}$ is a zero matrix excepting unity in the (j, k)th position $(j = 1 \ldots g(l-1); k = 1 \ldots n)$. Therefore

$$\partial R_1^*/\mathrm{vec}(\partial \Pi^*) = I_g \otimes (0 \vdots I_n) = D_1. \tag{A9.3}$$

Next

$$\frac{\partial R_i^*}{\partial(\Pi_2)_{jk}} = \Pi_1 \frac{\partial R_{i-1}^*}{\partial(\Pi_2)_{jk}} \text{ and } \frac{\partial R_i^*}{\partial(\Pi_1)_{jk}} = \begin{pmatrix} 0 \\ R_{i-1,k}^* \\ 0 \end{pmatrix} + \Pi_1 \left(\frac{\partial R_{i-1}^*}{\partial(\Pi_1)_{jk}} \right) \tag{A9.4}$$

using (7.3) and (2.6); where $R_{i-1,k}^*$, the kth row of R_{i-1}^*, has been placed in the jth row. From here

$$\frac{\mathrm{vec}(\partial R_i^*)}{\mathrm{vec}(\partial \Pi^*)} = AP^* \frac{\mathrm{vec}(\partial R_{i-1}^*)}{\mathrm{vec}(\partial \Pi^*)} + I_g \otimes (R_{i-1}^{*\prime} \vdots 0) \tag{A9.5}$$

where P^* is a permutation matrix such that $P^* \mathrm{vec}(R_i^*) = \mathrm{vec}(R_i^{*\prime})$, and

$$A = \begin{bmatrix} I_n \otimes \Pi_{1,1.} \\ \vdots \\ I_n \otimes \Pi_{1,g.} \end{bmatrix} \text{ given } \Pi_{1,i.} \text{ is the } i\text{th row of } (\Pi_{11} \ldots \Pi_{1l}).$$

Therefore the sequence of differentials in (A9.5) is given by

$$D_t = AP^* D_{t-1} + I_g \otimes (R_{t-1}^{*\prime} \vdots 0) \quad t = 1 \ldots T \tag{A9.6}$$

with D_1 from (A9.3). Finally, in (A9.2) $E_t = [D'_{t,1} \ldots D'_{1,1} 0 \vdots \cdots \vdots D'_{t,g} \ldots D'_{1,g} 0]$ where $D_{t,j}$ is rows $(j-1)n$ to jn from D_t (for $j = 1 \ldots g$ and $t = 1 \ldots T$). The zero blocks have $n(T-t)$ columns.

The last term in (A9.1) is given by Goldberger, Nagar and Odeh (1961) as

$$\frac{\text{vec}(\partial\Pi^*)}{\text{vec}\,\partial(\beta \vdots \Gamma)} = -(\beta)^{-1} \otimes (\Pi^{*\prime} \vdots I) \tag{A9.7}$$

for the system (2.6). Inserting (9.8), (A9.2) and (A9.7) into (9.18) gives the desired result.

10

The specification and analysis of preferences

10.1 Introduction

The specification of an objective function which adequately reflects the collective preferences of policy makers is perhaps the major unresolved difficulty in making economic planning operational as an optimisation problem. The selection and analysis of the most desirable policies becomes exceedingly difficult, particularly in macroeconomic planning where there are many who contribute to policy formulation and where individual preferences vary substantially.

Essentially we are concerned here with the qualitative, and potentially political, judgements which condition the behaviour of the policy makers in any economy. No description of an economy is complete without some modelling of the policy formation process. That means we must face the problem of describing the control of a self-managed system with co-operating policy makers. In our framework the selected policy values depend on the values taken for Q, q and z^d. These are values the policy makers must set. But since the true collective preferences cannot generally be known a priori, and may not even exist, we are compelled to work with approximations to them; approximations whose validity typically is restricted to a small subspace of the policy space. So to specify even an approximation, a priori, will be virtually impossible. The appropriate approximation partly depends on the policy choice, as well as vice versa. Instances of this difficulty abound. The inability of planners to handle relative penalties on deviations of the policy variables from their ideal values is no doubt the prime reason for their reluctance to entertain policy optimisation methods. The inability of researchers to select realistic penalties so that computed policies remain within the bounds of acceptability has often discredited these methods in the eyes of the planners. Yet the selection of one preferred policy package from a set of candidates involves the use of at least an implicit criterion.

In this chapter we investigate how these preferences and aspirations may be specified in a form precise enough to be used in any of the policy optimisation algorithms – or indeed for use in discriminating between the results of any of the earlier forecasting or simulation exercises. We emphasise this preference function problem is common to all the techniques, not just policy optimisation (sections 10.2 and 10.3). It may be convenient to represent the calculation of economic policies as an optimisation problem, but we need not assume that all policies are, in fact, chosen by optimisation. We do, however, suppose that planners make rational choices when selecting the values for the variables (instruments) under their control. The assumption of rational choices implies no more than that a preference ordering exists over values of all the variables of interest to the planners, and that this preference ordering should satisfy a minimal set of axioms of choice. Self-interested maximising choices are made on this basis. We continue to suppose that planners know their own ideal values for the instruments and targets, and that they know that they face certain constraints. It is not required that they necessarily know the constraints correctly, but that they at least have some perception of them and that they choose policies on that basis.

'Satisficing' might be a more realistic behavioural model for planners, but it is formally equivalent to optimising one's own perception of one's own self-interest. The implicit preference function used here (section 10.4) allows an appropriate blend of ideology and pragmatism. It provides a very general and non-controversial maintained hypothesis for the planning behaviour being modelled.

This chapter also indicates an efficient policy selection technique which avoids the necessity of specifying an objective a priori (section 10.5). This technique is developed from an interactive planning scheme (Hughes Hallett (1980)) which has two possible modes of application; either with the preferences implicit or explicit. It is made operational with an algorithm introduced by Ancot, Hughes Hallett and Paelinck (1982) to solve for a policy simultaneously with the implied preference structure (section 10.6). We review the restrictions and flexibility in the representation of collective preferences obtained this way (sections 10.7 and 10.9–11). The different ways of dealing with the specification of $w(\tilde{z})$ are drawn together by a numerical example (section 10.8).

10.2 The case for an explicit preference function

It is generally necessary to reach a compromise between the variables of our planning problem in terms of stochastic deviations from their desired values, even when under certainty those desired values could definitely have been reached, i.e. when $n \geqslant m$ and no instrument penalties apply. Again w has two, possibly conflicting, roles to play in policy selection. It sets the terms of trade between the a priori selectable 'failures' in each variable, meanwhile also setting the terms of trade between the potential random disturbances to those variables from the values we would select for them. The problem is that one may not wish to trade the former type of (known) error at the same rate as the latter (unknown) errors. The point can be illustrated with a simple example.

Consider an economy in real terms:

$$Y = C + G + A$$
$$C = aY \qquad 0 < a < 1 \tag{10.1}$$

where Y = GNP, C = consumption, G = government expenditure and A = other expenditures which may take one of two possible values A_i, $i = 1, 2$. Y is the target and G the instrument such that, under conditions of certainty, any ideal value of Y may be attained. But, given uncertainty over A_i, it will be necessary to trade the relative probable losses incurred by the potential, but unforeseeable, stochastic deviations from that ideal value. In other words, sketching the preference function associated with A_1, and A_2, $w(Y, G, A_i)$, $i = 1, 2$ (figure 10.1), we see that any policy G in the interval $G_1 \leqslant G \leqslant G_2$ dominates the rest in terms of $E(w)$. For some G in the interval (G_1, G_2), $\partial w/\partial G = w_1 > 0$ given A_1 but $\partial w/\partial G = w_2 < 0$ given A_2. If A_1 occurs with probability p then the expected loss to increasing G is pw_1 under A_1, and the expected gain is $(1 - p)w_2$ under A_2. The optimal policy under $E(w)$ is $\hat{G}$, the solution to

$$pw_1 + (1 - p)w_2 = 0. \tag{10.2}$$

The larger p, the more $\hat{G}$ tends towards G_1, and vice versa. We might compare $\hat{G}$ to G^* which has a certain outcome and is the minimax solution (minimising the maximum loss). Now, assuming the symmetric preferences of (7.12), $G^* \simeq \hat{G}$ if $p \simeq \frac{1}{2}$. But in this diagram G^* is a sensible policy, independently of p and $E(w)$, because the gain $L_1 = \min [w(G_1, A_1),$

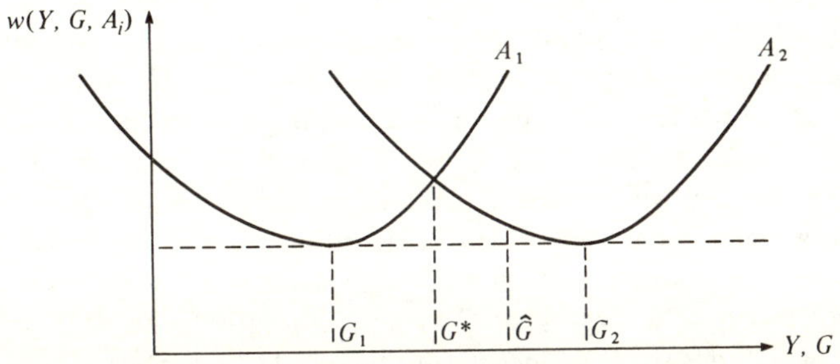

Figure 10.1 Preference functions under uncertainty

$w(G_2, A_2)] - w(G^*)$ is small compared to the loss $L_2 = \max[w(G_1, A_2), w(G_2, A_1)] - w(G^*)$. On the other hand G^* is less attractive if $|L_1/L_2|$ rises, either on account of potential gains forgone or because the losses risked are reduced.

This is an example with one target and instrument. It is sufficient to demonstrate that an objective function is necessary whenever there is uncertainty, and necessary for that reason alone if for no other. The use of an objective function, with an appropriate specification, also allows a qualitative input (represented here by different attitudes to risk) which is an essential ingredient of any planning problem.

Now $E(w)$ appears to be an appropriate criterion if the density function of the stochastic elements is highly skewed and if the preference function is relatively insensitive over the likely range of the policy options. If the density function is less 'compact' (skewed or not) *or* the preference function is highly sensitive (sharply curved) then other criteria might be preferred. But the difficulty is that we cannot generally know the density function of w, or of z; indeed we have gone to considerable lengths to avoid assuming any density functions for them on the argument that to do so was meaningless. Notice that our arguments over the correct criterion to be applied to w in the face of uncertainty are already leading to the consideration of the second, third and fourth moments of the distribution that governs w. That is likely to cause trouble, not only in terms of how to compute appropriate multivariate decision rules from those moments, but also over how to handle the uncertain components in such decision rules. The certainty equivalence type result, as we have seen, will not extend to this sort of situation; and without specifying a full density function we have no substitute for certainty equivalence.

Thus $E(w)$ as a criterion requires some justification despite its invariable use. It is of course one way of treating uncertainty and allows the computation of policies that are optimal on average, but it may not account for risk. There are several other simple criteria that might be considered; for example, a minimised variance $\text{Var}(w)$, or $\min c$ such that $p(w < c) = 0.95$, or a constrained variance $\text{Var}(\tilde{z}) = E(\tilde{z}\tilde{z}')$. We have been informally working towards criteria of this sort with the ad hoc rules for increasing robustness (Chapter 9). The techniques which follow may be regarded as an attempt at formalising those rules. But the actual replacement of $E(w)$ will, however, remain beyond our reach. Nevertheless, we must acknowledge that there is little point in going for a high benefit solution if it has a low probability of being realised, or if there is a reasonable probability of a large loss. One can rationally forgo some expected gain in order to have less uncertainty. It would be foolish to ignore the precision of the chosen policies.

10.3 On the scope for avoiding the a priori specification of preferences

Any particular explicit preference function is evidently an artificial construction – however convenient a concept academically for resolving conflicts between rival variables and rival planning periods. Almost all authors refer to the difficulties posed by the quadratic preference function introduced at (7.10), while continuing to use it. Its main drawbacks are:

(a) no single preference function exists; in fact (7.11) represents the compromise between the individual preferences of all the pressure groups both in and out of government, and possibly between aggregated and detailed objectives, or between economic and noneconomic targets;

(b) it is no more than an approximation of unknown validity to a more general preference function; an approximation which must be revised in the light of changing events, a changing perception of the feasible set, or in view of the performance realised so far;

(c) it makes precise, and explicit, preferences which are possibly imprecise and almost certainly imperfectly known over the domain of the arguments of (7.10),

(d) it is unlikely that anyone can specify truthful preferences for circumstances rather different from their recent economic experience; (7.10) refers to slowly changing circumstances and policies, and is intended to be used by an experienced policy maker.

If the specification of an acceptable, representative and truthful preference function poses such difficulties, it is expedient to decide if its use is both necessary and advantageous. Generalised inverses, as an extension to the simple Tinbergen theory of economic policy, are one way to avoid specifying an explicit criterion. Another popular suggestion is that repeated simulations in the hands of experienced planners will lead to a near-optimal policy selection. Such proposals are common enough in discussing applications, but have attracted little attention in the literature. With the aim of avoiding the a priori specification of an explicit criterion, we first consider these two possibilities as an alternative to a systematic numerical search over feasible explicit approximations to the true, but implicit, criterion used by the planners.

10.3.1 Generalised inverses and policy selection

Without preferences on $\tilde{x}$, we merely wish to obtain values of it to give $\tilde{y}^* = 0$. When $m = n$ and R is nonsingular, the required policies are

$$\tilde{x}^* = -R^{-1}b. \tag{10.3}$$

That is exactly the original Tinbergen theory of economic policy but adapted to a dynamic context, given each $\tilde{x}_t^*$ is recalculated sequentially using the adjustments to R and b in (7.31).

When $n \neq m$ a generalised inverse might be used in (10.3) without calling on a preference function. But generalised inverses are never unique, and different ones give different solutions for $\tilde{x}^*$. To get a unique solution is equivalent to selecting a particular generalised inverse which is conventionally done by choosing one to minimise some norm (see Rao and Mitra (1971)). Any indeterminacy in the recommended policies due to different computational techniques is then avoided. Suppose now R to be of full row rank when $n > m$ (when $RR^+ = I_m$), and of full column rank if $n < m$ (when $R^+R = I_n$), where R^+ is a generalised inverse. We have in place of (10.3)

$$\tilde{x}^* = -R^+b. \tag{10.4}$$

Thus, by (7.9),

$$\tilde{y}^* = (I - RR^+)b. \tag{10.5}$$

When $n > m$ there are an infinite number of possibilities for R^+ giving $\tilde{y}^* = 0$. If we try to shift $n - m$ instruments to b and use (10.3), we are using some preferences over $\tilde{x}$ since those shifted will naturally be set at their x^d values, while those remaining are those for which penalties are lowest. That may, in particular cases, be easier than specifying Q. More generally, each possible $\tilde{x}^*$ yielding $\tilde{y}^* = 0$ is associated with a different R^+ since R is not of full column rank. So we are back to a selection problem, which of course involves a criterion. A natural way to do that is to choose the 'most agreeable' $\tilde{x}^*$. The selection of a p-norm, $p \in [1, \infty]$, which is imposed on $\tilde{x}^*$ in a metric expressed by the positive definite and symmetric matrix A, defines what is meant by 'most agreeable'. We then seek R^+ to minimise $\tilde{x}^*$ of (10.4) in terms of that norm, $\|\tilde{x}^*\|_{p,A}$. Since[1]

$$\|\tilde{x}^*\|_{p,A} = \|R^+b\|_{p,A} \leqslant \|R^+\|_{p,A}\|b\|_p \tag{10.6}$$

we need R^+ to minimise $\|R^+\|_{p,A}$. The most popular norm uses $p = 2$ (Euclidean length). In that case (10.6) becomes

$$\|\tilde{x}^*\|_{2,A} \leqslant \|(R^+)'A^{-1}(R^+)\|_2^{1/2}\|b\|_2 \tag{10.7}$$

for which the minimum is $R^+ = AR'(RAR')^{-1}$. Other choices of p (with more complicated formulae for R^+), such as $p = 1$ or ∞ which measure the average absolute and largest absolute error respectively, are possible.

When $n < m$ no R^+ exists such that $\tilde{y}^* = 0$. Each 'solution' described

1 See Fröberg (1972). One special case is a metric A such that $n - m$ elements of $\tilde{x}^*$ are set to zero.

by (10.5) is associated, again, with each possible generalised inverse where now R is not of full row rank. So again we have a selection problem for R^+. Choosing R^+ with a minimum p-norm in the metric of a given B (of order mT) is equivalent to minimising $\|\tilde{y}^*\|_{p,B}$ because this time

$$\|\tilde{y}^*\|_{p,B} \leqslant \|I - RR^+\|_{p,B}\|b\|_p \leqslant (\rho(B)^{-1} + \|RR^+\|_{p,B})\|b\|_p \quad (10.8)$$

where $\rho(.)$ denotes spectral radius. For $p = 2$, $R^+ = (R'BR)^{-1}R'B$ is the solution to minimise the matrix norm of the first inequality. But, in each case, the generalised inverses have reintroduced implicit preferences.

Finally, the most interesting case is when we try to combine (10.4) and (10.5); that is to get $\tilde{y}^*$ as close to zero as practicable without letting $\tilde{x}^*$ get too large. Ignoring preferences this amounts to finding the generalised inverse $(H^*)^+$ as a solution to the simultaneous equations which replace (7.2):

$$\begin{pmatrix} \tilde{y} \\ e \end{pmatrix} = \begin{pmatrix} R \\ I \end{pmatrix} \tilde{x} + \begin{pmatrix} b \\ 0 \end{pmatrix} = H^*\tilde{x} + \begin{pmatrix} b \\ 0 \end{pmatrix}. \quad (10.9)$$

H^* is never of full row rank, so the solution is always of the form (10.8). A unique solution requires a minimum norm generalised inverse; e.g. for $p = 2$, and writing Q for B, (10.8) gives $(H^*)^+ = (H^{*\prime}QH^*)^{-1}H^{*\prime}Q$ which, put into (10.4), is exactly the optimal policies given by (7.18). This case contains the previous two examples as special cases. It is also the typical case in that failures to reach both ideal target and instrument values are penalised singly and jointly in all planning periods.

Hence the obvious requirement for a unique policy recommendation, as opposed to a set of possibilities dependent solely on the computational techniques, means a generalised inverse solution is indistinguishable from that using a preference function, (7.10), with z^d defined as the unconstrained minimum of (7.11).

10.3.2 The regression analogy

The formulae above bear an obvious resemblance to generalised least squares regression formulae. This is not fortuitous. Noting from (10.9) that $\tilde{z}^*$ cannot be set to zero by choice of $\tilde{x}^*$, we have until now minimised the sum of squares of the errors in some metric Q,

$$\min_{\tilde{x}} \begin{pmatrix} \tilde{y} \\ e \end{pmatrix}' Q \begin{pmatrix} \tilde{y} \\ e \end{pmatrix} \text{ s.t. } H\tilde{z} = b \text{ and } e = \tilde{x}. \quad (10.10)$$

In approaching the problem as one of least squares regression we set $\tilde{x}$ to minimise the errors $\tilde{y}$ of the model $b = -R\tilde{x} + \tilde{y}$. We also have the non-orthogonal prior information that x should approximate x^d; and the errors e of $x^d = x - e$ should be jointly minimised with $\tilde{y}$ in the metric Q. The Theil and Goldberger (1961) generalised least squares mixed estimator for non-spherically distributed errors is the well known solution, and it is displayed in (7.18) and (10.9) when $q = 0$. x^* plays the role of model parameters; $\tilde{y}^*$ the fitting errors; y^* the systematic part; and Q plays the role of the inverted error covariance matrix across equations and time. Since b is in fact stochastic, first period certainty equivalent $\tilde{z}^*$ values are conditional means for, respectively, the 'model's fitting errors' (i.e. the estimated residuals of a model with the constant suppressed, since $\tilde{y}^*$ has nonzero expectation) and 'the model parameters', $\tilde{x}^*$. The analogy does not, however, extend to questions of inference. For example, the normal parameter variance formulae are invalid since Q^{-1} does not actually equal the 'error' covariance matrix. Yet suboptimality is not implied for our policies since the risk function is finite when R is fixed (by counterexample in Harkema (1975)). So the criterion conforms to this analogy.

Thus if $[B$ and $C] \to 0$ the solution corresponds to that of absolutely certain 'prior knowledge' over $\tilde{x}$, relative to the penalties on $\tilde{y}$. Then $x^* = x^d$, showing that simulation is indeed a special case of optimal control. Therefore, every other simulation strategy, $x^* \neq x^d$, which corresponds to a point on the Pareto optimal frontier, is generated by altering the balance of B to A and varying the relative penalties within A (or equivalently within B); x^d fixed. These simulations could always be constructed, for example, from[2]

$$dz^* = (\tilde{z}^{*\prime} \otimes \Phi)(\text{vec}\, dQ) \tag{10.11}$$

where there are $\frac{1}{2}(n+m)T((n+m)T+1)-2$ unrestricted elements in Q but $(n+m)T$ in dz^*. But to set Q to pick that set of feasible deviations in $\tilde{z}$ which, at the same time, is also most desirable is extremely difficult. It could be done on a trial and error basis, which is equivalent to repeated and certainly very extensive simulations. Numerical search procedures would make this systematic but ultimately the most efficient method is the optimisation of policies, leading directly to the final point in that sequence of simulations. This is what we propose to do.

If, on the other hand $[A$ and $C] \to 0$, the solution corresponds to no instrument restrictions (no prior information) and we see the best solution available, in terms of $\|\tilde{y}\|_{2,B}$, given a free hand with the policies.

10.3.3 Simulation as a special case of policy optimisation

The suggestion that repeated simulations might substitute for policy optimisation implies that the experienced planner has only an idea

2 See equation (9.25). Symmetry, positive definiteness and a normalisation are required in $Q: n \geqslant 1$, $m \geqslant 1$, $T > 1$. A solution always exists despite Φ not being of full rank because both z^* and $z^* + dz^*$ are feasible if both are to be simulation results.

of his preference ordering and the feasible set for z, rather than precise knowledge of the appropriate specification for $w(\tilde{z})$. The planner may not always be so experienced. In this context 'experienced' means an intimate understanding of the government's priorities over the feasible set for various different economic circumstances. If these circumstances are rapidly changing, this kind of experience may not be available; and it requires a different insight from that acquired merely by long service. The complexity, interdependence and dynamics in most models can often leave the planner unable to correct, sequentially, his instruments in desirable directions. He may never approach an acceptable policy, or he may zigzag around the acceptable region.

If $w(\tilde{z})$ is known a priori, in the sense of giving acceptable policies, then policy optimisation is obviously preferable to searching among simulation results. When $w(\tilde{z})$ is not known accurately a priori, searching among the results of a few optimising exercises is still preferable. First, each candidate corresponds to the optimal result, obtained in one step rather than from a subset of simulations, given a trial version of $w(\tilde{z})$. Second, the set of candidates is restricted to points on the Pareto optimal frontier. Unnecessary and irrelevant candidates are removed from the decision process. Be that as it may, the real gains to efficiency are in the reduction of interactions between man and model. Typically 'man' is a committee, so simplified decision making, and error elimination, can be valuable. To constrain the number of optimisations required, a systematic search can be used to modify the outcome at each step towards preferred policies specified by the planner; and a start is made closer to the finish by using a version of $w(\tilde{z})$ implicit in the historical policies of the most similar set of recent circumstances. One scheme is described in section 10.5 below. To put numerical values on the preferred result (which will presumably still be infeasible by a small distance) some experimentation may be necessary to indicate what is and is not possible. Therefore, the start may be augmented with the results of the polar cases mentioned: simulation with ideal instrument values, and the lower bound to $\| \tilde{y}^* \|_2$.

10.4 Axioms of choice, implicit preferences, and the maintained hypothesis of planning behaviour

We have now established that it is effectively impossible to avoid some representation of collective preferences – either implicitly or explicitly – in describing the policy formation process. But an agreed criterion becomes problematic if there are many options to choose from. To make matters worse the set of policies acceptable to the policy makers is typically very restricted, as pointed out by De Wolff and Sandee (1959). That means the policy options are usually only clearly distinguished qualitatively rather than numerically.

In that case, it is best to start from scratch by reviewing what exactly the preference function can and cannot be expected to represent. So next we build up the preference function characteristics from an axiomatic base. Then in the following section we build up the specification of a particular $w(\tilde{z})$ to reflect the preferences implicit when certain policy options are chosen in favour of others. When $w(\tilde{z})$ is unknown, the only information we have on it is contained in such choices. And, in as much as the preferences remain implicit in those choices, we can at least avoid specifying any preference function a priori. Following this line leads to the interactive planning algorithm of the following section, extended to treat multiple policy makers and committee planning behaviour.

10.4.1 Individual preferences

If values are rationally chosen for $\tilde{z}$ then some index of economic performance can be associated with each $\tilde{z}$ value. The ability to do no more than rank $\tilde{z}$ values (which is the direct consequence of presuming rational choices as a behavioural theory for individual decision makers) implies the index is an ordinal preference function for $\tilde{z}$,

$$w = w(\tilde{z}) \tag{10.12}$$

which satisfies the minimal set of axioms consistent with rational choices. These axioms are *reflexivity* and *completeness* to yield a properly defined set of options; and *transitivity* so that a consistent preference ordering exists, plus *convexity* so that an optimal choice for z can be represented by minimising (10.12). Any agent may be said to follow an implicit preference function of this type. $w(\tilde{z})$ then represents preferences between rival targets and instruments, and the trade-offs between conflicting values over time. These preferences are expressed as relative penalties on failing to reach the desired values in each component of z. These relative economic priorities are traditionally displayed in the form of the decreasing marginal rates of substitution:

$$\frac{dz_i}{dz_j} = \frac{-\partial w/\partial z_j}{\partial w/\partial z_i} = \rho_{ij} \quad i, j = 1, \ldots, (m+n)T. \tag{10.13}$$

A rational choice is defined as picking x to minimise $w(\tilde{z})$ – or any monotonic transformation of it – while also satisfying the model (7.9). Agents therefore aim for the global unconstrained minimum of $w(\tilde{z})$, which, by definition, is given by z^d. We cannot exclude the possibility that z^d is infinite in some elements and finite in others. Consumption (more goods being preferred to less) is an example of the former; unemployment, inflation, or the balance of payments are examples of the latter. Economic theory suggests output and employment might be planned to grow at their 'natural' levels. Thus, monotonicity cannot belong to the axioms; $w(\tilde{z})$ is at most monotonic in the two half-planes defined by z^d. That, in turn, rules out linear programming (e.g. Cochrane (1975)) as a policy selection technique because wherever the coordinate policy axes (with z^d as origin) intersect the feasible set the optimal policies will be indeterminate. The minimisation of $w(\tilde{z})$, subject to (7.9), is only a legitimate characterisation of a rational choice *provided* z^d does indeed represent the ideal.

Rational choices, however, imply agents optimise their own perceived self-interest (including 'satisficing') in the form of $w(\tilde{z})$. The foregoing axioms of choice need not be extended further if a game theoretic approach is adopted to determine the best z value (as, for example, in Hughes Hallett and Ancot (1982)). But, and strictly only for convenience, we shall treat $w(\tilde{z})$ here as if it were continuous and smooth, and hence differentiable. The convenience is to avoid specifying the precise game theoretic strategy followed. The point is that it is necessary to avoid imputing any particular criterion of success, and thereby any specific preference functional form, to decision makers through the maintained hypothesis of the decision model. Moreover, differentiation is also neutral as to the process by which an optimal choice is derived, and therefore imposes no extra restrictions on the maintained hypothesis.

Whether we consider $w(\tilde{z})$ for an individual or collectively, the criterion of success is seldom clearly or simply defined. In macroeconomic planning the criterion is not just maximising some variables, and the minimisation or stabilisation of others. Nor is it just vote maximisation, vote share maximisation, the maximisation of the utility of politicians and administrators, maximising the tenure of office, or extending one's power base, etc. It is a combination of all these. Similarly market share maximisation, sales maximisation, growth, integration, and diversification as well as profit maximisation are all possible criteria in models of firm behaviour. For a commodity market, the aim may be redistributional as well as to raise or to stabilise the producers price. It is important not to restrict the maintained hypothesis a priori, or prejudice the model of planning behaviour by imputing any specific criteria when setting the form of the relative priorities in $w(\tilde{z})$. That is why it is necessary to relax the maintained hypothesis as far as possible by assuming no more than rational choices by the planners. So we impose the minimal set of axioms of choice necessary to guarantee a consistent preference ordering. Indeed the validity of $w(\tilde{z})$ as an objective, such as social welfare, 'national interest', etc., depends on such an interpretation. And only in this way can we be sure that any results, either for policies or for preferences, stand or fall with just those axioms rather than with any particular assumed objective function or any particular imputed (even if unintentionally) criteria of success.

10.4.2 Collective preferences

There is a second reason why a model of planning behaviour should be specified with implicit preference functions. In the economic context the specification of a $w(\tilde{z})$ suitable for formulating collective decisions can never generally be known perfectly a priori. There may be uncertainty as to the existence of collective preferences, doubt as to the precise specification of relative preferences particularly for areas of economic performance different from recent experience, or for larger subspaces of F, or uncertainty over the correct specification of preferences in a form acceptable to all contributors to the planning process. There are also issues in the qualitative design of policies to be incorporated into $w(\tilde{z})$ (e.g. the degree of risk aversion; measures of robustness, co-ordination, or continuity in policies, etc.) which do not admit a precise mathematical or numerical specification. But, the basic difficulty in specifying preference functions a priori is that no one person can fully know the preference sets of the other contributors to the policy process; that is before consideration of how they should, or could, be aggregated. Since planning involves several individual participants, either within one planning agency or through the interaction of bodies of decision makers, policies will emerge from the deliberations of those planners as a negotiated solution. Moreover, the relative influence of each participant may vary with events. Hence our representation of preferences must prejudge neither the bargaining process nor the route by which collective decisions are made.

These points are crucial in representing the behaviour of a self-managed system because decisions are scarcely ever taken (if ever at all) by one single omnipotent dictator without the influence of advisors and other contributors to policy formation, and without the influence of other interdependent interest groups also in the same 'policy game'. This applies to an aggregate view of organisational behaviour. At a national level decisions are influenced by the individual interests of the government, organised labour, the business community, the administrators, and national security, etc. At an industry level specific government agencies, particular trade unions and individual managements negotiate between and among themselves. This applies equally in a microview of organisations. A government is composed of individual cabinet (or politburo) members; trade unions have executive councils, and aggregate to a confederation; a firm has a board of directors, etc. Not only may these different decision makers have different variables and different priorities in their own preferences, but they may also judge success by altogether different criteria. Therefore our preference structures must not restrict the criteria which the different agents might apply.

10.5 A model of planning behaviour

As in Chapter 7, we take a second order approximation to (10.12) about some feasible $\tilde{z}^*$

$$w = \tfrac{1}{2}\tilde{z}'Q\tilde{z} + q'\tilde{z} + \text{constant} \tag{10.14}$$

where $Q = \left(\dfrac{\partial^2 w}{\partial z \partial z'}\right)_{\tilde{z}^*}$ and $q = -Q\tilde{z}^* + \left(\dfrac{\partial w}{\partial z}\right)_{\tilde{z}^*}$. The point made clear by (10.14) is that the relative penalties on the 'failures', $\tilde{z}$, appropriate for the specification of $w(\tilde{z})$ must generally depend on the trajectory chosen for evaluation. For reasons given below (section 10.8) and as the converse of the insensitivity found in Chapter 9, we should perhaps expect these penalties to be sensitive to small changes in $\tilde{z}^*$ values. And strictly $\tilde{z}^*$ should be the policy choice which we are trying to determine.

10.5.1 The inadequacy of the linear-quadratic decision model

Therefore we need (10.14) to obtain $\tilde{z}^*$, and also $\tilde{z}^*$ to obtain (10.14). That is the classical predicament in minimising nonquadratic functions analytically; and there are several well known numerical search procedures which solve this difficulty although the solution to, say, (7.13), when $w(\tilde{z})$ is nonquadratic but known, cannot be written algebraically in terms of $w(\tilde{z})$, H and b. Perhaps the obvious technique is a variable metric algorithm, since that introduces an explicit updating of a Hessian matrix which converges on the matrix of second derivatives of $w(\tilde{z})$ when the minimum of that function is reached.

Hence, the selection of optimal economic policies inevitably involves the simultaneous determination of the associated (approximate) preference structure; or, put another way, that policy selection is equivalent to solving a nonquadratic programming problem. That conclusion is reached either by arguing that $w(\tilde{z})$ cannot be known a priori and so cannot be assumed to be quadratic, or by arguing that any quadratic preference function over economic variables can only be realistically interpreted as an approximation to some more general function. In fact, even where quadratic preferences are the correct specification, being uncertain of the precise values for Q and comparing the policies from a few trial versions will lead to solving a problem which is equivalent to a nonquadratic minimisation. Therefore we would anyway face the logical difficulty of specifying preferences which are dependent on unknown values of the policy variables in order that they may determine what these values should best be. Hence, the linear-quadratic form of decision model is inappropriate for economic planning unless it is embedded within some search procedure for the optimal policy values.

10.5.2 The decision model: implicit preferences and the individual planner[3]

Consider first how a single planner would actually select optimal policies as his proposal. Suppose he takes some sequence of candidate policies $z^{(s)} \in F$; $s = 0, 1 \ldots$ His selection process is to rank the candidates according to

$$\| z^{(s+1)} - z_p \|_2 < \| z^{(s)} - z_p \|_2 \qquad (10.15)$$

where z_p is any *preferred*, 'second best', but generally infeasible policy while z^d remains the ideal. We can allow z_p to be updated during these comparisons, where necessary, in order to maintain it as preferred to all the candidates considered so far. The policy finally selected will be the final member of the $\tilde{z}^{(s)}$ sequence, $\tilde{z}^{(p)}$ say, introduced by (10.15).

Within each individual planner's scale of preferences we assume that some z_p exists preferred to $z^{(s)}$, and that the intersection of F and the set of z values acceptable to the planner is nonempty. If each member of the sequence $\{\tilde{z}^{(s)}\}$ is the constrained optimum of (10.14), corresponding to each member of the possibility set $\{Q^{(s)}\}$ for Q, then z_p is any point such that $w(\tilde{z}_p) < w(\tilde{z}^{(i)})$ $i = 0 \ldots s$. All that is required of z_p is that it be no less highly valued than the latest $z^{(s)}$, and preferred in at least one element. Thus z_p would probably be set by making modifications to $z^{(s)}$ in the direction of z^d; i.e. in terms of preferred mean levels or changes (frequency, size, direction, timing, etc.) or variances, for one or more policy variables to the planning horizon. Adjustments to $z^{(s)}$ in terms of covariances would probably also be included. The covariances reflect any requirements for coordination between two or more variables, at each planning interval or over different planning intervals. For example, expenditures and revenues must move up or down in step if a balanced budget is desired, or at least with a lag if imbalances are acceptable only in the short run. This example extends readily to firms, international trade payments, etc. Similarly movements in consumption and investment should be compensatory to stabilise aggregate demand. Thus to adjust policy levels in the specifications of any z_p is to change the priorities

3 Recall the sequence of simulations in De Wolff and Sandee (1959), discussed in Chapter 4, as a demonstration of this type of planning.

on achieving low values in $\tilde{z}$, or to remove extreme policy values. z_p can also be set to remove sudden or frequent reversals of policies, to reduce persistent failures in one policy or coincident failures of two policies, or to offset particular events.

The description of z_p suggests that it would also involve elements to induce robustness in both $w(\tilde{z})$ and $z^{(s)}$ against stochastic shocks from either model or information errors. These qualitative characteristics of preferences are in addition to the numerical adjustments mentioned above. Thus z_p will also be set to reflect the planners' own preoccupations with such things as risk, policy types, the importance of coordination and timing of policy impacts, the value of intervention or continuity in policies, or confidence, and so on. Evidently the policy maker must use his implicit, but unspecified, preferences to set z_p. The important point is that if it is difficult to specify the quantitative priorities in $w(\tilde{z})$ adequately, for the various qualitative characteristics it is impossible. These more subtle characteristics are less clearly distinguished in the planners' minds and seldom admit a precise or unique definition, let alone a numerical representation.

One final reason for stressing the difficulties in specifying an objective function a priori, and the value of introducing the more difficult aspects of preferences via z_p, is because risk aversion and political acceptability together may well be such that the qualitative design is more important in an economic environment than the precise policy values selected. The planner's first priority usually is to generate policies which incorporate these qualitative characteristics whatever their particular values. Indeed, the most common experience reported by planners involved in actual exercises run by planning institutions is that final decisions are made between relatively few options which are only clearly distinguished qualitatively or politically, rather than numerically. This makes clear what is demanded by those who face the uncertain and political nature of economic planning in practice; and so it is that which the objective function of a self-managed economic system must be capable of describing. To induce these characteristics via z_p and interactive planning, rather than in $w(\tilde{z})$ a priori, is essential not so much because that is easier but because it is almost certainly the only way to do so.

10.5.3 The decision model: the policy selection

We next suppose the policy maker picks a sequence of z_p vectors in order to sample the Pareto optimal frontier of F with respect to z^d. Each z_p is picked as one in a series of experiments to locate which feasible positions are preferable to each $z^{(s)}$; and therefore *ultimately* to locate the preferred feasible position (the policy proposal) while z^d remains the ideal. We define each z_p to ensure a systematic search of the frontier, but otherwise the switch from one z_p to another (when, and by how much) is unrestricted. The definition of z_p ensures the eventual convergence of any z_p sequence given the convexity of $w(\tilde{z})$. Our scheme now has an inner iteration in $z^{(s)}$, and an outer one in z_p; but that in $z^{(s)}$ need not be fully exploited. If the inner iteration is completed we obtain the solution, for a given z_p, to

$$z^{(p)} = \min_{z} \{ \|z - z_p\|_2 \text{ s.t. } Hz - s\} \tag{10.16}$$

$$\text{i.e.} \quad z^{(p)} = (I - H'(HH')^{-1}H)z_p + H'(HH')^{-1}s. \tag{10.17}$$

Evidently (10.17) is a special case of (7.16) with $Q = I$, $z_p = z^d$ and $q = 0$. Consider any point on the Pareto optimal frontier of F; say $z^{(0)}$ generated by (7.16) with $Q = Q^{(0)}$ and z^d. Now consider any other arbitrary point on that frontier, say $z^* = z^{(0)} + dz^*$. Since z^* is also feasible, $Hdz^* = 0$. The optimisation to give z^* would, if the appropriate Q were known, be (7.16), from which

$$Pz^d = z^* - Q^{-1}[H'(HQ^{-1}H')^{-1}(s + HQ^{-1}q) - q] \tag{10.18}$$

where $P = I - Q^{-1}H'(HQ^{-1}H')^{-1}H$. If z^d were altered, then

$$dz^* = Pdz^d. \tag{10.19}$$

Now $r(P) = nT < (n+m)T$ where $r(.)$ denotes rank. Thus $r(P, dz^*) \leqslant r(P) < (n+m)T$. Hence at least one solution exists for dz^d given such an arbitrary dz^* since $H(P, dz^*) = 0$. Yet $H \neq 0$ (having rank mT by construction). So every feasible policy, rationally chosen with respect to z^d and according to some admissible preferences, may be generated by fixing $Q = Q^{(0)}$ and varying z^d as necessary within (7.16). One particular case is given by $Q^{(0)} = I$ and with z^d replaced by the z_p sequence; i.e. (10.17). Therefore it is only necessary for the planner to experiment with different z_p values in order to sample the entire Pareto optimal frontier of F.

On the other hand, every feasible z^* can also be generated by varying Q over the set of positive definite, symmetric, normalised matrices while z^d is fixed (Chapter 9). One way of doing that is given below at (10.23) and (10.24). We therefore have two fully equivalent search procedures for policy selection. One keeps preferences implicit in the z_p values (i.e. Q fixed, z^d iterated); the other makes the preferences explicit (i.e. z^d fixed, Q iterated).[4]

4 Chow (1981) provides some interesting illustrations of tracing the best available unemployment–inflation trade-offs by varying either z^d or Q, other things remaining equal. Exactly the same information is provided by successive $z^{(p)}$ values. The advantages of (10.17) are: (a) only vector multiplications, rather than repeated optimisations, are involved; (b) the trade-off traced is from a directed rather than a grid search.

Again policy selection and the 'estimation' of preferences are two facets of the same problem, and the same interactive planning mechanism therefore permits the analysis of two interesting but separate problems. Given any policy selection $z^{(p)}$, where $w(\tilde{z})$ is unknown, the preferences implicit in that choice (up to a quadratic approximation at $z^{(p)}$) may be recovered by running pseudo policy iterations from an arbitrary start to $z^{(p)}$, through the 'preferences explicit' algorithm. Of course, this depends on establishing convergence and how far the results may be uniquely interpreted as preferences. Sections 10.6 and 10.8 take up those points. Alternatively, given any policy (z_p) preferred to the current situation or choice ($z^{(s)}$), where $w(\tilde{z})$ is imperfectly known, we can generate an improved policy recommendation by running actual policy iterations *either* through the 'preferences implicit' algorithm, *or* through the 'preferences explicit' one if the preference structure is also of interest. In other words, although we argued earlier that $w(\tilde{z})$ could never be accurately known a priori in economic policy problems, two important situations may still be examined. They are when $z^{(p)}$ is known but $w(\tilde{z})$ is not; or when neither is known completely but the implicit function $w(\tilde{z})$ is known at least to the extent that a 'downhill' direction can be specified from every $\tilde{z}^{(s)} \in F$. The former is the converse to the forward planning problem and is the classic situation for the estimation of revealed preferences. We have argued that the latter, rather than when $w(\tilde{z})$ is known accurately a priori, is the typical situation for the forward planning of an economy.

10.5.4 Collective decisions and individual preferences: planning by committee

It is in the nature of a participatory political system that planners propose but voters dispose. Within any policy committee there will be interactive 'bargaining' between individual proposals and the associated disposals, or rankings, accorded to them by the committee members. We need a model of committee decisions, in which members both propose and dispose. To base that model on a 'representative' planner is unlikely to be satisfactory; the implied aggregation errors would be the items of greatest interest, and they would not be mutually compensating.

The advantage of modelling policy decisions by the interactive bargaining approach of (10.17) is that it permits all candidate policies to be compared independently of any *explicit* preference specifications. Consequently, provided F and the segment which forms the Pareto optimal frontier remain fixed, *any* rationally chosen candidate policy proposal contributed by *any* participant to the planning process may be modelled by (10.17) despite the differences in the preferences which underlie those proposals, simply by inserting that participant's own considered choice of z_p. For this proviso to hold on F we need a unified view of the economic system (i.e. of R and s) and agreement on z^d. A considered choice of z_p means one arrived at by the process described above for the individual planner. Now agreement over R, s and z^d cannot be a foregone conclusion among any group of policy makers. But a wide measure of agreement will exist within the planning committees of one ministry, political party, board of directors, or pressure group within some planning structure, etc.; whereas it is certainly most improbable across the electorate or outside such groups. The fact that the planners agree to provide a unified plan is tacit admission that their views do not differ so much as to make a compromise on R, s and z^d impossible. A unified plan means that no individual attempts to force the implementation of any value for $\tilde{z}_i^*$ (under his control) in defiance of a solution agreed with the others. But it does imply that z may only cover policies which can fairly be said to be under the planners' control.

Therefore, within any planning group cohesive enough to agree on R, s and z^d, consider an interactive bargaining game in successive rounds between the individual planners and the model first, and then between the planners themselves. Each planner selects, as above, the best z_p and $z^{(p)}$ in terms of his own version of (10.14). If the set of $z^{(p)}$ values are not all the same, we move to the next round in which each player must replace his z_p by a linear combination of all the z_ps in play, with weights in the open interval $[0, 1]$ and summing to unity. This ensures each new z_p is an interior point on the hyperpolygon formed by the old z_ps. The game is repeated until the set of $z^{(p)}$s generated are all identical. That situation follows because if z_p in (10.17) is replaced by $A^*\lambda_j$, where $\lambda_j' = [\lambda_{1j} \cdots \lambda_{kj}]$ with $0 < \lambda_{ij} < 1$ and $A^* = [z_{p-1,1} \cdots z_{p-1,k}]$ for k planners, then each planner obtains his own proposal in the next round as

$$z_j^{(p)} = (I - H'(HH')^{-1} H)A^*\lambda_j + H'(HH')^{-1} s \qquad (10.20)$$

which is a linear combination lying interior to the set of previous proposals. The last remark follows because (10.20) is reproduced, and the same $z_j^{(p)}$ set obtained, if $A^{(p-1)} = [z_1^{(p-1)} \dots z_k^{(p-1)}]$ replaces A^*. Since the interactive scheme, which describes the choices of each player, operates with an arbitrary preference representation there is no loss in assuming that $Q_j = I$, $q_j = 0$ were applied. If in fact that were not the case, it would only be necessary to find an associated $z_{p-1,j}$ implied by $Q_j = I$ and the announced $z_j^{(p-1)}$. In other words, the same sequence of sets of $z_j^{(p)}$ proposals will be obtained from (10.20), provided $A^{(p-1)}$ replaces A^*, even if no player knows the Q and z_p values being used by other players. Hence, we get exactly the same contractions in $z^{(p)}$s as are implied for the z_ps; and eventual convergence is inevitable if $0 < \lambda_{ij} < 1$. So it is immaterial whether the players construct their new proposals from a combination of the $z^{(p)}$s or of the z_ps. The former is more natural, and may be less liable to tactical misrepresentation since it might be adopted at any stage. There is no attempt, however, to make the proposals 'tactics proof' since we are describing a bargaining game in which tactics are of the essence. They would be worked out in the voting procedure which follows.

The vector λ_j may be rationalised as the proportions, or probabilities, of a vote which that particular planner is prepared to allocate to each of the most recently declared proposals (including his own). The rules of the game specify that each proportion be strictly less than unity, which is justified by the necessity to force agreement over the proposals within a planning group in the face of potential competition in policy supply and by the necessity to act within given periods of time. In fact, if the jth planner optimised his vote distribution he would vote to produce his optimal combination of policy proposals. He would solve

$$\min_{\lambda_j} \{w_j(\tilde{z}) \mid e_k'\lambda_j = 1, \text{ and } z = A^{(p)}\lambda_j\} \tag{10.21}$$

to obtain

$$\lambda_j^* = (A^{(p)\prime}Q_jA^{(p)})^{-1}(A^{(p)\prime}Q_jz_j^d + f_je_k) \quad j = 1, \ldots, k \tag{10.22}$$

with

$$f_j = \frac{1 - e_k'(A^{(p)\prime}Q_jA^{(p)})^{-1}A^{(p)\prime}Q_jz_j^d}{e_k'(A^{(p)\prime}Q_jA^{(p)})^{-1}e_k} \text{ and } e_k' = (1, \ldots, 1) \text{ of length } k.$$

Notice that $\lambda_{ij} \leqslant 1$ is guaranteed if $\lambda_{ij} \geqslant 0$ holds. The latter may be verified independently. Indeed, strict inequalities will be forced unless $z_j^d = z_j^{(p)}$ or $z_j^d = z_{p,j}$ if each player works and votes in terms of z_ps. The former is impossible. The latter, however, implies $\lambda_{ij} = \begin{cases} 1 & i = j \\ 0 & i \neq j \end{cases}$. So $z_j^d \neq z_{p,j}$ supplies the required rules of the game. Convergence in this scheme follows despite differences in preferences (and without considering a 'representative' planner which would run counter to each proposing as well as disposing) because of the convergence in z_ps.

By virtue of its interactive nature, this model of planning behaviour is designed so that all points of the Pareto optimal frontier of F are implicitly sampled and evaluated by each of the planners. Policies then emerge from the committee's deliberations as a negotiated solution between the individual choices. That negotiated solution may be reached either by an interactive procedure (iterating z_p) or by respecifying the preference structure (iterating Q). So we may speak of a surrender of individual preferences or of interactive policy adjustments as being equivalent in the conversion of individual choices into a collective choice.

10.6 Estimating preferences: the 'preferences explicit' algorithm

It remains to define a numerical search which solves for (10.14) and (7.16) simultaneously, given some z_p. We apply the algorithm examined by Hughes Hallett and Ancot (1982). It supplies the inner iterations of interactive planning, for which (10.16) and the z_p sequence were the outer iterations; and it gives numerical form to the preferences implicit in z_p.

At convergence, a variable metric optimisation algorithm supplies a quadratic approximation to the objective function (Dixon (1975)). The variable metric algorithm requires only the 'downhill' property (i.e. $w(\tilde{z}^{(s+1)}) < w(\tilde{z}^{(s)})$), and knowledge of $[\partial w/\partial z]_{z^{(s+1)}} - [\partial w/\partial z]_{z^{(s)}}$ at each step s. Provided that $z^{(s)}$ is the constrained minimum of the current approximation to $w(\tilde{z})$, the latter can be approximated by $\phi_s Q^{(s)} \delta^{(s)}$ where $\delta^{(s)} = z_p - z^{(s)}$. The symmetric rank one version then implies

$$Q^{(s+1)} = Q^{(s)} + \frac{(\phi_s - 1)}{c^{(s)}} Q^{(s)} \delta^{(s)} \delta^{(s)\prime} Q^{(s)} \qquad (10.23)$$

and

$$z^{(s+1)} = z^{(s)} + \alpha_s P^{(s)} \delta^{(s)} \qquad (10.24)$$

where

$$\alpha_s = \frac{(\phi_s - 1)a^{(s)}}{(\phi_s - 1)b^{(s)} - \phi_s c^{(s)}}; \quad a^{(s)} = \delta^{(s)\prime} Q^{(s)} \tilde{z}^{(s)};$$

$b^{(s)} = \delta^{(s)\prime} Q^{(s)} (I - P^{(s)}) \delta^{(s)}$; and $c^{(s)} = \delta^{(s)\prime} Q^{(s)} \delta^{(s)}$. Finally $P^{(s)}$ is P evaluated at $Q^{(s)}$.

The fact that $\delta^{(s)}$ contains z_p in place of $z^{(s+1)}$ is a further approximation to the true symmetric rank one algorithm. However, the resulting differences between the direction vectors (and *hence* the iterates) in (10.24) and the true algorithm vanish at convergence, if that follows. These two approximations thus prevent any appeal to standard convergence results for variable metric algorithms.

The fixed points $z^{(p)} = \lim_{s\to\infty} z^{(s)}$ and $Q^{(p)} = \lim_{s\to\infty} Q^{(s)}$ are obtained from the iterations (10.23) and (10.24) given an arbitrary symmetric, positive definite $Q^{(0)}$, and arbitrary fixed values z_p and z^d. This may be shown as follows:[5]

5 See Hughes Hallett and Ancot (1982) for proofs. This use of (10.23) and (10.24) is developed from the respecification algorithm suggested in Rustem, Vellupillai and Westcott (1978).

(a) $0 < \alpha_{s-1} < 2$ ensures a strict inequality in (10.15)
(b) $Q^{(s)}$ is positive (semi) definite if $Q^{(s-1)}$ was also, and $\phi_{s-1} > 0(\geqslant 0)$.
(c) $\lim_{s \to \infty} \alpha_s = 0$ is necessary and sufficient to obtain these fixed points.
(d) If (a) and (b) are to be satisfied then $\alpha_s \in [0, \min(2, a^{(s)}/(b^{(s)} - c^{(s)}))]$ whenever $a^{(s)} < 0$ but $\alpha_s \in [0, \min(2, a^{(s)}/b^{(s)})]$ when $a^{(s)} \geqslant 0$.
(e) $\lim\{a_s = \lambda_s a^{(s)}/(b^{(s)} - c^{(s)})\} = 0$ if $a^{(0)} < 0$, provided only that λ_s is chosen in the closed interval $[\lambda_{\min}, \lambda_{\max}]$; where $\lambda_{\min} = \max\left[0, \dfrac{(b^{(s)} - c^{(s)})(2a^{(s)} + c^{(s)})}{(a^{(s)})^2 + b^{(s)}(2a^{(s)} + c^{(s)})}\right]$ and $\lambda_{\max} = \min[1, 2(b^{(s)} - c^{(s)})/a^{(s)}]$. Then $a^{(s)} \leqslant a^{(s-1)} < 0$. Moreover $\lambda_{\max} - \lambda_{\min} > 0$ if $a^{(s)} < 0$; and for $\lambda_{\min} \leqslant \lambda_s \leqslant \lambda_{\max}$ the interval is a non-decreasing function of s.
(f) If $a^{(0)} \geqslant 0$ set $\alpha_0 = a^{(0)}/b^{(0)}$. (10.23) and (10.24) give $a^{(1)} = 0$. Replace $a^{(1)}$ by d where $-c^{(1)} < d < 0$. (10.23) and (10.24) give $a^{(2)} < 0$. Proceed by steps (a) to (e) above, from $z^{(2)}$ and $Q^{(2)}$.

Simpler restrictions, such as $0 < \alpha_{s-1} \leqslant 1$ for example, are neither necessary nor sufficient for convergence. The point made here is firstly that convergence in $z^{(s)}$ coincides with that in $Q^{(s)}$; secondly that the positive definiteness of $Q^{(s)}$ is retained throughout; and thirdly that global convergence is implied.

Finally, pseudo policy iterations replace z_p with a given policy choice.

10.6.1 The necessity for convergence

We reiterate the necessity of converging as closely to the final z_p as possible. The reasons are as follows.

Without convergence, how is one $z^{(s)}$ to be recommended before another, and what is then the stopping rule? Any such policy recommendations are arbitrary and non-unique, even if z_p were unique. This basic point can be put more provocatively by citing the difficulties which would ensue:

(1) Without convergence the policy maker can be induced to accept a policy which reflects neither his preferences nor what is ultimately possible. Suppose he adopts the rule 'I accept the first $z^{(s)}$ in $\|z^{(s)} - z_p\| < \varepsilon$' for some $\varepsilon > 0$. Then an unscrupulous advisor could arrange to finish in whichever particular position best suits his own tastes and prejudices yet satisfies that rule, just by choice of $\alpha_s, s = 0 \ldots$ Likewise a coalition member may attempt to force his own preferred solution on his partners, not by voting strength or legitimate bargaining but by trying to control the convergence path (if not the stopping rule as well) via $Q^{(0)}$ and $\alpha_s, s = 0 \ldots$

(2) Since z_p can be approached from many directions there would still be grounds for disagreement between policy makers on the basis of their individual preferences.

(3) Alternatively the coalition partner or advisor might arrange to 'hang around' his own favoured area until the policy maker gives up and accepts $z^{(s)}$ as the best of a bad bunch in ignorance of what other options were yet available. An arbitrary stopping criterion is easily revised arbitrarily.

(4) The current objective function approximates an unknown, possibly non-quadratic, preference function. At best it is *locally* valid. We need $Q^{(p)}$ to get $z^{(p)}$, and $z^{(p)}$ to get the correct evaluation of $Q^{(p)}$. This is precisely the problem that variable metric algorithms solve when w, but not the quadratic approximation at the unknown minimum, is known. In our case w is not known but the necessary characteristics are represented by (10.15) and the normalisation, so we can imitate such an algorithm – provided we converge to the minimum as usual. Since $z^{(p)}$ depends on $Q^{(p)}$, and $Q^{(p)}$ on $z^{(p)}$, a legitimate policy recommendation is only possible at convergence.

(5) With w unknown, $[\partial w/\partial z]_{z(s+1)} - [\partial w/\partial z]_{z(s)}$ had to be approximated. Convergence is necessary so that this approximation becomes arbitrarily good. Point 4 shows that the fact that we need a variable metric algorithm also means convergence is essential for it to be legitimately used; while point 5 says that to get that variable metric algorithm at all we must go to convergence.

Thus convergence in interactive algorithms is vital. It is vital for the policy maker to know that convergence is possible and that any recommendation made does, in fact, incorporate it. Otherwise the recommendations contain too much arbitrariness, are subject to too much disagreement, and are prone to being gerrymandered by coalition partners or other interest groups. Unless he knows the recommendations cannot have been subverted by other parties, and feels that he has lost none of the power of decision, he will never agree to use the technique. In other words, an interactive algorithm can only prove acceptable if the policy maker is not at the mercy of the technique, nor of any interest group however well intentioned. It is necessary to take interaction to its limit in order to demonstrate that policy options rejected were indeed inferior; and that that recommended is neither arbitrary nor unduly favours any particular group. It is most important of all that policy makers should know this and be able to see it for themselves.

10.6.2 The game theory connection

We could cast this model of planning behaviour in the form of a mathematical game of planner against model. The game is implicit in the sequence of z_p values selected; as is the strategy followed. But in order not to associate our model with any particular method of selecting policies (since that would then impute some particular criterion of success to the planner in the way that each policy proposal or z_p vector was constructed) we have deliberately left the precise form of the strategy open – apart from the systematic search aspect.

The upshot is that the choices of z_ps are not structured in any way. Some would see this as an advantage; first because it ensures the planner need look only 'locally' for preferred policy adjustments (he cannot be expected to be certain of preferred adjustments 'globally' if he cannot specify $w(\tilde{z})$), and second because policy makers certainly resent being restricted by a technique not of their making (or understanding) and which (they think) inhibits the exercise of judgement. HMSO (1978) contains ample evidence on this point. This lack of structure may help 'sell' the technique, although from other points of view it could be a disadvantage. The obvious drawback is that the iterations may be slow if the planner has no clear idea where he wants to go and has to experiment extensively with z_p (although he is protected from repetition and inconsistency). In this connection, a good start, within a neighbourhood of the finish, can often be provided by using $Q^{(p)}$ from the last similar historical policy choice.

The description of z_p suggests that it would be constructed so as to combine exogenously selected trajectories for z, themselves designed to be more acceptable than $z^{(s)}$. To adjust policy levels in z_p is to change the priorities on achieving low values, or more acceptable values, in $z^{(p)}$. Likewise z_p can be set to mitigate frequent policy reversals, to reduce persistent failures in one policy or coincident failures of two policies, or to influence the timing of policy impacts (e.g. for elections). The choice of new z_p values would be facilitated if the optimisation exercise generated additional information about $z^{(s)}$, the best choice so far. For instance, a few alternative trajectories might be generated in which the weights on the more important variables (or time periods) were first sharply increased, and then decreased, in order to show what movements are possible. A sensitivity analysis of $z^{(s)}$ to model and information shocks could also be provided.

Having said that, any particular structured way of setting z_p can of course be attached to the interactive schemes described here. In this sense our scheme is completely general. Nearly all nonlinear optimisation algorithms require precise gradient (relative priority) evaluations, or precise objective evaluations, to provide search directions. The difficulty over setting z_p arises basically because in our context those evaluations are obviously impossible. Some approximations are therefore inevitable (such as those introduced at (10.23) or via a game). Although there are better and worse approximations, they cannot be avoided by structuring the choice of z_p. Geoffrion has a method (slightly modified by Zionts and Walenius (1976)) for adapting interview procedures to estimate these gradients which could then be used to determine each z_p. But they are still only estimates; and, being rather complex, approximations to those estimated search directions would have to be used in practice. Consequently, it is doubtful if an experienced planner would find these extensions for picking z_p useful.

10.7 On the existence of collective preference functions

Modelling planning behaviour by rational choices and a collective objective function inevitably raises the question of what precisely $w(\tilde{z})$ represents, and how far we may interpret it as showing 'preferences'. If so, whose preferences?

Obviously a collective preference function exists if we construct it, as we have done here. But the question remains whether the construction represents anything which is useful either to estimate or interpret. It seems to be universally accepted in models of this kind that planners should aim to optimise some index of performance. That index may not represent collective preferences exactly but rather any of the other possible allied interpretations – such as vote or utility maximisation, the maximisation of financial rewards, or office maximisation – which could be relevant objectives for any of the individual policy makers. It is therefore the planners' implicit collective preference criteria which we have here; not that of the 'voters' or policy consumers.

There is no doubt that collective preferences cannot exist in certain cases (for example, where Arrow's Possibility Theorem applies). But a collective preference function can only be said not to exist if certain strict conditions are met. These conditions are discussed in detail by Johansen (1969) and Bailey (1979). Basically, nonexistence requires the decision process not be the outcome of a cooperative mathematical game; nor may the domain of the choice set be restricted; and the choice set must be reducible to no more than two options. By the nature of economic planning these conditions cannot be met on the planners' side. For example, the condition that people prefer more goods to fewer will violate the requirement of unrestricted domains for the choice set. Since we must also decide on values for several variables (both in the list of policy variables, and at several points in time) any opportunity of structuring the decisions in a hierarchy, in which pairs of dichotomous options are considered sequentially, is likewise blocked because optimising all variables simultaneously involves at least a two dimensional search with four options to be decided upon at each stage ($m \geqslant 1, n \geqslant 1, T > 1$).

We should also argue that the outcome of decision making here is the outcome of a cooperative game. Final decisions are taken to reflect the 'coalition' view (a) between the cabinet members in the government, or the board of directors in an enterprise, etc.; or possibly (b) between government, administrators, trade unions, business community, etc.; or between management, shareholders or employees; and (c) in any case between economic and non-economic goals. In our model of planning by committee, bargaining has taken place in the iterative process leading to the final choice. But, the bargaining game is cooperative since once a final proposal is agreed, the participants in the planning group will abide by the outcome until the next planning period. Incidentally, this cooperation is often formalised with rules of collective responsibility, as found, for example, in cabinet or politburo decisions; and it may be reinforced with presidential or party patronage. Most frameworks for taking national economic decisions contain a forum where the necessary bargaining to produce a consensus can take place. A number of examples are described in Chapter 14.

Thus $w(\tilde{z})$ may represent the collective preferences of any one planning group whose decisions actually determine the subset of policy values studied. This is not to say that there may not be other noncooperating planning groups who control their own instruments. There may well be such groups – and this is the subject of the next chapter. What this does say is that it only makes sense to talk of $w(\tilde{z})$ and interactive planning *within* such groups, but not *between* them. How the groups then interact we shall see in the next chapter.

10.8 Is the quadratic function justified as a representation of preferences?

The quadratic preference function has been employed here largely because of its simplicity in optimisation, in search procedures, and in treating uncertainty. The fact that we treat it explicitly as an approximation prompts the question: is it not a very restrictive form?

10.8.1 Homogeneity

Given (7.12), w displays Euler's theorem for a function homogeneous of degree 2 in $\tilde{z}$ since $q = 0$. The priorities over correcting the failures in $\tilde{z}$ are linearly related to $\tilde{z}$ itself. And to the extent that the level of economic activity varies by scalar multiples of b, and this contains all the uncertainty, the true preferences will select failures for each policy variable in constant ratios to all the other optimal failures. That is to say that, along the linear expansion path, the marginal rates of substitution of $\tilde{z}_i^*$ for $\tilde{z}_j^*$ at the optimal solution are constant. If all the exogenous factors in b, such as world trade, import prices, agricultural conditions, etc., conspire to produce boom conditions with, say, 2% unemployment and 2% inflation, and if we accept falling short of the unemployment target by 100,000 jobs is tradeable without penalty for 1% less inflation, then the same rate of trade is also desired if 20% unemployment and 20% inflation were to be produced as a result of the same items in b taking other values. Clearly this is absurd. Every government would press somewhat harder on the inflation target in the former case and very much harder on unemployment in the latter. Such stylised examples would not occur in practice, but they make the objections to modelling the true preferences as homogeneous in failures, for more than the immediate neighbourhood of the final policy choice, obvious enough.

This example reminds us that even where no reference is made to (7.12) being an approximation to something more general – and this has been the case in the majority of policy optimisation studies – how restricted the validity of a particular Q and z^d specification really is. If we need to consider policies significantly removed from the economic conditions for which a particular set of preference parameters apply then new ones must be supplied.

The homogeneity problem is avoided to some extent if we use $q \neq 0$ with the true z^d. Then the marginal rates of substitution vary from q_j/q_i around the unconstrained minimum, towards the constant ones described for the homogeneous function. Naturally if the constrained and unconstrained minima are far apart this suggestion is ineffective.

10.8.2 The local nature of the approximate preferences

The difficulty with (10.14) is the restricted validity of one preference function specification. A large shock to the economy, a radical change in the political atmosphere, or just dissatisfaction with current recommendation may well lead policy makers to seek a preferred trajectory. Could the original preference specification still be used? The examples above suggest not. One result discussed by Hughes Hallett and Ancot (1982) is that for any given z_p the associated Q is unique only up to additive factors such that

$$\Delta Q\tilde{z}_p = 0 \text{ where } \Delta Q = Q_1 - Q_2. \tag{10.25}$$

If we take a set of vectors which form a basis spanning z space, we can regard each member of that set as a notional basic policy component mutually uncorrelated with the others. The observed $\tilde{z}_p$ is spanned by a subset of that basis. Then (10.25) shows we have no uniquely estimated preferences over those components which do not enter a basis for $\tilde{z}_p$ itself.

The latter policy components are, of course, those not chosen by the planners. Thus we have no estimate of preferences over subspaces orthogonal to that containing $\tilde{z}_p$ but a unique estimate for that in which $\tilde{z}_p$ lies. This is as it should be. Working from one $\tilde{z}_p$, it is unreasonable to expect to be able to infer relative priorities over policies or components which have been rejected. But in other circumstances these rejected components may contribute. Indeed, if we had more than $(n + m)T$ linearly independent observations on z_p (10.25) could not generally hold. However, this seems unlikely ever to be possible if only because identically repeated conditions will never be found. Thus, we can only claim an approximation to $w(\tilde{z})$ defined on the subspace of policy space spanned by a basis for $\tilde{z}_p$. Moreover, being normalised Q represents only relative priorities. However, we can extend Q to apply to all policies within a neighbourhood of $\tilde{z}_p$ for which that ranking (signs included) is invariant but where (10.25) no longer holds precisely. This is the extent to which we can generalise the local nature of the implied preferences. There is no disadvantage in practical terms to have the estimated preferences only locally valid: it is a special feature of particular significance in problems of social choice that the relative penalties on the policy failures $\tilde{z}$ are themselves heavily dependent on the values of those variables. In recognition of this we have specified $w(\tilde{z})$ as potentially nonquadratic.

Other studies in this field have attempted to obtain globally valid preference orderings by imposing prior zero restrictions and time invariance on Q. We relax the maintained hypothesis on Q, and trade global results for local ones since in any event no more generality is justified. Indeed empirical results suggest that these prior restrictions do not generally hold. A series of tests by Hordijk et al. (1976), in which these prior restrictions are varied while the implicit preferences of a fixed problem are calculated, show that varying the restrictions will typically produce greater changes between the results than seen within the preference structure itself.

Thus the main problem in specifying (10.14) a priori lies in its local nature. We can no more set z_p, compared to a current policy suggestion, without first being in the right neighbourhood with (10.14) than we can for any feasible $\tilde{z}^*$. Indeed to get z_p, as distinct from z^d which is 'more acceptable' from every position, the planner must discover what is and is not possible. z_p then depends on (10.14), just as any policy recommendation does, and is best set by interactive planning.

10.8.3 Other functional forms

Linear decision rules come from other functional forms – not just quadratic preferences. A well known example is the linear expenditure system of demand theory. But, as we saw in Chapter 7, there will be difficulties in treating uncertainty with nonquadratic preferences. Johansen (1981) provides a technique for the special case of exponential preferences; but for wider classes of preference functions no general solution is available.

10.8.4 The parameters in the preference structure

Our preference structure may be decomposed with respect to time:

$$w = \sum_{i=1}^{T} \sum_{j=1}^{T} \tilde{z}_i' Q_{ij} \tilde{z}_j \tag{10.26}$$

and with respect to the choice variables:

$$w = \sum_{i=1}^{T} \sum_{j=1}^{T} \left[\sum_{k=1}^{n+m} \sum_{l=1}^{n+m} (Q_{ij})_{kl} \tilde{z}_{ik} \tilde{z}_{jl} \right]. \tag{10.27}$$

Thus, we may examine the preference structure over variables within one planning period; or over planning periods for one variable; or both. Now $(Q_{ij})_{kl} = \partial^2 w / \partial z_{ik} \partial z_{jl}$ defines the *relative* penalty assigned per unit to the joint failure to achieve both $\tilde{z}_{ik} = \tilde{z}_{jl} = 0 (i, j = 1 \ldots T; k, l = 1 \ldots n + m)$:

(i) The diagonal elements of Q, $(Q_{ii})_{kk}$, $i = 1 \ldots T$, $k = 1 \ldots n + m$, show penalties assigned to squared deviations of variables from their desired values in each period. In particular we can look cross-sectionally to see how the implied preference ranking alters over time and how the relative gaps in that ordering increase or decrease. We may also look at the time series behaviour of those weights in order to rank preferences on any one variable over the planning exercise.

(ii) The remaining elements of Q_{ii} show penalties on joint failures, additional to penalties on the individual failures to reach desired values of two variables simultaneously at a given moment. Thus, with taxation and government expenditure, for example, pressure to maintain a balanced budget follows from a negative weight on their joint failures in each period. If taxation overshoots its desired value then the penalties are reduced below the weighted sum of their individual penalties whenever government expenditure also does so; but they are increased if it does not. In contrast, if consumption overshoots, penalties should presumably be reduced if investment does not, so as not to increase the pressure of aggregate demand unacceptably. Negative off-diagonal elements encourage complementary positions, and positive elements substitution between the policy variables.

(iii) Finally, the remaining submatrices $Q_{ij}, i \neq j$, contain penalties which perform a similar function but for the joint failures at different points of time. Intertemporal penalties may be assigned so that the *accelerating* penalties accrue to persistent failures, to penalise the timing with which a unit failure occurs, or to encourage substitutability or complementarity over time. This is in addition to the basic pattern of preferences in each time period as set up in the block diagonal components of Q. Examples of this are, respectively, penalising units of a balance of payments deficit proportionately more the longer they persist; penalising undershooting the employment target proportionally more the closer to an election it occurs; penalising consecutive consumption failures of the same sign; or rewarding a failure in receipts and a subsequent expenditure failure of the same sign when a balanced budget is desirable in the long run, but a deficit or surplus is permissible in the short run.

Intertemporal penalties play an obvious and important role in economic management. It is unsatisfactory that they are almost always excluded from planning exercises by making (10.14) separable with respect to time. In the case of demand models, Samuelson (1971) stresses the importance of avoiding time separable preferences. The standard Keynesian paradigm of short-term budget management is another case implying intertemporal penalties. The necessity of ensuring consistency within dynamic choices has long been recognised (under the various names of time complementarity, time consistency, coherent choices); but the desire to guarantee that consistency has meant that intertemporal penalties have been arbitrarily omitted from the objective function. Intertemporal penalties are theoretically necessary because otherwise the optimal policy rule can in fact be of the proportional plus derivative, but not integral, kind; (8.20) with $l = 1, k = 0$ provides one example. In Chapter 7 we pointed out that an integral rule is generally essential to solve control problems.

Of course, there are different ways of specifying the same joint or intertemporal penalties if different definitions of the policy variables are used. An identity defining the budget deficit allows an unbalanced budget to be penalised directly; and, if tax and expenditure variables are retained within z, we can separately penalise the way that balance is achieved. But we are unable to encourage particular outcomes, or to penalise the sign of a given failure. Defining the cumulated total of some variable as a target might approximate intertemporal penalties on the underlying variable; e.g. penalties both on capital and investment, or on the borrowing requirement and the budget deficit. But it is not an equivalent specification. First, a squared cumulative variable introduces t squares and

$\frac{1}{2}t(t-1)$ products of the underlying variable at time t. Here the T penalties on the cumulative variables must be equated to the $\frac{1}{2}T(T+1)$ penalties on the summed squares and products of values of the underlying variable, which is not generally possible. Second, in moving from period 1 to period 2, penalties are not adjusted to those appropriate to that part of the cumulative variable which now remains free for choice. If penalties are time varying not all parts are equally penalised. We saw intertemporal penalties involve implicit shifts in the aim points (ideal values), at each t, which depend on the states of that variable from 1 to $t-1$, and which are therefore unknown before t. These automatic adjustments to preferences, via the linear term, were noted at (7.32). Cumulative variables (whose ideals, for consistency, must be the cumulated ideals of the underlying variable) introduce no such adjustments. In other words, the cumulative variable approach may lead to time inconsistencies in the implemented plans (see sections 11.5 and 11.6).

The need for intertemporal penalties is, in fact, a consequence of working in discrete time. A preference structure in continuous time assigns no penalties for 'making the same mistake twice' because in any finite interval many minute policy revisions can be made, each being virtually costless. But if there are long intervals between decisions the system may have moved too far in the wrong direction for the adjustments to be minute. Indeed

$$\begin{aligned} w = \tfrac{1}{2}\tilde{z}'Q\tilde{z} &= \tfrac{1}{2}\sum_{t=0}^{T} \tilde{z}_t'Q_t\tilde{z}_t + \sum_{t}^{T}\sum_{j>t}^{T} \tilde{z}_i'Q_{tj}\tilde{z}_j \\ &= \tfrac{1}{2}\sum_{t}\tilde{z}_t'Q_t\tilde{z}_t + \sum_{t}\sum_{j}\tilde{z}_t'Q_{tj}\Delta^{t-j}\tilde{z}_t \end{aligned} \tag{10.28}$$

where $\Delta^{t-j}\tilde{z}_t = \tilde{z}_t - \tilde{z}_{t-j}$. Thus, in continuous time,

$$w = \tfrac{1}{2}\int_0^T \tilde{z}_t'Q_t\tilde{z}_t\,\mathrm{dt} + \int_0^T\int_{-\infty}^{\infty} \tilde{z}_t'Q_{tj}\,\mathrm{dz}\,\mathrm{dt} \tag{10.29}$$

and the terms in the second integral vanish being of 'second order of smallness'.

10.8.5 Asymmetric preferences

One obvious restriction of (10.24) is that it assigns equal penalties to unit failures of either sign about each element of z^d. However, we can set z^d at the unconstrained optima of $w(\tilde{z})$ while $q \neq 0$. Then $\partial w/\partial z = q$ at z^d, so the signs in q determine the form of asymmetry about z^d in $w(\tilde{z})$. If $q_i > 0$ is large, then the preference surface has steep sides at z_i^d and is sharply curved at the minimum. If $q_i < 0$ is large, it has shallow sides and the preferences are less sharply differentiated. Hence q indicates the flexibility of preferences in each dimension. Second, by (9.25) the difference between $\tilde{z}^*$, computed as if $q = 0$, and that in (7.16) is

$$dz^* = \Phi q \tag{10.30}$$

where Φ is singular. In order to overcome the symmetric penalties by choice of q, we must choose dz^* by (10.30) so that at least the signs within $\tilde{z}^*$ are the more desirable in each case. To add to $\tilde{z}_i^*, q_i < 0$ must be chosen sufficiently large relative to $q_j, j \neq i = 1 \ldots (n+m)T$. To subtract from $\tilde{z}_i^*, q_i > 0$, must be so chosen. In many cases this may be sufficient to obtain the desired shifts in $\tilde{z}^*$; but it is never possible to attain arbitrary adjustments throughout $\tilde{z}^*$ because of the singularity of Φ. This is a reflection of the fact that dz^* is restricted to leaving the new z^* feasible. This justifies our suggestion that we may use q to 'bias' (10.14) in order to give a preference structure unavailable from the strictly local approximation to $w(\tilde{z})$ and so as to leave the more desirable sign in each element of $\tilde{z}^*$. But to attempt to set q a priori, so that the same outcome will be achieved, is much more difficult since the frontiers of F will not then be known. Again interactive planning is required.

10.9 A numerical example

One purpose of these algorithms has been to suggest some interpretation of the information which can be obtained from observing interactions between planner and model, while iterating toward some acceptable policy trajectory. While we make no attempt to use the techniques to derive realistic results, it is useful to reinforce these ideas with an example which shows the techniques in action. To this end, results are given for a hypothetical planning exercise undertaken for the design of macroeconomic policy of the first Roosevelt administration in the United States, 1933–6; the example of Chapter 7. Here $Q^{(0)}$, $z^{(0)}$ and z^d were taken from the results of that example; the latter two are reproduced in table 10.1(a), (b).

We show how the techniques would have worked, had they been used in order to derive the historical policies of that period as optimal for that administration as it took office. That is we stand in the planners' shoes armed with all the information available to them at the start of 1933, plus knowledge of the model, and show how the interactions would have operated to give the historical policies as the final optimal selection. We suppose z^d in fact represents the planners' ideal values. Then we need the following: an arbitrary start, $Q^{(0)} = I$ and $z^{(0)}$; a historical simulation of the target values using this model; the instrument values actually

Table 10.1 *The policy vectors*

	1933	1934	1935	1936		1933	1934	1935	1936
(*a*) *The start* ($z^{(0)}$)					(*b*) *The ideal values* (z^d)				
C	47.36	51.77	56.37	60.73	C	49.69	53.78	57.88	61.97
I	− 6.23	− 2.38	0.90	3.59	I	− 3.1	0.0	3.1	6.2
D	8.25	5.02	1.91	0.05	D	11.25	7.5	3.75	0.0
W_2	6.13	6.26	6.20	6.36	W_2	5.038	5.254	5.469	5.685
T	8.62	8.45	7.64	6.99	T	7.396	7.635	7.874	8.113
G	14.26	13.92	13.20	13.30	G	10.438	10.868	11.298	11.727
(*c*) *The historical simulation* ($z^{(p)}$)					(*d*) *Preferred policies* (z_p)				
C	44.29	46.86	50.44	54.04	C	46.62	48.87	51.95	55.28
I	− 6.54	− 3.69	− 1.44	− 0.12	I	− 3.41	− 1.32	0.76	9.67
D	7.59	5.18	4.57	7.73	D	10.59	7.66	6.41	7.68
W_2	5.6	6.0	6.1	7.4	W_2	4.51	4.99	5.37	6.73
T	5.4	6.8	7.2	8.3	T	4.18	5.98	7.43	9.42
G	9.3	10.0	10.5	10.3	G	5.48	6.95	8.59	8.73

chosen; and expectations of the uncertain variables conditioned on the information set available at the start of 1933. This simulation provides the policy recommendation, $z^{(p)}$, which was adopted. It is given in table 10.1 (c). $z^{(p)}$ therefore represents an open loop policy choice, and any preferences derived from it will be those of the administration on taking office. By conditioning $z^{(p)}$ on alternative information sets we could get preferences at different points of the administration; e.g. using a closed loop $z^{(p)}$ gives preferences at reelection time.

The first step is to determine what preferred (possibly second best) but infeasible policy selection, z_p, could have led the planners to their observed policy selection $z^{(p)}$ – in the sense of (10.17) or (10.23) and (10.24). Evidently there is no unique z_p even if $z^{(p)}$, Q, z^d, etc. are unique. One such z_p is given in table 10.1 (d). We will suppose that this was the final z_p which the planners adopted. Indeed this seems plausible as it shows that, faced with the infeasibility of z^d, they went for a second best selection of a slightly slower and steadier growth in the target variables, with a spurt in the last (reelection) year; and less of an ambitious choice for D but with considerably more emphasis on I. There is some appreciation of the strong dynamics in the model which is absent from z^d. Such modifications to z^d are to be expected since predictions made with this model would have indicated that z^d was most likely to be overoptimistic. Notice, in particular, that D is a target which can be sacrificed if necessary. Among the instruments, lower activity, especially for G, in the early years and higher activity later is preferred to the steady growth of z^d. The administration appears to be working towards mild deficit financing in the first three years, but a balanced budget for 1936. Once again these figures have clearly been modified from z^d, towards what might have been accepted as feasible for the depression years.

Had the planners chosen this z_p as their final z_p value (after a suitable amount of experimenting with the policy recommendations available from other values) and inserted it into (10.23) and (10.24) together with $Q^{(0)} = I$, $z^{(0)}$ and $z^{(d)}$, they would have obtained, and accepted, $z^{(p)}$ after 17 iterations with $\lambda_s = 0.6$ and a convergence test of 10^{-6}. These are just the iterations of the inner loop for the last z_p value. At each iteration the planner can review progress so far and consider whether to reset z_p, etc. Each step also provides the associated preference structure. That obtained at convergence, $Q^{(p)}$, is given in table 10.2.

Table 10.2 offers a picture of the planned macroeconomic strategy of the 1933–6 Roosevelt administration assuming that the policies were rationally chosen. It therefore provides a rather interesting view of President Roosevelt's reelection ambitions. The penalties on failing to achieve the desired target values rise dramatically to 1935, and fall back in 1936 – especially for I and D. Clearly D is considered the most easily sacrificed, and C the least. In contrast the penalties on instrument failure start large and decline to 1935 before rising again. The evidence is consistent with a strategy of providing economic success in good time for reelection year; loosening the 'inessential' (long-run) targets I and D and tightening the instruments in a final effort to secure success. There is also evidence of intended budget imbalances throughout, but a balanced budget by 1936; that D can be sacrificed in favour of C; that taxation policy should encourage private expenditure (except in 1936), but at the same time government expenditures should be accommodating. There are rapidly accelerating penalties on all failures (except D and T) to 1935 (although the rate of acceleration slows in 1936). An unbalanced budget is only considered acceptable provided it does not persist.[6]

On the other hand, $z^{(p)}$ is obtained instantly by (10.17) after the z_p appropriate for either technique has been chosen. The intervening review and reconsideration steps are avoided, and a decision can be taken right away on whether to accept $z^{(p)}$. The point being stressed is that a respecification technique is likely to be impractical in that it can be laborious, involve a number of 'blind alleys', and be accident prone in the interaction and (committee) decision processes rather than in the algorithm itself. That difficulty is minimised in the more efficient calculations of (10.17). This point evidently worried the Committee on Policy Optimisation as it formed their main criticism of interactive policy selection techniques (HMSO (1978)).

6 Further examples from American and Soviet economic planning are given by Hughes Hallett and Ancot (1982), Ancot and Hughes Hallett (1982).

Table 10.2 *The preference structure*

		C	I	D	W_2	T	G			C	I	D	W_2	T	G
				1933								*1935*			
	C	1.00	0.10	0.21	0.17	1.05	1.62		C	3.66	1.77	− 2.31	0.05	0.23	1.68
	I	0.10	0.01	0.02	0.02	0.11	0.16		I	1.33	0.64	− 0.84	0.02	0.08	0.61
1933	D	0.21	0.02	0.05	0.04	0.22	0.34	*1934*	D	− 1.59	− 0.77	1.00	− 0.02	− 0.10	− 0.73
	W_2	0.17	0.02	0.04	0.03	0.18	0.28		W_2	0.19	− 0.09	− 0.12	0.00	0.01	0.09
	T	1.05	0.11	0.22	0.18	1.10	1.69		T	1.23	0.59	− 0.78	0.02	0.08	0.56
	G	1.62	0.16	0.34	0.28	1.69	2.61		G	2.91	1.41	− 1.83	0.04	0.18	1.33
				1934								*1936*			
	C	1.61	0.58	− 0.69	0.09	0.54	1.27		C	3.16	1.23	− 0.63	− 0.54	− 0.69	1.58
	I	0.16	0.06	− 0.07	0.01	0.05	0.13		I	1.14	0.45	− 0.23	− 0.20	− 0.25	0.57
1933	D	0.34	0.12	− 0.15	0.02	0.11	0.27	*1934*	D	− 1.37	− 0.53	0.27	0.24	0.30	− 0.68
	W_2	0.28	0.10	− 0.12	0.01	0.09	0.22		W_2	0.17	0.06	− 0.03	− 0.03	− 0.04	0.08
	T	1.68	0.61	− 0.73	0.09	0.57	1.34		T	1.06	0.41	− 0.21	− 0.18	− 0.23	0.53
	G	2.59	0.94	− 1.12	0.14	0.87	2.06		G	2.51	0.98	− 0.50	− 0.43	− 0.55	1.25

				1935								*1935*			
	C	2.28	1.10	−1.44	0.03	0.14	1.05		C	5.21	2.52	−3.28	0.07	0.33	2.39
	I	0.23	0.11	−0.14	0.00	0.01	0.11		I	2.52	1.21	−1.58	0.04	0.16	1.15
1933	D	0.49	0.23	−0.31	0.01	0.03	0.22	*1935*	D	−3.28	−1.58	2.06	−0.05	−0.21	−1.50
	W_2	0.39	0.19	−0.25	0.01	0.02	0.18		W_2	0.07	0.04	−0.05	0.00	0.00	0.03
	T	2.39	1.16	−1.51	0.04	0.15	1.09		T	0.33	0.16	−0.21	0.00	0.02	0.15
	G	3.69	1.78	−2.32	0.05	0.23	1.69		G	2.39	1.15	−1.50	0.03	0.15	1.09
				1936								*1936*			
	C	1.97	0.77	−0.39	−0.34	−0.43	0.98		C	4.49	1.75	−0.89	−0.77	−0.99	2.24
	I	0.19	0.08	−0.04	−0.03	−0.04	0.10		I	2.17	0.84	−0.43	−0.37	−0.48	1.08
1933	D	0.42	0.16	−0.08	−0.07	−0.09	0.21	*1935*	D	−2.83	−1.10	0.56	0.49	0.62	−1.41
	W_2	0.34	0.13	−0.07	−0.06	−0.07	0.17		W_2	0.06	0.02	−0.01	−0.01	−0.01	0.03
	T	2.06	0.80	−0.41	−0.36	−0.45	1.03		T	0.28	0.11	−0.06	−0.05	−0.06	0.14
	G	3.18	1.24	−0.63	−0.55	−0.70	1.59		G	2.06	0.80	−0.41	−0.35	−0.45	1.03
				1934								*1936*			
	C	2.58	0.93	−1.12	0.14	0.87	2.05		C	3.87	1.51	−0.77	−0.67	−0.85	1.93
	I	0.93	0.34	−0.40	0.05	0.31	0.74		I	1.51	0.59	−0.29	−0.26	−0.33	0.75
1934	D	−1.12	−0.40	0.48	−0.06	−0.38	−0.89	*1936*	D	−0.77	−0.29	0.15	0.13	0.17	−0.38
	W_2	0.14	0.05	−0.06	0.01	0.05	0.11		W_2	−0.67	−0.26	0.13	0.12	0.15	−0.33
	T	0.87	0.31	−0.38	0.05	0.29	0.69		T	−0.85	−0.33	0.17	0.15	0.19	−0.42
	G	2.05	0.74	−0.89	0.11	0.69	1.63		G	1.93	0.75	−0.38	−0.33	−0.42	0.96

10.10 Alternative specification methods: interviewing

The nature of the problem may be such that the specification of (Q, q) is obvious (Underwood (1977)), but this is the exception for most planning, particularly macroeconomic, problems. Of course in systems with an overriding ideology the specification may indeed be 'obvious'! Elsewhere, direct interviews with the government are suggested where planners are neutral experts in government service (e.g. Norway, see Johansen (1974)). If there are sufficient planning documents, committees, etc., imaginary interviews may be conducted (e.g. Holland, see van Eijk and Sandee (1959)). However, where government is decentralised, or vacillates in its commitment to organised planning, and particularly where there are few policy pronouncements or documents available, then this is not a feasible approach.

Johansen (1974) provides an excellent and detailed review of Frisch's scheme for direct interviewing. In imaginary interviewing we deduce the weights from estimates of acceptable trade-offs in policy variables made from observed behaviour, policy statements (intentions, and reasons for choice) and minutes of meetings between the parties to the bargaining which formed those policies. This could be fed into the interactive scheme as a way of determining z_p from $z^{(s)}$. As an example, from the transcripts of the meetings of the Social and Economic Council advising the Netherlands government in 1957 van Eijk and Sandee (1959) found the agreed policy recommendations accepted that a 100 million florin balance of payments surplus was tradable for 400 m. fl. extra government expenditure, 500 m. fl. investment, 2% extra real wages, 1.33% less inflation, $\frac{1}{2}$% more unemployment or a 200 m. fl. budget surplus. They then go on to construct a linear preference function. But these trade-offs also suggest $\delta^{(s)}$, and thus z_p for (10.23) and (10.24) or for (10.17).

There are a number of dangers in treating interviewing as a means of extracting a decision from the planner, rather than as a means for creating the policy experiments from which a decision may emerge (HMSO (1978)). It is most unlikely that any individual would be sure of his preferences over $\tilde{z}$ values far from his recent experience. He would be unable to specify exact relative penalties for hypothetical scenarios, and it would not be in his interest to reveal his preferences even if he knew them. We are dependent on that individual being able and willing to mimic realistically his role as a decision maker, but in a hypothetical situation. It is quite impossible for him to represent the preferences of other policy makers with any accuracy; nor can he then accurately assess and make allowances for the relative bargaining power of others. It is certainly revealing in this connection that, since econometric projections have become publically available, policy makers have been noticeably reluctant to commit themselves on specific economic developments in the immediate future.

10.11 Conclusions

In this chapter we have attacked one of the major difficulties in policy selection by optimisation. We have argued that the appropriate objective function can never be known a priori, but some representation of it is unavoidable. Moreover, the traditional quadratic objective function can generally be no more than a local approximation to the true preferences, just as any model approximates the behaviour of the real economic system about the observed levels of its variables.

In demand theory axioms of choice are introduced expressly to avoid explicit utility functions. The subjective nature of utility makes it impossible to specify the relative gradients of the utility function over values of the choice variables with any accuracy. Moreover, there is no obvious agreement on the appropriate functional form. Since we are in a similar situation here, we follow a similar strategy. But whereas the characteristics of demand behaviour may be estimated directly from consumption patterns, we have had to design policy experiments so that the characteristics of planning behaviour can be observed and estimated. This has led to an interactive planning scheme (with preferences either implicit or explicit). This scheme can be interpreted as a method of tracing the segments of the Pareto optimal frontier relevant in the eyes of the planners.

We are therefore emphasising that policy selection is a 'learning by doing' process. Optimisation is important because it is such an efficient way of picking the learning steps. Irrelevant and confusing simulation steps based on trial and error are removed, and the search is systematic. In fact, (10.17) has the advantage of simplicity and efficiency and would be used when policy proposals alone are the focus; and (10.23) with (10.24) when preferences are also of interest. The experimental content of these techniques should not be overlooked. Indeed, independently of optimisation, a final choice may be made from the two or three most promising candidates taken from the part of the Pareto optimal frontier investigated.

It is certainly true that we learn fastest when we ask the right questions. But which questions are the right ones depends on discovering what we wish to know – hence the gradient problem. (10.17) yields information about the model and feasible policies; (10.23) and (10.24) do the same but also indicate the preference structure.

11

Decentralised planning: anticipatory behaviour and multiple policy makers

11.1 Introduction

Perhaps the most constructive debate in the problems of economic policy making has been the challenge to the analogy between controlling physical and social systems. The ability of decision makers to anticipate developments, or other people's actions, and then adapt their own behaviour is of particular significance in economics. The difficulties in selecting economic policies when agents are hypothesised to have rational expectations is a prominent case in point.

In this chapter we deal with three issues: (a) what causes dynamic inconsistencies in policy selections where endogenous expectations and multiple noncooperating policy makers are part of the system; (b) how should optimal policies be chosen when rational expectations are present; and (c) are dynamic inconsistencies only avoidable with simple fixed (suboptimal) rules? Most of the definitions required will emerge during the chapter. However, we start by calling a choice *dynamically consistent* if there is no incentive to change its deterministic components at any decision point beyond the first. Preferences are *inseparable* if they are not weakly additively separable with respect to time over the whole feasible set (the marginal rates of substitution between periods have no invariance properties).

Our purpose is to describe policy selections between noncooperating groups in policy formation, in contrast to the cooperative selections within such groups described in the previous chapter. The crux of the matter is the implicit noncausality caused by anticipating behaviour, and the inability of dynamic algorithms to handle that because the necessary time-nested structure of the constrained objective function is lost. Noncausality is introduced in section 11.2. In section 11.3 it is shown how noncooperating policy makers are necessarily subject to noncausality. Section 11.4 describes the Lucas critique of policy making, and shows that the problem of policy choice now boils down to ensuring dynamic consistency. Then sections 11.5 and 11.6 illustrate why, in these circumstances, optimal policies can be provided by a static algorithm but not by a dynamic one. Those optimal policies are set out in section 11.7, with extensions in section 11.8 and a numerical example in section 11.9.

11.2 The dynamics of endogenous expectations and noncausality

11.2.1 Noncausality

The policy selection methods so far have been applied exclusively to *causal models*; that is to models having

$$\{\partial Y_i/\partial x_j, \partial Y_i/\partial N_j, \partial Y_i/\partial u_j\} = 0 \text{ for all } i < j \tag{11.1}$$

and $i, j = 1 \ldots T$. The block triangularity of R, K and S is implied by (11.1). That construction follows for any model whose entire dynamic structure can be summarised by (7.1); or equivalently by $\partial Y_i/\partial Y_j = 0$ for $i < j$ in the structural model $Y = f(Y, x, N, U)$. *Noncausal models* are those in which one or more of the partial derivatives in (11.1), or in $\partial Y_i/\partial Y_j$ of the structural model, are nonzero. These partial derivatives show the effects of expectations of future variables (exogenous and endogenous) on the system. Naturally those expectations must be conditioned on the information available to date, Ω_i. We distinguish noncausality introduced by endogenous expectations, $\partial Y_i/\partial Y_j \neq 0$, from that due to decentralisation (multiple policy makers), $\partial Y_i/\partial N_j \neq 0$. Both imply $\partial Y_i/\partial x_j \neq 0$, as we shall see.

Evidently there are no additional computational difficulties in allowing noncausal models. The policies (7.16), (7.18), (7.33) and the certainty equivalence theorem do not depend on R, K or S being block triangular. So our optimal policy calculations only require modifications: (i) to evaluate the appropriate partial derivative matrices for the upper triangular blocks; and (ii) to determine whether the adjustments in (7.32), which update the constrained objective function and the sequence of optimal policy choices at each reoptimisation, need be extended.

11.2.2 Policy models with endogenous expectations

Much of the literature on rational expectations and policy choice has been concerned with models of the type

$$Y_t = A(L)Y_t + E_tB(L^{-1})Y_t + CX_t + V_t \tag{11.2}$$

where L is the lag operator, and $L^kY_t = Y_{t-k}$ for $k = \ldots -2, -1, 0, 1, 2 \ldots$ $A(L)$ is a polynominal in positive powers of L and defines the conventional causal dynamics, or distributed lag, in Y_t:

$$A(L) = A_0 + A_1L + A_2L^2 + \ldots \text{and } A_0 = 0 \tag{11.3}$$

$B(L^{-1})$ is a polynominal in the forward shift operator L^{-1}, so that

$$E_t B(L^{-1})Y_t = E_t[B_0 Y_t + B_1 Y_{t+1} + B_2 Y_{t+2} + \ldots]$$
$$= B_0 Y_{t,t} + B_1 y_{t+1,t} + \cdots \tag{11.4}$$

where $Y_{i,j} = E(Y_i|\Omega_j)$ for $j \leqslant i$.

So (11.4) defines the noncausal dynamics. $Y_{t+j,t}$ is a rational expectation of Y_{t+j}, for $j \geqslant 0$, formed by taking the mathematical expectation conditional on the latest information set, including knowledge of (11.2) or, failing that, some estimate of it. In other words, each certainty equivalent employed since Chapter 7 has been the current rational expectation of the associated variable. That is why it has been necessary to update them for realisations *and* for any modified future expectations at every t, to ensure closed loop control rather than just feedback control. If expectations, other than those used, were superior predictors the optimality of the policies chosen would be lost. They would no longer be rational expectations of the *ex post* optimal choices (as claimed in (7.55)).

Now Y_t is determined by the final form equation

$$Y_t = [I - A(L) - E_t B(L^{-1})]^{-1}(CX_t + V_t) \tag{11.5}$$

provided the inverse exists. In that case (11.5) may also be written as

$$Y_t = \Phi_0 Y_0 + \sum_{k=1}^{t} \Phi_k(CX_t + V_t) + \sum_{i=1}^{t} \sum_{k=i}^{\infty} \Psi_{ki}(CX_{k,i} + V_{k,i}) \tag{11.6}$$

with known initial conditions Y_0. However, Φ_k and Ψ_{ki} are complicated functions of the coefficient matrices in $A(L)$ and $B(L^{-1})$. Evidently the presence of endogenous expectations in (11.2) has led to the noncausal model at (11.6); with noncausal multipliers Φ_k and Ψ_{ki}. A detailed analysis of the dynamics in (11.2) is no less complex. The complexities arise because of the interaction of the leads and lags in Y_t in (11.2) which blocks their elimination by repeated substitutions. Writing the inverse of (11.5) as a power series demonstrates the point. There is also the question of the conditions under which the inverse in (11.5) exists. The reader may refer to Hughes Hallett (1981b) for detail on these matters, and for a computational scheme to determine the matrices Φ_k and Ψ_{ki}.

The point here is to note the noncausal model at (11.6), so that we can move on to deal with a generalisation of it when X_t is partitioned between policy instruments in the hands of independent policy makers. Starting from (11.2) we can compute (11.6), which can in turn be rewritten as (7.2) where R and K are no longer block lower triangular. Then the policy vector, x, may be determined as usual.

11.3 Noncausality in multiple player policy problems

11.3.1 The two player case

Noncausal models arise in an obvious way even when no lead variables appear in the model, so $B(L^{-1}) = 0$ in (11.2). Suppose there are two separate policy making authorities each with its own set of policy instruments, say $x_t^{(1)}$ and $x_t^{(2)}$. Until now $x_t^{(2)}$ has been a subset of N_t. But in this case

$$y = R^{(1)}x^{(1)} + R^{(2)}x^{(2)} + s \tag{11.7}$$

where s has KN, of (7.6), replaced by the remaining noncontrollable elements K^*n_3; and each submatrix of K has been partitioned as $(R_{it}^{(2)} \vdots K_{it}^*)$ conformably with $N_t' = (x_t^{(2)'} \vdots n_{3t}')$. In this context, each y_t is the union of the sets of targets selected by all the decision makers.

Here we also have a case of noncausality although $R^{(1)}, R^{(2)}$ and K^* are all block lower triangular matrices. (11.7) would be derived from the complete model

$$Y_t = \Pi_1 Y_{t-1} + R_{tt}^{(1)}x_t^{(1)} + R_{tt}^{(2)}x_t^{(2)} + a_t \tag{11.8}$$

where $a_t = K_{tt}^* n_{3t} + V_t$. Suppose any policy rule of the form

$$x_t^{(1)} = G_t Y_{t-1} + g_t \tag{11.9}$$

were applied. If the other player also uses the rule

$$x_t^{(2)} = L_t Y_{t-1} + l_t \tag{11.10}$$

then the 'controlled' model behaves as

$$Y_t = (\Pi_1 + R_{tt}^{(1)}G_t + R_{tt}^{(2)}L_t)Y_{t-1} + (a_t + R_{tt}^{(1)}g_t + R_{tt}^{(2)}l_t). \tag{11.11}$$

These decision rules need not be optimal; they could just as well be of the type developed in simulation studies. Noncausality arises in the policy problem faced by each player individually because of the joint dependence between $x_t^{(1)}$ and $x_t^{(2)}$ in that they both determine the development of Y_t; and also because of the explicit multiperiod nature of the plans implying $x_t^{(1)}$ and $x_{t+j}^{(2)}$, $0 < j \leqslant T - t$, are jointly dependent through the determination of Y_{t+j}. So the setting of $x_t^{(1)}$ must be conditioned on the expected values of $x_{t+j}^{(2)}$ (and vice versa for $x_t^{(2)}$ on $x_{t+j}^{(1)}$). Consequently there is simultaneity between $x^{(1)}$ and $x^{(2)}$ as a whole, which must be accounted for if optimality is to be achieved in either player's selection. This simultaneity is both over players ($x_t^{(1)}$ and $x_t^{(2)}$, at each t) and over time($x_{t+i}^{(1)}$ and $x_{t+j}^{(2)}$, for $-t+1 \leqslant i, j \leqslant T-t$ and $i \neq j$). It means $x^{(1)}$ should be selected conditional on $x^{(2)}$, while $x^{(2)}$ is being selected conditional on $x^{(1)}$. Evidently it is convenient to use (11.7) and a static algorithm, since then the simultaneity over time is treated as contemporaneous simultaneity in all the choice variables outstanding in $x^{(1)}$ and $x^{(2)}$. Policies which fully account for this simultaneity are said to constitute a Nash equilibrium of the policy game. No player has any incentive to change his policies unilaterally.

Simultaneity (and noncausality) is absent only if *both* players operate rules such that $\partial x_t^{(1)}/\partial x_{t+j,t}^{(2)} = 0$ and $\partial x_t^{(2)}/\partial x_{t+j,t}^{(1)} = 0$ for every $0 \leqslant j \leqslant T - t$ and all $t = 1 \ldots T$. In terms of (11.8)–(11.10) these conditions imply $G_t = 0$, $L_t = 0$, plus $\partial g_t/\partial x_{t+j,t}^{(2)} = 0$ and $\partial l_t/\partial x_{t+j,t}^{(1)} = 0$, by backsubstitutions in (11.11) from T to t. Notice, we are not concerned with whether each player actually does account for the current and future actions expected from his opponent; but with whether he could benefit by doing so within the scope of a particular policy regime. Noncausality does not arise only if both players fail to react to each other, or to any endogenous or endogenised variable in the controlled system. Also they must be presumed not to learn from their mistakes, so policy revisions in terms of the equation residuals are ruled out (recall (7.38)). If these conditions do apply players are said to follow a Cournot strategy.

Thus noncausality is a wider condition than just something associated with policy optimisation or closed loop controls. Automatic stabilisers, simple fixed rules which account for changing circumstances (such as expanding the money stock in line with productive capacity), and most other realistic policy rules are all examples. But there is one interesting special case which escapes noncausality. That is where one player dominates because he knows (or thinks he knows) the policy rule of his opponent *a priori*. Then we have the recursive dependence, rather than simultaneity, of (say) $x_t^{(1)}$ on $x_t^{(2)}$ within each t. The dependence over time could be substituted out recursively from T to 1; and that between $x_t^{(1)}$ and $x_t^{(2)}$ within each step. An example is the Stackelberg game in which player 2 disregards player 1, and sets his instruments presuming that player 1 will optimise conditionally on that behaviour. However, unless player 2 actually knows player 1's choice with certainty, it must be demonstrated that it is not worth his while to improve on his initial assumption. In some cases that may follow because the costs to information gathering, or to changing the current policy, are substantial. However, the fact that governments do attempt to 'steer' the decisions of economic agents and that firms do engage in market research, suggests that the traditional examples of government vs the private sector, and of monopolistic firms vs consumers, are invalid.

Finally, the most interesting special case, policy selection by optimisation, does involve noncausality. We see, by (8.19), that $\partial g_t/\partial x_{t+j,t}^{(2)} \neq 0$ and $\partial l_t/\partial x_{t+j,t}^{(1)} \neq 0$ if both players optimise. The same points are seen directly from (7.16) by expanding s according to (7.6) and inserting the new partitioning in N.

A noncausal model has therefore been induced by the forms of the policy rules followed, although the model itself contained no forward expectations. Indeed, it is only avoided if the instruments of each player have no impact directly, or indirectly through a decision rule, on the targets of any other player.

11.3.2 The extension to multiple players

The generalisation of policy selection techniques to the case of multiple policy makers is straightforward once a methodology has been developed for the two player case. It is a matter of partitioning N_t between the various 'opposition' players and treating $x_t^{(1)}$ as the instruments of the player whose decisions we wish to describe. The matrices of multipliers in $R^{(2)}$ must be partitioned conformably. The remaining noncontrollables, i.e. variables which are exogenous but not the instruments of any player in the game, will be transferred to b as usual. Thus $N_t' = (x_t' \vdots n_t') = (x_t^{(1)\prime} \dots x_t^{(p)\prime} \vdots n_t')$ contains the set of instruments controlled by p players; and n_t are the remaining noncontrollable variables, whose values are 'acts of God', such as the weather, time trends, etc. Without loss of generality we can investigate the case of two players by taking $x_t^{(1)}$ as $x_t^{(j)}$ for $j = 1 \dots p$ in turn, and then treating $x_t^{(2)\prime} = (x_t^{(1)\prime} \dots x_t^{(j-1)\prime}, x_t^{(j+1)\prime} \dots x_t^{(p)\prime})$ as if it is a single opponent in each case. Notice putting each player in turn under scrutiny is symmetric. No special role is assigned to the player under scrutiny. He is not presumed to fulfill any particular function such as a dominant player, a market leader or follower; nor does he assume that a Nash, a Stackelberg, or a Pareto strategy is appropriate for the game.

11.3.3 The generality of multiple player noncausality

Multiple players are involved whenever there is a degree of decentralisation in the planning structure. An obvious example is where a monetary and a budgetary authority independently execute economic policy using separate instruments to do so (the United States is a case in point; see Pierce (1974)). Having control of separate instruments first involves them in a bargaining game, even if cooperation follows later. A well known example without cooperation is where the government and trade unions both try to influence the economy, each in their own interests. Unions have the money wage rate as their 'instrument'. A more widely discussed example is where the two players are the government and the private sector, again acting in their own interests.

On a wider stage, wage bargaining between employer and employee, or an exchange economy where producers and consumers use price and quantity as instruments, would also be examples. So we come to market behaviour with oligopolistic firms, monopolistic competition between buyers and sellers of goods or labour, the regulation of multi-national firms, etc. More examples come from open economies where, if trade is a significant component of GNP, internal policies are partially dependent on the policies of a major trading partner, and vice versa if the trade is also important to the partner. Trade between the countries of the European Economic Community is a useful example; or, again, policy selection for the regions and central government in a federal structure where the 'trade' is in budget receipts and allocations.

Of course, noncooperation does not automatically imply conflicting objectives. Whatever the objectives, if decision makers choose rationally they will unilaterally and selfishly maximise their own self-interests. No account will be taken of the objectives of any other agent, except in so far as to do so furthers their own interests. Policy problems with multiple players are therefore common enough. Moreover, the influence of the New Classical Macroeconomics on today's policies, where policy makers turn away from intervention in favour of private decision making, gives the analysis of individual choices a special interest.

11.4 The policy selection problem in decentralised systems: The Lucas critique and dynamic inconsistencies

Noncausality in a policy game raises difficulties for the selection of policy values by each player. We have seen that successful policy selection requires each player to determine his own choice simultaneously with his expectation of his opponents choice, for all periods together. For example, $x_t^{(1)}$ derived by (8.20) is only optimal conditional on $x_{t+j,t}^{(2)}$ being known since $(\partial w/\partial x_{t+j,t}^{(2)}).\ (\partial x_{t+j,t}^{(2)}/\partial x_t^{(1)})$ is set to zero; and that for $x_t^{(2)}$ similarly obtained is likewise only optimal when $x_{t+j,t}^{(1)}$ is known ($t = 1 \ldots T, j = 0 \ldots T - t$). Neither $\partial x_{t+j,t}^{(2)}/\partial x_t^{(1)}$ nor $\partial x_{t+j,t}^{(1)}/\partial x_t^{(2)}$ vanish, because each player can influence the decision expected from his opponent since the latter is conditioned on the decision expected from the first player. The opponent's decision must therefore be endogenised within the determination of the first player's choice.

We attempt to separate two aspects of simultaneity in order to examine what difficulties are implied for designing suitable policies for each player. The contemporaneous simultaneity between the players' choices at every t is a manifestation of the Lucas critique[1] of policy making (Lucas (1976)).

1 That a policy rule is invalidated by its own implementation because as soon as other players perceive it they react to it, thus altering the dynamic responses of the economy upon which the original rule was based.

The intertemporal simultaneity (that is noncausality superimposed on the time nested decisions implied by (8.6)) is a manifestation of the dynamic inconsistency critique[2] of policy making (Kydland and Prescott (1977)). These critiques have led to an apparent (but false) paradox between so-called 'consistent but suboptimal' policies and 'inconsistent but optimal' policies. (The former policies are obtained from one application of a dynamic algorithm to periods $T \ldots 1$; the latter by reapplying that algorithm at each t, for the interval $T \ldots t$.) Examination of the origins of these two critiques will suggest the means to resolve them (section 11.6), and will then lead to making policy selections which are protected from them (section 11.7).

11.4.1 On simultaneity over players

Consider two arbitrary (not necessarily optimal) decision rules which induce noncausality:

$$\left.\begin{aligned} x^{(1)}_{t+j,t} &= G_{t+j}Y_{t+j-1,t} + g_{t+j}(x^{(2)}_{t+j,t}, \ldots) \\ x^{(2)}_{t+j,t} &= L_{t+j}Y_{t+j-1,t} + l_{t+j}(x^{(1)}_{t+j,t}, \ldots) \end{aligned}\right\} \begin{aligned} &\text{for } j = 0 \ldots T-t \\ &\text{and } t = 1 \ldots T. \end{aligned} \qquad (11.12)$$

Player 1 must solve the system (11.12) for his current choice ($x^{(1)}_t = x^{(1)}_{t,t}$) and for *all* expected instrument values, $x^{(1)}_{t+j,t}$ and $x^{(2)}_{t+j,t}$, conditioned on his own current information set (where $Y_{t-1,t} = Y_{t-1}$). The reverse problem faces player 2; i.e. to solve (11.12) for $x^{(2)}_t = x^{(2)}_{t,t}$, and his set of $x^{(1)}_{t+j,t}$ and $x^{(2)}_{t+j,t}$ values. The simultaneity must be resolved at every point from $t = 1$ to $t = T$. But, at each t, the simultaneity must be solved out by simulating the pair of equations recursively (as given by $j = 0 \ldots T-t$) so that the result of the previous step, plus the current expectations for the genuine noncontrollables $a_{t+j-1,t}$, may be inserted into the model (11.11) to yield the $Y_{t+j-1,t}$ values. It is straightforward to examine the consequences of particular decision rules. But it is no longer possible for a player to choose between those rules. He lacks any description of how the other player will actually choose his rule and, more important, he lacks any indication of how his opponent would change that rule in response to any choices made by the first player. In general, he must assume that the opponent makes rational choices (inclusive of assumptions about the first player's choice), unless he knows for sure that he is in a Stackelberg game.

It is therefore obvious that each player can generally obtain a solution for his chosen instruments and the complete set of expectations ($x^{(1)}_{t+j,t}$ *and* $x^{(2)}_{t+j,t}$) consistent in expectation with those values obtained by the

2 Under conditions of certainty, multiperiod decision rules are invalidated by their own implementation since they are based on a predicted rule for the future. It will be found that there is a gain to revising that rule when that future arrives, thus invalidating the first period's rule just used.

other player only if: (a) they use identical sets of conditioning information Ω_t throughout, and (b) they use identical models, and (c) they know or have been able to correctly calculate the decision rule of the other player. But if, as is more probable, they use different information they will actually implement mutually inconsistent solutions. Since the satisfaction of condition (c) is also doubtful, and only yields an expectation in any case, it is important that each player should use a feedback closed loop control rule so that their future choices may be closed loop with respect to the other player as well as 'nature'.

However, whether or not both players compute identical solutions, the policies obtained by each individual player when solved out in this manner are necessarily *internally consistent*. That implies consistent selections for, say, $x_t^{(1)}$ and $x_{t,t}^{(2)}$ (for the player with $x_t^{(1)}$). Since his expectations $x_{t+j,t}^{(2)}$, $x_{t+j,t}^{(1)}$, for $j = 1 \dots T - t$, are consistent within (11.12), internal consistency implies *expectationally consistent* choices. Finally, for a fixed set of certainty equivalents in $a_{t+j,t}$ $(j = 0 \dots T - t)$, policies that are both internally consistent as well as dynamically consistent over all $t = 1 \dots T$ are *time consistent*.

11.4.2 The essentiality of time consistent choices and the Lucas critique

Mutually consistent policies require each player to know the exact policy rules followed by other players. That is an attractive property implying no player is, on average, surprised by the actions of another player. But lack of it does not imply suboptimality or irrational choices. Rather, it reflects a lack of knowledge of the information sets and decision strategies employed by other players. It is a desirable rather than an essential quality.

But it is essential for each player to compute internally consistent policies (unless no player reacts to any expectations for the policies of his opponents). Otherwise each player surprises himself, which does imply irrational choices, given any assumptions on Ω_t and the decision mechanisms of other players. Suboptimality is revealed in that reactions of other players (while restricted to (11.12)) differ systematically from those assumed in forming the first player's choice. Each player could improve his own policy selection by eliminating any internal inconsistencies. Indeed he would be unlikely to be satisfied until he had done so. That is to say, no policy equilibrium is generally possible until a technique has been found to accomplish that. Hence planning methods which can only offer the choice between the 'consistent but suboptimal' and the 'inconsistent but optimal' options are likely to prove poor forecasting tools, and will result in misleading policy prescriptions.

By rewriting (11.12) with repeated forward substitutions from (11.9) and (11.10), we can transform the simultaneity between both policies (and their future expectations) to a question of time consistency within each policy individually:

$$\left.\begin{aligned} x_t^{(1)} &= G_t Y_{t-1} + g_t(L_{t+j} Y_{t+j-1,t} + l_{t+j}(x_{t+j,t}^{(1)}, \ldots), \ldots) \\ x_t^{(2)} &= L_t Y_{t-1} + l_t(G_{t+j} Y_{t+j-1,t} + g_{t+j}(x_{t+j,t}^{(2)}, \ldots), \ldots) \end{aligned}\right\} \qquad (11.13)$$

for $t = 1 \ldots T$ and $j = 0 \ldots T - t$.

Now $x_t^{(1)} (= x_{t,t}^{(1)})$ is contained within the successive values of $Y_{t+j-1,t}$ for $j \geqslant 1$ by virtue of the dynamics of the model; and within $l_{t+j}(x_{t+j,t}^{(1)})$ for $j = 0$, and therefore within $l_{t+j}(x_{t+j,t}^{(1)})$ for $j \geqslant 1$, by virtue of the effects of the decision rule.

This means that the time consistency aspect of noncausality is the essential problem to solve. The discussion of mutual consistency, of the Lucas critique, and of the dynamic inconsistency of endogenous expectations are all just particular parts of that problem. Indeed (11.13) displays the essence of the Lucas critique. Any changes in the policy rules of one player (say in L_t or l_t) automatically induce changes in the rules of the other player (and hence in his chosen policy values). In turn, substitute these changed policy rules into the relevant behavioural equations of the model and we find changes in the behavioural relations emanating from each player – and thus in the model as a whole, (11.11). According to Lucas, even short-run policies which do not account for changes in the reactions of another player will be false and misleading because such changes generally take place rapidly. Notice that this point is symmetric between players in our framework because both players follow non-causality inducing policy rules. It would still follow for the player who was a follower in a Stackelberg game; but not for the leader.

This Lucas critique applies to any rules which account for some interdependence of either players or planning intervals. They do *not* have to be optimal rules; *nor* is this only a consequence of feedback, closed loop, or discretionary (fine tuning) rules. But one set of rules which is protected from this critique are the simple fixed rules which ignore all other players, such as those which have been advocated most vigorously by the proponents of monetarism in the New Classical Macroeconomics debate. That is not the same as to say that fixed rules are the only such rules. On the contrary, there are many other possibilities; among them the closed loop feedback control policy rule derived below which has all the characteristics of discretion and contingency, as well as stochastic optimality. Recognition of the force of the Lucas type critique gives us no cause to argue that therefore fixed rules should be recommended, or that feedback rules be abandoned. Robustness to information errors, or a desire for simplicity, may be a different matter (subject to the qualifications of Chapter 12); but robustness to the reactions of other players turns out to be no grounds for criticisms of properly computed policy rules of the closed loop form.

11.4.3 The problem of optimising policies

The policy rules (8.20) and (8.50) are suboptimal and suffer from time-inconsistencies because both (8.19) and (8.48) ignore the terms $(\partial w/\partial x^{(j)}_{t+k,t})\ (\partial x^{(j)}_{t+k,t}/\partial x^{(i)}_t) \neq 0$, for $i \neq j$. The second partial derivative cannot be evaluated until the control rule for $x^{(j)}_t$ is known, which itself depends on that for $x^{(i)}_t$.

Essentially we have to solve (11.13) for $G_{t+j}, L_{t+j}, g_{t+j}, l_{t+j}$ together. At $t = T$ one might solve for $x^{(1)}_T$ conditional on a value for $x^{(2)}_T$ to be determined, using the methods of (8.20). Then we could do the same for $x^{(2)}_T$ for some $x^{(1)}_T$ to be determined. Solving those two expressions simultaneously would produce rules for $x^{(1)}_T$ and $x^{(2)}_T$ individually. We might then insert those rules in the constrained objective function as seen from $T-1$, and repeat those steps. However, it is not clear that the set $(x^{(1)}_T, x^{(1)}_{T-1}, x^{(2)}_T, x^{(2)}_{T-1})$ would now be optimal for the 2 period problem. The difficulty is that $x^{(1)}_{T,T-1}$ affects $x^{(1)}_{T-1}$, as seen in (11.13), but then $x^{(1)}_{T-1}$ affects $x^{(1)}_{T,T-1}$ via $Y_{T-1,T-1}$. So we can no longer take $\partial Y_{T-1,T-1}/\partial x^{(1)}_{T-1} = 0$ in deriving the stepping stone rule for $x^{(1)}_{T,T-1}$ (as we did following (8.14) for example). This is the crux of the time consistency problem. In proposition 11.3 below, we will show that the dynamic algorithms cannot be adapted to give optimal policies in this situation of noncausality (although they can still be used to give suboptimal ones).

A simpler solution is to solve for the complete set of instruments in $E_t(x^{(1)})$ and $E_t(x^{(2)})$, at each t, simultaneously. In (7.18) the simultaneity of $x^{(1)}_t$ with $x^{(1)}_{t+j,t}, j \geqslant 1$, is already solved out; the policies to be implemented are calculated simultaneously with expectations of the future values conditioned on Ω_t. Moreover, the full simultaneity between $x^{(1)}$ and $x^{(2)}$ is also made explicit in that optimal rule; and a time consistent updating formula is used at (7.32). It remains only to solve out that simultaneity between $x^{(1)}$ and $x^{(2)}$; and then adapt the time consistency constraints for these modified optimal choices.

11.4.4 Policy selection with a dominant player

The optimisation difficulties are substantially reduced in the special case of a Stackelberg game. Suppose player 2 knows (or assumes he knows) the policy rule adopted by player 1. Then $x^{(2)}_t$ is conditioned on $x^{(1)}_{t+j,t}$ whether or not that is a correct assumption. Then $x^{(1)}_t$, but not $x^{(2)}_t$, is subject to noncausality. One branch of the simultaneity is broken. Now optimal values of L_t and l_t are obtainable (by either player) in terms of player 2's preferences and his fixed expectations for $x^{(1)}_{t+j,t}$, $0 \leqslant j \leqslant T-t$, by temporarily replacing each $a_{t+j,t}$ with $a_{t+j,t} + R^{(1)}_{tt} x^{(1)}_{t+j,t}$ and using, say, (8.20) in the usual way. Next we can substitute $x^{(2)}_t$ out of the model for all periods; from (11.8) and (11.10)

$$Y_t = \Pi^+_{1t} Y_{t-1} + R^{(1)}_{tt} x^{(1)}_t + b_t \tag{11.14}$$

where $\Pi^+_{1t} = (\Pi_1 + R^{(2)}_{tt} L_t)$ and $b_t = a_t + R^{(2)}_{tt} l_t$. Now player 1's policy rule follows in the usual manner where the optimisation is now constrained by the transformed model (11.14). Such a procedure has been put forward by Chow (1981). Evidently the policy rule followed by player 1 will have altered from the case where player 2 is ignored, but the technology required to derive his optimal policies requires no modification. This is only the first step in the general problem of satisfying the Lucas critique applied to both players. There a modification of the optimisation technology is certainly necessary.

11.4.5 The necessity of satisfying the extended Lucas critique

It may be that the original point in the Lucas critique – and therefore the conventional interpretation of it – was concerned with a Stackelberg game. Most explanations take player 1 as the private sector and player 2 as the government, and assume the government to be dominant. If the policy rule of the government is perceived to change, as indeed it will by a private sector with rational expectations, then the policy rule of the private sector will also change in response. Yet the government's rule is not supposed to change again in response to their perceptions of the private sector's latest reaction, which is equally predictable.

It is unsatisfactory to endow the private sector,but not the government, with rational expectations. It is the government, after all, which has access to more comprehensive information as well as a more sophisticated understanding of the economy. Rational decision makers will try to achieve a Nash rather than a Stackelberg equilibrium in the policy making arena, just as they do in the markets of an exchange economy. For that reason we have stressed the extension to simultaneity over players and time. But there is a further reason. From (11.13) we can see that noncausality – and hence the Lucas critique – is induced unless *all* players operate a rule of the $\partial g_t / \partial x^{(2)}_{t+j,t} = 0$ type. No player can be certain that all other players will continue to operate such a rule; and he cannot afford to assume that they will do so without first checking that the expected loss, if they do not, is acceptably small. Even if player 2 chooses to ignore the reactions of player 1 and accept suboptimal policies, for reasons of simplicity and economy, he should know that the gains from accounting for those reactions do not compensate for the extra costs. If player 1 assumes he is in a Stackelberg game as a follower, he should first satisfy himself that he does not stand to lose too much if it turns out that he is wrong and player 2 actually does react. It is therefore important for the players to have the technology to derive optimal policies for the Nash equilibrium, in order to measure the risks in any other strategy if for no other reason. It is reasonable to assume that agents without certain knowledge of their opponents' strategies, but with rational expectations for them, would presume the same for their opponents and would make rational choices on that basis.

11.5 Time inseparability and the sources of dynamic inconsistencies

One of the more confusing points raised by noncausal models (in particular those containing endogenous expectations) is that optimal policies may appear dynamically inconsistent while consistent policies can appear suboptimal. The difficulty of ensuring the consistency of dynamic choices over successive intervals is appreciated well in demand theory, and in optimal growth models, when preferences are not additively separable over time[3]. However, more recently, Kydland and Prescott (1977), and Calvo (1978), among others, have pointed out that similar difficulties also arise for the consistency of policies chosen for noncausal models. In this section we find that easily computed consistent and optimal policies do exist.

11.5.1 Dynamic inconsistencies and time inseparable preferences

As a demonstration that it is the adjustments set out in (7.32) which guarantee time consistency, consider a two period deterministic policy selection problem involving a causal model, a single player, but time inseparable preferences. Partition z, in the notation of Chapter 7, so that z_1 represents current and z_2 all future policy variables. The model is

$$\begin{pmatrix} \tilde{y}_1 \\ \tilde{y}_2 \end{pmatrix} = \begin{pmatrix} R_1 & 0 \\ R_2 & R_1 \end{pmatrix} \begin{pmatrix} \tilde{x}_1 \\ \tilde{x}_2 \end{pmatrix} + \begin{pmatrix} b_1 \\ b_2 \end{pmatrix} \tag{11.15}$$

which, for the purposes of generality in this example only, will be written as

$$\begin{pmatrix} \tilde{z}_1 \\ \tilde{z}_2 \end{pmatrix} = \begin{pmatrix} R_1 & 0 \\ R_2 & R_1 \end{pmatrix} \begin{pmatrix} \tilde{x}_1 \\ \tilde{x}_2 \end{pmatrix} + \begin{pmatrix} b_1 \\ b_2 \end{pmatrix} \tag{11.16}$$

3 Samuelson (1971). The term 'time complementarity' has also been used for this problem. More detailed arguments are given in Deaton and Muellbauer (1980), and references there. The arguments for time inseparable preferences were given in Chapter 10.

where $\begin{pmatrix} R_1 \\ I \end{pmatrix}, \begin{pmatrix} R_2 \\ 0 \end{pmatrix}, \begin{pmatrix} b_1 \\ 0 \end{pmatrix}$ and $\begin{pmatrix} b_2 \\ 0 \end{pmatrix}$ have replaced R_1, R_2, b_1, b_2 in (11.15). Let the objective function be

$$w(\tilde{z}|\Omega_1) = \tfrac{1}{2}(\tilde{z}_1' \vdots \tilde{z}_2')\begin{pmatrix} Q_1 & Q_{12} \\ Q_{12}' & Q_2 \end{pmatrix}\begin{pmatrix} \tilde{z}_1 \\ \tilde{z}_2 \end{pmatrix}. \tag{11.17}$$

Proposition 11.1: The list of the leading subvectors from $\tilde{z}^*_{(t)}$ of (7.33) for $t = 1 \ldots T$ form a time consistent policy.

Proof: Following (11.17), the optimised instruments for $w(\tilde{z}|\Omega_1)$ are

$$-\begin{pmatrix} R_1' & R_2' \\ 0 & R_1' \end{pmatrix}\begin{pmatrix} Q_1 & Q_{12} \\ Q_{12}' & Q_2 \end{pmatrix}\begin{pmatrix} R_1 & 0 \\ R_2 & R_1 \end{pmatrix}\begin{pmatrix} \tilde{x}^*_{1,1} \\ \tilde{x}^*_{2,1} \end{pmatrix}$$

$$= \begin{pmatrix} R_1' & R_2' \\ 0 & R_1' \end{pmatrix}\begin{pmatrix} Q_1 & Q_{12} \\ Q_{12}' & Q_2 \end{pmatrix}\begin{pmatrix} b_1 \\ b_2 \end{pmatrix}. \tag{11.18}$$

But the instruments which optimise $w(\tilde{z}|\Omega_2)$ are given by (7.18) and (7.32),

$$-(R_1'Q_2R_1)\tilde{x}^*_{2,2} = R_1'[Q_2(b_2 + R_2\tilde{x}^*_{1,1}) + Q_{12}'(R_1\tilde{x}^*_{1,1} + b_1)] \tag{11.19}$$

where $\tilde{x}^*_{2,2}$ (i.e. $\tilde{x}^*_2$ computed at the start of period 2) is constrained by the value of x_1 implemented in period 1, $x^*_{1,1}$. Now $\tilde{x}^*_{2,2} = \tilde{x}^*_{2,1}$ by comparison of (11.19) with the bottom of (11.18).

The point at stake here is no more than to demonstrate that 'dynamic inconsistencies' will be revealed in $x^*_{2,1}$ if either of the two adjustments of (7.32) are ignored in making up $x^*_{2,2}$ and thus in the reoptimised policies of (7.33). Expositions of dynamic algorithms, however, deal exclusively with the special case where $Q_{12} = 0$. That restriction therefore rules out the time inconsistency problem *a priori* since the first adjustment of (7.32) is automatically incorporated in Z_{t-1} of (8.20).

11.5.2 Dynamic inconsistency in noncausal models

Now consider a second example involving a noncausal model but time separable preferences, where a similar thing happens. Yet the inevitability of dynamically inconsistent and suboptimal policies has all too frequently been the conclusion drawn from this type of example in the literature.

In this case time inseparabilities will be introduced to the *constrained* objective function by the model. We write that model in the manner of (7.2):

$$H\tilde{z} = b \text{ where } H = \begin{bmatrix} I & 0 \vdots -R_1 & -D \\ 0 & I \vdots -R_2 & -R_1 \end{bmatrix} \text{and } z' = [y_1', y_2', x_1', x_2']. \tag{11.20}$$

The matrix $D \neq 0$ represents the noncausal influences. Now insert that into (7.17):

$$\frac{1}{2}\begin{pmatrix}\tilde{z}\\ \mu\end{pmatrix}'\left(\begin{array}{cccc|cc} B_1 & 0 & C_1' & 0 & -I & 0\\ 0 & B_2 & 0 & C_2' & 0 & -I\\ C_1 & 0 & A_1 & 0 & R_1' & R_2'\\ 0 & C_2 & 0 & A_2 & D' & R_1'\\ \hline -I & 0 & R_1 & D & 0 & 0\\ 0 & -I & R_2 & R_1 & 0 & 0 \end{array}\right)\begin{pmatrix}\tilde{z}\\ \mu\end{pmatrix}+\begin{pmatrix}q\\ b\end{pmatrix}'\begin{pmatrix}\tilde{z}\\ \mu\end{pmatrix} \tag{11.21}$$

Permute rows and columns to separate the choice variables with respect to time:

$$\frac{1}{2}\begin{pmatrix}\tilde{z}_1\\ \mu_1\\ \tilde{z}_2\\ \mu_2\end{pmatrix}'\left(\begin{array}{ccc|ccc} B_1 & C_1' & -I & 0 & 0 & 0\\ C_1 & A_1 & R_1' & 0 & 0 & R_2'\\ -I & R_1 & 0 & 0 & D & 0\\ \hline 0 & 0 & 0 & B_2 & C_2' & -I\\ 0 & 0 & D' & C_2 & A_2 & R_1'\\ 0 & R_2 & 0 & -I & R_1 & 0 \end{array}\right)\begin{pmatrix}\tilde{z}_1\\ \mu_1\\ \tilde{z}_2\\ \mu_2\end{pmatrix}+\begin{pmatrix}q_1\\ b_1\\ q_2\\ b_2\end{pmatrix}'\begin{pmatrix}\tilde{z}_1\\ \mu_1\\ \tilde{z}_2\\ \mu_2\end{pmatrix}. \tag{11.22}$$

No further reorganisation of the hessian matrix will clear the two non block-diagonal submatrices. The expression (11.22) has the same structure as the unconstrained objective function at (11.17) (i.e. not time separable) except that now R_2 and D control the nonseparable elements, rather than R_2 and Q_{12} as in (11.18). Collecting terms that are respectively quadratic, linear and constant in the variables still to be chosen, $\tilde{z}_2$ and μ_2, we find that adjustments of a form similar to (7.32) must be made. But in this case $\mu_1^{*\prime} D\tilde{x}_2 + q_2\tilde{z}_2$ and $\tilde{x}_1^{*\prime} R_2' \mu_2 + b_2'\mu_2$ are the terms linear in variables still to be optimised at the start of the second period. Hence, in terms of a multiperiod problem, we must add

$$\begin{pmatrix}0\\ \cdots\\ D_t'\end{pmatrix}\mu_0^* \text{ to } q_{(t)} \text{ and } R_t^+\tilde{x}_0^* \text{ to } E_t(b_{(t)}) \tag{11.23}$$

where $\tilde{x}_0^*$, R_t^+ and μ_0^* are defined by (7.30) – (7.32). D_t is rows 1 to mt and columns $nt+1$ to $n(T-t+1)$ of the noncausal R matrix above. Notice that (7.33) remains valid, with one modification to $q_{(t)}$. For reasons of simplicity we have taken separable preferences here. But inseparable preferences are easily handled by also including the first adjustment of (7.32) in $q_{(t)}$. Additionally, by (7.16), $H'\mu^* = Q\tilde{z}^* + q$. Hence $D_t'\mu_0^* = (C_{(t)} \vdots A_{(t)})\tilde{z}_{(t)}^* + R_{(t)}'\mu_{(t)} + q_{(t)}$. This adjustment is therefore a function of the anticipated (noncausal) policy variables and their penalties. Finally,

$\mu_0^* = (I_{m(t-1)} \vdots 0)[(B \vdots C')\tilde{z}^* + q]$ could be used in (11.23) to avoid computing any Lagrange multipliers. Hence:

Proposition 11.2: Incorporating the adjustments (11.23), and the first member of (7.32) as necessary, guarantees that the policies given by each of the leading subvectors of (7.33), for $t = 1 \ldots T$, are time consistent (i.e. $\tilde{x}^*_{2.1} = \tilde{x}^*_{2,2}$ only if (11.23) is used).

Proof: Obvious from proposition 11.1 applied to (11.22).

11.6 The suboptimality of dynamic algorithms when constrained objectives are not time-nested

The similarity of the constraints for time consistency in (7.32) and (11.23) suggests some relationship exists between time inseparable preferences and noncausality. We show the equivalence of solving for optimal instrument values when $w(\tilde{z})$ is time separable but the model noncausal to the same problem when $w(\tilde{z})$ is time inseparable but the model is causal. We also show that dynamic inconsistencies arise from a defect in dynamic algorithms when applied to noncausal models. This will make it clear that time inseparabilities, of any kind, force optimal policies to be computed by the simultaneous optimisation of all instruments in all outstanding periods.

11.6.1 The relation between time inseparable preferences and noncausality

Suppose that Q is such that (7.10) is additively inseparable with respect to time. Consider the possible application of dynamic programming. Suppose the model to be in an extended reduced form (or state-space representation) as given by (8.2):

$$Z_t = A_t Z_{t-1} + C_t x_t + a_t \tag{11.24}$$

where $A_t = \Pi_{4t}, C_t = \Pi_{5t}$ imply a time varying version of (8.2). Also uncertainty is permitted in a_t. Stack the equations up for $t = 1, \ldots, T$

$$\begin{pmatrix} Z_1 \\ \vdots \\ Z_T \end{pmatrix} = \begin{pmatrix} A_1 & & 0 \\ & \ddots & \\ 0 & & A_T \end{pmatrix} \begin{pmatrix} Z_0 \\ \vdots \\ Z_{T-1} \end{pmatrix} + \begin{pmatrix} C_1 & & 0 \\ & \ddots & \\ 0 & & C_T \end{pmatrix} \begin{pmatrix} x_1 \\ \vdots \\ x_T \end{pmatrix} + \begin{pmatrix} a_1 \\ \vdots \\ a_T \end{pmatrix} \tag{11.25}$$

or $Z = \hat{A}Z_{-1} + \hat{C}x + a$. Let $Q = V'\Lambda V$ be a similarity transform and Λ a diagonal matrix of eigenvalues. Let $Z^+ = VZ, q^+ = Vq$ and $a^+ = Va$. The conventional dynamic programming algorithm might then be applied without modification to the transformed problem, i.e.

$$\left.\begin{array}{l} \min w = \tfrac{1}{2}\tilde{Z}^{+\prime}\Lambda\tilde{Z}^+ + q^{+\prime}\tilde{Z}^+ \\ \text{subject to } Z^+ = A^+Z^+_{-1} + C^+x + a^+ \end{array}\right\} \tag{11.26}$$

where $A^+ = V\hat{A}V'$ and $C^+ = V\hat{C}$ in view of the orthogonality of V. This is the standard problem for a dynamic algorithm as far as w is concerned – but the transformed model is now noncausal. A^+ and C^+ are both full in that they are neither block diagonal nor block triangular. Consequently Z_t^+ is a function of $Z_{t\pm i}^+$ and $x_{t\pm i}$, $i = 0, 1 \ldots$ There are no stochastic complications. If $E_t(a_t) = 0$ and $E_t(a_t Z_{t-1}') = 0$, then $E_t(a_t^+) = 0$ and $E_t(a^+ Z_{-1}^{+\prime}) = VE_t(aZ_{-1}')V' = 0$. The problem has a form identical to the problem solved by the dynamic algorithms of Chapter 8 – apart from the noncausality. Hence modifying those solutions to handle noncausality will also solve the difficulty of time inseparable preferences. Conversely the difficulties encountered in a solution for the inseparable preferences case will also appear in the noncausal model case.

11.6.2 Inseparability and noncausality in static algorithms

The same points can be seen more clearly in the context of the method of Chapter 7; and therefore be used to confirm the above. Consider the instrument calculations of (7.18). If there are inseparable preferences, then take the similarity transform $Q = V'\Lambda V$. Replace H^* by VH^*, $\begin{pmatrix} b \\ \cdots \\ 0 \end{pmatrix}$ by $V\begin{pmatrix} b \\ \cdots \\ 0 \end{pmatrix}$, q by Vq and Q by Λ. Next apply (7.18) in terms of the transformed problem, and then premultiply the result by V' to obtain $\tilde{x}^*$. For the converse case of separable preferences but a noncausal model, we can always find a decomposition for R such that $R = UL$ where L and U are, respectively, an $n \times n$ lower triangular matrix and an $m \times n$ matrix. Then we can replace Q by $\begin{pmatrix} U & 0 \\ 0 & I \end{pmatrix}' Q \begin{pmatrix} U & 0 \\ 0 & I \end{pmatrix}$ in the inverted matrix but by $\begin{pmatrix} U & 0 \\ 0 & I \end{pmatrix}' Q$ in the remaining position of (7.18). Finally, replacing R by L in H^* leaves $\tilde{x}^*$ expressed as the optimiser of the transformed problem involving a causal model but inseparable preferences.

Clearly, if both time inseparability and noncausality occur we can choose which of these two transformations to introduce and thus which of the single problems to solve. Since static algorithms provide a general solution to the causal – inseparable problem, we are also assured of a solution to any noncausal problems. All the remarks made about (7.32) guaranteeing time consistency apply, pari passu, to (11.23).

11.6.3 The role of the principle of optimality

In the light of the argument so far, the principle of optimality (or more precisely its necessary condition, the Markov property) appears as a device for checking the optimality of any proposed sequence of dynamic policy choices. It plays two roles here. It must apply to the forward sequence of optimal policy revisions seen at (7.33) and (8.20). And, for each of those steps, it must also apply to any backwards sequence of recursive optimisations which may be applied to the constrained objectives outstanding; i.e. to (8.18) and (8.19) for example. It must therefore apply in the forward sense for any planning problem. But in the backward sense it need be checked only in the case of a dynamic algorithm. In fact without the time nested structure of the constrained objective, noted in (8.6), the necessary Markov property cannot be satisfied by the backwards recursions. Dynamic algorithms are thus suboptimal unless the restrictions of *both* causality *and* time separable preferences apply.

Proposition 11.3: Any application of a period by period recursive policy optimisation procedure does not satisfy the principle of optimality if *either* the preferences lack time separability, *or* the model is mixed causal and noncausal, *or* both.

Proof: Consider a noncausal optimisation problem, such as (11.26), at $t = 1$. The (forward) Markovian objective is

$$w = E_1\left(\sum_1^T w_t(\tilde{z}_t)\right). \tag{11.27}$$

The required solution is obtained by solving, for $\tau = T$,

$$\min_{\substack{x_t \\ t=1\ldots\tau}} E_1\left\{L_\tau(\tilde{Z}) = \sum_{t=1}^{\tau}\left[w_t(\tilde{z}_t) - \mu_t'(Z_t - A_t^+ Z_{-1} - C_1{}^+ x + a_t{}^+)\right]\right\} \tag{11.28}$$

where $A_t^+ = [A_{t1}^+ \ldots A_{tT}^+]$ and $C_t^+ = [C_{t1}^+ \ldots C_{tT}^+]$ are the rows of A^+ and C^+ corresponding to Z_t^+ in (11.26). But

$$\begin{aligned}
\min_{\substack{x_t \\ t=1\ldots T}} E_1[L_T(\tilde{Z})] &\leqslant \min_{x_1}[E_1\{L_T(\tilde{Z})|\Omega_{T-1}^*\}] \\
&= \min_{x_1}[E_1\{L_1(\tilde{Z}_1, E_1(\tilde{Z}_{(2)}^*))\} + E_1\{L_{T-1}^*(\tilde{Z}_1, E_1(\tilde{Z}_{(2)}^*))\}] \\
&= \min_{x_1}\{E_1(L_1(\tilde{Z}_1, \tilde{Z}_{(2)}^*)) + \min_{x_2}\{E_1(L_2(\tilde{Z}_2, \tilde{Z}_{(3)}^*)) \\
&\quad + \ldots + \min_{x_t}\{E_1(L_{T-t}^*(\tilde{Z}_t, E_1(\tilde{Z}_{(t+1)}^*)))\}\ldots\}\}
\end{aligned} \tag{11.29}$$

given convexity in w, where

$$L_{T-1}^*(\tilde{Z}_1, E_1(\tilde{Z}_{(2)}^*)) = \min_{\substack{x_t \\ t=2\ldots T}} E_1\{L_T(\tilde{Z}_1^0, \tilde{Z}_{(2)}) - L_1(\tilde{Z}_1^0, \tilde{Z}_{(2)})\} \tag{11.30}$$

is the result of the previous $T-1$ period optimisation (for any arbitrary $\tilde{Z}_1^0$ value), whose outcomes $\tilde{Z}_{(2)}^{*\prime} = (\tilde{Z}_2^{*\prime} \ldots \tilde{Z}_T^{*\prime})$ make up an 'information set' Ω^*_{T-1} covering the results of the $T-1$ earlier backwards recursions. Indeed the strict inequality holds in (11.29). Since (11.28) shows[4] that $\partial L_1/\partial Z_{(2)} = \mu_1'(A^+_{13} \ldots A^+_{1T}, C^+_{12} \ldots C^+_{1T})$, equality in (11.29) follows if and only if *both*

$$(A^+_{13} \ldots A^+_{1T}) = 0 \text{ and } (C^+_{12} \ldots C^+_{1T}) = 0 \qquad (11.31)$$

because $\partial L_1/\partial Z_{(2)} = 0$ is the necessary and sufficient (Markov) condition for the principle of optimality to apply to the selection of x_1 by means of (11.29) and (11.30). Therefore $\tilde{Z}^*_{(2)}$ was not the set of optimal future policies for an arbitrary choice of x_1 ; and x_1 and $\tilde{Z}^*_{(2)}$ are not an optimal pair. Finally, any optimisation problem with time inseparable preferences and a causal model can be transformed into (11.28) such that (11.31) is again violated (see the discussion at (11.26)). So equality in (11.29) also fails in those cases. In our notation, (11.31) rules out noncausality in any form (e.g. from multiple players or endogenous expectations). But if we reverse the time indices ($t = 1$ is the last period and $t = T$ the first) then (11.31) rules out causal models. This completes the proof.

11.6.4 Comments

(a) The right hand side of (11.29) contains the backwards recursions which define the dynamic algorithms of Chapter 8. The order in which the terms were taken is determined by the recursions due to the causal nature of the model. One can imagine a hierarchical Stackelberg game, structured in the opposite way. The index $t = 1$ could signify the lowest 'level' of decision, and $t = T$ the highest, in our attempt to find the overall optimum. Proposition 11.3 would then hold with respect to forward recursions, a purely noncausal model (no lagged causal elements)[5] and a reverse principle of optimality (Dreyfus (1965)). Therefore backward recursions are appropriate for causal, and forward recursions for noncausal models. They are only both appropriate if $A^+ = 0$ and C^+ is block diagonal. Neither are appropriate for achieving the overall minimum if we have a mixed causal–noncausal model or time inseparable preferences.
(b) The problems we have considered in this chapter were not presented in terms of a model such as (11.26). But the nonzero matrices A^+_t and C^+_t were implicit, and it was the purpose of sections 11.2 and 11.3 to demonstrate that.

4 Nonzero elements only.

5 The nonzero coefficients of x_t in an equation for Y_t are consistent with both a purely causal and a purely noncausal model. In the past the econometric literature has confined itself to either one case or the other (e.g. Wallis (1980), Ravenkar (1980) use purely noncausal models).

(c) The key concept here is the Markov property. If we select to use a dynamic algorithm, we can only guarantee the Markov property at each backwards step if we also have the special functional form indicated by $\partial L_i/\partial Z_{(i+1)} = 0$, for $i = T-1 \ldots t$.

(d) Dynamic algorithms suffer a clear loss of generality in being unable to handle problems with intertemporal penalties, or with multiple players, or with endogenous expectations. We have argued that these are typical features of economic planning. We saw that the static algorithm, with (7.32) and (11.23), gave dynamically consistent and optimal closed loop policies for noncausal models. That is in contrast to the 'consistent but suboptimal' policies derived from the right hand side of (11.29). The latter cannot be said to be time consistent because, once the planner notices the suboptimality of his selected trajectory and abandons that particular 'optimising' technique, he has an incentive to alter the deterministic component of his original choice.

(e) Most examples of dynamic inconsistencies show the advantages of reneging, in a later period, on contracts made in an earlier period (Prescott (1977), Kydland and Prescott (1977)). They do not allow either agent to predict this in advance, and then to alter his strategies to the more favourable course in advance. But if the authors of these examples can make such predictions, so can the agents. Obviously agents will look for a new selection technique, as we have done. In other words, nonequilibrium solutions to a policy game are of no interest as descriptions of planning behaviour, nor for making policy recommendations.

11.7 Optimal policy selections for dynamic policy games

We now come to the final topic of specifying private optimal (and time consistent) decisions for policy makers in a multi-player decentralised game of choice. These will be compared to socially optimal decisions in the following section. Then a numerical example will be given. We take this opportunity to sharpen the discussion of the topics of previous sections, and to use the derivation of private choices to summarise the properties of policies optimal for a dynamic policy game.

11.7.1 Individual policy choices

The game is noncooperative, and we seek the Nash equilibrium for the multiperiod dynamic choices where each player unilaterally maximises his self-interest. We start with a 2-player game in which both players believe they face the same expectations and constraint set. Generalisations then follow. Let the players have preferences

$$w^{(i)} = \tfrac{1}{2}\tilde{z}^{(i)\prime}Q^{(i)}\tilde{z}^{(i)} + q^{(i)\prime}\tilde{z}^{(i)} \quad \text{for } i = 1, 2 \tag{11.32}$$

where $\tilde{z}^{(i)\prime} = (\tilde{y}^{(i)\prime}, \tilde{x}^{(i)\prime})$ and $z^{(i)d\prime} = (y^{(i)d\prime}, x^{(i)d\prime})$, and the normalisation is the same for all i. At each t, player 1 has n_1 instruments, $x_t^{(1)}$; and player 2 has n_2 instruments, $x_t^{(2)}$. However, we write $\tilde{y}^{(i)} = y - y^{(i)d}$; so y represents the union of the individual targets. $Q^{(i)}$ has rows and columns of zeroes wherever members of that union do not enter the subset of targets considered by the ith player. Given no cooperation, no player has direct preferences or ideal values for the instruments of the other player. He has indirect preferences through his opponent's policy, which depends on his own choice and vice versa. Moreover, $y^{(1)d} \neq y^{(2)d}$ is allowed. In all other respects each $w^{(i)}$ conforms to the specification of w discussed in Chapter 10.

We return to the model at (7.9), transformed to

$$\tilde{y} = R^{(1)}\tilde{x}^{(1)} + R^{(2)}\tilde{x}^{(2)} + b \tag{11.33}$$

where $R^{(1)}$ is an $mT \times n_1T$ matrix, and $R^{(2)}$ is $mT \times n_2T$, and both have the same block triangular structure as R. In previous chapters x has been ordered by time periods: $x' = (x_1^{(1)\prime}, x_1^{(2)\prime}, \ldots x_T^{(1)\prime}, x_T^{(2)\prime})$. But here x will be permuted to an ordering by players: $x' = (x^{(1)\prime}, x^{(2)\prime}) = (x_1^{(1)\prime} \ldots x_T^{(1)\prime}, x_1^{(2)\prime} \ldots x_T^{(2)\prime})$.

As far as player 1 is concerned, the model in terms of the variables subject to his own choice is

$$\tilde{y}^{(1)} = R^{(1)}\tilde{x}^{(1)} + b^{(1)}. \tag{11.34}$$

Player 2, on the other hand, views his choice variables through the model

$$\tilde{y}^{(2)} = R^{(2)}\tilde{x}^{(2)} + b^{(2)}. \tag{11.35}$$

Notice $b^{(1)} = R^{(2)}\tilde{x}^{(2)} + c^{(1)}$ and $b^{(2)} = R^{(1)}\tilde{x}^{(1)} + c^{(2)}$ where, for $i = 1, 2$, $c^{(i)} = s - y^{(i)d} + \sum_1^2 R^{(j)}x^{(j)d}$. Hence the optimal decision for $x^{(1)}$ is structurally dependent on that for $x^{(2)}$; and vice versa.

The necessary conditions for solving the original policy problem, (7.13), were

$$\partial w/\partial\tilde{x} + (\partial\tilde{y}/\partial\tilde{x})'\partial w/\partial\tilde{y} = 0. \tag{11.36}$$

Inserting the relevant quantities from (7.9) and (7.10) yields (7.18). In a similar manner, the necessary conditions for an optimal choice of $x^{(i)}$ are now

$$\partial w^{(i)}/\partial\tilde{x}^{(i)} + \{(\partial\tilde{y}^{(i)}/\partial\tilde{x}^{(j)})\partial\tilde{x}^{(j)}/\partial\tilde{x}^{(i)} + \partial\tilde{y}^{(i)}/\partial\tilde{x}^{(i)}\}'\partial w^{(i)}/\partial\tilde{y}^{(i)} = 0 \tag{11.37}$$

for $i = 1, 2$ and $j \neq i$. Excepting $\partial\tilde{x}^{(j)}/\partial\tilde{x}^{(i)}$, all the partial derivatives required to evaluate (11.37) are given directly by (11.32), and (11.34) or (11.35). The difficulty will be to deduce values for $\partial\tilde{x}^{(j)}/\partial\tilde{x}^{(i)}$ and $\partial\tilde{x}^{(i)}/\partial\tilde{x}^{(j)}$. On the other hand, given knowledge or estimates of $\partial\tilde{x}^{(j)}/\partial\tilde{x}^{(i)} = D^{(j)}$, for $i, j = 1, 2$, and then solving (11.37) for $i = 1$ and $i = 2$ simultaneously, yields the optimal decisions

$$\begin{pmatrix} \tilde{x}^{(1)*} \\ \tilde{x}^{(2)*} \end{pmatrix} = -\left[\begin{array}{c|c} G^{(1)\prime}Q^{(1)}G_0^{(1)} & G^{(1)\prime}Q^{(1)}\begin{pmatrix} R^{(2)} \\ \cdots \\ 0 \end{pmatrix} \\ \hdashline G^{(2)\prime}Q^{(2)}\begin{pmatrix} R^{(1)} \\ \cdots \\ 0 \end{pmatrix} & G^{(2)\prime}Q^{(2)}G_0^{(2)} \end{array}\right]^{-1} \begin{bmatrix} G^{(1)\prime}\left\{Q^{(1)}\begin{pmatrix} c^{(1)} \\ \cdots \\ 0 \end{pmatrix} + q^{(1)}\right\} \\ G^{(2)\prime}\left\{Q^{(2)}\begin{pmatrix} c^{(2)} \\ \cdots \\ 0 \end{pmatrix} + q^{(2)}\right\} \end{bmatrix} \tag{11.38}$$

where $G^{(i)\prime} = \{(R^{(i)} + R^{(j)}D^{(j)})' : I\}$ and $G_0^{(i)\prime} = (R^{(i)\prime} : I)$ hereafter.

The policy selections in (11.38) constitute a Nash and noncooperative equilibrium of individual choices since the pair $(\tilde{x}^{(1)*}, \tilde{x}^{(2)*})$ satisfies

$$w^{(1)}(\tilde{x}^{(1)*}, \tilde{x}^{(2)*}) \leqslant w^{(1)}(\tilde{x}^{(1)}, \tilde{x}^{(2)*})$$

and $$w^{(2)}(\tilde{x}^{(1)*}, \tilde{x}^{(2)*}) \leqslant w^{(2)}(\tilde{x}^{(1)*}, \tilde{x}^{(2)})$$

for all $\tilde{x}^{(1)} \neq \tilde{x}^{(1)*}$ and $\tilde{x}^{(2)} \neq \tilde{x}^{(2)*}$ in F. No player has any incentive to deviate unilaterally from his own choice. As one would expect in a non-cooperative game, each player's optimal strategy depends on, and is determined simultaneously with, the optimal strategy of the other player. This simultaneity extends over the whole planning period; that is $\tilde{x}_t^{(1)*}$ depends on $\tilde{x}_{t+j}^{(2)*}$, and vice versa, for all $-t+1 \leqslant j \leqslant T-t$ and each $1 \leqslant t \leqslant T$.

The expressions (11.37) and (11.38) show that when $D^{(1)}$ and $D^{(2)}$ are unknown a priori (such as where we seek the relevant values for a Nash equilibrium) then, like $R^{(i)}$ and $Q^{(i)}$ before them, they depend on the choice of $x^{(1)*}$ and $x^{(2)*}$, while $x^{(1)*}$ and $x^{(2)*}$ themselves depend on $D^{(1)}$ and $D^{(2)}$. The point here is that this mutual dependence remains even when (11.32) and (11.33) contain known quadratic and linear functions.

But, despite the complexity of the dependence between $D^{(j)}$ and $x^{(i)}$ values, the existence of optimal values $D_*^{(1)}$ and $D_*^{(2)}$ to minimise $w^{(1)}$ and $w^{(2)}$ simultaneously is assured by the existence of a Nash equilibrium solution to any nonzero sum game with convex objectives and strategy sets.[6] The determination of those values, however, will require a numerical search. In principle, since (11.37) transforms the dynamic optimisation into an extended static form, any fixed point algorithm for constructing general equilibria could be adapted for this purpose. Those algorithms are well known, and can be reapplied at each t.

Nevertheless, we obtain some insight into the reciprocal dependence between $x^{(1)}$ and $x^{(2)}$ from the obvious (if inefficient) iterative scheme suggested by (11.38). Inserting trial values $D_s^{(1)}$ and $D_s^{(2)}$ implies new values. In fact the players would then best observe the policy reactions,

$$\begin{bmatrix} I & -D_{s+1}^{(1)} \\ -D_{s+1}^{(2)} & I \end{bmatrix}\begin{pmatrix} \tilde{x}_s^{(1)*} \\ \tilde{x}_s^{(2)*} \end{pmatrix} = \begin{bmatrix} E_{s+1}^{(1)}c^{(1)} + k_{s+1}^{(1)} \\ E_{s+1}^{(2)}c^{(2)} + k_{s+1}^{(2)} \end{bmatrix} \tag{11.39}$$

6 And, at least if (11.32) and (11.33) contain quadratic and linear functions respectively over F, a unique solution exists: see Aubin (1979), p. 271, theorem 1.

where for $i = 1$ and 2

$$D^{(i)}_{s+1} = -(G^{(i)'}_s Q^{(i)} G^{(i)}_0)^{-1} G^{(i)'}_s Q^{(i)} \begin{pmatrix} R^{(j)} \\ \cdots \\ 0 \end{pmatrix} \tag{11.40}$$

for $\quad G^{(i)'}_s = \{(R^{(i)} + R^{(j)} D^{(j)}_s)' \vdots I\}$

and $(E^{(i)}_{s+1} \vdots k^{(i)}_{s+1}) = -(G^{(i)'}_s Q^{(i)} G^{(i)}_0)^{-1} \; G^{(i)'}_s \left\{ Q^{(i)} \begin{pmatrix} I \\ \cdots \\ 0 \end{pmatrix} \vdots q^{(i)} \right\}$. These are the optimal decision rules in terms of the opponents' anticipated reactions implied by the current version of (11.38). The iteration (11.40) demonstrates the disequilibrium (and suboptimal) nature of any solution not guaranteed to correspond to the fixed points $D^{(i)}_*$, for $i = 1, 2$. But it is not certain that (11.40) as it stands will always achieve $D^{(1)}_*$ and $D^{(2)}_*$ from arbitrary starts $D^{(1)}_1$ and $D^{(2)}_1$; and modifications to that end may be necessary.

Now it is also straightforward, but tedious, to evaluate the step corresponding to (11.39) in terms of the policies in (11.38):

$$\tilde{x}^{(i)*}_s = -\left\{ G^{(i)'}_s Q^{(i)} \left[G^{(i)}_s - \begin{pmatrix} R^{(j)} \\ \cdots \\ 0 \end{pmatrix} (D^{(j)}_{s+1} - D^{(j)}_s) \right] \right\}^{-1} G^{(i)'}_s \left\{ Q^{(i)} \right.$$
$$\left. \times \left[\begin{pmatrix} c^{(i)} \\ \cdots \\ 0 \end{pmatrix} + \begin{pmatrix} R^{(j)} \\ \cdots \\ 0 \end{pmatrix} (E^{(j)}_{s+1} c^{(j)} + k^{(j)}_{s+1}) \right] + q^{(i)} \right\}. \tag{11.41}$$

Hence, by comparison with (7.18), the Nash equilibrium solutions, $\tilde{x}^{(i)*}$ for $i = 1$ and 2, can be derived as the optimal decision for a single player attempting to minimise $w^{(i)}$ subject to

$$\tilde{y}^{(i)} = (R^{(i)} + R^{(j)} D^{(j)}_*)\tilde{x}^{(i)} + d^{(i)}_*. \tag{11.42}$$

where $d^{(i)}_* = c^{(i)} + R^{(j)} (E^{(j)}_* c^{(j)} + k^{(j)}_*)$ and the subscript '$*$' denotes evaluation at the fixed points $D^{(1)}_*$ and $D^{(2)}_*$.

In conclusion, therefore, policies derived from imposed (or arbitrary) $D^{(i)}_s$ values will generally be suboptimal and induce disequilibrium into the economy. They are only optimal subject to further improvements and the disequilibriating tendency being wilfully ignored. If either player looked again at such decisions he would find that it pays him to alter his component unilaterally.

11.7.2 The zero option

There are two interesting special cases under the heading of imposed decision rules. First, there are many examples where one player's decisions are a fixed reaction to those anticipated from another. Fixed exchange rates, wage bargains linked to variables strongly influenced by government policy such as inflation or unemployment, social security payments being index linked, are some examples. Secondly, a player may introduce disequilibrium while recognising the interdependence of instruments. This arises when player 1 attempts to optimise $\tilde{x}^{(1)*}$ conditional on a value of $x^{(2)*}$ to be chosen by player 2: i.e. by (7.18)

$$\tilde{x}^{(1)*} = D_1^{(1)}\tilde{x}^{(2)*} + E_1^{(1)}c^{(1)} + k_1^{(1)} \tag{11.43}$$

where

$$(D_1^{(1)} \vdots E_1^{(1)} \vdots k_1^{(1)}) = -(G_0^{(1)\prime}Q^{(1)}G_0^{(1)})^{-1}G_0^{(1)\prime}\left\{Q^{(1)}\begin{pmatrix} I \\ \cdots \\ 0 \end{pmatrix}(R^{(2)} \vdots I) \vdots q^{(1)}\right\}.$$

If player 2 likewise optimises conditional on a value of $x^{(1)*}$ then

$$\tilde{x}^{(2)*} = D_1^{(2)}\tilde{x}^{(1)*} + E_1^{(2)}c^{(2)} + k_1^{(2)} \tag{11.44}$$

in obvious notation. The individual choices are then given by the 'reduced form' rule

$$\begin{pmatrix} \tilde{x}^{(1)*} \\ \tilde{x}^{(2)*} \end{pmatrix} = \begin{bmatrix} I & -D_1^{(1)} \\ -D_1^{(2)} & I \end{bmatrix}^{-1} \begin{bmatrix} E_1^{(1)}c^{(1)} + k_1^{(1)} \\ E_1^{(2)}c^{(2)} + k_1^{(2)} \end{bmatrix}. \tag{11.45}$$

The paradox between ignoring the policies' reciprocity while recognising their interdependence is that both players calculate values for $D^{(1)}$ and $D^{(2)}$ before choosing $x^{(1)}$ and $x^{(2)}$, but to do so they use $\partial\tilde{x}^{(2)}/\partial\tilde{x}^{(1)} = 0$ and $\partial\tilde{x}^{(1)}/\partial\tilde{x}^{(2)} = 0$ in (11.37)! Those calculated values must therefore be mutually inconsistent. Indeed (11.43) and (11.44) are just (11.39) with $G_0^{(i)}$ for $G_s^{(i)}$. Hence (11.43) and (11.44) can provide good starts for (11.40). But (11.45) is a clear illustration of the suboptimality and disequilibrium in a prior imposition of policy reaction functions. The reaction functions in (11.43)–(11.45) constitute the only kind of noncooperative policy game considered elsewhere (see, among others, Kydland (1975) or De Bruyne (1979)).

11.7.3 The noncausalities evaluated

There is a second potential source of suboptimality in the solution of dynamic policy games. Solutions which ignore the implicit noncausality facing each player contain an element of suboptimality which manifests itself in dynamically inconsistent choices.

Although the economy being modelled here is strictly causal, the decision facing each player contains a noncausal element. When $\partial y_t/\partial x_{t+j} \neq 0$, for some $j \geqslant 1$, anticipated future instrument choices necessarily affect current targets directly. But those targets also affect that anticipated instrument choice through the future economic state predicted by (11.33). The current and future choices are mutually dependent, not recursive. The noncausality cannot be backsubstituted out over time. In particular, any reaction to the anticipated future choices of another player will induce noncausality into one's own (current) choices. It transmits an impact from those anticipated future instruments to current targets via one's currently chosen instrument values, since the latter are themselves conditioned on their calculated future impacts as implied by (11.33), which in turn depend on the expected future targets, the opponent's anticipated decisions, and so on. If this is reciprocated, the noncausality is *symmetric* over players and cannot be substituted out recursively between them. That in turn blocks any backsubstitutions over time. The upshot is the joint dependence of instrument values over both time and players.

For the problem in hand, the noncausality implicit in a Nash equilibrium solution has already been demonstrated. Indeed it was made explicit by noting optimal decisions are given by minimising $w^{(i)}$ subject to (11.42). In fact, any imposed values $D_s^{(i)}$ imply each player should observe the model

$$\tilde{y}^{(i)} = (R^{(i)} + R^{(j)}D_{s+1}^{(j)})\tilde{x}^{(i)} + d_{s+1}^{(i)} \quad i, j = 1, 2 \text{ and } i \neq j \tag{11.46}$$

in order to allow for the anticipated reactions of his opponent when making his own choices. Since, by (11.40), neither $D_*^{(1)}$ and $D_*^{(2)}$, nor indeed $D_{s+1}^{(1)}$ and $D_{s+1}^{(2)}$ given *any* $D_s^{(i)}$ values (including $D_s^{(i)} = 0$ for $i = 1$ and 2), are generally block lower triangular, each player is using a noncausal model to evaluate the consequences of his policies. The degree of noncausality facing player i can be computed explicitly from the strictly upper block triangle of $R^{(j)}D_*^{(j)}$ (respectively $R^{(j)}D_{s+1}^{(j)}$).

Notice that $D_{s+1}^{(j)}$ causes the noncausality facing player i, and that $D_{s+1}^{(j)}$ is determinated by $D_s^{(i)}$. Thus, for $D_s^{(i)} \neq D_*^{(i)}$, the disequilibrium in (11.39) is due to player i allowing for player j's reaction but *not* for his own counter-reaction. So even if player i assumes it is acceptable not to react further to player j, he cannot afford to presume player j will make the same assumption.

11.7.4 Certainty equivalence, asymmetric information and rational expectations

In an equilibrium solution, the usual certainty equivalence result may be applied directly:

$$\min_{x^{(i)}} \left\{ E_t(w^{(i)}) \,|\, \tilde{y}^{(i)} - (R^{(i)} + R^{(j)}D_*^{(j)})\tilde{x}^{(i)} - d_*^{(i)} = 0 \right\}$$
$$= \min_{x^{(i)}} \left\{ w^{(i)} \,|\, \tilde{y}^{(i)} - (R^{(i)} + R^{(j)}D_*^{(j)})\tilde{x}^{(i)} - E_t(d_*^{(i)}) = 0 \right\} \tag{11.47}$$

for $i, j = 1, 2$ and $i \neq j$. In this case $E_t(d_*^{(i)})$, for $i = 1, 2$, involves inserting both $E_t(c^{(1)})$ and $E_t(c^{(2)})$ into the relevant expressions. Uncertainty with respect to 'nature' (i.e. over s within $c^{(1)}$) and with respect to the decisions of the other player (i.e. over $c^{(2)}$ itself) are both handled for player 1 by applying conventional certainty equivalence to $d_*^{(1)}$. Similarly, player 2 treats uncertainty as if he were in a single player game against 'nature' in the form of $d_*^{(2)}$. So, each player can independently evaluate $\tilde{x}^{(i)*}$, for $i = 1$ and 2, via (7.16) or (7.18) with $E_t(d_*^{(i)})$ for b and $R^{(i)} + R^{(j)}D_*^{(j)}$ for R.

Certainty equivalent decisions for any other $D^{(1)}$ and $D^{(2)}$ values are obtained by inserting the same expectations into (11.39), although naturally there is no optimal interpretation attached. Whether a player solves (11.47) or (11.39) his decisions will be consistent with his calculations of what he expects his opponent to decide. But that is not to say that player 1's evaluation of (11.47) or (11.39) is necessarily consistent with player 2's evaluation of (11.47) or (11.39). If the players work with different information sets the calculations made by player 1 will not coincide with player 2's own determination of what he himself should do. In order to allow asymmetric information sets, we shall use $E_{ti}(s)$ to make up $E_{ti}(c^{(1)})$ and $E_{ti}(c^{(2)})$, and thus $E_{ti}(d^{(1)})$ and $E_{ti}(d^{(2)})$, for $i = 1, 2$. $E_{ti}(.)$ denotes player i's expectations conditional on Ω_{ti} – his own information set at period t. Then player 1's view is obtained by evaluating (11.47) or (11.39) with $E_{t1}(c^{(1)})$ and $E_{t1}(c^{(2)})$. Then, or independently, player 2's view is derived from (11.47) or (11.39) with $E_{t2}(c^{(1)})$ and $E_{t2}(c^{(2)})$.

We can also obtain each player's own view of the optimal choices when they have different estimates of the model (each player has his own values for some or all of $R^{(1)}$, $R^{(2)}$ and s), or the preferences (i.e. each player has his own values *for all of* $Q^{(1)}$, $Q^{(2)}$, $q^{(1)}$, $q^{(2)}$, $z^{(1)d}$ and $z^{(2)d}$), by evaluating (11.47) or (11.39) based on each player's own information in turn.

One further refinement is possible. The extensions discussed in the previous paragraphs cover the case where each player either knew, or was totally ignorant of, the other player's expectations and estimates for s, $R^{(i)}$ and $w^{(i)}$ for both $i = 1$ and 2. But if, instead, those expectations and estimates were thought to differ across players, then player 1 would solve (11.47) in which $E_t(d^{(1)})$ contains $E_{t1}(c^{(1)})$ and $R^{(2)}$ from player 1's estimates, but $E_{t2}(c^{(2)})$, $D^{(2)}$, $E^{(2)}$, $Q^{(2)}$ and $G^{(2)}$ made up from his view of player 2's estimates. Likewise player 2 would make up the first two components of $E_t(d^{(2)})$ from his own estimates, but the factor multiplying $R^{(1)}$ from his view of player 1's estimates.

The generalisations above seem to be of considerable significance because in practice most noncooperative games, and economic competition generally, turn in the first place on differing information sets. Unfortunately, there are usually as many views on how the economy works (and the preferences to be applied) as there are contributors to policy formation. The set of decisions and the expected outcomes as determined by each player coincide if and only if *both* players use identical estimates and expectations for the model, both sets of preferences, both sets of ideal values, and $E_{ti}(s)$ for $i = 1, 2$. It is extremely unlikely that so many stringent assumptions would be simultaneously satisfied.

Finally, each policy selection is based on the mathematical expectations $E\,(d^{(j)}|\Omega_{ti})$, for $i, j = 1$ and 2. To the extent that uncertainty is confined to s, each player's own policy selection and his prediction of his opponent's selection are both rational expectations of rational choices. Rational expectations of the targets then follow by (11.33). Thus each player's decision depends on rational expectations of current and future decisions by his opponent, and therefore implicitly on rational expectations of current and future targets. But if uncertainty appears in any part of R, then the same is true up to a linear approximation.

11.7.5 Time-consistent policy revisions

The remaining problem is to determine how to revise each decision rule optimally, for each $t \geqslant 2$, in the light of unanticipated shocks ($s_{t-j} \neq E_{t-1}(s_{t-j})$ for $j \geqslant 1$), past achievements (y_{t-1}), and changed expectations of the future ($E_t\,(s_{t+j}) \neq E_{t-1}\,(s_{t+j})$ for $j \geqslant 0$). Returning to the technique used for the single player game in Chapter 7, we can try to repeat the steps (7.29) to (7.32) to obtain time consistency constraints for the optimal solution to (11.47). Equation (7.30) holds unchanged. But the counterpart to (7.31) no longer contains a zero subvector, except when $E_{t-1}(\tilde{x}^{(i)}_{(t)})$ is inserted. It is replaced by $\tilde{y}^*_0 - (R^{(i)}_0 + (R^{(j)}D^{(j)}_*)_0)\tilde{x}^{(i)*}_0 - (R^{(j)}D^{(j)})_t\tilde{x}_{(t)} - b_0$ which contains variables still to be chosen. Moreover the lower subvector of (7.31) has $R^{(i)+}_t + (R^{(j)}D^{(j)}_*)^+_t$ and $R^{(i)}_{(t)} + (R^{(j)}D^{(j)}_*)_{(t)}$ in place of R^+_t and $R_{(t)}$ respectively, where

$$R^{(i)} + R^{(j)}D^{(j)}_* = \left[\begin{array}{c|c} R^{(i)}_0 + (R^{(j)}D^{(j)}_*)_0 & (R^{(j)}D^{(j)}_*)_t \\ \hline R^{(i)+}_t + (R^{(j)}D^{(j)}_*)^+_t & R^{(i)}_{(t)} + (R^{(j)}D^{(j)}_*)_{(t)} \end{array}\right] \qquad (11.48)$$

is partitioned conformably with $y' = (y^{*\prime}_0, y'_{(t)})$ and $x^{(i)*\prime} = (x^{(i)*\prime}_0, x^{(i)\prime}_{(t)})$; similarly to R at (7.31). The constraints in the reoptimisation problem are therefore no longer just a modification of those outstanding from the original constraint set. However, writing the original constrained objective as the lagrangian

$$\tfrac{1}{2}\tilde{z}^{(i)\prime}Q^{(i)}\tilde{z}^{(i)} + q^{(i)\prime}\tilde{z}^{(i)} - \mu^{(i)\prime}[\tilde{y}^{(i)} - (R^{(i)} + R^{(j)}D^{(j)}_*)\tilde{x}^{(i)} - E_t(d^{(i)}_*)] \qquad (11.49)$$

and inserting (7.30), (11.48) and $\mu^{(i)\prime} = (\mu^{(i)*\prime}_0, \mu^{(i)\prime}_{(t)})$, leaves a reoptimisation problem of the same form where all quantities are again replaced by their counterparts subscripted (t). Indeed, expanding (11.49) and collecting linear and quadratic terms in variables still to be optimised, we see (7.32) applies again, but incorporating an extra linear term $\mu^{(i)*\prime}_0(R^{(j)}D^{(j)}_*)_t\tilde{x}^{(i)}_{(t)}$.

So the complete set of time consistency constraints are now to add

$$Q_2^{(i)}\tilde{z}_0^{(i)*} + \left[\frac{0}{(R^{(j)}D_*^{(j)})'_t\mu_0^{(i)*}}\right] \text{ to } q_{(t)}^{(i)}$$

and $$(R^{(i)} + R^{(j)}D_*^{(j)})_t^+ \tilde{x}_0^{(i)*} \text{ to } E_t(d_{(t)}^{(i)}) \qquad (11.50)$$

for *both* i and j ($i \neq j$). The value of $\mu_0^{(i)*}$ is obtained in the solution of (11.47), or as described at (11.23).

This set of adjustments ensures each player makes time consistent decisions. The terms not involving $R^{(j)}D_*^{(j)}$ are standard for sequential optimisations; the remaining term is simply the extension for a noncausal model. These adjustments constrain each reoptimisation to the previous (historical) decisions. By forcing the continued satisfaction of (11.37) at every t, they ensure that in the absence of uncertainty each reoptimisation reproduces the same solutions for the outstanding decisions. Hence these optimal strategies are time consistent (proposition 11.2).

11.7.6 Noncausality and the determination of optimal choices

It has been established that the conventional backwards recursive optimisation procedures for making optimal multiperiod choices (e.g. by dynamic programming, or by Pontryagin's minimum principle, etc.) fail to give optimal solutions when applied to noncausal models. Of course, such techniques may still be applied to yield suboptimal decision rules, but they cannot satisfy the conditions for the noncooperative equilibrium. Each player will have an incentive to seek alternative decision rules. That happens because, by construction, the first order conditions at each recursive step ignore the dependence of that decision on any decisions having an earlier time index. In other words, in the determination of $x_T^{(i)}$ the 'initial conditions' (y_{T-1}, x_{T-1} etc.) are assumed invariant to the decision being made, although the values of those 'initial conditions' still remain to be chosen. That assumption is justified if we are determining $x_T^{(i)}$ for use at T (i.e. $x_{T,T}^{(i)}$) since the 'initial conditions' are by then fixed by history. But it is false in a noncausal model when the decision rule for $x_T^{(i)}$ is being determined during period $T-1$ (i.e. $x_{T,T-1}^{(i)}$) as a stepping stone to the choice of $x_{T-1}^{(i)}$ itself. In that case, the mutual dependence between $x_{T,T-1}^{(i)}$ and $x_{T-1,T-1}^{(i)}$ violates the supposed invariance of $x_{T-1,T-1}^{(i)}$ to $x_{T,T-1}^{(i)}$ in the first backwards step. Hence, the first order conditions which determine the optimal rule for $x_{T,T}^{(i)}$ must differ from those which yield the optimal rule for $x_{T,T-1}^{(i)}$ to be used as a stepping stone for determining the rule for $x_{T-1}^{(i)}$. The rule for $x_{T,T}^{(i)}$ is therefore not interchangeable with that for $x_{T,T-1}^{(i)}$. But that interchangeability is built into dynamic programming.

The optimal rule for $x^{(i)}_{T,T}$ satisfies

$$\frac{\partial w^{(i)}}{\partial \tilde{x}^{(i)}_{T,T}} + \left(\frac{\partial \tilde{y}^{(i)}_{T}}{\partial \tilde{x}^{(i)}_{T,T}}\right)' \frac{\partial w^{(i)}}{\partial \tilde{y}^{(i)}_{T}} = 0 \text{ for } i = 1, 2. \tag{11.51}$$

That condition differs from the first order conditions which define an optimal $x^{(i)}_{T,T-1}$:

$$\frac{\partial w^{(i)}}{\partial \tilde{x}^{(i)}_{T,T-1}} + \left(\frac{\partial \tilde{y}^{(i)}_{T-1}}{\partial \tilde{x}^{(i)}_{T,T-1}}\right)' \left(\frac{\partial w^{(i)}}{\partial \tilde{y}^{(i)}_{T-1}} + \left(\frac{\partial \tilde{y}^{(i)}_{T}}{\partial \tilde{y}^{(i)}_{T-1}}\right)' \frac{\partial w^{(i)}}{\partial \tilde{y}^{(i)}_{T}}\right) + \left(\frac{\partial \tilde{y}^{(i)}_{T}}{\partial \tilde{x}^{(i)}_{T,T-1}}\right)' \frac{\partial w^{(i)}}{\partial \tilde{y}^{(i)}_{T}} = 0 \tag{11.52}$$

for $i = 1, 2$. The determination of an optimal $x^{(i)}_{T-1,T-1}$ itself depends on solving the latter simultaneously with

$$\frac{\partial w^{(i)}}{\partial \tilde{x}^{(i)}_{T-1,T-1}} + \left(\frac{\partial \tilde{y}^{(i)}_{T-1}}{\partial \tilde{x}^{(i)}_{T-1,T-1}}\right)' \left(\frac{\partial w^{(i)}}{\partial \tilde{y}^{(i)}_{T-1}} + \left(\frac{\partial \tilde{y}^{(i)}_{T}}{\partial \tilde{y}^{(i)}_{T-1}}\right)' \frac{\partial w^{(i)}}{\partial \tilde{y}^{(i)}_{T}}\right) + \left(\frac{\partial \tilde{y}^{(i)}_{T}}{\partial \tilde{x}^{(i)}_{T-1,T-1}}\right)' \frac{\partial w^{(i)}}{\partial \tilde{y}^{(i)}_{T}} = 0 \tag{11.53}$$

(for $i = 1, 2$) which are the first order conditions for $x^{(i)}_{T-1,T-1}$. We cannot replace (11.52) by (11.51) because the discrepancy between them,

$$\left(\frac{\partial \tilde{y}^{(i)}_{T-1}}{\partial \tilde{x}^{(i)}_{T,T-1}}\right)' \left(\frac{\partial w^{(i)}}{\partial \tilde{y}^{(i)}_{T-1}} + \left(\frac{\partial \tilde{y}^{(i)}_{T}}{\partial \tilde{y}^{(i)}_{T-1}}\right)' \frac{\partial w^{(i)}}{\partial \tilde{y}^{(i)}_{T}}\right)$$
$$= \tfrac{1}{2}[R^{(j)}D^{(j)}_{*}]'_{(T-1,T)}(I\,\vdots\,0)[Q^{(i)}_{(T-1,T-1)}\tilde{z}^{(i)}_{T-1} + 2Q^{(i)}_{(T-1,T)}\tilde{z}^{(i)}_{T} + q^{(i)}_{T-1}] \tag{11.54}$$

is always a nonzero function of $x^{(i)}_{T-1}$ (and $x^{(i)}_{T}$), even when $\Omega_{T-1} = \Omega_{T}$. The subscripts $(T-1, T-1)$ and $(T-1, T)$ in (11.54) indicate the relevant submatrices of Q and $R^{(j)}D^{(j)}_{*}$, partitioned with respect to time. So the leading submatrix contains the noncausality between periods T and $T-1$. If we banish uncertainty, and thereby any innovations in the information sets, then we can treat $E_{T-1}(x^{(i)}_{T}) = E_{T}(x^{(i)}_{T}) = x^{(i)}_{T}$. But even then, if we ignore the terms in (11.54), we necessarily still get a solution for $x^{(i)}_{T,T-1}$ which differs from that for $x^{(i)}_{T,T}$ despite no information changes.

In fact, (11.54) vanishes only if $D^{(j)}_{*} = 0$; i.e. when no player reacts to any other player. In that case (11.51) and (11.52) coincide, and (11.52) and (11.53) may be solved recursively (backwards) in the manner of dynamic programming. Thus ignoring the terms in (11.54) is one source of time inconsistencies. But another source is the neglect or inaccurate evaluation of (11.50), the time consistency constraints.

By their construction, dynamic optimisations presume that *both* $D_*^{(1)} = 0$ and $D_*^{(2)} = 0$. But the simultaneity between $x^{(1)}$ and $x^{(2)}$ destroys any time nested decision structure for $x_t^{(i)}$. We see this by rewriting (11.49), with time separable preferences, as

$$\sum_t \left[\frac{1}{2} \tilde{z}_t^{(i)\prime} Q_t^{(i)} \tilde{z}_t^{(i)} + q_t^{(i)\prime} \tilde{z}_t^{(i)} - \mu_t^{(i)\prime} \left(\tilde{y}_t^{(i)} - \sum_{k=1}^{T} (R^{(i)} + R^{(j)} D_*^{(j)})_{tk} \tilde{x}_k^{(i)} - E_1(d_*^{(i)}) \right) \right] \tag{11.55}$$

where $(R^{(i)} + R^{(j)} D_*^{(j)})_{tk}$ is the (t, k)th submatrix of $R^{(i)} + R^{(j)} D_*^{(j)}$ partitioned with respect to time. A time nested structure in the constrained objective, in the form of (8.6), is required to guarantee the necessary condition ('the Markov Property') for the principle of optimality to apply to each backwards recursion of a dynamic algorithm. Obviously the terms $\sum_{k=t+1}^{T} (R^{(j)} D_*^{(j)})_{tk} \tilde{x}_k^{(i)}$ violate that necessary condition ($R^{(i)}$ being block triangular) for each backwards step to $x_t^{(i)}$ $(t \neq T)$. Dynamic algorithms cannot be used to derive either individually or socially optimal choices, nor the equilibrium position, in multiplayer policy problems.

11.8 Extensions: private vs social optima

11.8.1 Private decisions in multiplayer games

The generalisation of private decision rules to the case of $i = 1, \ldots, p$ players is straightforward. Extend the notation so that each quantity superscripted (i) is now associated with player i. Permuting x once again to an ordering by players, and the columns of R correspondingly, the model becomes

$$\tilde{y}^{(i)} = \sum_{j=1}^{p} R^{(j)} \tilde{x}^{(j)} + c^{(i)} \tag{11.56}$$

with $c^{(i)}$ as before except that the summation extends to p.

Next define $D^{(i,j)} = -(G_s^{(i)\prime} Q^{(i)} G_0^{(i)})^{-1} G_s^{(i)\prime} Q^{(i)} \begin{pmatrix} R^{(j)} \\ \cdots \\ 0 \end{pmatrix}$ for $i, j = 1 \ldots p$, and $j \neq i$. Thus

$$\tilde{x}^{(i)} = \sum_{j=1}^{p} D^{(i,j)} \tilde{x}^{(j)} + e^{(i)}, \; i = 1, \ldots, p \tag{11.57}$$

with $e^{(i)} = (E_{s+1}^{(i)} c^{(i)} + k_{s+1}^{(i)})$. The private decision rules are now

$$\begin{pmatrix} \tilde{x}^{(1)*} \\ \vdots \\ \tilde{x}^{(p)*} \end{pmatrix} = \begin{bmatrix} I - D^{(1,2)} & \ldots & -D^{(1,p)} \\ \vdots & \ddots & \vdots \\ -D^{(p,1)} & \ldots & I \end{bmatrix}^{-1} \begin{pmatrix} e^{(1)} \\ \vdots \\ e^{(p)} \end{pmatrix} = D^{-1} e. \tag{11.58}$$

Moreover, any $p-1$ decisions can be expressed in terms of the remaining one

$$\begin{pmatrix} \tilde{x}^{(1)*} \\ \vdots \\ \tilde{x}^{(p)*} \end{pmatrix}_{(i)} = [D_{(i)}]^{-1}\{e_{(i)} + D_{(i)}^{(\cdot,i)}\tilde{x}^{(i)*}\} \tag{11.59}$$

where the subscript (i) implies the ith subvector has been deleted. $D^{(\cdot,i)}$ contains the columns of D associated with $x^{(i)}$. $D_{(i)}$ is therefore the co-factor of the principle minor corresponding to that subvector; and $D^{(i,i)}$ does not appear in $D_{(i)}^{(\cdot,i)}$. Consequently player i faces the constraints

$$\tilde{y}^{(i)} = [R^{(i)} + R_{(i)}(D_{(i)})^{-1}D_{(i)}^{(\cdot,i)}]\tilde{x}^{(i)} + d^{(i)} \quad i = 1\ldots p \tag{11.60}$$

with $d^{(i)} = c^{(i)} + R_{(i)}(D_{(i)})^{-1}e_{(i)}$ and $R_{(i)} = [R^{(1)}\ldots R^{(i-1)}, R^{(i+1)}\ldots R^{(p)}]$. Therefore the properties described for the optimal choices in the previous section carry over *in toto* to each individual decision; that is with respect to noncausality, asymmetric information, and certainty equivalence. Moreover, the time consistency constraints, given at (11.50), generalise directly by using $R^{(i)} + R_{(i)}(D_{(i)})^{-1}D_{(i)}^{(\cdot,i)}$ for $R^{(i)} + R^{(j)}D^{(j)}$ throughout. The vital point, however, is that (11.59) shows that the same properties may also be said to hold for each pair of 'individual' choices of $\tilde{x}^{(i)*}$ and $\tilde{x}_{(i)}^{*}$; i.e. with respect to player i's choice and that of his collected (but not combined, or cooperating) opponents as if they were an individual. It is not necessary to analyse each pair of decisions individually; a 2 player analysis repeated p times over all possible pairs $(\tilde{x}^{(i)}, \tilde{x}_{(i)})$ does the same job. Computationally this is remarkably simple. If we can evaluate D, with $D_s^{(i,j)}$ imposed or using (11.40) to obtain $D_*^{(i,j)}$, we need only make p passes, at each t, through a program for the case of a single player against nature using the transformed model (11.60).

11.8.2 Alternative strategies and the Lucas critique

(i) Cournot and Stackelberg games

Equilibria under alternative strategies for reaching a collective optimum, other than the Nash noncooperative equilibrium, are contained within the solution to (11.37). The two player Cournot equilibrium game (each player assumes the policy choice of his rival to be invariant to his own choice: perfect myopia between players but not over intervals of time) is where player 1 assumes his rival will choose, say, $\tilde{x}^{(2)**}$ and player 2 assumes his rival will choose $\tilde{x}^{(1)**}$. In that case $\partial\tilde{x}^{(j)}/\partial\tilde{x}^{(i)} = 0$ for $i, j = 1$ and 2; so (11.43) and (11.44) yield the required decisions directly with $D^{(i)} = 0$ and $b^{(i)} = c^{(i)} + R^{(j)}\tilde{x}^{(j)**}$ for $c^{(i)}$.

The Stackelberg equilibrium solution assumes one player (the leader) plays a Cournot strategy, and the other (the follower) conditions his choice on knowledge of that strategy. Taking player 2 as the leader we must insert $\partial \tilde{x}^{(2)}/\partial \tilde{x}^{(1)} = 0$, but $\partial \tilde{x}^{(1)}/\partial \tilde{x}^{(2)} \neq 0$, into (11.37). Then, making the Cournot type substitution above to (11.44) only, (11.45) becomes

$$\begin{pmatrix} \tilde{x}_s^{(1)*} \\ \tilde{x}_s^{(2)*} \end{pmatrix} = \begin{bmatrix} E_1^{(1)}c^{(1)} + k_1^{(1)} + D_1^{(1)}(E_1^{(2)}b^{(2)} + k_1^{(2)}) \\ E_1^{(2)}b^{(2)} + k_1^{(2)} \end{bmatrix}. \tag{11.61}$$

The recursive and asymmetric nature of the solution of a Stackelberg game is again made clear. Indeed that solution expressed in terms of the Cournot solution is:

$$\begin{pmatrix} x_s^{(1)*} \\ x_s^{(2)*} \end{pmatrix} = \begin{bmatrix} x_c^{(1)*} + D_1^{(1)}(x_c^{(2)*} - x^{(2)**}) \\ x_c^{(2)*} \end{bmatrix} \tag{11.62}$$

(ii) The Lucas critique

The final lesson directly concerns the joint dependence of all elements in $x^{(1)}$ and $x^{(2)}$. For any particular (either optimal or imposed) values of $D^{(1)}$ and $D^{(2)}$ inserted into (11.43) and (11.44) implies that this joint dependence is reciprocal over players. Repeated substitutions between $x^{(1)}$ and $x^{(2)}$ then show how a bargaining sequence works that dependence out, leaving (11.45) as the equilibrium position. For example, suppose each player accepts his opponents' last bargaining position as the best estimate of his opponents' next position and then conditions his own current choice on that. So both players play 'follower' and assume the other to be a 'leader' with respect to the latest position in some bargaining sequence. Using the Stackelberg solution in (11.62), the first position is

$$\begin{pmatrix} x_s^{(1)} \\ x_s^{(2)} \end{pmatrix} = \begin{pmatrix} D^{(1)}D^{(2)} & 0 \\ 0 & D^{(2)}D^{(1)} \end{pmatrix} \begin{pmatrix} x^{(1)**} \\ x^{(2)**} \end{pmatrix} + \begin{pmatrix} I & D^{(1)} \\ D^{(2)} & I \end{pmatrix} \begin{pmatrix} E^{(1)}c^{(1)} + k^{(1)} \\ E^{(2)}c^{(2)} + k^{(2)} \end{pmatrix}. \tag{11.63}$$

After r bargaining rounds they will reach

$$\begin{pmatrix} x_s^{(1)} \\ x_s^{(2)} \end{pmatrix} = \begin{pmatrix} D^{(1)}D^{(2)} & 0 \\ 0 & D^{(2)}D^{(1)} \end{pmatrix}^r \begin{pmatrix} x^{(1)**} \\ x^{(2)**} \end{pmatrix} + \sum_{j=0}^{r-1} \begin{pmatrix} D^{(1)}D^{(2)} & 0 \\ 0 & D^{(2)}D^{(1)} \end{pmatrix}^j \begin{pmatrix} I & D^{(1)} \\ D^{(2)} & I \end{pmatrix} \begin{pmatrix} E^{(1)}c^{(1)} + k^{(1)} \\ E^{(2)}c^{(2)} + k^{(2)} \end{pmatrix}. \tag{11.64}$$

If $\max(\rho(D^{(1)}D^{(2)}), \rho(D^{(2)}D^{(1)})) < 1$ this bargaining sequence converges to

$$\begin{pmatrix} x_s^{(1)*} \\ x_s^{(2)*} \end{pmatrix} = \begin{bmatrix} I & -D^{(1)} \\ -D^{(2)} & I \end{bmatrix}^{-1} \begin{bmatrix} E^{(1)}c^{(1)} + k^{(1)} \\ E^{(2)}c^{(2)} + k^{(2)} \end{bmatrix} \tag{11.65}$$

where $\rho(.)$ denotes spectral radius.[7] That reproduces (11.45) for the given $D^{(1)}$ and $D^{(2)}$; but the Nash equilibrium solution if and only if $D_*^{(i)}$, $E_*^{(i)}$, and $k_*^{(i)}$ are employed for $i = 1$ *and* 2.

The sequence of policy adjustments described by (11.64) is a demonstration of the Lucas critique of economic policy formation (Lucas (1976)). Each time a player perceives his rival to change policies, the rule which determines his own choice (and hence that choice itself) will alter in response; and so on until the equilibrium position of (11.65) is reached. The conclusion, however, is:

(a) this critique applies to both optimal and suboptimal (simple or fixed) decision rules employed by a player in a policy game;

(b) optimal decisions by (11.47), and those achieving the bargaining equilibrium of (11.65) with other $D^{(i)}$ values, are automatically protected from the Lucas critique. The existence of a game does not imply that optimal and contingent policy rules should be abandoned.

(iii) Strategy errors

We can likewise express the difference between the Nash and Cournot or Stackelberg solutions in simple forms: respectively

$$\begin{pmatrix} x_N^{(1)*} \\ x_N^{(2)*} \end{pmatrix} - \begin{pmatrix} x_c^{(1)*} \\ x_c^{(2)*} \end{pmatrix} = \begin{pmatrix} D_*^{(1)}[x_N^{(2)*} - x^{(2)**}] \\ D_*^{(2)}[x_N^{(1)*} - x^{(1)**}] \end{pmatrix} \tag{11.66}$$

or

$$\begin{pmatrix} x_N^{(1)*} \\ x_N^{(2)*} \end{pmatrix} - \begin{pmatrix} x_s^{(1)*} \\ x_s^{(2)*} \end{pmatrix} = \begin{pmatrix} x_N^{(1)*} \\ x_N^{(2)*} \end{pmatrix} - \begin{pmatrix} x_c^{(1)*} \\ x_c^{(2)*} \end{pmatrix} + \begin{pmatrix} E_*^{(2)}b^{(2)} + k_*^{(2)} \\ 0 \end{pmatrix}. \tag{11.67}$$

These two differences describe the error due to making the wrong assumptions about the strategy of the other player.

These formulae express the degree of frustration which would be experienced by each player in making the wrong assumption about the behaviour of his opponent. They contain important information because there are almost certainly heavy costs to gathering the information required to generate a Nash solution; the opponent's preferences, his model, his expections for s, all have to be inserted into the components of (11.47). If, on the basis of reasonable guesses or preliminary information,

7 Easily verified from the inverse of the partitioned matrix in (11.65). The spectral radius condition will hold at least for $D_*^{(1)}$ and $D_*^{(2)}$ because otherwise no equilibrium could exist for the game, contradicting the results quoted on p. 281

these differences are large then retaliation is required and the expenditure of effort on information gathering is justified. But if they are small the reactions of the opposition can safely be ignored. It is therefore essential to have the ability to analyse the Nash equilibrium even if its realisation is not anticipated.

11.8.3 On socially optimal policy choices

The Nash equilibrium is optimal for the individual player in that he cannot improve the game by unilateral action. But such policy choices are almost always socially inferior in the sense that they do not belong to the Pareto optimal set. A cooperative solution might achieve lower penalties all round. The pair of strategies $(x^{(1)*}, x^{(2)*})$ is Pareto optimal if and only if no other pair $(x^{(1)}, x^{(2)}) \neq (x^{(1)*}, x^{(2)*})$ exists such that $w^{(i)}(\tilde{x}^{(1)}, \tilde{x}^{(2)}) \leqslant w^{(i)}(\tilde{x}^{(1)*}, \tilde{x}^{(2)*})$, $i = 1, 2$, with strict inequality for one i.

Consider a simple two player game where private optimal choices are given by (11.45). Partition $Q^{(i)} = \begin{pmatrix} B^{(i)} & C^{(i)\prime} \\ C^{(i)} & A^{(i)} \end{pmatrix}$, $q^{(i)} = \begin{pmatrix} q_1^{(i)} \\ q_2^{(i)} \end{pmatrix}$ and $z^{(i)d} = \begin{pmatrix} y^{(i)d} \\ x^{(i)d} \end{pmatrix}$. (11.45) can be rearranged to give

$$-\left[\begin{array}{c|c} R^{(1)\prime}B^{(1)}R^{(1)} + R^{(1)\prime}C^{(1)\prime} + C^{(1)}R^{(1)} + A^{(1)} & R^{(1)\prime}B^{(1)}R^{(2)} + C^{(1)}R^{(2)} \\ \hline R^{(2)\prime}B^{(2)}R^{(1)} + C^{(2)}R^{(1)} & R^{(2)\prime}B^{(2)}R^{(2)} + R^{(2)\prime}C^{(2)\prime} + C^{(2)}R^{(2)} + A^{(2)} \end{array}\right]\begin{pmatrix} \tilde{x}^{(1)*} \\ \tilde{x}^{(2)*} \end{pmatrix}$$

$$= \begin{bmatrix} (R^{(1)\prime}B^{(1)} + C^{(1)})c^{(1)} + R^{(1)\prime}q_1^{(1)} + q_2^{(1)} \\ (R^{(2)\prime}B^{(2)} + C^{(2)})c^{(2)} + R^{(2)\prime}q_1^{(2)} + q_2^{(2)} \end{bmatrix}. \tag{11.68}$$

On the other hand the cooperative solution, from the general preferences expressed by

$$Q = \left(\begin{array}{c|c|c} \hat{B} & \hat{C}^{(1)\prime} & \hat{C}^{(2)\prime} \\ \hline \hat{C}^{(1)} & \hat{A}^{(1,1)} & \hat{A}^{(1,2)} \\ \hline \hat{C}^{(2)} & \hat{A}^{(1,2)\prime} & \hat{A}^{(2,2)} \end{array}\right), \quad q = \begin{pmatrix} q_1 \\ q_2 \\ q_3 \end{pmatrix} \text{ and } z^d = \begin{pmatrix} y^d \\ x^{(1)d} \\ x^{(2)d} \end{pmatrix}$$

partitioned conformably to $z' = (y', x^{(1)\prime}, x^{(2)\prime})$, is (7.18). We get now

$$-\left[\begin{array}{c|c} R^{(1)\prime}\hat{B}R^{(1)} + R^{(1)\prime}\hat{C}^{(1)\prime} + \hat{C}^{(1)}R^{(1)} + \hat{A}^{(1,1)} & R^{(1)\prime}\hat{B}R^{(2)} + R^{(1)\prime}\hat{C}^{(2)\prime} + \hat{C}^{(1)}R^{(2)} + \hat{A}^{(1,2)} \\ \hline R^{(2)\prime}\hat{B}R^{(1)} + \hat{C}^{(2)}R^{(1)} + R^{(2)\prime}\hat{C}^{(1)\prime} + \hat{A}^{(1,2)\prime} & R^{(2)\prime}\hat{B}R^{(2)} + R^{(2)\prime}\hat{C}^{(2)\prime} + \hat{C}^{(2)}R^{(2)} + \hat{A}^{(2,2)} \end{array}\right]\begin{pmatrix} \tilde{x}^{(1)*} \\ \tilde{x}^{(2)*} \end{pmatrix}$$

$$= \begin{bmatrix} (R^{(1)\prime}\hat{B} + \hat{C}^{(1)})b + R^{(1)\prime}q_1 + q_2 \\ (R^{(2)\prime}\hat{B} + \hat{C}^{(2)})b + R^{(2)\prime}q_1 + q_3 \end{bmatrix} \tag{11.69}$$

where $b = s - y^d + \Sigma R^{(i)} x^{(i)d}$. The set of Pareto optimal policy choices for this class of problem is generated by $\min(w = \alpha_1 w_1 + \alpha_2 w_2)$ subject to the model (7.2), for different values of α_i subject to $\alpha_i > 0$ and $\Sigma\alpha_i = 1$ (Da Cunha and Polak (1967)). So *Proposition* 11.4: the necessary and sufficient conditions for the private policy choices to be Pareto optimal, in general, are

(i) $B^{(1)} = (\alpha_2/1 - \alpha_1) B^{(2)} = B^{(2)}$; likewise $y^{(1)d} = y^{(2)d}$
(ii) $\hat{C}^{(i)} = 0$ for $i = 1, 2$ and therefore $C^{(1)} = 0$, $C^{(2)} = 0$
(iii) $\hat{A}^{(1,2)} = 0$.

Proof:
Compare (11.56) with (11.57), where $Q = \sum_i \alpha_i Q^{(i)}$, $q = \Sigma\alpha_i q^{(i)}$, $z^d = \Sigma\alpha_i z^{(i)d}$, and $\Sigma\alpha_i = 1$. Notice $\hat{C}^{(i)} = \alpha_i C^{(i)}$ for $i = 1, 2$.

The generalisation of proposition 11.4 to multiple players is straightforward. Let $w = \sum_1^p \alpha_i w_i$ such that $\Sigma\alpha_i = 1$. We use the fact that we can treat $x^{(2)}$ above as if it were $p - 1$ collected opposition players behaving as one 'individual'. Therefore we can compare (11.68) and (11.69) in the p versions obtained by rotating $i = 1$ to be each player and $i = 2$ to be his opposition. We subdivide $R^{(2)}$ as $(R^{(2)} \ldots R^{(p-1)})$ and $x^{(2)}$ conformably each time. Then proposition 11.4 parts (i) and (iii) immediately generalise to (i) $B^{(i)} = \sum_{j \neq i} (\alpha_j/(1 - \alpha_i)) B^{(j)}$, $y^{(i)d} = \sum_{j \neq i} (\alpha_j/(1 - \alpha_i)) y^{(j)d}$ and (iii) $\hat{A}^{(i,j)} = 0$. Part (ii) remains $C^{(i)} = 0$. All three parts are for $i, j = 1 \ldots p$ and $i \neq j$.[8]

Proposition 11.4 makes it clear that the conditions on preferences for the private policy choices to be socially optimal are extremely stringent:

(i) Individual preferences over the target priorities, the list of targets, and their ideal values, must all be identical or identically linearly dependent. Different goals in those three aspects are ruled out. The time profile of target penalties must also be identical across individuals, despite the different electoral time tables, contract periods, or other periods of account, which they will face in practice.

(ii) $C^{(i)} = 0$ states that there can be no envy (emulation, demonstration effects, etc.). No disutility is felt by any player as result of the joint values of his own instruments and the union of the targets. There is no extra penalty in any individual preferences (beyond that on an individual variable's failure) if a target is achieved by a disproportionate sacrifice by one player; as, for example, in organised labour having to forgo

8 Proposition 11.4 is similar in style to some results given by De Bruyne (1979). It is more general in that intertemporal penalties are encompassed here, and we see that time plays no special role. Moreover, De Bruyne's result corresponds only to parts (ii) and (iii). But the essential point is that De Bruyne's results apply to policies which are time-inconsistent, being derived from a dynamic algorithm. They are therefore suboptimal. They do not describe private optimal choices. Nor could they refer to a Nash equilibrium solution since generally $D_1^{(i)} \neq D_*^{(i)}$.

increases in money wages in order to achieve higher investment, or in entrepreneurs accepting higher taxation in the interests of an equitable distribution of the social wage. It also rules out dogma over 'means' to various 'ends' (dogma over 'ends' is contained in $B_i^{(i)}$ and over 'means' in $\hat{A}^{(i,i)}$) such as a preference for achieving particular policies through monetary rather than fiscal instruments.

(iii) $\hat{A}^{(i,j)} = 0$ states that there can be no externalities; the use of one player's instrument imposes no costs on the preference function of any other player.

To identify the conditions under which privately optimal choices provide a socially optimal solution is an obvious as well as a traditional concern. Indeed much economic theory, in the shape of Walrasian general equilibrium analysis, is designed to investigate that very question and to show that private rational decisions in an exchange economy under perfect competition will also be socially optimal. However, in terms of the private decisions investigated here, ruling out conflicts in tastes and all externalities to ensure a social optimum effectively makes a game (competition) hardly seem necessary. But it is obvious that for genuinely optimal private decisions by (11.47) – or even by (11.39) with $D_s^{(i)} \neq 0$ – there are *no* conditions under which they produce a socially optimal outcome. In fact, perfect competition is a special case in which $D_*^{(i)} = 0$ due to the large number of equally insignificant agents with very fast decision speeds. The results of this subsection therefore serve to point out the very specialised nature of the perfect competition assumptions, in addition to the restrictive conditions on preferences to ensure socially optimal decisions. In the more interesting cases, where competition is genuine but not 'perfect', private (Nash equilibrium) decisions cannot be socially optimal.

11.9 A numerical example

As an illustration of policy optimisation in a policy game, we have extended the policy optimisation example of Chapter 7. Although this is for illustration only, it does give some feel for the results obtained in a Nash equilibrium, as opposed to a Cournot or a cooperative solution. To avoid any convergence difficulties, the Nash solution will be estimated here by (11.45).

We partition the available instruments as W_2 for one player (organised labour), and T and G for a second player (the government, or budgetary authority). The union of target sets remains as C, I, and D. The remainder of the problem is as specified in Chapter 7 with the exception of the preferences. To add some extra realism we gave each player an objective

Table 11.1 *The nonzero preference structure*

Player 1: $C = 0$; $q = 0$; penalties on squared failures

Policy	1933	1934	1935	1936	preference matrix
W_2	1.0	2.0	1.0	5.0	A
C	1.0	0.1	1.0	1.0	B
I	0.01	0.3	0.5	0.5	B
D	0.5	0.5	2.0	5.0	B

Player 2: $q = 0$; from the upper triangle of Q:

Policy	1933	1934	1935	1936	preference matrix
T	1.0	0.1	0.1	0.8	A
G	2.0	1.0	1.0	1.0	A
C	1.0	2.0	5.0	3.5	B
I	0.1	0.3	1.0	0.5	B
D	0.5	0.4	2.0	0.25	B
T and G	0.25	0.25	0	− 0.8	A
C and I	0.05	0	1.0	0	B
C and D	0.3	0	− 1.0	− 2.0	B

Intertemporal penalties: T_{1935} and T_{1936} : − 0.1; T_{1935} and G_{1936} : − 0.1; G_{1933} and T_{1936} : − 0.5; G_{1933} and G_{1936} :0.5; G_{1935} and T_{1936} : − 0.2; G_{1935} and G_{1936} :0.3; C_{1933} and C_{1935} :0.5; C_{1933} and C_{1936} :0.5; C_{1935} and C_{1936} :2.0; D_{1935} and C_{1936} : − 1.0; C_{1933} and G_{1936} :0.5.

function to reflect the main points of the preferences revealed by the historical policy choices (table 10.2).[9] Table 11.1 shows the preferences finally set for the players. Their desired values are as in Chapter 7. Both players have identical information sets in Ω_t, covering the model, expectations and preference structures, for each t. For the Cournot solution each player presumes that the other sets his instruments at their desired values.

The idea behind this example is to examine the optimal policies in a noncooperative game between the Roosevelt administration and organised labour as the economic strategy of the New Deal was introduced to counter the great recession of that period. Those policies can be

9 We took the diagonal elements from table 10.2, and also the off-diagonal elements largest in absolute size. The latter were then adjusted to give a Cournot policy choice which at least uniformly dominates the historical choice in the targets. In this scheme, adjustments were only applied to the government preferences; labour had a diagonal Q matrix. The fact that the diagonal elements on their own were found to yield rather inferior choices shows that the small elements of Q, taken together, can play an important role in determining policies.

compared to the cooperative solution and the historical policies. Organised labour was one of the chief groups in the coalition which brought Roosevelt to power. It had suffered particularly from the recession and unemployment after 1929. So labour could have been expected to attempt to extract a price for its continued support. Its instrument would be power to influence wage demands (and hence D) as well as the industrial relations in both public and private sectors. Just how much bargaining power it in fact had will be revealed by how much it could force the administration to modify their policies from the government's preferred cooperative solution. It is perhaps unrealistic to presume that labour had literal control of W_2, the public sector wage bill. But W_2 may be taken as an indicator for labour's actual wagc bargaining power and as a proxy for the variable used in establishing the resulting wage contracts. Indeed a stable relation between private sector wage bargains and the proxy W_2 exists since public wages move in line with the general wage level in the economy at large, and W_2 is determined by fixed comparisons with the private sector.

The Cournot and Nash equilibrium solutions in terms of closed loop controls are set out in tables 11.2 to 11.5. The Nash solution shows many of the features of the cooperative solution of Chapter 7, and to some extent reflects the preoccupations of the two players in their preferences. The steady improvement in C and I, the steady values of W_2 (1934 apart), and the rapid improvement in D, all suit organised labour. The improvements in C, with an especially good performance in 1935 in time for the

Table 11.2 *Closed loop Cournot solutions: constant \$ billions*

	1933	1934	1935	1936	
C	44.68	47.95	49.92	53.91	organised labour
I	− 6.71	− 3.46	− 1.70	0.34	
D	10.48	6.96	5.94	5.37	
W_2	5.56	5.09	4.34	5.19	
w^* (open loop) = 191.8, w^* (closed loop) = 191.8. No improvements.					
C	45.93	53.03	57.62	60.84	government
I	− 6.09	− 0.88	1.95	3.91	
D	7.20	1.74	2.02	− 2.21	
T	7.54	7.83	7.76	5.28	
G	12.86	14.14	13.24	12.39	
w^* (open loop) = 58.1, w^* (closed loop) = 51.8. Improvement: 10.8%					

Table 11.3 *Closed loop Nash solutions: constant $ billions*

	1933	1934	1935	1936	
C	46.85	52.87	57.75	61.11	
I	− 6.19	− 1.19	1.68	3.66	
D	7.51	1.94	2.14	− 0.95	
W_2	6.71	5.85	6.42	6.06	organised labour
T	7.24	7.80	7.70	6.42	
G	12.50	14.06	13.23	13.37	government

Labour: w^* (open loop) = 30.77, w^* (closed loop) = 26.61. Improvement: 13.6%
Government: w^* (open loop) = 49.26, w^* (closed loop) = 28.91. Improvement: 41.3%

Table 11.4 *Policy revisions: constant $ billions*

	1934	1935	1936	1934	1935	1936	1934	1935	1936
C	− 1.58	− 0.18	− 0.17	− 1.15	0.01	− 0.02	− 0.96	− 0.01	− 0.02
I	− 0.98	0.09	0.19	− 0.74	0.45	0.12	− 0.77	0.40	0.12
D	0.37	− 0.48	− 0.58	− 0.75	0.11	− 0.15	− 0.70	0.08	− 1.00
W_2	0.37	1.11	0.19	government			0.38	0.10	0.05
T	organised labour			0.22	0.12	0.06	0.12	0.25	0.07
G				1.06	− 0.42	0.08	0.94	− 0.32	0.09

These figures are open loop less closed loop policy values. The first two sets are for Cournot solutions; the third for the Nash solution.

Table 11.5 *Coefficients of variation in instrument settings*

	Nash	Cournot	Cooperative optimal (table 7.2)	Cooperative historical
W_2	0.06	0.1	0.05	0.05
T	0.086	0.17	0.1	0.15
G	0.05	0.06	0.04	0.05
Budget deficit	0.1	0.16	0.13	0.19

next election, a steady improvement in I, and the sacrificing of D in 1934 and 1935 but its achievement in 1936, are all desired by the New Deal government. An expenditure-led reflation, similar to that in the co-operative solution, is present in the budget. But the budget deficit incurred is not now removed. Any pressure to balance the budget by 1936 has been overcome by other electoral considerations.

A comparison of Cournot and Nash solutions reveals some important features of policy games. The Cournot solutions are inferior to the Nash solutions in several respects for both players. Not only does the anticipated future look brighter for both if they recognise the role played by their opponent; but the results which each actually achieves are quite dramatically improved if each player explicitly accepts and exploits the role played by his opponent. There are definite gains to accepting the existence of a game, and playing along with it, as opposed to ignoring others in pursuit of one's own prejudices and ideology. This is not to say that cooperation would not yield even better results. But there are large costs to opting out of the system, or to refusing to work within it.

Secondly, there is no evidence here that the players should choose a strategy to spite his opponent. On the contrary, recognition of how one's opponent will use his instruments to improve his targets increases the scope of one's own instruments. That is to say, unless the players have diametrically opposed objectives, there is a kind of specialisation in the uses to be made of the instruments, which, if exploited, results in an all round improvement in the outcomes. Once again, however antagonistic the players may be it is in their interests to work within the system rather than destroy it. This result holds generally since any non-Nash policy (i.e. any policy not conditioned on the correct expectation of the opponent's policy selections) is suboptimal. The point here is to note the empirical significance of that observation.

Thirdly, there is some evidence here that the government dominates. This is to be expected since it has two instruments, and both of them tend to be more effective as measured by their multipliers (tables 4.1 and 4.2). So the gains to playing the game are more marked for labour. On its own, labour is quite unable to secure the two main targets in their preferences, C and D. And to do as well as they do, they must suffer lower and falling values of W_2 compared to the Nash solution. On its own, the government's final budget position is worse although they lose rather little in the targets. The fact that labour fares worse in their Cournot solution than in history (table 7.1) suggests that they did play the game in reality. On the other hand, the government fared considerably worse in history than in any solution here, which might suggest that they did not optimise.

Fourthly, table 11.4 shows that larger policy revisions are generally necessary in the Cournot compared to the Nash solution. In fact, the figures for w^* in tables 11.3 and 11.4 suggest there is considerable gain for the government, and some for labour, in being able correctly to allow for the uncertainty of the other player's reactions in their own policy settings. The Nash solutions exploit the possibility of revisions more effectively.

Finally, we see that both players (but particularly labour) have to use their instruments more vigorously in the Cournot solution. Table 11.5 shows the coefficients of variation for W_2, T and G in the various solutions available from tables 11.2, 11.3 and 7.2. Cournot solutions are uniformly highest and the two 'cooperative' solutions are lowest for W_2 and G but not T. The differences are not large (again excepting W_2), but they become much clearer when only nonelection years are considered.

11.10 Conclusions

We have now examined time consistent optimal policies where the choice variables are subject to implicit, or explicit, noncausalities. We have focussed on multiplayer policy games to provide a description of policy selection between (noncooperating) groups which influence policy formation. This complements earlier chapters which dealt with policy selection within any such group.

Optimal policies derived for each player are simply a transformation of those for a single player game. Further, the problems of dynamic inconsistencies and the Lucas critique only arise when anticipating behaviour is not correctly allowed for in the optimising techniques. There is therefore no call for simpler policy rules in these circumstances. In fact, this is a case where the analogy with physical systems is counterproductive because it obscures a feature typical of economic systems.

Brandsma and Hughes Hallett (1982) show greater losses may result from ignoring noncausalities (e.g. in table 11.3) than from ignoring the game altogether (as in table 11.2). Here, closed loop policy revisions are due exclusively to uncertainty, not to any dynamically inconsistent or disequilibrium solutions. Closed loop optimal policies are important precisely because players have rational expectations, but not complete knowledge, of their opponent's actions.

12

Optimal policies and degrees of uncertainty: policy rules vs discretion

12.1 The background

The relative merits of simple fixed policy rules, as compared to flexible or discretionary rules, is an issue which has caused a great deal of debate and disagreement.

A closed loop optimal policy is a discretionary policy which will, other things being equal, outperform any other, including fixed rules. Unfortunately other things are seldom, if ever, equal. Recently, this debate has concentrated on the argument that the uncertainty over the conditioning information – specifically on the impacts of anticipations terms, the reactions of other policy makers, the Lucas critique, collective preferences, and so on – generally makes the discretionary policy rule quite unreliable. In other words, it is argued that mistaken conditioning information produces a worse decision than the suboptimality of a fixed rule robust to such errors. We have met and effectively disposed of those arguments in the previous chapters.

An older and more general form of the same argument is that fixed rules are better in the face of extensive uncertainties over the model and noncontrollable variables – particularly the former. For example, a policy acting through a highly uncertain parameter may turn out to have an effect very different from that intended. This could actually lead to worse outcomes than no intervention (Friedman (1953)). So far we have clearly had least success in providing techniques to handle this kind of uncertainty. And we must recognise that, in the area of practical policy, these uncertainties assume great importance in the policy maker's mind; perhaps even dominating the other problems to which we have managed to find a solution. Consequently, ad hoc proposals are often made in the form of simple fixed rules, said to be 'good' if sub-optimal, in order to account for this risk aversion. For example, to take no decision is to take the neutral policy stance of constant rates of growth in the policy variables. But since the foundation for this kind of response to risk aversion is inadequately specified, its exact justification remains unclear. Lengthy debates over its relative merits are then inevitable.

We examine the possible justifications for simple, fixed and other suboptimal (or only approximately optimal) rules in two stages. In this chapter we investigate the theoretical case by analysing optimal policy choices under varying degrees of model and information uncertainty. This requires a complete analysis of an optimal policy for increasing uncertainty over the policy impacts (sections 12.2 and 12.3). Then we consider uncertainty over the forecasts used in the certainty equivalence theorem (section 12.4). The conclusion is that, although the choices are indeed affected by increasing uncertainty, there is no sense in which an optimal policy choice reduces to one of these simple rules as that uncertainty increases, unless such a simple rule was in any case implicit in the *ideal values*. Thus, the arguments in favour of fixed rules in fact reflect a prejudice for such rules as an ideal. They cannot be justified as a rational response to risk aversion, or to a lack of robustness in other techniques. Included in this class of fixed rules is, of course, the procrastinator's typical 'do nothing and play safe' policy response.

The following chapter takes up the empirical case for fixed and other suboptimal rules by evaluating the losses from using fixed rather than optimal policy rules.

12.2 Controlling systems with uncertain policy impacts

Since Chapter 7 we have handled multiplicative uncertainties by the first order certainty equivalence approximation. It was noted that this approximation depends on R and b having 'relatively small' variances and covariances. We need to examine the quality of this approximation in practice. In order to do that we must first derive the optimal choice to minimise $E_t(w)$ given both multiplicative and additive uncertainties.

Uncertainty in any of the structural model parameters will (with few exceptions) be reflected by uncertainty in all elements of R, K, and S. In practice each coefficient matrix of (2.2) will contain some uncertain elements. Moreover, since many of the same elements of the reduced form parameters go to make up R, K, and S, it is almost certain that R and b will be correlated. But that is the extent of the potential uncertainty in policy selections. The tenor of chapters 9 and 10 makes it clear that we consider the preference parameters, Q and q (or z^d), to be unknown because of the difficulty and effort involved in discovering their values accurately, but not because they are inherently random. In fact, we argue that it is inappropriate to derive optimal policies with random preferences because, if circumstances prevent the accurate specification of Q and q, they will also prevent that of $E(Q)$, $E(q)$. Therefore we go no further than to compute the disturbance to $\tilde{z}^*$ when the preferences are wrongly specified.

12.2.1 Optimal policy choices without learning

The optimal policy choice for $E_t(w)$ when the policy impacts are uncertain can be derived straightforwardly from the expectations of (7.19), bearing in mind that, in a static algorithm, we compute one first period certainty equivalent solution for each t:

$$\tilde{x}^* = -[E_t(M)]^{-1}E_t(m_1). \tag{12.1}$$

Now $E_t(M) = A + CE_t(R) + E_t(R)'C' + E_t(R)'BE_t(R) + E_t(dR'BdR)$ in the notation of (7.27). Likewise $E_t(m_1) = E_t(R)'q_1 + q_2 + CE_t(b) + E_t(R)'BE_t(b) + E_t(dR'Bdb)$. We then write

$$\tilde{x}^* = -(\bar{M} + F)^{-1}(\bar{m}_1 + f) \tag{12.2}$$

where $\bar{M} = E_t(H^*)'QE_t(H^*)$, $\bar{m}_1 = E_t(H^*)'[Q(E_t(b')\vdots 0)' + q]$ are the first order certainty equivalent quantities used until now; and $F = E_t(dR'BdR)$ and $f = E_t(dR'Bdb)$ are the covariances of R, and of R with b, respectively, both in the scale of target preferences. Finally, for calculation purposes, $F_{ij} = \sum_k\sum_l B_{kl}\sigma_{lk}^{(i,j)}$ and $f_i = \sum_k\sum_l B_{kl}\sigma_{lk}^{*(i)}$ where $\sigma^{(i,j)} = E_t(dR_{.i}dR'_{.j})$ and $\sigma^{*(i)} = E_t(dR_{.i}db')$ are the two covariance matrices measuring the relevant degrees of uncertainty. $dR_{.i}$ corresponds to the ith column of R, so $\sigma^{(i,j)}$ is the covariance matrix of multipliers attached to x_i and x_j. Obviously the updating scheme of (7.30)–(7.32) should be applied to (12.2) at each t to generate the policy revisions, except that now $E_t(R_t^+)\tilde{x}_0^*$ is added to $E_t(b_{(t)})$.

Thus a knowledge of the degree of multiplicative uncertainties does affect the optimal policy choice. We shall see what effects they have shortly. The calculation of the optimal policy choice in this case is just a simple modification to the first order certainty equivalent solution. It depends only on knowledge of the means, variances and covariances from the multivariate density function of $(R_{.1}, \dots, R_{.nT}, b)$, conditioned on Ω_t for each t. No other information on the character of the uncertainties – for example, higher order moments or the type of density function – is relevant.

In practical terms, the only problem with (12.2) is the evaluation of the necessary variances and covariances. Chapter 3 has highlighted many of the difficulties of deriving exact estimating formulae for those covariances. Fairly complicated asymptotic distributional results have been obtained by various authors for linear models, together with some only somewhat simpler approximations (Dhrymes (1973), Schmidt (1973), Gill and

Brissimis (1978)). For nonlinear models, where R, K, and S are made up as described in Chapter 7, Fair (1980a) has developed an estimation method based on stochastic simulation (noted following (7.25)).

The question of an effective optimal control algorithm under parametric uncertainty thus becomes a matter of estimating the necessary covariances.

12.2.2 Other techniques which allow for parametric uncertainty

Holbrook and Howrey (1978) discuss the differences between particular versions of (7.18) and (8.20) which allow for parameter uncertainty. However, neither corresponds to (12.2). Their counterpart to (7.18) uses $E_1(M)$ and $E_1(m_1)$ throughout (12.1). In contrast the updated conditional expectations in (12.2) ensure that each decision is taken with the intention that it will be revised, at each t, with respect to F and f.

Their counterpart to (8.20) uses (8.18) and (8.19) in the form

$$H_t = Q_t^+ + E_i(\Pi_4' H_{t+1} \Pi_4) + G_{t+1}' E_i(\Pi_5' H_{t+1} \Pi_4);$$
$$h_t = Q_t^+ \hat{Z}_t^d + E_i(\Pi_4 + \Pi_5 G_{t+1})'(h_{t+1} - H_{t+1}(E_i(a_{t+1}) + \Pi_5 g_{t+1})) \qquad (12.3)$$

and

$$G_t = -[E_i(\Pi_5' H_t \Pi_5)]^{-1} E_i(\Pi_5' H_t \Pi_4) \text{ and}$$
$$g_t = -[E_i(\Pi_5' H_t \Pi_5)]^{-1} E_i(\Pi_5' H_t (E_i(a_t) - h_t)), \text{ for } t = T \ldots i \text{ and each } i = 1 \ldots T. \qquad (12.4)$$

This is based on an approximate solution due to Chow (1975). For operational reasons it is necessary to recompute the sequence (G_t, H_t, g_t, h_t) based on $E_i(.)$ throughout for $t \geqslant i$, where i is the current period. It can be made time varying by inserting Π_{4t} and Π_{5t} throughout G_t, H_t, g_t and h_t.

To see the difference between (12.2) and this version of (8.20), repeat the steps of section 8.3.3 but applied to (12.2). The two techniques obviously give identical results at $t = T$. At $t = T-1$, (12.2) implies a version of (8.22) comprising $E_t(M_i)$, for $i = 1 \ldots 4$, and the expectation of the product of the last three terms. But now the leading term of (8.22) no longer equals the inverse in G_{T-1} and g_{T-1}. This is because $E_{T-1}(\Pi_5'\Pi_4' Q_T \Pi_4 \Pi_5) \neq E_{T-1}[\Pi_5' E_{T-1}(\Pi_4' H_T \Pi_4)\Pi_5]$ for use within $E_{T-1}(M_1)$ and G_{T-1} respectively (where the special structures of Π_4 and Π_5 have been used to express M_1 in those terms). Likewise $E_{T-1}(\Pi_5'\Pi_4' Q_T \Pi_4) \neq E_{T-1}(\Pi_5)' E_{T-1}(\Pi_4' H_T \Pi_4)$ for use within M_2 (or M_3) and G_{T-1}. For similar reasons it is impossible to identify the components of $E_{T-1}(\Pi_5' H_{T-1})$ with the matrix products in the expectation of the last three terms in (8.22). Thus the proof indicated in section 8.3.3 in general breaks down, unless Π_4 and Π_5 have zero variances and covariances.

The problem with this version of (8.20) is the failure to distinguish the calculation of G_T and g_T for use at T, from their determination as a stepping stone to computing G_{T-1} and g_{T-1}. The necessity to pick some values for G_T and g_T before determining G_{T-1} cuts through the covariances between the two policy rules as follows. Picking G_T and g_T first, at $T-1$, ignores the dependence of G_T and g_T on G_{T-1} and g_{T-1} (while recognising the reverse dependence), although the allowance made for parametric uncertainty in the latter determines how much uncertainty is handed on to period T via Π_4 and therefore conditions the allowance to be made for parametric uncertainty in the former. Hence, in terms of (8.6), one cannot completely substitute for x_T in $\bar{w}_{T-1}(x_T, x_{T-1})$ before x_{T-1} has been chosen, since the choice of rule for x_{T-1} will determine how much uncertainty will remain to be treated by the rule for x_T. In other words, if we choose (G_T, g_T) first, and then (G_{T-1}, g_{T-1}), we will generally need to revise (G_T, g_T) again because the uncertainties handed on will differ from those presumed in the first choice. Time-inconsistencies will emerge, and the original choice will be suboptimal, unless the covariance between rules is fully accounted for. Hence, conditional on $\Omega_{T-1}, \partial Z_{T-1}/\partial x_T \neq 0$ which specifies noncausality. The possibility of trading uncertainty between (G_T, g_T) and (G_{T-1}, g_{T-1}) requires their joint optimisation (as in 12.2) for allocating policy reactions between T and $T-1$.

12.2.3 Optimisation with learning: dual control

Equation (12.2) is not the only approach to controlling an uncertain economic system. It is appropriate if the uncertainty in R is irreducible random behaviour, rather than an expression of our lack of knowledge of the true distribution of R or of our inability to estimate R better with the available data. It presumes that we cannot generate observations which would yield more precise estimates of R and thereby reduce the degree of uncertainty. But, in fact, the act of implementing a policy disturbs the system in a way which yields further information on the parameters of the system's responses. The opportunity therefore exists to choose policy values in early periods which are designed, in part, to reveal more about R in order that more precise policies can be derived for use in the later periods.

To claim that (12.2) is optimal requires proof that sacrificing performance in early periods, to get better estimates of R, cannot be compensated for by improved performance in later periods due to the better knowledge of the system then available. That obviously depends on the time profile of the relative preferences, the degree of irreducible uncertainty in the system, the efficiency of the current estimates, and the size of

$\partial w/\text{vec}(\partial H)$, etc. The application of such techniques, called dual control, is reviewed by Bar-Shalom and Tse (1976) and Kendrick (1980). Even in a linear model, we are attempting to steer two multiplicatively related stochastic quantities (the instruments, and the parameter estimates). So we are faced with a nonlinear control problem which is difficult to solve and difficult computationally. As yet the calculations have only proved manageable with very small models. Moreover, the evidence is that there is little to be gained over (12.2) – unless the parameter uncertainty and the terminal period penalties are both very large (Wall and Bar-Shalom (1978), Kendrick (1981)). Dual control is therefore not considered further.

Dual control is sometimes called control with learning. Of course, there is also a passive learning process incorporated in (12.2) since the covariances should be reestimated, conditionally on Ω_t, at each t. The missing element is any *active* attempt to learn about R. There is no experimental design incorporated within the policy settings of (12.2), except in so far as sensitivity analysis and interactive planning may induce modifications to (Q, q) or the model.

12.2.4 Stabilisability revisited

Uncertainty in the parameters demands a reformulation of the stabilisability criterion (Chapter 6). The system (2.6) is said to be *stochastically stabilisable* if also

$$\min_{A_t} \Big\| \sum_{j=0}^{\infty} (\bar{\Pi}_1' + A_t'\bar{\Pi}_2')^j$$
$$E_t\{(d\Pi_1 + d\Pi_2 A_t)'(d\Pi_1 + d\Pi_2 A_t)\}\,(\bar{\Pi}_1 + \bar{\Pi}_2 A_t)^j \Big\|_2 < 1.$$

The parametric uncertainty is represented by $\Pi_1 = \bar{\Pi}_1 + d\Pi_1, \Pi_2 = \bar{\Pi}_2 + d\Pi_2$, where $x_t = A_t Y_{t-1}$, $\bar{\Pi}_i = E_t(\Pi_i)$, and Π_i are distributed independently of the structural errors, for $i = 1, 2$. This condition ensures the existence of the stabilisation policy (12.2).

12.3 The approximate optimal control of an uncertain system

For simplicity we drop the subscript t for the remainder of this section. Expanding (12.2)

$$\tilde{x}_s^* = -[I - (\bar{M})^{-1}F(F + F(\bar{M})^{-1}F)^{-1}F](\bar{M})^{-1}(\bar{m}_1 + f) \quad (12.5)$$

so that

$$\tilde{x}_s^* = P^*(\tilde{x}_F^* - (\bar{M})^{-1}f) \quad (12.6)$$

where $P^* = [I - (\bar{M})^{-1}F(F + F(\bar{M})^{-1}F)^{-1}F]$. $\tilde{x}_s^*$ is the optimal policy choice for an uncertain system, and $\tilde{x}_F^*$ the first order certainty equivalent choice. We shall now investigate the quality of x_F^* as an approximation for x_s^*.

We shall need the fact that both P^* and $I - P^*$ have eigenvalues in the open interval (0, 1). To see this, notice that F being nonsingular[1] implies $I - P^*$ is symmetric and strictly positive definite. In that case P^* must be of full rank; with roots $\gamma_i^* > 0$, say. Then $I - P^*$ has roots given by

$$|(\bar{M})^{-1}F(F + F(\bar{M})^{-1}F)^{-1}F - \gamma I| = 0. \tag{12.7}$$

But γ_i are also the roots of $|(F + F(\bar{M})^{-1}F)^{-1}F(\bar{M})^{-1}F - \gamma I| = 0$. (Dhrymes (1970), pp. 573, 574; there are no zero values of γ_i here).

Now let $(\bar{M})^{-1} = LL'$ where L is a nonsingular triangular matrix, so that we can write

$$\left| L'FL - \left(\frac{\gamma}{1-\gamma}\right) I \right| = 0. \tag{12.8}$$

Hence $\gamma_i/(1 - \gamma_i) > 0$; and therefore $\gamma_i < 1$, since $\gamma_i > 0$, all i. In that case P^* has roots $0 < \gamma_i = 1 - \gamma_i^* < 1$ as claimed.

12.3.1 Multiplicative uncertainty and fixed rules

In view of the symmetry of $I - P^*$ we have, for any norm, $\| P^* \| = 1 - \min_i(\gamma_i) < 1$, and $\| I - P^* \| = \max_i(\gamma_i) < 1$. Without loss of generality we can likewise take $\rho[(\bar{M})^{-1}] = \| (\bar{M})^{-1} \| \leqslant 1$ by adjustment of the normalisation constant in Q. We now have the following results when $f = 0$:

Proposition 12.1: $\tilde{x}_F^*$ approximates $\tilde{x}_s^*$ in the neighbourhood of $\Psi = E(\text{vec}(dR))(\text{vec}(dR))' = 0$, and only up to the first order in $\rho(\Psi)$.

Proof: $\| x_s^* - x_F^* \| \leqslant \max_i(\gamma_i) \| \tilde{x}_F^* \|$. But $\| F \| \leqslant \| B \| \; \| E(\text{vec}(dR))(\text{vec}(dR))' \| = \| B \| \| \Psi \|$. Let $\rho(\Psi) = \varepsilon > 0$; and $\delta_i = \gamma_i/(1 - \gamma_i) > 0$, $i = 1 \ldots nT$. Then $\max_i(\gamma_i) = \max_i(\delta_i)/(1 + \max_i(\delta_i))$ because $\partial\delta_i/\partial\gamma_i = 1/(1 - \gamma_i)^2$ shows δ_i is a monotonically increasing function of γ_i for $0 \leqslant \gamma_i \leqslant 1$. But $\max_i \delta_i \leqslant \varepsilon \| L \|^2$. Hence $\max_i(\gamma_i)$ is bounded above by a monotonically increasing function of $\varepsilon \geqslant 0$ such that $\max_i(\gamma_i) = 0$ when $\varepsilon = 0$.

Corollary: $|x_s^* - x_F^*| \to 0$ as the variance $\max_{i,j} V(R_{ij}) \to 0 \begin{cases} i = 1 \ldots mT \\ j = 1 \ldots nT \end{cases}$

1 This we assume. Since no constraints are redundant, F will be nonsingular in any system with one or more uncertain structural parameters. P^* is defined in any case, as is $(\bar{M} + F)$, because of the positive semi-definiteness of F.

Proof: The difference vanishes as $\varepsilon \to 0$. But $\max_k |\Psi_{kk}| = \|\Psi\|_1 = \varepsilon$ for $k = 1 \ldots mnT^2$.

Proposition 12.2: Let F be nonsingular. The optimal policy choice x_s^* exists and is unique when $0 \leqslant r(\bar{M}) < nT$.

Comments: By construction $r(H^*) = nT$. Proposition 12.2 therefore states that an optimal policy choice exists in an uncertain model when the preference structure is incompletely specified, and even when $r(Q) < nT$. There are better and there are worse decisions to be made even when very few variables enter the quadratic part of the preference function; or even when $n \geqslant m$ and no instruments attract any form of penalty. In the latter case all the instruments are needed to combat that uncertainty, whereas if R had been known some would have been superfluous. It is obviously possible to extend the proposition to cases where $r(\bar{M}) < nT$, $r(F) < nT$, but $r(\bar{M} + F) = nT$ to define policies in the former case. Proposition 12.2 may be regarded as an extension of the Tinbergen theorem and its generalisation to an optimal policy in (7.18). It confirms the strategy suggested in section 4.8.2.

Proposition 12.3: The optimal policy choice x_s^* is less active than x_F^* in the sense that *both* $\|\tilde{x}_s^*\| < \|\tilde{x}_F^*\|$ *and* $\|x_s^* - x_F^*\| < \|x_F^* - x^d\|$ for any norm; F nonsingular.

Proof: By (12.5) and the proof of proposition 12.1, since $\|P^*\| < 1$.

Comments: Thus, measured in any norm (for example, in terms of its length, or the element of largest absolute size, or the mean absolute size of the elements) x_s^* lies between x_F^* and x^d. But, apart from the fact that $E(w(\tilde{z}_s^*)) \leqslant E(w(\tilde{z}_F^*))$, we have no information on how y_s^* lies relative to y_F^* and y^d. All that can be said in general is that parameter uncertainty pushes the optimal policy choice towards the simulation solution ($x^* = x^d$) which always exists as a special case of policy optimisation (Chapter 10). Whether x_s^* is a less 'vigorous' policy choice, in the sense that it involves a smaller change between its starting value and its final value, or that it implies smaller policy variations during the interval (1, T), depends *solely* on whether x^d indicates that the ideal was more 'vigorous' than the most advisable choice (x_F^*) under certain 'knowledge' of the policy impacts. So we cannot say if there will be greater or smaller policy interventions, or more or less frequent interventions; except in so far as typical specifications of x^d place substantial political and administrative costs on deviations from the status quo, whence less intervention may be the usual case.

In terms relative to x^d, uncertainty over policy impacts clearly does lead to smaller (and possibly less frequent) interventions. So the optimal policy failures are indeed less active, or responsive, to the economy. But the interventions are, under any definition, of the same type as in the certainty case. Thus, far from encouraging either a fixed rule or a 'do nothing' policy, increasing uncertainty over policy impacts encourages us to stick closer to the original ideals for the instruments – that is 'to shut one's eyes and hold tight, hoping for the best'. Only when x^d is defined by constant growth rates can this also constitute either a fixed rule or a less vigorous policy.

This result is to be expected since the effect of parameter uncertainty is to add an extra term to the quadratic penalties on instruments. It is eminently reasonable to react less to movements in the economy if one is unsure of the impacts of those reactions. But that is often misinterpreted to mean: 'take no decision' or 'follow a fixed rule'. This is an interesting illustration of the poverty of the bureaucratic mind, in which increasing uncertainty about the outcomes is presumed to imply that it is best (safest) to do nothing at all. In fact, the best choice under any preferences is to have the courage of one's convictions and stick closer to one's initial judgement of the ideal instrument values, and ultimately to simulate x^d.

12.3.2 Increasing uncertainty

Next we allow for $f \neq 0$.

Proposition 12.4: Proposition 12.1, its corollary, and proposition 12.2 all carry over without modification for any $f \neq 0$. Proposition 12.3 holds good when $\tilde{x}_F^* - (\bar{M})^{-1}f$ replaces $\tilde{x}_F^*$ throughout.

Proof: Obvious from (12.6) and the proofs above.

Comments: When $f \neq 0$, the problem with proposition 12.3 is that x_s^* undergoes a shift of origin similar to that found in z^d caused by $q \neq 0$. It is therefore not possible to say that x_s^* lies between x_F^* and x^d as large covariances between R and b may place x_s^* 'outside' x_F^* and x^d. However, $f_i = \sum_k \sum_l B_{kl}(\widehat{V(R_{.i})}^{1/2} \Delta \widehat{V(b)}^{1/2})_{kl}$ where '$\hat{\ }$' denotes a diagonal matrix formed from the variances of $R_{.i}$ and b respectively, and Δ is the matrix of correlation coefficients. Thus, the most we can say is that proposition 12.3 holds good for small variances in R or b. If R and b have high co-variances the optimal policy shifts in such a way that its expected value is compensated for the biasing effects caused by the more probable joint outcomes of R and b.

Proposition 12.5: The larger the degree of uncertainty (as measured by variances) in any one (or more) multiplier associated with some x_i, the lower the value of $|(\tilde{x}_s^*)_i|$ in the optimal decision (each $i = 1, \ldots, nT$).

Proof: An increase in $V(R_{ij})$, for a given i and any individual $j = 1 \ldots nT$, implies $d\sigma_{jj}^{(ii)} > 0$. Then $dF_{ii} > 0$ because $B_{jj} > 0$. Now from (12.5)

$$d\tilde{x}_s^* = -[(\bar{M} + F)^{-1} dF]\tilde{x}_s^* \tag{12.9}$$

where dF is a null matrix excepting $dF_{ii} > 0$. Consequently the result follows from

$$(d\tilde{x}_s^*)_i = -(\bar{M} + F)_{ii}^{-1} dF_{ii} \tilde{x}_i^* \tag{12.10}$$

since $(\bar{M} + F)_{ii}^{-1} > 0$ by the positive definiteness of $\bar{M} + F$.

Corollary: Increasing uncertainty reduces the activity of x_s^* in the sense of proposition 12.5, but no sign changes appear in $x_s^* - dx_s^*$ compared to x_s^*.

Proof: $\| d\tilde{x}_s^* \| < \| \tilde{x}_s^* \|$ by applying the proof of proposition (12.3) to (12.9) since $dF > 0$ is symmetric.

Proposition 12.6: Increasing uncertainty about b_k, for a fixed degree of correlation with R_{ki}, implies a reduction (increase) in $|(\tilde{x}_s^*)_i|$ if $(\tilde{x}_s^*)_i \Delta_{kk} \geqslant 0 (\leqslant 0)$.

Proof: By the same argument as proposition 12.5 we have

$$(dx_s^*)_i = -(\bar{M} + F)_{ii}^{-1} df_i. \tag{12.11}$$

Consequently, since $f \neq 0$ is almost certain in practice, the failure to reproduce proposition 12.3 further weakens the case for fixed rules under increasing uncertainty over policy impacts. However, propositions 12.5 and 12.6 indicate the conclusion that we should stick closer to the ideal values (x^d), and thereby react less to movements in the economy, carries over – whether or not x^d itself represents more or less interventions than policies of no change, fixed rules, or other benchmark regimes.

12.3.3 Conclusions

The optimal policies in (12.2) present no extra difficulties once the covariances $\sigma^{(i,j)}$ and $\sigma^{*(i)}$ have been obtained. But computing those covariances may not be easy. Some computationally expensive techniques for evaluating the $\sigma^{(i,j)}$ matrices were mentioned earlier. But the calculation of $\sigma^{*(i)}$, and thus f, may present real problems because no corresponding techniques are, as yet, available. Indeed, as b contains Su, that calculation will probably be very difficult. Chapter 3 has shown some of the difficulties which will emerge, although stochastic simulation is always possible. In that case, (12.2) with $f = 0$ may form a useful approximation to the true optimal choice. It is the result of (12.2) in which the covariances between elements of R and b are assumed to be of an order smaller than those between elements of R. The use of (12.2) therefore raises a genuine conflict between simplicity and expensive precision.

On the other hand, at no point in discussing (12.2) has it been necessary to specify the probability density function of R and b; nor have we used moments of those distributions higher than the second. This is a consequence of the linear-quadratic nature of our policy choice problem.

It is important to realise that the increasing parameter uncertainty dealt with here covers *both* policy impacts *and* the impacts of the (uncertain) noncontrollable variables.

12.4 The use of forecasts in policy selection: degrees of additive uncertainty

The degree of uncertainty surrounding the additive information, b, has had no influence on the optimal policy selection. The certainty equivalence theorem of Chapter 7 established that $E_t(b)$ was the only information relevant to the optimal decision at each t; other moments (such as variances) of the density function were not involved.

The certainty equivalence result assumes, however, that $E_t(b)$ is known for sure. In practice that may well not be the case. Suppose we have to insert forecasts for N and u as estimates of $E_t(N)$ and $E_t(u)$, in order to make up $E_t(b)$. That procedure is correct (as we shall shortly show) for additive uncertainty, provided the forecasts consist of no more than single point estimates of the relevant expectations. But suppose we have interval estimates or more than one conflicting forecast of each quantity. How should this auxiliary information best be used to condition our policy choice? In view of the certainty equivalence theorem, it is only when some supplementary information on b becomes available, and which does not coincide with our prior estimate of that representative value, that the degree of additive uncertainty can exert any influence on the policy choice.

12.4.1 Forecast in decisions: optimal control without certainty equivalence–II

Suppose we have access to auxiliary forecasts $N^f \neq E_t(N)$ of the noncontrollables.[2] N^f can represent some forecast, more than a point estimate in that at least the second moment of its distribution is known, of the true but imperfectly known $E_t(N)$ value. Alternatively N^f and $E_t(N^f)$ can represent two competing forecasts, when the true expectation is unknown; and, for the sake of argument, we will take $E_t(N^f)$ as the 'benchmark' forecast.

Notice all our optimal policy choices have been conditioned on N in the form of a linear function of its realisation. We could therefore reformulate the optimal policy choice as

$$\tilde{x}^* = FN + f, \tag{12.12}$$

2 We continue to assume $E_t(u)$ is known for sure. There seem to be no exceptions to this case in the literature, and it is hard to imagine them even if u_t follows some autoregressive or moving average scheme.

for some matrix and vector, F and f, to be selected. Then insert N^f for N and determine F and f to minimise $E_t(w)$ subject to (7.2). Inserting (7.2), and then (12.12), into w leaves

$$L = \tfrac{1}{2}N^{f\prime}F'MFN^f + N^{f\prime}F'(m_1 + f) + \text{constants} \tag{12.13}$$

in place of (7.19). Hence

$$E_t(L) = \tfrac{1}{2}E_t(N^f)'F'MFE_t(N^f) + E_t(N^f)'F'(m_1 + f) + \tfrac{1}{2}\text{tr}F'MFV_t(N^f) + \text{constants} \tag{12.14}$$

where we have split (12.13) into its deterministic and stochastic components by steps similar to those used to derive w_d and w_s in (7.57). Write the covariance matrices $V_t(N^f) = E_t(N^f - E_t(N^f))(N^f - E_t(N^f))' = \Sigma_{ff}$ and $E_t(N^f - E_t(N^f))(N - E_t(N))' = \Sigma_f$. These two matrices describe, respectively, current estimates of the degree of uncertainty in the forecasts, and their association with the realised values. Typically we will be interested in cases where $E_t(N^f) = E_t(N)$, but to preserve generality we leave open the possibility of inequality.

Differentiating $E_t(L)$ with respect to F and f, we get (dropping the subscript t again)

$$MF\Sigma_{ff} + H^{*\prime}Q\begin{pmatrix} K \\ \cdots \\ 0 \end{pmatrix}\Sigma_f + MFE(N^f)E(N^f)' + MfE(N^f)' + H^{*\prime}Q\begin{pmatrix} K \\ \cdots \\ 0 \end{pmatrix}E(N^f)E(N^f)' + H^{*\prime}Q\begin{pmatrix} \sigma^* \\ \cdots \\ 0 \end{pmatrix}E(N^f)' = 0 \tag{12.15}$$

and

$$MFE(N^f) + Mf + H^{*\prime}Q\begin{pmatrix} K \\ \cdots \\ 0 \end{pmatrix}E(N^f) + H^{*\prime}Q\begin{pmatrix} \sigma^* \\ \cdots \\ 0 \end{pmatrix} = 0 \tag{12.16}$$

where $b = KN + \sigma^*$, which is a notational reorganisation of (7.6), has been used to decompose $m_1 = H^{*\prime}Q\begin{pmatrix} b \\ \cdots \\ 0 \end{pmatrix}$. Post multiplying (12.16) by $E(N^f)'$ and subtracting from (12.15) yields the optimal choices as

$$F^* = -M^{-1}H^{*\prime}Q\begin{pmatrix} K \\ \cdots \\ 0 \end{pmatrix}\Sigma_f\Sigma_{ff}^{-1} \text{ and } f^* = -M^{-1}H^{*\prime}Q\begin{pmatrix} I \\ \cdots \\ 0 \end{pmatrix} \times [\sigma^* + K(I - \Sigma_f\Sigma_{ff}^{-1})E(N^f)] \tag{12.17}$$

implying

$$\tilde{x}^* = -M^{-1}H^{*\prime}Q\begin{pmatrix} I \\ \cdots \\ 0 \end{pmatrix}(\sigma^* + KN^*) \tag{12.18}$$

where $N^* = E(N^f) + \Sigma_f \Sigma_{ff}^{-1}(N^f - E(N^f))$ are now the optimal replacements for the uncertain N values.

Thus, without prior appeal to any certainty equivalence theorem, the optimal policy choice is indeed conditioned on the forecast $E(N^f)$ if any of the following are known or can be assumed: (i) other forecasts are irrelevant (i.e. uncorrelated with N) so $\Sigma_f = 0$; (ii) $E(N^f)$ is a single forecast (if literally no other forecast information, represented by N^f here, is available then $N^f = E(N^f)$); (iii) only a point forecast, $E(N^f)$, is available (lack of information over the distribution of N^f implies $\Sigma_{ff} \to \infty$); (iv) there is no uncertainty, or $N^f = E(N^f)$ is guaranteed. In any of these cases we continue to use (7.16) or (7.18) with b made up from $E(u)$ and $E(N^f)$. It is not then necessary to say that our benchmark forecast is unbiased, i.e. $E(N^f) = E(N)$. Although it is hard to imagine the forecast remaining uncorrected for a known bias, we may not wish to commit ourselves on that point. In that case we have strictly only an estimated version of certainty equivalence. And in case that should seem inadequate, one should remember that supposedly unbiased point forecasting of exogenous information is the method most widely used in economics for estimating the means of the distributions of the associated variables.

In every other case b must be made up from $E(u)$ and N^* before insertion into (7.16) or (7.18). It is only in these other cases that the degree of uncertainty over the values of N can play a role. But then to use N^f optimally in practice, it is necessary to estimate Σ_f and Σ_{ff}. Now $\Sigma_f \Sigma_{ff}^{-1}$ are the regression coefficients of N and N^f. So N^* can always be constructed given N^f and a track record of past observations on N and N^f. That is the best single estimate of the imperfectly known $E(N)$ given the information available on the distribution of alternative forecasts of N. N^* is then used as if it were a known value of N.

12.4.2 The effect of increasing additive uncertainties

The expression (12.18) provides some insight to the quality of the decision taken, based on the degree of uncertainty in N. As a generalisation of certainty equivalence, it shows that the degree of uncertainty in the exogenous information only plays a role when we have two (or more) conflicting but relevant (i.e. nonorthogonal, $\Sigma_f \neq 0$) estimates of the value of N.

In (12.18) we have determined the weight to be given to each piece of information:

$$N^* = \Sigma_f \Sigma_{ff}^{-1} N^f + (I - \Sigma_f \Sigma_{ff}^{-1}) E(N^f). \qquad (12.19)$$

So the value of N to be entered into the optimal decision rule is a weighted average of our two estimates. The weights favour the forecast N^f, the more certain it is (as measured by smaller variances). But the more unreliable the forecasts, the less they influence the decision. In that case we increasingly rely on $E(N^f)$. Ultimately, when the forecasts are infinitely unreliable, we rely completely on $E(N^f)$. That explains why when only one estimate of N is available the degree of uncertainty in that estimate does not influence the policy decisions. Put formally we have

Proposition 12.7: Increasing uncertainty in any forecast of N_i^f leads, other things remaining fixed, to a reduction in $|N_i^* - E(N_i^f)|, i = 1, \dots rT$.

Proof: Consider two evaluations of N^* differing only by $d(\Sigma_{ff})_{ii} > 0$, in which the latter is a small quantity. Then $(\Sigma_{ff} + d(\Sigma_{ff}))^{-1} \simeq \Sigma_{ff}^{-1} - - d(\Sigma_{ff})' \Sigma_{ff}^{-1} d(\Sigma_{ff})$. Hence

$$dN_k^* = -(\Sigma_f)_{ki}(\Sigma_{ff}^{-1})_{ii}(d\Sigma_{ff})_{ii}^2(N_i^f - E(N_i^f)) \qquad (12.20)$$

Assuming N_i^f to be positively associated with N_i itself then, by (12.20), $dN_i^* < 0$ when $N_i^f > E(N_i^f)$, but $dN_i^* > 0$ otherwise.

Corollary: The certainty equivalent policy choice (7.18) is optimal in any event if any *one* (or more) unbiased forecast is diffuse (infinitely unreliable).

Proof: Obvious by (12.18) since $\Sigma_{ff}^{-1} \to 0$ when $(\Sigma_{ff})_{ii} \to \infty$ some i. We also have $E(N^f) = E(N)$.

Comments: We have presumed $(\Sigma_f)_{ii} > 0$ in proposition 12.7, as one would normally expect. It is unlikely that a forecasting technique known to have forecasts negatively related to the realisations would be used. If it were, we get the opposite conclusion from proposition 12.7 which is the correct response to a forecast that is typically 'wrong'. We may likewise apply proposition 12.7 to other components, N_k^*, for which N_k is positively correlated with N_i^f; and the converse holds for the remaining elements of N^*.

12.4.3 On judgement and the conditioning information

We must stress two particularly important cases where we have competing estimates of the values of N, and yet at least one of those estimates is a point estimate of the type where $N^f = E(N^f)$ is normally accepted for use in (7.16) without comment.

The first case is where we have combined two forecasts of N in the manner described in Chapter 3. Indeed (12.19) is a generalisation of the optimal combination of forecasts formula, (3.39). In (12.19) the weights $\Sigma_f \Sigma_{ff}^{-1}$ are such as to allow all forecasted variables at all periods to be combined, rather than being just a linear combination of each variable in each time period.

Secondly, in view of the foregoing interpretation, (12.19) can also represent that combination of 'mechanical' and 'judgemental' forecasts discussed in Chapter 3. We might tentatively take N^f to be a mechanical, econometric or other auxiliary forecast, and $E(N^f) = E(N)$ to be the policy maker's judgemental forecast. That is a very useful observation because criticisms are so often made by, and on behalf of, policy makers that techniques such as policy optimisation dilute their power to take decisions and reduce their ability to take the initiative or exercise their judgement. Such inputs are extremely important for the quality of the decisions; and here, as elsewhere, policy decisions should still exploit judgemental information. These inputs are, however, concerned with setting the scenario, the preferences and the ideal outcomes. The scenario includes the targets and their acceptable values, the types of instruments to be used and their acceptable values, the external events of interest, attitudes to risk, continuity or intervention, etc. Policy optimisation then merely aims to make better decisions based on whatever conditioning information has been supplied by the policy maker. It improves the decision making process, but does not aim to change the nature of the decisions.

12.4.4 The case for fixed rules

At this point it is natural to ask, once again, if increasing uncertainty over the noncontrollable influences on policy choice leads to a less active policy. And once again the answer is negative in general. Increasing additive uncertainty, in as much as it has any influence, means (12.18) tends toward the certainty equivalent policy choice (7.18). Thus, whether the policy choice is less active or not depends on whether $E_t(N)$ contains more or less variation than N^f. All that can be said in general is that increasing uncertainty about a forecast leads to a less active use being made of that forecast as conditioning information. Naturally particular cases may be constructed where a less active policy does result. Friedman's classic paradigm of the destabilising properties of too active a contracyclical policy is a case in point (Johansen (1972)). And there could be certain situations in which N^f should be expected to contain more variation than $E_t(N)$, although the result that the forecasts' variance is smaller than the realisations' variance (section 3.10) suggests this is not likely.

It is therefore not legitimate to conclude that increasing additive uncertainty is generally sufficient reason to recommend a fixed rule, in the interest of robustness, in place of discretionary policy choices. And even when a less active policy is introduced as a result of increasing uncertainty, there is still some gain to be made by using (12.19) in a discretionary policy. For example, (7.58) shows a monotonically increasing loss with respect to $|x^* - x|$, where x is a fixed rule and x^* is from (12.18).

The Friedman paradigm also shows there is always some gain to be made. The conclusion should therefore be that discretionary policies actually become more important under increasing uncertainty in order that whatever gains are available are in fact secured.

12.5 Conclusions

In this chapter we have formulated and analysed optimal policy choices under multiplicative uncertainty. This completes a topic started in Chapter 7. We have also analysed how those choices behave under degrees of additive or multiplicative uncertainties.

The inescapable conclusion is that (increasing) uncertainty about the model, or about the policy impacts and their dynamics, does not in itself provide any justification for adopting a fixed policy rule. The same point emerges from examining the effects of increasing uncertainty about the additive terms. In either case, one should hold closer to the values specified for x^d and $E_t(N)$, respectively.

However, all these results are predicated firmly on $E_t(w)$ as the appropriate criterion. It might be that a justification for simple rules as a rational policy choice will emerge if the selection criterion $E_t(.)$ on $w(\tilde{z})$ were changed to some other criterion. This is a matter which is not investigated in this book. So we finish up with the conjecture that simple rules may be rational choices under another criterion; and that proposing them in place of the optimal choices studied in this book is perhaps an implied criticism of the $E_t(w)$ criterion itself, but not a criticism of the choices which follow from it.

13

Evaluating the quality of policy choices: the indirect benefits of optimisation

13.1 Introduction

Whilst most texts on the policy selection problem focus on the determination of policy values, an important advantage of an optimising approach is the variety of extra information which it generates to summarise the salient features of the problem faced and the proposed solution. These indirect benefits provide valuable, if not essential, information for the successful implementation of the proposed policies.

We now survey some of these indirect benefits. In section 13.2 we use optimal policies as a yardstick for evaluating alternative policy regimes. One particular application is to evaluate the empirical case for simple and fixed rules versus optimal policies. To do this we must set the costs due to a lack of robustness in optimal policies against the losses due to the suboptimality of the simple rules. Direct measurement of the losses shows that simple rules can be very suboptimal – chiefly in the sense that they tend to cope unsuccessfully with the stochastic shocks; that is, with precisely those elements of the policy problems which motivated their introduction. Although this is perhaps not surprising, it does suggest that the main benefit of policy optimisation is to exploit the optimal policy revisions forced by the stochastic elements, rather than in the optimisation of the original open loop policies.

In sections 13.3 and 13.4 we extend the analysis to judging historical policies and different models. Then we consider the important problem of designing new policy instruments in order either to improve the effectiveness of the existing instruments (section 13.5), or to mitigate the larger costs and risks which can be identified with particular targets (section 13.6). Finally, section 13.7 introduces some measures of the relative contributions and effectiveness of different instrument sets for any given problem.

13.2 Measuring the benefits of policy optimisation

Perhaps the information of first importance for implementing a policy programme is an estimate of the gains to be secured through that programme. One of the more valuable contributions of policy optimisation techniques is to provide a yardstick for judging other policies, even when the details of the optimised policies are of no direct interest themselves. Given a model and preference set, one can measure the scope, *at most*, for improving policies. This provides a standard of comparison by which particular ad hoc, fixed, simple, or robust rules can be judged; also a standard of comparison by which historical policy making can be evaluated. On the other side of this coin one can measure how much is forgone by accepting any particular suboptimal policy.

One answer to such questions is almost trivial; we simply insert the two policies to be compared into (7.58). It is a basic prerequisite for implementation that there should be adequate room for improvement over the current strategy, so the value of this type of information should not be underrated. But of course (7.58) applies only to the comparison of two deterministic policies; e.g. comparisons with the first period certainty equivalent policies based on $\Omega_t, t = 1,\ldots,T$, and consequently also with closed loop policies. That would estimate the gains that were available through optimal stochastic control over deterministic optimisation in a particular set of circumstances, and through optimisation over other possible policies, given a model and preferences. Although that is one part of policy evaluation, it is not a complete picture.

From the point of view of implementation, we must be able to produce this sort of information *ex ante*; that is to evaluate the relative advantages of various candidate strategies for their success in controlling the stochastic parts of the economy (in addition to their deterministic success) in general and independently of the realisations in any particular case. The policy maker needs this information before he commits himself to any course of action, not as a post mortem exercise. He needs to know the importance of stochastic, relative to deterministic, optimal control; and the relative success of any particular proposed policy rule in meeting those two standards.

The answers to all these questions lie in comparing w_s^* and w_d^* of (7.57) with their counterparts for various alternative policies. The obvious comparisons will be with policies of nonintervention, historical policies, and various fixed rules or 'naive' policy models.

Policy optimisation therefore offers a standard of judgement on the scope for improving policies, and the relative importance of stochastic control. If either is substantial then the effort required to gather the necessary information (the data, model and preferences) and for successful implementation (making administrative decisions, enacting institutional changes, and monitoring performance), plus the effort involved in computing those policy revisions which monitoring reveals to be necessary, will be justified. For optimal policies we have to compare the likely losses in using an imperfect model, and the damage done by inferior forecasts of external events, to the benefits of reacting directly errors appear. Policy improvements should also be set against the costs of information gathering, the administrative costs and institutional disruption necessary to secure them. Among these potential costs is the damage caused by lack of confidence and continuity induced by the unpredictability of the frequent and large policy revisions necessary when stochastic control dominates.

13.2.1 A deterministic example: primary producer cartels

A straightforward example where the gains of policy optimisation techniques can settle a policy question is set out in Underwood (1977). Three aspects are noteworthy. First, in this example we are concerned with two commodity markets – those for copper and for tea. So the focus of attention is market management rather than macroeconomic planning. In view of the spectacular rise of about 500% in real earnings from oil enjoyed by the OPEC countries in the early 1970s, the question arises if the formation of other primary producer cartels could not achieve the same success for their member countries. Evidently this is a matter of measuring the scope available for improving current production policies in the particular markets for a given cartel composition. Second, this is an example in which the objective function is largely known a priori. Apart from setting the discount rate, the index of comparison is fixed beyond debate as total cartel earnings (over T periods). Third, the example clearly illustrates an important lesson in this kind of application; transversality problems must be explicitly accounted for, because the judgement of suboptimal policies over a horizon of T periods based on comparisons with optimal policies computed with the same horizon is necessarily biased to the extent that transversality conditions were not correctly imposed on the latter. In a commodity market there are no obvious horizon values for T. Several values were tried in each case here.

For this particular study Underwood constructs small and highly aggregated annual econometric models respectively for the world copper and tea markets. They comprise dynamic demand, supply and price determination relations. In the case of copper there are production relations for the main producing areas (the United States, Canada, Zambia,

Chile, and the rest of the world), and three production from scrap relations. These quantities depend on stock adjustment mechanisms, prices, autoregressive structural errors and the autoregressive development of variables exogenous to the model. Four consumption equations (for the United States, Europe, Japan, and the rest of the world) depend also on stock adjustments, prices, current and lagged industrial production indices, the price of aluminium (the main substitute), and the various autoregressive terms. Supply and demand variables, plus some dynamic terms, determine the market prices.

The tea model has a similar structure. Supply is split over India, Sri Lanka, East Africa and the rest of the world. Demand is determined as the sum of consumption by the United States, Britain, India, Canada, Australia and the rest of the world, together with an inventory demand. Supplies depend again on stock adjustments, and prices; and demands on prices, population, income levels, and the price of coffee. The tea price is determined within the model while the market is demand dominated.

The operation of a cartel is now modelled by optimising the respective commodity models through dynamic programming. The target of export earnings appears in the objective function as the product of price and total supply minus the product of price and domestic consumption. Thus $w = \sum_{t=1}^{T} \tilde{y}_t' B_t \tilde{y}_t$ where $B_t = \delta^t B$ and δ is the discount factor. B has $\frac{1}{2}$ in the off-diagonal positions corresponding to the former products, and $-\frac{1}{2}$ corresponding to the latter. The instrument variables attracted no extra penalties. The instrument (a proportional export tax) is inserted into the model by 'controlling' (positively is the desired direction) the constant in the price equations. The point of a cartel is that it allows a tax to be imposed on top of the market price. Without the cartel, the attempt to do the same merely erodes the producer's margin and thereby restricts production, as many countries have found to their cost (Sri Lanka's tea exports are a prominent example). Therefore the no cartel situation is simulated by solving the model under identical conditions but with the instrument variable set at zero.

In this study only deterministic policies (optimal and otherwise) were considered. Two alternative values of δ (0.95 and 0.90) were tried, but they produced insignificant differences in the results. The plans were compared for all horizons from 1 to 10 years. The expected gains in total export earnings to a cartel in the copper market were $2\frac{1}{2}\%$ in the medium term (after a 10 year interval), with a peak of 5.3% after 6 years. These comparisons contain no allowance for the biases due to the lack of transversality conditions since the policy optimisation horizon is the same as the policy comparison interval. When the optimisation horizon was stretched to 20 years, the gains over the 10 year interval fell to 1.3%.

In the tea market example the expected gains in total export earnings were substantially larger; at $28\frac{1}{2}\%$ after a 10 year interval, having been in steady decline from 98% after 1 year. Extending T to 20 years only cuts the 10 year gain to 24%.

These results suggest that the scope for improving export earnings through a cartel is rather limited, *at best*, for tea producers. For copper producers it is negligible. Certainly nothing resembling OPEC's success emerges. There are a number of further interesting issues in using policy optimisation not covered in this study. Some, such as allowing for the possibility of the reactions of other agents (e.g. producers who stay outside, or speculators) being affected by the formation of a cartel, or the case where the cartel operates a buffer stock for raising average earnings, require alterations in the structure of the model. But others, such as price stabilisation programmes, the reduction of earnings fluctuations, and the control of the effects of random shocks in the market, are concerned with the stochastic control aspects. Underwood notes that his results do not rule out benefits to a cartel concerned with stabilisation even in the copper market. The size and prevalence of random fluctuations in that market suggest that the stochastic control issue may be important here. Measurement of the gains, decomposed as w_d^* and w_s^* of (7.57), could be carried out in the same way; but to find examples of this we must turn elsewhere.

13.2.2 The importance of stochastic (closed loop) control

The possibility that optimal policy revisions are, ex ante, the essential part of policy making, suggests that a closed loop strategy is important precisely because of the large uncertainties typical of economic planning. Comparison of w_s^*, w_d^* and $v^* = \frac{1}{2}\mathrm{tr}\,B\Sigma_1$ (the open loop counterpart to w_s^*) demonstrates the relative gains and importance of implementing discretionary policies. These calculations may be made at any decision point to indicate the size and form of the policy problem faced, and the scope available for solving it.

In a standard application to Dutch economic policy over 1976–80, Brandsma, Hughes Hallett and Van der Windt (1981) find the uncertainty in an open loop strategy to be 9 times more damaging than in a closed loop one. However modest the actual optimal policy revisions may later appear, the importance of having an optimal error correction device is enormous in the planners' prior evaluation. Indeed, at the optimum, control of these stochastic components is still 40% of the problem. These uncertainties concern targets taken from official publications; namely, the balance of payments, output, inflation, unemployment, budget

Table 13.1 *The gains to stochastic control*

Context	w_d^*	w_s^*	v^*	horizon	seen from
Dutch macro-economic planning	241.3	154.4	1409.7	5 yrs	1976
Copper price stabilisation	31.4	77.9	155.1	40 qtrs	1971.1

deficit, real wages, and labour's income share. They were related to the instruments (taxes, government expenditure, incomes policy, investment incentives, and money supply) through a version of the annual model used to make the official forecasts and policy projections.

In a less conventional application, Ghosh, Gilbert and Hughes Hallett (1981) test the nature of the policy problems, and the scope for stabilisation, in the world copper market. The aim is to control the quarterly fluctuations of the market prices about long-run trend values by means of buffer stock purchases and sales. The planning period is 1971–80 inclusive, over which the buffer stock would ideally be constant. Hughes Hallett (1982b) reports lower bound estimates of the stochastic objective function components for this case. The dominance of the stochastic components (71% of the problem) shows the main job to be done is to control the impacts of stochastic events. Indeed, failure to do so via an open loop policy rule would cause, on average, twice as much damage. Since it also turns out that the optimal buffer stock over the period has a negligible net present value, the problem is really one of combating the impacts of random disturbances rather than alleviating market inefficiencies.

13.2.3 Evaluating alternative policy regimes: fixed rules

A different illustration of the gains to stochastic control can be found in the work of Chow (1972). A 9 equation annual macroeconomic model of the United States is used, from which consumption (C), producers' investment (I_1), construction investment (I_2), the rate of interest (R), aggregate demand (Y) and disposable income (YD) are taken in various combinations as targets. The two instruments are currency and demand deposits (M) and government expenditures (G). The model is estimated in first difference form, but control exercises are done both in that form and in levels. In these exercises $Q = I$, and the policy horizon is 10 years starting 1964. Desired values are given by 5% growth per annum in each variable (except the interest rate whose desired growth is zero). The ex ante evaluation of the optimal policies can be split into deterministic and stochastic components, w_d^* and w_s^*, according to (7.57).

Chow takes suboptimal rules of the type $x_t = Hx_{t-1}$, but we may consider the wider class of time varying rules $x_t = H_t x_{t-1} + h_t$. In each case the instruments follow an open loop rule, independent of the stochastic developments in the economy. The case of $H_t = H$ all t, and $h_t = 0$, is the widely discussed 'fixed rule' type of policy associated with the monetarists when the money supply grows at a constant percentage rate, or with the New Cambridge School when budget financing does so. For any of these policy rules, we compute the gains to optimisation in the deterministic components by comparison with the open loop strategy in (7.58). That takes care of w_d^*. Next, in the notation of (7.47), $V_t(\xi) = \hat{\Sigma}_t$ so $w_s^* = \frac{1}{2}\text{tr}B\Sigma_1$ at $t = 1$. But it is more difficult to evaluate w_s^* for an arbitrary (but sub-optimal) feedback rule of the type put forward by Philips (1954, 1957) or Liu (1963) among others; say $x_t = GY_{t-1} + g$ where G and g are known with certainty at $t = 1$. That could also represent the steady state, or equilibrium, policy rule of Chapter 8. The simplest approach is to insert this rule – now generalised to $x_t = GZ_{t-1} + g$ – in (8.2) and back substitute to obtain Z_t in terms of the initial conditions. Thus $z = \hat{R}s +$ constants,

where $\hat{R} = \begin{pmatrix} \hat{R}_1 & & 0 \\ \vdots & \ddots & \\ \hat{R}_T & \cdots & \hat{R}_1 \end{pmatrix}$ with $\hat{R}_i = (\Pi_4 + \Pi_5 G)^{i-1}$ and

$\hat{s} = [(\Pi_5 g + a_1 + V_1)' \ldots (\Pi_5 g + a_T + V_T)']$ in the notation of (8.2); and where all rows corresponding to nontargets and lagged variables have been deleted as in (7.2). So, in this context, $V_1(\xi) = \hat{R}E_t(\hat{s}\hat{s}')\hat{R}' = \hat{R}\hat{\Sigma}_1\hat{R}'$, say, from which[1] $w_s^* = \frac{1}{2}\text{tr}Q\hat{R}\hat{\Sigma}_1\hat{R}'$.

Chow takes the matrix H to be diagonal and, in order that the fixed rules strategies should be seen in the most favourable light, he minimises the objective function with respect to H, subject to the estimated model with this control rule inserted. Now the gains to policy optimisation may be computed: a sample of three results is presented in table 13.2. The deterministic gains are small (14–31%), but those to stochastic control are substantial (44–87%). These results are, of course, dependent on the particular model and objective function (although Chow experiments with different Q matrices without noticeably disturbing his results, as Chapter 9 predicts). Secondly, the clear dominance of the stochastic parts in these exercises suggests once again that, at an aggregate level, the important thing is not so much optimal open loop policies, but a

1 Recomputing w_s^* at each t, by inserting $\hat{\Sigma}_t$, gives the corresponding measure for each policy revision and thus for closed loop policies.

Table 13.2 *The benefits of stochastic policy optimisation*

Variables in $w(\tilde{z})$	Model in levels	
	w_d^*	w_s^*
1. C, I_1, I_2, YD, G	(a) 59.7	417.1
	(b) 69.9	778.8
2. I_2, R, G	(a) 7.3	487.0
	(b) 9.6	701.0
3. C, I_1, I_2, R, YD, G	(a) 64.1	520.3
	(b) 73.3	840.6

(a) optimal policy, (b) suboptimal policy, $x_t = Hx_{t-1}$.

policy regime with an explicit error correction mechanism which correctly revises its policies to counteract any disturbances.

13.2.4 Fiscal vs monetary instruments

These techniques extend to the comparison of two suboptimal rules. A familiar example is monetary and fiscal policies. We have already discussed dynamic *effectiveness* by means of multipliers. But we pointed out there that such comparisons took no account of the costs, political or administrative, in operating the instruments in question. They are also conducted in terms of single targets. Moreover, we discovered in Chapter 6 that the impact of a policy depends on the realisations of other variables. So to mount a proper comparison of these policies we need to operate them at their best. We could therefore devise a best or neutral policy rule for, say, the monetary instruments x_{1t} as $x_{1t} = H_1 x_{1,t-1}$, where H_1 could be set exogenously or optimised as above. Inserting this into the model, we can compute the optimal policies for the resulting constrained economy, and $w_d^{*(M)}$, $w_s^{*(M)}$ by (7.57) associated with those optimal policies. Next we repeat the exercise with reversed roles for the instruments, so that x_{2t} (the fiscal instruments) follow $x_{2t} = H_2 x_{2,t-1}$ and we finish up with $w_d^{*(F)}$, $w_s^{*(F)}$ for comparison. Finally, the calculation of w_d^* and w_s^* (obtained by using such rules but now derived without imposing any restrictions) is optional for further comparisons.

13.3 Judging history

Here, as before, the evaluation of any policy scheme requires an agreed criterion function, and an agreed model to indicate the outcomes of the possible alternative courses of action. Given these, optimal stochastic control may be used as a benchmark for judging performance. We might judge actual policies against optimal stochastic control ex ante, or against closed loop policies based on the information sets of the time, or against ex post optimal policies. The assessment must include several periods so the future consequences of each action are held to account. The essential point here is that policies should not be judged by actual realisations, but by the probability distributions of them and of the criterion. In order to separate good judgement from luck, we must assess policies against the background prevailing when that course of action was selected.

Comparisons with ex post optimal policies are unfair as a judgement on the policy maker's performance. But they are useful for checking on the efficiency and effectiveness of the decision making (and policy implementation) machinery in reacting to given circumstances. It does no harm to monitor that against the ideal, but it tells us nothing about the quality of the policies. Comparisons of actual policies with the closed loop optimal controls tell us about the quality of the policies compared to the best in particular conditions. An example was given in table 7.4. But the only technique which judges independently of particular events (realisations of the stochastic variables) is ex ante comparison. Both w_s^* and w_d^* (evaluated at any t) are free from whether policy makers were 'lucky' or 'unlucky'. The difficulty here is to determine what policy rule the policy makers actually followed, for without this only comparisons of the deterministic elements are possible. Chow (1981) suggests estimating reaction functions by fitting feedback relations between instruments and lagged targets. But Chapter 10 has taught us that this is unlikely to be satisfactory because the underlying preferences are typically so volatile as to imply very sensitive time varying coefficients in these relations. The danger of poor fits is little statistical discrimination between historical and optimal policies, resulting in tests of questionable validity. That can be a serious problem (e.g. as in Chow (1975)). Our suggestion is to estimate Q^* as a revealed preference structure by the algorithm of section 10.6; and then compute w_d^* and w_s^* from (7.57) based on that Q^*. This is not to suggest that the policy makers actually optimised. But it is intended to put the best possible interpretation on their decisions. Only if we also use Q^* in forming optimal rules, and associated w_d^* and w_s^* values as a scale of comparison, will they appear to have optimised. The judgements will be independent of whatever model the policy makers may have actually used. But the question of whether the model which we use is the best one for making these judgements is still open. We turn to that in the following section.

An illustration provided by the familiar question of whether government policies have in practice been destabilising is considered in Chow (1981).

Table 13.3 *Contributions to instability by policy types, US economy 1965–6*

	U	GNP	B	P	Total	
w_d components	4.3	71.8	12.2	17.4	105.7	historical
w_s components	5.7	37.8	5.6	37.2	86.3	policies
w_d components	3.5	62.2	11.9	17.7	95.3	fixed
w_s components	7.1	50.4	5.3	37.4	100.2	rule
w_d^* components	0.7	14.7	9.4	20.8	45.6	optimal
w_s^* components	2.9	18.0	5.7	40.6	67.2	policies

Of course the analysis will be a special case of section 13.2.3 above, once we have policy reaction functions and a criterion function. In this case fitted historical reaction functions and fixed rules of the $x_t = Hx_{t-1} + h$ form were compared to an optimal stochastic control solution, using a version of the Michigan model. The information sets assumed auto-regressive predictions of the noncontrollables rather than historical values. The criterion for judging stability was simply $\sum_{j=1}^{(n+m)T} \tilde{z}_j^2$ over 8 quarters (1965.1 to 1966.4) for unemployment (U), GNP as a deviation from its potential value (GNP), the balance of trade (B) and inflation (P). By (7.47) this decomposes to the sum of squared anticipated failures, plus the sum of target variances. Inserting the three rules into the model in turn gave table 13.3, showing each variable's own instability contribution. Evidently policy makers could have expected, a priori, significant reductions in instability had they optimised. Optimisation reduces both w_d^* and w_s^*; but w_s^* rises to 60% of the control problem. Thus the better the policy choice the more important is stochastic control. The improvements in GNP and U are bought at the expense of some 'loss of control' over P. The interesting feature is that historical policies fare somewhat better than fixed rules, seen ex ante. In fact their deterministic components are worse (which is a significant criticism); but, once again, fixed rules are very poor at controlling disturbances. Government policies were therefore not destabilising compared to fixed rules, but they were significantly inferior to optimal policies.

The weakness of this approach is the selection of a criterion. That given above is not everyone's idea of stability. Frequent policy reversals, or intervention itself, often generate instability in the reactions of others. A gradualist philosophy would penalise *changes* in policies as one component of the stability criterion. That implies intertemporal penalties, so that w_s^* is more than a sum of variances. Indeed variances may be a poor measure of stability; policies cycling with small amplitude about z^d have a small variance. Moreover, stability is often used to mean good coordination and timing. For example, we should be able to test whether instruments interventions would have exaggerated the movements in the targets but for other exogenous events. That requires a criterion which penalises the sign of products of policy failures, either contemporaneously or not. Nevertheless, all these points can be accommodated within the specification of Q at (10.27).

13.4 Judging the value of a model

Policy optimisation techniques play an equally valuable role in model evaluation. Policy analysis is one way of learning about the dynamic properties of a model, as part of the process of its respecification and improvement. Much of that process must proceed by experimentation, based on trial and error and past experience. Clearly those experiments must be as systematic and efficient as possible. As in policy selection itself, that requires one optimisation per experiment rather than an incomplete series of many simulations. Experimental design may be conducted through z_p of Chapter 10.

Nevertheless, one of the main criticisms of policy studies always is the weakness of the model's specification. Policies robust against model errors are indeed desirable; and so to be able to select the model which provides the most reliable policy prescriptions is a valuable advance. Discrimination between alternative models is possible based on a suggestion in Chow (1981).

Crudely put, the idea here is to recognise that at any moment all models will be imperfect. And they will remain imperfect because uncertainty over which specification is the most accurate is inevitable while economic and econometric theory cannot conclusively discriminate between them on the restricted and imperfect data available. If these putative model errors cannot be eliminated in the short term, then for policy analysis purposes it pays us to abandon the search for the ideal model. Instead, from those models at hand we should pick that model which, when used at its best, will incur the smallest expected losses had any of the alternative models been the true specification. So each model must be compared to all the others; and the set of models must contain each specification thought to be a possible representation of the true 'state of the world'. Using a model at its best implies policy optimisation. By choice of the model, we pick the most robust policy in the sense that we risk the smallest expected loss by using its prescriptions instead of the *available* alternatives which might, in fact, prove to be correct. But there is no guarantee that a unique recommendation will appear from this exercise.

We construct a pay-off matrix W^*, consisting of w_d^* and w_s^* elements from (7.57), for the policy rules derived from each model when each of the alternatives is true. Naturally each model appears best when it is taken to be true, so we specify pay-offs relative to these situations. Let W^* have typical element $W_{ij}^* = (w_s^* + w_d^*)_{ij}$. The $(w_d^*)_{ij}$ elements of that matrix are taken from (7.58) in the form

$$(w_d^*)_{ij} = \tfrac{1}{2}(x_i^* - x_j^*)' M_j (x_i^* - x_j^*) \quad \text{for } i, j = 1, \ldots p \tag{13.1}$$

where there are p alternative models and $M_j = (H_j^{*\prime} Q H_j^*)$ where H_j^* is defined by (7.18) for model j. Here $\tilde{x}_j^* = -M_j^{-1} H_j^{*\prime} Q \begin{pmatrix} I \\ \cdots \\ 0 \end{pmatrix} E_1(b_j)$ and $\tilde{x}_i^* = -M_i^{-1} H_i^{*\prime} Q \begin{pmatrix} I \\ \cdots \\ 0 \end{pmatrix} E_1(b_i)$, given $q = 0$ and b_i is b for the ith model, are optimal policies based on the jth and ith models. Next,

$$(w_s^*)_{ij} = \tfrac{1}{2} \operatorname{tr} Q[V_{ij}(\xi) - V_{ii}(\xi)] \tag{13.2}$$

where $V_{ij}^*(\xi) = [I - H_j^* M_i^{-1} H_i^{*\prime} Q] \hat{\Sigma}_1 [I - H_j^* M_i^{-1} H_i^{*\prime} Q]'$.

So W_{ij}^* is the relative loss in using model i when model j truly describes the economy. Chow (1981) considers two models with demonstrably different dynamic responses, reconstructed from the Michigan and Wharton models (models A and B) respectively, to represent the possible true states of the world; and compares the risks in policy optimisation to a no intervention policy (constant growth rates) in the instruments. To eliminate transversality effects the W matrix is computed for 12 period policies taken from 32 period optimal trajectories. The targets are GNP and prices; the instruments are defence spending and monetary reserves. The results according to (13.1) and (13.2) are shown in table 13.4. Evidently optimal policies derived from model B are the least risky on most criteria,

Table 13.4 *Judging a model's reliability*

	(w_d^*)		(w_s^*)	
True state:	A	B	A	B
Optimal policy based on A	0	2115	0	23999
Optimal policy based on B	142	0	383	0
Policy based on no intervention	1912	2361	2802	5542

and certainly on a minimax one – provided A and B represent the only 'true states' worth examining. The other policy rules run into serious problems in handling stochastic shocks; although all rules here find it harder to control stochastic shocks than to get the right average values. The table shows not only how sensitive optimal policies can be to model errors, but also that, if an optimal policy rule is not robust, the conclusion that a no intervention policy is safer does not necessarily follow. Some other 'wrong' optimal policy may be better.

The results from this kind of study can only be extended to implementation if the set of models considered represents the full range of 'true states' which we are prepared to contemplate. In other words, these results tell us nothing about the absolute usefulness of the policy rules when neither A nor B are true. For the same reason these results do not tell us much about the deficiencies of the models, for that also depends on the true state of the world. This sort of technique measures *relative* usefulness of what is available. We do not bother with what would be the ideal rule and model, but select the most reliable from those available. In Chapter 1 we argued that there will be no one ideal model, but one best suited to any particular problem.

13.5 On the design of new policies

The methods for experimenting with different policy selections discussed so far have all assumed both the list of policy variables and T to be fixed. If the policy maker is unsure of the relative priorities he wishes to assign to the policy variables, he may also be unsure which variables he should subject to his direct control. He would no doubt appreciate the opportunity to experiment with different lists of policy variables to see which serve his purpose best. Typical questions include: 'Would excluding an unpopular instrument entail serious damage to the results?'; or 'Which of two similar instruments can better be omitted?'; 'If a target presents a severe obstacle in one period, is it worth dropping for that interval?' In addition, if the optimal values of one instrument turn out to be highly sensitive to stochastic shocks whereas another's do not, then it becomes important for the successful operation of the plan to review the list of policy variables being used. It is pointless to attempt a plan which, in probability, cannot be successfully achieved. It is first necessary to find out if such sensitivities exist, and, if so, to investigate alternative lists for results which are less accident prone.

To be able to discriminate between policy strategies qualitatively, as well as quantitatively, is important in its own right since optimisation methods are frequently criticised for being of no help in the design of new instruments (HMSO (1978)). As long as the potential new instrument can be represented in a model, its potential is best evaluated by policy optimisation since that describes the benefits of its introduction, *when used to best effect.*

To experiment with including or excluding variables (targets or instruments) without indulging in extensive and repeated reoptimisations is a special case of assessing the effects of altering the preference structure with respect to those variables, where all candidates were included in the original optimisation. We can therefore use (9.25) to show the effects of creating a new instrument (or target). Assume that $\tilde{z}$ in (7.10) contains all the candidate variables, and z^d is correspondingly specified. Then the effects of removing a variable are given by setting $dQ_{ij} = -Q_{ij}$ and $dQ_{ji} = dQ_{ij}$, for $i = kt$ and $j = 1 \dots (m+n)T$, in

$$dz^* = \frac{\partial z^*}{\text{vec}\,\partial Q}\text{vec}(dQ) = \sum_{i=1}^{(n+m)T} (\tilde{z}_i^* \Phi) dQ_{i.} \tag{13.3}$$

where variable k (one, or several, but not all of $k = 1 \dots n+m$) is excluded in period t (one, or several, or all of $t = 1 \dots T$). On the other hand, in order to experiment with new variables, consider the use of (7.18) with the full set of candidate variables in z, but those not yet considered for policy selection associated with a row and column of zeroes in Q (and q). Now, (13.3) shows the effects of including an extra variable when $dQ_{ji} = dQ_{ij} = Q_{ij}$, the weight we now wish to impose.

Such calculations allow, quickly and cheaply, a lot of experimentation with alternative designs of the selection problem without resort to tedious and expensive reoptimisations. In fact, given a benchmark solution, $\partial z^* / \text{vec}(\partial Q)$ can be used as a table of ready reckoners to summarise possible policy changes. In practice, it may be easier to work with Φ itself as an incomplete table of ready reckoners. Since $dz^*/\tilde{z}_i^* = \Phi dQ_{i.}$ the changes, proportional to $\tilde{z}_i^*$, due to changes in the penalties on $\tilde{z}_i$ (ith row of Q) are given by Φ for each $i = 1, \dots, (n+m)T$. Since $dQ_{ij} = dQ_{ji}$ for $i \neq j$, if Φ_{ij} is involved we get the primary effects through dz_i^* and dz_j^* but not the secondary effects via the remainder of dz^*. In any case, ready reckoners of this kind will be important because changing the list of policy variables has three channels of influence:

(a) from the removal (addition) of a full row and column of Q;
(b) the immediate alteration to the optimal values of the other variables in $\tilde{z}^*$, and hence to w^*;
(c) the dynamic effects of the alterations in (b), and hence to w^*.

So the full consequences of changing Q may not be obvious. At the same time we can compute the changed sensitivities by (9.39), in the hope that a new policy design, which is sufficiently robust to stochastic errors, will emerge.

We may start from a benchmark solution with as few as one target in each period if necessary. But that means experimenting with lengthening horizons is not possible. Yet, in nonpolitical contexts, the appropriate T is often not clear. And even in the political arena, responsible politicians should be forced to look beyond the next election or plan completion date. Thus we must take the benchmark solution to have the maximum T.

Some special cases of this analysis are of immediate interest. The inclusion or exclusion of subsets of targets and instruments is likely to have quite different consequences than their inclusion or exclusion singly. This may apply for subsets consisting of one variable over different periods, or for subsets consisting of several variables at one period. By setting nonzero elements of dQ by blocks of variables or by blocks of time we get some measure, respectively, of the possible benefits of a proper coordination and timing of policy impacts.

Finally (13.3) may be good for experimenting with the general policy design; but as an accurate measure of the effects of including or excluding variables it will only be good for small dQ_{ij} values. $\partial z^*/\text{vec}(\partial Q)$ depends on z^* and Q which inevitably will be the pre-change values. For experimentation this approximation may nevertheless be acceptable because of the insensitivity of z^* to Q which we observed in Chapter 9.

In passing, note that we can use similar approximate techniques for assessing the effect of changing the model structure by means of (9.18) since $\text{vec}[d(\beta \vdots \Gamma)]$ is set up to accept new elements arising from a changed specification of each equation by inserting new columns. That only requires the new reduced form coefficients implied to be inserted into extra columns of $(\Pi^{*'} \vdots I)$ of the matrix E in (9.18). Thus we can approximately test the proposition that changing the model specification will materially alter appropriate policies. We can allow for time varying parameters, in particular in order to use parameter changes as instruments (tax rates, for example). Finally, and most important, we can test the efficiency of new legislation which is designed to alter the 'rules of the game' or the feasible economic responses – such as the introduction of the new rules on competition and credit into the British Banking System in 1971.

In all these cases, our tests are conducted so that the policies concerned perform to their best advantage. Simulation, for example, is an inadequate test procedure since the last property is not guaranteed. There is little point in 'auditioning' a new policy when it is not shown off to best advantage. Our argument is intended to suggest that policy optimisation can indeed help in the design of new policy instruments, or legislation, aimed at modifying economic responses in order to enhance the effectiveness of existing policies. A proper evaluation of those opportunities is one indirect benefit of policy optimisation. We have shown how to estimate the effects of introducing new instruments on optimal policy choices, but not how to identify which of the potential new instruments is most needed and which targets pose the greatest risk. To do that requires lagrange multipliers and a measure of the contribution made by each policy instrument to achieving the stated objectives. These are the next topics.

13.6 The uses of lagrange multipliers in policy selection

Directly or indirectly lagrange multipliers offer valuable qualitative information on a proposed programme of policies. They are an integral part of analysing the composition of the implied costs of 'near optimal' selections, and thus of errors in implementation. We cover three of these features: (a) the 'shadow costs' of each target, (b) the identification of new instruments, and (c) the robustness of the optimised objectives.

Information on potential implementation difficulties should in any case accompany a policy proposal; and the cost structure associated with near optimal policies may suggest suitable modifications. This kind of information is not available from other policy selection techniques.

13.6.1 Shadow costs and bottlenecks

In Chapter 9 we saw that $\partial w^*/\partial s = \mu^{*\prime}$, so that the lagrangian multipliers indicate which constraints are most important to the solution, in the sense of showing where a relaxation would make most contribution to improving the outcome. Similarly they indicate where a random shock would cause most damage. Mistakes in implementation, as well as the effects of model and information errors, can always be represented by an additive shock to the optimised system. Consequently lagrange multipliers are particularly useful for evaluating the costs associated with near-optimal choices.

The minimised cost of a policy programme, w^*, will be sensitive to some variables in some periods, but less so to other variables and other periods. Therefore these high risk variables must be very carefully kept on their optimal paths and their implementation very carefully monitored so that proper revisions can be made when necessary. But the relative neglect of the other variables (and the other periods) will be of little consequence to the success of the plan. The advantage of working with lagrange multipliers, and their sensitivities, is that one knows the bottlenecks and likely expensive implementation errors in advance for any policy proposal. Lagrange multipliers identify where modification of the

Table 13.5 *Lagrange multipliers for Dutch macroeconomic policies 1976–80*

Open loop targets	1976	1977	1978	1979	1980	Target penalties at each period
Unemployment	3.1	3.3	5.3	7.1	10.2	1
Real wage	– 27.9	– 19.9	– 16.4	– 9.2	– 8.9	100
Inflation	5.8	1.3	1.6	3.0	3.2	1
Labour income share	3.7	3.6	4.2	2.1	4.6	1
Balance of trade	– 2.6	– 2.2	– 2.7	– 2.5	– 0.5	1
Closed loop targets						
Unemployment	3.1	3.3	3.4	2.6	2.0	1
Real wage	– 27.9	– 28.6	– 15.5	– 2.8	– 2.1	100
Inflation	5.8	6.8	3.5	0.6	– 0.05	1
Labour income share	3.7	1.6	2.0	0.2	2.4	1
Balance of trade	– 2.6	– 2.4	– 5.6	– 3.6	– 3.4	1

Remaining multipliers were less than 10% of the dominant one.

proposed policies is most useful – or at least where the greatest effort in monitoring their performance should be concentrated.

The policies suggested by Brandsma, Hughes Hallett and Van der Windt (1981) for the Dutch economy over 1976–80 produced the lagrange multipliers set out in table 13.5. The shadow costs of any policies will reflect the preference structure – as indeed they should. The high penalty on real wages is designed to restrict policies to what is politically acceptable. So, from the point of view of open loop planning, maintaining the real wage target presents the most serious difficulty. But those difficulties are projected to fall steadily, and to be replaced by the unemployment target as the main bottleneck or danger to success. In fact, as the programme unfolds (see the closed loop values) the difficulties over maintaining real wages almost disappear in 1979–80, after increasing in 1977. And the danger to unemployment fails to materialise. Instead the balance of trade presents the main bottleneck over 1979–80.

13.6.2 Identifying new instruments

It is simple to identify those new policy instruments, from among the noncontrollable variables, whose introduction would most benefit and improve the current optimal policy selection. In Chapter 9 we discovered that

$$dw^* = \mu^{*\prime} K dN. \tag{13.4}$$

Therefore from $\mu^{*\prime}K$ we may pick out both the instrument and its timing which has the greatest potential (per unit) for reducing the current best performance index. All that is required in this scheme is that all existing candidate instruments be included in the list in N. On the other hand, the creation of totally new instruments alters the model. They must therefore be evaluated via the sensitivity (9.18)

$$dw^* = \mu^{*\prime} E[\mathrm{vec}\, d(\beta \vdots \Gamma)] \tag{13.5}$$

where extra elements have been created in the matrix E, and in $\mathrm{vec}[\beta \vdots \Gamma]$, to accommodate any necessary new variables. This possibility was raised at the end of the previous section.

In either case lagrange multipliers must be evaluated since the projected improvement is the sum of the impacts of the change on the targets weighted by the relative values, in this solution, of relaxing the constraint which governs each target. Naturally we wish to introduce that new instrument which produces the largest negative dw^* value. So these formulae also indicate how that instrument should be used; that is, in which direction it must change from its current value (which may be zero), and with what timing.

An application of the policy game described in Chapter 11 provides a simple illustration. The application is to a possible power struggle between the United States and the Soviet Union, in which each attempts to hinder the development of the opposing economy to its own advantage while continuing to promote progress in its own economy (Hughes Hallett and Brandsma (1980)). The targets over 1980–4 include profits; industrial production and wages; disposable income; capital stock; the trade, budget and demand–output balances; and labour productivity. The Soviet instruments are defence expenditure; industrial and agricultural investment allocations; and real wage adjustments. The American instruments are changes in Soviet agricultural, technical and machinery imports; their prices; and exports to the west. Based on the SOVMOD model (Green and Higgins (1977)), the Americans are able to induce only a deteriorating trade balance, with political costs to the Soviet leadership, through worsening foreign exchange, consumption, and budget deficits. These costs are shown in the lagrange multipliers of the optimal Soviet response in table 13.6. (The remainder are less than 2 in absolute value, although associated with unit penalties.) Two extra instruments are available to the Soviets: 'other' government expenditure, and the level of gold reserves held. In order to deflect American action in 1981 it would

Table 13.6 *The shadow costs of Soviet economic policy*

	1980	1981	1982	1983	1984	Target penalty
Balance of trade	– 18.9	– 27.1	– 31.8	– 27.4	– 36.5	1.0
Budget	– 5.9	– 7.9	– 10.3	– 7.5	– 11.1	0.5

be best to reduce gold reserves rather than nondefence expenditure; (13.4) gave – 16.22 against – 12.63. On the other hand, similar calculations also show that any induced autonomous increase in real wages would cause substantially more damage to the Soviet economy than would any export embargo.

13.6.3 Making the optimised objective robust

We can make use of the lagrange multipliers to help evaluate and manipulate the trade-off between inducing robustness in $w(\tilde{z})$ and minimising $|\tilde{z}|$. We know from Chapter 9 that the relevant sensitivities all depend on μ^*: i.e. $\partial w^*/\partial u = \mu^{*\prime}S; \partial w^*/\partial N = \mu^{*\prime}K; \partial w^*/\text{vec}\,\partial(\beta\vdots\Gamma) = \mu^{*\prime}E$. The object, then, is to engineer changes in the preference parameters, and possibly in any structural model components under the policymaker's control, such that μ^* becomes near orthogonal to S, K and E – or at least so the larger sensitivities are reduced in absolute value. We can pick dQ, dN and $d(\beta\vdots\Gamma)$ so that

$$d\mu^* = (\tilde{z}^{*\prime} \otimes \Theta')\,\text{vec}(dQ) + (HQ^{-1}H')^{-1}(E\ \text{vec}\ d(\beta\vdots\Gamma) + KdN) \tag{13.6}$$

shows changes of required sizes and signs. At the same time we should restrict $d\mu^*$ so that the implied policy changes, dz^*, are not excessive. But in practice it is easier to determine the desired $d\mu^*$, reoptimise, and insert the old z^* (unconstrained by the concern for a robust w^*) as z_p in the interactive algorithm of Chapter 10. Iterations in that algorithm allow the policy maker to determine his preferred position in the security–success trade-off.

13.7 The regression analogy revisited

In Chapter 10 we established a formal analogy between optimal open loop policy calculations and least squares regression. Specifically, (7.18) is the nonstochastic least squares mixed regression which minimises the mT 'errors' $\tilde{y}$ in the 'model' $b = -R\tilde{x} + \tilde{y}$. This regression involved 'observed regressors', $-R$, 'parameters', $\tilde{x}$, and is subject to the nonorthogonal prior information that $\tilde{x}$ should approximate zero. The inverted matrix of 'error covariances' for all $\tilde{z}$ over all periods supplies the metric for minimisation, Q.

The same analogy also offers a range of summary 'statistics', and other diagnostic information, which characterise the plan as a whole. However, the analogy only applies to each successive first period certainty equivalent policy, $E_t(\tilde{x}^*_{(t)})$. It does not apply to the closed loop solution which contains part of each $\tilde{x}^*_{(t)}$. Moreover, the analogy does not readily extend to the stochastic ex post optimal solution $\tilde{x}^*$. Our summary 'statistics' are therefore nonstochastic. Without probability distributions, formal inference and hypothesis tests become no more than indices of the proposed plan's characteristics.

13.7.1 Indices of achievement

A natural index of success is the R^2 analog. By (7.55) the certainty equivalent optimised policies (writing b for $E_t(b)$) are

$$\tilde{z}^* = [I - H^*M^{-1}H^{*\prime}Q]\begin{pmatrix} b \\ \vdots \\ 0 \end{pmatrix} \qquad (13.7)$$

with the result that $H^{*\prime}Q\tilde{z}^* = 0$. Thus $b'Bb = \tilde{z}^{*\prime}Q\tilde{z}^* + \tilde{x}^{*\prime}M\tilde{x}^*$ or

$$R^2 = 1 - 2w(\tilde{z}^*)/b'Bb = \tilde{x}^{*\prime}M\tilde{x}^*/b'Bb. \qquad (13.8)^2$$

The object of policy selection, according to this analogy, is to pick x to 'mop up' (account for) b – the unavoidable events in the economy. Our success, measured in the metric of Q, is divided between the controlled sum of squares ($\tilde{x}^{*\prime}M\tilde{x}^*$) and the sum of squared failures. Thus R^2 gives a standardised and dimensionless index of achievements over failures, defined on the interval (0, 1). At each t it can be computed for the remainder of the plan. It is a useful complement to $w(\tilde{z}^*)$ because it allows different proposals to be compared when the list of policy variables, or their relative priorities, are also varied. Otherwise it is hard to distinguish improvements due to changes in the policy vector from the improvements due to relative priorities changing in $w(\tilde{z}^*)$.

It is necessary to be careful in interpreting R^2. Changing the list of instruments in x will automatically change b – the quantities to be accounted for – unless we happen to remove some instruments by forcing them to take their ideal values. The task facing the new x selection will be more (less) difficult if $b'Bb$ increases (decreases). In either case R^2 may rise or fall. However, if we add (remove) targets while the instrument set is fixed,

2 The results of Havenner and Craine (1981) motivated much of this material.

we increase (reduce) the number of constraints in the model and elements in b. This, and increasing T, are both equivalent to extending (reducing) the sample in estimation. Whether R^2 rises or not depends on whether the new targets are easier, on average, to satisfy than the old set; i.e. on whether $b'Bb$ increases slower or faster than $w(\tilde{z}^*)$. Thus R^2 necessarily rises only if a new instrument not previously in the system is created, or if a dormant instrument is activated from its ideal value.

13.7.2 On the use of instruments: the importance of timing, coordination, and efficiency

As a measure of the precision, or reliability, of the calculated instruments we have M^{-1}, which is the inverse of the hessian (information) matrix of the constrained criterion function (see (7.19)). That is a conventional measure of solution sensitivity in optimisation and is, of course, the analog of the covariance matrix of a model's estimated coefficients. The diagonal elements of M^{-1} show how robust each policy value is to changed assumptions on $E_t(b)$ – with an eye to the likely future revisions. We can look at variables in one period, or a particular variable in all periods, to assess how much 'hard' information we actually have obtained on the best values of a particular policy in a particular period. The off-diagonal elements show whether errors in instrument values would be reinforcing or compensating; i.e. when $(M^{-1})_{ij} > 0 (< 0)$ changes caused in instrument i would be accompanied by similar (opposite) changes in instrument j. An instrument error may substitute for itself in different periods, or for other instruments in the same or different periods.

Probably M itself will be of greater interest. As the matrix of second derivatives of the constrained criterion with respect to $E_t(\tilde{x}^*)$, M describes the role played by each instrument in the optimal solution. Large diagonal elements indicate that a particular instrument is important in that period. Hence, we can see if one instrument or one period dominates in the sense that implementing the wrong values for those elements of the solution would cause serious damage.

Large off-diagonal elements show whether instruments are being used as substitutes ($M_{ij} > 0$) or complements ($M_{ij} < 0$). Once again an instrument can be a substitute (say) for itself in different periods, or for another instrument in the same or different periods. We can measure the importance of the correct *timing* in the use of instruments. If a particular instrument in a particular period is associated with a large M_{ii} value but that instrument is not a significant substitute for itself in different periods (or, worse, it is complementary), then the precise timing of its impacts is extremely important. But if those time substitutions are important, they will be used to compensate $w(\tilde{z})$ for any failures to get the right impact at the right time; either in the shape of large revisions to that instrument later, or of large precautionary values earlier.

Likewise where two instruments within one time period are associated with large diagonal elements in M but are strongly complementary, their *coordination* is important. If they have large diagonal M elements in different time periods and are complementary between those two periods then both timing and coordination, i.e. their *phasing*, is important.

Finally, if two instruments act as close substitutes (or complements) in the way we try to use them, then M will be nearly singular. Without extra information, optimisation is unable to say much about the best choice of those instruments. Since they are so similar it matters rather little how they are chosen, although vis-a-vis the remaining instruments that choice may still be important. By analogy with collinearity in estimation, (Gilbert (1978)), we might take $c = (nT)^{-1}\sum_{j=1}^{nT} M_{jj}(M^{-1})_{jj} \geqslant 1$ to represent the efficiency of the instrument set chosen for the job we are interested in (as defined by Q and z^d, and the individual policy effects available). For full efficiency $c = 1$; and it increases with increasing inefficiency. We can isolate where the instruments are ineffective, by period or by variable, if we compute c as

$$c = 1 + \sum_{i=1}^{n} \sum_{t=1}^{T} c_{it} \text{ where } c_{it} = [M_{it,it}(M^{-1})_{it,it} - 1]/nT \geqslant 0. \quad (13.9)$$

Thus we might refer to a problem as having nT/c effective instruments (or $n/(1 + \sum_i c_{it})$ in period t) rather than nT. A lack of efficiency implies little information is available on the best use of the associated instrument, and, consequently, that the computed values will be unreliable.

Thus, from M we obtain information on how each instrument should best be used in each period and overall; and from M^{-1} we learn how much we really know about the reliability of each calculated value in terms of the externally supplied information.

13.7.3 Indices of the contribution of particular instruments

Given the interest in the possibility of changing the list of instruments, the measurement of the contribution made by each instrument in each period to the optimal solution is an obvious concern. When all possible instruments have been used, we will want to know how well the economy could be controlled if one instrument were deleted. That is a natural question if one instrument is thought to be ineffective, either singly or in addition to other instruments (as indicated by c_{it}). More generally we will be interested in the contribution, or improvement, which could be made with an additional instrument, *after* the other instruments have done their best. For the inclusion (exclusion) of one instrument in one period both questions can be answered by the analog of the partial correlation coefficient:

$$r_j = [\tilde{x}_j^*/(M^{-1})_{jj}][(\tilde{x}_j^*/(M^{-1})_{jj})^2 + mT]^{-1/2}, j = 1 \dots nT. \quad (13.10)$$

More likely we shall be proposing to include (delete) an instrument throughout the period (1, T). An F index of the contribution of k instruments to the whole plan is:

$$F = \frac{(w^{*(k)} - w^*)/kT}{w^*/mT} \text{ for } k = 1 \dots n \quad (13.11)$$

where $w^{*(k)}$ and w^* are evaluations of $w(\tilde{z}^*)$ without and with the k instruments in the optimisation. But if this index is to be properly defined it must be calibrated for mutually exclusive events; and it must specify the reference, or origin, position. In this case the reference position specifies the values taken by the deleted instruments at $F = 0$. The problem is that removing (adding) a subset of variables from the x vector transfers them to (from) b. This is like trying to test the significance of a subset of explanatory variables, while at the same time varying the endogenous variable's data. We cannot discriminate unambiguously between non-nested non-disjoint alternative hypotheses. In our context, (13.11) would then attempt to index alternatives which are not mutually exclusive. On the other hand, the formal analogy holds good for the reference position of $\tilde{x}_{jt}^* = 0, j = 1 \dots k$ and all $t = 1 \dots T$. Thus, we have an index of the contribution made by those k instruments as they vary from their ideal values. This interpretation should also be kept in mind when using (13.10), or (13.11). The latter can also be used when $k = n$; which is to measure that contribution from all instruments together.

Once again, (13.10) provides information on the importance of timing if r_j varies when calculated for different time periods but only one instrument. Similarly, if (13.10) or (13.11) vary when computed for the same variable excluded but different instruments included, then we learn about coordination and phasing respectively. The trouble with (13.11) is that, being nonstochastic, there is no calibration against which it may be measured. Apart from looking for 'large' or 'small' values, we can only use it for comparing contributions made in different circumstances or in different plans.

13.7.4 Measuring the difficulty of a plan

There are many possibilities of extending these indices to gauge the difficulties inherent in different aspects of a policy problem. The loss caused by attempting to satisfy k *exact* restrictions among the instruments in t of the T planning periods, in addition to those in the existing model, is given by (13.11) with t replacing T. For example, we may wish to evaluate the costs (and benefits) of imposing a balanced budget on a plan involving government expenditures and revenues. That is evidently a special case of evaluating the contribution of k instruments since $w^{*(k)}$ will come from optimising a structural model with k instruments substituted out by their restrictions.

Inexact constraints of this form can be handled by incorporating them as k extra targets in the model's structural form, and then reoptimising to produce $w^{*(k)}$. That is a special case of increasing the list of a plan's targets. Generalising, we can use (13.11) to indicate the costs (or benefits) to changing the list of targets. In all these cases (13.11) provides an index of the difficulty of the extended policy problem relative to any proposed plan.

A direct measure of the difficulty inherent in a policy problem would be useful. The mixed regression analogy arises because we attempt to achieve y^d, while also setting x close to an x^d inconsistent with that y^d. Thus we may be interested in testing the incompatibility, or degree of infeasibility, of y^d and x^d in the scale of preferences. An index for this purpose is[3]

$$\gamma_0 = \tilde{x}^{0\prime}[(R'BR)^{-1} + A^{-1}]^{-1}\tilde{x}^0 \tag{13.12}$$

where $\tilde{x}^0 = -(R'BR)^{-1}R'b$ is the polar choice for x with no instrument penalties mentioned in Chapter 10. The other polar case was x^d itself. The extremes of γ_0 indicate the losses to using each polar case when the other would have been correct; i.e. by (7.58) if $A^{-1} = 0$ then $\gamma_0 = \gamma_1$ is the loss in implementing x^d when x^0 is optimal, while if $(R'BR)^{-1} = 0$ then $\gamma_0 = \gamma_2$ is the loss in x^0 when x^d is optimal. In fact $0 < \gamma_0 \leqslant \min(\gamma_1, \gamma_2)$; where γ_1 defines the complete incompatibility of x^d measured in terms of the y^d constraints, and γ_2 defines the complete incompatibility of y^d with the x^d constraints. The latter aspect is expressed, through x^0, as the best y value (without x^d constraints) because the system may not be statically controllable. Thus the degree of incompatibility, for a proposed policy problem, is given by γ_0 in relation to $0, \gamma_1$ and γ_2. If it gets too large we should consider revising x^d (if $\gamma_1 < \gamma_2$) or y^d (if $\gamma_2 < \gamma_1$), and possibly the relation of A to B in either case.

13.7.5 Some numerical examples

In the example of optimal policies for the American economy in 1933–6 (given in Chapter 7), the three instruments (public wages, taxes, government expenditure) make the contributions shown in table 13.7 to

3 If Q contains $C \neq 0$ then add $R'C' + CR$ to A and $\begin{pmatrix} 0 \\ Cb \end{pmatrix}$ to q. Then use (7.12) before computing γ_0 as given.

Table 13.7 *Indices of success in optimal policies for the American economy*

Horizon	1933–6	1934–6	1935–6	1936
R^2	0.717	0.783	0.782	0.719
F	2.53	3.61	3.59	2.56

Table 13.8 *The contributions of individual open loop instruments*

	1933	1934	1935	1936
W_2	0.43	0.38	0.29	0.26
T	0.74	0.58	−0.05	−0.61
G	0.90	0.83	0.76	0.55

The effective number of instruments is 4.6 where $nT = 12$.

meeting the targets of consumption, investment, and income distribution. Roughly 75% of the impact of b on target failures has been eliminated, which is a satisfactory, if not good, record of success. The contribution of the instruments, which is substantial, rises by nearly 50% in the midterm but falls back in 1936. Their individual contributions, (13.10), are set out in table 13.8. G makes the biggest contribution, and, excepting T in 1935, W_2 could most easily be discarded. It is rather important to time the impacts of W_2 and G for the start of the plan. Indeed, inspection of the larger elements of M showed that T_{1933} was a strong substitute for T_{1934}, as was T_{1934} for T_{1935}. But T_{1933} was a strong complement for G_{1933}, as was T_{1934} for G_{1934}, T_{1933} for G_{1934} and T_{1934} for G_{1935}. Hence, the careful timing of the tax policy over 1933–5, the coordination of T and G in 1933–4, and their phasing over 1933–5, are all important to the success of the plan.

The policy game version of this example, which was used in Chapter 11, provides a more interesting illustration (table 13.9). Here F refers to the contribution made by each player's instrument set, and F^* measures the extra contribution made by giving each player control of his opponent's instruments in addition to his own. In other words, F^* is an index of how much each player may expect to gain by cooperation. Recall that the preferences have changed from those in Chapter 7 both because each player uses his own preferences, and because of the loss of instruments to

Table 13.9 *Characteristics of the 1933 open loop policy games*

	Cournot solutions			Nash solutions			
Player	R^2	F	F^*	R^2	F	F^*	F^{**}
Government	0.89	12.1	0.59	0.91	15.2	0.04	0.18
Labour	0.06	0.19	4.42	0.09	0.3	0.86	5.23

each player. The Nash solutions here are estimated by (11.45). To the extent $D_1^{(i)} \neq D_*^{(i)}$, w^* is an upper bound estimate so that F and F^* are lower bounds.

The Government is clearly rather more successful in accomplishing an evidently simpler task. The new objectives are easier to satisfy despite the loss of an instrument. The remaining instruments make a bigger contribution, even in the Cournot cases where b is unchanged. Moreover, the Nash solution implies a further 25% improvement in their contribution. Labour, on the other hand, faces a much more difficult task. Not only has it lost any control over the only two effective instruments in the game, but the severe drop in R^2 suggests that the new preferences are no easier to satisfy. But the Nash solution offers nearly a 60% improvement in the contribution that manipulating wages could make to Labour's objectives. In view of (11.47), the Nash solution must be regarded as a least squares solution involving a transformed model; the matrix $R^{(i)}$ becomes $R^{(i)} + R^{(j)}D^{(j)}$. This means that, in the estimation analogy, comparison of F indices between the Nash and Cournot solutions is again equivalent to indexing nonnested alternative 'hypotheses', which are not mutually exclusive because of the different 'data sets' for R and b.

However, (11.39) shows the Nash solution may also be regarded as one in which each player chooses the value of all instruments in the game, but each instrument is subjected to a restriction in terms of the others. Thus for a proper comparison between Nash and Cournot solutions we use (13.11) for m targets, n instruments and n exact restrictions. The results are given as F^{**} in table 13.9. As expected, the gain for Labour is substantial, but that for the Government is slight. These results support our earlier observations on the potential value of exploiting a policy game, rather than ignoring it.

Finally, despite some surrender of individual preferences, the gain to cooperation is indicated by F^* – the contribution of extra unrestricted instruments. For the Government there is little to be gained over either the Cournot or the Nash solutions. For Labour, however, the gain over the Cournot solution is definitely worthwhile even if that over the Nash solution is slight. This amounts to saying that the Government probably does sufficiently well under any strategy to be indifferent between strategies – although there is some gain to cooperation over Cournot solutions. Labour, on the other hand, has considerable incentive to move from Cournot to either a Nash or a cooperative solution; but once the transfer is made to a Nash strategy the incentive for cooperation largely disappears. Therefore the chances of cooperation look poor since most of the gains can be made by exploiting the policy game within one's own preferences.

13.7.6 The possibility of stochastic extensions

Although reverting from $E_t(b)$ to b throughout leaves us with a stochastic policy, these regression analogies do not readily translate into conventional hypothesis tests. They therefore do not extend to questions of inference on the ex post policy choice to be resolved at, or before, implementation. For one thing, Q^{-1} is not the actual covariance matrix $E(bb')$ and so $E(\tilde{x}^*\tilde{x}^{*\prime}) \neq M^{-1}$. In fact $E(\tilde{x}^*\tilde{x}^{*\prime})$ was given earlier at (7.53). Second, the distribution of $\tilde{x}^*$ depends on that for b, which is unknown for reasons given in Chapter 7 and which we are unwilling to guess at. Third, the distributions of $\tilde{x}^*$, and b, are too difficult to determine when H^* is also recognised to be stochastic. However, if one were to make the (in our view unjustified)[4] assumption that b is distributed asymptotically as $N(\eta, \Sigma_1)$ say, then (13.11) would be distributed as $F_{kT,mT}$. It would test the null hypothesis $\tilde{x}_{jt}^* = 0$ against $\tilde{x}_{jt}^* \neq 0$, all t and $j = 1 \ldots k$, in the ex post optimal choice. That is to say it tests whether the k instruments, chosen optimally and ex post, would be significantly different from their ideal values. But setting $x_{jt}^* = x_{jt}^d$ is the simulation solution. It is non-stochastic, and not due for future revisions in the light of the realisations of the remaining stochastic variables. It is also part of the optimal solution given infinite uncertainty about the impacts of the policies for the non-controllables. In other words, $\tilde{x}_{jt}^* = 0$ implies x_{jt} contributes only to the minimisation of the deterministic objective $w_d(.)$, but not the stochastic objective $w_s(.)$, of (7.49). Hence we are also testing whether x_{jt}^* makes no contribution to reducing the effects of uncertainty, against the alternative that an active use of x_{jt}^* can significantly reduce uncertainty.

Now generalising to the case of all instruments, $(k = n)$, we can test if x^* differs significantly from x^d; and therefore can be used to reduce

4 Because it requires uncertainty to be purely additive, and all random variables to be asymptotically normally distributed.

the uncertainty significantly. In that case, of course, (13.11) becomes

$$F_{nT,mT} = mT(v^* - w_s^*)/(nTw_s^*) \tag{13.13}$$

given the definition of w_s^* in (7.57) and of v^* earlier in this chapter. On this basis, both examples in table 13.1 show very significant reductions in uncertainty by using $x^* \neq x^d$. In the Dutch planning case, $F = 11.4$ against a critical value of 2.4 for $F_{25,35}$ at the 1% level. In the copper market case, $F = 1.98$ against 1.86 for $F_{40,80}$ at the 1% level.

13.8 Conclusions

An important advantage of calculating optimal policy values is the supplementary information generated on the characteristics of the policy problem. The variety of examples surveyed here shows the potential for: (i) evaluating other policy regimes, and illustrating the possibilities for improving current policies; (ii) discriminating between models; (iii) designing new policy instruments and identifying which targets pose the greatest risk; (iv) measuring the contribution of instruments. The points to be stressed are: (a) most of this information is generated automatically during the calculation of the policy proposal; (b) it is information essential for the successful implementation of policies and it is unavailable from other selection techniques; and (c) the instruments in the policy problem faced are used to best effect. Implementation is a difficult, and perhaps slightly vulgar, topic for theoretical work; with the result that practical problems in policy making have tended to take second place to setting out the 'grand design'. Nevertheless, successful planning depends on coming to grips with these matters.

14

A summing up: econometric models and the decision structure

14.1 Epilogue

It is natural to ask the question: How much use is made, or should be made, of econometric models and the associated policy selection techniques by planning authorities?

The answers to such questions turn on how the information produced by the model can be used most effectively. It is as important that a sound decision making framework should surround the model as it is to have a good model. For the best of models will be valueless if the information it generates is mishandled or ignored. Yet, it is surprising how few econometric decision models actually endogenise the policy decisions. It is rightly argued that such models cannot provide reliable descriptions or prescriptions for any of their variables. The econometric model, the preference system, the information system, and risk allowance are all components in a decision making structure, each of them subject to many of the same specification and estimation difficulties. If all these components are to be properly treated it will be important to view policy optimisation as the objective from the start; that is as a generalisation of simulation and multiplier analysis rather than as just the next activity.

Ultimately, improved economic performance will not come from taking a different kind of decision because the models and techniques described here are employed; but because of better and more accurate judgements of the consequences of the combination and timing of adjustments to the available policies, because of systematic error corrections, and from a clearer understanding of where, and in what form, new policy instruments would be useful.

14.2 Models and planning systems

It can be extremely difficult to discover how much use is made of econometric models and formal policy selection techniques in practice. Information, available to the outsider, concerning the exact institutional structure and policy selection procedures surrounding the model will of necessity be sketchy and rapidly obsolete. In some cases the secrecy which must naturally cover the planning discussions is also found to cover the planning procedures.

Almost every country uses some form of forecasting model, simple or sophisticated. Centralised economic planning has long been practised by governments of the Soviet block nations. The planning techniques have been of a formal nature, and in general the models have represented nonbehavioural user and materials balances in an interindustry accounting framework.

In the developed western countries the models have been of the behavioural type (fitted to a national income accounting system) for decentralised indicative planning of aggregate demand, unemployment, inflation and the balance of trade. The concern over the unsatisfactory treatment of the supply sectors has led to some integration with interindustry accounting (Preston (1975) and references therein).

In the less developed nations, government economic planning often takes the form of solutions to a sequence of specific, often unconnected, 'one-off' problems such as urban unemployment, rural/urban income imbalances, foreign exchange shortages, or the management of particular products or commodities. This situation manifests itself in the many plans which are a series of public investment projects, neither linked to nor integrated with the general development of the rest of the economy.

14.2.1 The British and Dutch forecasting frameworks

(a) In the Netherlands, planning models are housed in the Central Planning Bureau. The models used are an annual one concentrating on supply and demand functions, employment and foreign trade for planning long-term developments; and a quarterly one for short-run forecasts and policy adjustments. As a rule, the short-run model is used for problems of stabilisation based on projections of exogenous events, and the long-run model to study the possibilities for growth compatible with a moving equilibrium in the goods, labour, capital and foreign trade markets. The projections of medium- and long-term events are undertaken at roughly five year intervals, and revisions to forecasts and plans based on each such exercise are contained within the short-run projection exercises which are undertaken each year with a horizon of up to two years. It appears that the short-run projections are intended to fit into the frame of reference provided by the long-run projections. Thus the short-run projections contain revisions in the light of the performance so far and the various exogenous influences; they provide a sharper and more detailed view of the expected performance over the next year or two of the current medium-term plan. However, there is no mechanism guaranteeing the mutual consistency of the two sets of plans, with the result that longer-run plans may lack the benefit of systematic revisions.

It is hard to detail precisely the administrative procedures followed in formulating economic policies in the Netherlands, because they have grown up in an informal way since 1945 and because they depend to a significant extent on individual personalities. The terms of reference are set by those Ministers most concerned with economic affairs, in agreement with other official consultative bodies and officials from the relevant ministries. Those terms include the favoured instruments and give some indication of bounds to acceptable policy changes. They are translated into a technical form and inserted into the econometric models by the Central Planning Bureau. In the recent past targets have included consumption, real disposable income, output, unemployment, inflation, the trade balance, public sector borrowing, and labour's income share. The instruments have been incomes policy, social security benefits and contributions, investment and construction stimuli, government employment, direct and indirect taxes, government expenditure, and the exchange rate. From here, multipliers are computed for policy changes about the central projection implied by terms of reference – the 'spoorboekjes' of Chapter 4. In practice there may be several central projections depending on alternative assumptions for the noncontrollables. But there are not several accompanying 'spoorboekjes' on the unsupported assumption of near linearity in the economy.

The policy advisors then review the central projection and suggest desirable modifications, to be simulated approximately by building up a suitable policy package from the set of multipliers. Repeating these steps, an agreed 5 year policy proposal is eventually reached after several iterations. A proposal may be submitted to Ministers either during or at the end of this iterative process. The Ministers may change the scenario and start off a new iterative process. When that is complete the projection is considered by the consultative bodies, who can recommend further modifications (and hence further iterations) before it goes on to be adopted by Parliament.

In a second phase, annual revisions with a one or two year horizon are made to that policy proposal by the same procedure but using the short-term model. The associated multipliers are now used to construct suitable revisions to the original policy proposal in order to regain its goals. The short-term revisions are supposed to be consistent with the original plan which is not revised as a whole.

At each stage a proposal is presented in the form of a central projection and variants about that, rather than as a set of alternatives for policy makers to choose between. Another unusual feature is the level of technical sophistication which is presumed for the Ministers, the senior ministry staff, and the members of the consultative bodies. This has led their discussions to be overly concerned with technical detail and to be based on a spurious idea of the accuracy and certainty of the plans.

The Central Planning Bureau plays a key role in the iterations which lead to the formation of economic policies. Through its directorate, the advice of the Bureau will be presented and argued at all levels up to, and directly into, the Cabinet; as well as in the major consultative bodies such as the Council of Economic Advisors, and the Social Economic Council, which include representatives of the Central Bank, business and labour.

(b) In the UK the main points of the Treasury's planning procedures have been summarised in the Report of the Committee on Policy Optimisation (HMSO (1978)). The Treasury has prepared routine forecasts since the Second World War, but an econometric model was first introduced in 1969. The model has been used to illustrate the possibilities for demand management, industrial strategy, fiscal policy, growth, foreign trade, etc. Monetary affairs are the concern of the Bank of England.

There is a deliberate and clear split between the model builders (technicians) and the policy makers who must analyse and decide between the available policy options. The reason for this split is that the former group understands the model, its statistical basis and its limitations, very well but the political and economic possibilities (i.e. what is acceptable and what is feasible) rather poorly. With the latter group it is the reverse. This split is designed to avoid misunderstandings and failures in communication. A Policy Coordinating Committee consisting of all Deputy Secretaries (Departmental heads) of the Treasury and chaired by the Permanent Secretary, and a macroeconomic group consisting of the Undersecretaries (responsible for each division within a department) concerned with macroeconomic issues, represent the policy makers. The technicians up to Undersecretary level form a Forecast Committee with two components (the short-term and model group; the medium term and policy group). These two committees do not meet together, but when each meets the Economic Advisory Section attends as well to act as liaison, as interpreters, and possibly as referees.

Short-term forecasts are made twice a year, processed through the following system. The initial assumptions for the forecast are usually based on unchanged policies and assumed exogenous events (in consultation with the home, overseas and industrial specialists within the

Treasury). These assumptions may be proposed by the forecasters, but they must either be laid down or approved by the Policy Coordinating Committee. A preliminary forecast is made from the model. It is then discussed, sector by sector, with the specialists from other Treasury divisions and other departments of government (e.g. Departments of Trade or Energy, the Bank of England, the Ministry of Agriculture, etc.). The information, comments and criticisms are then used to produce a first draft forecast from the model with adjusted assumptions, corrections, or even alterations in the model itself. This forecast generates further forecasts of foreign and domestic financing and industrial production detail, through sub-models which are linked to the main one and which need the collaboration of the specialist government departments. A two day seminar follows for reviewing these forecasts, and is attended by the technicians and the Economic Advisory Section. All decisions taken there are then reviewed again while a second draft forecast is made incorporating them. A report describing the forecast and the assessment of the uncertainties is made available to all Ministers, the Cabinet, and officials of some other departments. The Chief Economic Advisor and his closest colleagues thus produce one single forecast. But they are not bound to it. They may add their own advice and comments to it. Although the forecast is the best single estimate, it is essential that the uncertainties and difficulties associated with it should be properly explained to the policy makers.

The forecast goes to two committees of policy makers who discuss the policy implications (the macroeconomic group is consulted first on more technical matters). The secretariat of the Economic Advisory Section summarises the outcome of those discussions in terms of the policy implications. This passes to the Policy Coordinating Committee (now including the senior members of the forecasting group) who set the terms of reference for the examination of the policy options from the model. Some proposals will also come from an earlier consideration of the forecast by those concerned with policy analysis. An analysis of the policy options is then prepared from the nonstochastic simulations given by the model. Fully worked out variants in the effects of different policy packages are set out. This draft is considered again by the Policy Coordinating Committee, together with the original forecast and other comments from elsewhere in the Treasury. The Permanent Secretary may initiate further discussions to amend the picture and correct the advice presented to the Ministers in that draft. The final version is then sent to the Chancellor and through him to the members of the Cabinet. The choice between options remains theirs.

This whole exercise is kept distinct from the medium-term strategy. The latter is developed along very much the same pattern as the short-term exercise in policy analysis. The Policy Coordinating Committee exercises more control in setting the assumptions and simulations to be considered. The results and further simulations are considered by the Economic Advisory Section before a draft report passes to the Policy Coordinating Committee again for further discussion and amendment before going on to the Ministers. There is therefore a split between short- and medium-term policy analysis; neither of which are properly integrated, nor are they necessarily mutually consistent.

These policy and forecasting exercises also benefit from the advice of a panel of external consultants. This opening up to outside influences is in response to criticisms that the Treasury was too secretive and selective in its evaluation of alternative policies. Nevertheless, the point brought out by this discussion is that it is the policy making process as a whole, rather than the Treasury itself, which lacks openness. There is no formal provision for the views of other interested parties to influence the selection of options (or projections) presented to the Chancellor; and their views are implicit only in his decision between the options. At best, perceived versions of those views are incorporated at the discretion of the officials involved. Any criticism of a lack of openness in the policy evaluation process has been met by a typically British response: accommodate the criticisms within the Treasury but continue the process itself as before.

A lack of outside influence is inevitable in an information system containing its own 'in house' model. This is true of the Dutch, British and many other systems. There is naturally a strong vested interest in using one's 'in house' model and forecasts – not to mention the large investment of resources to be justified. Also the models are typically so large that it is extremely difficult for any outsider to comment or criticise constructively on the forecast, or for those comments to be accommodated. But, in the absence of such outside influences, one is unlikely to be fully aware of the uncertainties and problems in a projection, and it is hard to make due allowance for them. Indeed there is little incentive to do so. Nor will alternative views of the impacts of policy, or likely external events, be accounted for. One result is that the projections and policy recommendations made by the Treasury actually appear to take very little account of uncertainty, although the forecasters are doubtless only too well aware that large uncertainties do underlie them. As in the Dutch case, there is a spurious impression of accuracy in the results, and excessive concentration on detail.

But the most serious difficulty remains the short horizon of these exercises so that the policy measures cannot be integrated into a longer-term outlook. It is inevitable that frequent policy changes will be proposed.

14.2.2 Some other planning frameworks

The weaknesses raised by the planning systems above are the lack of integration of medium- and short-term plans; the lack of external consultation over desirable modifications to the terms of reference or policy proposals; and the lack of an explicit or systematic allowance for uncertainty. The Committee on Policy Optimisation (HMSO (1978)), for example, reported concern among policy makers over the appropriate time horizon for planning, and criticisms of policies advantageous in the short run but inconsistent, even destabilising, for longer-term objectives. Planning with econometric models, particularly if formal techniques are employed, will help eliminate these inconsistencies in so far as dynamic consistency is forced. Also, because uncertainties are so large, it is important that the longer-run plans be revised systematically. Generally, however, any revisions have been unsystematic and irregular.

In the USA the system is rather informal. There are no 'in house' models in government agencies concerned with policy making. Consequently the economic advisors base their projections and policy recommendations on the results provided by the models available outside. It is their responsibility to choose the model(s) and the technique for combining their results, and to ensure that all necessary policy exercises have been undertaken. With a large number of models, and many of them specialised, this means in practice that a consensus of model results, and a consensus of advisors' opinions, underlies any recommendations. This has the desirable effect of identifying, and perhaps cancelling out, the likely errors, as well as pointing out different views on future economic development.

In France, economic planning is centralised. Since 1971 a large nonlinear model has been used for simulations. Again the policy maker may commission studies and he must choose his own policy. The modellers only present a range of options. Three alternative rates of growth in GNP are considered to give the long-run framework. Outputs are broken down into agricultural, industrial and services sectors; and then further into individual industrial outputs. Rather detailed single equation models give a fine disaggregation of demand components under the headings of consumption, investment, imports, exports and committed government expenditure. Intermediate industrial demands are obtained by input–output methods, leading to employment demands; whereas labour supplies are estimated by demographic and other studies.

The policy decision procedure operates in two stages. The planning board makes a forecast using the econometric model for the final year of the next 5 year plan, based on exogenous assumptions for foreign trade and no changes in policies. This is a point forecast rather than a trajectory. It is debated by various committees of administrators, trade unionists, employers, and economic experts. From the results of these deliberations the planning board (which contains representatives of the same groups) designs several sets of policy options for each of the three possible GNP growth rates, and simulates their consequences. The government reviews these feasible states, and picks a growth rate and a policy option set. These are submitted to Parliament. Further iterations with the model give the preferred variant within the set of options, and this forms the Plan. The consistency of projections is obtained by iterating around the individual projections. Finally, detailed fiscal and monetary policies are set which are consistent with the balances just obtained. The plans may not be dynamically consistent, and are presumably difficult to revise.

The second stage is to construct the trajectories to that final year. Approximate trajectories are the implied average growth rates. A more precise picture of the feasible policies is given by optimising a short-run dynamic model derived from the main model. Extensive simulations are conducted to indicate the relative uncertainties, and their sources, in the projections. A preference function is deduced from interviews and inferred from decisions on the options, and the risks revealed in them. Then policies, optimal in being the best approximation to long-run plans, are computed together with the feedback rules as a revision mechanism.

The Belgian Economic Plan is a five-year plan, but each year the corrections necessary to guarantee the realisation of the Plan at the end of the five-year period are made in the economic budget. The Plan is regionalised. It is: (i) binding for the Public Authorities only in as far as investment expenditures are concerned; (ii) contractual to the extent that the state can get enterprises to agree to contracts which offer them benefits if they follow certain prescriptions provided by the Plan.

The Plan is built in two stages. In the first stage, the Planning Bureau evaluates and discusses the economic and social choices which are technically feasible with the social (trade unions and federations of Belgian enterprises) and regional councils. This results in a proposal of options from which the government makes a selection which is then submitted to Parliament. The latter amends and, eventually, votes the Plan. The second stage consists in the drafting of the Plan and in the determination of its concrete objectives in terms of the law. This strategy is illustrated in figure 14.1.

The Planning Bureau generates global macroeconomic projections by means of a regionalised, dynamic, nonlinear macroeconomic model of the Belgian economy. The model has no sectoral dimensions. It is essentially used to test different variants of economic policy, by means

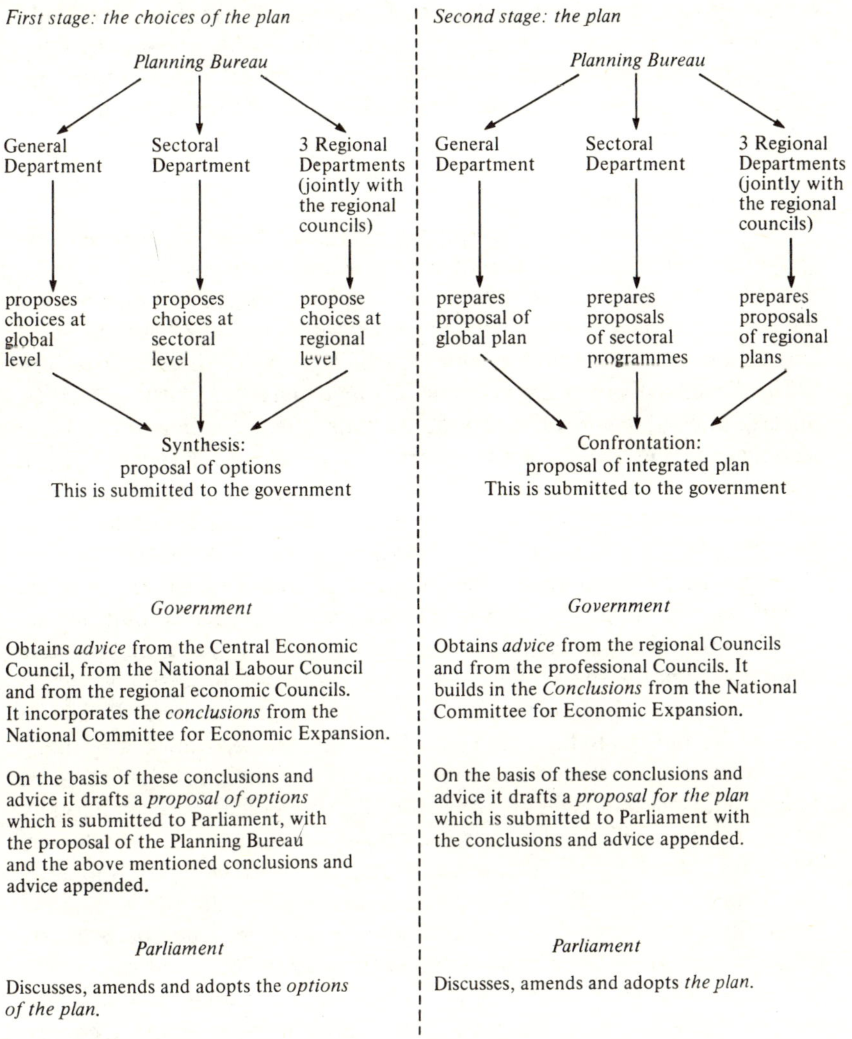

Figure 14.1 The above scheme summarizes the Belgian Planning System

of simulation techniques. Certain optimisation exercises have also been conducted.

Next, sectoral studies are obtained from input–output submodels whose predictions depend on the results of the central model. To guarantee the mutual consistency of the results of these submodels with the central model has caused problems of convergence. Various other submodels are used, or are being prepared, to study specific aspects of economic policy, energy use, the analysis of employment, demographic indicators, etc. Considerable use has been made of formal optimisation techniques here.

14.2.3 Comments

In most countries the policy makers and their technical advisors appear to agree on the advantages of an administrative system which maintains the distance of the policy makers from the technicians and their model. Policy makers are concerned with choosing between alternative plans but not with the techniques which generated those alternatives. While the aims of policy are not generally in dispute, the relative priorities, uncertainties and information requirements often are. It is not for the technicians in public service to insert their judgement into the political decisions. Nor is it for the policy makers to impose their judgement on the technical means of assessing the feasibility and consequences of possible plans (Peacock (1977), HMSO (1978) and Wass (1978)). The policy makers should retain the initiative in decision making, but the technicians the initiative in how best to generate the necessary information.

This separation seems to be a natural tendency in practice. Ministers generally do not wish to interfere with the projection process, even when the results are not to their taste, and in return they expect officials to offer advice but not to take decisions. However, this separation may interrupt the dialogue between the policy makers and their advisory services. That would make it difficult to ensure that the policies chosen actually reflect the planners' preferences. It would also increase the misunderstandings over the risk in those policies, and over what the model is (or is not) able to tell us. But perhaps the greatest danger is that the feasibility and consequences of candidate policies will not be properly debated with the policy makers (notwithstanding the usual claim that 'all serious options will be (politely) considered'). In that case, not only are the decisions likely to suffer from failing to heed sound technical advice, but also the quality of advice offered is likely to suffer and eventually become a series of mere platitudes. Note that we are dealing with feasibility and consequences of policy options, but not the taking of decisions. In this, two way communication is essential.

It is to minimise these dangers that some less time consuming and less error prone methods of planner – model interaction have been suggested in earlier chapters. These bring the policy makers into direct contact with the planning exercises, but without involving them in the technicalities. In this context, efficiency in reaching the best decisions means asking the right questions of, and supplying the right information to, the decision makers.

14.3 Why a model approach?

It is often said that forecasting and policy evaluation using econometric models is unreliable. The gap between the theoretical specification and the statistical assumptions made on behalf of the model and its data on the one hand, and reality on the other, is wide enough to undermine any inferences made from an estimated version of that model. The alternative is to use some informal and less checkable technique. But model or no model, the specification of any conditioning information (and the assumptions underlying it) will be as formal or informal as we care to make it. The desirable property conferred by a model is accountability for the feasibility, and for the assumptions in the maintained hypothesis, of projections or policy recommendations which are made mutually consistent as a solution to a simultaneous difference equation system. It is in order to make forecasts or policy proposals accountable to informed opinion, which must lie at the heart of any decision making system, that we consider only those planning techniques which presume a model, whether simple or sophisticated.

It is perhaps obvious that the successful planner must develop a feel for the constraints, the likely bottlenecks, and the opportunity for manoeuvre offered by the dynamic responses of the economy. This is emphasised often enough by the policy makers themselves: see, for example, Peacock (1977), Bray (1978), Richardson (1978), Wass (1978) and HMSO (1978). We have noted the large number of targets which have now been accepted by governments, and the depth of detail on policy impacts which is demanded in order that the means may be found to meet those targets. To generate realistic forecasts of targets and policy projections in sufficient detail, and to offer a framework for constructive outside criticism, should perhaps make the use of a model inevitable. But to guarantee that those forecasts and projections are mutually consistent and dynamically coherent means a model is essential. Potentially there are target inconsistencies (the achievement of one implies the partial nonachievement of another, as in the inflation–unemployment trade-off), sectoral inconsistencies (with finite resources the achievement of a target in one sector hinders the achievement of that in another; again there is a trade-off to be exploited), dynamic inconsistencies (when the natural dynamics of the economy are such that the achievement of a target in one period serves to undo its achievement in some later period), and policy inconsistencies (a policy introduced in order to achieve some target offsets, by way of side effects, the impact of another instrument designed to achieve another target). As a matter of fact, the policy optimisation approach ensures all four types of consistency.

Secondly, we have emphasised that uncertainty and errors play an especially important role in economic projections. Again it will be necessary to have some model of the economic system in order to make a systematic estimate of the probabilities of the set of possible shocks, to assess their combined effects on the projections, and to consider the appropriate policy instrument settings in the light of those potential disturbances. The potential for specification and estimation errors may raise questions about the reliability of the model. In addition, projections have to be conditioned on assumed values of exogenous events, and the uncertainty surrounding those assumptions can never be eliminated. But despite all the potential errors, given a model we can design ways of running the system so that these uncertainties do least damage. The policy optimisation schemes in Chapter 7 and Chapter 12 contain explicit examples of this.

In advocating the use of a model we take no position on whether that model should be large or small, simple enough to be analytically tractable or not, linear or nonlinear, etc. This is an empirical matter, depending in part on the user's requirements. But the criticism that the claims of many existing models are too extravagant should be taken seriously. The economy is a very complex dynamic system. Given inadequate data, poor specification methods and inadequate power in the available model testing techniques, it is unlikely that a completely satisfactory model will emerge. Even so, standard models tend to be large, not analytically solvable, and nonlinear. This means that it is very hard to get a proper picture of the model's characteristics with respect to policy responses. No one evaluation of the model's behaviour would be typical, since its responses vary with circumstances. Adequate tests to prove whether or not such models are suitable for general policy analysis are not usually available.

Therefore there can be no prejudice in favour of large, complex and highly developed models here. But we do say that explicit models, whether simple or sophisticated, are a necessary replacement for informal or implicit 'back of the envelope' type models which easily become self-contradictory. Explicit models need not be comprehensive in their description of the economy concerned; and they are seldom monolithic. The word 'model' may even cover a set of individual projection devices. An explicit model is necessary, but probably not sufficient, for what we have called accountability.

14.4 The case for policy optimisation

Policy makers appear to have accepted that a model of the dynamic behaviour of the economy is generally necessary for forecasting and policy analysis. Of course the models cannot be perfect; they may not even be particularly good. But after sufficient proving tests they may be considered the best available. When confronted with his chosen model, the policy maker's problem is simply to learn how best to use it in an uncertain world. There is a prima facie case for policy optimisation so that the model is exploited to best advantage. Indeed, if the policy maker believes his model to be the best available, then it is illogical to use it to generate policies which he knows to be suboptimal.

The practical importance of optimising policies should perhaps be self-evident. It is therefore remarkable that so many highly developed and sophisticated models exist apparently to be used in a naive and inefficient manner; as, for example, in the unsystematic and incomplete search implicit in simulation experiments chosen by trial and error. Simulation is unsystematic because it lacks experimental design: (i) an explicit and consistent set of priorities is not incorporated, so policy rankings are ambiguous; (ii) it does not suggest directions for modifying policies so whether we secure improvements is a matter of 'hit or miss'; with the result that decisions are accident prone, and the search may become bogged down or stuck in a blind alley; (iii) the treatment of uncertainty is not explicit, so both the allowances made for it (if any) and the intended policy reactions to stochastic shocks remain undefined; (iv) the trade-offs between policy goals (and time periods) are not properly examined for either deterministic or stochastic changes, so that we have neither hard information on the gravity of the policy problem faced, nor on the scope available for solving it. Simulation is incomplete as a selection technique because: (a) it fails to account for the benefits of future policy revisions; (b) given substantial uncertainty it is unrealistic to tie a policy maker to a course of action in which revisions, dependent on future realisations, are not made explicit from the start; (c) it may generate instability by failing to analyse and constrain the effects of a sequence of such revisions; and (d) it is an incomplete exploration of the alternatives in which the final choice depends on the start and steps taken. Given the complexity of the system, simulation is a rather inefficient method of policy selection and involves extensive interactions between man and model. It may imply the consideration of irrelevant alternatives since the search is not restricted to the Pareto optimal frontier. It is also risky since its success depends on the policy maker having already guessed the nature of a satisfactory policy, which in itself presupposes such a policy exists. In short, simulation, which is the general alternative to optimisation, is suited to adaptation rather than policy innovations. It replaces the question 'where, ideally, would we like to be and how close can we get to that?' by 'where do we go from here?'

Policy optimisation can be regarded as a generalisation of simulation experiments. It represents the final step in that infinite (but hypothetical) sequence of simulations which make up a systematic and complete search, *given* a fixed priority structure, risk aversion measure, model, and conditioning information on the noncontrollables. So if one is prepared to simulate policy options (or analyse multipliers) then one should also be prepared to optimise them.

Lest it should appear that policy optimisation has now been 'oversold', it is worth repeating that it is far from free of difficulties. The main drawback, in practice, is usually seen as the difficulty of adequately or accurately specifying the components of the decision structure beyond the econometric model; namely the information system, the preference system, and the allowance for risk. However, to recommend alternative selection techniques in order to avoid these difficulties is a false simplification. First, these three extra components are as integral a part of the decision structure as the model itself. If it is accepted that an *explicit* model is necessary for reasons of accountability and consistency of choice in projections, then a decision structure explicit in all four components is vital for exactly the same reasons. We are merely dealing with a generalisation of the conditional forecasting problem. Second, simpler policy selection techniques are, if anything, more susceptible to errors in the specification of all four components, so these difficulties will not go away if we ignore optimisation.

Again we shall take no position over whether an elaborate or simple ('large' or 'small') decision structure is appropriate. This is an empirical matter depending on the problem at hand. For some problems the simple certainty equivalent linear-quadratic form will be suitable. But for other problems we can accommodate the respecification of the preferences, interactive policy selections, risk averse choices, anticipations and adaptive behaviour, multiple policy makers of both the cooperating and noncooperating variety, uncertain policy impacts, multiple forecasts of the noncontrollables, nonlinear models, and so on, as required. Formal policy selections, whether simple or elaborate, are not intended as rigid instructions in place of discretionary guiding principles. Dynamic policy optimisation is the only technique which allows the discovery of a best set of such principles in a very complicated dynamic context.

It should be clear that policy optimisation only generalises simulation (or indeed forecasting) in the sense that we are forced to specify priorities, the information system, and risk allowances explicitly, in addition to the model, instead of allowing us to duck these issues. The case for optimisation is therefore that accountability for the policy decisions demands that these components should all be made explicit.

14.5 On policy experiments and policy decisions

Successful policy selection therefore implies experimenting in order to (a) define the objectives of policy more clearly; (b) make the circumstances under which certain policies become feasible better understood; (c) assess the desirability and associated risks of the various options; and (d) design policies, given an explicit error correction mechanism, which make the most of the limited opportunities and freedom to intervene without laying the economy open to large external shocks. We stress the inefficiency of simulation not only because it is an expensive method of producing suboptimal policies – although that is important. The greatest advantage of optimisation is that it forces us to concentrate on the specification of exactly those parts of the policy problem which cause the greatest difficulties. This means that now the whole decision structure – not just the model – must be explicit in terms of those parameters subject to policy experiments as well as those fixed by prior specification. Experimentation with the preference function is necessary either because it cannot be known perfectly a priori, or because it is an approximation whose evaluation varies rapidly with circumstances. The same will be true for the degree of risk aversion, or indeed parts of the model and, perhaps, the exogenous information. The required experimental design is achieved by going through the motions of an optimisation exercise.

This need to experiment shows that 'optimal' control is not optimal in any absolute sense. Moreover, interactive algorithms have now provided the means to convert experiments in the parameters of that specification to experiments in different policy options. Therefore the policy maker's decision making function and his ability to exercise his judgement certainly has not been supplanted. It is instructive that an economist's comments on econometric projections and policy analysis indirectly stress this same point: advice generated from econometric policy studies is no more than guidance (Samuelson (1975)). It is important to recognise that the combination of planner and model is more powerful than either alone; 'Models are to be used but not necessarily believed' (Theil (1971)).

So we have now come full circle. We may say of the specification and estimation of the model, or of information system and risk aspects, that we learn fastest when we ask the right questions – as we did earlier for the preferences. But which questions are the right ones depends on what we want to know, and that means conducting properly designed experiments so that the model is blamed only for its own demerits, not for those induced by inappropriate tests. So, even when policy values are not of interest in themselves, policy optimisation is important for checking and improving the model's specification; and, by implication, for our understanding of the economy. If this improves our view of how the economy works and of the scope and limitations of policy making in certain circumstances, while also pointing out the deficiencies in our model and the associated decision making framework, then the exercise is surely a success. To quote Samuelson (1975) again: 'I would no more dream of tackling the back of an envelope before I had looked at the Wharton, and Michigan and St. Louis models than I would dream of doing so on the basis of tea leaves or rereading Alfred Marshall's Principles. In other words, we dwarfs of judgement see as far as we do because we stand on the shoulders of computer giants.'

References

Adelman, I. and F.L. Adelman (1959), 'The Dynamic Properties of the Klein-Goldberger Model', *Econometrica*, **27**, 596–625.

Aitcheson, J. and S.D. Silvey (1960), 'Maximum Likelihood Estimation Procedures and Associated Tests of Significance', *Journal of the Royal Statistical Society*, Series B, **22**, 154–71.

Ancot, J.P. and A.J. Hughes Hallett (1981), 'The Determination of Collective Preferences in Economic Decision Models: with an Application to Soviet Economic Policy' in J. Gruber (ed.) *Econometric Decision Models*, Springer Verlag (Lecture Notes in Economics and Mathematical Systems), Berlin and New York.

Ancot, J.P., A.J. Hughes Hallett and J. Paelinck (1982), 'The Determination of Implicit Preferences: two Possible Approaches Compared', *European Economic Review*, **18**, 267–89.

Ando, A. et al., (1972), 'Equations and Definitions of Variables for the FRB–MIT–Penn Econometric Model' in Hickman, B.G. (ed.), *Economic Models of Cyclical Behaviour*, NBER Studies in Income and Wealth, No. 36, Vols. I and II, Columbia University Press, pp. 543–600.

Aoki, M. (1976), *Optimal Control and System Theory in Dynamic Economic Analysis*, North-Holland, Amsterdam.

Athans, M., E. Kuh, L. Papademos, R. Pindyck, T. Ozan and K. Wall (1977), 'Sequential Open Loop Optimal Control of a Nonlinear Macroeconomic Model' in M.D. Intriligator (ed.), *Frontiers of Quantitative Economics*, Vol. III A, North-Holland, Amsterdam.

Aubin, J.P. (1979), *Mathematical Methods of Game and Economic Theory*, North-Holland, Amsterdam.

Bailey, M.J. (1979), 'The Possibility of Rational Social Choice in an Economy', *Journal of Political Economy*, **87**, 37–56.

Ball, J. (ed.) (1973), *International Linkage of National Economic Models*, North-Holland, Amsterdam.

Ball, J. et al. (1975), 'The London Business School Quarterly Econometric Model of the U.K. Economy' in Renton, G.A. (ed.), *Modelling the Economy*, Heinemann Educational Press, London.

Barker, T.S. (1976), *Econometric Structure and Policy*, Chapman and Hall, London.

Bar-Shalom, Y. and E. Tse (1976), 'Caution, Probing and the Value of Information in the Control of Uncertain Systems', *Annals of Econ. & Social Measurement*, **5**, 323–37.

Baumol, W.J. (1961), 'Pitfalls in Contracyclical Policies: Some Tools and Results', *Review of Economics and Statistics*, **43**, 21–6.

Bellman, R. (1961), *Adaptive Control Processes: A guided tour*, Princeton University Press, Princeton, NJ.

Bernavie, A. (1972), *Mathematical Techniques for Economic Analysis*, Prentice-Hall, Englewood Cliffs, NJ.

Bhansali, R.S. (1974), 'Asymptotic mean square error of predicting more than one step ahead using the regression method', *Journal of the Royal Statistical Society*, Series C, **23**, 35–42.

Bogaard, P.J.M. van den and H. Theil (1959), 'Macro-dynamic Policy Making: An application of Strategy and Certainty Equivalence Concepts to the Economy of the United States, 1933–6', *Metroeconomica*, **11**, 149–67.

Bowden, R.J. (1972), 'More Stochastic Properties of the Klein–Goldberger Model', *Econometrica*, **41**, 87–98.

Box, G.E.P. and G.M. Jenkins (1970), *Time Series Analysis, Forecasting and Control*, Holden-Day, San Francisco.

Brainard, W. (1967), 'Uncertainty and the Effectiveness of Policy', *American Economic Review* (Proceedings), **57**, 411–25.

Brandsma, A.S. and A.J. Hughes Hallett (1982), "The Impact of Noncausality on Noncooperative Strategies in Dynamic Games" *Economics Letters* (forthcoming)

Brandsma, A., A.J. Hughes Hallett and N. Van der Windt (1981), 'Optimal Economic Policies and Uncertainty: the Case against Policy Selection by Nonlinear Programming', *Proceeding of the 3rd Symposium on Mathematical Programming and Data Perturbations* and forthcoming in *Computers and Operations Research*.

Bray, J. (1975), 'Optimal Control of a Noisy Economy with the U.K. as an Example', *Journal of Royal Statistical Society* (A), **138**, 339–373

(1978), 'The Making of Economic Policy', *The Times*, 19 April 1978.

Breusch, T.S. and A.R. Pagan (1980), 'The Lagrange Multiplier Test and its Application to Model Specification in Econometrics', *Review of Economic Studies*, **47**, 239–54.

Broomfield, P. (1972), 'On the error of prediction of a time series', *Biometrika*, **59**, 501–8.

Budd, A. (1978), *The Politics of Economic Planning*, Fontana/Collins, London.

Buiter, W.H. and M. Gersovitz (1981), 'Issues in Controllability and the Theory of Economic Policy', *Journal of Public Economics*, **15**, 33–43.

Calvo, G.A. (1978), 'On the Time Consistency of Optimal Policy in a Monetary Economy', *Econometrica*, **46**, no. 6, 1411–28.

Chow, G.C. (1972), 'How much could be gained by Optimal Stochastic Control Policies?', *Annals of Economic and Social Measurement*, **1**, 391–407.

(1975), *Analysis and Control of Dynamic Economic Systems*, J. Wiley, New York.

(1981), *Econometric Analysis by Control Methods*, J. Wiley, New York.

Christ, C. (1975), 'Judging the Performance of Econometric Models of the U.S. Economy', *International Economic Review*, **16**, 54–74.

Cochrane, J.L. (1975), 'Optimal Macroeconomic Policies', *Economic Journal*, **85**, 329–37.

Cooper, R.L. (1972), 'The Predictive Performance of Quarterly Econometric Models of the United States', in B. Hickman (ed.), *Econometric Models of Cyclical Behaviour*, NBER, Columbia University Press, New York.

Cramer, H. (1946), *Mathematical Methods of Statistics*, Princeton University Press, Princeton.
DaCunha, N. and E. Polak (1967), 'Constrained Minimisation under Vector Valued Criteria in Finite Dimensional Spaces', *Journal of Mathematical Analysis and Applications*, **19**, 103–24.
Deaton, A.S. and J. Muellbauer (1980), *Economics and Consumer Behaviour*, Cambridge University Press, Cambridge.
De Bruyne, G. (1979), 'Pareto Optimality of Non-Cooperative Equilibrium in a Time-Dependent Multiperiod Game', *European Economic Review*, **12**, 243–60.
Desai, M.J. (1973), 'Macroeconometric Models for India—A Survey', *Sanhkya*, **35**, 165–206.
De Wolff, P. and J. Sandee (1959), 'Recent Experiences in the Application of Econometric Policy Models in the Netherlands', Econometric Society Meeting, Amsterdam.
Dhrymes, P.J. (1970), *Econometrics: Statistical Foundations and Applications*, Harper and Row, New York.
(1973), 'Restricted and Unrestricted Reduced Forms: Asymptotic Distribution and Relative Efficiency', *Econometrica*, **41**, 119–34.
Dixon, L.C.W. (1975), 'Quadratic Termination and Second Order Convergence' in L.C.W. Dixon and G.P. Szegö (eds.), *Towards Global Convergence*, North Holland, Amsterdam.
Dorrington, J. and Renton, G.A. (1975), 'A Study of the Effects of Direct Taxation on Consumers Expenditure' in Renton, G.A. (ed.), *Modelling the Economy*, Heinemann Educational Press, London.
Dow, J.C.R. (1964), *The Management of the British Economy 1945–60*, Cambridge University Press, Cambridge.
Dreyfus, S. (1965), *Dynamic Programming and Calculus of Variations*, Academic Press, New York.
Duesenberry, J.S. et al. (1965), *The Brookings Quarterly Econometric Model of the United States*, Vol. I, North-Holland, Amsterdam.
(1969), *The Brookings Quarterly Econometric Model of the United States*, Vol. II, *Some further Results*, North-Holland, Amsterdam.
Eckstein, O. et al. (1974), 'The Data Resources Model: Uses, Structure and Analyses of the U.S. Economy' in *International Economic Review: Symposium on Econometric Model Performance: Comparative Simulation Studies of Models of the U.S. Economy*, Vols. 15 & 16, (1974/75), October 1974, pp. 595–615.
Eichhorn, W. and Oetli, W. (1972), 'A general Formulation of the Le Chatelier–Samuelson Principle', *Econometrica*, **40**, 711–17.
Eijk, C.J. van and J. Sandee (1959), 'Quantitative Determination of an Optimum Economic Policy', *Econometrica*, **27**, 1–13.
Evans, M.K. (1969), *Macroeconomic Activity*, Harper and Row, New York.
Evans, M.K. and L.R. Klein (1968), 'The Wharton Econometric Forecasting Model', University of Pennsylvania, *Economic Research Unit Studies in Quantitative Economics*, No. 2, University of Pennsylvania Press.
Evans, M.K., Y. Haitovsky, and G. Treyz (1972), 'An Analysis of the Forecasting Properties of U.S. Economic Models' in B.G. Hickman (ed.), *Economic Models of Cyclical Behaviour, NBER Studies in Income and Wealth No. 36*, Vols. I & II, Columbia University Press, 1972, pp. 949–1140.
Evans, M.K., Y. Haitovsky, G. Treyz and V. Su (1972), 'Short-Run Predictions and Long-Run Simulations of the Wharton Model' in Hickman, B.G. (ed.), *Econo-*

mic Models of Cyclical Behaviour, NBER Studies in Income and Wealth No. 36, Vols. I and II, Columbia University Press, 1972, pp. 139–91.

Fair, R.C. (1980a), 'Estimating the Uncertainty of Policy Effects in Nonlinear Models', *Econometrica*, **48**, 1381–91.

(1980b), 'Estimating the Expected Predictive Accuracy of Econometric Models', *International Economic Review*, **21**, 255–278.

(1981), 'Evaluating the Predictive Accuracy of Models' in Z. Griliches and M.D. Intriligator (eds.), *Handbook of Econometrics*, North-Holland, Amsterdam.

Feldstein, M.S. (1971), 'The Error of Forecast in Econometric Models when the Forecast Period Exogenous Variables are Stochastic', *Econometrica*, **39**, 55–60.

Friedman, B.M. (1973), *Economic Stabilisation: Methods in Optimisation*, North-Holland, Amsterdam.

Friedman, M. (1953), 'The Effects of a Full-Employment Policy on Economic Stability: A Formal Analysis', in *Essays in Positive Economics*, The University of Chicago Press.

Friedman, M. and D. Meiselman (1963), 'The Relative Stability of Monetary Velocity and the Investment Multiplier in the United States 1897–1958', in *Stabilisation Policies*, Research Papers for the Commission on Money and Credit, Prentice Hall, Englewood Cliffs, NJ.

Fröberg, C.E. (1972), *Introduction to Numerical Analysis*, 2nd Edition, Addison–Wesley, Reading, Mass.

Fromm, G. and P. Taubman (1968), *Policy Simulations with an Econometric Model*, Brookings Institution, Washington DC.

Gandolfo, G. and Padoan, P.C. (1981), 'A Continuous Time Macrodynamic Model of the Italian Economy', Paper presented to the Society for Economic Dynamics and Control; in *Journal of Economic Dynamics and Control*, **4**, 205–24.

Ghosh, S, C. Gilbert and A.J. Hughes Hallett (1981), 'Optimal Control and the Choice of Functional Form: an Application to a Model of the World Copper Industry', Econometric Society Meeting, Amsterdam, and 'Optimal Stabilisation of the Copper Market', *Resources Policy*, 1982.

Gilbert, C.L. (1978), 'A Diagnosis of Multicollinearity', *Bulletin of the Oxford University Institute of Economics and Statistics*, **40**, 87–92.

Gill, L. and S.N. Brissimis (1978), 'Polynomial Operators and the Asymptotic Distribution of Dynamic Multipliers', *Journal of Econometrics*, **7**, 373–84.

Godfrey, L.G. (1976), 'Testing for Serial Correlation in Dynamic Simultaneous Equation Models', *Econometrica*, **44**, 1077–84.

(1978), 'Testing Against General Autoregressive and Moving Average Error Models when the Regressors Include Lagged Dependent Variables', *Econometrica*, **46**, 1293–1301.

Godfrey, L.G. and M.R. Wickens (1981), 'Testing Linear and Loglinear Regressions for Functional Form', *Review of Economic Studies*, **48**, 487–96.

Goldberger, A.S. (1959), 'Impact Multipliers and Dynamic Properties of the Klein–Goldberger Model', North-Holland, Amsterdam.

(1962), 'Best Linear Unbiased Prediction in the Generalised Linear Regression Model', *Journal of American Statistical Association*, **57**, 369–75.

Goldberger, A.S., Nagar, A.L. and Odeh, H.S. (1961), 'The Covariance Matrices of Reduced Form Coefficients and of Forecasts for a Structural Econometric Model,' *Econometrica*, **29**, 556–73.

Granger, C.W.J. (1966), 'The Typical Spectral Shape of an Economic Variable', *Econometrica*, **34**, 150–161.

Granger, C.W.J. and Newbold, P. (1977), *Forecasting Economic Time Series*, Academic Press, New York.

Green, D.W. and C.I. Higgins (1977), *A Macroeconomic Model of the Soviet Union*, Academic Press, New York.

Grunfeld, Y. and Z. Griliches (1960), 'Is Aggregation Necessarily Bad?', *Review of Economics and Statistics*, **42**, 1–13.

Haitovsky, Y. and N. Wallace (1972), 'A Study of Discretionary and Non-Discretionary Monetary and Fiscal Policies in the Context of Stochastic Macro-Econometric Models' in Zarnowitz, V. (ed.), *The Business Cycle Today*, National Bureau of Economic Research, pp. 261–309.

Harkema, R. (1975), 'An Analytical Comparison of Certainty Equivalence and Sequential Updating', *Journal of American Statistical Assoc.*, **70**, 304–5.

Hatanaka, M. (1974), 'A Simple Suggestion to Improve the Mincer–Zarnowitz Criterion for the Evaluation of Forecasts', *Annals of Economic and Social Measurement*, **3**, 521–4.

Havenner, A. and R. Craine (1981), "Estimation Analogies in Control", *Journal of the American Statistical Association*, **76**, 850–59.

Hendry, D.F. (1974), 'Stochastic Specification in an Aggregate Demand Model of the United Kingdom', *Econometrica*, **42**, 923–37.

(1979), 'Predictive Failure and Econometric Modelling in Macroeconomics: The Transactions Demand for Money' in P. Ormerod (ed.), *Economic Modelling*, Heinemann, London.

Hendry, D.F. and R.W. Harrison (1974), 'Monte Carlo Methodology and the Small Sample Behaviour of Ordinary and Two Stage Least Squares', *Journal of Econometrics*, **2**, 151–74.

Hickman, B.G. (1972) (ed.), *Econometric Models of Cyclical Behaviour*, Columbia University Press, New York.

Hickman, B.G. and R.M. Coen (1976), *An Annual Growth Model of the U.S. Economy*, North-Holland, Amsterdam.

Hirsch, A.A. (1973), 'The BEA Quarterly Model as a Forecasting Instrument', *Survey of Current Business*.

HMSO (1978), 'Report of the Committee on Policy Optimisation', Cmnd 7148, H.M. Stationary Office, London.

Holbrook, R.S. (1974), 'A Practical Method for Controlling a Large Non-linear Stochastic System', *Annals of Econ. and Social Meas.*, **3**, 155–77.

Holbrook, R.S. and E.P. Howrey (1978), 'A Comparison of the Chow and Theil Optimisation Procedures in the Presence of Parameter Uncertainty', *International Economic Review*, **19**, 749–59.

Holly, S., B. Rustem and M. Zarrop (eds.) (1979), *Optimal Control for Econometric Models: An Approach to Economic Policy Formulation*, Macmillan, London.

Hordijk, L., A.P. Mastenbroek and J. Paelinck (1976), 'Contributions récentes à la étude empirique de Fonctions de Préferences Collectives', *Revue d' Economie Politique*, **4**, 505–34.

Howrey, E.P. (1967), 'Stabilisation Policy in Linear Stochastic Models', *Review of Economics and Statistics*, **49**, 404–11.

(1971), 'Stochastic Properties of the Klein–Goldberger Model', *Econometrica*, **39**, 73–87.

(1972), 'Dynamic Properties of a Condensed Version of the Wharton Model' in B.G. Hickman (ed.), *Econometric Models of Cyclical Behaviour*, Columbia University Press, New York.

Howrey, E.P. and Kelijan, H.H. (1971), 'Simultation versus Analytical Solutions' in

T.H. Naylor (ed.), *Computer Simulation Experiments with Models of Economic Systems*, J. Wiley, New York.

Hughes Hallett, A.J. (1979a), 'The Robustness of Optimal Policies to Parametric and Stochastic Shocks' in S. Holly, B. Rustem and M.B. Zarrop (1979).

(1979b), 'Computing Revealed Preferences and Limits to the Validity of Quadratic Objective Functions for Policy Optimisation', *Economics Letters*, **2**, 27–32.

(1980), 'The Qualitative Design of Economic Policies and Planner–Model Interaction' in J.M.S. Jansen, L.F. Pau and A. Strazak (eds.), *The Control of Dynamic Models of National Economies*, Pergamon Press, Oxford.

(1981), 'Some Extensions and Comparisons in the Theory of Gauss–Seidel Iterative Techniques for Solving Large Equation Systems' in E.G. Charatsis (ed.), *Procecdings of the Econometric Society Meeting (1979): Selected Papers in Memory of Stefan Valavamis*, North-Holland, Amsterdam.

(1981b), 'Policy Analysis in Models with Rational Expectations', Erasmus University, Rotterdam (mimeo).

(1982a), 'Alternative Techniques for Solving Nonlinear Equation Systems', *Journal of Computation and Applied Mathematics*, **8**, 35–48.

(1982b), 'Measuring the Importance of Stochastic Control in the Design of Economic Policies', *Economics Letters*, **8**, 341–47.

Hughes Hallett., A.J. and J.P. Ancot (1982), 'Estimating Revealed Preferences in Models of Planning Behaviour' in J.H.P. Paelinck (ed.), *Quantitative and Qualitative Mathematical Economics*, Martinus Nijhoff, Boston and the Hague.

Hughes Hallett, A.J. and A. Brandsma (1980), 'Time Consistent Optimal Policies for Non-Causal Models with Multiple Players: A Proposal for the Selection of Policies under Rational Expectations', Paper presented to the Society for Economic Dynamics and Control, Princeton University, Princeton, NJ.

Hughes Hallett, A.J. and J. van Sinderen (1980), 'Robust Iterative Solution Techniques for Non-Linear Econometric Models', Erasmus University, Institute of Economic Research Discussion Paper 8001/G, Rotterdam.

Hymans, S.H. (1968), 'Simultaneous Confidence Intervals in Econometric Forecasting', *Econometrica*, **36**, 18–30.

Hymans, S.H. and H.T. Shapiro (1974), 'The Structure and Properties of the Michigan Quarterly Econometric Model of the U.S. Economy', in *International Economic Review: Symposium on Econometric Model Performance: Comparative Simulation Studies of Models of the U.S. Economy* in Vols. 15 & 16 (1974/5), October 1974, pp. 632–53.

Johansen, L. (1969), 'An Examination of the Relevance of Kenneth Arrow's General Possibility Theorem for Economic Planning', *Economics of Planning*, **9**, 5–41.

(1972), 'On the Optimal Use of Forecasts in Economic Policy Decisions', *Journal of Public Economics*, **1**, 1–24.

(1974), 'Establishing Preference Functions for Macro-Economic Decision Models', *European Economic Review*, **5**, 41–61.

(1981), 'Parametric Certainty Equivalence Procedures in Decision Making under Uncertainty' *Zeitschrift für Nationalökonomie*, **40**, 257–80.

Jorgenson, D.W., J. Hunter and M.S. Nadiri (1970), 'The Predictive Performance of Econometric Models of Quarterly Investment Behaviour', *Econometrica*, **38**, 213–24.

Kendrick, D.A. (1980), 'Control Theory: with Applications to Economics', in K.J. Arrow & M.D. Intriligator (eds.), *Handbook of Mathematical Economics*, North-Holland, Amsterdam.

(1981), 'Caution & Probing in a Macroeconomic Model', University of Texas Discussion Paper # 80–6; in *Journal of Economic Dynamics and Control*, **4**, 149–70.

Kenkel, J.A. (1976), *Linear Dynamic Economic Models*, Gordon and Breach, New York.

Kleijnan, J.P.C. (1975), *Statistical Techniques in Simulation: Part II*, Marcel Dekker, New York.

Klein, L.R. (1950), 'Economic Fluctuations in the United States 1921–41', *Cowles Commission Monograph*, No. 11, J. Wiley, New York.

(1969), 'Economic Analysis of the Tax Cut of 1964', in Duesenberry et al. (ed.) (1969), *The Brookings Model: Some Further Results*, North-Holland, Amsterdam.

(1971), *An Essay on the Theory of Economic Prediction*, Markham Press, Chicago.

(1977), 'Economic Policy Formation through the Medium of Econometric Models' in M.D. Intriligator (ed.), *Frontiers of Quantitative Economics*, Vol. III B, North-Holland, Amsterdam.

Klein, L.R. and A.S. Goldberger (1955), *An Econometric Model of the United States 1929–52*, North-Holland, Amsterdam.

Klein, L.R. et al. (1961), *An Econometric Model of the United Kingdom*, Oxford University Press, Oxford.

Kmenta, J. and P.E. Smith (1973), 'Autonomous Expenditures versus Money Supply: an Application of Dynamic Multipliers', *Review of Economics & Statistics*, **55**, 299–307.

Kydland, F.E. (1975), 'Noncooperative and Dominant Player Solutions in Discrete Dynamic Games', *International Economic Review*, **16**, 321–35.

Kydland, F.E. and E.C. Prescott (1977), 'Rules rather than Discretion: The Inconsistency of Optimal Plans', *Journal of Political Economy*, **85**, 473–91.

Leenders, C.T. and T.J. Rothenberg (1964), 'Efficient Estimation of Simultaneous Equation Systems', *Econometrica*, **32**, 57–76.

Liu, T.C. (1963), 'An Exploratory Quarterly Econometric Model of Effective Demand in the Postwar U.S. Economy', *Econometrica*, **31**, 301–48.

Lucas, R.E. (1976), 'Econometric Policy Evaluation: A Critique', in K. Brunner & A. H. Meltzer (eds.), *The Phillips Curve and Labour Markets*, Carnegie–Rochester Conference Series on Public Policy, Vol. 6, North-Holland, Amsterdam.

McCarthy, M.D. (1972), Appendix p. 392 in B.G. Hickman (ed.), *Economic Models of Cyclical Behaviour, NBER Studies in Income & Wealth*, Vols. I & II, Columbia University Press.

Manove, M. (1971). 'A Model of Soviet-Type Economic Planning', *American Economic Review*, **61**, 390–406.

Mincer, J. and V. Zarnowitz (1969), 'The Evolution of Economic Forecasting', in J. Mincer (ed.), *Economic Forecasts and Expectations*, NBER, New York, pp. 1–46.

Mizon, G.E. (1977), 'Inferential Procedures in Non-Linear Models: An Application in a U.K. Industrial Cross Section Study of Factor Substitution and Returns to Scale', *Econometrica*, **45**, 1221–42.

Mizon, G.E. and D.F. Hendry (1980), 'An Empirical Application and Monte Carlo Analysis of Tests of Dynamic Specification', *Review of Economic Studies*, **47**, 21–46.

Mizon, G.E. and J.F. Richard (1982), "The Structure of Some Nonnested Hypothesis Tests", presented at the Econometric Study Group, University of Warwick, March 1982.

Morishima, M. and M. Saito (1972), 'A Dynamic Analysis of the American Economy 1902–52' in M. Morishima, U. Murata, T. Nosse & M. Saito (eds.), *The Working of Econometric Models*, Cambridge University Press, Cambridge.

Nagar, A.L. (1969), 'Stochastic Simulation of the Brookings Econometric Model' in J.S. Duesenberry, G. Fromm, L.R. Klein and E. Kuh (eds.), *The Brookings Quarterly Econometric Model of the United States*, North-Holland, Amsterdam.

Nerlove, M. (1964), 'Spectral Analysis of Seasonal Adjustment Procedures', *Econometrica*, **32**, 241–86.

Norman, A.L. (1974), 'On the Relationship between Linear Feedback Control and First Period Certainty Equivalence', *International Economic Review*, **15**, 209–15.

Ormerod, P. (1979), 'The National Institute Model of the U.K. Economy: Some Current Problems', in P. Ormerod (ed.), *Economic Modelling*, Heinemann, London.

Osborne, D.R. and F. Teale (1979), 'An Assessment and Comparison of two NIESR Econometric Model Forecasts', *Nat. Inst. Econ. Review*, 1979, **88**, 50–62.

Paelinck, J.H.P. and L.H. Klaassen (1979), *Spatial Econometrics*, Gower Press, Farnborough.

Peacock, A. (1977), 'Giving Economic Advice in Difficult Times', *Three Banks Review*, **113**, 3–23.

Pesaran, M.H. and A.S. Deaton (1978), 'Testing Nonnested Nonlinear Regression Models', *Econometrica*, **46**, 677–94.

Philips, A.W. (1954), 'Stabilisation Policy in a Closed Economy', *The Economic Journal*, **64**, 290–323.

(1957), 'Stabilisation Policy in the Time-Form of Lagged Responses', *The Economic Journal*, **67**, 265–77.

Pierce, D.A. (1975), 'Forecasting in Dynamic Models with Stochastic Regressors', *Journal of Econometrics*, **3**, 349–74.

Pierce, J.L. (1974), 'Quantitative Analysis of Decisions at the Federal Reserve', *Annals of Economic and Social Measurement*, **3**, 11–19.

Pindyck, R.S. (1973), *Optimal Planning for Economic Stabilisation: The Application of Control Theory to Stabilisation Policy*, North-Holland, Amsterdam.

Pindyck, R.S. and D.L. Rubinfeld (1976), *Econometric Models and Economic Forecasts*, McGraw-Hill, New York,

Prescott, E.C. (1977), 'Should Control Theory be used for Economic Stabilisation?' in K. Brunner and A.H. Meltzer (eds.), *Optimal Policies, Control Theory and Technological Exports, Carnegie–Rochester Conf. Series on Public Policy*, Vol. 7, North-Holland, Amsterdam.

Preston, R.S. (1975), 'The Input–Output Sector of the Wharton Annual and Industry Forecasting Model' in G. Fromm and L.R. Klein (eds.), *The Brookings Model: Prespective and Recent Developments*', North-Holland, Amsterdam.

Preston, R.S., L.R. Klein, Y.C. O'Brien, B.W. Brown (1976), 'Control Theory Simulations using the Wharton Long-Term Annual and Industry Forecasting Model', Wharton EFA Inc., Philadelphia.

Preston, A.J. and K. Wall (1973), 'Some Aspects of the Use of State Space Models in Econometrics', Prem Discussion Paper 5, Imperial College, London.

Rao, C.R. and S.K. Mitra (1971), *Generalised Inverses of Matrices and their Applications*, J. Wiley, New York.

Ravenkar, N. (1980), 'Testing the Rational Expectations Hypothesis', *Econometrica*, **48**, 1347–63.

Renton, G.A. (ed.) (1975), *Modelling the Economy*, Heinemann, London.

Richardson, G. (1978), 'Reflections on the Conduct of Monetary Policy', *Bank of England Bulletin* (February), 31–7.

Rustem, B., K. Vellupillai and J.H. Westcott (1978), 'A Method for Respecifying the Weighting Matrix of a Quadratic Objective Function', *Automatica*, **14**, 567–82.

Salmon, M. (1981), 'Error Correction Mechanisms', Paper presented at the Econometric Society Meeting, Amsterdam, Sept. 1981.

Samuelson, P.A. (1971), 'Turnpike Theorems although Tastes are Intertemporally Dependent', *Western Economic Journal*, **9**, 21–5.

(1975), 'The Art and Science of Macro Models over 50 Years' in G. Fromm, and L.R. Klein (eds.), *The Brookings Model: Perspective and Recent Developments*, North-Holland, Amsterdam.

Sargan, J.D. (1976), 'The Existence of the Moments of Reduced Form Coefficients', Discussions Paper No. A6, LSE Econometrics Program, London School of Economics.

(1980), 'The Consumer Price Equation in the Post War British Economy, An Exercise in Equation Specification Testing', *Review of Economic Studies*, **47**, 113–36.

Schmidt, P.A. (1973), 'The Asymptotic Distribution of Dynamic Multipliers', *Econometrica*, **41**, 161–4.

(1974), 'The Asymptotic Distribution of Forecasts in an Econometric Model', *Econometrica*, **42**, 303–9.

(1978), 'A Note on the Estimation of Seemingly Unrelated Regression Systems', *Journal of Econometrics*, **7**, 259–61.

Slutsky, E. (1937), 'The Summation of Random Causes as the Source of Cyclic Processes', *Econometrica*, **5**, 105–46.

Sowey, E.R. (1973), 'Stochastic Simulation of Macroeconomic Models: Methodology and Interpretation' in A.A. Powell and R.A. Williams (eds.), *Econometric Studies of Macro and Monetary Relations*, North-Holland, Amsterdam.

Suits, D.B. (1962), 'Forecasting and Analysis with an Econometric Model', *American Economic Review*, **52**, 104–32.

Tausky, O. (1964), 'Matrices C with $C^n \to 0$', *Journal of Algebra*, **1**, 5–10.

Theil, H. (1961), *Economic Forecasts and Policy*, (2nd edn), North-Holland, Amsterdam.

(1964), *Optimal Decision Rules for Government and Industry*, North-Holland, Amsterdam.

(1971), *Principles of Econometrics*, J. Wiley, New York.

Theil, H. and J.C.G. Boot (1962), 'The Final Form of Econometric Equation Systems' in A. Zellner (ed.), *Readings in Economic Statistics and Economics*, Little, Brown & Co., Boston.

Theil, H. and A.S. Goldberger (1961), 'On Pure and Mixed Statistical Estimation in Economics', *International Econ. Review*, **2**, 65–78.

Tinbergen, J. (1952), *On the Theory of Economic Policy*, North-Holland, Amsterdam.

(1968), *Statistical Testing of Business Cycle Theories*, Vols. I & II, Agathen Press, New York.

Turnovsky, S.J. (1977), *Macroeconomic Analysis and Stabilisation Policy*, Cambridge University Press, Cambridge.

Uebe, G. and T. Fischer (1978), 'Some Remarks on the Algorithm of Pindyck', *Econometrica*, **46**, 473–6.

Underwood, J. (1977), 'Optimal Rules for Cartel Managers with Empirical Applications to the Copper and Tea Markets' in *Annals of Economic and Social Measurement*, **6**, 231–43.

Varga, R.S. (1962), *Matrix Iterative Analysis*, Prentice Hall, Englewood Cliffs, NJ.

Wald, A. (1943), 'Tests of Hypotheses Concerning Several Parameters when the Number of Observations in Large', *Trans. of the American Mathematical Society*, **54**, 426–82.

Wall, K. and Y. Bar–Shalom (1978), 'Evaluation of the Caution and Probing Terms in Macroeconomic Models', Paper at 7th NBER Workshop on Control & Economics, Univ. of Texas, Austin,

Wallis, K.F. (1980), 'Econometric Implications of the Rational Expectations Hypothesis', *Econometrica*, **48**, 49–73.

Wallis, K.F. and M. Salmon (1980), 'Model Validation and Forecast Comparisons: Theoretical and Practical Considerations', International Symposium on Criteria for Estimating the Reliability of Macro Economic Models, Pisa, Dec. 1980.

Wass, Sir D. (1978), 'The Changing Problems of Economic Management', *Economic Trends* (March), 97–104.

Wonham, W.H. (1974), 'Linear Multivariate Control', Springer Verlag, Lecture Notes in Economics and Mathematical Systems, **101**.

Worswick, G.D.N. (1975), 'National Institute Experience with Econometric Models' in G.A. Renton (ed.) *Modelling the Economic*, Heinemann Educational Press, London.

Yamomoto, T. (1976), 'Asymptotic Mean Square Prediction Error for an Autoregressive Model with Estimated Coefficients', *Journal of the Royal Statistical Society*, Series C, Vol. 25, 123–7.

Young, R.M. (1979), 'Forecasting the U.S. Economy with an Econometric Model' in P. Ormerod (ed.), *Economic Modelling*, Heinemann, London.

Zionts, S. and J. Walenius J. (1976), 'An Interactive Programming Method for Solving the Multiple Criteria Problem', *Management Science*, **22**, 652–63.

Index